Everyday Life
in
South
Asia

Everyday Life

in

South

Asia

SECOND EDITION

EDITED BY

*Diane P. Mines and
Sarah Lamb*

INDIANA UNIVERSITY PRESS
BLOOMINGTON & INDIANAPOLIS

This book is a publication of

Indiana University Press
601 North Morton Street
Bloomington, IN 47404-3797 USA

www.iupress.indiana.edu

Telephone orders   800-842-6796
Fax orders   812-855-7931
Orders by e-mail   iuporder@indiana.edu

© 2010 by Indiana University Press
All rights reserved

∞The paper used in this publication meets the minimum requirements of the American National Standard for Information Sciences—Permanence of Paper for Printed Library Materials, ANSI Z39.48-1992.

Manufactured in the United States of America

Library of Congress Cataloging-in-Publication Data

Everyday life in South Asia / edited by Diane P. Mines and Sarah Lamb. — 2nd ed.
p. cm.
Includes bibliographical references and index.
ISBN 978-0-253-35473-0 (cl : alk. paper) —
ISBN 978-0-253-22194-0 (pb : alk. paper)
1. South Asia—Social life and customs. I. Mines, Diane P., [date]
II. Lamb, Sarah, [date]
DS339.E94 2010
306.0954—dc22
2009054114

4   5   15   14

CONTENTS

ACKNOWLEDGMENTS

We would like to thank each of our contributors—from both the first and the second editions—not only for their rich essays, but also for their invaluable suggestions and advice as the volume unfolded. We would also like to thank our students who, using this reader, educated us about how best to present readings to interested but novice students of South Asia. Gloria Raheja offered specific feedback about the first edition that helped us think about how to rethink some important issues for the second edition. Priyanka Nandy, Ph.D. student in anthropology at Brandeis University, provided very welcome administrative assistance. We thank with great warmth and appreciation our editor at Indiana University Press, Rebecca Tolen, for her patience and encouragement. It was she who instigated this project, encouraged us to put together this new edition, and provided good critical feedback on the contents while also giving us a free hand to develop the reader as we pleased. Any errors or omissions are our own and no one else's. We would also like to thank Laura MacLeod, Miki Bird, Nancy Lightfoot, Peter Froehlich, and Dan Pyle of Indiana University Press and freelance copy editor Carol Kennedy for their support and editorial wisdom.

Members of our families contributed to this volume in various ways. Rick Rapfogel, Diane's husband, provided critical assistance with technical and photographic aspects of the book, and gave not only his time but also emotional support to the project. He and daughter Lucy spent a lot of solo time so Diane could hide away in the office to complete the work. Lucy let Diane have this time with only a few sad faces at bedtime. Ed, Rachel, and Lauren were wonderfully generous in their lasting willingness to grant Sarah precious time to write and work while still always welcoming her home.

Boone, North Carolina   D.P.M.
Waltham, Massachusetts   S.L.

NOTE ON TRANSLITERATION

South Asians speak well over twenty major languages and even more minor languages and dialects. In transliterating terms from this rich diversity of languages, we have for the most part used accepted conventions. We have allowed for some variation, however, to reflect distinctive local pronunciations and to accommodate contributors' preferences. In most cases, terms appear in italics—with or without diacritics—only on the first usage in a chapter. Proper nouns—names of places, people, deities, and texts—have been left without diacritics. Some authors prefer to use diacritical marks in their translations to enhance accuracy. Others prefer not to use them at all, but rather use English spellings that closely approximate the term's pronunciation. South Asian terms are pluralized here in the English manner, by adding an "s." The names of some major Indian cities have been changed to spellings that more accurately reflect indigenous names and/or pronunciations that preceded British Anglicization of those same names. Thus Mumbai replaces Bombay; Chennai replaces Madras; Varanasi replaces Benares; and Kolkata replaces Calcutta.

Everyday Life
in
South
Asia

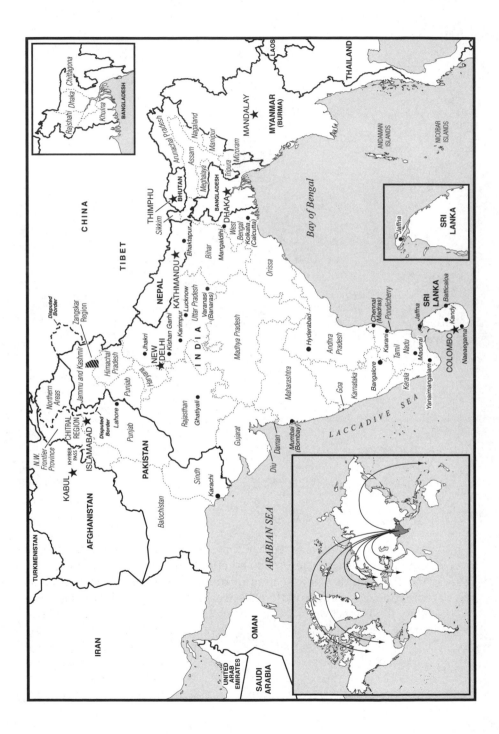

INTRODUCTION

Everyday Life in South Asia centers on the daily lives and experiences of people living in South Asia. Inspired by the focus on practice and everyday life in the work of social theorists,[1] we maintain that one can learn much about social-cultural worlds by examining the daily acts performed by ordinary people as they go through their lives. The book explores the ways people live, make, and experience their worlds through practices such as growing up and aging, arranging marriages, exploring sexuality, going to school, negotiating caste distinctions, practicing religion, participating in democracy, watching television, enduring violence as nations are built, and moving abroad for work. By focusing on the everyday life practices and experiences of particular people, the book conveys important dimensions of social-cultural life in South Asia that could not be imparted solely via abstract theoretical accounts or generalities.

South Asia has witnessed a great deal of social change over recent years, and this new, second edition of *Everyday Life in South Asia* highlights these changes. To design the first edition (2002), we approached leading scholars of South Asian studies (from the United States, Great Britain, and South Asia) to ask them what they would like, and find important, to contribute to a book on everyday life in South Asia. For this new, second edition, we kept many of those first papers—inviting the authors to update them when relevant—and solicited new ones from scholars whose work focuses on the kinds of critical contemporary issues that have impacted the region and grabbed the media over recent years, and attracted scholars' attention in new ways. These new essays, and the volume's new section introductions, explore topics such as the participation of young, middle-class workers in the flourishing call center industry; the impact on local gender systems of the massive out-migration of Sri Lankan housemaids to the oil-producing nations of the Middle East; the force and flavor of new Hindu nationalisms; the contemporary terrain of homosexualities and local "global gay" movements; return migration or "brain drain in reverse" of diasporic professionals to India; and the emergence of new middle-class lifeways amidst far-reaching processes of cultural and economic liberalization and globalization. Pakistan is also more on the radar in the global news media than ever, and this second edition includes several new essays focusing on everyday life in this crucial world nation.

The readings are organized into a series of topical parts—The Family and the Life Course; Genders; Caste, Class, and Community; Practicing Religion; Nation-Making; and Globalization, Public Culture, and the South Asian Diaspora. Although each individual piece can be read on its own, we, the editors, have written part introductions in which we introduce some background concepts and facts, draw out and reflect upon the common and uncommon theoretical and analytical themes that emerge, and briefly situate the papers in wider contexts.

The book as a whole is intended to serve as an accessible reader both for general readers and for students of South Asia at all levels. We hope also to make a valuable contribution to the academic field of South Asian studies. The papers clearly convey important facets of the history, diversity, and richness of the region's social-cultural life, as well as speak to theoretical questions and concerns viewed as vital by a range of contemporary scholars.

SOUTH ASIA

"South Asia," as we use the term in this book, refers to a geographical area— sometimes referred to as the South Asian "subcontinent"—that includes the contemporary nations of Pakistan, India, Bangladesh, Nepal, Bhutan, and Sri Lanka (see map on p. xiv). Sometimes Afghanistan—also part of British "India"—is included in South Asia, as well. The borders of any so-called cultural area such as South Asia (or Europe, East Asia, Southeast Asia, sub-Saharan Africa, etc.) are somewhat arbitrary, for the sharing of cultural ideas, practices, and materials is by and large continuous across a territory, not sharply demarcated by national (and, previously, colonial) boundaries. Indeed, the sharing of ideas, technologies, and material is now global in scope. In this book we do, however, retain the convention of defining South Asia as a cultural region. Because of a significant number of historical and cultural continuities, South Asians do share many practices and concepts even within the amazing diversity that also characterizes the peoples of that region.

The population of South Asia is quite large considering its relatively small territorial dimensions. India alone supports over one billion people, despite being in area only one-third the size of the United States. With the populations of Pakistan, Bangladesh, Nepal, Sri Lanka, and Bhutan included, the population of the region reaches close to 1.6 billion, nearly one-fourth of the world's population.

In the history of Euro-American scholarship, as well as in the popular imagination, South Asia has often been considered by European and American writers to be a part of the "Orient," an area and a concept that, as Said

(1978) has cogently argued, has been constructed as if it were timelessly traditional (instead of historical), basically religious (instead of rationally political), and characterized by Europeans as essentially weak and irrational (and therefore in need of governance by superior outsiders such as themselves). However, such stereotypes are untrue. There is no "timeless tradition." South Asia has its own history: cultural practices, religion, political structures, family structures, values—and all the similarities and diversities of South Asia—are nothing if not historically changing realities that respond to argument, action, and discourse among South Asians themselves.

The layers of history that have contributed to making and remaking the cultures and practices of South Asians are many. Often, textbooks on South Asia begin with the migration of "Aryans" from central Europe into the Indus River Valley (in what is now Pakistan) and then beyond. These migrations began around 1500 BCE. But of course, there were already people in South Asia before this. The Indus Valley civilization, for example, reached the peak of its urban development around 2300–1700 BCE. Others, perhaps the ancestors of the "Dravidians" whose languages still persist in southern India and other pockets across South Asia, were spread further throughout the area. Archaeological evidence shows the area to have been inhabited by humans since the Paleolithic age, as many as 400,000 years ago (Wolpert 1982: 4–28). Aryan culture—from whence came Sanskrit and some of the early rituals of Hinduism—spread over the subcontinent, and it was that culture which became hegemonic, that is, the powerful cultural norm, even as it was itself no doubt diverse and influenced by the practices and ideas of peoples already there.

Since as early as 300 BCE, residents of the Indian subcontinent were trading and exchanging ideas and material goods with merchants from Greece, other parts of Asia, Arabia, the Middle East, and, eventually northern Europe. Later, Mughal and Persian cultures, and with them the cultural and religious values of Islam, began to have a profound effect on South Asia. Muslim kings, first from areas now called Turkey and Afghanistan and later from Persia (now Iran), ruled much of the subcontinent from the twelfth to the seventeenth centuries, after which the British began to gain control of the area as they established colonial rule. During the centuries of Islamic rule, many South Asians converted to Islam, Islamic forms of art and architecture blended with prior styles, and many new Persian administrative concepts came to restructure South Asian society. When the British began to take control of what they defined as "India" (which then included much of the subcontinent), they, too, introduced new administrative concepts and practices, such as the census (Cohn 1987b), which had broad impact on the structure of Indian society. With the British (and, in smaller numbers, the Portuguese, Dutch, and French), Christianity in various forms also came to influence South Asia, as did the British structure of education, land administration, ideas of private property, and, of course, the English language. In the nineteenth century, when Indian nationalists began to challenge British control in hopes of taking back control of their own political destinies, they, too, altered some of the structures and values of the society (see Chatterjee 1993; Metcalf and Metcalf 2006).

Contemporary global economic and cultural values continue to shape South Asia: Microsoft has offices in Hyderabad; global customer service lines are staffed by Indians who have been trained to speak in American accents so no one will know they are Indian; economic liberalization encourages new consumption habits and cosmopolitan values; and South Asians respond to and refashion these influences in diverse and creative ways. South Asia, in turn, has shaped other peoples' practices in other parts of the world: Mahatma Gandhi's resistance techniques were used by Martin Luther King, Jr., in the civil rights movement in the United States; yoga is an everyday part of the lives of many people worldwide; Hindu temples are built in suburban U.S. neighborhoods; Sikh temples abound in English towns; clothing styles, music, and food from South Asia can be found in shops from Paris to Tokyo to small town U.S.A. Further, many South Asians live in other places, including the Middle East, Europe, Africa, and North America. These migrants both influence and are influenced by the styles, structures, and values of these places as they move back and forth across continents transnationally.

What we hope to convey with this all-too-brief outline of some phases of South Asian history is that South Asia has always been a changing, growing, diverse culture area. There is no "authentic" South Asia. There are people living their lives and making changes in the structures of their societies as they live every day. The papers in this volume, as well as the part introductions, clue us in to these lives as well as to some of the changes and histories that the living continue to make in South Asia today.

EVERYDAY LIFE

Why focus on "everyday life"? As Bowen and Early point out in their book *Everyday Life in the Muslim Middle East* (2002: 1–2), to focus on the "everyday" is to focus on the ways people actually live their ordinary, day-to-day lives, rather than on generalities or averages or abstract theories about those lives. Some theorists (e.g., de Certeau 1984) have argued that everyday life is where we can see the actual production and transformation of structures and cultures as people actually "make use of and operate with the categories, cultural routines, spaces, and structures" (Raheja 2002: 199) of given social life. Generalizing analyses and abstract theories tend, in contrast, to "freeze" or "freeze-frame" culture, as Pradeep Jeganathan points out (2002). But culture is not a frozen set of rules that people merely enact. Nor do all peoples in a culture abide by the same cultural principles or concepts: the activity of people is heterogeneous, contentious, emotionally charged, creative, and often surprising (see Bakhtin 1981). Our activity is always potentially cultur-ally transformative and historically relevant. In other words, culture *is* as culture *does*. And culture only *does* through active, living human beings. The discourses that are culture may come out not only in words, but also in the way a person walks, where they choose to walk, how they wear their hair, how they dress, with whom they gossip, how they worship, and so on. All of these everyday activities are part of the heterogeneous and always changing discourse that we call culture.

In keeping with some of these ideas, all of the authors in this volume were invited to write on some aspect of the everyday life of the South Asians among whom they worked. Therefore, while being at the same time analytic and theoretical, each paper gives primary concern to some aspect of the lives of real living and acting people who not only enact culture but also repro-duce and change it as they act.

HOW TO READ THIS BOOK

There are at least two ways to read the book. One is to focus on the essays in each part as a group. The other is to read across the parts to follow one of the many themes that wind through the whole volume. First, within each of the major parts the individual chapters cover different aspects of the topic named in the respective headings, and as such convey something of the di-versity of life in South Asia but within a common theme. In themselves these individual parts make extremely valuable contributions to specific topics in South Asian studies. For instance, "Genders" brings together new research and diverse perspectives on women's, men's, and transgendered lives. This part offers not only revealing explorations of the ways women have been made relatively subordinate within families (via arranged and patrilocal marriages, lack of access to schooling, attributions of bodily impurity, and the like), perspectives which have played a dominant role in existing litera-ture on women in South Asia; "Genders" also offers pieces on masculinity, same-sex love, the experiences of transgendered *hijra*s and global "gays," and some of the ways gender relations are changing in both rural and urban South Asia as women pursue increasing opportunities for education and work.

The part on "Practicing Religion" likewise brings together a diversity of materials, from Hindu, Buddhist, and Muslim traditions, exploring phenom-ena such as why women in remote Kashmir fight to join Buddhist monas-teries, how lower-caste Hindus use temple rituals to protest existing social orderings, how Muslims in Pakistan's Northwest Frontier discuss and prac-tice culture in the context of a region undergoing intense Islamization, how a devout Muslim family in Lahore lived with a powerful jinn, or spirit, who possessed their young daughter in a rather friendly way, and what it's like to be a young anthropologist unintentionally intoxicated and caught up with the fervor, ardent devotion, and seeming social chaos of a village festival of the Hindu god of love, Krishna.

Because so many of the papers touch on multiple intersecting themes, our section headings must not be read as compact, neat, and closed categories for thinking about South Asian lives. They merely point to a few among many possible ways to conceptualize aspects of social lives depicted in the readings. The reader may wish to think about alternative ways of organizing their reading by tracing one or more of the key themes that wind in and out through the different sections. These themes include how South Asians define modernity in diverse and unique ways; youth culture and the lives of young people; education and the role of schools in creating citizens; the power and the stigma of women's work; the differences between "ideals" and "realities" of life; competing notions of persons as sociocentrically bound to their families or as individuals pursuing their own, independently defined goals; violence in the constitution of modern nations; globalization; and the impact of economic liberalization on South Asia today.

So, for example, someone interested in the ways "modernity" is experienced and produced in South Asia might focus on the readings by Wadley, Liechty and Lamb (part 1), Gold, Gamburd, and Reddy (2), Dickey and Lukose (3), Marsden (4), Lynch (5), and Pandian and Mankekar (6) These pieces offer various views about how family structures, gender relations, entertainment, and ideas of self and society are impacted by the kinds of forces people see as constituting modernity, such as consumerism, economic development, global popular culture, education, religious nationalism, women's labor, and urbanization. Someone interested in youth might string together Liechty, Kapur, Gold, Lukose, Lynch, Pandian, Trawick, Hall, and Narayan—who examine young people's lives across a wide swath of the South Asian world, from middle-class "punks" in Kathmandu, to working-class Sikh migrants in England and middle-class migrants in the United States, to uneducated girls in rural Rajasthan and college kids in Kerala, to young women who work in textile factories, to children growing up in the war zone of northern Sri Lanka. Another cross-cutting theme is the invocation of religion, morality, and ethnicity in the constitution of nations. Here one could group Lukose's discussion of caste, religion, and secular citizenship with Lynch's discussion of "good" Buddhist girls in Sri Lanka, Menon's paper on female Hindu nationalists, Ring's discussion of women's exchange practices as foils to ethnic strife in Pakistan, Bate's paper on democratic politics in South India, and Butalia's search across borders for the meaning of Partition to one family.

The point here is that there is no single way to understand people's lives in South Asia. Together these pieces—detailed descriptions of lived realities—hope to convey something of the richly varied, historically shifting, and intensely experienced nature of life as lived, and made, in South Asia.

NOTES

1. Scholars such as Pierre Bourdieu (1977a), Michel de Certeau (1984), Lila Abu-Lughod (1993), Michael Jackson (1996), and Sherry Ortner (2006).

PART ONE

The Family and the Life Course

The family is a central site of everyday life in South Asia. It is an arena through which persons move through the life-course passages of birth, youth, marriage, parenthood, aging, and dying; it can be a place of love and conflict, material sustenance and want, companionship and painful separations. One term for family in several Indian languages is *samsāra*, which means literally "that which flows together," and also more broadly connotes worldly life in general. In its sense as family, samsara refers to the assembly of kin and household things that "flow with" persons as they move through their lives.

One common assumption held by many both within and outside South Asia is that South Asians live ideally in "joint families," consisting of a married couple, their sons, sons' wives and children, any unmarried daughters, and perhaps even grandsons' wives and children. We see in the following selections that this assumption is both true and not true, and that family relationships and structures are richly complex and varied. In general, urbanites tend to live in smaller, more nuclear households than those in rural areas, and poorer people (with less land and smaller homes to their names) tend to live in smaller households than the wealthier. National and transnational migration also affects household structures, as many across South Asia are moving to cities or abroad for work, only sometimes bringing the rest of their families with them.

Children are highly valued and loved. The births of boys are often even more elaborately celebrated than the births of girls, but this is not because girls are not equally loved. Parents often worry about the burden of providing a dowry for a daughter's marriage, and they know that a daughter will move away from them when she marries—unlike a son, who could remain with his parents for their lifetime. Most children in South Asia spend at least some time in school (although this school education can be very minimal, as Gold examines); many also play vital roles by helping their parents with work; and they also play with friends and receive affection and indulgence from seniors. Liechty explores how many urban youth (in this case in Kathmandu, Nepal) are participating in what is becoming a globalized, cosmopolitan youth culture, with shared forms of popular music, media, slang, dress, and sometimes drugs.

Although not all people get married (see, for instance, Seizer's account of actresses' lives and Reddy's exploration of same-sex relationships in part 2), marriage is considered by most in South Asia a crucial part of a person's and family's life. Young people—rural and urban—spend much time thinking about their marriages and chatting among themselves about whether traditional arranged marriages or romantic "love marriages" are better. Arranged marriages have long been the most widely accepted marriage practice across South Asia, where the parents and other family members make the match, taking into consideration the background and character of not only the bride and the groom but also their families, considering matters such as caste endogamy, family status, community reputation, wealth, occupation, education, potential business alliances, physical attractiveness, and perceived compatibility. Even when a marriage is arranged by parents and other senior kin, the young person will usually face the event with, along with some trepidation, a degree of eager anticipation and romantic expectation, having perhaps met the future spouse on one or more occasions, or at least having seen and admired a photo. The distinction between "arranged" and "love" marriages is in fact becoming increasingly blurred, especially among the urban middle classes, where it is common for young people to participate in choosing their potential partners within the framework of parental approval in one of two ways: Parents or other kin may introduce the two, who then might spend some time getting to know each other by phone or email, in meetings in the parents' homes, and even by dating a few times, before agreeing to a match. Or the couple might meet each other on their own in, say, college or the workplace, or by growing up in the same village, and then—if the family backgrounds seem compatible—broach the topic of a match to the parents, who may then assume the responsibility of arranging the marriage. Extensive socializing between the sexes before marriage is still widely discouraged, however, and single women employed in mixed-gender workplaces can be criticized for opposite-sex fraternizing, as the selections by Kapur (this part) and Lynch (part 5) explore. Divorce rates in India are among the lowest in the world, especially among Hindus (within Islam, divorce is accepted under appropriate circumstances), although divorce is on the rise within professional, cosmopolitan circles in India, as Kapur's chapter examines.

Aging and dying tend to be accepted as natural parts of life and family flows for many South Asians. The expectation or ideal (one that is not always realized) is that intergenerational ties will be close and reciprocal throughout life and even after death, as parents care for their children when young, and children (especially sons and daughters-in-law) in turn support their parents in old age and as ancestors (Lamb). Much public discourse in India—in newspapers, television serials, gerontological texts, and everyday talk—is currently concerned with the decline of multigenerational family living for the aged, in the face of the growing prevalence of nuclear family households, living alone, old-age homes, and the transnational dispersal of families amidst global labor markets. Nonetheless, the vast majority of India's elders continue to live in multigenerational family homes: of persons aged sixty or older, just 4 percent in 2000 lived in single-person households, for instance, and just 7 percent as an elderly couple.[1] These figures present a stark contrast to those in the United States, where among those sixty-five and over, 30 percent live in single-person households and 53 percent with only their spouse, and where it is widely considered entirely normal and even desirable for people to live singly and especially with a spouse in late life.[2]

For the most part, older South Asians practice fewer attempts to fight the bodily changes of age—through the hair-dyeing, face-lifting, anti-aging exercise routines, life-prolonging medical technologies, and the like that are so dominant now in Europe and America. (Such techniques are, however, becoming popular among the cosmopolitan South Asian elite.) Hindus, as well as Buddhists, Jains, and Sikhs, view death as not an end but a passage on to new forms of life; the body is discarded and cremated, while the soul moves on to new births, deaths, and rebirths. Muslims bury their dead and imagine an afterlife with the possibility of suffering or bliss depending partly on how much merit or sin one has accumulated. Some Muslims believe that death should not be loudly mourned, for the timing and circumstances of death are in Allah's hands, and one would not want to insult Allah.

One significant theme running throughout several of this part's chapters is the idea that belonging to a family whole is more important than pursuing individual aspirations (see also Radhakrishnan, part 6). Susan Wadley quotes a Brahman man using the imagery of the broom to explain the value of a large, interdependent family: "Say there is a broom. If you have one straw separate, it can't sweep. But when all are together, it can sweep." Patricia and Roger Jeffery's examination of a Muslim woman's life in rural north India illustrates how the ideal of a harmonious joint family does not always work out neatly: Sabra's marital family suffers bitter disagreements, separations, poverty, and death. Yet in significant respects Sabra's interdependent extended family ties endure, and it is only through remaining part of her husband's family that Sabra is able to survive as a widow with young children. Sabra's story also demonstrates the importance of a woman's natal ties. Although she moves to her husband's home, her ties to her natal parents and brothers remain valuable lines of material support and affection.

Another theme that appears in these chapters surrounds the nature of modernity. Many in South Asia interpret problems in contemporary families, such as a youth drug culture (Liechty), divorce (Kapur), neglected elderly (Lamb), and a general decline in family values, as modern afflictions, stemming from forces such as consumerism, urbanization, individualism, colonialism, a globalizing political economy and media, and the back and forth of transnational migration. Some view such features of modernity as coming principally from the "West" and/or from "globalization." In such discourses, the intimate extended family can stand as a sign of "tradition" and a morally superior national culture (see Chatterjee 1993; Lamb, Lynch, Radhakrishnan). Yet, the chapters in this part also highlight crucial dialectic processes of interchange between more local and global cultural forms, as people forge family lives while striving to maintain older needs, desires, and values, and also producing and fulfilling and sometimes resisting new ones, wrestling strategically with what they see as the conditions of their modern society.

*   *   *

The chapters in this section together aim to portray the richness and diversity of everyday experiences of the family and the life course in South Asia. Susan Wadley begins by examining the ideology and practice of the joint family in the largely Hindu community of Karimpur in rural north India. People of Karimpur express the idea that power comes through numbers and that those who wish to sustain a family's honor and vitality should remain together as one whole under a unifying male head. Wadley further examines how, contrary to expectations, the joint family is more prevalent now in Karimpur than ever before, although the nature of some relationships within the family is changing.

Patricia and Roger Jeffery's vivid account of the life of Sabra, a rural north Indian Muslim woman, portrays the phases of a woman's life as she moves from girlhood, to marriage, to motherhood and widowhood; the quest for sons; and the afflictions and sustenance that derive from extended family ties.

Mark Liechty focuses on youth culture in urban Nepal. Middle-class youth, while waiting—often in vain—for white-collar employment, have the leisure time to join gangs, consort with foreign tourists, sell and take drugs, and consume foreign media—participating in the intermingling of global and local worlds, creating images and fantasies of foreignness and modernity.

Cari Costanzo Kapur explores the ways call center employees in India negotiate their sense of identity as young, income-earning professionals at a stage in life when both career growth and decisions about marriage and family are paramount. She asks how the intersection of global labor, gender ideologies, and class in contemporary India are shaping ideas about, and options for, courtship, marriage, and divorce, and enabling new ways of thinking about kinship.

Sarah Lamb moves on to examine the ways Bengalis think of aging as a time to loosen ties to family, things, and their own bodies, to prepare for the myriad leave-takings and journeys of dying. She explores the experiences and perspectives both of those living in families in a large West Bengali village and of those in the rapidly emerging old-age homes in India's middle-class cosmopolitan centers, institutions that are replacing for those who live in them the more conventional multigenerational co-residential family that many have long viewed as central to a proper way of aging and society in India. To some, such old-age homes signify not merely a new form of aging and family, but also much broader social, cultural, and national transformations.

NOTES

1. See Census of India 2001: "Data Highlights: HH-5: Households with number of aged persons 60 years and above by sex and household size," pp. 2–4, www.censusindia.gov.in/.

2. U.S. Census Bureau, www.census.gov: Single Person Households Age 65 and Older in 1999: 2000 Census, Tables No. 60 and 61; and "A Profile of Older Americans: 2003," www.aoa.gov/prof/Statistics/profile/2003/6.asp#figure3.

1

One Straw from a Broom Cannot Sweep: The Ideology and Practice of the Joint Family in Rural North India

Susan S. Wadley

The Indian joint family is built upon the idea and reality that power comes through numbers, and that those who seek to be most powerful, especially in India's village communities, should remain in joint families in order to successfully sustain a family's honor and position. A second, but equally important, component of the success of joint families in practice is the training that children receive that marks their interdependence, their sense of belonging to a group that is more important than individual goals and aspirations. The ideal joint family is made up of a married couple, their married sons, their sons' wives and children (and possibly grandsons' wives and great-grandchildren), and unmarried daughters. In the community of Karimpur[1] in rural Uttar Pradesh, some 150 miles southeast of New Delhi, some joint families extend to four generations and include more than thirty members. For Karimpur's landowning families, which are more likely to be joint than are poor families, separating a joint family is traumatic, rupturing family ties, economic relationships, and workloads, as well as necessitating the division of all of the joint family's material goods (land, ploughs, cattle, cooking utensils, stocks of grain and seed, courtyards, verandahs, rooms, cooking areas, etc.). Separation (*nyare*) is, in fact, most comparable to an American divorce. It also brings dishonor to one's family.

The paradigm most frequently used to regulate social life in Karimpur is that of the ordered family, implying the authority of a male head, a number of adults working together under that authority, and respect for all of those higher in the family (or village) hierarchy. As in many north Indian communities, Karimpur residents use fictive kin terms toward all nonrelated

Parts of this essay are reprinted from *Struggling with Destiny in Karimpur, 1925–1984*, by Susan S. Wadley. Copyright © 1994 The Regents of the University of California. Used by permission of the University of California Press.

village residents of whatever caste group; and traditionally, they have seen
the village community as one family.[2] As one elderly Brahman man put it
in 1984:

> Where there is cooperation (*sangṭhan*), there are various kinds of wealth and
> property. And where there is no cooperation, there is a shortage of each and
> every thing or there is an atmosphere of want. Where there is cooperation
> there is no need [of the ambition] to pile up wealth. "The minor streams or
> rivers go into the ocean but they do not have the ambition [to be big]." So, in
> the same way, property and comfort accrue without being sought after when
> there is cooperation: property comes to the properly regulated (*kāydā*) man.

Hence the family is dependent upon a man who has himself, and his family,
under his control. This control is attained through a variety of daily practices, as well as a clearly articulated ideology of male superiority. The same
elderly Brahman male spoke of women in this way:

Q: How does the man *control* her?[3]
BM: *Control*? They [women] don't have much knowledge (*gyān*). How is
the lion locked in the cage? It lacks reason (*vivek*). Man protects her from
everything.
Q: If a woman progresses, then she would be knowledgeable. Then how
can you shut her in a cage?
BM: I say that if the sun begins to rise in the west, then what? It is a law of
nature.

At another time, he added that "a woman cannot think as much as a man"
(even though, he went on to state, she might be more powerful). A Brahman widow concurred with this assessment, saying, "The woman is inferior
(*choṭī*, literally 'small'). A woman can only work according to the regulations
(*kāydā*). She can never leave the regulations." Hence a woman who follows
the laws and customs of her family will be controlled and bring honor to her
family.

A male gains honor by having land and wealth, by being kind to others,
by keeping his word, and by having virtuous women who maintain *purdah*
(seclusion). Families can lose honor through their women by having daughters or daughters-in-law who elope, become pregnant prior to marriage, or
are seen outside too often. Men may bring dishonor to a household by stealing, gambling, drinking, and eating taboo foods, as well as by being unkind
and miserly. A family also loses honor by not remaining joint, in part because control is easier in a joint family.

Karimpur's residents believe that joint families are able to maintain better
control of their members, especially young adults. Shankar, a Brahman male
and village headman of Karimpur in the early 1980s, suggests that self-con-
trol, particularly sexual control, is more easily maintained in a joint family.
Several aspects of joint family living relate to his remarks. First, as he notes,

no one has his/her own room or even space in the traditional household. In fact, through the 1960s in most joint families, the mother would assign sleeping places on a nightly basis; this gave her immense control over the sexuality of her sons and daughters-in-law. If she felt it appropriate, she would arrange for them to have a place where they could meet at night. A young man, newly married, once complained that he and his wife were being forbidden to sleep together because he had had a bad cold for some time and his grandmother (female head of his joint family) thought that they should remain apart for the good of his health. This raises a second point: many South Asian Hindu men believe that male health is threatened by too much sex, for a man loses vital energy through his semen. Hence controlled male sexuality is especially important. On these issues, the headman remarked:

> But if society lives together (*samāj ikhaṭṭhe*), your self-control (*sanyam āpkā*) is maintained. If you live separately, you lose your self-control. You get a separate room. You get a separate cot. You have separate food. Everything becomes separate. This affects your health (*tandurustī*). But when you live together—you have your mother at one place, sister at another, *bhābhī* (older brother's wife) somewhere else, or a servant at some place—then self-control is not difficult. You don't have any place to indulge yourself [implied is food or sexual indulgence]. This is the greatest factor in good health. That is why it is essential for the family to live together. Now it is important to understand that all this is a gift of nature (*kudarat*). If it is not in men, then how can we blame others? This tendency to live separate is very dangerous. They say that if a young daughter is alone in a room, then even her father should not go into that room. She is the girl whom you have produced out of your own seed, out of your own body, and she is young. So you should not go into that room. So when our family lives together, then we get less time, and we get more opportunities to work. We would not even be able to think about it [sex]. That is why our health used to be good.

Aside from the physical surveillance that is implied in joint family life, other forms of control are vital to the success of a joint family. These include such means as the silencing of women and children (or even adult males younger than the head of the household) through rules that deny them the opportunity to speak, through the seclusion of women (purdah), through rituals which mark the superiority of male kin and the importance of the family unit, and through daily practices such as eating routines that mark the male as superior. For example, a woman should speak only in a whisper, if at all, to her husband's father or older male relatives. A man should not talk with his wife in front of his parents, nor should he do anything disrespectful before his father (such as smoking a cigarette). A woman should keep her face covered before all men senior to her husband, and she should not leave the family home unless accompanied by another woman or male relative and her head and body are covered by a shawl. The yearly ritual calendar is filled with celebrations in which women pray for healthy sons, for long-living husbands, and for their brothers. There are no annual rituals where they pray for their mothers or daughters. Finally, a Hindu wife should never eat a meal before her husband and other male relatives have eaten as this would be enormously disrespectful: the result is that women often eat late at night, after the last men have returned from the town or fields.

These factors are dependent upon and support the powerful male head of the family. The unified, cooperating joint family demands both a trustworthy leader and the respect of the sons. The most powerful Brahman family in 1984 achieved the ideal more successfully than any other Karimpur family: the family was composed of four brothers, the widows of their two dead brothers, their wives, children, children's wives, and grandchildren, who had lived together for over twenty years since the death of the parents. One of the brothers attributed this success to the male head, his older brother, saying, "We understood that he is wise, older, more sensible, would do every kind of good work, but would not do bad work." The family is now separated, but the brother heading the largest portion was described as thinking ahead, having understanding, and seeking peace.

If the family stays together, its power increases. One young Brahman man used the imagery of a broom to explain the need for a large, cooperating family: "Say there is a broom. If you have one straw separate, it can't sweep. But when all are together, it can sweep." One elderly Brahman man used the example of a family with four sons. All have different habits. But the family's power would increase if all four were under the control of one person.

> I am telling what I understand. A family must have one thing. That is, a family is strong when all remain in the control of one [person]. Whatever is said, they must accept that. In other words, having accepted the words of Brahma [the Hindu deity], they have become firm and constant in that, whether it is right or wrong. But the family must be controlled by one, whether or not he has money. Unless there is selfishness [on the part of the leader], the power [of the family] will endure.

On another day, this same man added, "If the family goes every which way, then the whole house is ruined."

Equal treatment of all the members within the family and unchallenged decisions by the head are necessary to the smooth functioning of the united family. I learned this lesson soon after beginning fieldwork in Karimpur in 1967. I was living in a family that included four married sons, along with their wives and children. Whenever I brought sweets or fruits for treats, I was required to give them to the grandmother, who would distribute them among her sons, daughters-in-law, and grandchildren. Her decision as to who got what amount carried weight: mine did not (although I find that thirty years later, I am allowed to make the distribution myself). Further, if

I bought saris for the women, they had to be identical, apart from color, for the women at each tier: the brothers' wives all should get one kind, their sisters should get one kind; the daughters all should get one kind, and so on. Likewise, frocks for the young girls or sweaters for the boys should differ in color only, unless I wanted to instigate fights and high levels of tension among the women. So I learned the appropriate buying patterns, those used by heads of households. Thus it is easy at holidays or at more public events like the district fair to identify family groupings, because of the clusters of girls in identical dresses or boys in matching shirts.

My elderly Brahman friend once told his (somewhat idealized) version of the rule within his family:

> In the United States, when people get married, a man becomes master for himself and feels that his duty is to his wife and children. But here in India, whenever there is a guardian and we make the bread in one place [meaning that they cook together], we cannot say, "My wife does not have bread. Bring some for her." Or that "she has no blouse." Whether she has no clothes or she changes into a new sari every day, I do not have the right [to give clothes to her or to complain]. . . . We are either oppressed by the older people or we have respect for them. There is another thing: we cannot say that she does not have a sari so why don't you bring one for her. And I cannot bring another either. The time never came when I had to think about whether she had clothes or not. No one [namely his wife] ever said to me, "I have no clothes or other things." No one ever told me this problem. If she had, what could I have done? That rule has been in my mind till now. But for the past five or six years we have become separate. Now I do all of this that the family wants—saris and clothes for the children. Before, my brother was master of the family and I was always behind. I never was concerned whether my children were in trouble or were happy. I never worried about this.

The unity of the joint family depends, too, on the wife's first duty being to her parents-in-law, not to her husband. As one young man, a Water-carrier by caste, explained:

> First of all she should think about the family. Then me. . . . First of all she should take care to feed them. My mother is old, so my wife should massage my mother. It is her duty to eat the food after my mother, my older brother's wife, and sister. If my parents want her to clean the pots, she must clean them. Even if she feels that she is a new *bahū* (wife/daughter-in-law) and she need not clean the pots now, her duty is to clean the pots.

Another man remarked that the women must also see to equality, not giving bread rubbed with ghee (clarified butter, a prestige item) to one person and plain bread to another. Above all, the good daughter-in-law is one who serves and obeys her father-in-law/mother-in-law (*sās-sāsur*). As a poor Cultivator said, "She should accept what the father-in-law and mother-in-law say, whether they are right or wrong." The authority of the parents-in-law is key, because if a woman seeks favoritism through her husband, the unity of the family is threatened. I vividly remember a young man in his twenties telling us that his mother and aunt (his father's sister) used to like his wife very much, but that he hadn't liked her. (It was an arranged marriage, as are all marriages in Karimpur.) Now he loved her, so they no longer liked her. Without his affection for her, the unity of the family was secured and the power structures unchallenged. Once his affection developed, the power structures that allow for the ideal unity and cooperation were threatened.

Behavior within the family marks the hierarchies. Respect for those senior is demanded: sons respect fathers and older brothers and obey their mothers, with whom a more affectionate relationship exists. Sons cannot smoke, play with their children, or talk with their wives in the presence of their fathers. The Flower Grower's wife says that sensible (literally "understanding," *samajdhār*) boys show respect to their fathers, but some, like one of her sons, refuse to listen to the advice of their parents. Women must also show respect within the household. A bahu asks her mother-in-law what to cook, how much spice to add, whether she can go to the fields, and so on, even when she is forty and the mother-in-law sixty or more. Bahus also show respect through veiling, by touching the feet of senior women on ritual occasions, and through eating patterns, always eating after both the men and the women senior to them.

The rule of those senior is not always benign, however, and decisions are regularly enforced with physical punishment. The household head (or more senior person) has "understanding" that the others lack. If they do not accept that understanding, that wisdom regarding right and wrong, the message can be reinforced through physical punishment. Husbands can beat wives; fathers can beat sons (and, more rarely, daughters). The Flower Grower's son, a young man then in his early twenties with an eighth-grade education who did construction work in Delhi, explained the roles of husbands and wives thus: if a wife erred but did so in public (sitting with her friends, for example), she should not be corrected, for that would be an insult. But in private, a husband could say something or beat her. "In other words, you should scold her, if she makes an error. You must make her understand that she must not do so." A Sweeper woman said, resignedly, "If we don't work well, we're bound to get a beating." A young Water-carrier man told of the time he hit his wife:

> At that time I was studying in high school. It was 1978. One day the food wasn't cooked. On that day, I said nothing. On the following day, I was also made late because the food wasn't ready. Again I didn't speak to her. On the third day again I was made late. In this way, I was late each day. On the fourth day, I went again [to eat, late]. It was summer. I sat on the roof in the air. Then after eating, I hit her four or five times.

So a husband's duty is to make his wife understand things through physical coercion if necessary. A wife can also correct her husband: if he drinks or gambles, she should try to forbid him. But given the limits on female mobility, due to rules of seclusion, she has no real way of intervening in these matters. Moreover, she cannot beat him, although everyone knew of wives who did in fact hit their husbands when angry.

Children should be physically corrected as well. The Flower Grower said, "If he [a son] does some wrong work, beating is a duty." The goal is to teach through fear. My elderly Brahman friend captured the essence of control as understood in Karimpur: physical punishment and verbal abuse are used to instill fear.

> A child who fears that when the parents come, they will shout at me, [that child] won't play in the dirt, won't use foul language, won't fight with anybody. But if he has no fear, he will play in the dirt the whole day. Because he has no fear, he will use bad language toward others. So there should be control—for every man and every woman.

Without fear, according to Karimpur residents, there can be no control, and elders in one's family have the right and duty to "cause understanding." Similarly, those who are senior in the village can beat "understanding" into those of lower status.

In many ways, the village is perceived as one large family. The fictive kin ties that link everyone are one mark of this "family writ large" conception, although there are other ways in which the fictive kinship of one large family is marked. When someone dies, the whole village shares in the grieving by canceling music events or other celebrations. In 1968 a Leatherworker named Horilal died on Holi, the popular spring festival characterized by the throwing of colored powder, raucous play, and role reversals. Within minutes of the news of his death, all Holi celebrations throughout the village came to a sudden halt.

The perceived unity of the village was further articulated when a fire swept through the Brahman section of Karimpur in April 1984. People claimed that the fire was caused by the accumulated sins of the village as a whole, but especially by its Brahman leaders. Just as the sins of a family are ultimately the responsibility of the head, so too the sins of the village are the responsibility of the dominant caste, in this case the Brahman landlords. Here again individuality is muted. Whereas an individual can sin and hence affect his own life course by altering his destiny (*karma*), he also alters that of his family, lineage, caste, and village, for an individual is not a unique entity but shares substance and moral codes with all of those with whom he or she is related, in ever larger circles. All those belonging to the nation of India also share in the same way.

If a family should be united, so too should the dominant group. A retired Accountant by caste attributed the power of Karimpur's Brahman landlords to their unity:

Those people [Thakurs, commonly landlords throughout northern India] used to understand that they were landlords. Also those [Brahmans] because they were wealthy. Above all, there was unity [*sangthan*] among them where-as elsewhere there was no unity. Everything depends on unity.

By the 1980s that spirit of cooperation was felt to be missing, and hence Brahman domination had lessened. In the election for headman in June of 2000, sixteen men ran, including four Brahmans. With no unity amongst the Brahmans, none of their candidates was successful; one garnered all of eight votes of some three thousand cast.

THE CHANGING FAMILY

Numerous factors have begun to put stress on both the united family and the united village. These include increased education, migration, and con-sumerism. Contrary to expectations, however, the joint family is more preva-lent than ever before, although internal arrangements differ from those of the 1960s and before. As table 1 shows, the percentage of all Karimpur fami-lies that are joint is greater than at any time in the twentieth century. There is also a marked caste difference in joint families, so that in 1998, the richer Brahmans had 22 joint families and 24 nuclear families, while the poorer Cultivators had 25 joint families and 46 nuclear families. With the average size of the Brahman joint family at 12.2 persons while nuclear families aver-aged 4.7 persons, twice as many Brahman individuals lived in joint families (269) as in nuclear (112). For the Cultivators, joint families averaged 9 persons while nuclear families averaged 5 persons, and the numbers of persons in joint and nuclear households was almost equal.

The increase in joint families is related to demographic changes as well as to economic changes. In the 1920s, the average life span in India was about twenty-five years, while now it is over sixty.[4] With many not living past their

Table 1. Family types in Karimpur

| | Number of Families (percent) | | | |
Type	1925	1968	1984	1998
Single Person	13 (8.1)	9 (3.7)	7 (2.1)	13 (3.3)
Subnuclear	33 (20.4)	11 (4.5)	26 (8.0)	23 (6.0)
Nuclear	36 (22.4)	107 (43.5)	143 (43.7)	159 (41.3)
Supp. Nuclear	42 (26.1)	33 (13.4)	58 (17.7)	60 (15.6)
Joint	25 (15.5)	81 (32.9)	91 (27.8)	130 (33.7)
Other	12 (7.5)	5 (2.0)	2 (0.6)	0

twenties, joint families were often impossible, because many families didn't include two intact married couples. As table 1 shows, in 1925 families tended to be either supplemented nuclear families (a married couple with one related adult and their children) or subnuclear families (having no married couple). So whereas over 20 percent of Karimpur families in the 1920s were subnuclear, in the 1990s, with greater life spans, only 6 percent are subnuclear. Likewise, joint families have gone from 15 percent of all families to almost 34 percent of all families.

This increase in joint families runs contrary to the expectations of Western social scientists, who anticipated that family structures in the developing third world would follow the pattern of those of the West, with nuclear families predominating. Many elements work to keep joint families intact, including the role of maintaining honor. But economic factors are also important. The temporary migration of men out of the village to seek jobs in nearby towns or Delhi or Mumbai has increased dramatically in the last fifteen years. Frequently the migrant leaves his family with his parents or brothers in the village, though he may eventually bring his wife and children to join him. Even then, the family may be economically and emotionally joint, as the migrant brother contributes cash to buy fertilizer for the family fields or to pay doctor bills, while also providing housing so his brother's children can attend the better schools found in urban areas. Likewise, the brother managing the family lands contributes food to the migrants and may house young unmarried adults or nieces needed to help with women's household chores. Moreover, it is to the advantage of the migrant to have a trusted relative rather than a land-poor sharecropper working his portion of the family lands. So while much of the time there may be two separate households, one urban and one rural, in fact there is a constant flow of people between the parts of a joint family, as workloads are redistributed around childbirth, holidays, labor needs, and so on. Joint families, whether village-based or split between village and city, also benefit from having one adult male freer to manage other family needs such as getting the sick proper medical care, dealing with officials, arranging marriages, or being involved in village politics.

Families with no or little land are most likely to be nuclear or supplemented nuclear households. Here poverty overwhelms the desire for honor, and without land to work and its proceeds to share, with little motivation to enter politics, with no money for complicated medical care, families split more readily. As one woman from the poor caste of Midwives said:

> My mother-in-law separated [from us] because of my children, saying, "You have lots of children. You live hungry. We will live with the other son. That son is in service [has a job]." So because of my poverty, we separated. . . . Now that son is in service. He sends money home. At my place there is nothing. Now that she has left, I have to raise the children alone. Before she used to

look after them [while I went with the grazing animals to make cow-dung cakes].

In this instance, a mother chose to live with her more prosperous son, creating a supplemented nuclear family. What had once been a joint family, with parents, two married sons, and their children, is now one nuclear family and (with the father dead) one supplemented nuclear family. Most families move through a cycle of at least brief joint status, while sons and their wives are young. As sons achieve differential success in the workplace, and have more or fewer children, the momentum to separate grows. Yet as the same Midwife said, "Living alone is not right." But only those with land, political ambitions, and more favorable economic circumstances can ward off separation.

But even in the joint families, other forms of "separation" are now occurring. Karimpur families are becoming increasingly couple-oriented and challenging the authority of their elders. One manifestation of this change is the use of space. In 1968, only one couple, a young Brahman and his wife, had their "own room"—and only over the strenuous objections of the man's mother. But by the 1980s, many couples in joint families were allocated their own space to set up and use as they liked. This space, often a room of their own, was clearly off-limits to the mother-in-law, who thus lost her control of her son's sexuality. Indeed, I was frequently told that the result of both separate families and "rooms of their own" was a shortening of the time between children, from over three years in the 1960s and earlier to barely over two years in the 1980s.

With these changes came challenges to the authority of those senior. Songs in the 1980s continually spoke of new kinship patterns. For example, in one song a bridegroom is described as very clever because he took his bride to see a movie without asking any of his kin. The following excerpt is from a woman's song that directly challenges the authority of the mother-in-law by reversing roles:

Mother-in-law, gone, gone is your rule,
The age of the daughter-in-law has come.
The mother-in-law grinds with the grinding stone,
The daughter-in-law watches.
"Your flour is very coarse, my mother-in-law,"
The age of the daughter-in-law has come.

While the mother-in-law may still retain authority, songs such as these point to contentious issues in modern joint families, where the daughter-in-law is likely to be much better educated than her mother-in-law and more willing to demand some independence and mobility, as well as consumer goods unavailable in earlier decades. With her closer ties to her husband, as symbolized by their personal space, these tensions, though always present in joint families, are greater than ever.

One response to the changing family is the enormous popularity of the goddess Santoshi Ma, the goddess of peace and benevolence but also a goddess whose story speaks directly to women whose husbands are working outside of the village or to women having in-law troubles. In the story told as a rationale for her worship, a young wife has a worthless husband who finally leaves home to seek his fortune. She is left alone with his family. As his absence grows longer, she is treated more and more cruelly, forced to gather firewood from the forest and given rags to wear. On one of her excursions into the forest, she comes upon a group of women worshipping Santoshi Ma. Hearing the story of the goddess, she too begins to worship her every Friday. The husband thus begins to prosper and eventually returns home. When the husband discovers how his wife has been treated, he builds a lavish home for her with the help of the goddess. So those who worship the goddess will prosper, as did the young wife.

The village community is also threatened by similar changes—by democracy, by migration, by education, by right-wing Hindu movements which have pitted Muslim against Hindu in ways unknown in the past, and by new ideas and wants conveyed through films and television. As one of the Carpenters said, "Now there is a headman in every house." In village opinion, what is most damaging is a loss of the village morality that was based on a complex web of mutual obligations between kin and between caste groups. Speaking of the village, people repeatedly spoke of the lack of caring that exists now. While speaking of the family, people lamented the lack of love and of care for one's elders. The cultural code that supported a hierarchy whereby the high had knowledge and might and the right to control the low is now continuously challenged. Thus far, Karimpur's joint families have adapted and met the challenge, so that their unity remains. Meanwhile, the unity of the village is fragile and rapidly disappearing.

NOTES

1. The research on which this paper is based took place between 1967 and 1998 in the village of Karimpur in western Uttar Pradesh. Our knowledge of Karimpur social life is extensive: William and Charlotte Wiser, missionaries with the Presbyterian Mission, conducted research on Karimpur farming practices and social life beginning in the 1920s (see C. V. Wiser 1978; W. Wiser and C. V. Wiser 2001; W. Wiser 1958). I began doing fifteen months of research in Karimpur in late 1967 and have been there twice more for extended research trips and numerous times for short visits: I was most recently there in 1998 (see Wadley 1975, 1994, 2000). Funding came from the National Science Foundation, the American Institute of Indian Studies, the Smithsonian Foreign Currency Program, the National Endowment for the Humanities, and Syracuse University. Portions of this paper are taken from Wadley 1994 and

Wadley 2000. A Web site devoted to Karimpur with photos and a text by Charlotte Wiser is located at www.maxwell.syr.edu/southasiacenter/karimpur/.

2. India's village communities are facing enormous social change due to economic shifts and other factors related to globalization. The extent to which the village is still a "little community" varies considerably, but in most places is surely less than even two decades ago. "Tradition" is also a term that implies a lack of change over long periods of time: I do not use it in that sense here, for change is a fact of life in India as elsewhere. But there is a sense of a confluence of factors that before the past two decades was more stable than what exists now.

3. Two asterisks surrounding a term indicate that the speaker used the English word in his/her Hindi sentence.

4. See Wadley and Derr (1993) for a fuller explication of this argument.

2

Allah Gives Both Boys and Girls

Patricia Jeffery and Roger Jeffery

Since 1982, we have been doing research in rural Bijnor district (western Uttar Pradesh), particularly in two villages, Jhakri (a Muslim village) and Dharmnagri (a Hindu and Scheduled Caste[1] village). Throughout our research, we have focused on various aspects of gender politics, especially at the household level.[2] After a year-long field trip in 1990–91, we began thinking about how to portray aspects of domestic life through brief narratives and life stories. In view of the increasing salience of communal politics in India, we were especially concerned with highlighting the notable parallels between the everyday lives of Hindu and Muslim women in the area. This endeavor resulted in *Don't Marry Me to a Plowman!* from which the following story about Sabra is extracted.[3]

Sabra and her husband, Suleiman, were Muslims living in Jhakri, and they became key informants during our research on childbearing in 1982–83 and again in 1985. When we first met her in early 1982, Sabra was about thirty years old and her oldest child was a girl of about eight. Suleiman's father, Bashir, was one of three brothers who had been among the most wealthy farmers in Jhakri. After Bashir's second marriage, however, Suleiman and his older brother, Razaq, had watched helplessly while their father sold land to pay his debts, and their youthful stepmother continued to bear sons who would be entitled to share what might remain of Bashir's land.

Being the son of a wealthy farmer was no guarantee of economic security, and Suleiman and Razaq were compelled to seek other sources of income. For Suleiman and Sabra, though, the issue of security in old age also loomed large because they had no sons to support them when they were old and infirm. Not only that, but the line of daughters born in the quest for a son created worries about arranging their marriages and providing them with dowries. By the time we returned in 1990, however, the significance of these

An earlier version of this essay appeared in *Don't Marry Me to a Plowman! Women's Everyday Lives in Rural North India,* by Patricia Jeffery and Roger Jeffery. Copyright © 1996 by Westview Press. Reprinted by permission of Westview Press, a member of Perseus Books, L.L.C.

issues had altered in ways that we had not at all expected, for Sabra had been widowed a couple of years earlier.[4]

*   *   *

When we first went to Bijnor in early 1982, people could vividly remember the political Emergency of 1975–77, especially its high-profile coercive population control program. In Jhakri, many people initially suspected that we were somehow associated with the government, and that we had come to pressure them into being sterilized. From the start, though, Sabra had given us a friendly welcome. She would often come through the fields from Jhakri to the Dharmnagri dispensary, where we were living. There was frequently some reason for seeing the doctor. And when she had finished, she would generally take a few minutes to chat with us. Sometimes, too, we would talk to her while she worked at home.

On the first sunny day we had had for a while during the 1982 monsoon, Sabra wanted all the clothes to be dried before nightfall, so she carried on pounding her laundry as she chatted.

"You haven't been in Jhakri for a while," she complained, though with a smile.

"We've been going to other villages and getting women to fill out forms for us. And do you know, the people there haven't been as frightened as the people in Jhakri!"

"I've filled out one of your forms without worrying about it. But I can't say why other people in Jhakri are afraid," she replied.

Indeed, not only did she willingly respond to our requests for information but she was more tenaciously curious about life in Britain than many of the other people we met. One time, Sabra wanted to hear about marriage ceremonies in Britain. Before Patricia could get a word in, our research assistant, Swaleha Begum, said that weddings in Britain were very simple and that the bride and groom simply exchanged rings. Sabra's response was instant:

> That sounds like a good custom. For us a girl seems burdensome. Her parents have to give her a dowry with jewelry, utensils, and so on. They have to give several pounds of silver and gold. And when the girl goes to her in-laws' house, her parents have to fill a whole trunk with clothes. It's a dreadful thing how much has to be given to get a girl married. Nowadays, people want to arrange their son's marriage only into a house from which they'll get a splendid dowry. Meanwhile, who knows how a girl's people will be able to marry her? They just have to get the dowry and jewelry ready. There ought to be a law that dowry should neither be given nor taken.[5]

Another day when Sabra was visiting us at the dispensary, the ANM (auxiliary nurse-midwife) came to confirm that we would take Bhagirthi to the hospital in Bijnor in our jeep.[6] Bhagirthi had been married into a rich-peasant Rajput Hindu household in Dharmnagri. In 1979, she had had a stillbirth because she was given three labor-accelerating injections by the dispensary pharmacist. She was now about to give birth again, and the ANM had told her that the baby's head was large. The ANM did not want to be held responsible for any further calamity, and Bhagirthi was anxious enough to want a checkup in Bijnor. Sabra asked who we were talking about. The ANM retorted:

> Whoever it is, I don't want to be blamed for any problems. Nor do I want people to think I get women dragged off to hospital to be sterilized by compulsion. Have I ever told you to be sterilized, you with your four girls? And haven't I had you treated for TB [pulmonary tuberculosis] without any pressure for sterilization? And aren't you all right now? And didn't I get treatment for Asghari for TB so that she'd become pregnant? And didn't I help Dilshad's sister Gulistan when she nearly died in childbirth?

Sabra nodded rather sheepishly. Then the ANM asked Patricia to make sure that Bhagirthi had clean cloths prepared for her baby. She turned to Sabra again: "Do you know, when I went [to Jhakri] to help with Zubeida's delivery, there wasn't even a piece of cloth the size of a pocket handkerchief clean enough to wipe the baby off."

Sabra again assented, and the ANM departed, leaving Patricia and Sabra exchanging rather bemused grins as she went. Yet Sabra was a good deal more prepared to seek the ANM's services than many others in Jhakri. She had indeed obtained considerable relief from TB, though it was not completely cleared up.

Some time later, Sabra again came to the dispensary, this time to obtain some medication for her daughter, whose head was covered in boils. As we chatted, we were once more joined by the ANM, who began asking about various pregnant women in Jhakri. She then launched into complaints: "Jhakri women are so unwilling to have prenatal tetanus injections. I give the injections free before the birth. That's much better than having to pay for them afterward. I give freely what comes here free from the government. But I don't give anything from my own pocket. People would become suspicious. But people don't listen to me."

"That's because people are afraid of you," said Sabra, alluding to local people's belief that the ANM would pressure them to be sterilized.

The ANM pursed her lips. She had no answer to that. As she started to leave, Sabra began asking about tetanus injections. Sabra said that she was in the fourth month of pregnancy. Some months later, it was Fatima from Jhakri who told us about Sabra's delivery in early 1983: "She's had another girl, poor thing. That's the fifth."

* * *

When we talked to Sabra about her childbearing career, it became very clear why she was so vocal about the problems parents faced in providing dowries for their daughters. Sabra was married to Suleiman in about 1969 when she was seventeen or eighteen, she reckoned. Her first pregnancy had ended in a miscarriage. Sabra thought she must have been three or four months pregnant, though she was not sure. She had missed three periods.

> But I was young and I didn't know what that meant. I didn't know why pe-
> riods stopped coming. Nor did I ask anyone. I'd been spreading wheat out
> on the roof to dry in the sun with my sister-in-law [Razaq's wife]. But in the
> afternoon, clouds began to appear and we collected the wheat into sacks in
> case it rained. Then we put the sacks in the grain store in the house. That
> night I was tired and slept heavily. In the morning, I had stomach pains and
> bleeding began. I told my sister-in-law that I hadn't had a period for three
> months and now suddenly one had begun. But she said that I must be preg-
> nant and she called the *dai* [traditional birth attendant] who was living in
> Jhakri then. The dai said that the bleeding had started because I'd been lift-
> ing heavy weights. She gave me some pills and told me to eat pulses without
> chili pepper or spices. But even so, I still had pains and the blood continued
> to flow. In the evening the baby itself came out. It was just a ball the size of
> my fist. We called the dai again. She said it was hard to stop that happening,
> as I'd been lifting heavy things, so she gave me some medicine to clean me
> out properly. The dai told my husband the names of the things he had to
> bring from the bazaar and she ground them and gave them to me to drink.[7]

We asked what had happened in the next pregnancy, but true to form, Sa-bra reprimanded us for not going on to ask her what food she had eaten after the miscarriage or what she had paid the dai. We obediently noted down the details and then asked what had happened in her other pregnancies. "Well, after that baby fell, I had a girl without any trouble," she told us. "But the next time, because I had so little sense, I caused an abortion at five months."

We were astonished at her willingness to mention such a sensitive sub-ject and hardly dared to press her for more details. But after a few moments, we asked—somewhat diffidently—if she would tell us about it. Sabra told us what had happened with hardly any further prompting:

> You see, it was partly that I was lacking in sense, partly that my mother-in-
> law and my husband's sisters didn't explain things to me. Five months had
> been completed and sometimes I had spotting like at the end of a period,
> when just a small amount of blood comes out. At that time I was fighting
> with my sister-in-law [Razaq's wife]—we weren't speaking to one another.
> So I talked to a neighbor about the spotting, and she said the baby certainly
> wouldn't stay in place, it would miscarry. So having listened to that woman,
> I went to a doctor and told him that I wanted an abortion.

What doctor had agreed to do such a late abortion, when surely she could have died? Did the doctor not even ask why she wanted an abortion? Did he not suggest that Sabra bring her husband with her?

> No, he didn't ask me anything. He simply gave me the medicines—just tablets, nothing else. And I took them to my mother's house. My husband didn't know anything about it. You see, a man wouldn't like the idea of an abortion. And also, I was very young at the time, and I just panicked. Now I have five children, and I could cope with another baby, but I didn't think I could then. So I was afraid of my husband, and I took the pills to my mother's house. It was there that I ate them. I didn't tell anyone there first. I just ate them, and the baby was cleaned out. No one was with me at the time. I got pains in my belly, and so I went outside to crap. It was then that the baby fell, and I became unconscious. Sometime later my mother found me, and she carried me inside.

The baby was a boy. Sabra's mother wrapped him up in cloth and buried him. Sabra herself became very weak. Her mother was furious with the doctor and said he should not have done such a dangerous thing. For as long as Sabra's husband was still alive, she told him, he was not to do another abortion for Sabra or he would have to face the consequences.

> And out of fear of my husband, I stayed with my parents for a week afterward. But someone had told him about it before I got back to Jhakri. He was very angry. When I got back from my mother's house, he asked me why I was lying down. He said, "Go outside and do your work!" I managed to walk slowly out into the courtyard. But I couldn't work or even sit. So I went back inside. He said some more angry things, and he swore at me. But then he became silent. Having an abortion at five months is dangerous. It's also a sin. It's wrong to kill something with life in it. But I was young, and didn't know any better. Now I'm able to think. Now I'm afraid. I worry about what will happen after I die.[8]

After that, Sabra gave birth only to girls. And yet, when we asked her after the fifth girl was born if she had ever taken medicines to procure a son, she was adamant: "I've never taken any medicine like that. If Allah wants to give me a boy, He'll do so without any medicine. Allah gives both boys and girls, so what's the point of taking any medicine?"[9]

She had not been altogether happy that she had become pregnant again, however, though she had felt she should do nothing about it: "I caused an abortion once and was very troubled after that. And now my health is not what it was then. Anyway, I'm afraid of Allah. Previously, I didn't understand so much." On balance, even though she had no son, she did not want any more children. It would be hard enough to bring up the five girls she now had. "My health is bad. We don't have enough to eat because we don't have enough land from which to obtain grain. These children are too many.

It's hard to feed the children and ourselves. Five children are a lot." Not surprisingly, she and Suleiman did not organize any celebrations in 1983 to mark this latest arrival.

* * *

Sabra's situation in Jhakri was in marked contrast to that into which she had been born. Her parents and three brothers lived in nearby Badshahpur, where her brothers shared the operation of a farm of over eighteen acres. There was, as Sabra put it, no need for them to seek jobs elsewhere, as the farming kept them fully occupied.

> My father arranged my marriage. My mother also agreed to it, but it was my father who'd seen the boy. I must have been eighteen or so at the time. There were other offers of marriage for me—I can't remember how many—but my father liked only this one. The go-between was a Julaha [weaver] from Chandpuri.[10] He used to go to Jhakri and Badshahpur selling cloth, and he told my father that if he wanted to get me married, he'd show him a boy in Jhakri. The Julaha told my father-in-law about me, and then an offer of marriage was sent to my father. Parents don't ask the girl anything about her marriage. And out of embarrassment the girl doesn't say anything. The parents alone make the decision.

At the time, Suleiman's father, Bashir, operated about thirty acres jointly with his two brothers. He had two adult sons, of whom Suleiman was the younger. Sabra's parents gave her a dowry consistent (as Sabra put it) "with their own standing and the expectations of the time": some fifty-five pounds of brass and copper utensils, eleven pieces of jewelry (silver and gold), thirteen suit lengths of cloth for herself and eighteen for the people of her in-laws' connection. There was also a cycle and watch for Suleiman and the customary bed and stool. Sabra's in-laws had presented her with twelve pieces of jewelry and fourteen suits. Further items of clothing and foodstuffs came from her parents when Sabra went to Jhakri for the second time after the marriage. A year later, her parents sent a buffalo. The clothing and foodstuffs were rapidly used up, as was to be expected. But Sabra was soon forced to succumb to her father-in-law's financial demands.

> There were utensils in my dowry, but I can't remember how many separate items. You see, my father-in-law sold the lot. He also sold two pieces of the jewelry that my parents had presented to me. That was before I'd been married for even a year. My father told him that it had not been his right to sell the things. My father asked him to say where he'd sold the things so that he could get them back. But my father-in-law just asked my father to say how much everything had cost and he'd repay the sum. He still hasn't done so. I even told my mother-in-law that I'd give some other jewelry to them if they'd return the utensils from my parents' house. But they didn't. Then a little later, my father-in-law forcibly took the jewelry that he himself had pre-

sented me—apart from two pieces that I hid. At that time, we were still living jointly, and one of the bullocks died. So he [her father-in-law] sold my things and bought another bullock and made all the arrangements to cultivate the crops. And even those two pieces of jewelry that I managed to hide didn't remain with me. My husband's brother needed money one time and he asked for them, and I've never had them back. And the jewelry from my parents' house got broken, so I sent it to the goldsmith for repair; but he disappeared with it all. So nothing has remained with me.

Sabra's father-in-law's propensity to cheat his relatives and cause them financial worries was widely commented upon in Jhakri, and several people told us about the bad blood it had caused in her husband Suleiman's wider family. It also seems that Suleiman and his brother, Razaq, were hardly paragons themselves. They had reputedly been involved in several thefts in the village. One man alleged that this had prompted Bashir to oust them from his house and refuse them access to most of his land and its produce. Suleiman and Razaq received just one acre between them. A different—though not wholly incompatible—account was given by Sabra. Just before Sabra was married, Bashir had made a second marriage to a woman much younger than himself. Sabra believed that Suleiman's exclusion from his rightful due had been instigated by his stepmother, who wanted to preserve the land for her own children:

> We were all joint with my parents-in-law until after my first daughter was born. But then my mother-in-law made us separate. That was about three and a half years after my marriage. You see, my mother-in-law is a stepmother-in-law. She'd been fighting with me from the day I was married. She didn't want to have her daughters-in-law with her. She began saying that even more often around the time my husband's two sisters were being married. And then my father-in-law joined in all the squabbling, and he made us separate.

This had had several consequences. For one thing, Sabra was deprived of help that she might otherwise have expected, particularly after childbirth:

> My mother-in-law gave me no help with my first baby, and that was when we were still living jointly! She hasn't helped me with any of my other children either. And I can't call my husband's married sisters, since my mother-in-law gets angry that they're helping me. It's a father's job to call his daughters, but my father-in-law rarely calls the older one and he never calls the younger one. His wife doesn't want them to come. And I have nothing to give them, so how could I call them myself?

Sabra had found this particularly trying before and after the birth of her fifth daughter. For most of the pregnancy, Sabra was severely incapacitated with a fever and chest pains (almost certainly TB), yet she was compelled to work right up to the end: "Women should stop lifting heavy loads or making dung cakes, but I had no respite at all. The girl was born at night and I'd worked right into the evening. If I'd had someone to help me, I'd have stopped working, for I wanted to lie down and rest."

Such little help as Sabra had after delivery came from Razaq's daughter and from her own oldest daughter, then eight years old. Suleiman's sister happened to be in Jhakri but could help for only a day in the face of her stepmother's ire.

Perhaps more serious than this, however, were the implications of being cut off with hardly any land. For some time after her fifth daughter's birth, Sabra ran a fever and had pains throughout her body, especially in the pelvic region. After a couple of weeks of treatment from a private doctor in Bijnor—costing Rs 120—Sabra felt somewhat better. But she still had the sensation of "ants walking all over the body." Over the next two months, the medical expenses mounted to Rs 1,500, and Suleiman had to borrow money to pay the bills. "My medical treatment is consuming money that should be spent on food. Sometimes we've had to stop the treatment because we were short of money. But then we get medicines when the pain gets too bad again."

Suleiman's brother, Razaq, had not been so short of resources. His mother-in-law in nearby Chandpuri told us she had not wanted her daughter married to Razaq, but her husband had given his word and would not break his promise. After the marriage, her husband frequently gave Razaq financial help for the sake of their daughter. This had enabled Razaq to save some money, and he had bought about two-thirds of an acre of land on his own account before his father cut him off. Razaq's wife died in 1980—according to her mother, during premature labor after Razaq had beaten her severely. Even after this, Razaq's father-in-law continued to provide for his grandchildren's schooling and other expenses.

Suleiman, however, had not had such comprehensive support from his in-laws. Sabra's parents continued to send her the customary gifts of clothing and foodstuffs on festivals and after she gave birth, but they did not send substantial cash gifts. According to Sabra, "Our girls see children in other compounds with toys, but we can't afford to buy things like that. We can afford to eat, but not much more. My father-in-law hasn't given us our share of land, so my husband has to do laboring work."

Was Suleiman not able to rent land or take some land on a sharecropping basis? "He [Suleiman] doesn't have enough money to buy land at Rs 20,000 per acre," Sabra told us. "For one year, he rented nearly two acres from someone in Dharmnagri. That cost Rs 900 for the year. But then we didn't have enough money for the rent, so we'd sharecrop and get half the crop instead."

What was going to happen that year? Did people in their own compound not give out land to people who wanted to sharecrop?

We haven't been able to get any land that way this year. The people of our compound won't help anyone. They prefer to get work done by laborers if necessary. That way they can keep all the crop themselves. We used to have a buffalo that gave ten pints of milk a day. But the children got none of it to drink because we used to sell all the milk. With that income and anything my husband could earn from laboring sometimes, we could manage to buy our food. I had to breast-feed the girl older than this baby for longer than I wanted, as there was no other milk in the house to give her. But that buffalo died last year. So now we're very worried about money, as we used to rely greatly on the income from the milk. My three brothers and my father have nearly twenty acres. It's a matter of fate that there's nothing for me in Jhakri.

Suleiman's rights to his father's land and Sabra's control over her dowry had been seriously infringed, with the result that Sabra had grave worries about the future: "Whatever a girl's parents give and whatever clothes and jewelry come to a daughter-in-law from her in-laws belong to her alone. But my in-laws left me with no jewelry and they even sold the utensils that my parents had given. Now I have five daughters, and I'm very worried. If I even had utensils and jewelry, they'd be of use to me. But my parents-in-law left us with nothing. We're just like rats in an unused water pot."

* * *

Suleiman and Razaq, however, were not content with such a position, and they decided to go into business together. They began buying tree plantations—mostly eucalyptus, a cash crop introduced a few years earlier. Then they would fell the trees, sell the wood, pay the debts incurred in buying the plantation, and use the profit to meet their families' needs. Slowly, the business began to flourish: "Whatever profit they earned from the business, the two brothers put to some other use," Sabra explained in 1985. "They saved some money and bought some land. They bought nearly two acres from their own income. We get grain from it; but we also have to buy grain, since we can't be fully fed from the grain that comes from our own land."

By the mid-1980s, things seemed to be promising. Sabra was not so constantly short of money, though they were still living in a single room in the corner of her father-in-law's courtyard. But the children were still a worry. The girl born in 1983 had died, but another one had come to take her place. And there was still no son. As Suleiman put it:

I don't want any more girls—we already have more than enough. I'd like a little bit of a boy. But it's not good to have too many. Two boys are enough; otherwise they'd fight over their shares of land. I can't say that large numbers of children are necessary. In any case, there's a big difference between boys and girls. A man with twenty acres might like a lot of children, but a small person like me needs only two boys and a girl. Then I could give my girl in marriage, and my two boys would each bring in a bride. The boys would be able to help one another, but the land wouldn't be split up too much. God has chosen to give me five girls, and there was one other who died. Parents love boys and girls the same—but a girl goes to her own house after she's married. Boys stay with their father. They do cultivation and animal husbandry, so their father can get some rest when he's old. Girls are fine, but the name of boys is greater. This is the reason: Boys make money for their father.

* * *

Every time we returned to Jhakri, new houses had sprung up. People were shifting from cramped quarters in the center of the village to new sites on the outskirts, where they were constructing kiln-brick houses with higher walls than the older-style houses and with flat roofs instead of thatch. On our return in 1990, one such house was nearing completion. It consisted of a line of three sizable rooms set back from the pathway that had earlier marked the edge of the village. It had yet to be plastered, and several of the windows did not have their wooden frames and shutters. The boundary wall had not been built, and one room was currently being used to house some livestock. The building turned out to be Sabra's.

Our immediate supposition that Sabra's life had changed for the better was dispelled as soon as we met her again. Suleiman had died in a road accident about two years earlier. "He was on his way to Bijnor on his Vikki [motorcycle]. He was hit by a minibus at the crossing with the road from Bijnor to the Ganges. The bus didn't stop. Later a police vehicle came past and they saw him. They took him to hospital but he died later. And now I have six girls and a boy. The boy was in my belly when my husband died. He was born three months after his father died."

Even without being widowed, Sabra would have had great problems in settling six daughters in marriage. Now, there was not enough land to feed the family, and Sabra herself could not cultivate it. Nor could she contemplate engaging in Suleiman's tree business. Without the goodwill and generosity of others, she and her children faced a bleak future.

Razaq had remarried shortly before Suleiman's death. Immediately after, he and his wife established a joint household with Sabra.

> My father-in-law never gave his two sons by his first marriage their proper share of the land. But they'd managed to buy land. They'd bought nearly three acres altogether. They used to work it separately. But since my husband's death, the land has been operated jointly, and the cooking hearth is also joint. We also had the Vikki mended, and we sold it. My brother-in-law has bought a new one. My brother-in-law has also taken over my husband's work in Bijnor, checking the men who fell trees.

Since then, Razaq had taken full responsibility for Sabra and her children. In order to lighten the task, his first wife's father had arranged and paid for the marriage of Razaq's daughter by his first marriage. Razaq's daughter explained what had happened one time when she was visiting Jhakri:

I've been married now for just over a year. My grandfather [mother's father] paid for my marriage. He married me from Jhakri and gave me a very good wedding. There were twenty suits for me and twenty for my in-laws. He gave all the things in the dowry. And the bed was a double one. When the wedding party was departing with me, my grandfather gave my husband Rs. 10,000 and told him to find himself a job. My husband is studying in tenth class [roughly equivalent to tenth grade] at the moment, but he's also searching for employment. After my uncle died, my father began caring for my uncle's children. There are six girls and a boy, so my father couldn't have paid for such a wedding as I had.

Meanwhile, Sabra's oldest daughter was now about seventeen. She had studied only the Holy Qur'an, for when she had suddenly reached puberty, Sabra had stopped sending her to the *madrasa*, the mosque school in nearby Begawala, where she might have learned some Urdu and Hindi. The girl herself commented that she had been unwilling to attend the madrasa since she was the only "big" girl going. She had remained at home for several years, helping with the family's work. But now she had reached the age to be married.

Razaq had taken the matter in hand. He viewed a boy in a nearby village and decided on the match. There was land in the boy's family, but the boy did not work on the land. He had studied to about fifth class, but he was also *Hafyz Qur'an* (able to recite the Holy Qur'an by memory) and he was teaching the children in his village. Given Sabra's daughter's education, it was a good match. The marriage was to take place in late spring 1991. Sabra, however, had no jewelry to present to her daughter. "A few years ago my younger sister died, but my father had already set aside jewelry for her marriage," Sabra told us. "My father gave all that to me because I had nothing left. I presented that jewelry to my husband's brother's new wife—but that too got stolen. When my husband's funeral procession was waiting at the cattle byre and everyone was there, there was a theft at our house and all the jewelry was stolen."

Fortunately, Razaq also took responsibility for all the details of the marriage arrangements, including the dowry. Sabra's brothers also played their part, for this was the first of Sabra's children to be married and it was incumbent on them to provide the *bhat*. Sabra received Rs 3,000, fourteen suits (two for the bride, one for the groom, and the rest for Sabra and her other children), and three pieces of jewelry for the bride—a gold nose stud and nose ring and a silver necklace.[11]

This was all a great relief to Sabra, who proudly displayed all the items to us on the wedding day while the wedding party from the boy's village was being received by the Jhakri men at Sabra's new house on the village outskirts. The bride and her female relatives were inside the village, waiting in one corner of the compound of Bashir, Sabra's father-in-law and the bride's grandfather. But when we asked if Bashir was making any contribution to the marriage expenses, Sabra denied it vehemently. "My mother-in-law," she told us, "made a curse that these children of mine would end up in a desolate place with no one to care for them. But did Allah forget them?"

"A person who has killed off someone else's money and land cannot live happily," commented Razaq's wife.

"Yes," said Sabra nodding, "just look how much land our father-in-law has sold. And still one or another person who has lent him money is standing up and demanding his money back. Stealing someone's entitlement isn't right. He'll never be able to live properly. He didn't even give two acres to us out of the ten or twelve acres he used to have."

* * *

Bashir's behavior caused no surprise in Jhakri. The role taken on by Razaq, however, was a source of wonder in the village. One young man reminded us of the thefts that Suleiman and Razaq had perpetrated years back and commented that Razaq was transformed. Maybe the deaths of his first wife and his brother had chastened him; maybe he was afraid of what punishment Allah might bring him next. One woman reported that Razaq had not let his niece sit on the ground during the seclusion before her marriage but had insisted that she sit on a bed. Another woman told us that Razaq had responded to his niece's tearfulness by saying that he would make good directly any shortages she felt there were in the dowry. But she also added a note of caution: "Sabra has six girls, and her brother-in-law has arranged the marriage for one of them. There are still five others. I don't know if he'll do all the other weddings. Uncles like that are rare. But his second wife is from the city, and she's very good."

The future, then, was uncertain for Sabra and her children: "The younger girls are still studying. I want them to study reading books as well as the Holy Qur'an. But then that'll be enough. What, are they to be made to go out for employment? If there were a school or madrasa in Jhakri, I might let them study more. But no one in Jhakri teaches children. I'd like them to be married into farming families so that they can eat from their own land. But beyond that, it's a question of their destiny what sort of husband they get."

As for the boy, Sabra would also like to see him educated: "There's so little land. What can come from it? If he's willing to study, I'll send him to the madrasa in Begawala to become Hafyz Qur'an. Then I'll send him to the government school in Dharmnagri. If he wants to continue further, I'll send him to Bijnor. If he studies, he could get an educated wife, somewhat schooled, too. I want him to study and then get service. But beyond education, Allah is the master."

ACKNOWLEDGMENTS

The research on which this account is based was funded by the Economic and Social Research Council (U.K.), the Hayter Fund at the University of Edinburgh, and by the Overseas Development Administration (U.K.). We are grateful to our research assistants: the late Radha Rani Sharma, Swaleha Begum, Swatantra Tyagi, Chhaya Sharma, and Zarin Ahmed. This research would not have been possible without the warm welcome and willing involvement of the villagers of Dharmnagri and Jhakri, and we are well aware of the debt we owe them.

NOTES

1. Scheduled Castes are castes listed in a schedule of the Indian Constitution as previously having been "untouchable" and therefore in need of protection and positive discrimination.

2. See P. Jeffery, R. Jeffery, and A. Lyon (1989); R. Jeffery and P. Jeffery (1997).

3. See P. Jeffery and R. Jeffery (1996a), in which Sabra's story is chapter 16. All personal names here are the pseudonyms used in our other publications on rural Bijnor.

4. For more discussion of widowhood in India, see Chen (1998) and (2000); Chen and Drèze (1992); Chen and Drèze (1995a) and (1995b); Chowdhry (1994: 74–120, 356–77); P. Jeffery and R. Jeffery (1996a), especially chapters 14 and 15; Kolenda (1987a) and (1987b: 288–354). Vatuk (1990) and (1995) discusses widows' fears of dependency on their sons, while Wadley (1995b) presents an account of a woman who overcame some of the difficulties of widowhood; see also Wadley (1994: 25–29, 154–62) and (1995a).

5. There are, in fact, several pieces of legislation relating to the curtailment of dowry, but they have been ineffective in combating the rise in dowry in north India.

6. ANMs had an eighteen-month training, and were employed by the government and posted at dispensaries and clinics. They were primarily responsible for maternal and child health, including prenatal and postnatal care, immunizations for children and pregnant women, and family planning.

7. See P. Jeffery, R. Jeffery, and A. Lyon (1987) and R. Jeffery and P. Jeffery (1993) for further discussion of the dai.

8. In local understandings of conception and pregnancy, the life or spirit enters the baby only at the end of three months, at which point its sex is also fixed. Only then do women talk unequivocally about "pregnancy" rather than having "periods in arrears." The terms "abortion" or "medical termination of pregnancy" cover actions that are distinguished by women in rural Bijnor: an abortion at five months is considered problematic (and sinful) in a way that one at two months is not. See P. Jeffery, R. Jeffery, and A. Lyon (1989: 74–77) and P. Jeffery and R. Jeffery (1996b).

9. Women may take so-called *seh palat* medicines at the end of the second or third month of pregnancy to ensure that the baby's sex becomes fixed as male. Many of our informants were skeptical about the efficacy or appropriateness of seh pal-at medicines, but their existence (and the lack of comparable medicines to obtain

daughters) reflects the importance of having sons. See P. Jeffery, R. Jeffery, and A. Lyon (1989: 191–193) and R. Jeffery, P. Jeffery, and A. Lyon (1984: 1210).

10. Many castes were associated with occupations. Julahas were generally associated with weaving, although they did not necessarily earn all their income that way. Chandpuri was a mixed Hindu-Muslim village near Dharmnagri and Jhakri, and many of the Julaha homes had working looms.

11. The bhat should be given by a woman's brothers at the first marriage of one of her children. It is one of many continuing obligations that men have to their out-married daughters and sisters.

3

"Out Here in Kathmandu": Youth and the Contradictions of Modernity in Urban Nepal

Mark Liechty

Kathmandu's Thamel tourist district is a place where imaginations meet. Every year hundreds of thousands of people from around the world pass through Thamel on visits to Kathmandu and Nepal's "adventure tourism" hinterlands, each carrying with them images of Nepal—mediated memories of an "exotic" and "mysterious" place they have never known outside magazines, books, films, and travelers' tales. At the same time Nepalis—often young people on the margins of society—come to Thamel with their own mediated images of foreignness. For them the bustling, cosmopolitan streets of Thamel provide the window through which to slip, even if only momentarily, into the imagined pleasures of modernity that they know through magazines, books, films, and travelers' tales. In Thamel Nepalis and foreigners interact, playing roles (wittingly or otherwise) in each other's imaginings of "other" places.

Although Thamel is often so crowded with young tourists that Nepalis sometimes refer to it as *"kuire* country"—using a derogatory term for fair-skinned foreigners—those *Nepalis* one sees in Thamel are mostly young men, the majority of them workers from rural districts around Kathmandu who put in long hours for low wages as cooks, waiters, and dishwashers in the dozens of Thamel tourist cafes and restaurants. But those young men one sees "hanging out" on the streets and in certain cafes and bars are often representatives of two categories: tourist hustlers (who are often drug users) and "*punks*"[1]—middle-class young men who cultivate a tough but suave and fashionable persona. Few tourists are aware of Thamel's unsavory local reputation for drugs, danger, and assorted illicit activities. For many Kathmandu young people, to frequent Thamel is to claim a vaguely sinister tough-guy reputation associated with drug use and/or violence. Most of the city's middle- and upper-middle-class young people congregate in other parts of town; to be in Thamel one should be tough and ready to prove it.

DOWN AND "OUT HERE" IN KATHMANDU:
DRUGS AND DREAMS FROM THE BOTTOM

Although a generation ago drugs were an important part of Kathmandu's tourist allure, by the 1990s drug use among tourists was not that common. One Thamel dealer in his thirties remembered "better times" but noted that now maybe only two or three out of a hundred tourists showed any interest in his whispered offers of "hash, real cheap." Ironically Kathmandu's drug market is now mostly propelled by local demand, and the substances of choice are often "harder" drugs like heroin and various commercially produced (and unregulated) pharmaceuticals.

Thamel's reputation for drugs is only indirectly related to tourism; tourists help finance local users. White heroin from Thailand and Burma is too expensive for Kathmandu users; the brown or unrefined heroin from India and Afghanistan makes up most of the local market. In the early 1990s a gram of "*brown sugar*'" cost 400 Nepali rupees (compared to Rs 1,200/gram for white).[2] At this rate, an "average" habit of one-half grams per day required a monthly cash outlay of at least 6,000 rupees, close to double the monthly salary of most civil servants. With the prospects for getting *any* job, let alone a high-paying one, abysmally low for even privileged young people, it is not surprising that most addicts eventually ended up pursuing tourists on the streets of Thamel. Taking profits on hashish or pot, changing hard currency on the black market, or acting as a tour guide, in Thamel a skilled hustler can make enough for a daily fix in a matter of hours.

Ramesh was one such person. Although I had encountered Ramesh several times in previous years, when I met him on a Thamel street one chilly spring morning in 1991 his gaunt and tired appearance seemed to confirm reports that he had relapsed into a heroin habit. As we walked together through Thamel in the months that followed, Ramesh threw light on a dimension of reality around us which was completely new to me. In Ramesh's company places I knew well would suddenly evaporate as glimpses of other (and others') places came briefly into view. Sitting together in a Thamel garden cafe that I had frequented for years, Ramesh opened my eyes to a parallel reality: drug transactions, police surveillance, schoolboys drinking codeine cough syrup, a junkie tottering out of the bathroom, his face flushed from retching, unable to keep down any food. Here was a kind of violence—usually quiet and self-destructive—that, once seen, shattered the tranquil image that I and other foreigners imposed on that place: our imaginations rendered this violence invisible and inaudible.

Ramesh introduced me to friends and fellow street hustlers. For these young men supporting addictions meant maintaining the precarious balance between presenting a "clean" and nonthreatening image to potential tourist clients, and successfully procuring a daily fix. Losing one's composure meant losing customers, which meant missing a fix and further damaging one's ability to make money. One victim of this truly vicious cycle was Tamding, a Tibetan refugee and former monk with a severe heroin addiction. When I met him, Tamding was in his late twenties and sleeping on the streets: thin, filthy, and with a full-gram-a-day heroin habit, he was close to death. Reduced to begging and unable to support his habit, he used what money he had on incredible "pharma-cocktails"—seemingly deadly combinations of powerful sedatives, synthetic opiates, and psychiatric drugs that would temporarily induce sleep and mask the effects of heroin withdrawal. In tears, Tamding described how a few months earlier his younger brother had died after eating refuse out of a Thamel tourist restaurant dumpster. It was clear that Tamding himself would not survive the next intestinal parasite he encountered.

Ramesh was in better shape, though his personal background would not have suggested his current condition. Ramesh's parents had moved to Kathmandu from an eastern hill district when he was in his early teens. He had attended a respected English-medium high school in the valley and learned to read and speak English. He had first tried heroin as a high school student, but over the course of a few years in which his mother died and his father married a woman with several sons, Ramesh developed a habit that grew out of control. Through a combination of mistrust between him and family members, a slow-burning resentment over his father's remarriage, and an increasingly disruptive heroin addiction, Ramesh began to spend more and more time living with friends and, eventually, on the streets. The previous year, after he went through a detoxification program, his good English had landed him a coveted (though typically low-paying) sales job in a retail shop catering to tourists. He swore to me that he had stayed clean and would still be working had not someone told the manager that he was a former junkie. (Others claimed that he had been caught trying to sell drugs to tourists.) By the early 1990s Ramesh had been in and out of drug rehabilitation seven times and had little more than the clothes on his back and the few rupees in his pocket. He lived by his wits day to day, hustling tourists, selling drugs, taking profits on petty commodity transactions, and running a variety of scams like sewing foreign labels into locally produced garments.

Being from a middle-class family, the product of an English-medium school, and a heavy consumer of imported Hindi and English mass media, from videos to detective novels, Ramesh had much in common with his peers. As with many others, consuming foreign media had made Ramesh painfully aware of the limitations of his life as a Nepali, a life that he constantly compared to lives lived in distant power centers. Ramesh constantly evaluated his Nepaliness through his media awareness of life in the West and Far East even though he himself had never traveled farther than North India. In my presence, he repeatedly brought up images of "America" compared to which he found his own life one of extreme deprivation.

R: Out here young people like me, we want a *fast* life, not this slow life.

M: What do you mean a *"fast"* life?

R: I mean like in the States where you can stay out all night until you drop. Here there's nothing, no [late-night] bars, and we can't even go anywhere to play video games.

When I asked how he knew about bars and video games, he explained that he had learned all about these things from movies and novels.

Indeed Ramesh was a special connoisseur of films, books, magazine articles—anything he could find—especially those having to do with New York City. He knew all the city's boroughs and landmarks, but he was especially intrigued by "the Bronx," a place he brought up again and again in our conversations. From dozens of tough-guy movies and gangster novels, Ramesh had constructed a detailed image of a New York street culture full of drugs and gangs. He frequently compared Kathmandu's street life with that of New York, like when he explained how Kathmandu "gangs" take "tabs" (specific prescription drug tablets) before going to a fight, "just like in the Bronx." Ramesh could quote lines from Mafioso novels, and he frequently spoke of how one's face should never show feeling, a lesson he learned from *The Godfather*. Ramesh's ultimate goal was to move to "the States" and live in New York City. He often spoke in vague terms of a cousin living in Seattle who might help him get there.

Ironically, it seemed sometimes as though Ramesh already lived in New York. "The Bronx" in particular seemed to be a kind of shadow universe where his mind roamed while his body navigated the streets of Thamel. "The Bronx"—with its street-smarts and anti-heroic codes of valor—was often the standard of reality against which he measured his own existence. At times it seemed that Ramesh was only imagining his life in Kathmandu against the reality of "the Bronx," not vice versa. For Ramesh "the Bronx" seemed to offer a way of understanding his own life, a life that he hated, yet that he could link with a way of existence at the modern metropole. Ramesh's vision of "the Bronx" allowed him to identify his own existence as at least some version of "modernity," even if it lacked the all-night bars, video games, and a host of other modern accoutrements that he had never seen in more than two dimensions.

Like many other young adults I met in Kathmandu, when speaking in English Ramesh constantly referred to the place he had spent most of his life as "out here." "Out here in Kathmandu" prefaced so many of his comments that in the course of time the words barely registered in my mind. This persistent self-peripheralization is almost unimaginable outside the context of global media and a host of other marginalizing transnational cultural forces, including tourism and commodity imports. Mass media (as well as tourists and foreign goods) act like a lens which situates the local in an implicitly devalued and diminished "out here" place, while at the same time seeming to provide a window onto modern places that are distant in both time and space. But if the video screen is like a window, it is one with bars that keep viewers like Ramesh outside: "out here" looking in.

THAMEL TOUGH GUYS: FIGHTING BOREDOM

While Ramesh struggled with images of a seemingly foreign modernity on the streets of Thamel, other young Kathmandu men came to Thamel to live out fantasies that were much more localized. If part of Thamel's reputation for "toughness" and danger is tied to its drug culture, the area is also infamous for its gang activity and violence. Ramesh often starred in his own internal dramas, but other young men are tied into a variety of loosely organized, hierarchical factions or "*gangs*" which occasionally enact group dramas of toughness that may become violent. Though by no means the only spot in town that sees gang activity, Thamel is known for having more, and more serious, violence.

For Europeans and North Americans "gangs" and "idle youths" hanging out on street corners ("corner boys") are usually associated with lower- or working-class backgrounds, but in Nepal the poor do not have the luxury of becoming what are known in Nepali as *punks*. Ironically, in Kathmandu the "tough-guy," "street-fighter" persona is the privilege of a kind of "leisure class." They are members of a middle class that, while not wealthy by first-world standards, would rather have its educated young people unemployed than engaged in anything but white-collar labor. In an enormously glutted middle-class labor market, young people are more or less idle for years between high-school graduation and the beginning of any meaningful employment (Liechty 1995, 2003).

Leading lives of essentially forced inactivity and boredom, young people, especially young men, often experiment with fantasies of "action" with scripts loosely based on the media images that fill much of their day-to-day lives. Of the many "action" fantasies available, some are more active and potentially violent than others. Thamel is a popular hangout for a certain kind of middle-class action seeker willing to "*fight* khelnu"—literally "to play at fighting."[3] A Kathmandu journalist in his early thirties described a fight he had recently witnessed in Thamel:

> I saw those people and they weren't the types who have nothing, you know. They were like me, just a little younger, that's all. I didn't see anyone who didn't look like [their family owned] a house in Kathmandu. It's all these people who at least have a house and their parents are working—basically middle-class types.

Said another young man, only half sarcastically, "The poor kids have gangs in America then they make movies about them and it's the rich kids who watch them here!" In Kathmandu the areas that have the worst reputations for juvenile violence—where taxi drivers hesitate to go at night—are usually the middle-class neighborhoods in the suburbs, not the poverty-stricken areas in the old city.

In many respects the young men who hang out in Thamel are similar to the Japanese *bosozoku* described by Ikuya Sato (1991). Bosozoku are young middle-class men who live for the thrill of dressing up in tough-looking clothes and driving their modified cars and motorcycles at suicidal speeds (known as *"boso* driving") down the city streets of Japan. As with the young *punks* in Kathmandu, in certain times and places becoming an antisocial and dangerous bosozoku offers young people an expressive experience in what would otherwise be "extraordinarily boring and purposeless" lives (Sato 1991: 4). Yet whereas bosozoku culture revolves around modified vehicles and the potential dangers of hot-rodding, Kathmandu *punks* are much more likely to fixate on what one might call "modified bodies"—disciplined through regimens of martial arts and bodybuilding—and the potential dangers of fighting. Bosozoku idolize characters from films like *Mad Max* and fantasize about the "fierce-looking Kawasaki 1000 vehicles they use in the movie" (Sato 1991: 77), while Kathmandu tough guys are more likely to be avid kung-fu film consumers, and focus on the moves and bodies (of both heroes and villains) depicted in those movies.

More than just a recent media-generated fantasy, the "toughness" projected by these young men in Thamel has an important history in Nepal. From Gurkha soldiers to Sherpa mountaineers, many Nepalis literally make a living off the now global image of the fearless, robust, and tireless Himalayan hill man.[4] Indeed "Gurkha" and even "Sherpa" are now essentially professional titles, as often as they designate ethnic or regional identities. Although the image and rhetoric of the brave Gurkha soldier is more than simply a colonial fantasy, the fact that British colonizers identified several populations in west-central and eastern Nepal as among the subcontinent's innately warlike "martial tribes" is an important factor in both the historical construction and the continued salience of an essentialized image of the *bahadur* (brave and courageous) Nepali male. For centuries the British and Indian armies have recruited Nepali Gurkha fighters, and many parts of rural Nepal are dependent on this form of mercenary labor (Des Chene 1991).

It is perhaps no coincidence that among those young men in Thamel with the toughest reputations, many are from those very "martial tribes" that have traded in toughness for centuries (Gurung, Rai, etc.). Precisely where and how "toughness" as a colonial artifact articulates with new media-generated images such as the kung-fu hero is difficult to say. But perhaps most important is how a deterritorialized global media genre such as the kung-fu film becomes embedded in a highly idiosyncratic local history that is itself already inflected by centuries of transnational cultural processes.

In informal interviews conducted in a Thamel restaurant, two young men talked about (among other things) their tastes in films. The first—a twenty-year-old Gurung with long hair, fashionable clothes, and a muscular build—explained which kind of "*English*" films he liked most:

> G: I like certain kinds, like *Rambo*, *commando* films, and the *kung fu,* *karate* films, you know, Bruce Lee, Jackie Chan, and all that stuff.
> M: Why these kinds?
> G: Now, while I'm a youth, I like to be brave and active. This is what I like to do.
> M: How did you get into watching English films?
> G: My friends all watch only English films and at first I didn't really like them but after a while, I got into the habit and I could understand what was going on. At first I didn't like them. But now I like them a lot.

His friend, a few years younger but also well-dressed and extremely fit, also claimed English films as his favorites.

> M: For example, what kind?
> F: Let's see . . . Well, there's *kung fu.* I like Bruce Lee *so* much. If I feel *bored,* like if there is some really *boring* time,[5] I like to go watch a Bruce Lee film.
>
> If I do, *automatically* I begin to feel very energetic, very strong and eager. All these feelings start to rise up! I've probably seen six different Bruce Lee movies already. There was *Enter the Dragon,* *Way of the Dragon,* and others too.

For both of these young men film preference had to do with imagining themselves as particular kinds of youth, ones who are tough, active, brave, and eager.

Part of the tough-guy persona involves adopting a studied presentation. In addition to fashioned bodies and fashionable clothing, young *punks* in Thamel cultivated a kind of expressionless countenance (like Ramesh), slow, fluid body movements, and a variety of striking postures and actions. A tricky way of lighting a cigarette, smoking in a sensual and suave manner, a sophisticated demeanor, effortlessly performing intricate dance movements: in Thamel young Nepalis often surpassed first-world visitors in cosmopolitan sophistication.

In addition to the often-mediated fantasies of toughness, bravery, and violence, perhaps the ultimate fantasies pursued in Thamel are sexual, and in particular, fantasies of sexual relations between Nepali men and foreign women.[6] An essential part of any claim to distinction in the "play world" of the Thamel tough guys is the ability to attract foreign women (or at least a reputation for doing so). With its bars, music cafes, and hotels, Thamel is the prime location in Kathmandu for engaging in these transnational sexual fantasies. Even if many tales of sexual prowess are exaggerated, there is no doubt that out of the over one hundred thousand Euro-American women who visit Nepal each year, a few bring with them romantic fantasies of a kind that complement those of some young men in Thamel.[7] Compared with male fellow-travelers, young female tourists from Europe and North America seemed more interested in having a "local experience" that included friend-ships with Nepalis. Because the Nepali people they encounter are likely to be in Thamel, there are fairly frequent opportunities for young *punks* to meet foreign women. What for these women may seem like a pleasant local friendship may, for the young men involved, be very sexually charged. Even if there is no sexual contact, these relationships may be the stuff of erotic fantasies and boasting among friends.

One young man I met came close to epitomizing the Thamel sophisticate. When I met Pradip, the friend of a friend, he was only in his late twenties and already owned a restaurant/bar and a small lodge in a prime Thamel location. Having owned land in Thamel, Pradip's family was able to cash in on the tourist boom of the 1970s and '80s (Liechty 1996, 2003). Pradip had re-ceived a first-rate English education, had grown up around foreigners, could converse in several European languages, and was a refined and engaging conversationalist by any standards. His reputation for sexual conquest was probably based more on speculation than evidence, but on several occa-sions he spoke of his relationships with foreign women. Pradip identified one woman in particular as his "girlfriend"—an American from California, whom he had met several years earlier. She came to Nepal at least once a year, and they were in regular phone contact. Clearly they had a sincere relationship, but, Pradip confessed, deep down, he knew it could not work. He described how one evening on her most recent visit she had been out smoking hash with friends and did not return to the lodge until the early morning. When Pradip angrily demanded an explanation, she exclaimed, "You don't own me! I can do what I like." Furthermore, his girlfriend as-sumed that he would eventually move to the United States. "Why should I go to America?" Pradip asked.

> There I couldn't get a very good job but would just have to work all day for little money. Here I have plenty of money and I don't have to work! Here I have my bar and my lodge. They are both in profit. Why would I want any-thing different?

In the meantime Pradip introduced me to a young woman from the con-sular affairs office of the French Embassy whom he had been "dating for the past six months." It was clear that ultimately Pradip was not interested in marrying a Western woman, even though he greatly enjoyed such company. Pushing thirty, Pradip was thinking of "settling down" and had realized that while Western women—witty and unreserved—were good to have in a Thamel restaurant (and possibly in a hotel room), a Nepali woman—obedi-ent and demure—was good to have at home. For Pradip different kinds of imagined women belonged in different imagined places.

"STARS OF ACTION": THE POLITICS OF DESIRE

During the early 1990s Star Beer (produced in Nepal) staked its claim in the increasingly competitive Nepali national alcohol market with an interesting jingle that ran frequently on Radio Nepal. Even though almost all of Radio Nepal's programming is in Nepali, the Star Beer jingle was in English:

> It takes a star of action, to satisfy a man like you,
> Smooth reaction, to satisfy a man like you,
> Men like you who want to see, men like you who want to be,
> Stars of action with Star Beer.

It struck me as no coincidence that advertisers would wish to capitalize on the desire to "see" and "be" "stars of action." The ad seemed to capture, in caricature, the "smooth reaction" of the suave, Thamel tough-guy persona, and then play on the related longing for "action." "Men like you" not only "want to see" the media stars of imaginary action, but also "want to be" those "stars of action."

For the young Nepalis who navigated its streets, Thamel seemed to encapsulate the anxious yearning for "action" and "satisfaction" that the Star Beer advertisement sought to capitalize on. For young men such as Ramesh and Pradip, Thamel was a place with a distinctive ethos, a quasi-foreign place in which to *experiment with* and, for those "lucky" enough, to *indulge in* images and fantasies of foreignness and modernity. For Ramesh—the heroin addict who came to Thamel to hustle tourists and dream of life on the streets of New York—dreams of foreign places made Nepal a place to flee. For Pradip and other Thamel sophisticates who successfully enacted the ethos of the Thamel transnational "play world," Thamel was a place to escape from local dramas into the mediated fantasies of a foreign modernity. Thamel was a fantasy space where a global traffic in images of "traditional" Nepal and foreign "modernity" flowed through and past one another, perpetuating the ideological economy in which "Nepali modernity" remained not just a paradox, but an oxymoron.

In places like Thamel, first and third worlds ("modernity" and "tradition") implode into one another; both tourists and locals come to Thamel to find the "others" they imagine. Although brought together in Thamel by a now global economy of desire for "other" meaning—whether the tourists' nostalgia for the "exotic" periphery or the Nepali youths' desire for the "modern"—the distance between their imagined places (and the fact that only one group may actually indulge their fantasies *in* the others' space) not only reflects but reinforces the global contours of power and privilege that keep Nepali youth "out here in Kathmandu."

ACKNOWLEDGMENTS

I am grateful to the International Institute for Asian Studies (IIAS) of Leiden, the Netherlands, for a postdoctoral fellowship during which I wrote much of this essay. Parts of this essay were originally published in Liechty 1996.

NOTES

1. Words appearing between asterisks in quoted material designate use of English in colloquial Nepali.

2. In the early 1990s, 400 Nepali rupees was equal to roughly 10 U.S. dollars. In 1991 Nepal's average annual per capita income was only 180 U.S. dollars (Central Bureau of Statistics 1994: 260).

3. Unlike *kusti khelnu* (to wrestle), *muṛki hānnu* (to punch), or *jhagaṛā garnu* (to quarrel, or tussle), "*fight* *khelnu*" is a term/concept that entered local language and practice via films. "*Fight* *khelnu*" refers both to the surrealistic choreographed fight sequences in South Asian potboilers and East Asian kung-fu films and also to the dramatic role acting between individuals and *gangs* which occasionally escalates into serious physical violence, especially when weapons are involved.

4. Adams (1996) and Ortner (1999) are two important recent studies of the historical and cultural construction of Sherpa identity.

5. When used in spoken Nepali, various forms of the English word "bore" can have meanings slightly different from common usage in the West. In addition to tedium or monotony, in Nepali feeling "*bored*" can imply sadness, depression, and frustration. In fact, the two sets of feelings are not antithetical and seem to be common features of life for many middle-class youth in Kathmandu.

6. As I discuss in detail elsewhere, these sexual fantasies of "other women" are at least in part tied into the heavy consumption of Euro-American and East Asian pornography in Kathmandu (Liechty 1994 [chapter 14]; Liechty 2001).

7. Because Nepali women have far fewer opportunities to interact with foreign men, there seems to be very little sexual contact across this divide. Unlike Bangkok, Kathmandu is not a destination for Euro-American or East Asian male sex tourism, even though it has an active prostitution scene. According to my sources (social workers, medical personnel, journalists, hotel managers), the only foreigners that employ Kathmandu prostitutes are Indians (truckers, businessmen, tourists).

4

Rethinking Courtship, Marriage, and Divorce in an Indian Call Center

Cari Costanzo Kapur

Every night in India, while the rest of the country sleeps, tens of thousands of call center employees engage in "real-time" business transactions by computer and telephone with American and European customers half a world away. Many of the large-scale labor schemes that mark today's global economy offer unskilled, low-paying, gender-segregated daytime factory work.[1] Call centers, by contrast, employ educated, upwardly mobile men and women who work side by side throughout the night, earning about Rs 10,000 per month—the equivalent of approximately $250 U.S. dollars. Although this is double the salary that most other Indian industries pay college graduates, call centers have stirred controversy throughout India. First and foremost are concerns over women's safety. While both male and female employees are ferried to and from work via car services retained by call centers, the rape of a twenty-four-year-old woman in Bangalore by her driver has prompted public outrage. In response, some call centers have instituted new policies whereby male employees escort female colleagues home in a company car, making certain that a woman is never left alone in a vehicle with a driver. Still, in a society that frowns upon the presence of women in public spaces after dark, concerns regarding the safety of women traveling to and from night jobs continue (see also Seizer, this volume).

The mixed-gendered environment of call centers has also raised the issue of opposite-sex fraternizing on and off the job. In India, where socializing between the sexes before marriage is widely discouraged, single men and women who work shoulder to shoulder throughout the night have been reprimanded for "dating" during the day. Recently, young professionals in Delhi were detained by police for displaying affection in city parks, while others "bore the brunt of police harassment" for socializing in public with members of the opposite sex (Sengupta 2006). Another concern is the postponement of marriage, as well as rising divorce rates—lifestyle trends that strongly correlate with growing numbers of salaried female professionals. India boasts one of the lowest divorce rates in the world, estimated at about

1 percent, compared to approximately 50 percent in the United States (Parry 2001).[2] However, divorce rates in India's urban areas, where more women earn advanced degrees and work outside the home, are rising rapidly: approximately 7 percent of marriages in India's metropolitan cities now end in divorce (Giridharadas 2008).

In light of such social shifts and cultural concerns, my research investigates the ways in which call center employees in India—the majority of whom are college students or recent college graduates—negotiate their identities as members of a transnational labor circuit at a stage in life when both career-growth and personal transitions, such as decisions about marriage and family life, are paramount. In particular, I explore the ways in which new forms of globalized labor, gender ideologies, and class intersect in contemporary India to inform ideas about, and opportunities for, courtship, marriage, and divorce.[3] Conversations and observations about courtship and marriage suggest that while call centers carve out new spaces for opposite-sex socializing, dating may not necessarily translate into widespread resistance to traditional, arranged marriages among upwardly mobile professionals.

In order better to understand these issues, I conducted fieldwork in the summer of 2005 in the city of Hyderabad. The capital of Andhra Pradesh, Hyderabad is often referred to as a cultural meeting point between "North" and "South" India. Hyderabadis boast an eclectic social milieu that draws from Telugu culture, Hinduism, and Islam. Just as diverse as its population is a landscape on which one finds juxtaposed the spectacular sixteenth-century Charminar monument, sparkling air-conditioned skyscrapers, international retail chains, and mega malls which emerged in the wake of the information-technology (IT) boom of the 1990s. The ubiquity of IT and IT-enabled services, such as call centers and other BPO (business process outsourcing) firms, have given birth to the city's nickname of "Cyberabad," and to unprecedented challenges associated with such rapid growth. For example, in the last five years, Hyderabad has witnessed the addition of one million new cars to its already crowded roadways. American and multinational corporations such as Bank of America, Dell, GE Capital, and Microsoft, as well as Indian software giants such as Infosys, Wipro, and Tata Consultancy Services, employ not only young Hyderabadi professionals, but also thousands of upwardly mobile transplants from other parts of India searching for career opportunities in this teeming metropolis, with its population of more than six million. Fifteen years ago, less than one-third of India's gross domestic product came from its cities; today India's largest cities produce some 60 percent of the country's GDP (Srinivas 2001: xxi). Factors such as these make cities like Hyderabad exciting ethnographic sites for urban anthropologists.

I interviewed approximately thirty employees at a two-hundred-person call center serving Australian, British, and American clients.[4] Some interviews took place at the call center itself, others in neutral social spaces away from work, where neither supervisors nor family members would be privy to our conversations. I also engaged in participant observation at social events, in company break rooms, and at language training classes. I used a split headphone to listen in on outbound and inbound calls between Indian employees and their Western customers.[5] English is a prerequisite to working in a call center, so all conversations I listened to were in English. Likewise, the interviews I conducted with employees were in English. In social settings, workers often spoke a form of English peppered with Hindi, a hybrid conversation style sometimes called Hinglish. I promised confidentiality to all of my interlocutors; therefore the names in this article are pseudonyms.

I was both surprised and delighted with the ways in which my inquiries were met with great candor, which I attribute not only to the outgoing nature of most of the employees I interviewed, but also to the fact that, as an American, I was viewed as an outsider who could serve as a repository of romantic tales and personal entanglements without posing a threat to the moral reputations of the single men and women with whom I spoke. Several informants even suggested that certain scenarios which might be considered scandalous in their own communities were probably everyday affairs in my part of the world! Whether or not this is the case, one thing is clear—many informants acknowledged that I was not judging them by their own cultural standards, and they could therefore freely open up to me about their lives.

LAMENTING THE "LOVE MATCH"

Call centers offer new hybrid spaces for young, educated professionals that are conducive to both professional development and courtship possibilities. Unlike IT and software engineering jobs, which are staffed primarily by young men, the gender ratio favors women at most call centers. Women comprised some 60 percent of employees at the call center where I conducted research, creating a unique social environment where single professionals meet numerous peers of both genders at work—a fairly uncommon social landscape in India. As a result, some multinational call centers are reconfiguring the way they do business, demonstrating the dialectical nature of local and global processes. One supervisor told me that the large American-owned call center where he previously worked decided to replace its annual overnight employee retreat with a daytime luncheon after parents expressed alarm at the possibility that their daughters would be spending the night in hotels, with male colleagues just down the hall. Separate break rooms for male and female employees have been introduced at several call centers in Hyderabad to assuage family concerns about opposite-sex socializing. Vikram, a company manager, told me that while employees would soon have the option to "hang-out" in single-sex break rooms currently under construction, many would likely not choose to do so: "Some of what we do, we do for the parents. Young people have their own minds. They want to hang out together, get to know each other. Work is their one chance to do so. . . . But we don't like to advertise that fact, especially to parents."

Employees suggested that their parents' concerns had mainly to do with "Indian" standards of appropriate female behavior. Inappropriate behavior displayed by daughters, particularly socializing with men, goes against accepted gender norms and reflects poorly upon the daughter in question and her entire family. In India, a society known for its strict control over female sexuality, the honor of a family is directly tied to the honorable actions of its daughters (see also Das 1995; Gold and Gujar 2002; Mankekar 1999; Narayan 2004).

Socializing between the sexes has raised questions about the sustainability of arranged marriages in contemporary India. Ashima, Anand, and Shalini shared their thoughts with me on this issue. Ashima, a nineteen-year-old woman who had been working in a call center for eight months when we first met, opened up to me over a meal of idli and sambar at a restaurant in Hyderabad. While discussing the challenges of sartorial decisions for professional women, Ashima explained that "looking good" enabled her to feel more confident while speaking on the telephone. "And, of course, you never know who you might meet at work, so it's important always to look your best," she exclaimed with a grin. Ashima indicated that she was interested in a few boys at work. When I asked her how she felt about the introduction of single-sex break rooms, she said that she was looking forward to them: "My girlfriends and I are thrilled that we will have a place to gossip about the boys! Girls like to chat, about who has eyes for whom, and all that." Ashima continued, "There are things I love about my job. The paycheck, for one, and having a bit of freedom to meet friends, and boys. What I really don't like are the hours." Ashima explained that her body's natural rhythm had been compromised by the night hours of call center work. She lives at home and finds it difficult to sleep during daylight hours, even though she is exhausted at the end of her shift. While she continues to find new ways of adjusting to night work—practicing meditation at the encouragement of her mother, for example—she also feels she is missing out on fun with her family of nineteen, which includes her grandmother and her parents, as well as five siblings—four of whom have spouses—and six nieces and nephews. Currently, only Ashima's twenty-one-year-old sister lives at home with Ashima, her parents, and her grandmother. Her other siblings, along with their spouses and young children, often pop over for visits in the afternoon—a time when Ashima must force herself to sleep. Working night hours also means socializing with friends in the morning, before going to bed, which can sometimes be difficult. Still, on balance Ashima enjoys her job. She typically makes arrangements to go out for breakfast with friends at the end of a shift, although her parents believe that only girls are present on such outings:

My parents would not understand the idea of going out with a boy. And if anybody saw me out alone with a boy, it would be a big problem, so I date in a group. We [the girls] invite the boys we like to come out with us. We try to get the same shifts so that we can see each other at work and make plans there. We get each other's mobile numbers. It doesn't always work out, but really I would have no way of getting to know so many people if it wasn't for work. [Ashima pauses as her cell phone rings.] And for my mobile!

The youngest of six children, Ashima explained that her older siblings did not have mobile phones back in their "single days." If they received a call at home, there was always someone hovering over to listen in on the conversation. The combination of her job and cell phone affords Ashima unprecedented social opportunities. While Ashima plans to continue "dating" boys from work, she believes that in the end she will task her parents with the important job of finding her a marriage partner. "One thing is that I really don't know the families of the boys I work with. And we cannot just show up at each others' homes. In fact, some of the families don't even live here, as the boys have come just for the work. So in the end, I cannot know for sure who is truly a good match. It's such a big decision, really."

While Ashima wants to date boys, she repeatedly emphasized the importance of what she described as an "informal" courtship process—dating without the "stress" of marriage decisions. Several other employees echoed Ashima's sentiments, indicating that the social spaces they enjoy at work may actually prevent them from jumping into "impulsive" marriages. Such responses reflect shifting notions of marriage throughout South Asia. Whereas marriage was once widely thought of as an institution geared toward the reproduction of an extended or joint family, today transformations around ideas about love increasingly place the conjugal couple at the core of a marriage (Ahearn 2001; Dwyer 2000). However, this "democratization of intimacy," in which individual happiness often trumps ideas about the good of the family, may actually render marriage more precarious (Giddens 1992). Thus, when it comes down to finding a lifelong partner, many employees insist that they still want their parents to handle the monumental matter of marriage.

When I asked informants to characterize the difference between love matches and arranged marriages, many explained that the boundaries between the two have in some ways become quite blurred. Today, in a match "arranged" by parents—typically through family networking or the use of matrimonial advertising in newspapers—prospective brides and grooms meet in a supervised setting, affording them the opportunity to determine whether they have the "right chemistry" to move forward with marriage. Efforts to confirm "compatibility" and "chemistry"—terms used by several informants—reflect the centrality of both emotional and physical compatibility for conjugal couples today.

In a love match, on the other hand, the betrothed "find" one another, independent of their parents. Some informants described love matches as much more spontaneous, and even a bit risky, while arranged marriages were characterized as "heavily researched"; the scrutiny of an individual's personal and professional "resume" is central to an arranged marriage. Parents' efforts to arrange the marriages of their sons and daughters may take months, or even years, as either the potential bride or groom repeatedly rejects proposed matches, or requires multiple meetings with a "match" before agreeing to the nuptials. In other cases, "arranged" matches are solidified in a matter of days, as was the case for Anand, a twenty-eight-year-old call center manager. Anand sees his growing call center success as an important step towards fulfilling his traditional duties as a son and husband.

> It is my turn now to care for my parents. They are aging, and I am the only son. . . . Yes, I met many girls at work. But when it was time for me to marry last year, I told my parents, please pick someone whom you will get along well with because she will be here taking care of you at night while I am gone to work.

Anand explained that his aging parents are in need of medical care and nurturing at home, and while his income allows him to pay for their medical needs, his work hours mean that he is not home during most of the night and early morning. As a call center manager who was sent by his company for two months to America for training, Anand was in the position to offer a young bride a very good future. His parents were able quickly to find him a match by posting an ad in the matrimonials describing Anand's career trajectory, which resulted in a plethora of responses. Anand met his prospective bride only once, when she and her family joined his family for tea. Anand agreed to the match that very night. While Anand plans to send his new wife to college next year, he also believes that it will be her duty to care for his parents as he builds his career. He hopes eventually to move his entire family to Canada. In the meantime, his salary and a new credit card have enabled Anand to buy durable household goods that will make his wife and parents more comfortable, including a new refrigerator and television—a reflection of their upward mobility.[6] While the idea of buying on credit is not popular in India, Anand has spent a considerable amount of time dealing with American credit-card holders through his call center work; he therefore has a level of comfort with the idea of credit that other Indians may not. For Anand—who earns a relatively high wage and is willing to experiment with consumer credit—membership in a transnational professional circuit translates into his ability to fulfill certain "traditional" duties—including marrying a bride selected by his parents, and earning enough income to support his wife and his parents. Anand has also raised the class standing of his family through his engagement with new forms of consumerism.[7]

Although Anand was eager to marry as soon as his parents found a match, not all of the call center employees with whom I spoke were ready to dive into marriage. Some young professionals who can both earn a relatively good salary and socialize with their peers are happy to extend this scenario for as long as possible. This was particularly true of employees who felt they were supporting themselves on their call center salaries. Self-support runs the gamut from living at home with parents while contributing to the economic needs of one's family to living completely on one's own—sometimes a necessity for employees who must relocate to secure a call center job in cities such as Hyderabad, Bangalore, or Delhi. While living independently has become common practice for young working males, the development of this "liminal" living space for women is new to India (Sengupta 2007). Traditionally, women went directly from their natal home to their husband's house. Women's hostels—popular among female college students in recent years—have become options for young professional females as well. However, most female hostel dwellers with whom I spoke yearned for their own apartments, explaining that early evening curfews at hostels made it difficult for call center employees working night shifts. Others complained about the food, indicating that hostel meals left much to be desired. And many women were frustrated by the fact that they could receive only visitors who appeared on a pre-approved list set by their parents. Furthermore virtually every hostel in the city insisted that these visitors be exclusively female.

Some women have been able to escape the restrictions of hostels by securing their own private apartments, although not without difficulty. Landlords do not want to rent to single women—particularly call center employees—often claiming the hours are disruptive to neighbors. When I discussed this with Shalini, a twenty-four-year-old living on her own, she felt that resistance among landlords had more to do with their inability to monitor a woman's "comings" and "goings," rather than with disruption to neighbors. Shalini explained to me that she has been careful not to raise eyebrows in her building, especially since four of her female colleagues were handed eviction notices after boys were seen leaving a dinner party at the apartment they shared across town. "The bottom line is that people think we are promiscuous because we work night shifts. Some matrimonials even say they don't want female BPO (business process outsourcing) employees! It's outrageous! The boys [BPO employees] are sought after. They earn good salaries and have possibilities to travel and work abroad. But if a woman works for a BPO, no one wants her," she explained.

Fortunately, Shalini is not worried about the matrimonials since she already has a boyfriend, whom she met at the call center where she works. They have been dating for almost a year, and are discussing whether or not to take the "next step," which would require divulging their relationship to their parents.

My parents have no idea! They would really freak if they knew he'd been to my apartment. We've had to sort of sneak around. I've successfully managed to hide him, even from my landlord. . . . But if we decide to get married, I will have to move back home until the wedding, because [my parents] will just begin worrying, wondering if he might be coming over, raising everyone's suspicions. That's the way it is here. Everyone becomes suspicious of an unmarried woman living on her own.

When I asked Shalini whether she would continue working after she was married, she said she was not sure. She would have to think about how to balance the myriad obstacles associated with starting a family and building a career, common pressures felt by "pink collar" workers around the globe (Freeman 2000). Shalini and some of her other colleagues who expressed apprehension about marriage were all well aware of the rising Indian divorce rates. For the women in particular, there was a deep sense of anxiety around the idea of a broken marriage. Divorce is not an easy path for Indian women, but as we shall see below, working in a call center may in fact provide emotional and psychological support for some divorcees.

DECISIONS ABOUT DIVORCE FOR A "VIRTUAL MIGRANT"

Scholars have described Indian call center employees as "virtual migrants" (Aneesh 2006). Unlike embodied migrants, who physically leave their home to work in other countries, virtual migrants work for another country without ever crossing their own national borders. As Aneesh explains, the labor production of call center employees, BPO workers, and engineers in tech centers throughout India is deposited in another country, through a sale over the telephone or through data processed and sent electronically thousands of miles away over the internet. The concept of virtual migration can also be applied to new ways of thinking about the convergence of multiple cultural norms in specific localities. Call center employees, for example, work within spaces marked by social values that are often quite different from those governing their own families, or their wider communities. As Meena, a twenty-eight-year-old language trainer explained:

In India, divorce is not accepted. Women have to hide the fact that they are divorced. When I talk to clients from the U.S. on the phone, they are very open about divorce. They will call and say, "Since my divorce I have had to switch my accounts and so I need to set a new password," or "I am going through a divorce and need my name put on a separate account," or whatever it might be. Very straightforward. It is part of everyday life there. Nothing to be ashamed of. . . . It really made me think about my own life.

One year into her call center career, just after a big promotion, Meena sought a divorce from her husband, whom she described as abusive. She explained to me that while she has felt an immediate sense of relief since leaving her husband, life for a divorced woman in India is not easy:

> It has been difficult in many ways. Landlords don't want to rent apartments to divorced women because they think we are fast, they think that we are forward, we might try to lure married men into our rooms, or we might bring stray men into our apartments at night. Basically, if you admit you are divorced, people think two things. First, they think you are available [for sex]. Then they think you are strong-headed and you cannot adjust to a man. Divorce here is always seen as the woman's fault. They say maybe she couldn't cook, or she couldn't satisfy her husband, or she was too stubborn.

Meena went on to explain to me that because divorce is perceived to be the result of a failure on the woman's part, dissatisfied wives who have the ability to support themselves economically outside of marriage often choose not to ask for divorce. Nonetheless, divorce has more than doubled in Indian metropolitan areas over the last decade, due in part to the increasing ability of professional women to support themselves. Fortunately for Meena, her parents supported her decision to leave her husband, and they welcomed her back into their home. Meena, however—who holds a master's degree—wanted to live on her own. Smartly dressed in a red and black salwar kameez, Meena spoke to me at work, in an empty language-training classroom. She explained that working for a "global" call center at the time of her divorce made life possible for her as a single woman. While she is paid relatively high wages, Meena emphasized that her ability to live independently since her divorce is not simply a matter of income. Although finances are a big part of the equation, living on the fringe of "accepted" social norms requires a strong support structure, and the call center where Meena works provides her with that. In her previous jobs teaching English to university students and working in the front office of an Oberoi Hotel, Meena says she did not experience the same sort of "open mindedness." She attributes the "broad perspective" on life among her fellow employees to their place as "professionals" in a new transnational industry. As call center employees, Meena and her co-workers are influenced by customers and clients from America, Europe, and Australia.

> What I like about my job is that I don't have to hide who I am. People here are open-minded. If I wanted to work elsewhere—almost any other job—the fact that I am divorced would be a problem. But not here. Our rep on the Australian account has an MBA from Melbourne University, and he is no stranger to divorce. He sees it every day in Australia. And no team leader here has propositioned me just because I am divorced. We are professionals here. We have a more global understanding of the world, much more so than

your average person, even educated person, in India. We get callers from the U.S. who tell us that they are gay, or that they are suffering from AIDS. Suddenly, our workers here are exposed to these concepts—gay, lesbian, AIDS. When the new trainees come in and hear these terms for the first time on a call, I say, "Let's get on the Internet. Let's learn about these issues." We work in an environment where we are talking to people every day who live these realities, so we have to become more understanding of such things. Divorce. AIDS. Whatever it is. That's what makes our work unique.

For Meena, there is a direct connection between her position in a "local" transnational labor force and the "global" moral economy of that professional environment. Virtual migrants like Meena enter the cultural and moral economy of other countries through their work, developing a transnational professional identity grounded in a wider understanding of the values and social processes of the various countries with which they do business. While this identity requires the recognition of multiple social norms, it does not necessarily require the abdication of certain "local" cultural values. For example, after explaining to me that she enjoys learning about the lives of her customers, Meena also told me that Indian women do not live with boyfriends before marriage, the way American women do. "For us, family is important, and we are more traditional in that sense. We do not just move in with our boyfriends. It's not done in India," she stated.

Meena's ability to shift seamlessly between her identity as a transnational professional (*"we* have a more global understanding of the world") and as an Indian woman (*"we* do not just move in with our boyfriends") illustrates well the multiple identities she navigates in her position as a call center employee serving Western clients and as an Indian middle-class woman enveloped by the complex cultural norms of her country. For women like Meena, divorce has become a possibility, not just because she earns a good salary, but because she is part of a transnational labor circuit through which she is exposed on a daily basis to the simultaneous existence of multiple social norms.[8] However, other things are not possible: Meena's position as a middle-class South Asian woman employed by a Western call center results in her tenuous freedom to live without a man as a divorced woman, but not with a man as an unmarried woman.

* * *

Of course, freedom, imagination, and identities are developed differently for different call center employees; socioeconomics, gender, and family circumstances all play a role in shaping possibilities for, and engagement with, the multiplicity of social norms encountered in transnational labor circuits. Everyday experiences within call centers also construct views about multiple cultural norms. As women in call centers are propositioned by Western men on the other end of the phone—some of whom instigate "phone sex" with their female Indian interlocutors—many BPO employees are witnessing a fanning of the fear of "cultural others." In light of such transgressions, the female body and female sexuality have increasingly come to function as a central terrain upon which globalization is debated (Shome 2006); women must be "protected" from new dangers made possible through global processes (Mankekar 1997; Oza 2007).[9] In some cases, Indian men must also be protected from "tainted" women who fall prey to the questionable moral environments in which they work. Hence, as we saw earlier in this chapter, the plethora of matrimonials discouraging potential brides employed by BPOs from answering marriage advertisements.

The cultural politics of Indian call centers are wide and varied. Call centers provide new ways of thinking about hybridity, identity, belonging, sexuality, family, xenophobia, and (post)colonialism in South Asia (Shome 2006). Call centers have also forced a reevaluation of the role of the state in the development of educational and economic policies that bring outsourcing and other forms of transnational labor to countries such as India (Sharma and Gupta 2006). Despite such factors, or perhaps precisely because of them, both the "real" and "virtual" environments in which call center employees work have the potential to facilitate enormous cultural shifts in India—particularly shifts around the social and professional roles of women, influencing new ways of thinking about kinship, courtship, marriage, and divorce.

NOTES

1. See Collins 2003; Cravey 1998; Fernandes 1997; Fernandez-Kelly 1983; Mills 2003; Ong 1987.

2. Jonathan Parry argues that divorce rates in India are skewed low by different forms of marriage. In India, both conjugal and jural marriages are common; in the latter, couples do not necessarily live with one another, and may not see each other for years, rendering a formal divorce unnecessary. Furthermore, customary divorce laws are still recognized by the Hindu Marriage Act of 1955, although India's official divorce rates do not calculate these less formal separations (see also Uberoi 1996). Also, Indian national divorce averages aggregate both urban and rural statistics, yet most instances of divorce occur in urban families. Only one-third of Indian households are in urban areas, while a full two-thirds are in rural areas. The 2005–2006 National Family Health Survey of India (NFHS-03), in which 124,385 women between the ages of 15 and 49, and 74,369 men between the ages of 15 and 54 were surveyed, reports very low rates of divorce. According to the NFHS-03, 0.1% of men and 0.3% of women participating in the survey were divorced, while 0.8% of women and 0.3% of men were separated. Respondents in the survey came from both rural and urban areas in twenty-nine Indian states (www.nfhsindia.org).

3. Susan Seymour (1999) suggests that contemporary social changes in India have had a much more profound impact on the lives of women than the lives of men, which makes the feminine experience particularly valuable for understanding the implications of globalization in South Asia. To better understand the effects

of transnationalism on women in Nepal, see McHugh (2004). For an interesting analysis of Sri Lankan migrant housemaids, see Gamburd (2000). Ahearn (2001) and Dwyer (2000) demonstrate that the dialectic between "global" processes and "local" popular culture is contributing to new ideas about love and romance, transforming middle-class marriage values in South Asia.

4. Call centers run the gamut from small, locally owned operations with fewer than 100 employees serving a variety of clients to large-scale Western-owned companies that provide services solely to that company's captive client base. Additional support staff is also required. For example, GE Capital's Hyderabad office employs 5,000 BPO (business process outsourcing) professionals, as well as approximately 100 drivers to shuttle employees to and from work, 30 security guards, and some 50 chefs who work the "canteens," or on-campus catering service. Larger operations are generally marked by increased surveillance, due to the wide circulation of private financial information within their facilities. A manager at one such firm explained to me that work spaces are often equipped with security cameras, and employees are prohibited from bringing scraps of paper or writing instruments with them into their cubicle area, where they type sensitive customer account information into their computers during shifts. Personal emailing from work is also forbidden, and all computer activity is tracked, including viewing of non-work-related websites.

5. An inbound call is one in which a customer dials a company's toll-free number seeking a particular service—be it to book a flight or secure assistance with an online transaction. An outbound call is marked by the call center employee dialing a person in the United States, Australia, or Europe in an attempt to sell a product or service. Most employees find such outbound telemarketing calls stressful, as rates of rejection, rude responses, and outright hang-ups are more likely to result than a successful sale.

6. For an interesting discussion of the ways in which upward mobility and middle-class aspirations in India have increasingly been marked by consumerism, particularly of durable household goods, see Mankekar 1999 and Mazzarella 2003.

7. Scholars suggest that with very few safety nets in place for the lower classes in India, upward mobility can be a precarious journey. Often it takes little more than the temporary illness or injury of a primary wage earner to throw his or her entire family off of their economic path (see Dickey, ch. 15 in this volume).

8. Increasing divorce rates and acceptance of remarriage within some communities in India has given birth to websites such as www.SecondShaadi.com (second marriage), an online matchmaking service for Indian divorcees (Giridharadas 2008).

9. For discussions of the ways in which patriarchy, globalization, and modernity collide, see also Bhattacharjee 1997, Freeman 2001, Grewal 2005, Mohanty 1997.

5

Love and Aging in Bengali Families

Sarah Lamb

Early on in my days in the West Bengali village of Mangaldihi, I met a woman called Mejo Ma, or "Middle Mother," sitting in the dusty lane in front of her home. She could not stop complaining about clinging. She worried that her ties to her children, to her grandchildren, to her own body, to the pleasures of this life were so strong that they would keep her soul shackled to her world beyond the appropriate time for moving on and dying. "How will I cut my ties to all these kids and things and go?" she lamented. The oldest woman of Mangaldihi, Khudi Thakrun, did not herself worry about clinging, but rather seemed to embrace her many involvements. She lived in the crowded households of her three sons, which were replete with three generations of descendants, the comings and goings of numerous visitors, and the smoke from several cooking fires. She wandered the village daily to spread news, to lend out money at high interest rates to increase her wealth, and to seek the best plums, mangoes, and papayas. Others, however, worried about her eagerly attached ways, saying that her soul could certainly end up as a lingering ghost after death.

These and other older people's stories and predicaments illuminate what many Bengalis see as an inherent dilemma of the life course: its fundamental intensity on the one hand and its irrevocable ephemerality on the other. Life, with all of its pleasure and ties, seems so real and lasting and vital and important as we live it, and yet ultimately it cannot last—a truth that Bengalis say becomes ever more salient in late life. This chapter takes a look at the ways Bengalis in Mangaldihi, and in a few Kolkata old-age homes, think about aging, and how their experiences of aging tie into views of love, family, and the life course.[1] Mangaldihi is a large, predominantly Hindu village of about 1,700, in the gently undulating terrain about a hundred kilometers northwest of Kolkata.

HOUSEFLOWS: AGING AND INTERGENERATIONAL TIES

Aging for Bengalis is defined not so much in terms of chronological years but rather via one's place in a family cycle. Most rural Bengalis do not keep careful track of or celebrate their birthdays; and few count the particular number of years passed in their lives as markers of identity or of life stage. It is the marriage of children, especially the bringing of a daughter-in-law into the home, that initiates the beginnings of the "senior" or "grown" life phase (*buṛo bayas*). Bodily changes—such as graying hair, weakening, and "cooling"[2]—can also be regarded as signs of aging.

It is at this point, when one's children are married and one's body has perhaps grown weaker and cooler, that seniors often shift to a new phase of life and place in the family. The family heads initiate their transition to becoming "senior"—often over a period of several years of competition and ambivalence—by gradually handing over the responsibilities of managing household funds, decision making, cooking, and reproducing children to sons (or a son) and their wives. In this way, the seniors move increasingly to the peripheries of household life. At the same time, the expectation is that their juniors will care for and serve them. Bengalis say that children have a profound social-moral obligation, in fact, to care for their parents in old age, in part because they owe their parents a tremendous "debt" (*ṛṇ*) for being produced and nurtured in infancy and childhood. Khudi Thakrun's oldest son, Gurusaday, strove to care for his mother assiduously, and explained his practices:

> Looking after parents is the children's duty. Sons pay back the debt to their parents of childbirth and being raised by them. The mother and father suffer so much to raise their children. They can't sleep; they wake up in the middle of the night. They clean up their [children's] bowel movements. They worry terribly when the children are sick. And the mother especially suffers. She carries the child in her womb for ten [lunar] months, and she raises him from the blood and milk from her breasts. So if you don't care for your parents, then great sin and injustice happens.

Another man, whose frail mother was incontinent and bedridden, reflected similarly:

> Caring for parents is the children's duty; it is *dharma* [moral-religious order; right way of living]. As parents raised their children, children will also care for their parents during their sick years, when they get old. For example, if I am old and I have a bowel movement, my son will clean it and he won't ask, "Why did you do it there?" This is what we did for him when he was young. When I am old and dying, who will take me to go pee and defecate? My children will have to do it.

Women often provide much more care for their parents-in-law, inheriting obligations toward their husbands' parents, than they do for their own parents. Parents with only daughters and no sons, however, sometimes choose to keep a married daughter with them, bringing a "house son-in-law" (*ghar jāmāi*) to inherit their property and to care (with their daughter) for them in old age.

Providing care for parents entails both material support (food, shelter, clothing) and *sevā* (respectful, loving service)—such as massaging tired limbs, combing hair, serving food, reading aloud, offering loving companionship, and (if necessary) cleaning up urine and excrement. Caring for seniors also extends beyond old age, as children (particularly sons) reconstruct ancestral bodies for and ritually nourish their parents as ancestors.[3] Such a system of long-term intergenerational reciprocity contrasts with practices in the United States, where among the white middle-class in particular, the dominant expectation is that parent-child gifts will flow "down" from parent to child in a lifelong unidirectional manner. It would make the child and the parent equally uncomfortable if the child were called upon to provide material support or intimate bodily care for his or her parent.

Intimate, smooth, and mutually supportive intergenerational relationships do not always come to fruition, however. Not only can children neglect their parents, but elders can refuse care in various ways. Some people have no children, and other children may be too poor to provide support. Rabilal, an elderly beggar of the leather-working caste, replied pessimistically when I asked him what happens when one grows old: "When you get old, your sons don't feed you rice." He lived in a small hut right next to his two married sons, but they were poor agricultural day laborers and could not spare enough to support their father. A young girl, Beli Bagdi, replied when I asked her what would happen to her in her old age, "Either my sons will feed me rice or they won't; there's no certainty."

Khudi Thakrun's several sons, daughters-in-law, and grandchildren all professed their desire to care for the elder woman. She lived alternately in the three separate homes of her sons, all within about a stone's throw of each other in the same village neighborhood. At each meal, she was served before all others and had the propensity to eat so many of the treats—milk, cottage cheese, sweets, fruit—that sometimes her juniors confessed (privately, but never to her face) to feeling that not enough was left for them. I would come to one of her homes and see her daughter-in-law massaging her dry skin with mustard oil, or a grandson reading to her from the Bhagavad Gita. But she herself did not seem to wish to become the peripheralized (though served) older person whom others expected her and other elders to be—one who received care mostly from family members and relinquished control of her own property to them. Khudi Thakrun, at about age ninety-seven, continued to maintain a considerable amount of property and money in her own name,[4] and, as mentioned above, she would roam the village to lend out her money to needy villagers, earning interest to increase her wealth. She would also commission people who worked in or visited cities to bring back treats for her, and since it was regarded as a great sin and moral injustice to repudiate the request of one as senior as Khudi Thakrun, most complied. I myself became a favorite recipient of her requests, and she would ask me to bring back small things, often sweets, from my trips to town. However, once when I brought her a requested bedsheet from Kolkata, her juniors found out and chastised her, "Why are you asking some girl who has come here from a foreign country to give things to you? You have three sons. They can give things to you." A neighboring woman exclaimed to me, "Such an old woman with three capable sons is still going around pestering others for food! Chi! Chi! An old woman with three sons like that is not supposed to ask others for things—her sons are supposed to give them to her."

Khudi Thakrun's juniors *wanted* to care for her—out of their sense of dharma and for the honor of their family. And in fact they *did* care for her: She lived with and was largely supported by them; she received their seva, or service and loving care. But Khudi Thakrun rejected some of their seva, and continued in part to support herself—a matter that somewhat concerned her kin and neighbors, though apparently not her.

Mejo Ma, on the contrary, lived as people expected, very well embedded in her family web, with her two married sons, daughters-in-law, one married grandson, and other grandchildren—happily receiving their seva and love as the family's most senior member. Perhaps this was one reason why she felt so close to them and worried about how she would leave them all to depart in death.

Transactions of intergenerational reciprocity are practiced and enjoyed to varying extents. But Bengalis say that it is through such transactions—the gifts and services of food, love, and daily care parents and children provide each other at different phases of life—that family ties are created and sustained across generations.

FLEETING LIVES AND THE PROBLEM OF MĀYĀ

The ties binding seniors and juniors across generations are part of what Bengalis call *māyā*. Maya is a polyvalent term found in all Indian languages, often translated by scholars as "illusion." In its sense as illusion, maya refers to the everyday, lived world of experience (known as *samsāra* in Sanskrit and *samsār* in Bengali)—a lived world that is not ultimate or everlasting (and is thus illusory) but which people feel very tied to and perceive in their daily lives as being "really real." In its more common, everyday sense for Bengalis, maya means love, attachment, compassion, or affection. A mother has maya for her child and a child has maya for her mother. Husbands and wives have maya for each other. People have maya for their homes, the plants they have

Figure 5.1. Khudi Thakrun (right) and her daughter.

tended carefully in their courtyards, the possessions they have gathered. People feel maya when they see a tiny calf bleating for its mother, or when a beloved sari is torn. If a grandmother calls her little granddaughter to her to feed her a sweet (even as she may lie dying), that is maya. When parents weep, seeing their newly married daughter depart to her husband's home, they are crying from maya.

Maya consists not only of what we might classify as emotional ties, but also of physical or bodily connections. Bengalis refer to maya as taking the form of "bindings" (*bandhan*) or a "net" (*jāl*) in which people, and all living beings, are enmeshed. It is created through experiences such as drinking a mother's breast milk, sharing food, spending time together, engaging in sexual relations, touching, and owning something for a long time. Persons see themselves as physically and emotionally *part* of and *tied* to the people and things that make up their selves and lived-in worlds. These ties, for Bengalis, are all part of maya.

On the one hand, maya is something that is valued and sought after by people at any stage of life. Strong family ties, for instance, are highly prized by most Bengalis, and people will say that a person has had a "good" old age if he or she is closely surrounded by loving kin with whom he or she has created ties of maya over a long life of living together and giving and receiving things.

On the other hand, having a lot of maya is problematic, because the more maya one has for people, places, and things, the more difficult are the separations that inevitably ensue. Once when I was talking with two younger villagers, Hena and Babu, about the meanings of maya, Hena added, "Maya is a very bad thing." I was surprised and countered, "*We* don't think of maya [comparable in my mind here to the American 'love'] as bad at all." "Then you must not have much maya," they both replied straightaway. I came to appreciate how maya is regarded by Bengalis as problematic, one of even the six human "vices" (along with anger, greed, jealousy, pride, and passion), because it can cause immense pain and suffering. Nothing that one loves, or has maya for, can last forever. Daughters grow up and marry, beautiful clothing becomes faded and worn, a wonderfully sweet mango is consumed and gone, a strain of lovely music fades into silence, a beloved parent dies, and even one's own place in this lived-in world will soon be gone. Old age in particular poses problems with regard to maya. Bengalis believe that the ties of maya tend to grow stronger and more numerous as life progresses, and yet at the same time old age is when one's ties are the most ephemeral, for one will soon be moving on in death.

Bengalis offer several reasons for why maya tends to increase with the length of life. First, because the number of one's kin increases as life goes on, maya necessarily increases as well—for all of these kin. As Hena put it: "When you are young, you have maya and pull only for your mother, father, and older sister. But then when you marry, maya increases—for all of the people of your father-in-law's house. And then you have kids, and then they have kids. You see, from all of this, maya is increasing." "Look at Khudi Thakrun," she added. "Almost everyone in the village is her relative! She will never be able to abandon maya—never."

Further, as life goes on one has the opportunity to accumulate more and more pleasurable experiences. Khudi Thakrun's middle-aged son, Gurusaday, reflected on how maya increases with age: "For old people, maya and desire increase and increase! . . . At the time of death, however many possessions [a person] has, that much maya and attachment will he have—for all of those things." He went on to explain, "If you throw ghee in a fire, then the fire increases. In this way, desire and maya increase and increase as one gets old. People should think, 'I've received and done [things] all of my life. I won't do any more.' But instead they think, 'Let more happen, let more happen!' You see, it's like adding ghee to a fire. The more he gets, the more he wants!" He then went on to repeat this phrase enthusiastically several times in English, seemingly proud to have come up with such a wise statement in my native language. "The more he gets, the more he wants! The more he gets, the more he wants!" And his mother, Khudi Thakrun, was certainly one who evinced such an eagerly attached demeanor in old age.

As death approaches, one's awareness of impending separations can also cause feelings of connection or maya to intensify. On another occasion when

I asked Gurusaday whether maya increases or decreases with age, he answered definitively: "Maya increases." "Why?" I asked. "Because [in old age a person] realizes that he will have to leave everything in this earth and go away," and as he responded, tears rose in his eyes. He added, "When I die, then I will have to leave everyone and everything—my children and everything. Then all of the love and all of the affection that I will have—that is all maya. It will make tears come."

One of the dangers of having such a lot of maya in late life is that it can make the process of dying very painful. One older woman, Mita's Ma, who was blind in one eye and lame in one leg, described the process of dying for a person with much maya as like pulling a deeply embedded thorn from the body. The emotional-physical ties of maya keep the soul, or *ātmā,* literally "bound" to the body, making it difficult—emotionally and physically—for the soul to leave. Having a lot of maya in old age can also cause one to linger on in a decrepit body past the natural time for dying. People say in general that it is much better to die while still "moving" (*calte calte*), that is, while the body is still in good working condition, and that it is just maya that keeps some people vainly striving to preserve their naturally aging bodies through tools like false teeth, hair dye, and anti-wrinkle creams that are so popular now among the cosmopolitan elite. "What need do I have of such things?" one toothless woman said to me when I asked her about dentures. "They are just unnecessary forms of dressing up. It is now time for my body to go." Too much maya at the end of life can also cause the soul to linger on in frustration as a ghost around its former habitat, seeking vainly to be reunited with the scenes of its previous life.

For these reasons, some strive to loosen their ties of maya in various ways *before* dying, engaging in practices that many associate with old age—practices meant to counteract the natural tendency for maya to increase. For instance, older Bengalis tend to wear white, a "cool" color associated with detachment, old age, asexuality, spirituality. Once their children are married, they generally refrain from engaging in sexual relations, which serve as an intimate means of creating bodily-emotional ties. Older people often sleep alone for the first time in their lives, and they may take their meals separately and before others. For those who can afford it, old age is also viewed as an appropriate time for going on pilgrimages, a process that helps loosen daily ties to home as one wanders beyond to mingle with holy places and divinities. Some elders, people say, become quarrelsome or petulant, which also (purposefully or not) can help slacken ties of affection with kin. Some strive to loosen ties to their own bodies with denigrating epithets, saying that their bodies have become like old clothing ready to be discarded, or like a rice plant at the end of its cycle, withered and gray. Others prepare their souls for the transition to a more heavenly abode[5] by chanting God's name every night as they fall asleep.

In Mangaldihi, efforts to loosen ties of maya tended to be of greater concern among the higher castes than among lower-caste and poorer people, for the poor often had to worry simply about getting enough to eat and thus did not have the luxury to become preoccupied with achieving a smooth and peaceful old age and death. Lower-caste people in Mangaldihi also told me that they didn't have as much reason for maya as Brahmans do anyway, because they owned fewer material things, had smaller families, and possessed frailer bodies from lifetimes of hard work.[6]

Other people, like Khudi Thakrun, a well-off and well-connected Brahman matriarch, simply did not wish to focus their final years on cutting ties to their worlds, so much were they enjoying the pleasures of life. Still others did strive to cut maya, but felt ambivalent about the process. One man went on a pilgrimage expressly in order to diminish his worldly ties, but confessed to me on the way home, tears coming to his eyes as he sat next to his wife, "I left everything to come, but I couldn't leave her." Most admit that no matter how much one strives to reduce the bodily-emotional ties of maya in old age, maya cannot easily be cut. Thus Mejo Ma moaned in the lane in front of her home, "How will I cut my ties to all these kids and things and go?"

People feel contrary pulls. One's life in this world is full of pleasures and experiences that bind the self to cherished people, places, and things. It is also inherently fleeting, only a temporary stopping place on the way to something else.

THE RISE OF OLD-AGE HOMES

I have concentrated so far on village life, but I wish to look briefly at the phenomenon of old-age homes springing up in India's cities. Until the past few decades, old-age homes scarcely existed in India, save for a handful established by Christian missionaries, largely catering to the Anglo-Indian community and the very poor. Now there are hundreds across India's cities, the vast majority having been founded over the last fifteen years (Lamb 2009; HelpAge India 2002). Viewed as predominantly Western-style institutions, the homes are commonly referred to in English—"old-age homes." Bengali alternatives include *briddhāśram*—"shelter" (or ashram) for the aged or "increased" (*briddha*), and *briddhābās*—"abode" (*ābās*) for the aged. These new elder residences are largely for the Hindu middle and upper-middle classes. Run by both nonprofit organizations and private entrepreneurs, the homes' rates range from about 1,000 to 5,000 Indian rupees per month (a little over US$20 to $100), and often require a sizable joining fee or security deposit of anywhere from about 5,000 to 300,000 rupees (or about $100 to $6,000)— sums affordable only to those with retirement pensions, considerable savings, and/or professional children (who often cover the fees). The residents come from a range of family situations: some are childless; others have only daughters (most Indians say it is improper or awkward to live with a daughter, especially if she has parents-in-law in her home); others' children are all abroad; and others have sons and daughters-in-law living right nearby but in "modern" nuclear-style households.

Navanir, "New Nest," one of many Kolkata old-age homes I spent time in as a researcher in 1990 and in the early 2000s, is one of India's very first non-Christian homes for the aged; it was founded in 1978. It is a spacious, comfortable home for about a hundred residents, with three or four women sharing a room, shuttered windows open to the airy outdoors, an attractive front courtyard of scented flowering trees, a central meeting room where people gather to watch TV or chat, a dining hall where Bengali home-style food is served. Those who are mobile can freely wander in and out, taking walks in the neighborhood, perhaps visiting a local tea stall or simply strolling for exercise.

I was keen to understand how the residents felt about living in such a home, being part of a society in which it is so highly valued that seniors will be cared for by their children. Most expressed a relief that they *had* a place to stay and they were very grateful to the woman who had founded the institution. "It's better to be here than on the street," several commented. "I didn't like living in someone else's household," another said of her earlier years with her daughter and son-in-law. "I wanted to get away from the signs of my husband in my home," another explained, "after he died. Here [in Navanir], everything is open and empty—it gives some peace of mind."

However, moving beyond personal life circumstances, residents, staff, and the public in Kolkata interpret the need for such institutions even more centrally in terms of the conditions of modernity. To many, old-age homes signify not merely a new form of aging, but also much broader social, cultural, and national transformations. In Kolkata, modernity is perceived as entailing a cluster of concepts and terms, including the English "modern," or *ādhunik* in Bengali, and other terms conveying the temporal present, such as "these days" (*ājkāl*) and "nowadays" or "now" (*ekhankār, ekhan*). As such, modernity is regularly associated with Western values, lifeways, and processes, as well as with features of "globalization" (a term commonly used in English), such as the global spread of Western values and lifeways, a (Western-dominated) global economy and media, and transnational or diasporic living. Modernity entails as well a host of other facets of contemporary life, including frequently urban residence, nuclear families, small flats, individualism, consumerism, materialism, careerism, a persistent lack of time, weak family ties, waning patriarchy, and old-age homes. Retired psychiatrist and old-age-home resident Dr. Ranjan Banerjee asserted to me: "Old-age homes are not a concept of *our* country. These days, we are throwing away our culture. The U.S. is the richest nation in the world and therefore has won us over." Soumil Chowdhury, a retired engineer who had just made plans, with mixed feelings, to move into an old-age home with his wife, similarly narrated:

> We are experiencing a clash between the Indian era and the Western era. We [Indians] want to live jointly, amidst our relatives, not alone. . . . In European culture, everyone does want to live separately. . . . [But] we don't want old-age homes. We want joint families—sisters and brothers, daughters and sons, granddaughters and grandsons, all together. . . . This is Indian culture.

Yet some argue that India's old-age homes are perhaps not so radically "new" or fundamentally "Western" after all. In fact, the elderly women of Navanir at times interpreted their old-age home as a new kind of *Indian* institution, drawing here on Hindu textual traditions to make their case. The classical Hindu ethical-legal texts, or *dharmasastras*, present a series of four life stages through which a person (specifically, an upper-caste male)[7] ideally moves over a lifetime. A person begins his life as a student, moves on to become a married householder, and then, as he sees the sons of his sons and his own gray hair, he becomes first a "forest-dweller" and ultimately a "renouncer" (Manu 1991). During the forest-dweller phase, the person passes most of his property down to his descendants and moves away to dwell in the forest or countryside in a hermitlike state of relative freedom from ties. Several people in Navanir and other Kolkata elder residences interpreted their stays in the homes as being comparable to the traditional Hindu forest-dweller life phase, and thus as having its own advantages, helping to facilitate a peaceful old age of relative freedom from the binding ties of maya. Like those in Mangaldihi, however, Navanir residents said that reducing ties of maya in late life cannot be easily done. The widowed mother of an only daughter reflected as we spoke of her life at Navanir, "For me, maya hasn't completely left yet." She laughed a sheepish, almost apologetic laugh. "I've only been here for a short time—three years—and I was with [my daughter and son-in-law] for so long. So that's why I still have it. But I'm trying to turn my mind toward God. Because what need have I for maya now? It's time for me to go. So what need is there for maya? I try to keep my mind strong. But maya does not go away easily."

Further, elders in old-age homes are often the recipients of quite a bit of sustained seva, or service to and respect for the aged—a key component of perceived traditional Indian ways of aging. Although offered by hired staff and proprietors rather than one's own junior kin—a not insignificant distinction—the residents of most homes nonetheless do enjoy the receipt of seva—in the form of the faithful arrival of daily 5 AM bed tea, meals served, oil massaged into hair, bathwater warmed and delivered. Several of the homes I encountered centrally figured the concept of seva in both their names and

Figure 5.2. Lady residents gathered at the temple
of an elder ashram organized around the notions
of "forest-dwelling" and spirituality, Hindu values
appropriately pursued in late life.

their mission statements; and founders told of being motivated to open their
old-age homes precisely in order to provide seva to elders who deserve to
receive it, but who are not able to find it within their modern families.

CULTURAL MODES OF "SUCCESSFUL" (NON-)AGING

While some biological processes of growing, aging, and dying are common
to us all, the meanings we give to these processes are social constructions
tied to the beliefs and values of specific cultural-historical settings. People
in West Bengal and in North America have interpreted and dealt with, in
varying ways, one of the paradoxical dimensions of the human condition—
its compelling intensity, seeming really-real-ness on the one hand, and its
irrevocable transience on the other. As we have seen, many Bengalis deal
with this paradox by striving to embrace transience and process in late life
(though such striving is laden with ambiguities). A dominant European-
American strategy is to fight against the changes of age, endeavoring to construct in their place a façade of permanence. In closing, I wish to make just a
few reflections about these contrasts.

In the United States, scholarly and popular cultural representations of aging have recently sought to define "successful aging" as a process that entails, ideally, no *new* changes or characteristics at all. This "successful" (what I would call) *non*-aging or "permanent persons"[8] perspective on aging is nowhere so apparent as in the American proliferation of technologies for disciplining and reconstructing aging bodies. We are witnessing a surge of new techniques to remake bodies so that they are no longer visibly marked as old—through age-calibrated exercise routines, special diets, hair dyes, anti-aging skin creams, and cosmetic surgery. Our contemporary system of biomedicine (which some are resisting, through living wills and "right to die" initiatives) sustains as well a "permanent persons" mode, with its fundamental aim of prolonging life as long as possible, through ever more successful and elaborate technology. Byron Good reflects on the key soteriological role that biomedicine plays in American culture, where death, finitude, and sickness are found in the human body, and "salvation, or at least some partial representation of it, is present in the technical efficacy of medicine" (1994: 86). "[I]n this country, we spend an astounding proportion of our health care dollars on the last several weeks of life," he observes, "so great is our commitment and our technological capacity for extending life" (p. 87). The *New York Times* and *Esquire* report that American biologists are working furiously to defeat the genetic process of aging (Hall 2000; Dooling 1999). We see here a hoped-for model of the body as a machine that can be repaired and maintained on a youthful plateau until, ultimately, even death is defeated.

My purpose in bringing up such contrasts between Bengali and American perspectives is not to deride the "permanent persons" cultural constructions of aging and the life course. Much of the scholarly and popular contemporary discourse of "successful" (non-)aging has been intended to combat what had been viewed as the purely *negative* alternatives, late life as a period of decline, decay, meaninglessness, and ageism. If later life processes of change are not viewed as meaningful transformations on the way to something else positive, then no wonder people (we) would fight against the changes of age. Bengalis strive in certain ways to take apart the self and its ties in late life, as part of a purposeful process of moving on and of acknowledging our fundamental impermanence. Both the Bengali and American modes work as cultural ways of striving to make meaningful the end of a life span.

ACKNOWLEDGMENTS

Research for this paper was generously funded by Fulbright-Hays, the American Institute of Indian Studies, and the Wenner-Gren Foundation for Anthropological Research. I am especially indebted to McKim Marriott and Diane Mines for their contributions to my thinking. And of course my deepest gratitude is reserved for the people of West Bengal, especially the residents of Mangaldihi, who enabled me to live among and learn from them.

NOTES

1. For a more in-depth look at Bengali aging and the themes covered in this chapter, see Lamb (2000, 2009). Cohen (1998), van Willigen and Chadha (1999), and Vatuk (1980, 1990, 1995) also examine aging in India.

2. Bengalis associate being "cool," *ṭhāṇḍā*, with social-bodily conditions such as old age, death, widowhood, and asexuality. Marriage, sexuality, passion, and anger are all "hot" states.

3. Bengali Hindus say that after death a person's soul (atma) ordinarily moves on *both* to be reincarnated *and* to become an ancestor. The two passages can happen at the same time and do not strike most people as incompatible.

4. Although Bengali women tend not to own much property in their own right, Khudi Thakrun was unusual in that her well-off father had not had any sons and had therefore left his land to his daughter. She had married within her own village, so now in old age still lived and owned land in her natal place. Most of her husband's property had gone to their sons, as is most common, upon his death.

5. Hindus tend to think of "heaven" (*svarga*) as a temporary abode where souls can remain for some time before being reborn or achieving ultimate "release" (*moksha*) from the cycle of births and deaths.

6. See part 3 for further discussions of caste and class. Higher-caste people are not necessarily economically better off than lower-caste people, although they often are, and in Mangaldihi the highest-caste Brahmans were also the economically most prosperous group.

7. In the Dharmasastra texts, the life stage (*āśrama dharma*) schema applies specifically only to an upper-caste man's life. Little attention is devoted to defining the appropriate stages of a woman's life, which are determined by her relationships to the men on whom she depends for support and guidance—her father, her husband, and finally her sons (Manu 1991: 115). Both Bengali men and women, however, not infrequently refer to this classical life stage schema to make sense of their own lives.

8. I use the term "permanent persons" to refer to what I see to be a prevalent desire among many Americans to *be* permanent as persons; that is, to stave off decline or life's end even as one ages (see also Lamb 2009: 137–40).

PART TWO

Genders

Gender is, for all of us, a part of our identity and how we are socialized. It is implicated in the ways we approach action in the world and make judgments about those actions. It is part of how we organize ourselves into social groups. Experiences and attitudes about gender and what it is to be male, female, or transgendered are an aspect of almost anything we do—a central dimension of everyday life.

Important diversity, of course, exists in experiences of gender across South Asia. New social and economic realities impacting gender have emerged especially among India's urban middle classes, in part spurred by the economic liberalization policies of the early 1990s: there has been a sizable increase of women in the professional workforce, a perceived decline in joint family living, and a widespread sense that younger women—especially if highly educated, older at marriage, and working—do not wish to move in with their in-laws. As we saw in the previous section, "love" marriages are also becoming more common. Many young South Asian women will marry someone of their own choosing, or never move in with their parents-in-law, or move abroad for professional work. Nonetheless, in rural and even urban South Asia, it is still very common and normal for a woman to progress over her life from being a daughter in her natal home, to a wife and daughter-in-law in her husband's and in-laws' home, to a mother of young children, to a mother-in-law, and finally to an older woman and, frequently, a widow.

If one speaks with older women, one will often hear them nostalgically describe their lives as young girls in their natal homes as the time when they experienced the most freedoms and pleasures, receiving love and affection from their elders, and playing with their neighborhood friends. As a young wife and daughter-in-law in a multigenerational household, a woman is often most constrained. She becomes the newest and perhaps most junior person in an unfamiliar home and must learn to exhibit deference to her husband and his senior kin. As a woman bears children, she often begins to feel more and more invested and significant in her marital home and can derive rich fulfillment from being a mother. As a mother-in-law in a joint family household, a woman is at her height of authority in the domestic sphere. She will often be the female head of household (with her husband as the male head), in control of much of the decision making about domestic matters.

As a woman becomes even older, juniors often gradually take over the position of household head. This means that an older woman loses much of her domestic power and authority but gains in other freedoms—to wander beyond the household, to visit faraway temples or married daughters, to play cards with friends, to watch the public performances that come to town, or to expose without care parts of the body, such as calves or breasts, that were once carefully protected from public view (Lamb 2000). A woman who becomes a widow when she is already at an advanced age with married sons often faces few social and economic consequences, although she may of course profoundly mourn the loss of her husband. In communities where widow remarriage is not practiced (that is, among many upper-caste Hindu groups, and even among many lower castes if the widow already has children), becoming a widow at a young age can have drastic consequences—ranging from poverty, to feelings of being unwanted in either natal or marital home, to being regarded as inauspicious, or to facing a precarious old age with no children to support her (see Chen 2001).

Many women work outside the home, in addition to carrying out their domestic roles as mothers, wives, cooks, and so on. The degree and nature of women's work depends profoundly on caste and class. In rural areas especially, upper-status women are often pressed to confine their movements largely to the home and are thus discouraged from taking on outside work. All over South Asia, though, other women can be seen laboring in the fields, or on road construction sites, or in others' homes as domestic servants (Gamburd). Well-educated urban women pursue a full range of professional careers, as professors, physicians, politicians, travel agents, and the like. Recently, working-class and upwardly mobile women are taking up jobs in factories (Lynch, part 5) and transnational call centers (Kapur, part 1). Some move between the information technology (IT) circuits of Silicon Valley and Bangalore, striving to balance high-powered global-oriented careers with what they regard as intimate "Indian" family lives (Radhakrishnan, part 6).

Compared to women, men do not necessarily experience as many marked transformations over the life course. A man may move for the purposes of work, but marriage does not generally necessitate his moving away from his natal to his wife's home and community, in keeping with patrilocal residence preferences across the region. Men inherit property and continue the family line; many in South Asia describe the parent-son bond as the most strong and long-lasting of all family ties. Men are generally expected to marry, to have children, to be economically productive, and, as the senior male in a household, to assume the role as central authority figure (see Wadley, part 1). Like women, when men grow older, they are expected to relinquish much of their authority to juniors (Lamb, part 1). Men at any age are generally free to move as they wish in public spheres—working, congregating with friends, hanging out at tea stalls, making journeys to markets, and the like.

Any examination of gender in South Asia must consider the presence of patriarchy. Dominant expectations are that a wife will be subservient to her husband. Hindu ideologies, for instance, proclaim that a husband is in some ways to his wife like a god, and his wife should serve and respect him. Islam also accords men a higher status. In South Asia, sons are generally preferred to daughters for a variety of reasons (see Dube 1988; Jeffery and Jeffery, part 1), and because of instances of preferential treatment of sons and the selective abortion of female fetuses following amniocentesis, India is one of the few nations in the world in which there are significantly more males than females in juvenile age groups (Arnold, Kishor, and Roy 2002; Miller 1981, 1987; Sudha and Rajan 2003). In many communities, women are regarded as more "impure" than men (e.g., Lamb 2000: 183–87; Rozario 1992: 96–102). Many Muslim and upper-caste north Indian families also expect their women to practice purdah (literally, a "curtain") or veiling, keeping their faces covered when in public and around senior male kin, and striving to confine their activities as far as possible to the inner domains of the home (Jacobson 1982; Mehta 1981; Ring 2006; Rozario 1992). However, veiling is not only about or a sign of patriarchy; it can signify religious devotion, pride in a Muslim or upper-caste Hindu identity, class distinctions, a self-consciously cultivated modesty, and even a flirtatious attractiveness.

Over the past few decades, reports of "dowry deaths" in India have made it into the world media—cases of newly married women murdered (usually burned to death) by their husbands and/or in-laws over the issue of inadequate dowry (Stone and James 1995). The practice of *sati*, or the burning of a widow alive on her husband's funeral pyre, has also long attracted Western attention; in colonial times, the British were both dismayed by and in awe of women as satis (Mani 1998). Highlighting dowry death and sati has the potential danger of contributing to sensationalist misconceptions about India. In discussing these issues—which are of vital concern to South Asians as well—it is important to realize that these are not the norms of South Asian practices, and are certainly no more typical of all South Asians than school shootings or rape are of all Americans.

Earlier studies of gender in South Asia tended to focus on the submission of women to such patriarchal "traditions." This collection of chapters, however, fits with recent trends in gender studies in South Asia and elsewhere (e.g., Abu-Lughod 1993; P. Jeffery and R. Jeffery 1996a; Mahmood 2005; Raheja and Gold 1994) in that it looks not only at dominant ideologies but also at the diverse ways such ideologies are experienced, negotiated, made sense of, and reinterpreted in women's and men's daily lives. Ann Gold's chapter, for instance, explores uneducated girls' own perspectives on why they remain outside school walls, and Susan Seizer's examines how actresses in Tamil Nadu both violate and conform to the idea of a "good woman."

Most previous studies of gender in South Asia have also concentrated on women, and on marriage and married women in particular. Marriage is indeed a crucial dimension of most South Asian women's lives. The dominant expectation is that all women will marry. Girls are taught at a young age to prepare for marriage (Dube 1988, Gold), and even highly educated, cosmopolitan, working women often strive to fit their professional lives into what they regard as traditional marriages (Radhakrishnan, part 6). But a unique and important contribution of this collection of pieces on gender is that—along with depicting more conventional expectations regarding gender and marriage—the chapters also examine those who do not marry (e.g., Seizer); women who assume the primary role of breadwinner in their families (Gamburd); constructions of masculinity (Gamburd); those who love others of the same sex (Reddy); and *hijras*, an important group of neither-male-nor-female transsexuals (Nanda).

A final note should be made regarding constructions of gender in South Asia: although South Asian societies are patriarchal in considerable respects, South Asians have long recognized significant female forms of political and spiritual power. In fact, every major nation of contemporary South Asia save Nepal has elected a female prime minister (while the United States cannot yet boast a female head of state)—Indira Gandhi in India, Benazir Bhutto in Pakistan, Khaleda Zia in Bangladesh, and Sirimavo Bandaranaike in Sri Lanka. Hindu religious traditions also include important, powerful, and beloved female deities, such as Kali, Durga, Lakshmi, Parvati, Sita, and Sarasvati (see Kinsley 1986).

*   *   *

Ann Gold opens this section by exploring why so many female children in rural Rajasthan do not go to school, focusing primarily on uneducated daughters' own perspectives. Some girls, in fact, do eagerly attend school, but others stay home for a variety of complex and compelling reasons—sometimes because their fathers won't let them go, and also because their visions of schooling do not fit with many of their own local values. The messages promulgated by women's development organizations and literacy campaigns seem unfortunately to be pitted hopelessly against local cultural views of family, home, tradition.

Susan Seizer richly portrays the ways unmarried female actresses in Tamil Nadu struggle to conform to the dominant terms of gendered respectability and virtuous domesticity, even while venturing out into the public sphere. They find creative means to configure themselves as "good women," and in so doing subtly reorganize the category itself and throw it into question.

Michele Gamburd examines how the prevalence of women's migration from Sri Lanka in response to high unemployment has forced villagers to rethink gender norms and, for unemployed husbands of working women in particular, generate new ways of expressing masculinity. The vast majority of Sri Lankan migrants to the Middle East are women, serving as domestic workers while sending money home to husbands and children. Their husbands, stripped of the role of breadwinner, resist taking over the "women's work" of child care and cooking, and grapple with local representations of their emasculation and delinquency.

Serena Nanda focuses on the life story of a hijra, an alternative neither-male-nor-female gender role in India. She depicts vividly the way Salima, born in a Muslim neighborhood in Mumbai, is as a child first considered male, but later becomes a hijra. As a hijra, she alternately experiences the warmth of being part of a community of other hijras, a marriage-like relationship with a man, and ultimately poverty and degradation on the streets. Salima's story powerfully conveys the potential ambiguity, fluidity, and not-strictly-binary nature of gender.

Gayatri Reddy explores several different intersecting sexual identity categories in Hyderabad, South India, including those of hijras, of *kotis*—female-identified men who desire and engage in receptive same-sex intercourse and adopt "feminine" mannerisms—and of "gays," who occupy marked public gay social spaces and belong to a growing number of gay/sexual rights organizations established in various cities across the country. Reddy examines the ways actors in Hyderabad engage with transnational discourses of a "global gay" movement, while arguing importantly that so-called traditional koti/hijra and "modern" gay identities and practices cannot be neatly dichotomized along lines of temporality and geography, of a gay/West/modern versus indigenous/non-West/traditional binary.

6

New Light in the House:
Schooling Girls in Rural North India

Ann Grodzins Gold

Early in 1997, I spent two months living in the village of Ghatiyali, District Ajmer, Rajasthan. I stayed in the home of Bhoju Ram Gujar, my friend and frequent co-author. Bhoju was at that time a government middle-school teacher (he is now a headmaster); his wife, Bali, is not literate. At that time they had three daughters, ranging in age from about ten down to four, and a two-year-old son. During this stay in Ghatiyali, Bhoju and I were engaged in two separate research projects: one on oral histories of environmental change and the other on environmental education, both formal and informal. For the latter project I sat many whole days in classrooms and school-yards, but spent others trekking long distances outdoors as I followed and talked with children between the ages of about ten and sixteen who worked herding goats and sheep, for their families or sometimes for wages. Originally I had no specific focus on the gender gap in literacy, but the more I spoke with children who herded and children who attended school, the more interested I became in the reasons so many female children remained outside the school walls.

In rural Rajasthan, low school attendance and low literacy rates persist in spite of government commitment at national, state, and local levels to universal education. According to statistics drawn from the 1991 Census of India, taken several years before my 1997 fieldwork, the statewide literacy rate in Rajasthan was 38.55 percent; broken down by gender, for males it was 54.99 percent and for females it was 20.44 percent. Of the total rural population only 30.37 percent was literate; and the literacy rate for rural females in 1991 was a startlingly low 11.59 percent (Sharma and Retherford 1993; Sharma 1994).

I have spent much of my anthropological career recording, translating, and interpreting oral traditions, and gathering many kinds of knowledge from unlettered persons of both sexes. In the course of that work, my profound respect for the richness and complexity of oral knowledge has been ever increasing.[1] Through nearly two decades of interacting with Rajasthani women, I had failed to contemplate or to conceptualize the disadvantages of being nonliterate—as were most all of my female village acquaintances. Village women to me had always seemed remarkably competent, and confident of their mastery of all skills necessary for their lives. It was they who instructed me, and gently mocked my multiple ignorances.[2] It was only in 1997 when I traveled to Jaipur city with Bhoju's wife, Bali, that I was hit by the difficulties and embarrassments of being nonliterate in a literate world. While in village and countryside, it was always I who was lost and she who led; now she had to ask me where we were. I could read the signs in Hindi and English.

A few weeks before this excursion, I had a painful encounter that provides a kind of anecdotal context for this chapter, as it highlights the intractable nature of some cultural obstacles that continue to slow the process of schooling girls in Rajasthan, and elsewhere in India. Bhoju and I had gone to interview the father of Arami, Bhoju's cousin Shivji's wife. Arami, like Bali and most young women of the Gujar community in the mid-nineties, was totally uneducated. Gujars' traditional occupational identity is raising dairy animals.[3] In her girlhood Arami had herded family livestock while her brothers studied. After her marriage to Shivji and before the births of her two daughters, she had worked as a laborer to supplement her husband's household income. Now she stayed at home with the baby and the toddler. Arami's father had been in the army, and had a partially transformed perspective on the world that seems to come to farmers with military experience.

Our recorded interview with Arami's father began well. He talked with us at length, very articulately, mostly about changes in agricultural technology. Eventually, we switched to the topic of education, as was our frequent pattern. Bhoju asked him about the choices he had made in educating his children. He told us of financial sacrifices undertaken to prepare his sons for cash-earning jobs by sending them to costly boarding school—an unusual step for a rural Gujar. I then casually inquired whether he had ever sent his daughters (of which he had several) to school. This affable man bluntly replied, "If I send them to school, they might run off, and then I would have to set them on fire, or take my rifle and shoot them!" Our conversation pretty much screeched to a halt, and Bhoju and I soon departed.

Later Bhoju summarized this rough moment, saying to me, "First his brain went bad, and then your brain went bad." Bhoju himself, as a teacher who has seen something of the world, knows the value of educating daughters. As a Gujar, he also well understands how other Gujars feel. Among Bhoju's and Bali's relatives and neighbors, a familiar pattern of sending boys to school and girls to herding prevails.[4] Bhoju was able eloquently to explain Arami's father's position. A family's entire social status is demolished by one wayward daughter. There are disastrous cases at which it is possible to point. What about the other children? No decent marriages can be arranged for the siblings of a girl who elopes with a school classmate.

Listening to Bhoju, I could not judge Arami's father to be a patriarchal monster or a dull-witted, ignorant man. Like most human beings he wants the best for his children, whom he loves—daughters as well as sons. He makes choices as wisely as he is able, in a society that is rapidly changing but nonetheless socially conservative. For Gujars and other agriculturist communities in Rajasthan, to educate girls is not only to gamble with the family honor, but to do so without visible potential winnings. If Arami's father stressed the dire risks entailed in girls' education as significant disincentives, many others, as we will see, stressed the lack of positive outcomes to be anticipated. This combination leaves little in the balance on the side of schooling daughters.

In this brief chapter my primary focus is uneducated herd girls' own perspectives on school, expressed in recorded interviews and songs. Then I shall turn to the ways some adult Rajasthani women who have awakened to the value of education articulate their views in slogans and moving lyrics. Nita Kumar has suggested in her study of educational history in Banaras (Varanasi) that to cooperate seriously in a process of modernization means necessarily to question existing practices and beliefs (2000: 194). Modernizing projects undertaken by women in Rajasthan not only question but challenge and often denounce existing practices. Such projects metaphorize their aims as "to dispel darkness" or "to climb aboard an accelerating train."

I have one main aim, and one secondary expectation. Most importantly I present female viewpoints: What do daughters, wives, and mothers think of the skewed literacy and school attendance ratios for girls and women? How does lack of education affect their lives and hopes? What do they wish for their own futures or for their children's? Along the way, I hope to reveal something of the existing conditions in which schooling for girls and local values may seem to clash so discordantly that Arami's father—a decent and reasonable man—would be led to take so extreme a position. Attitudes such as his are rooted in complex social and economic conditions, against which girls' education is realistically portrayed in women's consciousness-raising efforts as bringing "new light" into the house.

SCHOOLING FROM THE HERD GIRLS' POINT OF VIEW

One day a very old woman described the sufferings of her youth to me and Bhoju, and contrasted these with modern times (*nayā zamānā*)—"like in the song." She was a member of the Mina community, farmers sometimes described as "settled tribals" and understood to be indigenous to the region. Like Gujars, Minas had been slow to pursue educational opportunities. Her granddaughter, who had been listening, knew the song to which she alluded, and gave us a few lines. I was arrested not so much by the words—which are rather banal compared to many women's expressive lyrics—but by the song's opening image of a flood: two well-known rivers overflow their banks and wash away a major city. This suggests a tide of radical and irrevocable change, although the innovations described in the following lines will strike urban readers as far from revolutionary.

> The Chambal broke, the Banas broke, and Udaipur flowed away,
> Indira got down at the station, what did she have to say?
> I've installed electricity, faucets, street lamps too,
> And installed your sister-in-law's brother [husband] in a salaried job![5]

Electricity means women do not have to grind grain; water taps mean they no longer have to go to the well; streetlights may imply greater freedom of movement. Rural Rajasthani women have experienced these technologically implemented conveniences as a flood sweeping away previous structures of daily existence. But note that the song grants wage-earning careers only to husbands—presumably literate ones.

According to the young singer, this song was still popular among Mina girls, over ten years after the assassination of its heroine, former prime minister Indira Gandhi. Like many Mina girls, this woman had spent her childhood and early adolescence herding. Totally uneducated, she told us that she attended night school in her marital home, where living conditions were more comfortable than those in her natal village. She was proud of her better life in modern times, with nothing like the hardships her grandmother had endured.

Not all nonliterate or marginally literate wives are content with their situations. Other songs, recorded from women and girls, speak of domestic and emotional problems resulting from the skewed education system. These reveal that young women perceive the gender gap in schooling as leading directly to marital trouble. Illiterate brides are badly treated, even abandoned, by literate husbands seeking companionship.[6] Two songs I recorded in 1993 and published in other contexts revolve around this problem. One of these I heard from a group of unschooled preadolescent herd girls of the Mali (gardener) caste.

> In the school the parrot speaks; in the garden the peacock speaks.
> Over there, husband's sister, your brother went to study,
> From one side comes the motorbus, from the other comes the car,
> Your brother is dancing with the girls. (Gold and Gujar 1994: 80)

Uneducated females married to educated males fear their husbands will go astray in the world of modern transportation and foreign "dancing." While the Hindi word for "dance," *nāchnā*, evokes veiled women bending and twirling gracefully among themselves with no males present, the English "dance" that appears in this song represents the Westernized disco scene, of which villagers are aware from media images. Forlornly, the uneducated herd girl complains to her sister-in-law of their brother/husband's desertion to that alien world.

The second song is of a genre called *khyāl* ("feelings"), said to be, among other things, a medium through which women may complain about their husbands. I recorded it from adult women of the Nath community (farmers, temple priests, and gurus):

> Sold my nose ring and brought books,
> Went and sat in the school,
> Studied fine Hindi, and studied English,
> Became a respected railway clerk.
> Oh stifle my hiccups and stifle my soul!
> "Just now I'll meet with my pretty one."
> Mother is happy, my father is happy,
> but in the bedchamber, pretty one's sad. (Gold 1996: 18–19)

The young wife is emotionally abandoned by her husband, who has achieved success at her expense. He sold her valued ornament, and no longer seems to care for her. Women joke and tease one another about hiccups: "it means your husband's thinking of you." According to exegesis given me in Ghatiyali, the wife here admonishes herself to cease hiccuping and to keep her soul patient—in other words, to repress her desires. Her husband casually promises his immediate presence, but evidently his words do not console her much. He is just the kind of educated, salaried husband her parents wanted, but for her there is no conjugal satisfaction.[7]

Such songs voice the fears and anticipate the sorrows of unschooled women paired with literate men. Another song, performed by preadolescent Mali girls on the night of the harvest festival of Holi in 1993, is the only performance I happened to record in the village that speaks of secondary schooling for girls. The young singers had just done a song about Holi, the female demon, about to be consigned to a joyful bonfire.[8] They then spontaneously broke into a rousing tune, its lyrics proposing new, perilous, but thrilling possibilities for women:

> O innocent Shivji, my younger sister is going to school while riding on a
>   motorbike.
> O Shivji, she studied to the sixteenth class and joined the army.
> She beat the policemen with four sticks and hurt them, and the police
>   grabbed her and took her away.

Girls in Ghatiyali have yet to mount bicycles, let alone motorbikes, except as veiled, sidesaddle passengers. Careers in the military and the police are highly respected, desirable, and competitive professional options for educated young village men. This fanciful song seems uncertain where women's educational and professional achievements might lead. It sounds an adventurous note, but also warns of chaos and punishment. It seems to give voice simultaneously to girls' hopes and parents' fears.

Bhoju's niece Kali was an incredibly high-spirited, independent-minded, bright-eyed girl. People shook their heads and said she should have been born a boy. I interviewed her in 1993 when she was probably no more than nine years old. Her pragmatic attitude was already crystallized.

Ann: So, do you go to school?
Kali: School, never! I never went to school, never.
[She talks about her work helping to graze the family's sheep.]
Ann: Is grazing good or is studying good?
Kali: Grazing sheep is very good.
Ann: Why?
Kali: Sheep give us income, what does reading give? Sheep give us income. Suppose I do go to study, so, I'll hardly get a job!
Ann: So what is good about sheep?
Kali: Our own house's sheep? They give lambs, so we sell them; they give dung, and we sell it.

By 1997 Kali, maybe thirteen, was married but was still living in her natal home, where her work is valued. Her parents will demand that her in-laws give her some hefty silver ornaments before they relinquish their claims on her energetic labor and cheery company. Kali continued to emphasize the economic aspect of her non-education. It struck me, though, that she was well aware now of what she was losing. If not bitter, she was just slightly acid when she spoke of it.

Ann: Your brother goes to school—why not you?
Kali: If I went to school then who would do the housework?
Ann: Do you go to the night school?
Kali: My mother doesn't send me.
Ann: Why doesn't she send you?
Kali: She says, "What's the use of sending you? What kind of master will you become?" [*tum kaun sā māṛsā ban javelī*].

Kali's older brother, Shankar, is in school, in eighth grade. He dresses well, but is not very good at his studies. Kali never directly expressed envy of Shankar, but when the girls of Bhoju's extended family prevailed on me to take pictures of them posing in their finery on the roof, Kali disappeared, then returned triumphantly transformed, wearing Shankar's clothes.

Kali's mother's taunt, "What kind of master will you become?" is a painful one, but it reflects perfectly the way families such as hers gauge the potential worth of school education. Even at the younger age, she produced the line "I'll hardly get a job" to justify not attending school. Abraham and Lal, in their excellent account of female education in Jaipur district, confirm this to be a widespread attitude on the part of Rajasthani parents: "Envisaging the future of their children, all the parents saw education as a path to success." And success is defined as "gainful employment in the service or business sectors" (1995: 132–33). In numerous interviews with parents, teachers, and students, Bhoju and I systematically pursued this issue and found education consistently and firmly linked in all minds with the world of jobs (naukarī). Yet jobs are scarce, and women's opportunities are especially limited.[9]

THE STICK OF MODERNITY, BROKEN HEARTS, AND WISHES FOR DAUGHTERS

I want to turn now to messages of modernity—specifically of mahilā vikās, or "women's development," as transmitted in activist pamphlets in the local language. I draw largely on one particular booklet, which I first encountered in the hands of men. Anticipating a visit from a district-level officer, Bhoju's fellow teachers in the village of Palasya had decided it was necessary to paint slogans about literacy on every available wall. A pamphlet—not their minds—was their source for slogans, many of which were rhymed couplets in the original. I give a few examples, of which the first seemed to be the most popular in Palasya and environs.

1. One daughter will be educated, seven generations will be liberated!
   ek beṭī paṛhegī sāt pīṛī taregī
2. Every daughter has a right to health, learning, respect, and love.
   har beṭī kā hai adhikār sehat, śikṣā, mān aur pyār
3. If we educate our daughter, we increase knowledge and honor.
   beṭī ko ham paṛhāye jyān aur mān baṛāye
4. Just one vow is to be made: give your daughter an education.
   ek pratijyā lenī hai beṭī ko śikṣā denī hai
5. Let brothers do the housework too, so girls can go to school!
   bhāī bhī ghar kā kām karāye tabhī to bahnā paṛhne jāye
6. Girls and boys one and the same, be it health, education, or virtues!
   laṛkī-laṛkā ek samān, hom svasth, śikṣit guṇavān
7. When a daughter goes to study, our own knowledge will increase.
   beṭī paṛhbā jāvelī apṇom gyān baṛhāvelī
8. Daughters' education is the family's protection.
   beṭīyom kī śikṣā, parivār kī surakṣā

At my request, Bhoju later obtained a copy of his colleagues' source book. Its title, Prerṇā gīt aur chetan nāre, translates into something like Inspirational Songs and Consciousness-Raising Slogans. The book is authored and produced by members of a women's collective, working under the auspices of the well-known and successful Jaipur-based Women's Development Program (WDP).[10] An eloquent introduction begins, "The work of awakening human society to women's issues is a very heavy challenge." It ends with a wish for women who read the book to "make these songs and slogans your own," so that "Joining our voices and melodies, . . . one day we will be successful" (Upadhyay et al. 1995: i–ii). Although the introduction is written in Sanskritized Hindi, the songs are in the Rajasthani vernacular, the only language in which most unschooled village women of this region feel comfortable.

Girls are taught to perform such songs for school assemblies. On Republic Day at the big government middle school in Ghatiyali, the spacious courtyard had a single row of chairs for parents to watch their children recite, sing, and dance in honor of the national holiday. On these chairs sat a handful of men—fathers, all in Western clothes. Clustered outside the walls, peering over them, were larger numbers of parents in Rajasthani dress: men in loincloths and turbans; women in skirts and wraps, often with veils pulled over their faces. This voluntary and spontaneous segregation by gender and class, or profession, is indicative of ways the school remains an alien space. Nonliterate parents of both sexes feel no sense of belonging there.

Bhoju's own wife, Bali, stayed home, claiming child-care burdens, although Madhu, her oldest daughter, was in the show. Girls on the stage sang songs such as this one, which Madhu and two classmates beautifully performed:

> Don't get me married when I'm young,
> Let me study, let me study!
> My sister Kajori is un-schooled, she has eight children,
> and doesn't know how to raise them, so the lot of them are sick.
> Let their sickness be less!
> Don't get me married when I'm young,
> Let me study, let me study!
> Many literate sisters go to work at jobs, but
> The illiterate sit, their veils pulled down,
> In their homes, darkness and shadow.
> Let me bring the new light into my house!
> Don't get me married when I'm young.
> Let me study, let me study!

Self-defined consciousness-raising songs and slogans—heartfelt productions of already mobilized women—hurl themselves melodically against the surrounding culture of gender discrimination, to which uneducated herd girls' songs sorrowfully allude.

Notice that this song unites the idea of education with health, good housekeeping, and even jobs for literate young women. Yet among the herding and farming communities, at least, it is quite likely that the mothers and grandmothers of these girls are happily plotting weddings. Like Kali's family, and even Madhu's female relations, they believe good marriages to be more essential for their well-loved daughters' future well-being than any schooling.

I found many songs in the booklet to be unexpectedly moving, genuinely "inspirational," even when I had never seen or heard them performed. Some have individual named authors, while others were apparently composed by the collective. They carry powerful emotions, persuading me that at least some parts of the modernity project have been fully internalized. I shall give two of these texts in full. One speaks sadly of discrimination between daughters and sons; the other is about the imminent danger, and tragedy, of girls "missing the train" to literacy.

The first is titled "This Evil Custom Goes On (of Discriminating between Daughters and Sons)" [*rīt burī ye chālī (beṭī-beṭe meṁ bhed bhāv)*]:

> *Listen, Listen, O my company of girlfriends,*
> *this evil custom goes on, O sisters,*
> *without knowledge, she remains empty!*
> When I was born, a broken potsherd,
> When brother was born, a nice plate,
>   *O sisters, knowledge.*
> They send my brother to study at school,
> but they have me do the herding work,
>   *O sisters, knowledge.*
> My brother wears pants and a sports-shirt,
> but I'm wearing only a thin cloth wrap,
>   *O sisters, knowledge.*
> My husband's brothers' wives read books aloud,
> But they make me scrub the plates,
>   *O sisters, knowledge.*
> When a gardener plants two trees,
> That gardener alone is the one to water them,
>   *O sisters, knowledge.*
> All sisters, go and study!
> I too shall not stay empty,
>   *O sisters, knowledge.*
> (Upadhyay et al. 1995: 116)

This song aims a direct reproach at parents who practice multiple forms of daughter-neglect and son favoritism, leaving their girls hungry for knowledge, among other things. It is one among many with similar themes.[11]

The upbeat closing refrain of the "discrimination" song is absent in another composition titled "Daughters' Education: The Learning Train." This one, which has a named author, expresses a mother's acute personal sorrow at seeing her daughter kept away from school due to household needs.

> *The learning train is going along,*
>   *Oh, the learning train is going along.*
> See the rich boys slip right inside,
> See the children of the poor remain outside.
>   *How many girls are climbing in?*

Figure 6.1. Madhu Gujar and friends at school assembly, Ghatiyali, January 26, 1997.

But half of them descend again.
The learning train is going along,
Oh, the learning train is going along.
Everyone comes to the station when the train halts there.
But sometimes money, sometimes marriage get in their way.
How many girls are climbing in?
But half of them descend again.
The learning train is going along,
Oh, the learning train is going along.
My beloved daughter says, "Please register me at school."
I say, "I'd really like to but how can I register you at school?
When I go to do labor work, and you go to your school,
Then when we're both outside the house,
Who looks after baby brother?"
My daughter's tears flow, my heart just breaks,
Before our eyes the Education Railroad pulls away.
My daughter's tied down at home,
But the learning train is going along,
Oh the learning train is going along.
(Upadhyay et al. 1995: 98; song by Kamalesh Yadav)

Figure 6.2. The "stick of modernity": Chinu Gujar plays school.

Another of the pamphlet songs is called "Times Have Changed!" (*jamān badal gayo*). It begins by promoting literacy, and goes on to praise famous Indian women. This lengthy song then addresses just about every aspect of tradition that modernity rejects, admonishing people to renounce black magic, cease child marriage, reduce population, and live in happy small families, as well as to educate their daughters. Such is the package deal, imposed by what Nita Kumar has called the "stick of modernity" (2000: 199).

School itself is aptly associated with an authoritative stick intended to coerce young persons into new and unfamiliar behaviors and modes of thought. Chinu, Bhoju's middle daughter, decided to play schoolmaster to her younger sister and cousin one day while I was living there (fig. 6.2). She was about six years old at the time, and her pupils were three or four. She separated herself from them with a table and took up a stick, doubtless wielding it in imitation of teachers at the village primary school she attended. I have heard teachers harangue village students at morning assembly to "forget" everything they had in their minds before arriving at school, to sweep their brains clean, to erase them like slates. Education thus explicitly pits itself against family, home, and tradition.

In women's activist compositions the New Light prevailing in the New Times shines upon near inversions of familiar gender hierarchies, and not without good reason. As we have seen in the case of Arami's father and throughout this chapter, resistance to girls' education is stubbornly embedded in slow-changing social and economic patterns. It is easy to agree that all the factors disadvantaging women are linked. Child marriage, for example, works directly against keeping girls in school—as Madhu's Republic Day song recognized. Preference for sons, based on their potential future contributions to household income, means that girls are given herding chores so boys can study. Were we determined to pursue root causes, surely (as many others have argued) the fundamental sources of gender discrimination lie in property rights, patrilineal descent, and patrilocal marriage.[12] It is also my hunch that a major fount of many invidious gender practices I encounter in Rajasthan is the ineffable but palpable culture of honor, or *ijjat*. Fear of lost honor is what caused Arami's father to make his terrifyingly matter-of-fact statement about the mortal peril of schooling girls.[13]

Women's development organizations are probably correct in perceiving that multiple changes will have to precede gender equity in education, or at least to accompany it. Yet this stand, however logical, in the arena of gender perpetuates the split between home and school that has sabotaged efforts for universal literacy in India for well over a century.[14] Hence, I find myself wondering what would happen if the literacy campaigns in Rajasthan were to renounce their attacks on child marriage, child labor, household sex roles, brother favoritism, and all the rest of it. Could we just have initiatives for nothing but reading, writing, and arithmetic, and miraculously produce literate child bride goatherds? Even as I write this I realize it sounds not only heretical but absurd. Yet I remain troubled, as do many thoughtful authors on education in India, by a situation in which the school system is hopelessly pitted against the culture. Women's development groups—with all the best intentions—redouble this opposition.

One auspicious sign for future female literacy may be found in the wishes expressed by mothers for their daughters' education. Not only activists but women fully enmeshed in the present gender web sometimes express these aspirations, revealing that even those unable to decipher slogans may nonetheless read the writing on the wall. If change comes slowly to the farming communities of rural Rajasthan, similar processes took place among urban upper classes fifty and one hundred years ago in other regions.[15]

In concluding I turn to words I recorded at the end of an interview with women laborers, young wives cheerfully doing the work of breaking and carrying rocks. A program under the auspices of Rajasthan's accelerated "Total Literacy Campaign" for Bhilwara district in 1997 made participation in adult literacy classes a condition of obtaining work as laborers for the state government. Moreover, laborers' wages were to be withheld until they could successfully sign their names. These women disparaged their own success at the modernizing project, asserting that "wet clay won't stick to a baked pot" (*pākā haṇḍā kā gār na lāgai*).[16] But, like the author of the education train song, they had different aspirations for their daughters' lives. The last words I heard from an authoritative voice among them, as they scattered back to their hard work, were these:

I may not be literate (*paṛī lihkī*) but you should teach my daughter! . . . Our lives are half over, but our daughters [have a future], so take care of them.

ACKNOWLEDGMENTS

I am grateful to the Spencer Foundation and the American Institute of Indian Studies for research support in 1997. Bhoju Ram Gujar participated in every stage of this project, and I also owe enormous thanks to many women and girls who gave me their time and words—especially Bali, Madhu, and Kali Gujar. Many thanks also to Madhu Kishwar for encouraging me to publish this in India in *Manushi*, and to Diane, Sarah, and Indiana University Press for agreeing to let this happen.

NOTES

1. See, for example, Gold 1992; Raheja and Gold 1994.

2. In Ghatiyali I encountered nothing like the self-disparagement of nonliterate women reported by R. Jeffery and P. Jeffery (1996) from Bijnor, U. P. Regional differences are evidently of enormous importance.

3. There are castes called Gujar throughout North India. In Ghatiyali, and generally in eastern and central Rajasthan, Gujar identity—both in folklore and in practice—is bound up with livestock and often most specifically with dairy production. For pastoralists in Rajasthan, including Gujars, see Kavoori 1999.

4. Most boys also drop out relatively early. Young men educated to ninth or tenth grade are often unable to find jobs that suit their educated status, or to feel comfortable herding and farming. This chapter focuses on particular problems for girls, but keep in mind that total male literacy also remains a remote goal.

5. "Sister-in-law's brother" is a common circumlocution for "husband" in Rajasthani women's songs.

6. On girls' education explicitly defined as the production of companionable wives, see Forbes 1996: 32–63.

7. Women's songs recorded in other regions of north India include those in praise of wage-earning husbands and criticizing farmer husbands (P. Jeffery and R. Jeffery 1996a), as well as those that identify employed husbands with the sorrows of separation (Narayan 1997).

8. For the context of Holi in which this song was recorded, see Gold 2001.

9. These days competent, literate women are such a rare commodity that many of them do find minor wage-earning opportunities as workers in numerous development programs. These are often part-time positions they can hold without leaving their homes; as such, they garner neither the prestige nor the income of outside full-time employment.

10. For the WDP, see Abraham and Lal 1995; Unnithan and Srivastava 1997.

11. A number of activist songs critique discrimination against girls. These songs include in their litany not only the reaction of the family at birth and unequal access to education—as does this one—but also disparities in the distribution of food and clothing and differences in marriage age as well. Abraham and Lal describe teach-

ing a very similar song to women in a village in Jaipur district. They write, "And soon the whole village was humming the song" (Abraham and Lal 1995: 79–80).

12. For a masterful discussion of gender and property issues, see Agarwal 1994.

13. Manoj Srivastava's recent study offers a new angle on honor from the advantage of his experience as a government administrator in another low-literacy state, Bihar. Srivastava suggests that honor's motivating power may be harnessed and redirected to abet the cause of literacy. Speaking of some success stories in literacy campaigns, he writes, "[P]eople felt a sense of honor through a vicarious identification with the prestige that got symbolically, but intensely, associated with achieving a total literacy for the community" (1998: 143).

14. For two illuminating discussions of this, from different perspectives, see K. Kumar 1991; Illaih 1996.

15. See for example many of the writings in Tharu and Lalita 1991. Raman 1996 offers a fascinating portrayal of women's education initiatives, mostly among upper castes, in colonial Tamilnad. Among other things, we learn from her case study that marriage need not impede education and that daughters in families with a "reverence for learning" are likely to be educated. In other words, if schooling is valued it may easily trump gender discrimination, as it has done in Bhoju's own household.

16. See Srivastava for a similar saying used with similar import: "Can an aged parrot be ever domesticated?" (1998: 137).

7

Roadwork: Offstage with Special Drama Actresses in Tamil Nadu, South India

Susan Seizer

> The event was absolutely unique, and it was repeated every year.
> For the event (any event) unfolds simultaneously on two levels: as
> individual action and as collective representation; or better, as the
> relation between certain life histories and a history that is, over and
> above these, the existence of societies.
> —Marshall Sahlins, *Islands of History* (1985)

MISE-EN-SCÈNE

Roads and streets are a common mise-en-scène for enactments of the Tamil popular theater genre known as Special Drama. The obligatory opening comedy scene of these live performance events always begins with a young woman dancing in the middle of a road, a fantastic suspension of Tamil norms of conduct for women. The painted canvas backdrop for this scene displays a wide, generic road stretching off vertically into the horizon. The comic enactment that unfolds rapidly develops into an exploration of illicit love. An unknown young bachelor appears on the road, and all manner of shady business unspools between the young man and woman, including lewd banter, flirtatious spats, boasts laden with sexual innuendo, coy one-upmanship, cooing love songs, and, eventually, elopement.

This opening scene is a dramatization, in a comic mode, of the proverbial bad road for women. Its narrative content perpetuates and encourages a dominant association between public roads and the bad reputation of ac-

This is an abridged and amended version of a paper entitled "Roadwork: Offstage with Special Drama Actresses in Tamil Nadu, South India" that originally appeared in *Cultural Anthropology* 15, no. 2 (2000): 217–59. Reprinted with permission.

tresses as public women. This essay concerns how such an association of ideas shapes Special Drama actresses' offstage lives, and in turn, how their practices "on the road" potentially refigure that dominant discourse.

"Special Drama" (*Special Nāṭakam*) is a contemporary Tamil theatrical genre that began around the turn of the twentieth century. Its hybrid English-Tamil name refers to the practice of hiring each artist "specially" for every performance event. Special Drama is performed outdoors in small towns or villages, either in the village commons or, equally often, at the intersection of two roads. In 1993, sixteen cities and towns throughout the state of Tamil Nadu had actors associations, run by the artists to facilitate a statewide network of Special Drama performers (see fig. 7.1).

The participants in Special Drama—performers as well as audience members—are predominately working class. In my interviews and conversations with artists, the explanation most performers gave for entering this line of work was "due to poverty." Some Special Drama artists begin performing in childhood, others as young adults; about half come from families that are already involved in some way in the drama world. Though the work is only seasonal, the pay is relatively high when available. For example, a woman who works as a cook or a maid might earn Rs 75 *per month,* whereas working as an actress she might earn Rs 300 *in one night.* Such relatively high wages are virtually the sole compensation, however, for the loss of social standing that results from entering this profession. And this cost, to be sure, most severely affects women.

Becoming a Special Drama actress generally means forfeiting any chance of a "normal" marriage (by which I mean a legally sanctioned marriage arranged between the bride's and groom's families), as no self-respecting groom's family will agree to have a son marry an actress (and this often includes families of male actors!) because of a standard view of actresses as public women, a.k.a. prostitutes. Indeed, several common Tamil words for "actress" simultaneously denote "whore" or "prostitute." *Kūtti, kūttiyāḷ, tāci,* and *tēvaṭiyāḷ* all mean "dancing girl or prostitute" (Fabricius 1972: 505), "(derogatorily) mistress; concubine" (Cre-A 1992: 349), or "dancing girl devoted to temple service, commonly a prostitute; harlot, whore" (Lexicon 1982: 1825). The combined effect of such stigmatizing terms and the discourses that fuel their existence is to keep most "good" Tamil women from daring or desiring to be actresses at all, and ensuring that most actresses will become "second wives," a euphemism for concubines or mistresses—a lived rather than a legal category.

At the core of this essay are five fieldwork narratives.[1] These retell specific experiences I had while on the road with Special Drama actresses. Each experience helped me to better understand actresses' actions offstage; these were the settings in which I learned, in particular, how and why actresses create private, exclusive spaces in the midst of the Tamil public sphere. Each narrative speaks of one leg in the journey to or from a Special Drama. To-

Figure 7.1. Map of the State of Tamil Nadu, showing the location of the sixteen towns and cities in which actors associations are located.

gether, the five narratives thus make up a single composite journey that begins in a calendar shop in town (the first narrative), then heads out by van (the second) or by bus (the third), to the site of a Special Drama stage and its backstage spaces (the fourth), and finally returns home, on foot, to town (the fifth and final narrative).

Through these narratives I aim to convey a sense of the actresses' *road-work* as a set of lived, adaptive practices that operate to foil the dominant notion of actresses as "bad women." When actresses manage to make their behavior indistinguishable from that of good women—in other words, when they appear to comply with these dominant norms—might the norms be somewhat altered by being stretched to accommodate these women? With this question in mind, I suggest that actresses creatively *expand* the category of "good woman" to include themselves. I see this *expansion* of given, exclusive categories of social acceptability as a particular strategy for dealing with social stigma. The theoretical import of this study, then, concerns the larger issue of the effective redress of stigma: I detail a strategy that operates under the appearance of collaboration with social norms while simultaneously refiguring the norms themselves.

THEORETICAL GROUNDS

In her preface to *Imaginary Maps*, Gayatri Spivak uses the metaphor of an intractable obstacle, a roadblock blocking women's movements all over the world, to convey what she calls a "difficult truth": that "internalized gendering perceived as ethical choice is the hardest roadblock for women the world over" (1995: xxviii). In Spivak's vision, internalized gender norms and constraints block both the movement of individual women down particular roads and the progress of collective women's movements worldwide.

Partha Chatterjee similarly stresses the historical importance women's internalization of a properly gendered self-image has had in building the new Indian nation. He argues, however, that women's ability to internalize gender constraints eased rather than blocked their travels out into the world. Chatterjee suggests that it is precisely through their internalization of a self-image of virtuous domesticity that middle-class women have been able to maintain respectability while venturing out into the public sphere; these good women were able to carry their "home" identities out into the "world" with them. This amounts to an ingenious nationalist strategy for resolving "the women's question": the middle-class woman had simply to become so identified with the spiritual and moral sphere of the home that it remained intact wherever she went. As Chatterjee writes: "Once the essential femininity of women was fixed in terms of certain culturally visible spiritual qualities, they could go to schools, travel in public conveyances, watch public entertainment programs, and in time even take up employment outside the home" (1993: 130). Moving in public, the respectable woman carries with her an inner strength forged indoors.

The case is quite the opposite for those worldly women against whom nationalism's model middle-class women were explicitly defined—those women, that is, whom Chatterjee calls "sex objects" for the nationalist male, precisely *because* they are seen as "other" than his mother/sister/wife/daughter. Likewise, in Tamil Nadu today, while middle-class women are able to displace the boundaries of the home from its physical confines onto a more flex-

ible psychic domain, Special Drama actresses, who hail from among the urban poor in Tamil Nadu, never had such a proper middle-class home in the
first place. For these actresses, the task of attaining the qualities of the good
woman—still defined by the virtues of domesticity—requires that they constantly, vigilantly strive in their daily practice to erect those very physical
confines the new middle-class woman has left behind. Actresses attempt
to better their reputation as women by acting on the dominant script quite
literally, throughout their public journeys, by seeking to recreate domesticity
in its material form.

In this essay I focus on the problematic mobility of women who do *not*
properly internalize gender constraints. I write here about stage actresses in
Tamil Nadu, women stigmatized precisely for being too public, and for moving out into the world beyond the bounds of proper, modest feminine behavior. As such, this essay is literally about women and roads; more specifically,
it is about my own experiences traveling certain roads, and encountering
certain roadblocks, with certain women.

In these travels I began to develop my own embodied sense of actresses'
roadwork, of its system of signs and dispositions, indeed of the "imaginative
universe within which their acts are signs" (Geertz 1973: 13). I now understand my feelings during our travels as a set of diagnostic signs, signifying
to me that I had begun to understand viscerally something of what is at
stake for actresses when traveling through the public sphere. I was engaging
in the famous ethnographic work of "deep hanging-out" (Rosaldo, quoted
in Clifford 1997: 188), through which I began to understand "the character of
lived experience" among actresses. That is, I treat examining my own experiences moving with Special Drama actresses on their turf and in their terms
as a classically ethnographic way of gaining insight into their experiences of
being "other" in the context of the contemporary Tamil public sphere. "Ethnography . . . has always meant the attempt to understand another life world
using the self—as much of it as possible—as the instrument of knowing"
(Ortner 1995: 173).

THE STIGMA OF INAPPROPRIATE MOBILITY

Throughout India, as elsewhere, theater actresses have long been the
very definition of "bad" women. Unlike the chaste loyalty of the good wife,
who reveals herself to only one man, the actress's profession requires that
she willingly expose herself to the gaze of many unfamiliar men. This blatant step into the limelight of such mobile relations is largely what brands
actresses as bad.

There are three highly interconnected dimensions to the stigma of mobility accruing to actresses in Tamil Nadu. The first is a problem with acting itself, the fact of mimetic fluidity—that acting involves illusion and not
reality, and offers false selves, making mobile things that ought to be fixed.

The second involves the overly fluid offstage behavior of actors in employing fictive kin networks, rather than maintaining normal, orderly, sanctioned kin relations. Actors use kin terms across caste, class, religious, and ethnic boundaries, creating socially expedient relations between them where in reality no blood or marriage relations exist. Such identity shifts onstage (mimetic) and off (in kin relations)—both of which concern normative relations between men and women—taint the reputation of the acting community as a whole, and stigmatize it as excessively mobile and uncontainable.

I restrict my focus here to the third dimension of the stigma that accrues to actresses, their publicity and mobility as they move about conducting their business. The form of this mobility—the very public nature of the actress's line of work—threatens to expose the fragility of the culturally naturalized division of gendered spheres into home and world, as actresses move onto public stages to enact what are meant to be the most private of relations. While the other two dimensions of stigma haunt the acting community as a whole, this third dimension of stigma affects actresses far more than actors, as men have the freedom to move outside publicly without censure in Tamil Nadu. Stigma hits the actress hardest, as it is she, finally, who is most unsettling precisely in her unsettledness. Her battle for reputation against this unsettledness is constant, since the very organization of Special Drama depends on performers' mobility. Each artist is contracted individually for each performance. There is no troupe or director for Special Drama. Instead, there are repertory roles, such as Hero and Heroine, Buffoon and Dancer, in a set repertory of plays. It is each artist's responsibility to get to and from each venue on time. During the drama season, the hot summer months of March through August, actresses may appear on a different stage in a different town or village every night. These women travel all across the state to perform night-long shows that begin at 10 PM and end at dawn. The primary challenge for these women is how to accomplish their public artistic business with as little tainting publicness as possible.

In moving with Special Drama actresses through the streets of Tamil Nadu, I experienced how they created structures of enclosure even in the most public of places. I experienced viscerally how a dominant "inside/outside" dichotomy of "good/bad" morality informs their every journey. And I grew to appreciate their patient, understated, and expansive response to this oppressive climate. As we traveled, actresses erected enclosures that were their own exclusive, interior spaces, spaces that slyly appropriated for themselves a dominant strategy of exclusion everywhere we went. They strung together little islands, havens of familiarity, and hopped from one to the next as a means of remaining protected while moving through the outside.

Narrative One: Regarding the Gender Dimensions of Booking a Drama

The arrangement of bookings and dates for Special Drama is a side of their business from which actresses often distance themselves, especially because such negotiations concern their own public mobility. Instead of taking bookings directly, an actress hangs her calendar in a booking shop. In 1993, there were five such shops in the city of Madurai, the long-established center for Special Drama.[2] All were very male public spaces; several were printing shops in which booking artists' calendars were a side business, while for others such calendars were the main business. While the calendars of both male and female artists hang in these shops, only men are present physically—in the flesh, that is—sitting around talking, checking on the dates of their next performances, or drumming up business for new bookings. Male representatives from a village or town interested in booking a drama come to the city of Madurai to peruse the posted calendars, check on the availability of specific drama artists, and converse with those in the know about the current crop of artists.

Men who, for a living, help these local sponsors make their drama arrangements are known as drama agents. Together, drama agents, drama sponsors, and male drama actors regularly hang out in and around the five booking shops in Madurai, all of which are located within a small two-block radius in the center of town, a little business district in which actors are kings of the road but through which actresses only briskly pass on their way to and from performance venues.

Inside the shops, the walls are lined with individual artist's calendars. These calendars have a separate thin page for each day of the year. The pages make a square packet, which is stapled onto a cardboard backing where the artist's name is pasted as a heading, and beneath which the artist's bust photo provides further identification and allure. Every artist's calendar provides a book of days that opens out under its personalized headboard like a skirt—or so it appeared to me.

Men interested in hiring an actress do not approach her directly, but rather approach her calendar. An actress's calendar is in this way a material stand-in for her. It provides sponsors with a way to contract an actress without direct interaction, and simultaneously allows the actress to absent herself from the negotiations. Similar to the process by which good Indian girls become brides, here men engage in negotiations in which a woman's person is implicated, but not dialogically involved.[3] While he books an actress, she stays at home; an effigy of her (her personalized calendar) circulates in her stead.

Any man approaching an actress's calendar to book a drama may pick her effigy off the wall, handle it, peruse it, flip through its skirt, and read therein the unfolding story of the actress's public life: where she will be when in the coming days, where she has been in the recent past, how busy this season looks, how in demand (or not) she is this season. Penned onto the back side of her calendar is the actress's performance fee, which is a private note from her, hidden from public view. If he selects her, he pens his name, and his place name, directly onto the front of her calendar. Without her ever having to meet with him, he has arranged for her to come to his place, when he chooses, for a fee.

The shop owner, who functions as a booking agent, has a certain financial stake in these negotiations, as he earns a fee (three rupees was the going rate in 1993) every time an artist whose calendar he posts is booked for a drama. Being financially implicated in this way, the shop owner wants the calendars of popular artists in his shop. He needs to know whether or not a particular artist will actually attract sponsors' bookings; he needs to know each artist's value and reputation. When I asked one shop owner, Mr. Jeyaraman, how he ascertains this, he answered: "I'll ask them to sing. 'Show me how you sing,' I'll say, and they'll sing right here in the shop. I ask many people to sing before I put their calendar up." This surprised me because it was the first I had heard of such a practice. Our conversation continued:

> *Susan:* Really? So, imagine that I want to hang my calendar here. Would you ask me to sing?
> *Jeyaraman:* Oh no! No I won't. I won't ask this of women.
> *S:* Why is that?
> *J:* We can't ask a woman to come here and sing. Can we ask a woman to come sing in a public place? If this was a house, we might ask her; here we can't.

I was intrigued. We were talking about professional performers, stage actresses, the very women who *do* sing in public places—public women par excellence—were we not? I sat there in my sari with my black box of a tape recorder, asking him endless questions, feeling like a gender freak and a bit of a boor. Actresses might be public women professionally and by night, but in their local day-to-day lives, close to home, they tried to maintain a reputation as proper women.[4] In the daytime, in their daily local life, actresses would not come out to a public shop—the very shop where I currently sat and quite publicly acted the anthropologist, asking questions about these very gendered norms and practices—and perform publicly. I realized belatedly and somewhat sheepishly that, when he spoke about asking them to sing, Jeyaraman had been referring only to male artists, the kind of people who *should be* in shops like his.

Before I could even ask how it was, then, that he did ascertain the talents of an actress without asking her to sing, he volunteered the following: "Regarding women, if we want a critical assessment, that's easy: many people will be going to see her and will be knowing about her. We can learn from so many people: they'll be saying, 'this is how she talks; this is how she acts.' So therefore I can guarantee her to any town."

Even her booking agent, then, learns of an actress's talents only indirectly, through the eyes, ears, and words of other men who have seen and heard her onstage. Other men speak to him directly about her voice, or else they speak in and around his shop to other men hanging out in and around his shop. It is men, speaking among each other, who determine an actress's reputation, while she sits, quietly or not, at home.

Figure 7.2. Jeyaraman's calendar shop, Madurai, February 10, 1992, near the beginning of the drama season. (Mr. Jeyaraman standing at left.)

Narrative Two: Regarding Traveling to a Drama in a Private Conveyance

Whenever they can, Special Drama artists travel to their performance venues in private rather than public vehicles. Older artists recall with nostalgia the days when they traveled in the pinnacle of secluded, enclosed, and luxurious worlds: they rode in "pleasures." "Pleasure" is the English word artists still use to refer to the private automobile, the rented Ambassador "pleasure car" that used to pick up actresses at their own door and take them directly to the performance site.[5]

Very rarely are "pleasures" used by drama parties today. Instead, quite often artists pool their resources to hire a private van, the current means of avoiding public buses. Such drama vans are crowded. Sometimes sixteen people squeeze into a space designed for ten, where in addition the back seat is entirely taken up with artistic provisions: a large wooden foot-pedal harmonium, several drums, multiple rolls of painted canvas backdrops for scene settings, not to mention each actor's costume-filled suitcase. People have to sit practically on top of each other in these vans, often for many hours.

Nevertheless, the question of why artists adamantly prefer crowded private vans to public buses is obvious: public-private distinctions as markers of prestige and social status in Tamil Nadu long predate both vans and buses. The reigning logic is familiar: more prestigious persons occupy both more (and more private) personal space, while less prestigious persons occupy both less (and less private) space.

To me, traveling with drama artists in a van always felt risqué. Suddenly the strict women's side/men's side rules of public conveyances were lifted. The two requisite actresses in any Special Drama party would often sit side by side in the van in a two-person seat, but equally often they did not. My own presence could easily instigate multiple shifts: a woman certainly had to be seated next to me for reasons of propriety (so that I would not be forced to sit beside an unknown man), but then what about the other actress? She suddenly had increased mobility, without ever seeming to ask for it. Inside a van, other sorts of allegiances and alliances, even intimacies, emerged easily.

Van interiors provide drama artists a means of moving through and across public roads while carrying a collective interiority, a protective group cohesiveness, with them. The world internal to the drama community creates a bubble of familiarity that stretches to the contours of every space they fill together, and in these cases it was the size of the interior of a van. I felt included in that "inside" familiarity when I rode with them. I felt freer there than almost anywhere else in Tamil Nadu, engaged in a daring squeeze of closeness that was largely invisible to the outside world. I felt inside a family, of sorts, and it was a pleasure too.

Narrative Three: Regarding Traveling to a Drama in a Public Conveyance

Bakkiyalakshmi and I had finally settled on a date for me to accompany her to a drama. Bakkiya is a seasoned actress in her fifties, and we were going to a village in an area well known to her from decades of performing throughout the region.

As this village was accessible by main road, we were traveling by public bus (as there is less excuse for the luxury of hiring a van when a venue can be reached by bus). All Tamil town buses, like those we took that night, have a women's side and a men's side. The words indicating which side is which are stenciled directly onto the walls of the bus. When traveling in a pair, two women need have very little interaction with unknown persons on a public bus, least of all with unknown men. We had none.

We left from Madurai in the early evening and traveled into the night. To reach the sponsoring village we had to change buses at two different stations. In the first station our change was quick and easy, as the next bus was already loading when we arrived. We simply got up from our two-person seat on the women's side of the bus from Madurai, and switched to another two-person seat on the women's side of the bus from Sivaganga.

At the second station our bus was not waiting. Bakkiya told me it would not come for another half an hour. We got off the bus and she led me to a little food stall, one among many lining the road on the side of the bus station. There a man was making a common flamboyant dish, a specialty of the region called "egg parota" (parota is a deliciously thin bread layered in a flat spiral). Its preparation involves terrific energy on the part of the chef. He holds two metal tools—they are shaped more like axes than knives—and bangs them down onto a wide, flat metal skillet, over and over, rhythmically mixing and chopping parota and egg. It is the noisiest manner of food preparation I have ever encountered, entrancing as only an intensely loud barrage of sound can be, starting for a spell of deafening decibels at each new order and abruptly stopping again in equally deafening silence.

The chef at the stall we approached flashed a big smile at Bakkiyalakshmi. They knew each other, though I didn't catch exactly how. He was at least twenty years her junior. She introduced me and he immediately put down his tools and led us back through his stall into a small back room. In it was a desk, a chair, and a cot. The walls were painted royal blue. He made sure I was comfortably seated in the chair and returned to his metal axes and metal skillet. Bakkiya asked me whether I would like to eat, encouraging me to do so here rather than wait for whatever food the villagers had prepared. I agreed. She left the room, and I was alone.

I sat in that little room for what felt like a long time but couldn't have been more than fifteen minutes. The wall of sound just beyond unmistakably delimited inside from outside. Where I was sitting was inside: blue walls swimming around me, a tide of deafening sound reaching me in waves. The other noises and voices and commerce beyond the walls of that room were all outside.

I realized that even on this most public of routes, taking a public bus from a public bus stand two towns away from home, Bakkiya had secured a little private space, which that night she lent to me so that I could disappear into a respite of invisibility. I sat there feeling safe and tiny, and simultaneously out of the loop and bored. How, I wondered, does Bakkiya feel when she sits there?

Narrative Four: Regarding Spatial Arrangements at a Drama Site

When artists reach their performance venue, an outdoor stage has already been erected at the site. The stage is a raised rectangular platform, often with a dirt floor, with palm-frond thatching for three walls and the ceiling. Specifications for the stage require a large playing area and an equally roomy backstage to which the actors may retire when they are not onstage. Actors call the playing space onstage "outside" (*veḷiyē*) and the backstage resting space "inside" (*uḷḷē*).

A central feature of all Special Drama venues is thus that there is a definite demarcation between inside and outside, between a public space where actors are visible to all, and a private space into which they may disappear. This demarcation is provided by the painted canvases known as "scene settings" that stretch from ceiling to floor and are rolled and unrolled for scene changes throughout the night.

Actors change costumes, touch up their faces and hair, sleep in catnaps between scenes, chat, and snack together "inside" throughout the night. They prepare themselves in this collective space of inside before each stint outside. Inside, they generally maintain the decorum of women's side and men's side arrangements, though not rigidly; inside feels, in short, much like being in a privately relaxed Tamil domestic space, a home, where gender determines behavior somewhat more flexibly than in public.[6] This ability to create a familiar domestic place in the midst of the otherwise unknown and unfamiliar, an inside place where they are shielded from the public gaze and can feel and act in familiar ways, is a skill actresses employ everywhere they go.

Even inside the inside itself, for example, actresses maintain these familiar distinctions. Backstage, they carve out a private space by tying a string across one corner and hanging a sari over it, creating a modest one-woman changing corner.

I found out just how useful a shield from the outside such an inside place could be one night when I needed to empty my bladder and my actress friends directed me to their changing corner. Squatting inside that little triangular women's space, I realized the other obvious resonance of the terms "inside" and "outside," at least in the rural context. Where there is no restroom—and the majority of people living in rural India have none—"going outside" (*veḷiyē pōka*) means literally that. To have to go outside to relieve themselves would have put the actresses on par with the lower-class rural women in the audience, rather than allying them in bodily practice with middle-class women's use of an indoor toilet. Creating inside spaces such as changing corners that double as privies enables actresses to avoid all variety of unsavory outside experiences, and exposures to inclement outside environments, by fashioning inside spaces to meet their private needs.

Narrative Five: Regarding Traveling Home in the Morning

In Madurai I lived with an actress named Jansirani. The apartment building where we lived was smack in the middle of that little two-block radius of a Special Drama business district. Most Madurai actresses try to live as near as possible to this center, which minimizes the distance of their daily travels between home and a van, or home and the central bus stand.[7] Living in the center of town reduces their traversal of outsides, and shortens the distance between insides.

The majority of male actors, on the other hand, still live in their natal villages most of the year and only stay in Madurai during the drama season, when they rent rooms in lodges in the center of town. Lodges are notorious "bad" nightlife spots, such that for a woman with an eye to her reputation, being seen in one (let alone actually staying the night in one) is not a viable option.

Jansi and I returned together from a drama one morning by bus, sleeping against each other in our seat. We arrived at the Madurai station just before 7 AM, tried surreptitiously to unrumple ourselves, smoothed down our saris, and began walking from the central bus stand to home, a distance of about five blocks.

We walked briskly through the streets. Jansi was moving very purposefully toward home. I stepped outside myself for a moment to wonder what we looked like: Does Jansi look like a woman who simply rose early this morning? Do I? (Not that I ever look simply like any woman here.) Tamil women rising early at home do things around their house, sacred ritual things, the most visible to passersby being making *kolams*, geometric patterns in rice powder that are negotiations of light lines and dark ground at the entranceway of the houses, where street touches home. Kolams are one of so many respectable female daily efforts to keep the street from contaminating the home, to order and purify inner space and separate it from the disorderly outside.[8] Were we, at that moment, the embodiment of the chaotic, disorderly, outside element? The very fact that we weren't at home making kolams suddenly seemed yet another proof of this same distinction. Was it obvious that we had been riding a bus, sitting up all night, our faces bearing as many pressed wrinkles as our saris? What did people think when they saw us?

This felt to me like a particularly vulnerable moment, though at the time I couldn't understand why. Rationally, the kind of danger I was familiar with from generic travels as a woman was over: night was over, we were back on familiar territory, and it was a properly respectable hour of the morning to be out and about. But I saw too how tired Jansi was, and how she had that barely containable kind of morning giddiness that comes from staying up all night. I felt scared that everything we'd gone through was apparent on us—or was I perhaps picking up her fear, as she walked, fast, not stopping to say anything to anyone? I realize now that this was a particularly vulnerable moment for her, a moment of separation from the group: we were no longer in that cocoon of sorts created by all the actors together, inside the inside spaces of their night world and their street-side network of known people. Suddenly we were two tired women alone on the street in the broad daylight that glinted off the stray specks of green and pink glitter still stuck to Jansi's eyelids, and I felt exposed and confused, hurrying after Jansi, who was heading home so fast.

CONCLUSION

My own feelings when traveling with actresses reveal an unexpected sense of relief bordering on euphoria at finding havens of invisibility and familiar interiority, as well as a concomitant growing trepidation at being caught alone in public, day or night. In narrating these tales from the circuit of actresses' travels between booking shops, vans, buses, backstage spaces, and roads home, I have spoken of instances where I felt uncomfortably "other," as well as of times where I felt included like family; occasions when I felt invisible but somehow safe, and still others where I felt exposed and confused. While some of the sense of marginality and dislocation that pervaded my travels with actresses may have stemmed from my own psychology and cultural baggage, I have been interested here in how I began to experience their roadwork as a sensible embodied practice.[9]

My main aim for the narratives, however, has been to use them to illustrate the artistry of actresses' roadwork. Actresses attempt to resignify and resituate their own social position within a dominant system that persistently casts them as stigmatized other. I have attempted to show how Special Drama actresses struggle to conform to the dominant terms of gendered respectability while also suggesting that in so doing, they subtly alter—by refiguring—these organizing terms themselves. Their struggle readily exposes the extent to which the internalization of a model of femininity based on domestic virtues affects women differently in respect to their class and social status. Femininity based unproblematically on a securely domestic identity is a class-based privilege to which actresses by definition do not have access. Their roadwork is a response to that reality, simultaneously complicitous and resistant: in figuring themselves as "good women," actresses begin to throw that category itself into question.

NOTES

1. These narratives represent the "raw data" of my participant-observation. In a longer version of this essay (Seizer 2000) I have analyzed these experiences in light of the Tamil classificatory schemes that inform them, and it is only through such analysis that I came to the conclusions I offer here. The actresses' roadwork must be understood within the context and in the light of these broader classificatory schemes, especially that key distinction between complementary spheres of life—known as *akam* and *puram* in Tamil classical literature (Ramanujan 1975, 1985)—that shapes the distinctions interior/exterior, domestic/public, inside/outside, known/unknown, and invisible/visible (cf. Dickey 2000). I urge readers interested in understanding how I reached my conclusions here to read the longer essay in which I develop these arguments.

2. Madurai is an inland city in the south of Tamil Nadu. It is an ancient temple city that still figures largely as a Hindu pilgrimage site. Ramanujan coined the term "rurban" to describe the notion, emergent in both classical and modern Tamil literature, of "a center continuous with the countryside" (Ramanujan 1970: 242). Madurai, a city frequently described as "an overgrown village," is the paradigmatic example of such a Tamil rurban center.

3. In marital negotiations, mothers actively participate. In drama negotiations, as this narrative seeks to illustrate, only men participate. Nevertheless, in both cases the woman whose life is at the center of the negotiation is markedly silent.

4. As the remainder of this essay should make clear, even these women who are the apotheosis of public women care intensely that they not be seen as such, especially locally *where they live,* as is the case for this shop in Madurai for actresses who live in Madurai. For example, many actresses will not perform unless the venue is considered far enough away—generally, at least ten kilometers—from their domestic lives, from where they are known, local women.

Why should women who perform publicly, whose reputations for modesty have already largely been shattered, nevertheless attempt to conform to normative codes of gendered virtue? It seems these are the only codes that matter and that a woman must deal with these in some way. For many actresses, the public sphere seems to be divided into a differentiated continuum of publicness, either relatively more or relatively less proximate to her domestic sphere. Thus there is a proximate public sphere, relatively close to home, wherein a woman's reputation is reflected directly in her domestic life as well as affected by it. In that more proximate sphere a woman attempts to be seen as not an actress at all. In the less proximate public sphere where the woman is known primarily as an actress, she will then attempt to stave off the bad reputation through all the "roadwork" techniques and strategies I speak of in this essay. Thus, the same principles of womanly virtue affect her wherever she goes, though distancing herself from her own home allows her to more easily create a fictive self "on the road" whose modesty is then signaled by her "on the road" actions.

5. Ambassador is the brand name of the first model of automobile manufactured in India.

6. Some gender separations are also maintained in most Tamil homes; for example, women eat separately, after men. Likewise, backstage at a Special Drama event, women and men arrange their suitcases of costumes on separate sides of the available space, and sit behind their open suitcases, each with a hand mirror propped in its lid, to apply their makeup.

7. The towns and cities in which Special Drama artists live function as regional centers for the dense population of villages that surround them. Artists invariably live, and establish their actors associations, near central bus stations so that they can easily be contacted by villagers who travel to these regional centers, on public buses, to engage their services. The occupational need to live close to the central bus stations means that Special Drama artists generally live in the "first" postal code area of their respective cities: the oldest urban neighborhoods, those established around public transportation lines. Ramanujan's term "rurban" (see note 2 above) captures well the way artists live in urban settings precisely because they are continuous with their rural surroundings. Likewise, Oscar Lewis's description of the network of human exchange and interconnection that links persons in different villages in India as "a kind of rural cosmopolitanism" (Lewis 1955: 167) captures the centrality of links repeatedly forged and secured through the continued exchange of services between village, town, and city roads.

8. One account of the function of kolams stresses how they mark the threshold of the house as a boundary between the pure and the chaotic: "The mistress of the house, or a daughter, or perhaps a trusted servant, has laid out this pattern upon arising in the morning: she may have selected a traditional design of geometric shapes intertwined, or, if her intentions are more elaborate, two peacocks, perhaps, emerging from a maze. One cannot enter the house without passing through this man-made [*sic*] focus of auspicious forces, which sets up a protective screen before

the home. Of course, one cannot see the screen itself, but only its focal point at the threshold, the point at which it emerges into form—a complex form at that, carefully planned and executed, a reflection of some inner labyrinth externalized here at the boundary, the line dividing the inner and the outer, the pure from the chaotic" (Shulman 1985: 3).

9. I have written about certain of the complexities of my own subject position and identity in Tamil Nadu in an earlier essay (Seizer 1995).

8

Breadwinners No More: Identities in Flux

Michele Ruth Gamburd

"He's good-hearted guy, but what a fool!" Priyanthi exclaimed, laughing, as we sat in her living room three days after her return to Sri Lanka from two years' work as a domestic servant in the Middle East. Any money her alcoholic husband had, she told me, he spent right away: "Today he's like a white man, tomorrow like a beggar." Every time she came home from abroad, she found only the four walls of their house remaining; during her last trip, he even sold the kitchen knives. Nonetheless, Priyanthi radiated an affectionate, good-humored conviction that she could reform her husband and build a better life for her four sons with the money she had earned abroad.

When Sri Lankan village women like Priyanthi leave their families to work abroad, their men remain at home, often unemployed and subsisting on the money their wives remit. The migration of these married women has expanded common notions of motherhood in Sri Lanka to include long absences from home. At the same time, female migration has reconfigured male gender roles in an often uncomfortable fashion. Many men feel a loss of self-respect and dignity when their wives become breadwinners. Such men only reluctantly take over the "women's work" of child care and cooking; if possible, they arrange to have female relatives assume these duties instead, in accordance with strongly felt local gender roles. Scenarios that circulate in television shows, newspaper articles, and local gossip suggest that uneducated, slothful husbands waste the money their wives earn abroad and turn to alcohol to drown their sorrows. Representations of delinquent, emasculated men appear in these stories in tandem with images of promiscuous, selfish, pleasure-seeking women who neglect their husbands and children.

The prevalence of migration, itself a response to high unemployment in Sri Lanka, has introduced new social and economic realities in villages such as Naeaegama, where Priyanthi lives. In so doing, migration also forces villagers to violate old gender norms and to generate new ideals. This sort of change affects the gut-level, commonsense conceptions of how the world is organized that Raymond Williams calls "structures of feeling" (1977: 132).

In Sri Lanka, many people believe that women should stay at home and tend their families while men earn a living for the household. Local poverty and scarce job opportunities for men, however, drive many women to migrate for work. In the Naeaegama area in 1997, 90 percent of all migrants were women. Of the migrant women, 30 percent were single, and 70 percent were married, separated, or divorced. Most of the women in this latter group had at least one child, and approximately half had husbands who contributed regularly to their household income; the other half had husbands who were under or unemployed. Despite the relatively high proportion of employed husbands, many villagers lump together all the husbands of migrant women as lazy spendthrifts.

Common local stereotypes devalue these husbands' competence as breadwinners and as lovers. A number of housemaids in Naeaegama told me that "Arab people say that Sri Lankan men must be 'donkeys' because they send their wives abroad." The phrase carries two sets of implications. First, it emphasizes Sri Lankan men's inability to provide for their families. Second, the phrase implies that Sri Lankan women are not sexually satisfied with their husbands; if they were, they would not travel to the Middle East (and, presumably, sleep with Arab men). These images of Sri Lankan men rest on certain popular assumptions about migrant women: "If they can't eat grapes and apples, they go abroad. If they can't eat cheese and butter, they go abroad" runs one common adage. Grapes and apples, luxury fruits imported from abroad, signify a life of leisure and affluence. Cheese and butter, also luxury products, signify a rich and satisfying sexual life. This remark suggests that migrant women, dissatisfied with their lives and husbands in Sri Lanka, travel abroad in search of more gratifying economic and sexual situations.

When my research associates, Siri and Sita, and I repeated the story about Arab men calling Sri Lankan men "donkeys" to people I interviewed, it often sparked a lively conversation. Many people, after a moment's contemplation, replied by detailing their financial situations. Some slightly shamefacedly, some matter-of-factly, cited poverty as the reason women went abroad. A family, they explained, could not make ends meet on a man's wages as a casual laborer. Migrant women did not seek anything as fancy as "grapes and apples"; they merely hoped to support their families above the poverty line. Fewer respondents addressed the implicit suggestion of sexual impotence. Pradeep, an articulate young man, bounced his two-year-old son on his knee and replied that he knew and trusted his wife. Despite his hard work, his family could not afford to buy land, build a house, and start a business on his salary alone. If he could save the money his wife sent from abroad and build a house, and if she came home without being unchaste, that would prove he was not a donkey.

Despite the widespread awareness of such pragmatic concerns as local poverty and economic opportunities abroad, negative stereotypes continue to circulate, stigmatizing local men whose wives migrate for their inability to live up to older gender ideals. Both the stereotype of the Sri Lankan man as a "donkey" and the pragmatic discussions of poverty reflect the slow, difficult, and often painful negotiation of changing gender roles and family structures.

ALCOHOL: GROUP BONDING AND MASCULINITY

In Naeaegama, alcohol is a business, a medicine, a pleasure, a necessity, and a mark of masculinity. Drinking, an exclusively male activity and a sign of wealth (however fleeting), preoccupies many of the under- and unemployed village men. When families do not prosper from female migration to the Middle East, villagers often blame husbands who quit work and take up drinking in their wives' absence. At once scornful and tolerant of such husbands, villagers commonly tut, "He sits idly, drinks, and wastes." Asked why these men indulge in such behavior, several villagers suggested that the men sought to emulate the rich landowners of the previous generation. One village notable explained to me: "It is good to be rich and look idle; in the absence of riches, looking idle will suffice." Hard work, particularly physical labor, carries significant stigma in the village; light skin, clean white clothing, and a sweatless brow indicate leisure, high status, or at the very least a respectable office job out of the burning sun.

Alcohol is the despair of many a wife, and the basis of community among drinking buddies. When a migrant woman comes home, her husband often demands money to buy drinks for himself and to improve his status by buying rounds for poorer male friends and relatives. Some Naeaegama women anticipate these requests by bringing home prestigious foreign liquor they purchase at duty-free shops. Although they enable their husbands' drinking, these women nevertheless seek to limit it. Blame for bad male behavior such as gambling, smoking, drinking, and womanizing often falls on the absent wife, without whose control a husband, considered constitutionally incapable of controlling his baser urges, drifts helplessly into bad habits and bad company. Frequently, however, patterns of drinking, wasteful spending, and failure to prosper predate, and even prompt, female migration. While women are considered responsible for disciplining their families and regulating household finances, they often have little authority to enforce their will, especially while they are abroad.

Drinking norms in Sri Lankan villages do not resemble Western norms of social drinking or before-dinner cocktails. At weddings, funerals, and other mixed-sex get-togethers, the host often "runs a bottle" of hard liquor out of a

back room that most of the male guests visit surreptitiously, becoming pro-
gressively drunker as the event proceeds. While drinking, men do not eat,
because food reduces the "current" or high. This style of drinking spans social classes. I once attended a university dinner party where I learned (a little
too late) that respectable unmarried women rarely lingered at such functions
past seven or eight in the evening. While their wives (and two uncomfortable female Western academics) huddled together in one room, married and
unmarried men drank one bottle after another until, around ten or eleven in
the evening, the host decided to serve dinner.

Immediately after eating, the visitors departed, most in cars driven by
drunken men. Men strove to get as drunk as possible as quickly as possible;
drinking to excess was the norm, not the exception.

The production, distribution, and consumption of alcohol form a significant component of the village economy. A bottle of the legal hard liquor,
arrack, costs roughly what a manual laborer might earn in a day; in 1994 a
bottle of the officially distilled arrack cost Rs 118 (US$2.36) while a laborer's
daily wage was between Rs 100 and Rs 125 (US$2–$2.50). In 1994, one village outfit that offered wages of 150 Sri Lankan Rupees (Rs)—US$3.00—a
night, with free food and drink, went into production twice a week, running
three stills all night, each requiring six people's constant attention. Including production crews, complicit landowners and law enforcement officers,
and distribution networks, this distillery, one of several in the area, directly
involved more than fifty people. Women, who rarely if ever touch liquor,
constantly pressure their husbands to spend money on items for family
consumption rather than on alcohol. To save money, most local men drink
kasippu, the local moonshine. A bottle of kasippu, a fruit-, yeast-, and sugar-
based fractionally distilled liquor, cost about Rs 60 (US$1.20) in 1994. Despite
their families' debts and hunger, many men spend a great deal on alcohol,
and some work for local kasippu manufacturers who operate stills at night
in remote, wooded places.

Alcohol provides a strong basis for social allegiance and identity. Drinking groups often form around a particular kasippu producer. Heavy drinkers adopt the values and norms of their groups, which tolerate, even encourage, such activities as gambling, stealing, rape, and assault. Anthropologist
Jonathan Spencer glosses *lajja* as shame, shyness, and social restraint—all essential ingredients of good public behavior. He glosses *lajja-baya* as "shame-
fear"; particularly the fear of ridicule and public humiliation. Those who
drink are thought not to know lajja or baya. Spencer notes, "It is assumed
that people who drink alcohol will no longer be in control of their actions
and [will be] easily aroused to anger, which would be likely to spill out in
physical violence, given the opportunity" (1991: 169–72). Shifting groups of
local men, usually of similar age and status, gather regularly to drink, surreptitiously visiting a distribution center or purchasing a bottle to take to a
private location. Often those with money spot drinks for those without, who
return the favor at a later date.

Although they are rarely acknowledged by respectable village leaders, drinking groups form influential axes of political power. Outsiders occasionally employ such groups to assault opponents and to burn enemies' houses and property. Villagers fear the men in drinking groups, especially those with histories of thuggery and intimidation. And yet, drinking men remain integrated into village kinship and friendship networks. Alcohol producers provide generous support and protection to individuals and to village institutions, including schools and temples. Kasippu production groups maintain guardedly friendly ties with some law enforcement officers, and they often lend financial support to local politicians. For reasons ranging from loyalty to fear, villagers rarely challenge drinking groups or report their misdeeds to higher authorities—some of whom are complicit in the network anyway.

For men whose incomes are eclipsed by those of their wives, or who fail to make the most of their wives' salaries, alcohol provides relief from personal responsibility. An extenuating condition that can be entered whenever needed, drunkenness provides the perfect alibi for poor judgment or socially unacceptable behavior. Responsibility falls on the alcohol for any foolish actions and on the absent wife for the drinking itself. With prosperity in the village resting primarily on female migration to the Middle East, involvement with kasippu production and distribution provides poor men with alcohol, money, community, political clout, and a means to reassert the male power and respect lost in the face of women's new economic role. Drinkers thus emulate the idle rich of prior generations and reject the work ethic of the contemporary wealthy.

MEANING IN THE MAKING: RUKMINI AND RAMESH

Although many families hope to save a female migrant's earnings for large purchases, such as buying land and building a house, in many cases supporting the family on the husband's wages while putting the wife's earnings aside proves difficult. Men can pursue sporadic, grueling physical labor for very low wages—or they can dip into their wives' remittances. Many men in the Naeaegama area choose to rely on the money their wives earn abroad to finance their daily needs. The following case presents a fairly typical example of voluntary male underemployment and the concomitant use of a migrant woman's wages for family consumption. In a series of interviews, family members struggled to explain to me and to themselves their lack of improvement despite seven years of work abroad. In the process, they wrestled with the meaning of their continued poverty, and with its effect on individual and family identity.

Siri and I interviewed Hema, an elderly woman of a lower caste, and her son Ramesh. Ramesh's wife, Rukmini, was then working abroad as a housemaid. Rukmini, about thirty years old, had spent most of the previous seven years abroad. During the four years Rukmini worked in Jordan, she sent her money to her mother, who was supposed to look after her daughter. But Rukmini's mother had no stable home. She visited all of Rukmini's siblings, staying roughly six weeks with each, and spending lavishly with the checks Rukmini sent. The next time Rukmini went abroad, she left her daughter with Hema, her mother-in-law, instead. While Siri, Hema, Ramesh, and I sat in the shade of Hema's unfinished cement house, Siri half-jokingly explained to me in Sinhala that Rukmini did not send money to her husband Ramesh, an infamous drinker and gambler. Once the ice was broken, Hema took over the story, explaining that she had told Rukmini not to send the money but to keep it herself. Ramesh's gambling and drinking left nothing even to support himself and his daughter, Hema recounted. Ramesh had taken credit with many local stores, and he now owed interest-bearing debts to several moneylenders.

Hema suggested that if Ramesh could earn money for himself and his daughter, his wife could save all of her salary, and the family could then buy land and build a house, as they had originally planned. Sober and embarrassed, Ramesh said nothing to contradict his mother. I asked him about his work. He said he made about Rs 125 (US$2.50, considered a good salary locally) a day doing physical labor, and more than that when he drummed for ceremonies. Silently contradicting the impression that all of his wife's earnings had evaporated, Ramesh took me into the two-room clay house where he, his mother, father, daughter, and several brothers all lived, and he showed us a crowded collection of furniture he had bought with Rukmini's remittances.

When she returned to the village in mid-April 1994, I asked Rukmini to come meet with me at Siri's house for an interview. Usually I spoke with people in their homes, but at that time Rukmini and Ramesh were living in a six-by-twelve-foot lean-to built against the new cement wall of Hema's unfinished house. Unexpectedly, Ramesh accompanied his wife to the interview. Moreover, he was drunk. Siri tried to take Ramesh aside while Sita and I talked to Rukmini. Occasionally, however, Ramesh approached or interjected. When he did so, palpable tension pervaded the interview. Rukmini seemed barely able to finish a sentence. When I asked her about the gifts she had brought back from the Middle East, Ramesh declared that Rukmini had given him a shirt but that he had gotten his sarong for himself. She replied that she had given him a shirt, shoes, and cigarettes.

The full story explained Rukmini's barbed remark. Rukmini had given Ramesh a new pair of sandals, a pack of prestigious foreign cigarettes, and a new shirt. But when the police raided the illegal coconut beer brewery where Ramesh had gone to drink, he ran through a drainage canal toward the ocean. The canal muck claimed his new sandals, and the salt water ruined the pack of cigarettes in his shirt pocket. Rukmini mentioned that she had also brought her husband twelve beers and two whiskey bottles, all of which he had already consumed. But even if he drank, Ramesh retorted to Rukmini, at least he saved her clothing. Siri, Sita, and I assume that he was comparing himself favorably with the husband of another village migrant, who had sold his wife's dresses during her absence.

When Siri had persuaded Ramesh to walk in the garden, I asked Rukmini if she planned to go back to the Middle East. She intended to go back "no matter what," Rukmini replied. She said she was fed up with her husband's habits. There was no use earning money when he was drinking, she lamented, speaking very quickly. Some of the money Rukmini had just brought home had gone to settle Ramesh's debts and to finance drinking and gambling binges. Although she liked to come home to see her daughter, problems with her husband "unsettled her mind." Ramesh never listened to her, Rukmini complained; instead "he breaks things and wastes and drinks."

Her variation on the common trope—"He sits idly, drinks, and wastes"—emphasized her dismay at Ramesh's destructive behavior, which she judged worse even than indolence and dissipation.

Ramesh returned to the porch. Reaching for a neutral topic, but inadvertently stumbling into a minefield, I asked Rukmini what had been the worst time in her life. It started after she got married, she replied. Ramesh exclaimed, "Really?" They talked heatedly about a fight several years earlier that had ended with both of them filing separate complaints at the police station at the junction—a common conclusion to serious village disputes. Ramesh accused his wife of abandoning their daughter and neglecting her wifely duties. Silenced, Rukmini picked up an umbrella from the table, examining it with great care. Center stage and unchecked, Ramesh delivered a monologue about himself and how hard he had been working for the family's sake. Siri and Sita made no effort to translate his tirade, and I stopped taking notes. Rukmini slouched low in her cane armchair, turning slightly away from her husband. I caught her eye and winked. Suddenly she sat up straight and relaxed physically, telling Ramesh to go home so that she could answer my questions.

I am not versed in the cross-cultural connotations of winking, and this was my only use of the wink as an interviewing tool, so I can only guess how Rukmini might have interpreted my gesture. I think she might have worried that I would accept at face value everything I heard about how she had neglected her family and about how hard Ramesh had worked to make up her shortfall; maybe my wink positioned me with many local women, who listened to men talk without interrupting or contradicting them, but also without believing all they heard. Aware that Ramesh was drunk, but also recognizing his male prerogative to dominate the conversation, no one on the porch that afternoon directly challenged his assertions beyond Rukmini's initial protest that her married life had been hard. Perhaps Rukmini, caught between the desire to defend herself and the embarrassment of arguing with her drunken husband in front of a foreigner and two higher-caste villagers, chose silence as her best defense until my unvoiced support assured her that none of us took Ramesh's drunken ramblings seriously. That leverage allowed her not to confront his representations directly but to ask him to leave. (In other situations where men or more powerful people dominated conversations, I often found that others approached me later with contradictory information they had not wanted to voice in public.) Although for the most part they accept men's right to dominate the public transcript, women make ample use of other opportunities to communicate their opinions. That afternoon on the porch, Rukmini and Ramesh each attempted to control the narrative, influence judgments, and shape appraisals. Theirs was a struggle over meaning in the making, as each attempted to define his or her own agency, identity, and self-worth with respect to the story of their family's failure to prosper. By including himself in my invitation to talk, and by excluding Rukmini from the conversation when he could, Ramesh sought to prevent his wife (and me) from portraying Rukmini as the household's decision maker and breadwinner. Ramesh wanted to be thought of as part of a team, even as a leader, instead of as deadweight, or as someone who "sits at home idle, eating while his wife works." In his monologue, he sought to retell the story of what happened to all the money Rukmini had sent home, reworking his own image simultaneously in my eyes and in his own.

Three years later, Sita and I crowded into a trishaw (a covered, three-wheeled motorcycle) with Hema and her nephew so that Hema could show us the way to Rukmini's new house in a village ten miles from Naeaegama. Some months after the interview related above, Rukmini had gone to work abroad again, this time in Jordan, where she stayed for about a year. When she returned, she and Ramesh bought land and built half of a house. Deciding that they would rather live elsewhere, they sold that property and bought a different one. Their second house, much smaller than the one they had first started, had two rooms and a tin roof. Rukmini had spent Rs 5,000 to add a toilet to their tiny land plot. Bouncing her one-year-old daughter on her lap, Rukmini said that she would like to go abroad again, but neither her mother nor her mother-in-law would look after the girls, because their father would "come fighting" to the house, causing trouble, as he currently did for his wife.

Rukmini had asked a doctor for medicine to stop Ramesh's drinking, but the doctor would write a prescription only to Ramesh himself. Hema suggested asking the alcohol distributors not to sell Ramesh liquor. Although Rukmini still had some money in the bank (and she and her baby both wore gold necklaces), she said that the family had trouble making ends meet on Ramesh's earnings. She did not want to dip into her savings for daily expenses because she wanted to have a large coming-of-age ceremony for her oldest daughter. Fanning herself and her baby under the hot tin roof, Rukmini said that sometimes she thought she would have been better off not going abroad at all; if her husband "had a brain" she could have "brought the family up," but Rukmini wondered if her small plot of land and modest house were worth eight years of hard work abroad.

Back in 1994, I had asked Rukmini how she envisioned her life in another ten years. She said that she would like her whole family to live in a nice house of their own. My research associate greeted this aspiration with skepticism. In 1997, however, villagers voiced different opinions. Despite adversity and a wasteful husband, Rukmini did indeed live in her own home. Although small, the land and house counted as improvement in the eyes of the Naeaegama villagers, and they demonstrated that despite his heavy drinking, Ramesh had not wasted all of the money his wife earned abroad.

WOMEN'S WORK

Migration has forced men and women in Sri Lankan villages to renegotiate gender roles regarding not only whether a woman can respectably work abroad but also who will take care of a migrant woman's duties and responsibilities in the home she leaves behind. Despite the large number of under- and unemployed husbands in the village, only four or five families of around ninety I interviewed admitted that men had taken over more than the bare minimum of housework. In all but one of these cases, the men in question held other jobs as well, and they shared the domestic duties with female relatives.

In Sri Lankan villages, the gendered division of labor clearly marks child care and cooking as female activities. Most men would feel their sense of masculinity threatened if they took on household chores or cared for young children. Carla Risseeuw (1991: 271) writes of a rural Sri Lankan village near Naeaegama:

> Men cannot "stoop down" in the widest sense, without experiencing severe emotional stress. . . . The principle that he is "higher" than a woman, and more specifically his wife, permeates the actions, thoughts and emotions of both men and women. . . . Handling dirt, feces, cleaning toilets, being impure, doing repetitive, relatively less prestigious work, which often lacks the status of work as such or "prestige" of the proximity of danger, is the female expression of the principle of gender hierarchy.

Most of the men and women in Naeaegama accept this division as just, and they judge themselves and others according to it.

Migrants generally told me that they left their children in the care of their mothers or mothers-in-law, but in my daily interactions in the village, I noted more male participation in child care than people reported. Priyanthi, the Naeaegama migrant introduced earlier, left her four sons in the care of her husband and his father while she was abroad. Such men and their families often glossed over men's housework in order to preserve a masculine image. Since Priyanthi's husband, Ariyapala, held a well-paying job at the hospital, he was somewhat sheltered from village ridicule when he took on his wife's work. But in an interview, Ariyapala somewhat defensively explained his assumption of domestic duties as a pragmatic solution to Priyanthi's absence. Ariyapala's heavy drinking also reaffirmed his masculine identity. The few men who did take over their migrant wives' domestic chores both challenged and reaffirmed older gender roles.

JOKER, SIMPLETON, FREETHINKER: LAL

Indrani and her husband, Chandradasa, belonged to a new elite in the Naeaegama area. They were considered one of the most successful village families involved with the migration of labor to the Middle East. Indrani worked for the same family in Doha, Qatar, for twelve years, earning a very generous salary. Chandradasa worked as a security officer at a hotel near Colombo, returning home for two weekends a month. The couple saved and spent both spouses' salaries wisely. In Indrani's and Chandradasa's absence, Chandradasa's mother and brother took care of their five children and supervised the construction of their new house. Although Indrani named her mother-in-law the primary guardian for her children, the older woman's arthritis severely restricted her movements. The children's uncle Lal, a colorful village character, did the lion's share of the cooking and housekeeping.

Lal lived across the road from Siri's house, where I stayed, and he drew drinking water from the well in our garden. Members of our household replied to the greetings Lal called out every time he entered the compound with teasing comments and questions. About the state of the meal Lal was preparing, Siri invariably asked, "Is the [cooking] course over?" For a man to study cooking in school would be only slightly more astounding than to find him cooking at all. In a world of simple structural reversals, when the house-worker leaves to earn a living, one might expect the former breadwinner to do the housework. In Naeaegama, however, in most cases other women, not men, took over "feminine" chores, with grandmothers and aunts looking after the children. Lal, a man who for the past twelve years had cooked, kept house, fetched water, done laundry and shopping, and taken care of children, was the source of some astonishment and amusement in the village.

Many villagers associate full male adulthood with having a wife and a stable job. Lal had neither. At his mother's insistence, Lal had reluctantly married some years before I met him. His beautiful wife asked him to move to her relatives' home in the capital; when he refused, she found work in the Middle East and never returned to the village. Although he was fairly sure that she had come home safely, Lal had no desire to visit her relatives in the city or to see her again.

Lal had worked as a laborer and as an office clerk, but he had not held a job since he was hit by a van while walking on the side of the road a number of years previous. He had no wish to return to work and no ambition to start a business. His mother, who had persuaded him to marry in the first place, thought that he should do so again. Quoting a proverb, Lal said, "The man who is hit with the firebrand from the fire is afraid even of the firefly" (the local equivalent of "Once bitten, twice shy"). When his mother died and all of his family duties were fulfilled, Lal figured, he would become a priest. In the meantime, when his sister-in-law Indrani left for Qatar, Lal and his mother moved in with Chandradasa to look after the couple's children. The fact that Lal was single, lacked a salaried job, and devoted attention to chores often thought of as women's work caused a number of chuckles in the village. Curious about Lal's sexuality, two village notables arranged to question him informally. One afternoon Lal, who was nearly illiterate, asked Siri's father, the local justice of the peace, to help him write a letter to the *graama seevaka*, the local government administrator, asking to be put on a list to receive aid from a local nongovernmental organization. In jest, the justice of the peace wrote a completely unsuitable letter, telling the graama seevaka the stark truth—that Lal lived in a good cement house with electricity and a television set. (Lal's official residence, a collapsing clay hut, formed the basis of a subsequent, successful application.) Unable to read the letter, Lal took it to the graama seevaka, who laughed and said, "This won't do at all" and suggested that he and Lal both go talk to the justice of the peace.

Siri overheard the conversation. The justice of the peace and the graama seevaka teasingly but somewhat cruelly peppered Lal with questions about his long-absent wife, asking if he had sent her cards and sweets in the Middle East. They also asked about Lal's sex life. In a village where everyone knew everyone else's business, there was not even the hint of a rumor suggesting that Lal might be actively homosexual; several other men were known to be so. The justice of the peace and the graama seevaka merely determined that Lal did not know "which end was up." Having satisfied their curiosity, the justice of the peace wrote a suitable letter for the graama seevaka and gave it to Lal, who went home to start the evening meal.

Lal's calm, slow, joking manner made him a hard target for teasing. Of the male recipients of government aid, he was the only one who waited in line with the women to collect food at the local cooperative store. When villagers mocked his feminine behavior, Lal regaled them with humorous stories about his finicky taste in groceries; those who attempted to laugh at him found themselves instead laughing with him about the dead gecko in the rice bag and the dried fish so smelly it must have been fertilizer. He met comments on his domesticity with exaggerated stories about the latest crises in the kitchen, the rough quality of a new soap, and the price of beans. His complaints were uniformly within his domestic role, not about it. He created an ambiguous self-image, as something between a simpleton with no understanding of his failure to fulfill a man's proper role and a freethinker, impervious to criticism, who held a singularly different set of values. That opacity, along with his nonstop wit, allowed Lal to carve out a unique space for himself as a man whose sole job was women's work. The good-humored probing of the graama seevaka and the justice of the peace indexed at once the community's awareness of Lal's unusual behavior and its baffled but amused acceptance.

When I spoke with Lal in 1997, he expressed some ambivalence about his domestic role. At one point he said that he needed to be "bailed out of jail" and set free from the kitchen; a little later, he noted with pride that his family preferred his cooking to Indrani's. When Indrani cooked, Lal recounted, Chandradasa and the children could tell. "*Bappa* [uncle] didn't cook this," the children would say, with gestures that indicated that they did not like the food. Lal said that his sister-in-law made coconut milk by machine; he scraped coconuts the old-fashioned way, generating a richer milk. Her curries had a foreign taste; his had a better flavor. Neighbors had asked Lal why he still cooked when Indrani was home for a visit. He said that he would like to find a job, but Indrani and his mother had asked him not to leave. If he no longer took care of the family, Indrani would have to give up her job and look after her mother-in-law, a prospect neither of the strong-willed women viewed with pleasure. I asked Lal if he were ashamed or shy (lajja) about the work he did. Suddenly completely serious, he held his head up very straight and said that one should never be ashamed of the work one does to eat or drink. He took care of his mother, the house, and the children, and he did not try to hide what he did. He said he was ready to do any job that came his way, either men's work or women's work. He was not ashamed.

While Indrani's migration had changed household gender roles for both Lal and Chandradasa, only Lal's behavior drew extensive village comments. Although Chandradasa took over some of the household chores during his infrequent visits, for the most part his job as a security guard kept him out of the domestic sphere, at the same time reaffirming his breadwinner role. In contrast, Lal's daily routine included many activities commonly thought of as women's work; he lacked any other form of regular employment to reaffirm his masculinity; he had no wife or family of his own; and he did not drink alcohol. When a local committee arranged to resurface the paved road that led into the village, Lal, who had worked in road construction in the past, eagerly volunteered for the overtly masculine job. I believe he sought both the modest paycheck and the highly visible change of gender role.

Lal's ambiguous gender position complemented the new status and prestige Indrani's accumulated wealth gave her in the village. Indrani and Chandradasa contributed yearly to a large ceremony at a popular local shrine, spending over Rs 5,000 (US$100) on food and decorations. Contributing lavishly to community projects elevated the prestige and social standing of villagers; for Indrani and Chandradasa, this entitled them to positions of authority in community politics and temple decision making formerly monopolized by wealthy, high-caste, elite families. Several days after her return from the Middle East in 1993, Indrani received an invitation from three village youths to "open" a community food distribution event. Indrani accepted the offer and also made a generous contribution. Indrani's financial capital metamorphosed into prestige, symbolic capital, respect, and renown. Watching each other cynically for signs of returning poverty, villagers often recognized that wealth was difficult to maintain. Patrons who sustained their positions for a significant length of time, as Indrani and Chandradasa had, were recognized in the village as people who had truly prospered.

How Lal and Indrani would negotiate the transformation of their roles when Indrani returned permanently to the village remained to be seen. In 1997, returning home for a vacation for the first time in four years, Indrani displayed no desire to relieve Lal of the household chores. Having spent lavishly for her daughter's coming-of-age ceremony, Indrani insisted (against her husband's will) on returning overseas to continue earning money for the family. Many villagers felt that she should have stayed home to look after her daughter instead. Indrani countered that she had spent all of her money on improving her house and holding a grand ceremony for her daughter. Now that they were older, her children needed money for their schooling. She added that she had promised to fund the construction of a new cement house where Lal and his mother would move when Indrani returned from abroad for good. The family also needed money for further improvements on their own house and to start a business, perhaps a small shop.

Indrani's prolonged absence changed not only Lal's social position but also her own. Like many migrant women, she no longer fit into village society the same way she had before she left. Though her primary motivation for migrating was economic, issues of identity, independence, and torn loyalties also impinged on her decision. Like Lal, Indrani seemed ambivalent about assuming the housewife's role in her Sri Lanka home.

CONCLUSION

When women migrate to the Middle East, gender roles and power relations change in the villages they leave behind. The preceding cases illustrate both the world that could once be taken for granted and the challenges that now face older patterns of behavior. Ramesh, Lal, and Chandradasa, three village men associated with female migrants, all asserted their masculinity differently: Ramesh through idleness and alcohol, Chandradasa through work and wealth, and Lal through a playful self-parody of his feminizing housekeeping role.

Ramesh's drinking, his braggadocio, and his deliberate cultivation of the idle life challenged Rukmini to prosper despite her husband, not with his help. Membership in the drinking group affirmed Ramesh's masculinity, assuaged his shame or guilt (lajja) for not improving his family's social status, and provided the economic and social community he may have missed in his wife's absence. Chandradasa, by comparison, found his identity in hard work away from home. The cooperative and trusting relationship he shared with his wife gave him control not only of his own salary but also of the money she earned abroad. Willingly remitted for the construction of their house, her pay enhanced both spouses' standards of living and prestige in the village.

Lal, who took on all of the domestic chores in Indrani's absence, encountered daily teasing about his cooking and household work, but he met these remarks with unfailing good humor. Because he lacked other employment, Lal brought villagers face to face with the possibility of men taking over not just individual chores but entire social roles vacated by migrant women. Lal's behavior projected a crisis in gender categories. He generated a powerful mixture of laughter and unease by assuming a traditionally domestic role as his sister-in-law moved out into the international labor market.

9

Life on the Margins: A Hijra's Story

Serena Nanda

Hijras in India are defined as an alternative gender role, neither man nor woman. The cultural sources for the hijras as a powerful and meaningful gender derive from both Hinduism and Islam (see Nanda 1999). Hijras are born males, and become hijras by adopting women's clothing and behavior, formally joining the hijra community, and (except in the case of born hermaphrodites) undergoing emasculation, or surgical removal of the genitals, as part of their identification with the Mother Goddess. This identification gives hijras the power to bless newlyweds and infants with prosperity and fertility, which is the basis of their traditional occupation as performers at marriages and births.

As devotees of the Mother Goddess, and vehicles of her power, hijras claim to be ascetics, a claim ambivalently regarded by the public. Sometimes, when hijras perform or beg for alms, someone will try to lift their skirts to see if they are truly hijras, or fakes, in which case they will be reviled and chased away.

Hijras are an organized social community with local, regional, and national structures. Basic elements of Indian society such as the extended joint family, the caste system, the hierarchical relationship in Hinduism between gurus (spiritual mentors) and *chelas* (disciples), and local caste and neighborhood councils are all part of hijra social structure. Hijras can be Hindu, Muslim, or Christian, and come from all castes and social classes. Within the community there are no castelike rules pertaining to purity and pollution.

The most important element of hijra social organization is the guru-chela relationship. The hijra guru is both mentor and parent; the chela's role is as a dependent and obedient child and student. Each recruit to the hijra community is sponsored by a guru, who pays the new member's initiation fee and takes responsibility for her material subsistence, receiving a portion of the chela's earnings in return. The gurus in each city form a *jamat,* or council of elders, who regulate the working conditions of the city, act as a dispute resolution forum, and serve as the authorizing body of community membership and exclusion.

Hijra stories compellingly illustrate a basic anthropological theme, most prominently enlarged upon by Ruth Benedict (1934), that the margins of a culture are intimately related to its center and that understandings of the abnormal and the normal reciprocally reinforce each other. The hijra role, both as experienced and as conceptualized by others, also challenges us in many ways, demonstrating the construction of gender dichotomies but also the possibilities of gender diversities. And ultimately, the everyday lives of hijras inspire us, as they reveal the myriad ways that human beings, even under the most adverse conditions, become agents in shaping their own lives, creating meaningful identities and resisting, in small and large ways, the oppression of stigma, poverty, and marginality.

*   *   *

Salima is a Muslim, born in Byculla, a Muslim neighborhood in Mumbai, where she has lived her entire life. She is a "real" hijra, *born* intersexed, and not, as she says, "converts like those others." When I first met Salima, in November 1981, she was in her early thirties. She was living on the street, sleeping on a tattered bedroll with only a plastic lean-to to protect her from the monsoon rains that fall so heavily in Mumbai. Her clothes were dirty, as were her hands and feet, and she had a beard of several days' growth. We talked about her life over many weeks and, on my subsequent visits to Mumbai, over several years.

In her talk about her childhood Salima emphasized the sad fate of her birth:

> I don't remember much of my early days and only remember the days after my mother married her second husband. I consider this man my father. My parents felt sad about my birth, but they realized it was their fate to have me born "neither here nor there." From my birth, my [male] organ was very small. My mother felt it would grow as I grew up, but it didn't. She took me to doctors and all, but the doctors said, "No, it won't grow. Your child is not a man and not a woman. This is God's gift." My mother also took me to various holy places and made many vows but nothing turned out fruitful. It is God's will—some women give birth to lame children, some to blind children, it is God's will, even the gift of God. My father also made many vows but it was all futile. If I were a boy, I would have had a good job and brought a daughter-in-law into the house, but like this I have been of no use to my parents. They did what they could for me; the rest is my *kismet* [fate].
>
> From the beginning I only used to dress and behave as a girl. I would run off to Chowpatty and beg and fool around. I only enjoyed playing with the girls, even though I got my hair pulled and thrashed for it. I never thought of myself as a boy or that I should behave like a boy or dress like a boy. I would sit with the girls [in school], playing with them, playing with girls' toys, sweeping the house, cooking, doing all these female activities. My parents gave me a boy's name, but if anyone called me by that name, I would

say, "Get lost! Don't call me that! Call me by any girl's name and only then I will come; otherwise, I won't listen to you." I would put on girls' clothes and do up my hair nicely and put on *kajal* [eyeliner] and rouge. People thought of me as a girl and would give me girls' clothes. Even today, my neighbors still laugh and joke with me and the childhood bond is still there. They say about me, "We are childhood friends. It is not her fault—God made her that way."

In school I would never talk to the boys, but only to the girls. The neighborhood boys would tease me and I used to abuse them, as a girl would, and complain to their mothers. Their mothers would say, "Don't complain to us; when these boys tease you, thrash them yourself." So I would abuse and beat them, and these boys stopped teasing me. These boys would call me, "Hijra! Hijra!" My mother would tell them, "Why do you tease like this? God made him like this, and if you tease him, he can make your food go bad. So just leave him alone."

I was sent to my mother's womb by God, like any child; I am a gift for her. When I got older and the children would tease me, I would tell them, "See, today you are doing like this; tomorrow God will punish you for this." When the children would throw stones at me, I would tell them, "This is not good, God will punish you." I would want to abuse them more harshly, but my mother would calm me down, saying, "Never utter anything bad from your mouth, just let it go. Judgment will be given by God."

At around the age of ten or eleven, Salima joined the hijras:

The hijras already knew me and they used to take me along with them when they went begging. At that time my family was in financial trouble, and I helped them by giving them the money that I got on my begging trips with the hijras. One day the hijras came to beg for food at my house. They inspected my body and said, "You're neither a man nor a woman, but you are born this way." So they started accepting me; they would come to see me, bring with them various foodstuffs and other things. They wanted me to come with them, to be a chela (disciple) of their guru. My mother said, "All right, since you are born this way, go wherever you want to go, do whatever makes you happy."

In the beginning I was very scared of the hijras, but they used to talk to me so kindly and gently. I used to run away and hide sometimes, and I never used to listen, but then they were so kind to me, and they didn't beat me or ill-treat me, like I had heard they do, so whenever they called me, I would go running to them. The pain in my heart was lessened and my heart opened up to them.

They took me to live with their guru at Factory Compound and treated me very well. In the beginning they never let me go out; I only worked in the house, like sweeping, cleaning, and cooking. Sometimes I would miss my parents, and even when I was working I would sit and start to cry. I would say, "I'm missing my parents. I want to see my mother." They would take me to meet my mother and would give me 100 or 150 rupees to give her, along with a sari. Like this they looked after me. They kept me like a girl, protected.

Until my initiation, they didn't want me to go out of the house. I wasn't allowed to talk to men or other people. When I first went to the hijras my hair was very short. When my hair grew long enough for it to be tied into a small braid, then the jamat [council of elders] came and sat for my [initiation] ceremony. My guru distributed cardamom in my name. Everyone was to know that my guru Sona was taking Salima—that was the name my guru gave me—for her disciple. On a Sunday everyone collected—all the hijras and *naiks* [chiefs or elders]. My nose and ears were pierced. I wore a sari, and they applied turmeric and *mehndi* [auspicious henna designs] to my hair and hands and feet. They dressed me up just like a bride, gave me a name, and pierced my nose and ears.

From three days before the ceremony they made me sit in the house; they wouldn't let me go out or do any work at all. Everything was brought to me; my movements were restricted. I was not allowed anything salty or too spicy to eat; only I could eat milk, curds, yogurt. On the appointed day they made me wear a green sari, green blouse, and glass bangles. The Marwari jeweler himself came for my piercing ceremony. They made a paste out of rice, and in front of the rice they put plantains, betel nut leaves, betel nuts, and some flowers on a silver plate. Then on another silver plate, they kept one needle made out of gold and some gold wire. I sat on a low stool just like a bride. All the hijras who were there gave some money—five or ten rupees. Whatever people feel like giving they put on the rice. After this was over, the rice was taken by the jeweler along with the coins. The next night all the rich, important people came and gave presents, which were all given in my name, but I must give them to my guru. They garlanded me and all the naiks gave something; one gave silver anklets, others gave a sari, bangles, or eight *anna* coins, whatever they felt like. In this way they celebrated with so much pomp and show. After this I started going out for the singing and dancing and everyone came to know that I was Sona's disciple.

This was a good period in Salima's life. She and her "sister" hijras went out to beg and to perform. Salima played the *dholak* (two-sided drum), a prestigious role in the group. All day, every day, the group went to Byculla Market to beg cash and kind from the stall keepers or roam their exclusive territories in Mumbai, seeking out weddings or births where they could perform. They made good money, all of which went to the guru, but they were given everything they needed by their guru, "so what need was there for money?" Salima was her guru's favorite because she was a "real" hijra and had been with her guru since childhood.

This was Salima's life for about ten years. During those years she found herself a husband, Ibrahim, a man who was Muslim, like herself.

Only after leaving my house and joining the hijras did I meet Ibrahim. It was at the market where I used to go to beg vegetables and things that my eyes and those of Ibrahim got locked with each other. He used to run a fruit stall. As soon as my eye caught his, he started to give me things—oranges one day, sweet lime the next, one or two kilos of apples, or sometimes a grapefruit. In that same bag that he put the fruit, he would also put twenty or twenty-five rupees. He put it in the bag so that no one would know he gave so much. He did not want me to go from shop to shop. He would say, "In going from shop to shop no man should tease you; you are very young." We would sit together in a tea shop. I would tell the hijras to take the things for the guru so she would think I also was at the market. I told Ibrahim, "If you don't let me beg, then when I go home and the shares are divided up, then won't my guru ask me, 'Where is Salima's share? What did you bring?' I will be caught in my dishonesty."

So, initially, Salima saw Ibrahim on the sly. Gurus disapprove of hijras having boyfriends or "husbands," who compete for a hijra's earnings. Salima's guru did soon discover the relationship, but Salima was able to convince her that the relationship with Ibrahim was no threat to her earnings for the hijra group. The guru then arranged a "marriage" ceremony for Salima and Ibrahim and gave her blessings for them to live together in a separate house. Salima continued to work with the hijras and earn for them.

Ibrahim had told me, "Even when you die, I will pay for your shroud. Don't think that I have taken a young person just to fool around; I'll stay with you until the end." But I used to say, "You're saying all this, but your mother and father will never let you abide by your words." So Ibrahim used to say, "Even if my parents force me to leave you, I won't listen to them." So everywhere they tried to fix a marriage for him, he used to go and attempt to break off the marriage arrangements. But then his brother, that bastard, and his parents, they came and took him away. They told him, "You are not giving us money to run the house; all these years you have spent in Bombay, you never sent any money and we had no news of you." His parents had come from his native place to check on him. When they learned that he got married to me they took him away. Our house was sold, along with everything else. I just took my household belongings and tied them up and brought them back to my guru's house. Again I had to do all the singing and dancing, as well as looking after the dholak and looking after my guru's house. I did all that—I settled down in my guru's house.

At this time the guru was living with a husband of her own. At some point the guru fell ill and went to her native village, leaving Salima living in her guru's house with the guru's husband. Not surprisingly, difficulties developed. Salima's story was that the guru's husband made improper sexual advances toward her, while spreading the story that Salima seduced him. His intention, Salima said, was to undermine her credibility among the hijras and to replace her in her guru's affections so that he could eventually inherit the guru's considerable material assets. He was evidently successful, as on the guru's return, Salima was thrown out of the house and cast out of the hijra community.

This was a serious business: any hijra who would work with Salima, talk to her, or even so much as give her a drink of water, would be exiled from the community herself. In order to gain reentry, Salima had to pay a 500-rupee fine to the jamat. Unable to earn, much less save, this amount, Salima lived on the streets, where I first met her. Occasionally she begged in Victoria Railway Station but was chased away if other hijras saw her. Sometimes Salima joined a group of *jankhas* (non-hijra female impersonators), looking for work performing or begging alms. This meant long hours traveling on buses or walking to the outer suburbs of Mumbai in the extreme heat and rain of the monsoon season, for the most meager income. As a real hijra Salima was useful to these jankhas because she legitimated their performances. But then she came to owe them money that she could not repay, so she began to avoid them also.

Salima now lived on a street corner under a makeshift tent in the Mumbai Muslim neighborhood of Byculla. She occasionally earned a few rupees caring for some neighborhood children and was given some food by her neighbors. In the monsoon season, she slept under a bus or truck. She sometimes borrowed money from her parents but more often had to lend them money. As a hijra, Salima was the target of harassment from local rowdies. She considered prostitution, but as she so pathetically told me, "No customers are coming." Her general dishevelment, three days' growth of beard and dirty hands, feet, and clothes, made this easy to believe. Salima now talked bitterly about Ibrahim's abandonment, and she was also still hoping to raise the 500 rupees she needed to pay her way back into the hijra community.

These days I am begging and earning these small sums of money; when the hijras pass by and see me, they turn their face away. I ask Allah, "Have I come to this condition that I am like an insect in a dirty gutter?" Nobody wants me. I don't want to live such a cruel life. If I get a little money, then I can lead a proper life. I can't go on leading this cruel life. Just last night I was sleeping out and at three in the morning four urchins came to harass me. I was fast asleep, and this boy woke me up. He said, "We've been watching you for years. We want to know what your price is—what is the price of your virtue?" I said, "So you want to play with my virtue, do you? Well, while I have breath in my body, you people cannot touch my virtue. If you want to play with my virtue then you will have to kill me."

I have not been feeling well and had to go to the government hospital. If my guru were here, or if I had a protector, I would not have had to go to this hospital; I could have gone to a private one instead. Never mind, that is life; one minute it's like this, the next minute it's different. So I still pray only to Allah, "If this is the way you want me to live, it's all right, but never put me in such a condition where I'll have to go to the hijras for help. Even if I die on the road, the municipality people will pick me up and take me away." It's all right. . . . I've run my life and it's through.

Salima was at a loss as to what to do to make her life more bearable. It was in this condition that I left her when I departed from Mumbai. When I returned to visit her again about four years later, in the winter of 1986, Salima's life had taken yet another turn. I found her in her usual place on the street, along with a small group of people, which included one hijra and two men. She was dressed nicely, much better than when I had seen her on my previous visits, and she looked in much better health. She gave me a big smile, and very shyly turned to the handsome young man behind her and said, "This is Ibrahim." Salima told me that she had written Ibrahim a letter calling him back to Mumbai and he came.

> Now he wants to do some kind of business, maybe selling fruits, as he did before. But for the past couple of months he is not well; his leg is troubling him so he is not able to go out and do any business and he is not able to earn. He doesn't have any money to start some business. I manage by borrowing a little money, two rupees here, two rupees there. If Ibrahim has earned a little money, he gives it to me to buy food. And now, why hide it, I comb my hair and get ready and go out for business [prostitution]. I have to try for something because my husband is ill and I have to look after him. I ask the customers for twelve rupees; some nights I get two or three customers, but sometimes I just stand there without any business. Thieves and prostitutes, you'll never know what you make in a day. Sometimes in the end I have to borrow money from someone. For the place itself, I have to pay two rupees to do business, even my clothes, I borrow from my friend. I make a little money also from begging, but mostly I stay and pass my day here only. People say to me, "This guy doesn't work, he just sits and eats your earnings. Why doesn't he work for a living?" But how can he? How can my husband go and work? His life is in trouble; do you think he likes to just sit and eat? He would earn money for me himself; how could he just sit and eat but for this trouble? He has a problem, so I have to consider that, too. How can I neglect his trouble? If, by the grace of Allah, he gets some money, to start some sort of business and earns enough money to support us, it will be good. For now, I earn enough to fill our stomachs.

In 1992, six years later, I again returned to India, looking forward to seeing Salima. When I met her I found that her luck had again changed for the worse. Ibrahim had again abandoned her to marry a "real woman," and her health had deteriorated. Because of the Hindu-Muslim riots in Byculla at this time, I did not stay long in Mumbai. When I returned to Mumbai in 1995, I immediately went to look for Salima but could not find her in any of her usual places. I inquired among the neighbors and they informed me that she had died!

When I tried to find out more details I was told to look for her good friend, Rekha, who lived nearby. Rekha was one of Salima's "sister-chelas," that is, they were both chelas (disciples) of the same guru. Rekha was an older hijra who herself was living outside the hijra community. When I tracked her down, Rekha told me that Salima had died "of a broken heart" after Ibrahim left her. She had started to drink heavily and that, combined with her extreme poverty and depression, "led to her end." Rekha spoke warmly of Salima's character, describing how Salima had "saved her" from the streets, taking her under her wing. Her guru, whom I met the next day, also spoke of Salima's kindness to everyone, the help she had provided to Ibrahim, and his callousness in leaving her. The guru, who was very elderly, was now depending for support on Rekha, who, although lame, was full of vitality and hope.

It was a sad visit for me. I liked Salima very much and had great admiration for her strength in trying to fashion a meaningful life out of the barest of resources. But even with all of her survival skills, Salima was ultimately no match for the hurdles of poverty and marginality of life on the streets of Mumbai.

10

Crossing "Lines" of Difference: Transnational Movements and Sexual Subjectivities in Hyderabad, India

Gayatri Reddy

It was early evening in Hyderabad, the South Indian city where I did my fieldwork. The sun was just about to set, lifting the heavy torpor of the afternoon heat. You could hear a low hum of activity, as people were gradually emerging onto the streets and public spaces of the city. Public Gardens was one such centrally located place—a garden, once the property of a Hyderabadi nobleman and now a popular meeting ground (and well-known cruising area)—that was slowly coming to life. I was sitting on a low wall adjoining the tea stall in the "Garden," as most people refer to this area, having a cup of *chai* with Suresh, a young, self-identified gay man, when we had the following conversation.

"Is it true that in America there is a book that tells you specific locations across the country where you can find other *gays*?" Suresh asked me eagerly.[1]

"Where did you hear that?" I asked in turn.

"This friend of mine went for a *homosex* party in Bombay, and there was a *gay* man who had just come from abroad. He told my friend," Suresh replied. "It would be so great if there was one like that for India also, because then easily, we could go enjoy with other people in this *line*," he added wistfully.

In this article, I want to highlight two related notions circulating within what Suresh referred to as "this line": The first notion refers to the usage of the "gay" or "homosex" label and the construction of sexual subjectivity implied by this usage. The second notion refers to one potential source of this "gay" subject-position and the narratives associated with "this line," namely the heightened transnational traffic in images, commodities, and in this case people, circulating between India and abroad. I explore these notions in relation to a set of images articulated by *hijras* (introduced in the last chapter by Serena Nanda), delineating, in this process, the proliferation of sexual identity categories or subjectivities called forth by globalization in contemporary India.

At first glance, Suresh's invocation of homosexuality, and specifically gay subjectivity,[2] in urban India appears to be a vindication of prophecies of an emerging "queer planet."[3] In the past ten to fifteen years in India, there appears to have been a veritable explosion of people—and especially men—who refer to themselves as "gay," occupy marked public gay social spaces, and belong to a growing number of gay/sexual rights organizations established in various cities across the country. Indeed, it would appear that urban India instantiates the position, as some scholars have argued, that a "global gay identity" has come into existence. The premise of this globalizing narrative is, in Dennis Altman's terms, "the emergence of a 'western' style homosexuality in 'non-western' regions of the world, characterized by a modern invention, namely the creation of an identity and a sense of community based on (homo)sexuality" (1997: 425; cf. Altman 2001). With the increased transnational flow of images, narratives, and people, this modern invention, which developed as a result of particular historical specificities in the West, has apparently diffused to emerge as a variant of a universal, "global gay" identity in other regions, including Asia. Although Altman and other proponents of this view might recognize that this pattern is not a simple diffusion from west to east, replacing "traditional" sex/gender formations in a linear, sequential pattern, such formulations perhaps inadvertently perpetuate the somewhat sterile and culturally marked binarisms of gay/West/modern versus indigenous/non-West/traditional.

This article is an attempt to problematize this easy invocation of globalization and modernity with respect to emerging gay subjectivities in urban India, and its apparent opposition to traditional sexual subjectivities such as the hijras. Drawing on two years of ethnographic fieldwork among hijras in the South Indian city of Hyderabad to construct my argument, I will first sketch the outlines of these two subjective "imaginaries"—the so-called traditional hijra imaginary, and the modern gay imaginary—as if they were static, separate, and exclusive scripts of identity. Then, I will problematize their depiction as either coherent definitional fields or mutually exclusive markers of "tradition" and "modernity." Ultimately, I argue, both these processes of subject formation—hijra and gay—draw on multiple and uneven appropriations of modernity, even as they engage with, appropriate, and sometimes resist it, *always* altering it in this process. It is only in delineating the particularities of this process of meaning making that one can theorize the point of identity-formation where, to quote Stuart Hall, "the stories of subjectivity meet the narratives of history and culture" (Hall 1992).

TRADITIONAL HIJRA/KOTHI SUBJECTIVITIES

I start first with the so-called traditional model, as one of my interlocutors in the field referred to it. This model, fluid and shifting in response to the vicissitudes of history though it might be, is widely believed to have originated from hijra articulations and worldviews (Cohen 2006; Reddy 2005), and hence I draw in large part from the model that hijras delineated in conversation with me. First, hijras categorize all sexually sentient individuals into one of three identities, *kothis*, *panthis*, and *narans*. The central axes of subject-formation in this model are the act of penetration in sexual intercourse and the performance of gendered work. In this performative understanding, the sex/gender system is divided into, on the one hand, panthis, penetrative "masculine" men, and, on the other hand, (1) kothis, or receptive "feminized" men, defined by their public expression and enactment of desire—liking to do "women's work" and desiring the receptive position in same-sex encounters with other men—and (2) narans, or all women, an undifferentiated category based primarily on anatomy (naturalized as reproductive capacity) and gendered practice. Panthis (masculine men), in this system, are the partners of kothis (receptive, feminized men) and/or narans (women), bounded not merely by the form of their penetrative sexuality but also *against* the constellation of putative gendered practices and desires openly embraced by these other subject positions. In other words, in this model, the gender system in India appears to be divided on the basis of practice rather than anatomy, into "men" (panthis) and to use Don Kulick's phrase, "not-men" (kothis and narans) (Kulick 1998; Reddy 2005).

Second, there are a range of self- (and hijra-) identified kothi subjectivities—including hijras, *zenanas*, *kada-chatla* kothis, *jogappas*, and *siva sathis*—differentially positioned along a hierarchy of authenticity and respect. The criteria of differentiation among these various subjectivities include a whole host of axes that include genital excision, religion, clothing, kinship, and class, with each axis often varying in importance, depending on speaker, context, and audience.[4] In the eyes of the hijras I engaged with in Hyderabad, the most important criteria, by and large, are kinship, lack of sexual desire or practice, and the degree of non-normative (including sartorial) visibility in the public sphere. Very briefly, kinship is defined in this context as affiliation and social obligation to one of the hijra houses or lineages in the community. By deploying the marker of kinship, or the *rith*, individuals signify their membership in that house as well as within the wider community of hijras and kothis. The rith not only denotes membership in the wider community but also hierarchizes kothis along this axis of kinship. There are kothis who are "officially" kin (those who "have a rith with hijras") and those without a rith who are not kin. While this does not prevent the latter from identifying as kothis, it clearly places them lower in the kothi/hijra hierarchy of respect.

In addition to the rith, all hijras define themselves in opposition to the overly licentious and much disparaged kada-chatla kothis, that is, kothis-who-do-not-wear-saris,[5] or *gandus*, as they more commonly (and pejoratively) refer to these individuals. According to hijras, gandus, or men who enjoy anal sex, are defined not only by the *form* of their sexual desire, but more importantly, by its *excess*. According to hijras, excessive sexual desire is a marker of inauthenticity that both defines gandus and by that token separates them from the supposedly authentic, asexual hijras. An active symbol of hijras' essential asexuality that is deployed for this purpose is the physical excision of their genitalia, what they refer to as the *nirvan* (enlightenment) operation. Apparently, having had this operation (that is, surgically removing both the penis and testes) not only signals respect within the kothi community and indicates the possession of the necessary strength and courage to acquire seniority, but also provides a measure of respect, or *izzat*, in the social world. One becomes resolutely and irrevocably a "real hijra" following this operation. In hijra constructions, this corporeal symbol instantiates their greater authenticity and respect, serving simultaneously as an indictment of their more libidinous fellow-kothis.

MODERN GAY SUBJECTIVITIES

Against this kothi/hijra model of same-sex desire and subjectivity is the model delineated by self-identified gay individuals such as Suresh in the opening vignette. Not only does the classificatory grid that these gay individuals outline create a subjectivity based primarily on sexual object choice, but this reconfiguration of identity apparently involves different criteria from those employed by the kothi sexual paradigm. Although this model of same-sex sexuality was clearly not beyond contestation, by and large the contours of this grid conformed to certain rules.

For one thing, much like the production of the homosexual as a distinct species of person in the nineteenth-century West, gay men in Hyderabad see themselves in opposition to the heterosexual population, with the boundary defined explicitly by their sexual orientation rather than anatomical sex or gendered (feminine) practice. In Suresh's wistful fantasies, "this line" of homosex/sociality was squarely opposed to "that line" of heterosexuality. In this modern sensibility, sexual subjectivity is construed in the idiom of consumption, as a function of object choice and of practice defined in those terms. Rather than accept the penetrative/receptive kothi/panthi model described above, both partners in this modern same-sex relationship are reconfigured as gay, a move that elides the focus on public displays of femininity that apparently define "lower-class" kothi identity.

A case in point is Pratap, a handsome middle-class man who prided himself on straddling both worlds—that of self-identified gay men as well as kada-chatla kothis (kothis who do not wear a sari). During my fieldwork in Hyderabad, I heard frequent rumors that Pratap was the partner or panthi of at least one kada-chatla kothi. In fact, one of the kada-chatla kothis I spoke to claimed that Pratap had been her panthi before he abandoned her for someone else. Given kothis' sex/gender differentiated world wherein panthis' desires and proclivities are different from kothis', how is Pratap's dual positionality reconciled within this domain? When I asked Pratap about the rigidity of the division, he answered, "Not like that. It is not fixed like that. It is not that panthis cannot become kothis and vice versa. After all, we are all *gays.*" Other gay men I spoke to articulated similar beliefs even if they did not use kothi terminology. "You know like top/bottom or bottom/top as some people say? The same way the active partner can sometimes be the passive partner and sometimes be the active. It depends on various things you know," Rajeev told me in a conspiratorial whisper, not wanting to be caught divulging these embarrassing details to a woman.

Given the classificatory grid I outlined earlier, this non-differentiation between penetrative and receptive practice is not a notion that appears to sit easily with all kothis. For them, kothis are defined by their publicly acknowledged enactments of "female" desires/practices—including being receptive partners in male same-sex intercourse, with panthis being the exclusively penetrative partners. However, as Kishore, a self-styled gay spokesman stated to me, "Those are all different, old-fashioned ideas—this kothi, panthi and all this top/bottom business. It is not fixed like that. Some like to do this way, some like to do another way. But we all like to go with another man. That is the difference. Only those hijras and people talk in that kothi/panthi language like that. Here, we are all just *homosexuals* or *gays*," he added. In this scenario, "this line" of homosexuality, marked by its modernity as compared to the "old-fashioned" subject-positions of hijras and other kothis, is defined in opposition to "that line" of heterosexuality.

Further, the criteria of membership for this subject-position require neither official kinship in the manner prescribed for hijras nor any rhetoric/public display of either femininity or asexuality. Identifying the pattern of desire—that is, occupying the gay public space of gardens and bus stations in Hyderabad—and acknowledging a desire for other men makes all such individuals *equally* gay, as Kumar implied, without the hierarchical positionings that are so vital to hijra community structure. In addition, within this sexual paradigm, the very definition of the players seemingly centers explicitly on their sexual object choice rather than other aspects of identity such as gendered practice, ritual performance, hierarchical kinship, or asexuality, as with hijras.

A new class of individuals appears to have been invented in urban India, for whom sexuality indeed seems to have become the defining feature of subjectivity. The conjuncture of three facilitating conditions, among others, hastened the creation and acceptance of this sexual paradigm. One was the establishment, in the early 1990s, of popular, often English-language magazines (such as *Bombay Dost, Trikone, Shamakami*) and other forms of mass—primarily print—media, as well as gay and lesbian support groups, resource centers, and organizations, both in India and within the South Asian diaspora in the United States and the U.K. These key institutions (and the public personas of figures associated with them), enabled the circulation of knowledge and symbols relating to homosexuality/same-sex desire and practice, as well as allowing for the potential recognition of similitude, and the possibilities this opened up for multiple forms of sexual subjectivity.

The second facilitating condition was the liberalization of the economy that was initiated in the early 1990s in India. This move heralded the entry and circulation of global capital, greatly increasing the transnational traffic in persons, signs and images and facilitating the emergence of an increasingly wealthy and larger middle-class populace who now not only had ready access to previously out-of-reach objects and narratives, but also, for the first time, saw themselves as affording them. As the *New York Times* columnist Edward Gargan noted in one of the earliest articles chronicling this development, "most of the homosexuals [in Bombay] are young professionals who work in this city's expanding private sector and whose standard of living is well above the national average" (Gargan 1990). This point is key to the "evolving gay culture" in India, according to Ashok Row Kavi, one of the widely acknowledged founders of this culture in India. "There have always been opportunities for gay sex," he stated to the reporter, "but the point is that it is now a movement, that it is an evolving gay culture" (Gargan 1990).

The third set of facilitating conditions that impacted the proliferation of sexual subjectivities was the onset of HIV and the subsequent flow of AIDS-related NGO capital into India. Given the public health imperative to identify "target communities" or "communities of those at risk," the discursive elaboration of "homosexual" identities in India and the delineation and sedimentation of communities unified on that basis is at least to some extent an *effect* of mobilizing around the HIV/AIDS epidemic, rather than a prior commitment to a "line" of sexual difference.[6]

THE INCITEMENTS OF GLOBALIZATION

It would appear, then, that this commitment to gay identification (and the political-economic liberation premised on this construction), does appear to be somewhat different from the hijra/kothi conceptualizations of sex/gender difference and subjectivity delineated earlier. But, as I discovered over the course of my fieldwork, despite their heuristic value, these differences are far more complex, and cannot be neatly dichotomized along the axes of temporality, modernity, and geography.

For one thing, the evolution of this gay culture in urban India, despite its commonly perceived transnational origins and ongoing connections, is not isomorphous with its global label. As scholars have highlighted recently, coining new concepts such as "dubbing culture" in Indonesia (Boellstroff 2005) and "doubling" in China (Rofel 2007) to theorize this process, self-identifying gays and lesbians in non-Western sites are constantly engaged in appropriating *and transforming* "Western" discourses and values as they locate themselves meaningfully within local cultural contexts. A similar process of meaning making is at work in the Indian context. At the most literal level, some of the casual partners of gay individuals do *not* acknowledge themselves as "gay," being more comfortable with "traditional" labels such as panthi or kada-chatla kothi. In addition, it is polysemic images of the *yaar* or the *dost* (very loosely translated as "friend" or "buddy") that condition many gay individuals' quest for and subsequent relationships with other men. In 1999, for instance, a "conference of gays in the country" entitled Yaarian (for the plural of yaar, or friend/buddy) was held in Hyderabad. One of the self-conscious agendas of this conference was to "try and identify an indigenous or *desi* terminology for the concept of gay," as the statement at the end of the conference claimed. One of the participants quipped that future conferences should be referred to as "Yaarian-Sari/an," to include a broader spectrum of gender identities and practices specific to India. In fact, as one theory for the history of the kothi construct indicates, the "rift" between "kothi" and "gay" identities is an artificial one, apparently created by "foreigners" interested in dividing the indigenous community on the basis of class, according to several posts on the popular *khush* listserv (cf. Cohen 2006). Prior to this globalized power play, these terms and their multiple meanings were somewhat more fluid lexical codes that indexed playful (and campy) language usage rather than a compartmentalized code for fundamentally different identities. The very construction of the kothi category, in this understanding, is a product of the modern matrix of politics and class/ global privilege, not to mention the impact of the AIDS enterprise and its classificatory imperatives (Cohen 2006), reflecting neither a categorical rift on the ground nor a pristine indigenous category and hierarchy of "authentic" Indian sexual subject-positions.[7]

Clearly, there are individuals attempting to carve out a unique space on the "gay" platform by claiming "local" self-referential labels and invoking culturally inflected images of the dost (friend) in their self-fashioning as national subjects, gay *Indians*. Equally clearly, there are those, such as Suresh in the opening vignette, who are given tantalizing glimpses of this modern sexuality but do not embrace this mode of sexual subjectivity in its upper-middle-class form. This class of people who refer to themselves as both gay and kada-chatla kothi draws on globally circulating narratives of gayness while simultaneously constructing themselves within local networks of meaning and traditional subject positions within the hijra/kothi model. Suresh has friends who frequent the *homosex* New Year bashes in Bombay, apparently attended by "gay men from [various cities across India], as well as those from San Francisco, New York and London" as he informed me, at the same time that his other friends are "adopted" into hijra kinship networks as daughters and disciples in their hierarchical community structures. Bhabi, for instance, was officially Vasundara's daughter in the hijra kinship network, while simultaneously constructing himself both as a ka-da-chatla kothi and as gay in the Public Gardens of Hyderabad. Likewise, Vikas, although now a "full-time hijra" in Mumbai, considered himself a kada-chatla kothi in Hyderabad, actively cruising for male partners with his "*homosex* friends" as he referred to them, in the Garden. Similarly, Srinivas, his friend and fellow Mumbai hijra, hosted parties for self-identified gay men, in addition to other kothi identities such as jogappas, zenanas, and kada-chatla kothis—his previous forms or subject-positions—every time he returned to Hyderabad for a visit.

To further complicate the discursive production of a stable and coherent global gay identity, one can point to the differences apparent within the so-called modern gay community in India. As a recent vituperative exchange on the lgbt_india online listserv between two South Asian self-identified gay activists revealed, not only were there radical differences in their respective constructions of what it means to be gay in India, whether one should come out and confront one's family, and how one should go about doing so, but also differential investments in nationalism versus a globalizing rhetoric and the "need for recognition" by the global gay community. Likewise, the ideological differences between the two gay advocacy/sexual health groups in Hyderabad in their constructions of sexual identity, and the meanings of Indian "tradition" and "modernity," quite apart from the politics and practice of activism, militate against the emergence of a universal "western-style . . . homosexuality in Asia" (Altman 1997: 421). "To see oneself as 'gay' is to adhere to a distinctly modern invention, namely the creation of an identity and a sense of community based on (homo)sexuality," Altman states (1997: 423). But clearly, identifications and differences between similarly positioned actors are not as coherent or stable as a global gay identity would presume.

On a recent trip to Hyderabad, I was entrusted with the task of finding out more about the medical clinic that was apparently established by "one of our kothis [living] in [a] foreign [country]," as hijras described a well-known London-based gay activist. "Last month, one of my *customers* from Saudi [Arabia] told me about it. I believe this clinic is only for us—kothis here and in the Garden," Shanti, my hijra friend, explained to me, including in her lexical label both her fellow-hijras living in Secunderabad and the gay men frequenting the Public Garden. Later that week, when I spoke to some of these self-identified gay men in the garden, I was reassured that indeed, the clinic was for "all gays . . . but please tell hijras to come only on Sundays." On further inquiry, I was told that this was because their izzat (respect) was at stake: "If hijras come during the day, what will people think? Everyone will know this is a *homosex* clinic then, and our izzat will go. You can understand how this will look. . . . So you tell them," Rakesh told me, somewhat apologetically. In the same discursive move, hijras are being included as a recognizable gay-identified subjectivity/community on the one hand, while simultaneously differentiated by the apparently traditional kothi criterion of izzat and (sartorial) visibility, on the other hand. Interestingly, this differentiation is posited as one that someone like me, perceived by Rakesh as a woman outside "this line," could easily appreciate and thereby convey to others "in this line." Clearly, lines of identification/difference are not merely sexual but can shift along local frames of reference, revealing varying alignments of sociality.

In addition, not only are the particular articulations of the Indian gay male refracted through different lenses, but so-called traditional subject positions such as hijras also construct themselves creatively within this apparently modern matrix. For instance, when an Indian cosmonaut went into space along with a Soviet crew in the 1980s, the president of a hijra organization in Delhi wrote to Indian and Soviet leaders, requesting that in the interests of parity, the "sexually underprivileged" such as themselves be sent into space in future ventures (*Hindustan Times* 1994).

Likewise, in their recent election campaigns, hijras have begun to position themselves as authentic cultural signifiers beyond the factional and corruptible politics of gender, sexuality, and caste (Reddy 2003). But at the same time, they are also asserting this citizen construction as a collective identity and are developing a "public political consciousness" in Dennis Altman's (1997) terms. This invocation of a hijra community and its group rights culminated in a movement to declare a "World Eunuch Day," and a few months later, in the proposal by the recently elected hijras to launch a national political party for hijras (alongside their launch of a national fashion show). More recently, in 2005, hijras moved the Chennai High Court to grant them not merely voting rights and the right to education, employment, and marriage, but also "legal recognition as a third gender," a move that influenced the decision by the Tamil Nadu government to establish a special Welfare Board, catering exclusively to the contemporary concerns of *aravanis*/hijras.

These developments raise several questions in terms of the dichotomy between "tradition" and "modernity." For instance, within what "local" and "traditional" frames of reference do we accommodate the recent linkages forged between hijras and some members of the transgendered community in the United States—including numerous visits back and forth, as well as the establishment of formal kin ties (or the rith) between members of these communities? Such factors surely complicate the discursive production of *both* a pristine local or traditional hijra identity *and* a stable, coherent global and modern gay identity.

NOTES TOWARD A CONCLUSION

In his deservedly well-known treatise, *History of Sexuality*, vol. 1 (1978), the French philosopher/historian Michel Foucault popularized the axiomatic understanding of the birth of homosexual *subjectivity*—from "sodomite as temporary aberration" to "homosexual as species" (43)—in the modern West. According to Foucault, this process of subject-formation resulted from an epistemic disjuncture—or rupture—in the nineteenth century in which sexual identity was produced by the disciplining knowledge of the sexual sciences and the dividing practices of modern states. Since then, Eve Sedgwick (and several other queer scholars) have criticized this and related aspects of Michel Foucault's early work, namely his emphasis on the formation of sexual identity, as a "unidirectional narrative of supercession" in Sedgwick's terms (Sedgwick 1990: 46; cf. Boellstroff 2005; Butler 1993; Donham 1998; Manalansan 2003; Morris 1995; Rofel 1999, 2007; Wilson 2004; among others). As Sedgwick contends, we need to relinquish this narrative of rupture that has sustained the discourse on sexuality in the wake of Foucault.[8] She states: "Issues of modern homo/heterosexual definition are structured, not by the supercession of one model and the consequent withering away of another, but instead by the relations enabled by the unrationalized coexistence of different models during the times that they do coexist" (Sedgwick 1990: 47). This is increasingly accepted as a truism, with recent work emphasizing the conjunctures of different modes of subjectivity, *all* transnationally influenced and cohabiting in today's modern social field.

The social field in present-day India is perhaps an example par excellence. Whether attributable to the politics of HIV/AIDS funding (Cohen 2006), to heightened legal and media visibility in the public domain, or, as some scholars have argued, to a neo-colonial sexual globalization (Altman 2001), there is no doubt that today, perhaps more than at any other time in recent history, the current sexual landscape in India is a complex, shifting terrain, with a proliferation of categories and communities—hijra, kothi, males-who-have-sex-with males, TG or transgendered—each drawing on multiple, simultaneously deployed registers of "tradition" and "modernity" and with their own, if overlapping, investments in emphasizing and maintaining "sexual difference" even as they articulate these investments and identifications within similar terms of state and public-health recognized discourse. Further, these categories of difference and subjectivity are not rigid domains but are shifting and constantly *becoming* in contexts of relationship—with each other, with NGOs (non-governmental organizations), and with the state. Hence, at the very least, the "unrationalized coexistence," in Sedgwick's terms, of these so-called traditional and modern models questions the facile dichotomies between these terms, calling for a historicization and grounded contextualization of *both* kothi and gay identities in India. Such a perspective also blurs the boundaries that define gay identity, both in India and in the imaginary location of the West, and exposes the limitations of *all* dichotomous grids of intelligibility. Ultimately, it would appear that the refraction of "this line" in Hyderabad to reveal several competing paradigms of sociality, with the concurrent deployment of multiple bases of identification, militates against an epistemic rupture of any one "line" or model in favor of another.

ACKNOWLEDGMENTS

This essay is based on research originally published in the book titled *With Respect to Sex: Negotiating* Hijra *Identity in South India* (University of Chicago Press, 2005). It is a revised version of one chapter of that book (chapter 9). We thank the University of Chicago Press for permission to publish it.

NOTES

1. Our conversation was in Telugu but for a few English words noted by asterisks. This will be the notation used in the rest of the article—asterisks for English words used in non-English conversations, and double quotation marks to note problematic terms or direct quotations.

2. A caveat is in order here: I realize, of course, that a vast body of literature addresses itself explicitly to the differences between "homosexuality as we know it today," and previous arrangements of same-sex relations (Weeks 1981; Halperin 1990; Sedgwick 1990; among several others). Although recognizing that the terms "homosexual" and "gay" may refer to distinct periods and contexts in the history of this phenomenon, I use the terms interchangeably, drawing primarily on my informants' articulations and use of the terms.

3. See Boellstroff (2005), Manalansan (2003), Rofel (2007), Stoler (1995), among others, for analyses of globalization in relation to modes of sexual subject formation. See also Michael Warner's book, *Fear of a Queer Planet: Queer Politics and Social Theory* (1993), for this and other interpretations of "planetary" expansion.

4. See Reddy (2005) for a detailed elaboration of these criteria and the differential axes of kothi subjectivity.

5. Saris are the clothing hijras and other (adult) women wear in India. The term "chatla" in the hijra lexicon refers to a sari. Hence, a kada-chatla kothi is one who does not wear a sari, and instead wears regular male clothing, i.e., pants and shirt.

6. See Lawrence Cohen (2006) for an analysis of the kothi vis-à-vis the gay concept in India, and competing articulations of authenticity, subjectivity, and risk in relation to the politics of HIV/AIDS funding.

7. Importantly, this is not the only theory relating to the history of the category/lexical label of kothi, nor is this particular construction devoid of political maneuvering. The potential rifts or identity politics within the self-identified gay community in India are well known, speaking both to the refraction of a unitary gay (or kothi) identity and to the multiple, positioned nodes in the crafting of modern sexual identities, both gay and/or kothi. In this context, further research is necessary to explore the emergence and contextual deployments of *both* gay *and* kothi signifiers, given their increasingly complex and fluid circulations within the semantic fields of AIDS and sexual rights discourses. In this chapter, I have attempted to demonstrate the hybridity of gay and kothi sex/gender systems. But perhaps, as Lawrence Cohen

suggests, future iterations of this argument and further research on these issues need to go beyond merely highlighting fluidity, to challenge the "adequacy of viewing kothi and gay as different systems, however interlinked" (Cohen, personal communication; see also Cohen 2006).

8. "Axiom 5: The historical search for a Great Paradigm Shift may obscure the present conditions of sexual identity" (Sedgwick 1990: 44).

PART THREE

Caste, Class, and Community

All humans today participate in and perpetuate forms of social differentiation and inequality. Such social distinctions exist even within families and certainly within gender relations, as previous chapters illustrate. In this section the chapters focus explicitly on some of the predominant forms of social differentiation that impact everyday life in South Asia. These include caste, class, and religion, especially as religious differences relate to power relations and politics. In the lives of ordinary people, these three forms of social distinction sometimes overlap and interpenetrate in complex ways, as Ritty Lukose's chapter in this section demonstrates.

CASTE

Caste means more than one thing, and it means different things to different people in South Asia. Further, its meaning has changed over time, and varies from place to place. Here we wish to outline in broad strokes some of the many perspectives through which scholars have approached the study of caste, in order to provide some context for understanding this complex mode of social differentiation.

"Caste" is a term of European origin that is used to describe the social groupings that many South Asians recognize as distinguishing different kinds of human beings from others. The term *jāti*, which is the Sanskrit-derived term that most South Asian languages use to refer to these groupings, in fact means "kind" and is applied not only to kinds of humans but also to kinds of other things as well: animals, minerals, vegetables, genders, seasons, etc. Human jatis, or castes, are endogamous; that is, people tend to marry only within the caste to which they were born, although as recent research shows, the definitions of caste boundaries are increasingly expanding, allowing increasing flexibility in marriage choices (Fuller and Narasimhan 2008). And while many people today are also more flexible about commensality, that is, about eating together, still many upper-caste people avoid eating with those of lower castes, for reasons that will be addressed below. In a limited number of cases, caste names correspond to occupational groupings. That is, people may be born into a Barber or Potter or Blacksmith caste and *may* follow that profession as well. However, most castes names do not designate occupation, and even among those that do, people may and often do engage in occupations other than that suggested by the name of their caste. Caste is sometimes confused with *varna*, which is a common term used to describe an ancient textual—and for north Indians at least a contemporary practical—four-class division of humans into *Brahman*s (priests and scholars), *Ksatriya*s (warriors and kings), *Vaisya*s (commoners, including merchants and farmers), and *Sudra*s (servants of the other three). While there are four varnas, castes number in the thousands, with different ones in different parts of the subcontinent. And while caste is often associated with Hinduism, in fact caste distinctions have been and continue to be recognized among South Asian Muslims, Christians, Sikhs, Jains, and others as well.

Probably the first word that comes to mind for most readers when they see or hear the word "caste" is "hierarchy." Indeed, social rank is an important aspect of caste distinctions. It is not, however, the only aspect of caste recognized by South Asians. Here we will outline some of the main aspects of caste as the phenomenon has been studied over the last several decades.

Anthropological Models

Some of the first anthropological models recognized that caste was based on a form of non-monetary, non-market agricultural exchange found in many villages throughout India. In 1936, William Wiser coined the term "jajmani system" to describe this pattern as he found it in a north Indian village. He found that the non-Brahman landholders (*jajman*) in this village gave shares of their grain harvest as well as cooked food and other goods to other occupational castes, such as Barbers, Potters, Washermen, Carpenters, and Blacksmiths, in return for long-term service. Wiser characterized these exchanges as "mutual" or "symmetrical." That is, Wiser saw the jajmani system as a division of labor where landholding castes exchanged—tit for tat—grain for the services of the other castes, exchanges that apparently worked for the mutual benefit of all involved.

Wiser's characterization of these exchanges as mutual and reciprocal aroused debate among a later generation of researchers. These later researchers, influenced in part by a Marxian model, saw such exchanges to be coerced and asymmetrical, where services were given to the powerful landholders, who then redistributed grain in return. That is, while Wiser saw the landholders engaged in reciprocal, tit-for-tat relations with occupational service castes, others realized that the landholders were politically and economically powerful groups, with privileged access to the food supply, who controlled these exchanges using their power as the "dominant" castes (e.g., Harper 1959; Gould 1958; Beidelman 1959). Whether viewed as "mutual" or asymmetrical, however, all of these researchers shared a view of the jajmani system as a more or less bounded, interdependent, and self-sufficient village exchange network among permanent, hereditary occupational groups, or castes. This was their "caste system." It was primarily an economic system of non-market, non-monetary exchange at the village level.

A second, and subsequent, set of studies on caste concentrated on analyzing caste as primarily a religious, as opposed to an economic, mode of social organization. The most influential theorist to propound this model of caste was Louis Dumont (1970). He argued that Indian society is fundamentally hierarchical in form. He chose a single dimension of contrast—pure to impure—as the framework for this hierarchy, and located castes along this scale depending upon their relative involvement in biological or organic substances (the impure). Thus, those who were scholars and never ate meat (e.g., Brahmans) ranked above those who tilled the soil and were involved in the life-and-death practices of cultivation. They, in turn, ranked above people who washed the soiled—including bloodied—clothes of others (Washermen) or shaved their hair or cared for corpses at death (Barbers), who in turn ranked above those who made leather goods from the carcasses of dead animals (Leatherworkers) (see Parish, chapter 12 in this volume). This hierarchy was seen as "religious" because the valuation of substances, and categorizing people as "pure" or "impure" was seen to come from priestly, Brahmanical Hindu texts, beliefs, and practices (see introduction to part 4 for a discussion of Brahmanical Hinduism).

Ethnosociological Models

Another approach to caste rankings was put forward by McKim Marriott and some of his students. Marriott's models were based not only on textual ideas, but also on observational data he and his students collected doing field research, primarily in rural areas throughout India. Most of these studies have had as part of their aim to understand India as Indians themselves talk about it. That is, they have worked to construct their models about social life out of the terms and categories that Indians themselves use to discuss their lives. One of Marriott's over-arching aims has been to understand how Hindus understand the concept of "person." Caste was part of this inquiry, because caste—or rather jati—is an aspect of person. Indeed, jati is simply the "kind" of person one is.

According to ethnosociological models derived from Hindu concepts, humans are thought to differ from one another as well as from other kinds

of creatures and things in the universe because they all have different proportions of the same set of substances. These substances include the elements (fire, water, earth, wind, and ether), the humors (bile, phlegm, and
wind), and the three qualities of *sattvas* (goodness and light), *rajas* (action),
and *tamas* (darkness or inertia) (Daniel 1984: 3–4; Marriott 1990: 6–12). Marriott and Ronald Inden (1977) argued further that many Hindus understand
themselves not as "individuals" in the post-Enlightenment European sense
of bounded, integral wholes. Rather, they argued that Hindus operate as "di-
viduals," that is, as divisible persons made up of particulate substances that
can flow across boundaries, and thus be shared, exchanged, and transferred.
Much of the energy of personal action is devoted to maintaining one's own
"nature," in part by not mixing with things, places, or persons that might
alter you in a disagreeable manner, and, conversely, by seeking out transactions—such as with pure and beneficent gods—that might at least temporarily enhance your qualities, or "polish" them (*samskāra*). Hence some Indians,
for example, saw their own bodily nature to be affected by the soil on which
they lived and from which they ate food (Daniel 1984: 84–85), as well as by
their proximity and intimate exchanges with others (e.g., Trawick 1990: 99;
Lamb 2000: 31–35). Marriott further showed that different kinds of jatis use
different kinds of strategies to maintain their varied natures: central, landowning castes engage in many different transactions with all sorts of different people, while being careful to avoid polluting substances; Brahmans
tend to give much more than they receive, hence sending out their relatively
pure and cooling (sattvas-containing) substances but not taking in the substances of others. Lower castes tend to receive more than they give, partly
because the higher jatis do not wish to receive from them because of their
chaotic, hot, and impure natures, and partly because they require more in-
puts from others in order to survive. And some jatis seem to avoid transact-
ing with others in any direction, setting themselves apart almost as islands
in the otherwise flowing seas of inter-jati transactions (Marriott 1976).

An Aspectual Model

Writing and researching in the wake of all these approaches, Gloria Raheja
(1988) developed a comprehensive model to explore some of the dimensions
of meaning surrounding caste as it played out in Pahansu, a village in north
India. Raheja brought together (and altered) many of the ideas outlined
above, and identified three intersecting *aspects* of intercaste relations that
helped make sense of villagers' actions. These three aspects she named mu-
tuality, centrality, and hierarchy, or rank. No one aspect alone expresses the
realities of caste for the villagers, yet one aspect or another may be contextually foregrounded at one time (or place) or another.

    "Mutuality" refers to those reciprocal exchanges identified by Wiser. In-
deed, Raheja found, village residents did talk about their interrelations this
way: the Farmer who owns the lands gives grain in return for services pro-

vided by hereditary occupational castes such as Washermen, Barbers, and Brahman priests. "Rank" or "hierarchy" refers to those vertical relations of relative purity, where persons of castes that are more "pure" rank higher. Concerned with maintaining their own, purer bodily natures, members of relatively high jatis will regulate quite carefully whose substances they will consume in the form of cooked versus uncooked food, or exchanges of bodily fluids through sharing a pipe or a sexual relationship. "Centrality" is perhaps the most complex aspect of all. Centrality has to do with the fact that the powerful landowning castes are at the "center" of a distribution network, but that this distribution is not only political and economic. It is also a ritual distribution, where the landowners send out to other castes on the "periphery" (all the so-called service castes listed above, *including* the high-ranking Brahmans) their negative karma, their faults, evils, and inauspiciousness. Those on the periphery accept these negative substances in part because they are able to and in part because they must: if the central landowners are to succeed in growing the food that the whole village eats, they must be relatively free of these incapacitating karmic substances. D. Mines (1997b) has reported similar concepts at work in south India, where Brahman priests, Washermen, Barbers, and others receive evil-bearing gifts from dominant landowners. Evils are transferred from the landowners to objects and foodstuffs through rituals and mantras, and these items are then passed on to the "peripheral" castes, who are thought capable of absorbing or digesting them (see also Good 1991; Parry 1994).

Critical Studies

While many of these meanings and functions of caste persist today, other perspectives and debates enliven the discussion of caste in both scholarly and popular discourse. First, many critical academic studies of caste have highlighted the ways that anthropologists have sometimes treated caste ideas as "traditional" and "frozen" forms of meaning. In fact, caste—like any conceptual and social reality—is historically constructed, variable, and changing. Some have cogently argued that many scholarly concepts of caste have been, in part, influenced by British colonial categories, not to mention by anthropologists who themselves "construct" more than "reveal" knowledge of caste. Bernard Cohn (1987: 195–96), for example, argues persuasively that even Indians' own concepts of caste were altered historically by British colonizers who, in attempting to control the Indian population through the census, actually concretized caste into a frozen set of ranked groups that became, subsequently, real social and political categories within which Indians had to operate (see also Dirks 2001 and Bayly 1999). Chris Fuller (1989) has revealed how the so-called jajmani system neither was universal in South Asian villages, nor was nearly the closed and self-sufficient system that anthropologists imagined it to be. Others, especially those influenced by subaltern studies, a field that focuses on the histories of the non-elite, have pointed out that many anthropological models of caste derive from textual, Brahmanical models of caste, thus ignoring possible alternative understandings of the non-elite (see Dube 1998; Kapadia 1995; Prakash 1991; Trawick 1988). Indian fiction has for many years offered its own critique of caste in South Asia (e.g., Anand 1990; Bardhan 1990; Mistry 1997; Murthy 1989).

Of concern to many South Asians today, especially in India, are the ways that caste has become implicated in contemporary political life since (and in part due to) colonialism. For example, over the last several decades, caste groups often organize into associations that form the constituencies of political parties. Hence, caste identity has come to be defined as political identity—like religion is often now defined somewhat euphemistically as "community"—and now plays an important role in Indian forms of democracy (for an overview of the rise of caste associations, see Bayly 1999 and Metcalf and Metcalf 2006: 137–44). As castes come to define their identities as political ones, they also re-define their membership to include more and more people (which translates into more and more votes) who might previously have been considered to be different castes. Another important political and social movement that defines itself in relation to caste is the *Dalit* movement. "Dalit" is a politicized self-referential term used by many persons and groups that have otherwise been labeled "Untouchable." At least since the beginning of the twentieth century (Saurabh Dube's 1998 work demonstrates much earlier beginnings), Dalits have organized forthright resistance movements to protest caste-based inequities in Indian society. They have agitated for structural change as well as for changes in cultural values in an effort to move India toward egalitarian structures and values (see Zelliot 1992; Omvedt 1994; Moon 2001). These movements have resulted sometimes in violent confrontation between Dalits and the powerful caste and economic interest groups that would oppress them.

One issue that currently rivets attention all over India is the fallout from the Mandal Commission Report of 1980 and attempts by the government of India to implement its findings. The Indian Constitution of 1947 set forth several provisions to compensate for caste discrimination, including "reserving" a certain percentage of government jobs and university admissions for historically underprivileged caste groups. The Mandal Commission was a constitutionally mandated panel assigned by the government to review these constitutional provisions. As Lukose reports in her chapter, the Mandal Commission recommended that the number of such reservations be almost doubled, to nearly 50 percent of educational seats and government jobs. Attempts to implement this plan have led to many demonstrations and to a society-wide debate on the issue. Do such reservations merely perpetuate caste identities, or are they in fact needed to redress historical and ongoing "casteism"? This issue is argued with vigor, passion, anger, hope, and even despair, and is one of the most powerful social and political debates in India today. Indians are asking themselves, is caste still a relevant social real-

ity? If so, how now and to what extent? (See the Indian journal *Seminar*, nc
549 (2005), available at www.india-seminar.com, www.india-seminar.com/
semsearch.htm, and Pankaj 2007).

CLASS

Finally, in many places all over South Asia, class is in some respects and for
some people more important than, or in some cases replacing, caste as the
dominant mode of social ranking in everyday life. While class analysis has
long figured in studies of land tenure and peasant labor (e.g., Epstein 1973;
Gough 1989; Béteille 1965; Kapadia 1995), in recent years historians as well
as anthropologists have accelerated our understanding of class relations
in South Asia by analyzing labor relations in colonial history (Basu 1994;
Chakrabarty 2000; Daniel 1993; Gupta 1994), factories (Parry, Breman, and
Kapadia 1999; Lynch 2007; Hewamanne 2008), and domestic service (Adams
and Dickey 2000; Gamburd 2000; Ray 2000; Tolen 1996).

The rise of the new middle class and its attendant consumerism is particularly pertinent to analyzing class relations in India today (see, e.g., Liechty 2003; Sridharan 2004; Fernandes 2006). In recent years, this middle class
has expanded significantly due to several overlapping trends, including the
opening of borders to commerce and consumer values that come with global
economic liberalization, the region's own economic growth, outsourcing
and remittances from expatriates, and the substantial entry of women into
the professional workforce. As Sridharan reports, the number of persons
considered to be part of the fast-growing category of the middle class rose to
somewhere between 100 and 250 million (depending on the criteria used to
define middle class), from figures two to five times lower, over just ten years
from 1989 to 1999 (2004: 412–13). Many chapters in this volume, including
this section (Dickey, Rashid, and Lukose), discuss the impact of economic
class on experience and on definitions of self and other in South Asia (see
also chapters by Liechty, Kapur, Lamb, Lynch, Ring, Mankekar, and Radhakrishnan).

* * *

The chapters in this section reflect some aspects of caste, class, and community as these personal-cum-social distinctions affect people in their daily
lives. After a brief look at some of the major misconceptions of caste, Steven
M. Parish starts us off with a portrayal of the city Bhaktapur in Nepal. In
Bhaktapur, caste, city geography, and ritual all work together to make and
remake a set of caste values that provide residents a way to think about who
they are relative to one another. As Parish describes the city as a template for
caste relations, he also illustrates at least three of the aspects of caste defined
above. He fleshes out some of the everyday realities of caste rank based on

purity and impurity, he shows how the so-called Untouchables who live on the periphery of town serve as the repositories for the city center's impurities, and he shows that Untouchables are not uncritical of their position in society.

Viramma offers us a first-person account of caste relations in her village in rural South India. A Dalit (formerly "untouchable") woman who labors in others' fields, Viramma describes the different castes in her village from her own point of view. She tells stories of real events in her life. Some are humorous and reveal easy interactions between people of different castes, and others reveal some of the harder inequities of everyday life in a village where both caste and class matter.

Sabina Faiz Rashid focuses our attention on class as she analyzes adolescent married women's health in a slum of Dhaka, Bangladesh. Rashid argues that the political-economic realities of class are embodied as illness. She shows that young women are not mystified by this relation between economic class and bodily conditions. Rather, they understand their "white discharge" not only in medical terms but also in economic ones; they know that their poverty conditions their bodily experiences.

Sara Dickey's portrayal of the life decisions of Anjali, a young woman in Madurai, also focuses on class. Dickey shows that in urban settings today economic class and the cultural signs thereof are often more salient considerations than caste for many people as they struggle to make their way through life in the city. In Anjali's case, we see her poor, but high-caste, family struggle and work to achieve the signs of middle-class achievement.

Finally, Ritty Lukose brings the discussion of caste together with class and religion as she discusses how all three of these concepts play into contemporary definitions of both community and citizenship in India today. She focuses on how caste and religion participate in the construction of the "modern" citizen in a college that on the face of it denies both caste and religion as salient categories in contemporary, "secular," life.

11

Seven Prevalent Misconceptions about India's Caste System

1. *The caste into which one is born determines one's occupation.* False. People in the same caste engage in (and historically have engaged in) a wide variety of different occupations. Confusion arises in part from the fact that according to the mythical "varna" system of the idealized law books, everyone is supposed to carry out occupations that match their "varnas." While there are a handful of caste designations that point to particular occupations (Barber, Washerman, etc.) even these few occupations that correlate with caste names are not mandatory or inevitable.

2. *Caste designations are changeless.* False. There are many historical instances of castes changing (or trying to change) their caste names and behavior in order to receive advantageous treatment. Some of these efforts have succeeded; others have failed. There also are instances of caste groups moving to a different area and being given a new caste name in that area, for example, Chettiar (merchant), Brahman (priest), and Pahari (mountain people).

3. *Castes relate to each other in mutually accepted hierarchical patterns.* Frequently false. In any given locality some castes are likely to differ from other castes in their perceptions of what the "correct" local hierarchical patterns are. Disputes regarding the "correct" local hierarchy occur (and have occurred) frequently. Caste rankings can also change over time. And for many people today and in the past, hierarchical ranking is not even a primary concern.

4. *Everyone called by the same caste name is related to everyone else called by that same caste name.* False. Castes are assigned names by other castes living around them or have been so named in the past. Labeling coincidences frequently occur. Thus there are numerous castes, some of whose mem-

Adapted with minor changes from *Ghanta* 3, no. 2 (Spring 1992): 7.

bers perform priestly functions, that are called "Brahmans" by those around them. However, they are not related to all other castes that are called "Brahmans." Similarly there are castes that are called "Patels," "Deshmukhs," or "Rajputs" (honorific civil titles) by those around them that are not related to all other castes called "Patels," "Deshmukhs," or "Rajputs." Similarly, there are numerous castes, some of whose members make (or did make) pots, that are called "potters" by those around them that are not related to all other castes called "potters." Every "Gandhi" is not related to every other "Gandhi."

5. *Castes are uniquely Hindu.* False. In India castes exist among Christians, Jains, Sikhs, Buddhists, and Muslims. Frequently the rules about marrying within one's caste and avoiding interactions with other castes are as strict among Christians, Jains, and others as they are among Hindus.

6. *Hinduism legitimizes preferential treatment according to caste.* Occasionally false. Throughout history, Hindu movements and individuals have denounced preferential treatment according to caste (these include some Hindu devotional bhakti movements, sects such as the Lingayats, and certain Hindu philosophers and intellectuals including to an extent Mahatma Gandhi). Additionally, alternative religious and nonreligious movements and individuals have also critiqued (though not necessarily abolished) preferential treatment according to caste. These include Buddhism, Jainism, and Sikhism, as well as individuals such as E. V. Ramaswamy Naicker and B. R. Ambedkar, among many others. Since the late colonial period and continuing today with much debate, governmental affirmative-action-like "reservations" have worked to compensate for historical inequities by reserving government jobs and university admissions for individuals from historically lower castes.

7. *Castes have been abolished.* False. India's constitution declares that "untouchability" is abolished and anyone discriminating against "untouchables" can be prosecuted. However, India's constitution says nothing about abolishing castes. Similarly, in the United States discrimination on the grounds of race or gender has been declared illegal. However, the United States has no laws abolishing race or gender.

12

God-Chariots in a Garden of Castes: Hierarchy and Festival in a Hindu City

Steven M. Parish

My Kingdom is the Garden of the Four Varna and the Thirty-Six Castes.

— King Pṛthvī Nārāyana śhāha of Nepal

THE CITY

The Hindu city of Bhaktapur in Nepal's Kathmandu Valley is a place where caste and religion came to dominate much of everyday life. Located on an ancient trade route to Tibet, Bhaktapur sits on a rise above a river. Viewed from the south, from the fertile rice fields on the other side of this river, the city presents a face composed of four- and five-story redbrick houses thrust up like a kind of urban cliff, breached by narrow streets that climb up and into the interior. The great pagoda temple of a goddess towers above the rooftops, and beyond the city rise the snow peaks of the Himalaya.

Inhabited by an ethnic group called the Newars, the city was once the royal center of a small Hindu kingdom. Later it was conquered and made part of a larger multiethnic Hindu state. Throughout its history, it has been shaped to religious conceptions of the moral and cosmic order. Today, it remains a harvest of much of the meaning, much of the sense of reality, generated in South Asia over the centuries. The city embodies Hinduism in urban space and form, and makes it part of everyday life in myriad ways. Dense, compact, stratified, Bhaktapur is not just a city, built of bricks and timbers alone; it is a sacred city, a Hindu city, a city of castes—built of rituals and religious meaning within an encompassing social hierarchy.

Parts of this essay appeared in *Hierarchy and Its Discontents: Culture and the Consciousness of Politics in Caste Society* by Steven M. Parish. Copyright © 1996 University of Pennsylvania Press. Reprinted by permission.

THE JOURNEY OF THE CHARIOT, I

In Bhaktapur, myth comes to life with the music of drums and the clash of cymbals. A festival marks the turning of the year. To celebrate it, the gods and goddesses of the city leave their temples to journey through its streets, to rest beneath the eaves of their god-houses, to receive offerings from their worshippers.

Each spring, in rites that mark the passing of the year, the people of Bhaktapur pull two Hindu divinities, Lord Bhairav and the goddess Bhadrakali, in chariots through the streets of the city, and then out to the edge of the city. Before these set out, expectant crowds begin to gather in the square of the five-storied temple where the journey begins, several days before the new year. The celebration fills the town with joyful crowds, with a sacred tumult, as other divinities are also taken in procession.

During these festivals, I have seen the deities associated with various quarters carried in torchlit processions on the shoulders of ecstatic, intoxicated men. Carried away, they sometimes surge through the crowds that have gathered in the narrow streets; the rush of the men carrying the litter holding the divinity adds to the general commotion and excitement. Those who live along the procession's path crowd into their doorways and lean out the windows of their multi-storied houses to watch the gods go by.

The festival's main event, however, is the journey of Bhairav. At rest, waiting for its ceremonial progression to begin, his chariot is an echo on wheels of the two monumental pagoda temples that flank the city square where it sits. Standing motionless, the chariot rises into the air above the heads of the crowd. It is a mobile temple, a god-house on wheels, several times the height of the people who gather around it to watch and worship.

Moving, the chariot of the god surges through the crowd like a ship on the ocean, parting swirling masses of people, who stream away from it on nimble feet to avoid being crushed beneath its great wooden wheels, each taller than a man. The wheels have painted eyes. The chariot has a kind of prow that stretches forward and up, where an image of another god is attached, a mask that stares outward with blind eyes. The men of the city pull the chariot by ropes attached front and back. In one of the central acts of the festival, they pull it first forward, then back, chanting the rhythm of their efforts, in a sacred tug-of-war. The men of one half of the city vie with those from the other half, each group attempting to pull the chariot and the god it houses into their section of the city. Each side wants the blessings of the god, and the honor of being the first to take the god through the streets of their part of Bhaktapur.

Having the chariot pass through the city is a form of *darśana*, an opportunity to witness the god, offering people a way of coming into the presence of divinity.

The priests do not always have an easy ride during the journey of the god through the streets, either during the tug-of-war or afterward. I have seen the chariot pulled with such energy that it collides with houses along the street as it does not quite make a corner, gouging holes in brick walls, damaging the chariot itself. Bhairav is a dangerous god of force and motion, and the force with which his chariot is drawn through the city seems somehow appropriate, as a kind of metaphor for social and psychological forces that pulse just beneath the surface of Bhaktapur. Composed of human emotions and dissatisfactions, these forces sometimes break through the redundant constructions of reality and common sense that help establish a cultural and political order for Bhaktapur.

The chief Brahman priest of the Taleju temple rides the chariot, carrying a sword that represents the royal power of Bhaktapur's long-vanished kings. Another Brahman rides with the king, representing the king's own Brahman priest and royal adviser, his *guru-purohita*. Thus, the apex of the caste hierarchy is represented in the (symbolic) persons of king and Brahman. They ride with divinity: their proximity to the god declares their status, and lends it an aura of legitimacy.

Their importance is dramatized in the way they make an entrance onto the scene, with pomp and ceremony, before the ritual tug-of-war and hauling of the chariot through the streets begins. Shaded by a ceremonial umbrella carried by an attendant, accompanied by music, they march from the Taleju temple in the old royal palace complex to the temple square, where the chariot waits. Arriving in the square, the priest-king commands that Bhairav's image be brought. The image of the god is placed in the chariot and "the king" worships it. The Brahman representing the king takes a seat on the god's right. The Brahman representing the royal priest takes a seat on the left. Members of other castes take positions in the chariot that reflect their positions in society. Four Carpenters stand at the four corners. An Astrologer and a non-Brahman priest seat themselves behind the priests representing the king and his royal adviser. A *jyāpu*, a member of the farming castes who make up a majority of Bhaktapur's inhabitants, also takes a seat behind the king, the royal Brahman priest, and the god. In this way, a kind of self-image of caste society is composed, and then pulled through the streets of the city.

THE CASTE HIERARCHY IN BHAKTAPUR

While the festival offers a tableau of the caste order, the practical organization of the festival depends on the cooperation of many of the castes of the city. The division of labor that makes the festival possible reflects the division of labor, and the division of symbolic roles, that underlie the social and symbolic order of the city.

Caste is integral to the city. Nurtured by Hindu kings over the centuries, caste civilization flourished in the Kathmandu Valley. Cities, towns, and villages became extravagant flowers in royal gardens of caste, representing a cultural efflorescence of the idea of hierarchy, as caste practices were propagated and cultivated as the essence of the body politic. Society came to embody the ideal that humans are unequal. The propagation of ideas and images of inequality as legitimate and sacred values shaped not only the structure of society, but also the intimate consciousness of men and women, giving them both a fixed place in society and ways of thinking and feeling about themselves and others.

After the defeat of the Newar Malla kings and Bhaktapur's incorporation into the larger kingdom of Nepal, the early Shaha dynasty and the succeeding Rana regime continued to give legal support to caste hierarchy. By the middle of the twentieth century, the larger social and political context was quaking with radical structural change, but change tended to come later to Bhaktapur than to other places. In Bhaktapur, caste continued to be one of the key cultural axioms of local social existence even as the legal and political foundations for caste were swept away. By the early 1980s, when I arrived, some castes had vanished or abandoned their symbolic roles, but the caste system as a symbolic and moral system survived in Bhaktapur, and continued to grip people's minds, to define their social identity.

What we term "caste," Newars call *jāt*. However, although "jat" denotes those hierarchically organized divisions of society designated by the word "caste" in English, it refers also to occupational and ethnic groups and to gender—or to any other distinct category. It is used broadly to mean "kind." When it is used in the sense of "caste," Newars say there are as many as thirty castes in Bhaktapur. Some of these may recently have disappeared as families left Bhaktapur, and a few may be present only cognitively and symbolically—they are there in thought, not as actual groups. In terms of ethnic identity, most of these castes are considered Newar, but some belong to other ethnic groups.

No one—not I, and not any of the Newars I know—would deny that the opposition of pure and impure is one basis for the caste hierarchy (Dumont 1970), one of the key models for social relations, although it is only one among several. States of purity and impurity separate Newar castes, and purity is one key idiom of rank: higher castes are relatively more "pure" than lower castes. Among Newars, this is expressed concretely in a number of ways. As in much of South Asia, food is one medium—patterns of sharing and not sharing food and other items have hierarchical implications. High-caste Newars will not accept boiled rice or certain other foods from individuals of any caste lower than their own; they will accept nothing, not even water, from members of some still lower castes.

Some castes are dangerously impure or untouchable. Members of these castes cannot enter the upper stories of houses of high-caste Newars (the bottom story being conceived either as outside the house or as impure in its own right). They perform stigmatizing roles: accept polluting offerings in death rites, handle excrement, kill animals for a living.

In the past, exclusion was practiced in a variety of ways. For the most part, the higher castes lived in the center of the city while lower castes lived on the peripheries. Some of the more stigmatized castes lived in separate neighborhoods; the untouchable Sweepers, the Pore, lived outside the traditional boundaries of the city, in an area near the river, across from one of the city's cremation grounds. This location resonated with their symbolic association with filth, decay, and death. Certain occupations were reserved for certain castes; occupational mobility was limited. Education was limited to members of high castes. Members of the lower castes were required to wear distinctive dress. Among other legal disabilities, the untouchable Sweepers could construct only one-story houses with thatch roofs. They were barred from entering certain temples, though some Untouchables had the right to act as attendants at certain other shrines. Untouchables could not use the same water taps as "pure" castes. Untouchables could not enter the city after sundown. This was enforced by royal will, by state power. In the past, many still recalled, any wealth Untouchables might accumulate would be seized by the old kings. Power and force kept Untouchables in their places in the caste hierarchy.

The state no longer enforces this system of exclusions, which so powerfully symbolizes hierarchy, but the basic pattern persists, suggesting that it is not only the actions of the state that sustain caste. Given the social, economic, and political changes in Nepal, the persistence of the caste system is remarkable. In Bhaktapur, untouchable Sweepers still live outside the city. Untouchables now use water taps once reserved exclusively for use by the traditional "high" and "pure" castes, but they may still be met with verbal abuse, and be made to feel unwelcome and inferior. Members of the traditional "pure" castes of Bhaktapur object to Untouchables entering tea shops in their neighborhood. Traditionally they could be served outside, and would wash their own utensils. They would risk being beaten if they did not accept these exclusions, if they did not conform to expectations held by members of other castes. Many high- and low-caste persons recalled such incidents of violence for me.

Practices that exclude or stigmatize people, that put or keep them in their place in the caste hierarchy, may no longer receive the active support of the state, but groups, households, and individuals remain under pressure to conform to such practices or else leave Bhaktapur altogether. Although legal and political constraints have eroded, the social and cultural constraints of caste life continue to have power, to be central to people's lives.

Much of the ritual life of the city still rests on its complex caste system; the caste system constitutes a division of labor, not only for economic activity, but for citywide ritual activities (Levy 1990). Brahmans and other religious specialists have essential roles in the temples of the cities, and officiate at some of the domestic rites of families. Several castes have symbolic roles that are stigmatizing, but essential to the traditional social and symbolic life of the city. The impurity and inauspiciousness of untouchable Sweepers, for example, is necessary to the purity and the fate of the city; the impurities, misfortunes, and suffering of the city are conceived to flow into the Untouchables, who live in a separate area outside the old boundaries of the city. Their impurity thus defines the purity of the city.

In a sense, they suffer for the city: they absorb in a symbolic way the suffering of the city. Their symbolic presence helps relieve the existential anxieties of higher-caste actors; through some process of symbolic displacement they become living symbols that condense meanings and possibilities that high-caste actors want to cast away, reject, throw off, keep away from self. In the words of one high-caste Newar, Untouchables "soak up" impurities and inauspiciousness "like a sponge." They are seen as having a "nature" that fits them for their work of collecting dirt, feces, and garbage.

In a set of conventional stigmatizing stereotypes, the people of low and untouchable castes are seen as dirty, disgusting, and impure; as highly sexual and promiscuous; as ignorant and lacking the discipline and mastery of language that would make them truly human. In total, they embody an "otherness" that for high-caste individuals is disturbing and yet reflects a natural order that is necessary, ordained by the very structure of the universe. High-caste actors view low-caste actors, individually and collectively, as deserving their fate. The low castes are polluted, that is, naturally defiled, a notion based on a complex physical theory of the flow of person-defining substances. They are also viewed as realizing the fruits of the sins of previous lifetimes—their fate is justified by *karma* (one's destiny based on one's actions in this or previous lives) and ordained by the *dharma* (moral and religious law) which caste society embodies.

In sum, a hierarchy constituted by power (the king and state) fuses in experience and in practice with a ritualized hierarchy constituted in terms of purity and impurity. This fusion in turn interacts with other formations of hierarchy. It blends with a moral hierarchy of action and knowledge, of sin, virtue, and fate, and finds expression in a religious hierarchy of proximity to sacred values and access to spiritual power. In my view, caste hierarchy is all these, locked together in a dynamic propelled by struggles for domination and emancipation.

Lower-caste actors (Farmers and below) often resent the way they are stigmatized and excluded in the caste system. For them, the garden of castes yields a harvest of discontents. In the past, however, there was often not much they could do about their discontents, since the power of the state weighed in on the side of keeping them in their place. Despite the formal removal of legal sanctions, there is still not much they can do to escape being stigmatized, to escape the life chances offered by that caste system.

Overcoming the initial set of life chances determined by their caste standing remains exceedingly difficult, and for most perhaps virtually impossible. Since caste standing is linked to subsistence and survival, the historical reality is that very few could readily act on whatever critique of caste society some of them may have developed. Furthermore, since caste life generates a sense of moral community, shapes personal identity, and offers a number of satisfactions and meanings, it is not surprising that people are ambivalent about caste society. As we will see in testimony from several participants in the system, moral discourse in caste society does not reflect ideology alone; it expresses profound ambivalence.

Caste practices are potent forms of life and thought; they help constitute lived worlds for actors. It is as such that they pose quandaries for the moral imagination. Some actors find their social position and identity disturbing, and reject the reality and justice of the system that positions them in society and shapes the way others perceive them. They are disquieted by cultural life, even as they live it. Such perplexities and quandaries haunt the imagination of any complex society, including my own racially polarized and class-divided society of North America.

Perhaps the symbolic action of Bhaktapur's chariot festival helps quiet the moral imagination disturbed by the inequities of the caste hierarchy. Perhaps it helps reassure some social actors that the way things are represents the way they ought to be, affirming their identities and practices, guaranteeing privileges and compensating for subordination—perhaps. In any event, the festival does display, for social actors to see, images of a sacred and moral order. These images affirm hierarchical interdependence as the basis of social reality.

THE JOURNEY OF THE CHARIOT, II

At one point, the ritual progression of Bhairav and Bhadrakali takes them out of the city; at least, they leave the city's symbolic core as high-caste actors define it. After their progression through the two halves of the city and certain other events, the chariots descend the hill on which the greater part of the city is built, down a steep, crooked street, down to a wide field on the edge of Bhaktapur, near the river that passes by the city.

This passage to the edge of the city is not difficult for the smaller vehicle of the goddess, but can be a dangerous process with the larger chariot of Bhairav. Two special ruts have been built of stones in the surface of the street to guide the wheels of the chariot and keep it on track. Even with this, the chariot sometimes rushes out of control, endangering bystanders.

I used to watch from the window of one of the houses that line this street. I once observed the chariot break away and rush with great speed and force down a stretch of the road. A man ran alongside the chariot as it crashed down the street. He sped downhill in the narrow space between the chariot and the houses lining the road. Running all out, he virtually bounced off the walls of the houses, and careened back into the chariot, pumping his legs fiercely all the time to keep up with the chariot. I had no doubt that he was at risk: that he could fall and be killed.

I am not sure what he thought he was doing, although he may have been one of those responsible for seeing the wheels did not get stuck in the ruts built into the road for them. (They were in no danger of doing that in the moment I saw him.) I am even less sure how he managed to survive. He looked out of control, pacing the chariot as it accelerated out of control. Running along with the chariot seemed to have taken possession of him.

Caught up in the moment, he appeared in the grip of an adrenaline rush, caught up in some state of palpable religious enthusiasm. Others are swept up in the excitement of the festival as well, are pulled out of their everyday lives and mundane selves, if not as intensely and dangerously. In a variety of ways, festivals offer excitement, danger; they generate palpable sacred thrills. Experienced actively or vicariously, these are encompassed in a religious context, making the body's arousal a sensual chord in the mytho-sacred performance, a felt sign of the presence of the sacred.

At the bottom of the hill, where the street issues into the open area on the edge of the city, a crowd will have gathered to watch the chariot arrive. It emerges suddenly, bursts out of the city, plunging down the hill, rolling with great force and speed. The part of the crowd nearest it scatters to avoid being run over.

The chariot rolls to a halt in the broad field at the foot of the hill that spreads out toward the river. One corner of the field adjoins the segregated ward of the untouchable Sweepers, the Pore. When the chariot rolls to a stop, men again pick up the ropes to pull it into position for the next stage of the festival. Bystanders toss coins at it as it passes, offerings for blessings.

Robert Levy, who has also observed Bhaktapur's chariot festival, describes the selection and raising of a god-pole, which now becomes the focus of events on the edge of the city. The god-pole is made from a tree, which may be as tall as seventy feet, cut in the forests east of the city. The pole is treated as a god itself; the life or force of divinity is awakened or installed in it. Envisioned as a kind of body, the tree is stripped of branches, except at the very top, where some are left to represent the god's hair. A crossbar made of part of another tree is attached near the top of the pole, representing the arms of the god. Branches and leaves are tied to the arms to represent the god's hands and fingers. Two banners are tied on to the god-pole. The chariots of the god and goddess are pulled near the site where the god-pole will be raised in celebration of the passing of the old year and the coming of the new, "so that the two deities can watch" (Levy 1990: 476).

Thousands of people gather for the taking down of the god-pole, going first to take a ritual bath in the river. After esoteric and secret rituals are performed in the Taleju temple, the surrogate for the king, carrying the royal sword, and his Brahman adviser leave the temple and go out through the golden gate into the royal square. Joined by their charioteers and musicians, accompanied by an attendant carrying the royal umbrella, they return to the field where the chariots have been left and the god-pole stands. After some preliminary rites, they take their seats in the chariot. From there, they watch the god-pole lowered.

Levy's account describes the process this way: "First the god-pole is rocked back and forth in an east-west direction, in motion called 'rocking to sleep.' The god is said to be tired . . . for 'he has been standing all year'" (1990: 485). The ropes represent the city's protective goddesses. Seeing the god-pole now as Bhairav himself and these goddesses as his consorts, Bhaktapurians interpret the rocking of the pole and motion of the ropes as sexual intercourse between the god and the goddesses. Levy goes on: "The pole is slowly rocked back and forth, and finally, after perhaps ten minutes to half an hour of swaying, eased down to the west. . . . When the pole falls, the new year begins."

This is a high point of the festival, one of its key moments as a signifying practice. While the festival has many meanings, it is crucially a ritual construction of order. The order it constructs has universal dimensions: it is social and moral, cosmic and sacred. These aspects of order are linked; the ritually declared connection to the cosmos and divinities helps give legitimacy to the royal and caste order. Human and divine actors witness the beginning of the new year, participate in it. The festival is, among other things, a pageant of hierarchy and a spectacle of order, in which, as Levy says, "the king and his entourage and the god Bhairava are moved by immemorial ritual order, as the sun moves through the year" (1990: 493).

Much of the ritual activity of the festival takes place not far from where Bhaktapur's untouchable Sweepers live. What part do they play in this pageant of hierarchy, this construction of the order that subordinates and stigmatizes them? The traditional terms of their participation have them enact their own subordination; yet on occasion they have attempted to turn the event against itself through symbolic acts that disrupt it. Levy (1990: 486) describes an event that seems to signify much about dominance and subordination, inclusion and exclusion:

> Now some of the [Untouchables] take hold of the ropes at the back of the chariot, and other men, mostly Jyapus [Farmers], take hold of the ropes at the front. Again a tug of war begins. . . . The Jyapus are trying to pull the chariot back toward the city, while the [Sweepers] are trying to keep the deity in Yasi(n) . . . the area where they live, just outside the symbolic boundaries of the city. This struggle does not (at least in the memory and expectation of present informants) lead to fights, and gradually the more numerous Jyapus with the advantage of the two extra ropes at the front of the chariot prevail. (Levy 1990: 486)

In contrast to the tug-of-war between the city halves, where one side or the other might prevail, it seems unlikely that the Untouchables could ever "win" this tug-of-war. They are less numerous and they have fewer ropes to pull: the deck is stacked against them. We should perhaps see this as a ritual of social positioning that acknowledges their existence but asserts their subordination and marginality. They were not allowed to participate in the other tug-of-war, in which only men from higher castes pulled on the ropes. Unlike the two halves of the city, they do not get to draw the chariot through their quarter, which is symbolically "outside" the city. The unequal contest asserts the power of the castes of the city over those outside the city, the Untouchables. The god and goddess are pulled away from the Untouchables, back into the city.

Untouchables do not always permit the construction of hierarchical order to go unchallenged. In one of the years I observed this event, the pole broke as it was lowered. Rumors quickly spread of how a group of Untouchables—who were supposed to pull on only one of the ropes used to lower the pole—had grabbed more than one, and pulled in such a way that the pole snapped. In breaking out of the place assigned them, and in breaking the god-pole, the Untouchables disrupted the construction of the unity of the social, moral, and cosmic order. High-caste actors argued that this had ominous implications. They felt that the disorder that had taken place at the event would be repeated in a variety of misfortunes and disturbances in the coming year. They blamed the Untouchables for this in advance of any actual misfortune, and turned this blame into another layer of stigma to attach to Untouchables, who were called an unruly mob and denounced as sources of social and cosmic disorder. As this suggests, the symbolic construction of the dominant order does not always proceed smoothly; it may be disturbed by protests and disquieted by the social anxiety such protests release. Even such disruptions, however, may be turned by high-caste actors into reaffirmations of hierarchy, stigmatizing Untouchables as a source of disorder and legitimizing the caste hierarchy as necessary to prevent chaos.

SOME PEOPLE

In Bhaktapur, I lived on the upper floors of a house owned by a Brahman. The entrance was on the second floor; to get to the door you had to walk up a flight of stairs. In Newar culture, this is a walk up to a state of purity; the upper stories of a house are considered purer than the ground floor. Low-caste people are barred from entering the upper floors of a high-caste house. I had two friends who would sometimes come to see me, to help me by talking about their thoughts and experiences, by discussing a variety of cultural topics. They had very different ways of making their presence known when they arrived at my house, and I believe this expresses, in a small way, the reality of caste differences. Shiva Bhakta, a high-caste man, would run confidently up the steps, pound vigorously on the door, call out my name in a loud voice. Kancha, an Untouchable, would come into the tiny courtyard of the house, and sit down on a stack of lumber. He would quietly smoke a cigarette, waiting until I came down or poked my head out the window to see if he was there. I asked him to come to the door and knock, so that I would know that he was there, but he refused. He did not refuse directly—he always bobbed his head affirmatively when I explained to him that he should do this—but he would not make the journey to the top of the stairs. I would poke my head out the window the next time we had arranged to meet, and would find him sitting at the bottom of the stairs, smoking.

The contrast was striking. Some of Kancha's behavior was a public presentation, intended for a possible high-caste audience; when he got to know me, he would in private let much of the diffidence drop. In our interview sessions and conversations, he usually voiced his opinions in a direct and self-confident manner. He did not possess the self-assurance and authority that characterized Shiva Bhakta, but he was not at all passive. He felt it necessary to present himself as yielding—as unchallenging—in public. What we see in his behavior is the culture of dissimulation that develops in caste society and perhaps in any stratified society where power may be used in arbitrary ways.

Kancha did not, dared not, assert himself in public. I did not observe such a radical split in high-caste friends and acquaintances, although they too had public faces and private selves. Shiva Bhakta, far more than Kancha, could both assert himself and embed himself in historically determined patterns of group behavior—without radical self-contradiction. Positioned in society in different ways, and having different kinds of meaning in social life, people of different castes experience life and view the world in rather diverse ways that reflect their place in the caste order.

Let me sketch in the life circumstances of several individuals, beginning with Kancha and Shiva Bhakta.

Kancha, an Untouchable. Kancha is a middle-aged man, usually dressed in dirty, ragged clothes and carrying the tools of his trade as he goes about his business. He is a member of the Sweeper caste, the Pore. Sweepers like Kancha are employed by the Bhaktapur Town Committee (Nagar Panchayat) to clean the streets, and by private householders to clean their courtyards or latrines. As an Untouchable who does such work, Kancha exists on the margins of society, lives on the underside of hierarchy, in its stigmatizing depths.

This is expressed by where he lives: not near the center, where the highest castes are concentrated around monumental temples, but on the very edge of the city. The Sweepers live in a separate quarter, which is considered to lie outside the city. Unlike the houses of others, many of the houses in the Untouchable quarter have thatch roofs. In the old days, these Untouchables were not permitted to have tile roofs, or to live in houses as tall as those of other castes.

Kancha undergoes a social metamorphosis as he leaves his home and goes up "into" the city to work, walking up the same street the god-chariot came rolling down and "out" of the city during the festival. In the social gaze of high-caste actors, who bring a hierarchical sensibility to what they see, he undergoes a transformation. They see an Untouchable.

At home, he finds meaning in domestic life, finds a measure of psychological security—"my caste is good for me," he will tell you. There, he sees himself (and wants to be known) as a good father, a husband, a head of household, and a person with aspirations for himself and his children; but he must leave this psychological cocoon to make a living. As he leaves the Untouchable quarter and enters the city, he enters a world where his presence and being have other meanings. He walks the streets as a living symbol of the caste hierarchy. Here, in contrast to the domestic scene, he has no active role in constructing his own meaning: he simply exists for others as a living symbol of hierarchy. High-caste people view him as a member of a functional and symbolic category that performs needed, but degrading, work. In the symbolic social ecology of the city, they see him as a remover of pollution—of physical filth, but also of impurity and inauspiciousness. They see that his hands and clothes are dirty from contact with feces and filth. I have seen people shrink away, assume disgusted faces in the presence of Untouchables. Being harangued, ordered around by words hurled across the social distance that separates them, may be Kancha's dominant experience of interacting with high-caste people.

Arguably, for the high-caste community, the Sweepers have a special, psycho-symbolic value—the Untouchable is one of many "others" who define "self" through contrast and complementarity. Kancha is a source of impurity, a polluting presence; but perhaps even more critically, he absorbs—soaks up—the most disgusting, dangerous, contaminating residues and effluents of higher-caste bodies and selves. He is a receiver of impurity, of inauspiciousness, of what others reject and seek to keep away from themselves. Newar Sweepers have a multiple sociocultural identity, since they are conceived of as polluting in themselves, serve as removers of polluting and disgusting filth, and receive or control inauspicious qualities or forces that bring ill fortune to others. Kancha's caste is associated with an inauspicious celestial demon, Rahu, responsible for eclipses and human misfortune. Some say that the goddess of cholera used to dwell in the Untouchable quarter, near one of the cremation grounds.

Kancha does not seem bitter about his status. At times, he even defends the caste system; indeed, at times, he defends it more vigorously than some high-caste Newars. How, he wants to know, would he survive without it? But he wants something else for his children, and there are moments when he denies that the caste hierarchy has any moral reality, any ultimate justification.

Shiva Bhakta, a high-caste merchant. If Kancha is a marginal man living on the margins of the city, Shiva Bhakta inhabits the center, in a physical and social sense. Indeed, Shiva is a man of many centers, within a lived world that contrasts sharply with Kancha's world. Some of Shiva's many centers—his personhood and status, his prospects and possibilities, his class and caste position—are defined in part by where and how Kancha lives, by what Kancha is. Shiva is not Kancha—this is an existential and social fact of no little significance.

Shiva is a dweller in the city, the head of household of one of the large houses in one of the central neighborhoods of the city. In the local status system, only the Brahmans are higher in status, and even they may not be more central to the social and economic life of the city, although they are to its religious and ritual life.

Befitting his status and prosperity, Shiva dresses neatly, with a kind of precision, in traditional fashions. With a formal black hat settled on his graying hair, there is nothing diffident about Shiva. He is a merchant, and relatively prosperous, with a social network radiating out through and beyond the community. He lives in a larger social world than Kancha, who has few contacts outside of the city.

One center of life for Shiva is the modern economy and the opportunity it represents; he tells me life is getting better, that you have to seize the day. He applies this philosophy to business and pleasure. He has a certain zest for life.

If one center of Shiva's life is commerce, the effort to generate wealth and through it prestige, he is also centered in a moral world, in the traditions of family, religion, and city; he identifies with the dharma, the moral order and rightness, integral to each of these. I believe this gives him what Erik Erikson called an ordering core; for Shiva this ordering core is socially and psychologically attuned to the moral order of his city, his family line, integrating past and present, himself and significant others through whom he integrates self and culture. As the key concept of the Hindu moral order that Shiva identifies with, dharma offers Shiva a firm basis for his sense of self, and yields him moral insights for living his life, yet also helps constitute a society that oppresses others, such as Kancha.

Shiva's confidence also, I think, reflects a sense of position and entitlement, based not just on relative wealth and power, but also on caste status and family history. This is combined with the sense of purpose and fulfillment that doing dharma gives. Shiva characterizes himself as *calak*—vocal, articulate, clever—and I think he is right. Language, the power to use it to express social values and achieve goals, is another one of his centers; he is a man of words and means, grounded in dharma and family, who speaks and acts from the center of a community and tradition.

Kedar, a low-caste man who rejects caste. A member of the Jugi caste, Kedar is an angry man, unafraid to voice his fear of and loathing for the caste system—his contempt for what he sees as the bad faith and illusions involved in it. He voiced rage and a sense of powerlessness, too, in a less veiled fashion than some others. Unlike many other low-caste informants, he consistently rejected caste, stressing its oppressiveness and his impotence to change it. He often spoke with irony and sarcasm, pointing out what he felt was bad faith and hypocrisy, insisting on a kind of dual perspective. The caste order had no moral reality for him, but it nonetheless formed a social reality that he could neither ignore, nor deny, nor totally break free from. His goal was clearly freedom: he wanted to break from caste interdependency, to become a man of independent means. He expressed great pride in a small entrepreneurial business selling chickens and goats that he felt had made him relatively free of his caste's former dependency on caste roles. It may be this relative capacity to support himself that made him feel free to scorn the caste system in ways that others somewhat shared, though they would temper and hedge, worried about what others might think and about their own need to perform caste roles in order to survive. Perhaps it is because he has come to think of himself as a man of independent means that he also insists on defining himself through his own independence of thought. He was willing to concede, even underscore, his powerlessness in the face of the realities of caste. Why would he stress this, if he has achieved more independence than many? Perhaps because in his "inner" world he imagines and strives to create himself over and against the caste system. By claiming that he did not make the world of caste, he emphasizes that he did make himself, in defiance of the caste system and the place it allotted him. He values his hard-won relative independence, the freedom of choices he has earned, in contrast to his sense that he lived in a world that he did not make and would never have chosen.

Krishna Bahadur, a low-caste ritual dancer. Krishna Bahadur dances myth in the city, as a member of a ritual troupe that visits each neighborhood to perform rites that protect the city and its inhabitants. He has danced in the streets of Bhaktapur as a divinity. This role is his center, offering him an ordered and ordering core, a sense of identity. He wishes for his son to follow him, to share this identity, to dance for the city, to have a sacred role. Yet this identity is not without its cost, for it cannot be separated from his low-caste status. He is highly critical of the "closed" hierarchy of caste and proposes an "open" hierarchy based on knowledge—such as he himself possesses of sacred dances and Tantric divinities, knowledge of the kind he knows he has the capacity to master. A thin and intelligent man, brooding and yet gentle, he has given some thought to these matters, and speaks with some rhetorical force. Yet I do not think he can be said to have resolved anything; perhaps this is why he broods.

Dharma Raj, a Brahman priest. A priest and a reflective man, Dharma Raj sees the city in terms of the religious symbols and meanings that compose and integrate it. He supplies others with interpretations of cultural tradition, of religious reality. He performs domestic rites for people, using Sanskrit texts, as he was taught by his father. Like Shiva Bhakta, he sees the city as his; his caste provides the chief priest of Bhaktapur's main temple, in the old royal palace complex. In the days when Bhaktapur was the capital of an independent kingdom, members of his priestly caste served as advisers to the kings. In that role they shaped the ritual cycle and religious landscape of the city. Indeed, as we've seen, Brahman priests have in some ways been amalgamated with the old Newar kings, blending the symbolism of king and priest together in ways that help sustain the Hindu core of Bhaktapur.

Dharma places himself in a line of teachers and students, predecessors and successors, those from whom he received the knowledge of tradition (including secret religious knowledge), and those who will receive that knowledge from him. His most important teacher was his father, but other Brahmans also shared their knowledge and helped shape his view of the world.

His concern about change runs deep. He foresees that Hinduism will become more and more a private matter—religion will be confined to the household, and no longer centrally involved in the life of the city, as it is today, as it was in his father's time. Caste is the focus of some of his concern: to be what and who he is, he needs other castes. People will still need Brahmans for domestic rites but they will not care about the web of rites that link divinity to the life of the city, with many castes working together to please the gods and goddesses and perform the obligatory rites. While the caste system is still a powerful social reality, a breakdown of caste relations seems inevitable.

With this withdrawal of commitment, the means of maintaining the public ritual system of the city will vanish. He does not expect the caste system to vanish, only to change; it is the citywide ritual system based on caste specialization that he sees as threatened. Rather, he expects, with some reason, that the caste system will survive as the basis for identity and exclusion, competition and politics, but will no longer unite the city into a religious community. Already, gaps have grown where special castes once performed symbolic roles; so far, the system has enough resilience to absorb these losses. Dharma Raj lives in a state of quiet, anticipatory mourning, grieving for what is passing, and for what is still to pass.

AFTER THE FESTIVAL

The god and the goddess return to their temples; the people return to their homes; the chariot is dismantled and stored by the side of the Bhairav temple. The passing of the old year and the coming of the new has been celebrated. The order of life has been displayed. People have had their chance to come into the presence of divinity, and to view a kind of tableau vivant of the caste order, a living symbolic display of the caste hierarchy in which members of certain castes get to pose as themselves. The tableau presents an eternal, unchanging image of the way things are—hierarchical, fixed, sacred. It proposes that actual life is no different, that each actor is also a symbol in everyday life, an element in the cultural order. If this display cannot actually contain reality, if disturbing elements and ambivalences enter stage left, nonetheless life must go on. Having seen world-images and visions of themselves, people return to their routines, settle back into the habits of everyday life. Krishna broods, Dharma reflects, Kancha goes up into the city to sweep in the morning. The farmers work in their fields, and Brahmans perform rites.

13

High and Low Castes in Karani

Viramma, with Josiane Racine and Jean-Luc Racine

*Editors' note: Viramma is a member of the "untouchable" Pariah
caste, working as a midwife and agricultural laborer in the small
Tamil village of Karani near Pondicherry. Like the rest of her family, Viramma is bonded to Karani's richest landowner, the "Grand
Reddiar."* Viramma: Life of an Untouchable *records Viramma's
life story as told to Josiane and Jean-Luc Racine over a period of ten
years. She describes her brief, happy childhood; the ordeal of marriage as a young girl and her subsequent fulfilling relationship with
her husband; her experiences as a mother of twelve children, nine of
whom died; and her days of hard work under the burning sun. She
tells of the mutual support the untouchable castes provide each other in their* ceri—*the low-caste residential quarters separated from
the main village* (ur) *of the higher castes—as they lend each other
rice, sing together, and share confidences. She witnesses as well the
growing politicization of caste in her community, as various political party members come to encourage the local low castes to fight
the caste system and call themselves "Harijan" (people of God) and,
subsequently, "Dalit" instead of "Untouchable." (Indeed, in India,
the title of her narrative has been rendered—perhaps more appropriately—as* Viramma: Life of a Dalit.) *In this selection, Viramma
tells of the various castes making up her village of Karani. Being
"high" or "low" is tied here to owning land versus working on others' land; giving cooked food to others versus being regarded as so
low or impure that one may only receive it; and possessing money
versus having none. One can see in her narrative that it is possible
to be "low" in terms of caste purity, and at the same time be "high"
in terms of possessing wealth and power. Viramma's wit, strength,
and sense of pleasure in life also come through in her story, even as
she describes many of the hard inequities she has faced.*

All my family is employed at the Grand Reddiar's. My husband takes care of the pumps. The Reddiar owns two which irrigate every day. I collect the cow dung and clean the stable. My daughter Miniyamma helped me until she got married. Sundari has done the same and now it's my daughter-in-law Amsa who works at the Reddiar's. Anban started by looking after the cows. Now he does the important cultivation work with my husband. The reason is that we don't own any land. God only left us these eyes and these hands to earn our living. By working hard at the Reddiar's we've been able to lead our lives in the proper way. We've been able to give Miniyamma and Sundari away in marriage with silver ankle chains and some clothes. We've paid our share of funeral expenses when we've had to. I've been able to buy these jewels for my ears. And when we married Anban, the Reddiar gave Amsa her gold *tali* [marriage necklace] and her sari. Thanks to the Reddiar, thanks to his fortune—and it's a great one, especially in land—we have enough to eat without worrying. The Reddiar is an important man. Every day or nearly every day he goes to Pondy. The serfs who work at the Reddiar's have their rice guaranteed!

Of all the castes in the *ur* [village], the Reddiar caste is the highest. They have no equals. The others come after them: the Mudaliar, the Naicker, the Gounder. The Reddiar are the people who don't go to work, they put others to work: fifty, sixty, ninety, two hundred people. Their women don't work and they never go out.

I take twenty Paratchi [women Dalit laborers] to plant out the Grand Reddi's paddy fields, and they are paid by the day: it takes four Paratchi to plant out four hundred square yards. When we work for the Reddiar, there's no question of us singing. We keep our mouths shut out of respect for the Reddiar, because they're always there in the field watching over us, sitting on their cord bed under a coconut grove or even closer, on the dike under the shade of an umbrella. Their serf—for the Grand Reddi, that's me—directs the work and checks to see that everything is going right, 'Hey, plant out here! Hey, Saroja! That corner over there's not done!' But towards midday, as soon as the Reddiar goes home to eat, I start up with the first song. After our husbands, the Reddiar are the people we respect and fear the most. We are their serfs. It's different with other landowners, we sing as much as we want and anyway, they like it. Sometimes when we work for the Naicker, we joke with him. We can even make fun of him. We shout, 'Yennayya! You never stop giving your wife children! She's pregnant every year like a bitch and you'll lose your strength, you won't have anything left, even if you eat melted butter and curds. Come over here a bit, ayya, come and see if your strength is a match for us beef eaters when it comes to real work like this!' It makes him laugh to hear us going on like that! That's how we joke with him, Sinnamma, and with the other landowners for whom we're not serfs. The Naicker own lots of land. They've got some rented out, and pumps and stables full of animals: cows and goats, and they make plenty of milk.

We make fun of Brahmins as well, Sinnamma. When the *pappan* [Brahman priest] is about to walk past on the dike, we quickly make up a little song about him like this:

It's the *pappan, adi-pappan* [top Brahman]
Who irrigates by digging a hole,
Who fishes in there for a dish of crabs,
Who fishes in there for a dish of crabs,
While drinking the juices of a young girl
That very night, there was no moon
And his sleep was troubled,
That man with the *pottu*[1] in the shape of the moon,
Wants to welcome Virayi so much!!
Nanna, nanna, nanana,
Nanna, nannana, nananana . . .

The bile wells up in his mouth when he hears that. It disgusts him, he spits on the ground, wipes his lips and hurries on. Have you seen Brahmins eat crab? Even just hearing about it makes them want to throw up! Brahmins own nothing or almost nothing apart from the temple land. We never go and work for them, they only employ Kudiyanar. That's why we can make fun of them. The pappan are the Reddiar's priests for marriages, the *puja* [worship] of the ancestors, for this or that rite and for the funeral ceremonies on the sixteenth day as well. They are lower than the Reddiar and like the other servants, they get uncooked food from them. They take it raw because they're in contact with God and they must be pure: they have the food cooked at their homes. We prefer to get it cooked: it saves us the time and cost of cooking. One day at the Reddiar's, I heard the Brahmin mumbling his prayers as he raised the sacrificial fire. (*Laughs.*) I was looking through the window when the Grand Reddiar's mother saw me and chased me away: 'Eh, Velpakkatta! Get out of here! Get out of here! Don't look at that!' And it's true that we mustn't see any of it. The Reddiar and the Brahmins speak both languages, Tamil and Telugu. They are vegetarians, they eat lots of melted butter, yoghurt and fruit, and they drink milk. In the country there are no other castes that can match them.

But Karani has definitely got castes! Reddiar, Mudaliar, Gounder, Udaiyar, Tulukkan, Vaniyan, Ambattan, Komutti, Vannan. In the ceri [low-caste residential quarter] there are Koravan, Sakkili, Vannan as well, *talaiyari* [assistant to the village accountant]. There are Tomban towards Selvipatti and Pakkanur. No one accepts them into the castes.[2] They're pig rearers. They live with their animals. The Tomban is very low, but I've already told you, Sinnamma, he's become very rich. His pigs breed fast, he feeds them on abandoned ground, it costs him nothing and he earns plenty of money selling them. One year we had a big argument when I had rented a plot of land near the temple of Aiyanar from the Reddiar and I'd sowed it with *ragi* [grain]. One afternoon I was at my door oiling my hair when Sinnappayya ran up to tell me, 'Aunt! Aunt! Tomban's pigs are wrecking your *ragi* field! Come and see, quickly! Quickly!' I put up my hair, tying it up on one side, and followed Sinnappayya who ran ahead. The kids who used to graze the cows over there had discovered the pigs and sent Sinnappayya to tell me. 'You know, aunt, when the Tomban kids saw there was nobody in the field, they brought their pigs right up to it and went swimming in the river. When we were going past with the cows and saw the pigs in the field, we let you know straightaway, aunt!' I was boiling with rage. I told the kids to catch the pigs, but those dirty beasts, they're smart! They made us run all over the place and they kept on getting away. The Tomban kids saw what was going on from a distance and quickly got out of the water to round up their pigs but even so Sinnappayya managed to capture a piglet which we tied to a stake. Then the Grand Tomban arrived and beat his little pig-keepers. I said to him, 'Innappa! Your pigs got into my field. They've ruined part of my crop. What are you going to do?'

'Please don't get angry,' he answered, 'I didn't know what was happening. We didn't let them loose in your field on purpose. I'll be very careful next time!'

'Ah! That's what you think! You think we're going to let it drop. A crop ruined, a crop filled with such beautiful ears! I want compensation. I'm going to appeal to the Reddiar: he'll decide for himself!'

That's how I answered the Tomban and Sinnappayya ran to tell the Reddiar but he was having a rest. Sinnappayya waited for the Reddiar to get up and told him the story and he told him he'd come after he'd drunk his milk. Meanwhile we'd left the piglet tied up and gone into the shade. I had enough time to make myself a chew of betel. When I heard the Reddiar arriving on his motorbike, I got up and spat out my betel. I went towards him and said, 'Innanga! I've had my grain ruined! How do you expect us to pay you rent now? What do you think of that?'

The Reddiar turned to the Tomban and said, 'Innappa! What do you have to say to that? I see only two answers: either you let her have the piglet or you compensate her in money for her losses.'

The Tomban, squeezing together his legs and hugging his chest with both arms, begged the Reddiar, 'It's my fault but what's to be done? I didn't do it on purpose. I can only give ten rupees. Next time I'll make sure the kids don't bring my pigs this way, Sami!'

But I didn't want to hear any of it and I argued, 'How do you expect me to pay you the rent, Sami? How could I give you five sacks of *ragi* after this damage? I want thirty rupees in compensation!'

The Reddiar calmed both of us down by suggesting twenty-five rupees. Then the Tomban said, 'Have that pig untied and give it to the woman who cultivates your field. I cannot pay that amount!'

And that's how I came home with a piglet. I gave half a rupee to Sinnappayya and ten *paice* to each kid. They went and bought doughnuts at Kannimma's. As for me, I raised the piglet, and he grew big and fat very fast. My husband and Selvam the cobbler killed it, quartered it and sold it at Tirulagam market. We got twenty-five rupees—the same as Tomban's fine—and on top of that we treated ourselves to a pork curry—and Selvam too: of course we gave him a helping. Because we like pork very much, Sinnamma! Sometimes we club together to buy one on the days of festivals, for Dipavali, Pongal or for the festival of Kartikai, and we share it.[3] There's a little song about it:

> The one who's bred the pig is the Raja Pandya
> The one who's made the most of it is the Chetti-who-burps . . .

It's pork eaters who know how tasty it is and not the people who breed them on their land. Anyway the Tomban have got rich. They're farmers now: they grow rice, sugar cane, aubergines, chillis and they all get me to hire the manual labour. But in the end, even if they're rich, they're still very low. The Kudiyanar agree to work for them but they don't get any cooked food. Although all that's changing in this *kaliyugam* [Kali Yuga, the degenerate age]. Now you see Tomban living in the *ur*. They used to be only just a little bit above us and now they're much higher thanks to their money! Or rather, we've stayed poor and we find ourselves even lower than before, still accepting cooked food from the Tomban.[4]

In this *kaliyugam*, money's the master and when you know how to earn it, you make yourself higher than you were the day before. It's the same in the city—everywhere it's a question of money. Look at the Kudiyanar. In the past they only worked at the Reddiar's. They did housework, they cooked the gruel for the serfs and the agricultural workers, they did the washing up, they helped in the kitchen. Always at the Reddiar's. Nowadays they'll do hard work in the fields like us, at our side, and they'll even do it for the Tomban. Because you have to fill your stomach and so you'll work for anybody as long as he pays! But one of these Kudiyanar families moved to Madras and a girl from our caste has been doing their housework for a while. It's a different world far away from the village where you were born, especially in the city.

Just as there are the rich high castes, so there are the poor low castes. God gave the land to the rich high castes and he gave the poor low castes the duty of cultivating the land. The duty of the rich high castes is to employ us, us the Palli, the Pariahs, the Kudiyanar. But there are some Kudiyanar who own land, sometimes as much as twelve acres: they don't go and work. Other low castes have their particular trade. They are a little higher than us because they don't eat beef. They eat eggs, vegetables, fish, poultry, they drink milk like you. But meat is unclean, it's waste. Milk is pure. And as we eat waste, we're unclean. That's the difference between low castes and high castes.

There are all sorts of low castes in Karani that are higher than us. There are three families of barbers, brothers, who moved in next to the temple of Perumal. They're barbers for the Reddiar and the Gounder. They cut their hair, shave their armpits, cut their nails, massage them with oil. Generally they work on the steps of the lotus pond and for our Reddiar they move to his house and do their work on the *tinnai* [verandah]. These families work as barbers for the people of the *ur*, but the Sanar and the hunters sometimes go and borrow their scissors or razors secretly. We do that as well when our barber is away. We quietly borrow a razor from a barber in the *ur* and we quietly give it back to him, because if people ever knew that the same razor had shaved a Pariah and a Reddiar—ayoyo! there would be one of those arguments! That's impossible! But all the same, a barber agrees to it for some money or a little bit of grain. Those barbers are the temple musicians as well and they get some grain for that during the year. They play at puberty ceremonies, engagements and marriages; only auspicious celebrations. It all gives them extra income. Each of them plays a different instrument: the eldest plays the *ottu* [oboe], the youngest the *nadesvaram* [large wind instrument], and the youngest child the drum, dum, dum, dum, dum . . .

Two families of potters live opposite the barbers. They're not high or low, because everybody needs them, from the Reddiar to us. In the past the potter used to make enormous jars which contained thirty or forty measures of *kanji* [gruel]. If you knew how long it took to move those! If anyone carried them on their heads out to the fields, that made the shit come out of their hole! Nowadays the *kanji's* put in a big aluminium pot which is fixed to a pole. Two men on each side carry it and it's much easier. The potter makes much less crockery than in the past; he mainly makes jars, tea sets for celebrations and dolls. I had all the crockery for my children's marriages made by him. The jars for Anban's marriage were very prettily decorated! I paid the potter in cereals: he's higher than us, but he accepts our grain.

The joiners have built their houses behind him. They are lower than the Gounder and they only marry amongst themselves. Next door there are the carpenters as well. Who else is there? If you come out of their houses and go straight ahead, two blacksmiths have moved in near the Reddiar's quarter. They're never short of orders and they work for us as well. Before the harvest they're asked for thirty to forty sickles. They sharpen old blades and repair carts. One also forged the trident under the banyan tree and the one in our house: you saw how well I decorated it! I never forget to perform the *puja* to that trident, to light some camphor for it. When a house is built in the *ur*, the blacksmiths are asked to make bars for the windows, hinges and bolts for the doors, pulleys for the well, all that sort of thing. The blacksmiths aren't low caste, they're free to go into the Gounder's and Reddiar's houses. They even get to eat with the Grand Reddiar, I've seen them there for a wedding.

One of their sons is in teaching now. He married a girl from Pondy where he works and he lives there.

Opposite the blacksmiths are the goldsmiths. There were two families in the past, the big and the small goldsmith. The first made *tali* for the Reddiar and the Gounder. The small one made them for other castes, including us. But he wasn't very honest, that one. I could see that for myself when I gave him an earring to mend. He gave it back much shinier but it was very light. Danam took him her *tali* and she got it back much lighter as well! But we didn't dare complain. They say he cheated a lot of people in Karani and stole a little bit of gold dust from each of them. He got rich that way and chose to leave the village to flaunt his wealth somewhere else. Apparently he set up in his wife's village but sister Virayi who comes from there never saw him again. No one knows what country he's in, that thief! The big goldsmith stayed. Since he had more work than before, he went and got a little shop on the main street of Tirulagam: now he employs three people. Goldsmiths are lower than the Reddiar but, like blacksmiths, they can go into their houses and eat there.

Near the pond, at the entrance to the *ur*, there are two families of traders, they're Komutti. That caste has no other trade apart from business, you can see them in any town. The Komutti speak Telugu, like the cobblers and the Reddiar. But they don't mix either with the Reddiar or with us. We never go to their houses and we don't get food from them. When they celebrate a marriage, they only give betel to the cobblers and even then it's behind their house. They get married discreetly, without making a big noise. Unlike all the other castes, they marry in the month of Adi. I like them a lot, because their wives are always very friendly when they talk to us.

I'd forgotten that the launderers are one of the low castes in the *ur*! They live in four or five houses next to each other and they own a donkey. We have launderers in the *ceri* as well. They're lower than us and we take turns giving them the evening meal. They are pretty poor, but they still manage to hold their yearly festival. They worship Mayilaru and their god resides in their laundering oven. On the day of the festival of Mayilaru, the one in the family who carries out the *puja* takes a bath, puts on new clothes, changes the oven and lights camphor in front of the stone for beating linen. The families cook four jars of *pongal* [a special rice dish] with rice flour and coconut. Some slit the throat of a chicken or—less often—bleed a pig. There's never any shortage of betel, bananas and flowers. Everything is handed out between them. We don't get anything, even though we contribute to their festival, just as the Reddiar contributes to our own festival of Periyandavan. It's the same, anyway: the launderers work for us and we have to give them something for their festival. No one can refuse. When Arayi, the launderer's wife, arrives with her basket to collect what she's owed—a measure of grain or a cup of oil—we give it to her but we don't miss the chance to have a moan, 'Those people, they're always ready to worship Mayilaru but they haven't even brought our clothes back yet! They're nothing like the launderers in the *ur:* now *they* work!' Then Arayi goes into a corner, scratches her head and always comes up with a reason: it's rained and the linen hasn't dried: or it hasn't rained and there's not enough water in the river: or any old thing. We don't get a share of their offerings but sometimes our kids do. They always want to know what's going on and if they're there when the *puja*'s performed, the launderers give them a little *pongal.* As it's sweet and tastes good, the little ones eat it without thinking or realising that the launderers are lower than us. Don't forget that the launderers of the *ur* are higher than us as well as lower than the Gounder. I always speak with respect to the launderers of the *ur.*

The Sanar are also people of low rank. They're only just above us. A Sanar ought to act pretty much the same as us when the Reddiar goes by: he should stand up and speak to him humbly. Sanar and Pariahs talk to each other almost like equals in the fields. We call out to each other and say, 'Hey, big sister Kuppu! Ho, big brother Kannan! Uncle Viran!' You know my friend Vanaroja well, the palm juice seller. We love each other. Every day in the summer she goes through the *ceri* shouting, 'Palm juice! Palm juice!' She gives me a glass of it and in return I leave her a measure of paddy each year. Sometimes if the harvest looks like being scarce and I think our share is going to be small, I pinch one or two measures of paddy which I go and drop off at her house. Vanaroja keeps them well hidden for me and gives them back to me the next day without anybody seeing. To thank her I leave her a little share. We get on well, the two of us, even if our castes are different!

There's also the Sakkili, the cobblers. They're much lower than us. You know Selvam, the horn player: he gets cooked food from us. When there's a marriage, we give him a measure of rice and a rupee. His duty is to play the horn for us every time it's needed. We never go and drink or eat at his house, but we talk together normally, and we're warm to each other when we meet. He also often comes and sits on our *tinnai* to talk and joke (but never in a crude way) or simply to chew. Then he asks us, 'Give me some betel, aunt' or 'uncle' or 'big sister'—that's how he talks to us. That reminds me, Sinnamma, I'm going to stop for a bit. I want to chew some betel as well. Hey! Look: your little Rajini has two spirals on her head. That means she'll have two husbands! (*Laughs.*)

NOTES

1. A *pottu* is the mark many Hindus wear on their foreheads.
2. Viramma's list is not exhaustive and needs a certain amount of explanation. Of the castes in the *ur,* the Udaiyar are farmers and landowners like the Reddiar and Gounder, the Reddiar being the most powerful caste of landowners and the Gounder the largest. There are no Mudaliar in Karani in the main sense of a high caste of landowners, but the Kepmarithe caste of thieves give themselves this title.

Tulukkan is a general name for Muslims and Viramma is probably thinking either of the civil servants sometimes appointed to the village or the tradesmen from Tirulagam. Viramma leaves out the main caste in the *ceri*—the Paraiyar, with their two sub-castes, the Vettiyan and the Pannaiyar—and she describes them in the next chapter. The Vannan here are the launderers of the *ceri* and the Sakkiliar the very low caste of cobblers. There are no Koravar—members of the Nari Korava tribe in the *ceri* as such, but some pass through and the Sakkiliar are often treated as being like them. *Talaiyari* is more a profession than a caste—the position of assistant to the village accountant—and the Tomban are misleadingly described as being completely outside the caste system. Their low rank confines them to the outskirts of the *ur*, and Viramma's exaggeration could be due to her argument with a particular Tomban which she goes on to describe.

3. Kartikai, the eighth month of the Tamil calendar (mid-November to mid-December), is when the festival of Kartikai dipam is celebrated. Lamps are lit in every house to evoke the ceremony to Siva at Tiruvannamalai on the same night.

4. The rules governing the exchange of food are an essential aspect of the caste system. The orthodox view is that cooked food can only be accepted from someone of an equal or higher caste. So, although the Kudiyanar are economically dependent on the Tomban, they assert their caste superiority by refusing cooked food. Raw food and basic foodstuffs, like grain, are exchanged more freely—as Viramma goes on to say, the potter accepts grain from her.

14

Weakness, Worry Illness, and Poverty in the Slums of Dhaka

Sabina Faiz Rashid

Dhatu roge [discharge] can happen because of lack of food in the body. It is because of our poverty. If one does not eat properly, then calcium [nutrition] comes out of the bones and leaves the body. From poverty comes *chinta* [worries], and then from that discharge will start coming out much more from the body.
—Hasina, 18 years old, two children, abandoned

Structural and social inequalities, a brutal political economy, and neglect by policy makers and the government have left the urban poor in Bangladesh marginalized socially and economically. Little is known about the combined effects of macropolitical and economic conditions and social and cultural factors on urban slum women's understandings of reproductive illnesses.

In Bangladesh, adolescents constitute more than 22 percent of the population; 13 million adolescents are girls, and 14 million are boys (Nahar et al. 1999).[1] Because of their sex, age, and poverty, married adolescent girls are an extremely vulnerable group in the Dhaka slums. The importance placed on fertility for newly married adolescent girls results in high birth rates and low rates of contraceptive use. The current fertility rate of those aged 15–19 is 147 per 1,000 girls, ranging from 155 in rural areas to 88 in urban areas. This is the highest fertility rate for this age group in the world. Only about 30 percent of poor married adolescent girls use any method of contraception, compared with the national figure of 49 percent for all women (Arifeen and Mookherjee 1995). Bangladesh has also one of the highest maternal mortality rates in the world, estimated to be 320 per 100,000 live births (Government of

Bangladesh [GoB]–UN 2005). One consequence of early marriage and child-bearing is a higher death rate among adolescent girls than boys aged 15–19: 1.81 compared with 1.55 per 1,000 (Bangladesh Bureau of Statistics 1997).

It is reported that as of 2002, slum dwellers constituted 30 percent of the 14 million population of Dhaka.[2] Most urban migrants cannot afford housing and live in insecure tenure, setting up or renting small rooms in shacks with tin or polythene roofs on vacant government or private land. It is unofficially estimated that as of 2005, there were 4,500 slum settlements in Dhaka (BIP and CUS 2005). About 30 percent of Dhaka's population can be defined as "hard-core poor" (i.e., having a per capita monthly income of $43 or less), and 50 percent as poor (i.e., having a per capita monthly income of $65 or less; GoB 2004). The health indicators are worse for the urban poor than for the rural poor (Ministry of Health and Family Welfare 2001).

Phulbari, the slum in which I conducted this research, had a high proportion of squatter households, with most of the poor having been resettled after being forcibly evicted in 1975 from different parts of the city (Afsar 2000). The alleyways were tiny and congested; rooms had no fans; and drains overflowed with water, sewage, and excrement, particularly during the rainy season. Skin infections were rampant. During interviews with young women, I often saw rats and cockroaches run across the floor. The young women had few possessions, sometimes only a jute mat to sleep on and utensils for cooking. As slums are considered illegal, they are not entitled to basic government services, and residents face eviction at any moment. In Phulbari, some NGOs provided tube wells, and the community set up some illegal lines to access piped water. Water was available for only twenty to thirty minutes, which resulted in long lines, tension, and heated exchanges among the women who waited in the hot sun, fighting to get access to it. There was electricity but no gas for cooking, so most women burned paper, cloth, plastic, or wood to cook on mud stoves. The rent for a room in Phulbari ranged from taka 200 to taka 600 ($3–$9) a month.

Popular understandings of weakness and *chinta rog* (worry illness) among the young women of Phulbari describe it as a cause of vaginal discharge. For many, weakness was seen as a cause and consequence of discharge, and it was commonly believed that the discharge coming out of the body led to a loss of calcium and essential nutrients, resulting in the body wasting away. The urban poor spoke of chinta rog, which translates as "worry illness" in English, a condition associated with a wide range of both emotional problems and physical complaints. In everyday conversations, men and women spoke of chinta (worry) causing sleeplessness, loss of appetite, shaking, aches and pains, vaginal discharge, and more serious conditions of cancer and reproductive illnesses. The urban poor blame the origins of chinta rog on the harsh conditions of life, brought about by rapid socioeconomic transformations, poverty, and the breakdown of society and family, which have increased their suffering and led to increased chinta (worry) and all kinds of sicknesses. Explanations of *durbolata* (weakness) and chinta rog are metaphors for the economic, social, and political deprivation in poor women's lives.

I did fieldwork from December 2001 to January 2003. Case studies, repeated in-depth interviews, and long-term participant-observations provided rich empirical data. A small structured survey questionnaire was used to gather general background information, including young women's reproductive histories in the slums.

MARRIAGE AND ADOLESCENT WOMEN'S LIVES

In the slums, poor, married adolescent women articulate that the existing pressures of poverty and other everyday pressures can result in white vaginal discharge leaving the body. When young women spoke of their experiences of white discharge or weakness, it was within the context of a difficult political economy; disparate gender, class, and power relations; and injustices in the household and in the patriarchal and hierarchical society. Poor married adolescent women, because of their age and gender, tend to have limited power and often remain under the social and economic control of others, mainly males and family members. In a survey of 153 adolescent women, the average age of marriage was 13.5 years. In Bangladesh, marriage is the only acceptable option for a large part of the population. It allows individuals to have sexual relations without risk of social sanctions and confers social identity, particularly on women. An adult woman who is unmarried is seen as a deviant. Adult men are also expected to marry. In poor families, marriage is expected to take place soon after a young girl menstruates (Jesmin and Salway 2000; Khan et al. 2002). During discussions with community members and parents, common reasons given for early marriage were insecurity, poverty, and avoidance of the burden of dowry payments. Dowry is money paid to the groom at the time of marriage, an illegal but widely accepted practice. A common refrain in the slum was, "The younger the girl, the lower the dowry."

Another reason given for early marriage by parents is the fear that their daughters may become "spoiled" (i.e., indulge in sexual relations) in the slum environment. Many parents believe that the availability of a male guardian as a husband will protect their daughters from being sexually harassed by gang members in the slums. Although families often arrange marriages, more than 81 (out of 153) young women had a love marriage. Many factors, including acute poverty, have forced young girls to work outside the home in garment factories and interact with young males in the public domain, resulting in love affairs and marriages, sometimes against the wishes of parents and in-laws. In the close confines of slum households, many young girls fall in love with boys who live nearby and within the slum. Most of the love marriages involve little to no dowry. In the initial honeymoon period of the relationship, men are not interested in any cash. However, as reported, over time, some husbands or in-laws begin to feel cheated and begin to mistreat the young girl until her family is forced to pay some money.

Marital instability is a widespread concern among the women in the slum, and poverty, unpaid dowry demands, unemployment, and drug use were all blamed as contributing factors. In the 153 structured surveys, 17 young women said they were separated from or abandoned by their husbands. In addition, in 50 repeated in-depth interviews, another 7 young women revealed this was their second marriage. From this group, four women were found to be sharing their husbands with a co-wife, and another three young women suspected their husbands had another woman, possibly a co-wife.[3] In most discussions with young women, it was apparent that a certain amount of anxiety existed because of fear of abandonment and separation.

HUSBANDS OF THE ADOLESCENT WOMEN

Urban employment for men living in the slums is constrained by their lack of qualifications. The only work available tends to be labor intensive, stressful, low paid, and at times dangerous (Kabir 1998). Many unskilled laborers remain unemployable or get jobs primarily in the informal labor market. Twenty-nine young women initially reported that their husbands did not work regularly, with many either working erratically or periodically unemployed. More than 53 married adolescent women worked off and on sewing or working in the garment factory to support their families. This shift in men's culturally acceptable role as rice winners and females' role as homemakers has an effect on gender relations, creating tensions in the house hold. Of 153 young women, 89 said they experienced occasional to regular domestic violence at home. Twelve married young women volunteered that their husbands were heroin users or addicted to alcohol and gambling. Although the actual number of users is not known, observations revealed drug use and gambling to be a common problem among young men in the slums.

Patriarchy and social and cultural pressures force many adolescent women to tolerate their husbands' behavior, for their own protection, for social recognition, and to avoid the stigma of being single. A common refrain was, "Men can marry ten times, and no one comments; but if a woman marries even twice, everyone will talk. That is why we stay with the man!" Moreover, chronic poverty, competition for scarce resources, and disruptions in family life in slums are affecting the kind of support young women can rely on from their own families. Young women made comments such as, "You can't rely on anyone, including your own family these days"; "No one cares unless you have money"; and "This is a new era, and we have to cope on our own."

CHINTA ROG (WORRY ILLNESS), WHITE DISCHARGE,
WEAK BODIES, AND POVERTY

A majority of young women in Phulbari complained about their difficult
lives in the slums. Out of 153 young women, 69 blamed the causes of their
general ill health—such as weakness, dizziness, fever, headaches, body
aches, palpitations, and gastric pain—on chinta (worry), tension, and *moner
oshanti* (sadness or unease in the heart). Other causes mentioned were violence in the household, reproductive pressures, infertility, abuse by in-laws,
and poverty. Both young women and health workers repeatedly mentioned
that chinta rog (worry illness) in particular was both a cause and consequence of white vaginal discharge (*dhatu*), which they viewed as a problem
of physical and emotional depletion.[4]

Monsura (16 years old) said:

> My sister-in-law informed me that "from chinta (worry) one has headaches,
> severe headaches, and then from tension one loses discharge [*dhatu bhangey*]
> from the body." From chinta the head becomes hot with worry, and then
> if one's stomach and body becomes hot, then discharge will come out. . . .
> Apa, for me when I go to sleep at night I feel the world is breaking down and
> the entire body's burden is on my head. . . . I feel like my head is breaking,
> and I don't want to lie down, and I don't feel like working, and my body is
> weak. . . . From hunger my breasts are dry, and I don't have any milk to feed
> my baby.

For Monsura, life was difficult because her husband worked erratically and
liked to drink and gamble. She worried a lot because they had a ten-month-
old baby boy and her husband would not allow her to work outside the home.
He also beat her frequently. In addition to her discharge, she complained of
suffering from palpitations and shakes in her body from the violence and
from going without decent meals for days at a time.

Jharna (17 years old, with two boys) discussed her discharge problem.
She said:

> I am in tension and worry all the time. We are in difficult times now. My
> sons' father cannot work. He is sick at the moment [he was suffering from
> hernia and could not work]. How will we afford to pay rent? I need to eat
> more, but we don't have food, and what about my sons? From so much wor-
> rying my head becomes hot! . . . I can't sleep and have lost my appetite. . . .
> Won't all this affect me? My discharge is coming out like water, and I feel
> weak, and my hands and feet feel like they are breaking inside.

Parveen (15 years old, abandoned by her husband, and mistreated by her
family) said, "I live in my father's home. I don't have a husband. He left me.

If a girl does not have a husband, then you can understand what sort of situation the girl is in? Having no husband means no power, and I have to live with my parents." Parveen had no support and felt totally dependent on her parents. She said, "My health problems are that my body feels weak and my heart is filled with worries and unhappiness, and that is why I have constant discharge. . . . These are my health problems, and beyond this I have no other health problems. Worries, sadness, and weakness . . . this is what I suffer from!"

Living in a slum and having nowhere else to go—because a single woman cannot live alone as it is too insecure—Parveen moved back to her natal home. She was immediately asked to look for work by her father to contribute to the household. Her father had three wives, and her mother, stepmother and five siblings (including her stepfamily) lived together in the same compound. When Parveen moved back home with her young daughter, she was often the target of anger from her step relatives and father because she was occupying a room that could have been rented out to someone else for cash. For Parveen, her job at the garment factory was unstable and unsatisfactory because her employers were withholding the salaries of many of the young factory workers. During this period in 2002, periodic fluctuations in the import quotas allocated to ready-made garments from Bangladesh by the United States, European Union, and other major industrialized economies led to corresponding cycles of job losses and reemployment among workers, who are primarily female (*Dhaka Courier* 2003).

Asma (16 years old) was living with her sister and family because her husband was a heroin addict. When talking about Asma's discharge experiences, Asma's sister remarked, "What is in her home, sister, only unhappiness! Today her husband works, and tomorrow he does not work. Then why won't her body waste away? One's body has so many nice and good things. But from worrying the good things in Asma's body are all drying up inside her. She does not eat less. But her insides are becoming *khoi* [wasting away]!"

Asma was very dependent on the support of her natal family to manage but felt she was a burden on her sisters and brothers-in-law. She had a baby girl who was only three months old, and she was not in a position to work. Her husband often disappeared for months, leaving her to cope alone. To add to her sorrows, her father, whom she relied on for support, had recently died of a heart attack, and one of her brothers-in-law resented her living with them. The recent slum eviction (in July 2002) had also meant that her natal family had lost their home in the slum, and all of them were currently renting a room in a new slum settlement and paying much higher rent.

In discussions between two health workers, they disagreed on explanations of discharge but drew on popular folk explanations to understand the discharge experience. Sayeeda-apa (a health worker at a local clinic) spoke about her own daughter's discharge problem:

When Shaheen was healthy and fat then she didn't have *dhatu bhangey* [white discharge]. But now look at her, she is so thin now, and she is getting thinner. She has lost her job in the garment factory, and she has so many worries. I know that she worries a lot about money. There is no peace at home for her. Everyday Shaheen is getting weaker and becoming khoi [wasting away], and more discharge is coming out.

Sayeeda and her children lived with Sayeeda's older sister and family, who mistreated them. There were constant arguments and fights in the household about less food being given to Sayeeda's children and favoritism being shown to the older sister's children. During this discussion, Sufia (another health worker) piped up: "I don't know if chinta (worry) can cause discharge, but what I have heard is that discharge happens because of the lack of food in the body. You know when there is weakness, then from the bones calcium leaves the body."

The preceding accounts illustrate how social, cultural, and political-economic realities are embodied and incorporated into explanations of discharge by adolescent women and their families. Kielmann (2002) suggests that the body is not merely a site of suffering but the space and medium through which one can articulate the experience of the self. Many of the statements by the young women make references to bodies breaking, wasting away, tension and burdens, and the loss of well-being because of a lack of food.

For many young women in the slum, the family unit, particularly one's spouse, provides the basis for survival, and a breakdown of support can trigger an enormous amount of stress on the individual. Concerns were expressed about strained relations with husbands and family members, unemployment and insecurity, substance abuse, and the pressures of being a good mother and wife.

In the young women's narratives, "loss of discharge" spoke of their marginal position and how this was mirrored in their weak, worried, and increasingly thin bodies, a core indicator of ill health. The gradual deterioration of their bodies communicates the social, structural, and physical inequalities in their lives.

UNDERSTANDINGS OF DISCHARGE: LOSS OF NUTRIENTS
AND CALCIUM—SCARCITY AND HUNGER ANXIETY

The perceived relationship between *durbolata* (weakness) and discharge is so close that adolescent women in the slum used the terms interchangeably in discussions. This interchangeability also occurred because most young women in the slum were ashamed to use the term "dhatu bhangey" openly because of not only embarrassment but also the social stigma attached to this condition. Young women worried that people in the slum would mix up this illness condition with discharge that is caused by sexually transmitted diseases. As one young woman, Roshonara (18 years old), explained:

> I feel ashamed to tell my sister. I am embarrassed. What if she tells someone else, and then that woman will tell someone else. Then they will say, "Look, this is what she talks about, she has no shame!" Many women call it *goponi roge* [secret illness]. If people hear of it, they will say that I am *kharap* [bad]. But it can also happen because of poverty and hunger. . . . If the body is lacking of nutrition and if it is weak, then this can happen.

Similarly, a pharmacist informed us that women were reluctant to openly use the term "dhatu" because of its various sexual meanings: "Most women come to see me for *durbolata* [weakness problem]. Then I ask them, 'Does your discharge come out?' The women have never come out and said that they have white discharge. They say, 'I can't work, and I can't sleep. I feel very weak!' I understand what they are trying to say to me."

Young women spoke of needing calcium and nutrients for the body's energy, as it is believed that any loss can weaken the person considerably.[5] They shared stories of one's face becoming "discolored and darker" and of women losing their "beauty and vigor," with "bodies becoming dehydrated and skinny" because of the "loss of discharge." It was commonly heard that discharge resulted in the body losing blood, an essential life element. One of the health workers explained: "We believe that for every three drops of discharge that come out, one drop of blood leaves the body." These understandings can be traced back to the Ayurvedic and Hindu belief system, which states that "one drop of *dhatu* [male and female fluids] is equivalent to one cupful of blood" (Bang and Bang 1994: 84), and "any loss connotes loss of power, control and productive power" and strength (Nichter 1981: 390, 1989).

In the Ayurvedic medical system, it is believed that dhatu is an essential body humor associated with vitality and the regulation of body processes; it controls heat and strength and is a positive source of health. Women as well as men are believed to have semen (Nichter 1981). According to Ayurvedic ethnophysiology, the body is perceived to be in a state of "ceaseless flux within the natural and supernatural environment"; the body's boundaries are permeable, and a body in flux that loses too much dhatu can become sick (Trollope-Kumar 2001: 262).

Discussions with young women and health workers reveal that a majority viewed long-term loss of dhatu as damaging for their health, because it is understood as the loss of blood and essential calcium and nutrients from the body. Shohagi (15 years old) explained, "White discharge is the kind of illness that makes a standing person sit down. It makes a healthy person unwell. If the body is empty and without food, then won't discharge happen? How will my body stay okay? If I can't eat one meal and then if I can't afford to eat the second meal, how will my body stay okay? Slowly the body becomes weak and thinner."

These explanations and discussions are not surprising as Bangladesh is one of the poorest countries in the world and has one of the highest malnutrition rates (Bangladesh Country Brief 2006).

The experience of discharge-weakness was more than just symbolic for young women in Phulbari slum. Arguments would usually break out over food and money, both of which are extremely scarce commodities in the slum. For example, a young married adolescent moved out when her landlady accused her of trying to steal food from her kitchen one night. Fights broke out over unfair food distribution, with accusations of favoritism toward certain family members and individuals who contributed more money to the household compared with those who gave less. There were arguments between tenants and family members (in-laws, step relatives, siblings, parents) over who ate the last egg, got the biggest piece of fish, or was given stale rice and water. It was not uncommon for some family members and tenants to go without food while others ate dry bread or stale rice and water and chilies. One particular story highlights poignantly the effects of food deprivation on individuals. Jahanara (15 years old) said: "The landlady fed my sister rice, but I saw a rat come out of that rice before it was cooked! She saw it too. Who would tolerate and let their sister eat that rice? I am telling my sister don't eat that rice, she is giving you free rice out of which rats lived in. What does my sister do? She ignores me and gobbles the food down her throat."

Young women's explanations were influenced by the Ayurvedic system, but their understandings had shifted beyond just talking about "loss of blood" and reproductive health to incorporating the larger social and political-economic conditions that they perceive as affecting their bodies. Thus, the reinterpretation of white discharge as a loss of calcium and nutrients (*pushti*) from the body can be attributed to the fusion of Ayurvedic understandings with the grounded reality of their everyday lives of chronic poverty and food scarcity. This is further influenced by nutrition campaigns in the country.

In the past few decades, the media, development agencies, and the government have used billboards, messages on the radio and television, and health workers to promote an understanding of the link between poor diet and various illnesses. The overwhelming message is that pushti is necessary for healthy bodies and bones (Tontisirin et al. 2005). Yet the institutions that promote the nutrition messages overlook the political-economic reality of poor people's lives. They blame poor diet and ignorance, rather than the glaring disparities and asymmetrical power relations that are the root causes of the problem. In response to this, young women who are extremely malnourished covertly transform hunger anxiety into an illness condition and thereby indirectly express "disallowed feelings and sensations" (Scheper-

Hughes 1992: 195) through the idiom of white discharge—weak bodies and loss of calcium.

TREATMENT AND SERVICES

A popular understanding in Phulbari slum was that in addition to—or separate from—antibiotic medicines routinely prescribed by doctors and local pharmacies for discharge, there was a need to "rehydrate and replenish" the body by drinking cooling liquids or tonics to replace the body's loss of calcium and other nutrients. In discussions, young women said they preferred self-treatment and homeopathic care because they were affordable, but some of them also said that they visited local pharmacies and healers for this illness. According to most of the young women, only when the discharge became "abnormal," "smelly," or "thick" did one need to resort to treatment from doctors and pharmacists, who also advise women to drink cooling liquids, tonics, vitamin syrups, and tablets to treat white discharge and weakness. Below is an interaction between me and a local pharmacist:

> SFR: Do women come to see you for *dhatu bhangah* [discharge]?
> Pharmacist: Yes, they do come to the shop for treating their dhatu bhangah problem. They come to see me with all sorts of dhatu bhangah problems.
> SFR: When they come to you, what do they say initially?
> P: Some of the women say, "My body is becoming weaker," while others remark, "I am losing vitamins from my body." Some of them openly say they are suffering from *shada syrup* [white syrup] and say, "It is coming out like water," while others say, "It comes out like starchy rice," and a few say, "It is coming out *chakka chakka* [chunky]." But this is rare; and most women prefer to say their body is getting weaker.
> SFR: Why does a woman become weak if she loses discharge?
> P: Won't people become weak if they lose discharge? This is the body's essence. We have all sorts of organs. There is a reason for each thing inside the body. Therefore the discharge coming out means something is going wrong. Nothing should be thrown from inside of the body.
>   . . . [T]hese people in the slum have no end to their suffering. . . . [T]he body is like land, if you need to reap crops, then you need to fertilize it and sow seeds. . . . [T]here is so much poverty in our country, and that is why women's discharge comes out.

The danger lies in the fact that the treatment of discharge-weak bodies with tonics, syrups, and vitamins leads to the legitimacy of "false treatment" as well as the medicalization of young women's suffering and hunger anxiety. Attention is diverted from the complexity of their experiences and the factors involved in the maintenance of this illness or disorder. Poor families struggle and compete with one another over scarce resources, and the buying of tonics instead of food is a cruel irony.

However, we must not overlook the psychosocial importance and meaning the purchase of tonics, syrups, and saline has for poor, married, adolescent women in the slum. Unlike the meager quantities of food that young women are forced to ration and share with others, bottles of tonics and saline drips do not need to be shared with anyone else. If a woman buys a glucose saline drip or two bottles of syrup, she can afford to indulge herself without fear of retribution or guilt. Furthermore, the buying and use of tonics or syrups serve as "nonverbal markers of life problems" for young women (Nichter and Vuckovic 1994: 1516). Young women appear aware, though, that tonics will not take away the root cause of their problems: "When I drink this [tonic] I do feel better, but my worries and weakness will not go away. There is no cure for that. Those who chinta [worry] all the time can never be well and healthy." In some ways, accessing tonics and syrups by poor married adolescent women is an effort to cope with the oppression, "the hidden and overt injuries" of class and other forms of powerlessness (Baer, Singer, and Susser 1997).

CONCLUSION

A harsh political economy, rapid social transformations, chronic poverty, and the cultural construction of illness converge in the meanings, interpretation, and treatment of white discharge and weak bodies, and in turn influence adolescent women's health behavior. The general political-economic and social conditions in the slum community—with its violence, gang warfare, and police raids, and insecurities of home ownership and living situations—together with the larger external forces affecting unemployment, both locally and internationally, are some of the broader macro-environmental factors that affect young women's individual experiences of white discharge and other symptoms.

In the narratives, we see the contextualization of the experience of general deprivation, insecurity, and deteriorating social relations as embodied in the individual, social, and body politic among poor married adolescent women (Scheper-Hughes and Lock 1987). The weak bodies–worries model of white discharge reflects the lived experiences of poor young women in the slum. The young women and their health providers, who speak of weak bodies and white discharge, are conscious of the social, personal, biological, and economic contexts that make young women ill. For married adolescent women living in slums, white discharge has many levels of meaning linked to the broader social, political, and material inequalities in their lives.

ACKNOWLEDGMENTS

This study was supported financially by the Special Programme of Research, Development and Research Training in Human Reproduction, World Health Organization, Geneva. I thank all the married adolescent girls and their families for their time, kindness, and patience. I am very grateful to Nipu Sharmeen, my research assistant, for her valuable assistance during this fieldwork. I would like to thank Dr. Diana Gibson, Amsterdam University, for her critical feedback and valuable comments, which improved the article. I am indebted to Dr. Andrea Whittaker for her encouragement, support, and guidance. This chapter is drawn from my Ph.D. dissertation in medical anthropology-public health, awarded in 2005, from the Australian National University, Canberra.

NOTES

1. The World Health Organization defines adolescents as between ten and nineteen years of age, and this is the definition used to calculate the number of adolescents in Bangladesh.

2. UNICEF sets the number of slum dwellers across Bangladesh at 15 million as of 1996 and has forecast that the urban poor population may rise to 30 million by 2020 (Bangladesh Institute of Planners [BIP] and Centre for Urban Studies [CUS] 2005).

3. It is difficult to provide the actual number of marital breakups because of the sensitivity of the information, as marital disruptions and divorce are seen as a social stigma.

4. Studies of ethnomedical understandings of white vaginal discharge in both India and Bangladesh reveal common patterns of belief and strong perceived links between discharge and weakness in the body, poor nutrition, anxiety, stress, reproductive tract infections, and bodily and emotional depletion (see Rashid 2007; Bang and Bang 1994; Chaturvedi et al. 1995; Gazi and Chowdhury 1998; Mahbub and Ahmed 1977; Pachauri and Gittelsohn 1994; Patel and Oomman 1999; Ross et al. 2002).

5. An ongoing qualitative study at BRAC found that many sex workers also perceive white discharge as a loss of calcium from the body, which could be very detrimental to one's health.

15

Anjali's Alliance: Class Mobility in Urban India

Sara Dickey

In 1985, I took my first research trip to Madurai, a large city in southern India. After moving into an apartment in a downtown neighborhood, I started walking through the nearby streets, wondering how I would ever get to know my neighbors. In this densely built part of the city, brick and plaster houses are constructed wall-to-wall, and doors open right onto the street. Through those doors, I could sometimes glimpse passageways that led back to other homes. Late one afternoon, in front of such an entryway, I saw a group of children playing. A small boy and girl called me over, and all the children crowded around asking me to take their picture. The mother of the boy and girl heard the clamor, looked out, and invited me in. I followed her into their one-room house, which was long and narrow and ran along the street. There were several similar homes in the compound, all linked by a single roof, adjoining walls, and a central courtyard.

Anjali and Kumar, the two children, turned out to be seven and five years old. Their father was out working that day, driving a cycle rickshaw, and their three older siblings were still on their way home from school. From that day on, over the next fifteen months, Anjali and Kumar taught me Tamil proverbs and stick games and movie plots, and were delightful companions. We have remained close. Each time I return, we smile over a favorite photograph of the two children sitting on a windowsill in my old apartment, reading a picture book together. Then they pull down another photo from the same time, in which I am typing field notes for my dissertation, and they point out that back then my hair was long and braided, as a woman's should be. All of our lives have changed since then. I have short hair and a college teaching position and a child of my own. Anjali became the first person in her family to go to college, and then she became a computer graphics designer. With the wages that she and her siblings make, her parents have been able to pay off old debts and buy a television. But Anjali's father was injured recently and can no longer drive a rickshaw, and as his children marry and start to use their earnings for their own new households, his family's hard-won financial security becomes threatened. At the same time, his wife is trying to arrange Anjali's marriage. Yet despite all these changes in our lives, most of us are living out predictable life cycles and circumstances. The only one of us whose material circumstances may eventually be substantially different from her parents' is Anjali.

In both the United States and India, myths of upward class mobility are common and important. In both countries, most families actually maintain similar socioeconomic circumstances from generation to generation (e.g., Featherman and Hauser 1978; Driver and Driver 1987: 39–52; Rao 1989: 24; Béteille 1991; Solon 1992; Conley 1999). Movement out of the lower strata is especially difficult. Yet many of us know someone whose class is dramatically different from his or her parents', and in India there is other anecdotal evidence to support the myth. For one thing, economic circumstances often do vary within a single generation. As in Anjali's family, household income can rise and fall significantly according to how many children are employed, while daughters' marriages or family members' illnesses can require huge expenditures that deplete savings and increase debt for years. Changes like these are usually cyclical. The formal liberalization of the Indian economy in 1991 created potentially longer-term social change. Loans for small business enterprises are now more easily acquired, newly available consumer goods serve as investments as well as signs of class achievement, and new technological sectors provide a host of skilled jobs. All of these changes have contributed to noticeable growth in the Indian middle class (Kulkarni 1993; Mankekar 1999; Desai 2007). Nonetheless, significant upward class mobility remains elusive for most people.

Class is one of numerous systems of hierarchy that shape everyday life in India. Social hierarchies such as class, caste, gender, and age help a person determine, among other things, how to interact with other people: how to act toward and speak to them, what responsibilities might be had for them, and what kinds of help might be requested from them. Of course, like any other system of rules, these are frequently broken or manipulated; but they are followed more often than not, and they help people know what their ideal behavior should be—at least according to a particular set of rules.

Of these different forms of hierarchy, class has arguably received the least attention from scholars, and is often ignored in favor of caste. Caste is a form of rank that, like class, has social and economic aspects, but also carries ritual implications. It is embodied—embedded in the substance of people's bodies—and is passed on from parents to children. While caste provides a group membership that people retain throughout their lives, class standing can change both upward and downward. Although there is some correlation between class and caste rankings (Desai 2007; Deshpande 2003), and people of higher castes are generally wealthier than people of lower castes, there are numerous exceptions. There are many people like Anjali (who belongs to the high-ranked Pillai caste) who are high-caste but not wealthy, and many lower-caste people who are economically well-off.[1] There is no straightforward correspondence between class and caste rankings, and any person can at least theoretically be or become a member of any class.

Class is one of the most salient idioms of identity in contemporary India, especially in urban areas, and wealth and education provide two of the most direct means to social and political power (Kumar 1988; Dickey 1993; Kapadia 1995; Fernandes 1997). While class is not the only source of power in Madurai, it is a primary determinant of respect and of the distribution of social, cultural, and economic resources, and class is recognized as a potent social force by Madurai residents. All of the people I interviewed during my research in 1999–2000, 2001, and 2009 said that class had a greater impact on their life opportunities than did caste. Such impressions are a sign of the salience that class holds in the everyday lives and imaginations of urban residents.

One reason that class is so significant in urban life is that class standing, unlike caste membership, is highly visible. This makes it an important indicator of social position in the relatively anonymous setting of the city. Unlike villages and small towns, where families have generally known one another for generations, and where the number of castes to be identified is relatively small, in more urban areas it is difficult to judge caste accurately by looking at or speaking briefly with a person. Many symbols of class, on the other hand, are immediately evident upon meeting someone, including clothing, hygiene, speech, manners, and movement; and sometimes education, occupation, and housing. If you speak for a while with people or visit their homes, you may also learn which books and newspapers they read, whether they drink tea or coffee, how they decorate their homes and what kinds of consumer goods they display, what kind of cooking fuel they use, and which vegetables they cook with it. All of these are signs of class.

Such symbols are important to understanding the nature of class because class is both an economic and a symbolic system. By this I mean that economic and symbolic factors work together to produce an individual's class. In my view, class derives not only from income, material assets, and occupation—the economic sources that usually come to mind when we think of what determines our class—but also from such cultural and social "capital" as education, consumption habits, fashion, and ways of speaking (see Bourdieu 1984, 1986; Caplan 1987; Deshpande 2003; Fernandes and Heller 2006; Liechty 2003; Ortner 2003; Tolen 2000). As I have argued elsewhere (Dickey 2000: 467), what makes class a distinct form of hierarchy, and not just a variation on caste, is its more fundamental basis in economic power, combined with the status markers that financial resources can produce—such as education, honor, and conspicuous consumption—which themselves become sources of economic power.

Moreover, as these points suggest, it is also important to recognize that class is not simply a static structure of ranked differences, but a *process* in and of itself. Sherry Ortner has noted that "we may think of class as something people are or have or possess, or as a place in which people find themselves or are assigned, but we may also think of it as a project, as something that is always being made or kept or defended, feared or desired" (2003: 13–14). The value of examining symbolic and material features as interlinked tools in the production and representation of class is demonstrated by Anjali's case, in which the construction of class is a highly conscious project.

What is the locus of class? Put another way, where does a person's class come from? I contend that, in India, the family is the source of an individual's class.[2] This argument counters some of the only other discussions of the locus of class in India, such as those by Karin Kapadia (1995) and Selvy Thiruchendran (1997), both of whom argue that class is an individual phenomenon and must be defined for each person separately from the family. Kapadia, for example, argues that family members in the same household can be of vastly different classes, since in her assessment class derives from occupation and education, which can vary widely within each family (Kapadia 1995: 251–52). This is a provocative argument that, among other things, helps to highlight the widening gap in the opportunities available to women and to men, but it does not isolate the locus of class effectively.

I contend that the family serves as the source of an individual's class in two ways. First, other people judge an individual's class standing by looking at the individual's family, using signs such as family members' occupations, education, housing, and consumer goods. Second, it is primarily the family that provides and decides upon the resources and opportunities available to each individual (Béteille 1991). Family members share a pool of material resources, and the family head makes decisions about how to divide those resources. Family members also play a large part in deciding how much education individual members receive, and which if any jobs or careers they should aim for. Finally, each generation passes on cultural and social as well as economic "capital"—including knowledge, values, and social networks—to the next generation (Peace 1984; Béteille 1991: 16–19).

Unlike most other urban residents, Anjali appears poised to move up in class standing. How might this happen? How does class mobility occur in urban India, and how secure is it? The story that Anjali tells helps to answer these questions. It reveals the importance of education, the role that family plays in passing on class and making decisions that affect its members' class, and the role that both symbolic and economic features play in determining a person's class and the chances of improving class standing.

What is Anjali's class? Most visitors from affluent foreign countries, along with well-to-do Indians, would look at Anjali's natal family and judge them to be poor. They would probably base their judgments on the parents' occupations and education, on the size of the family's house, and on the work the children do. But Anjali's family, like other people of similar means in Madurai, do not view themselves as poor. They describe themselves as "in the middle" (*naṭuttaramānavarkaḷ*) or, using the English word, "normal."[3] (Although the Tamil term "natuttaramanavarkal" is similar to the U.S. English phrase "middle class," in Madurai this category denotes a position of significantly less financial security than it usually does in the United States.) They use indicators such as the children's education, types of food eaten in the household, consumer goods, the family's financial security and debts, family members' clothing and neatness, and the sturdiness and location of the housing. According to their categories, people who are poor, for example, have only enough money to buy food and other necessities for a single day at best, live in cheaper housing (made of mud, metal sheets, or cardboard), eat fewer meals and less nutritious and less high-status food, have less education, and have almost no "modern" consumer goods such as cassette players, televisions, or refrigerators. Some of the difference in our respective judgments lies in varying perceptions of the status of occupations, and some of it lies in uneven knowledge of which signs to use and how to discriminate between what seem to outsiders to be fine gradations but are in fact significant cultural distinctions.

When I first met Anjali and her family, Anjali was in the third grade and very interested in reading and in language. Her parents, like most parents without much money, decided how long to keep their children in school by balancing each child's interest and success in school against the expenses of sending them there. They were also typical in seeing education as the single most important factor in improving their children's chances for the future. Educating children is expensive, however. Private schools, especially English medium, are popularly viewed as providing the best education and the strongest chances of succeeding on standardized examinations (which will eventually determine entrance to and scholarships for postsecondary educational institutions), and the fees for these schools can be extremely high. Even government schools, which do not charge high fees, still require additional expenditures on uniforms, books, paper, pens, and other school supplies. In addition, children who attend school cannot work for the small wages that in some families are crucial for meeting housing, food, and medical expenses.

Anjali's family's income was small, but it was enough to get by on without sending the young children out to work. Anjali in particular was very interested in studying. She completed secondary school, a relatively high level of education at that time. Her parents had studied only through the fifth grade, but had educated all of their children through the ninth to twelfth grades. It is rare for a daughter to receive more education than her brothers (her sister, for example, finished the tenth grade and then married a doctor's assistant and moved to another city), but from the tenth grade onward, Anjali began hoping to go to college. She told me, "I was interested in studying computers. I wanted at the minimum to finish a degree. I thought that at least I should study, since no one else in the family has gone to college. And my older

brothers told me that they would help since I was their only younger sister."
When she finally told her parents, however, they resisted.

> A.: They said, "We don't have the money—how can you possibly go to col-
> lege?" So after completing +2 [the final year of secondary school], I went
> to take a typing course. My parents had said, "All right, go ahead and
> learn typing. We will support that." The director at the typing center
> asked me—he said, "You have a tough situation. There is a job open
> here. Would you like to work while you are studying?" So I took the job
> typing and was able to study for my B.Com. [Bachelor of Commerce]
> degree.
> S.: Your parents didn't continue to say you couldn't study?
> A.: No. Because I was so interested, they said, "Okay, you can study. We will
> adjust [financially] and help you."

Anjali was able to cover most of the costs of her studies with her typing income, and her parents accommodated the loss of her income toward
other household expenses. She worked full time, and completed her entire
degree through a three-year correspondence course from the university. She
would work at her job all day, study at home in the evenings while the rest
of the family was socializing in the same room, and then get up early in the
morning to attend two hours of "tuition" (tutoring) with dozens of other
students in the nearby home of a university professor, before going to her
job again. Anjali said that the time in a day was "just exactly long enough"
to fit everything in. She did find studying difficult. It wasn't just that she had
no quiet place to read, but also, as she said, "There was no one at home who
could teach me; they are all uneducated." No one could help her study, or
empathize with the problems and pressures she faced in finishing a college
degree.

Anjali was interested in working with computers, and her parents agreed
that the computer field was promising for her future career and marriage
prospects. After finishing her B.Com. in 1993 Anjali took a six-month computer certificate course that taught her the rudiments of computer hardware
and software. This training made her part of the growing (but then still tiny)
minority of computer-literate people in Madurai. With it she obtained a position in a small graphics design office near her home, where she was taught to
create the calendars, business cards, and invitations produced by the company. When I saw her a year into this work, Anjali confided that her dream
was to obtain a degree in computer programming, work for a technological
firm, and eventually run her own business, but her family's limited economic resources, as well as their lack of the social contacts that are so crucial to
gaining placement in competitive professions (cf. Béteille 1991: 19 and pas-
sim), appeared to prevent her from taking any of these steps.

Anjali's position gave her family an additional Rs 1,000 per month. It also
placed her in a social environment that would have been inaccessible if she,

like most other women of marriageable age, had stayed at home after finishing her education. The office on the floor above hers held a small videography business specializing in wedding and party videos, and down the corridor was a computer and Internet center. She made close friends with people her age working in these offices. Puri, who worked next door, taught her how to find affordable stylish clothing and to groom her hair in new ways. Both women became close friends with Murugan, one of the videographers. Until recently, such a friendship with a young man was unheard of for proper young women. Anjali's work gave her a new sophistication, which derived not just from her contact with computers, but also from her knowledge of fashion, casual friendships with men her age, a confident way of speaking, and an awareness of the world outside her family and neighbors. She was experimenting with modernity, an important element of a higher-class image (Hancock 1999: 25–27; Mankekar 1999: 48– 49, 74–89).

Anjali's arrival at this point had not simply been an individual accomplishment; it required the joint efforts and support of her family members. Her parents kept all their children in school through high school, despite their difficult financial circumstances. Anjali's parents and elder brothers had the authority to say whether and what she could study. They allowed Anjali to go on to college and get computer training because they felt these courses would be good for her intellectually and economically, and because she was able to finance her studies by working full time. They too contributed financially. Anjali herself was an agent in this project, persuading her parents to let her study, working full time as she carried a full course load, and shouldering the pressure of a college education largely alone. Her family was willing to support her because of her academic interest and success, but also because her education and computer-related career gave the family prestige and enhanced Anjali's prospects of making a "good" marriage. Through everyone's efforts, Anjali gained the education, work skills, sophistication, modern sensibility, and even social connections that could make her eligible to join a higher class.

In the meantime, with Anjali and her three brothers working, her family had become more comfortable financially. For a brief period, her mother—who managed the household finances—felt secure enough to stop worrying about how to make ends meet. She paid off debts, put money aside for her eldest son's wedding, and began to consider what kind of groom to find for Anjali.

But then Anjali's father was seriously injured. One day, about six months after Anjali began her new job, her father had picked up a heavy parcel from an office for a delivery and was carrying it down several flights of stairs. He slipped on a step and the box struck him on his upper spine. That night he began to have seizures. His frightened family rushed him to the Government Hospital, which offers free care to all patients. When they arrived, however, they found there was a strike at the hospital, and felt forced to take their father to a private clinic. X-rays there showed nerve damage that required surgery in order to avoid paralysis. Because like most Indians Anjali's family has no medical insurance, they knew they would be liable for all medical costs. The surgery alone amounted to well over a year's income for any member of their household, and X-rays and medications were also prohibitively expensive. But as Anjali said, "We thought, 'We have to get him treatment even though it means going into great debt. Our father has to be there for us.'" Without telling their father, they used the money that had been put aside for the eldest son's wedding, sold the mother's jewelry, and borrowed the rest from neighborhood moneylenders at the high rate of 10 percent interest per month.[4] According to Anjali, the physician they consulted was shaken by the extremity of their circumstances and would not charge them for his or his clinic's services. He cautioned, however, that they would have to pay the surgeon, "otherwise he will not come." This same surgeon, Anjali said, would have treated her father "for free at the [Government] Hospital, but because he treated him outside, he wanted Rs 15,000" before he would begin the surgery. For years, one person's wages—a third of the household income—went to paying off the interest and principal on the loans each month. Their father recovered somewhat, but he has never been able to return to paid work.

Anjali was then twenty-three, older than most unmarried women of her caste and class. Marriage, which is almost always seen in India as an alliance between families rather than a romantic partnering of individuals, is a key point at which family statuses are negotiated, effected, and displayed to the social public. Anjali's parents had decided to delay her marriage until after her oldest brother's so that they could augment her dowry with the money the new daughter-in-law would bring.[5] As it turned out, the money that her brother's wife brought offset only a small portion of their father's medical expenses. Anjali's parents were faced with looking for a husband for her at a time when they had not only lost the father's income, but had also incurred significant debt.

Searching for a groom is always a complicated business of finding the best combination of a "good" family (one that is sufficiently respectable, financially secure, and good-tempered) with a "good" son (someone who has the proper personality, job prospects, and horoscope), and then attempting to provide the dowry that such a family demands. Dowries vary according to caste and the earning potential of the groom, but in general they represent a very large outlay, usually at least five years' worth of income among the middle classes and mid- to high-level castes. Anjali's parents hoped to find her a "government servant" (a member of the civil service or other branches of the government), or at least a business owner. These positions were a large step up from Anjali's father's occupation as a rickshaw driver, and the class standing of such men's families is ranked much higher on the local scale. Anjali was educated, sophisticated, and personable enough, however, to attract a family with such a son.

I asked Anjali about the differences between these types of grooms.

> S.: When I was talking with your mother about your marriage, she said that your life would be better with a husband who has a government job. What would the differences be between marrying someone with a government job and someone with his own business? Do you know what I mean?
>
> A.: Yes. For a person employed by the government, things [i.e., his salary and position] can only improve, they can't get worse. And after retirement, he will get a pension and all that. If he dies suddenly, his children or wife will be given a position. They will get a pension. Throughout their lives, there will be something [i.e., some income to rely on]. For someone in business, sometimes things will be good, sometimes there will be losses. When they lose money, they can't look after the family. It will be hard. So people prefer government jobs.[6]

I asked Anjali whether her parents would look for a groom of their own class, or perhaps of a lower or higher class. Whereas most people I interviewed said that parents prefer to find grooms from families of similar means so that their daughters will be comfortable in the social setting of their new home, Anjali replied, "My parents will look for a little higher level. They'll think, 'So far she has lived in hardship. At least her life could be different after her marriage.' They will do that with the hope that at least after marriage, I can be comfortable compared with the hard life I have led so far." I asked, "Won't it be hard for you to live in such a place?" She answered philosophically, "I will have to change to fit with the way they are. That's all. It will be a bit difficult in the beginning. But I can observe what they are like, and I can change." This is the stock response of young women as they prepare for marriage in an unknown household, but in Anjali's case it also evoked the difficulty of adjusting to the material surroundings, consumption practices, manners, and social assumptions of people raised in a different class. As Tamils say, she would have to learn to "move" in such company, speaking and dressing and behaving appropriately.

As Anjali points out, government servants in India have secure employment for life and are guaranteed a pension. Yet government servants ask for such high dowries—in the Pillai caste that Anjali's family belongs to, the rate was then 20 "sovereigns" of gold jewelry (160g, 5.5 oz.) and Rs. 15,000–20,000 in cash, according to Anjali's mother—that such a groom was likely to be out of reach for her family. Families of young men who have their own businesses ask for about half of these amounts, still a huge expense for a family whose primary wage-earner made Rs 1,000 per month when he was working, and which had no savings remaining. Yet if Anjali could marry someone with financial security, she would not have to worry about poverty herself, and she might eventually be able to help her parents and her siblings. Given Anjali's skills and the immense security such a marriage could bring her, the step was worth taking if at all possible. Before her father's injuries, with five household members working and her brother about to be married, this goal seemed realizable. After the accident, it seemed farther off, but it remained something they might still work toward.

Shortly thereafter, the family made another decision that kept Anjali's prospects open. When Anjali's employers decided to move their business across town, Anjali suggested to her parents that they get a bank loan to open her own design business in the old office. Anjali had plenty of experience both with design and with managing the company's daily affairs, and those skills, along with the advantage of retaining the same office—and therefore the same customer base—made her confident that she could run a successful business on her own. She could also employ her brother Kumar, whose screen-printing skills would add to her output. The last time I saw Anjali and her family before her marriage, they had refurnished the small office, completed most of the arduous process of securing a bank loan for computer equipment, and obtained a new computer from one of Anjali's old classmates who sells computer hardware. The classmate's father happened to be the manager of the bank where Anjali's family applied for the loan, and as he knew that his father had already promised to provide the loan, he was thereby assured that the purchasing price would be forthcoming. In the meantime, Anjali's mother had stopped talking about finding a groom. When I asked why, she said they were waiting to get the business well established because they hoped its income would substitute for a portion of the dowry. In the meantime, Anjali and her two unmarried brothers would continue working, and every rupee left over from household maintenance and loan repayment would be put toward the rest of her dowry—at least until another emergency struck.

In the United States, middle- and upper-class people tend to think of class mobility as an individual endeavor. If you work hard enough at getting an education or earning a living, you can get ahead. In India, the vision tends to be one of group effort: if you educate your children and pick the right careers and then the right marriage alliances for them, their lives will improve and so might yours. Through a combination of joint financial effort, careful strategizing about Anjali's education and career, effective use of social networks, and Anjali's own talents and drive, Anjali's family seems poised to attain this ideal.

At the same time, the family's own history shows how difficult reaching this point is. Simply *maintaining* current resources can become impossible when illness strikes, or when a wage-earner dies or is incapacitated, since there are few "safety nets" of health and disability insurance, retirement plans, or even low-interest loans. Such events can immediately wipe out a family's savings in cash and assets, and plunge them into debt. Even children's marriages can increase financial hardship, since they may remove wage-earners from the household, and daughters' weddings often require an extremely high outlay of cash and goods. Expensive marriages also bring honor to the family, by demonstrating the family's resources and indicating the type of people willing to create an alliance with them; but like the losses incurred by illness or unemployment, they reduce the savings and other financial capital available to the family for making other long-term investments or for providing a safety net when other tragedies strike.

Anjali's potential gains have also been limited by her family's lack of cultural and social, as well as economic, resources. Their lack of experience with higher education, for example, made Anjali's college experience more challenging than many of her peers', and their lack of contacts in prestigious professions and institutions limited Anjali's ability to obtain a high-status and lucrative career.

Even education, that most vaunted social, cultural, and economic resource for upward mobility, is itself insufficient as a means of entering a higher class. A degree must be accompanied by other symbolic attributes that make one a proper member of a higher class. To be seen as an appropriate addition to a civil servant's or business owner's family, Anjali must adapt her dress, grooming, speech, and manners. She had already been able to learn much of this as a result of her education—by reading, by learning about computers, and by adapting to the social environments she observed among fellow students at "tuition" and her peers at work. People in Madurai frequently ridicule those who use their money or educational attainments to act "high-class" but retain the values and behaviors of the lesser class in which they originated. If Anjali does marry into a higher-class family, she will have to continue to mold herself into the proper image.

Moreover, she will be viewed by friends and acquaintances as a member of a higher class not merely because of how she presents herself—although this will suffice for casual encounters—but primarily because of the circumstances and image of the family she has married into. Before her marriage her natal family has determined her class, and as a married woman her marital family will provide the context by which others will judge her. Thus Anjali's class standing, like other people's, comes from her family in two ways: her class is judged on the basis of her family's circumstances, and the opportunities she has to change or maintain those circumstances are determined and decided upon primarily by her family members, rather than by Anjali herself.

Even with the economic opportunities provided by the contemporary Indian economy, upward class mobility remains difficult to achieve because of the barriers to financial security faced by lower- and middle-class people. When class mobility is realized, education, family contributions and status, and the acquisition of both symbolic and economic criteria are critical to its achievement and maintenance. Anjali's family provided financial and emotional support that allowed her to gain an education and other symbolic attributes of a higher class status. Anjali and her parents may be able to consolidate these gains through marriage with a more socially prestigious and economically secure family. Whether they are finally able to overcome the odds against her long-term upward mobility, however, remains to be seen.

EPILOGUE

A decade later, Anjali and her family's efforts to gain her entrance into a higher class have proved fruitful against the odds, although not in precisely the way her parents had planned. In 2001, when Anjali was twenty-five, she married a businessman who was the son of a retired civil servant. While this was just the type of groom her parents had hoped for, he was not of their choosing. Instead, Anjali had what is called an "arranged love marriage." She met her future husband on her own, and both sets of parents eventually approved of the match. Anjali's husband, Sundaram, was a friend of Anjali's older brother, and he worked in a building across from Anjali's office. They met one day when Anjali's brother visited them both, and they soon became interested in each other. They had no private place to meet, but developed their relationship secretly for several years by talking on their cell phones while at work. In the meantime, Anjali's parents began looking for a suitable husband, and Sundaram's parents were searching for a bride. After both had rejected several proposed matches, Anjali and Sundaram finally told their parents about their interest in each other. At first their parents resisted (especially Anjali's), but after many discussions they acceded, which qualified this as an "arranged" marriage as well as a love marriage. Indians often characterize the passions of romantic love and desire as the opposite of the careful planning and concern for the future that motivate marriage arrangements, but in this case, the two young people chose partners with the kinds of economic resources and educational attainment that their parents were looking for.

Sundaram's family owns a house on the southern outskirts of Madurai. Sundaram, who has an M.A., had started a bag-making business that was less profitable than he wished. Three months after he and Anjali married, he closed his company and began working in Anjali's design business, adding his typing and computer skills to hers. They renamed the enterprise after their two fathers. Today, their partnership appears to be both economically and personally successful. Working together in their own office means they can travel to and from work together (so there is no difficulty, for example, with Anjali coming home alone late at night), and they bring their children to the office with them. Murugan, whose well-regarded videography business has expanded into a larger office nearby, stops by every day to play with the children and take them for "rounds" on his motorbike. Anjali's son is studying in one of Madurai's most prestigious English-medium grammar schools, and they plan to enter their two-year-old daughter in the same school a year from now.

Anjali's father-in-law died three years ago, and her mother died last year. In her in-laws' home, she now lives with her mother-in-law, her widowed sister-in-law and her son, and an unmarried sister-in-law, along with Anjali's husband and children. When I visited Anjali shortly after her marriage, she was clearly in the position of new daughter-in-law; she never sat down when she was in a room with adult members of her husband's family, and she did most of the cooking, along with her office work. Now, nearing a decade into the marriage, she is more relaxed, and has more help with household responsibilities.

So Anjali was indeed able to move up in class—dramatically so—in terms of economic stability, housing, and social and cultural capital. Although she chose her own husband, her family agreed to the alliance largely because Sundaram's family had the economic security and social standing they had hoped to attain for their daughter; Sundaram's family agreed because of Anjali's education and earning power. Both families also made sure that the other one had a reputation for responsible behavior among neighbors and kin. Although Anjali did not bring cash as dowry, her family gave her numerous kitchen supplies to take with her, and she had 20 sovereigns of gold, one of the primary forms of durable wealth in Tamil Nadu. (Anjali said poignantly that her father had saved for her gold over twenty years by "putting aside a small amount of money every day after he finished carrying schoolchildren home from school.") The family she married into has been able to use Anjali's resources to further stabilize their own economic position. Her family of origin has benefited as well. They gained prestige from the alliance, and Anjali's younger brother Kumar continued to work for the design business for several years. Later, Murugan taught him the rudiments of still photography, and helped him get a job in another photo business. When Kumar's own marriage occurs, his professional credentials and Anjali's marital family's reputation may help him consolidate his attempts at upward mobility as well.

Despite the overall improvement in income and consumption spending in India, it remains very difficult for people who are poor to make significant improvements in their material and social conditions. Even for those people who have been part of the limited growth in the middle class, mobility like Anjali's is unusual. It is all the more so since she comes from a family with very limited economic means. Her family's success in overcoming these challenges, for at least one child, brings into relief the mutually constitutive roles that economic and symbolic capital play in the construction of everyday experience and class-based opportunity.

ACKNOWLEDGMENTS

I am grateful to Susan Bell, Stephanie Dickey, and the editors of this volume for their close readings and thoughtful comments on this chapter. Mary Hancock also provided suggestions that helped refine my concepts and arguments. A version of this essay was presented at the Women, Culture, and Development Colloquium of the University of California, Santa Barbara. I especially thank Anjali, Sundaram, and their families for their willingness to let me record their lives in print.

NOTES

1. These exceptions also appear at the aggregate level. The Nadars, for example, have a low ranking in the caste system but are one of the wealthiest groups in Madurai, while Brahmans, the highest-ranked caste, are not among the very wealthiest castes. On the other hand, the lowest castes do tend to be the poorest ones. Dalits in particular face significant challenges in attaining quality education, and in entering high-paying occupations when they do gain sufficient education (Da Costa 2008; Jeffrey, Jeffery, and Jeffery 2004).

2. By "family" I refer specifically to a person's family members who live in the household and to other members who may live away but still make regular financial contributions to the household. I do not include the larger extended family of kin who live separately and do not contribute financially to the person's household.

3. At this time, people of Anjali's family's socioeconomic standing and higher generally used a three-part model of class, including poor people, middle people, and wealthy people. Poorer people usually employed a two-part model, composed of poor people and rich people. Now, a three-tier model is widely shared, signaling both economic and cultural changes in Madurai. Because all of these class categories include people with a wide range of socioeconomic circumstances, when Anjali wants to be precise she qualifies her family's "middle-class" ranking by saying they are "between the low rank and the middle rank."

4. Lower-interest loans from a bank were then generally available only to government employees and others who had the necessary social connections. In addition, because they required a long application process and were targeted for specific needs, such as business equipment or housing finance, they were not useful for emergencies.

5. There are two components to what is popularly referred to as "dowry" in India (*varataṭciṇai* in Tamil). The first includes gold jewelry, cooking vessels, and other gifts of household items bestowed upon a daughter. The other consists of cash, jewelry and other gold items, and large consumer goods given to the groom and/or his family. Giving the second type of dowry is illegal in India, but the practice is almost universal (see Caplan 1984).

6. Preference for government jobs decreased in the late 1990s and early 2000s as private-sector incomes and opportunities surpassed those of the public sector. Recently, however, as corporate employment has become more insecure, government employment has regained some of its attraction for college-educated people.

16

Recasting the Secular: Religion and Education in Kerala, India

Ritty Lukose

Religion is a matter of the mind. . . . Don't think that my religion is
true and yours is false. This is the place where people live together
as brothers and sisters, irrespective of caste, creed, and religion.
—Sree Narayana Guru

The "place" referred to in this quotation is a college in the South Indian
state of Kerala, where I conducted fieldwork. Painted on a building at the
entrance of the college campus, the quote signals the formation and location
of this college within the movement for caste upliftment and social reform
that began in the late nineteenth century among the formerly untouchable
Ezhava caste community, spearheaded by the spiritual leader Sree Narayana
Guru. Part of a broad and far-reaching set of changes that transformed caste
relations in the region within the context of colonial modernity, Narayana
Guru's anti-caste politics recast religion as a privatized "matter of the mind,"
one that cleared the way for the creation of a place for secular tolerance, such
as the colleges and schools created by *Ezhava*-based community organizations.

Anti-caste politics articulate with understandings of secular tolerance
that the college seeks to instantiate at a time when secularism is being challenged and reworked by Hindu nationalism. The everyday instantiations
and negotiations of secularism in educational institutions form an important
context for understanding caste in contemporary India.

Dominant narratives of modernity assert the expulsion of religion from
the public secular spaces of the state, democratic politics, and civil society.
The presence of caste, conventionally understood as a traditional, religious
system (albeit with economic and other consequences) within modern India
has variously been regarded by scholars, politicians, and the public as evi-

dence of the unfortunate persistence of the traditional within the modern, and of the private (religion) within the public (secular). Yet in fact, caste is a complicated and messy product of the secular and the modern that needs to be explored within the spaces of contemporary, public life in India.[1] I argue for an attention to the everyday cultural politics of caste, one that problematizes the production of caste identities within the larger context of secular, democratic citizenship within India. I do this through an exploration of the politics of caste, religion, and secularism as it is negotiated in the college context.

CASTE, SECULARISM, RELIGION

Within the postcolonial context, caste as a crisis of contemporary politics emerges in the wake of the Mandal Commission Riots of 1990. The Mandal Commission was established by the Government of India in 1979, headed by parliamentarian B. P. Mandal, to review the quota or "reservation" system mandated by the Constitution of India. This reservation system is an affirmative action program intended to redress caste discrimination by reserving a certain portion of government jobs and university slots for members of lower castes (known as Other Backward Classes, Scheduled Castes, and Scheduled Tribes). The 1990 protests—which closed schools, businesses, government services, and transportation systems in many regions across India—came in response to Prime Minister V. P. Singh's government's decision to implement the Mandal Commission's recommendations, which would have almost doubled previous reservations to just under 50 percent of government jobs and university admissions for this highly differentiated set of categories of people based upon social, educational, and economic "backwardness."[2]

Within a week, anti-Mandal, anti-reservation violence spread throughout North India, eventually bringing down the V. P. Singh government. It is important to note that the main participants in the Mandal riots were students; some were elementary and high-school age, although most were college students. The riots, centered in cities such as New Delhi, involved middle- and upper-class and caste students who, fearful of lost job opportunities, blocked traffic, burned buses, fought police, and forced stores to close. Two forms of protest were particularly striking. First, students pretended to sweep streets and sell vegetables at roadside stands, emulating low-caste traditional occupations to indicate what would happen to them if crucial government jobs were taken away from them. The second set of protests, which spread throughout North India, involved attempted self-immolations by students, often preceded by the burning of academic diplomas and certificates, to dramatize the supposed devaluing of their educational achievements. These protests and the more general rhetoric were ridden with the language of "merit" and "efficiency." It was argued that if the quotas were implemented, the jobs would not go to those who truly deserved them, that is, college students who had worked hard and were best qualified to do the jobs efficiently. Others cautioned that the implementation of the commission's recommendations would lead to a further entrenchment of caste feeling and distinctions and would eventually lead to a caste war.

The question of reservations and caste re-emerged in May 2006 as a highly contested and fractious issue. The current Congress-led government of Manmohan Singh required reservations for institutions of higher education, including medical colleges. This prompted a widespread protest by medical students and doctors, which was later joined by a wider constituency. It has also led to a wide-ranging set of debates in the popular media and press that vacillate between support for reservations and a rejection of reservations as a divisive and populist measure on the part of politicians—one that is out of step with the needs and aspirations of a dynamic and globalizing market economy. Some favor a middle position, arguing that reservations are necessary at the primary and secondary levels of education, but should not be necessary—and are quite ineffective—at higher educational levels.

These protests highlight the centrality of education to the contemporary politics of caste and the ambiguous and contentious role of caste in the production of the modern, secular citizen-subject in India. Opponents of reservations regard the protesting students as appropriately rejecting caste as a principle of differentiation in favor of a language of meritocracy, while supporters of reservations argue that the protestors are merely defending their caste privilege, using meritocracy as a smokescreen.

The question arises then, just how *is* caste manifest within the institutional spaces of secular modernity? The Mandal riots and more contemporary reservation politics, the rise of lower-caste-based political parties in North India,[3] the persistence of violence against Dalits,[4] and the newer forms of critique of Indian politics and society by Dalit intellectuals such as Chandrabhan Prasad and Kancha Ilaiah all make clear that caste in contemporary, postcolonial India cannot be relegated to the realm of privatized tradition, nor simply displaced by other categories of analysis such as class. Examining caste in terms of the larger horizon of secular, democratic citizenship in India goes some way toward resisting the tradition-modernity binary within which discourses of caste have been located.[5] I am interested in interrogating the ways in which caste emerges as a site of contestation at the fault lines between notions of public and private, tradition and modernity, the religious and the secular.

However, it must be noted that the discourse of secularism within India is dominated less by the question of caste than by that of communalism, referring to tensions between religious "communities," notably Hindu and Muslim. The rise of political and militant versions of Hindu nationalism that are violently directed against religious minorities within India, in particular against the Muslim community, has led to an anxious and difficult reckoning about the status of India as a secular nation-state (see Menon, this volume). The Hindu Right's attack on the Indian state for being "pseudo-secular" and for "appeasing" religious minorities has resulted in a far-reaching discourse among academics and public intellectuals about the limits and possibilities of secularism in India.[6] One strand within this exploration has been an attempt to understand the ways in which dominant forms of nationalism, and the secularism that it is founded on, are tied to ambiguous and ambivalent assumptions and deployments of a majoritarian Hindu identity—what one might call a "Hindu secular." This assumption that the secular is Hindu in character makes secular nationalism in some ways complicit with contemporary Hindu nationalism. The production of a Hindu secular requires not only the boundary between religions, but the containment of caste politics in the name of a unified Hindu identity. In this sense, the common phrase "upper-caste, upper-class Hindu" as a reference to the normative citizen-subject of Indian modernity needs to be understood more deeply than this simple list of identity markers suggests. All of this points to a dynamic relationship between the production of caste and the production of religion (as Hindu) that requires exploration. The college in question here is one place that aims to produce modern secular subjects while also catering to a caste-based community. Here, we will be able to explore some of the contradictions and complexities of the imbrication of caste, religion, and secularism.

BETWEEN HINDU TRADITION AND SECULAR MODERNITY

Just beyond the entrance gate that breaks up the campus wall enclosing the college, which is gaily painted with all manner of advertising billboards, is a small, round building that houses the "watchers" or guards who monitor the entrance to the college. The outside of the building, which was paid for by the Parents and Teachers Association, is covered with painted Malayalam text, quotations from the writings and sayings of Sree Narayana Guru. At the top is painted his most famous saying: "Oru Jati, Oru Matham, Oru Devam" (One Caste, One Religion, One God).

The Sree Narayana Colleges are the products of a social-reform movement, begun in the colonial period, which sought to transform the social position of the untouchable Ezhava caste, the largest caste group in the state, constituting about 25 percent of the population (Rao 1979). Within the bureaucratic language of the state, they are considered "OBC" (Other Backward Classes). The organization that ran many activities of the movement was and is the Sree Narayana Dharma Paripalana (Society for the Propagation of the Religion of Sree Narayana), otherwise known as the SNDP, which was founded in 1903. Started by Dr. Palpu, considered the political father of the Ezhava community, the organization had as its first president Sree Narayana Guru, himself an Ezhava, who preached the abolition of the caste system under the well-known motto "One Caste, One Religion, One God." The SNDP established methods of anti-caste social activism such as reforms of internal caste practices; challenges to higher-caste practices, including temple-entry agitations; and actions for the general "uplift" of the caste through access to education and jobs. One of the movement's postcolonial reform projects was the establishment of fourteen colleges in the 1950s and 1960s. Although the Sree Narayana Colleges are controlled by the more elite, middle-class members of the community, they nevertheless cater to a wide spectrum of the Ezhava caste, many of whom are from the lower classes. Because it is one of the major colleges in the area, it also draws a variety of students from different religious communities, primarily Muslim and Christian, and from both upper and (other) lower castes.

The Sree Narayana anti-caste movement is part of a larger and important reworking of caste relations within Kerala under the impact of colonial modernity. As many have noted, Kerala had a particularly repressive caste system (R. Jeffrey 1976, 1993; D. Menon 1994; Dumont 1970: 82). Within the context of lower-caste reform and struggle in colonial Kerala, there were many fault lines and fissures that significantly vacillated between the demands and opportunities of secular modernity—particularly colonial education and Christianity—and the reimaginings of Hindu tradition in the vein of Sree Narayana Guru. The question of conversion to Christianity, Buddhism, and sometimes Islam among lower castes sat alongside powerful new conceptualizations of Hindu tradition, as well as assertions of atheism and rationalism. Narayana Guru's writings and teachings demonstrate a complex and mutually overlapping relationship between understandings of tradition and modernity, the religious and the secular, in the context of developing an anti-caste politics grounded in tolerance of religious difference.

Drawing on a variety of philosophical strands, Sree Narayana's message combined individual perfectibility and community improvement. It was a potent message that was taken up at the turn of the century by a rising Ezhava elite, embodied in the SNDP, which, through missionary education and the opportunities of a new cash economy, was eager to shed its untouchable status. As Kumar (1997) has noted, in Sree Narayana's philosophy, knowledge (arivu) occupies the structural space for Brahman, the only essential reality. Individual, bodily perfectability emerges as a way to achieve knowledge. This focus on bodily perfectability also allows a link to be made between spiritual and worldly existence. Narayana Guru takes this further by moving from individual perfectability to community improvement to the well-being of the human race. In this context, caste as a set of distinctions that differentiate the human race is understood as a false principle. Fundamentally, Sree Narayana relies on a biological essentialism to argue that those who procreate are members of one jati (caste or birth group), one he distinguishes from religion (madam) and community (samudayam) (see also Kumar 1997). First, according to Sree Narayana's thought and writing, untouchability is erased as the Ezhava "caste" transforms itself from being a particular grouping within a Hindu caste system to becoming a separable "community" that is modernizing through education, transformations of rituals, and other such projects. However, the secular community of Ezhavas intersects with ambiguous understandings of other notions of community. In the first instance, while community refers to a collectivity defined by the term "Ezhava," it also refers to the human community and the human race, representing a kind of universal humanism. Second, the movement, at various moments in its history, entertained the possibility of conversion to either Christianity or Buddhism, but Sree Narayana resisted that move. Despite Sree Narayana's proclamations that he did not belong to any caste or religion and that his temples did not belong to the Hindu religion, the redefinition of Ezhava as a caste community rests ambivalently within the horizon of a larger Hindu world.

POLITICS OF THE SECULAR

The presence-absence of caste within the life of the college is palpable. Caste is quite literally unspeakable, a direct result of Sree Narayana's teachings. Crucial to this unspeakability are the norms of naming. All students were officially known, within the documents of the college and in the ways they were referred to in everyday talk, by their first names followed by an initial, for example, "Niju P." or "Geetha S." This is part of the common practice of erasing names as markers of caste, which has a long history within the anti-caste movements of the region. One was not supposed to know what caste anyone belonged to because caste was a false principle of differentiation. However, this explicit erasure of caste as a form of social criticism is entangled with the ways in which the secular represses caste—pretends it isn't there when in some ways it really is—as reflected in strategizing relations in the college context. In the college, informal interaction and sociality involves a complex structure of knowing and not knowing caste backgrounds; some mixing and transgressing of (known but not named) caste hierarchies within friendship networks and romantic relationships within the spaces in and around the college; as well as avoidance of each other's homes, where violations of caste regulations or the desire to conform to them might become more explicit and embarrassing.

The ways in which the private spaces of one's family and home were made or not made available to the public world of college life was a very important way in which caste was marked without being named. When I first started my research, I had imagined that it might be possible, some time relatively soon into the research, to be able to visit students in their homes. When I asked students about their family backgrounds, answers were deliberately vague and general. It took me some time to realize that this vagueness about one's family was, at least in part, a deflection and avoidance of caste in the space of the college.

A study of the students who did initially invite me home reveals the ways in which caste and religion are negotiated within the college. The first day she met me, Sunita, a bright, articulate, English-speaking student of politics, took me to her home, a middle-class house in a middle-class neighborhood on the outskirts of town. Her family came from one of the prominent upper-caste Nayar families in and around the town. Her upper-caste background did not seem to necessitate the politics of evasion that often constituted the production of the "casteless" person for someone from a formerly untouchable caste. Given my gender, she was quite open and hospitable to me. She did not know conclusively on that first day that I was not an Ezhava, as my American English and status as a Ph.D. student produced a sense of novelty, enthusiasm, and affiliation (she was one of the few students at SN who spoke fluent English) that trumped the ambiguity of my background.

A second student, Meena, also readily invited me to spend the weekend at her family home, a small village two hours by bus from the college. She came from a poor fishing community, where her father was a fisherman. By asking me where my family was from in Kerala and hearing me mention my cousin's name (Annie), she recognized me to be a Christian. Since she came from a Christian community, this seemed to create some sense of affiliation that made it relatively easy for her to invite me home. The politics of caste and religion affects the ways in which the public of the college and the private of the home are negotiated.

This general and ambiguous erasure of caste within the space of the college broke down in an incident during the middle of the academic year during my stay. The dynamics of this incident reveal the complex articulations between caste, religion, and secularism within this college. The ambivalence of the community—in particular, the ambiguous association between "Ezhava" and "Hindu"—occupied a political space that in the 1990s was increasingly besieged by a more exclusivist notion of Hindu nationalism, reflected in the increasing popularity of the student political party, the Akhil Bharatiya Vidyarthi Parishad (ABVP), which was affiliated with right-wing Hindu political parties. If the dominant Student Federation of India (SFI) student party, affiliated with the Communist Party of India-Marxist (CPI-M), demonstrated by shouting "Inquilab Zindabad" (Long Live the Revolution) through the corridors of the college, the ABVP marched in the opposite direction, singing the militant nationalist song "Vande Mataram" (Hail to the Motherland). And in the everyday life of the college, the ambiguous status of the Hindu within the space of the secular was increasingly tested.

At the insistence of the school's principal, the student union was asked to organize a celebration of Onam—one of the most important holidays in Kerala. It had never before been celebrated at the college.[7] As the principal and teachers stated, the celebration was intended to bring the student community and teachers closer together. This intent, of course, was a reference to the highly charged presence of student politics, one that had kept colleges closed for months (Lukose 2005). The celebration of Onam was one attempt, among several others, to institute a kind of "civic culture" within the college that would counter and contend with the politicization of campus life, by subsuming and unifying the fractious student body within a larger cultural celebration that coheres around a regional Malayali identity. Understood less as "religion" and more as "culture," Onam nevertheless emerged out of a Hindu secular lexicon that has been given new meaning with the rise of Hindu nationalism within the region, as the incident to be discussed reveals.

The celebration was organized as a series of competitions, two of which prominently featured women, most of whom came dressed that day in Kerala *saris.* In one competition, every academic department entered its version of a *pukulam,* a round design on the floor made out of flower petals, which were created by the women students. The second competition featuring women called for the best rendition of *thiruvathirakali,* a regional dance in which female students, from each department, dressed in traditional saris with jasmine flowers in their hair, and performed the circular dance in the campus's wide-open central area. Under the protection of a "cultural program," this afforded the most visibility that women students had been granted in the public spaces of the college.

The most popular event of the festival was the "fancy dress" competition between half a dozen male students. This competition involved students dressing up as famous and popular personas. One student dressed up as Veerappan, the famous Tamil bandit who occupied the forests that straddle Kerala and Tamil Nadu. Dressed in tattered khaki clothes, his face painted in camouflage, and his head covered with leaves, the student entered the makeshift stage, a space in front of the college office where the principal, teachers, and students stood. He pranced around menacingly, but seemed to point his toy machine gun only at the principal and teachers, much to the amusement and goading of his fellow students. Next came the competitor who elicited the most excitement. He/she was a poor, lower-caste woman dressed in a cheap cotton sari that was half falling off, a begging bowl on her head, a pile of firewood under her arm. Coarse, loud, vulgar, and hyper-sexualized, he/she seductively sidled up to the principal and each male teacher who was present, licking his/her lips, making eyes, and swinging his/her hips.

The final contestants performed various enactments of the role of King Mahabali, whose benevolent, mythic reign is celebrated at Onam. Kerala is often depicted as the land of Asuras (demonic demi-gods), ruled by the demon-king Mahabali, who defeated the Vedic gods (the gods of the early Hindu texts) only to in turn be tricked by the god Vishnu, in his avatar as the dwarf Vamana. Within the textual tradition, Mahabali makes a transformation from an enemy of the gods to a demon-devotee, who through charity and religious rectitude finds liberation at the feet of Vishnu. Within the larger context of the Bali tradition, interpretations that stress Mahabali as a Dravidian, lower-caste-affiliated demon who contests the Brahmanical pantheon are rife (Omvedt 1998). Within Kerala, Mahabali is a sort of cultural hero. He is most significantly portrayed, through the sponsorship of the state government and the tourism board, as a good and righteous ruler, charitable and generous toward his subjects. The festival celebrates the return of King Mahabali to visit his adoring and appreciative subjects but also re-enacts his defeat. After being fed and taken care of, Vamana (Vishnu) is offered a boon by King Mahabali. Vamana asks for three paces of land, and the king readily agrees. Soon, the dwarf begins to expand. With the first step, he covers the sky, blotting out the stars. Next he straddles the nether world. One more step and the earth will be destroyed. Realizing his defeat and being the dedicated king that he is, Mahabali offers his head as the last step. The dress competition had two sets of Mahabali contestants. First, there was a "modern" Mahabali, dressed in a pair of shorts, a T-shirt, sneakers, and sunglasses, strutting and carrying a brightly colored umbrella to shade himself. He pranced around to much amusement and laughter. The second rendition consisted of two contestants, one portraying Mahabali and one Vamana (Vishnu in his dwarf form), dressed in traditional attire. They enacted the three paces, with Vamana finally stepping on the head of Mahabali.

Within celebrations of Onam, the right to appear as King Mahabali on *tiruvonam*, the last day of the ten-day festival, historically went to members of lower-caste performing groups such as Malayans, a practice that speaks to the non-Brahmanical origins of King Mahabali.[8] Although the return of King Mahabali was being re-enacted within the secular and playful context of a fancy dress competition at a college, one in which the identity of the role players should not matter, the complexities of caste and religion within the space of the secular emerged.

While the "modern" Mahabali was playful and innocuous, the "traditional" Mahabali and Vamana duo found themselves in trouble. By the end of the day, Saiju, who played Vishnu's incarnation as the dwarf Vamana (he was thought to be eminently suitable as he was so short), was in the hospital, in need of three stitches. He had been beaten up after the day's activities had wound down. Rumors abounded, with the consensus being that Saiju had been beaten up by students sympathetic to the ABVP, the Hindu nationalist-oriented student group. The consistent explanation was that he had been targeted because he had allowed his best friend Hasar, a Muslim, to play the role of Mahabali, an ostensibly Hindu king. While it was too contentious and provocative to attack Hasar, attacking Saiju was seen as a more acceptable warning.

Within the ambivalence of a caste-based—yet also caste-erased—college, the ambiguities of being Hindu in public are revealed as the celebration of a cultural program gets elided with that of specific bodies understood to belong to specific "communities." The seemingly innocuous celebration of

Kerala's culture, in the form of a putatively Hindu festival, becomes problematic when a Muslim student takes on the persona of a Hindu king. So far, we have a situation in which "Hindu" is pitted against "Muslim" within the context of a politics of Hindu nationalism that transforms the cultural figure of King Mahabali—understood in the "Hindu secular" sense as being Hindu, tolerant, and inclusive—into an exclusively Hindu one in the intolerant, exclusive "Hindu nationalist" sense. While the marking of modernity within the space of the secular in the form of "modern Mahabali" is a playful gesture that simply elicits laughter, the marking of tradition (caste and religion) within the space of the secular becomes problematic and contested. We see here that the "Hindu secular" celebration of Onam makes possible the assertion of exactly that which the secular ostensibly would exclude, namely the fact that caste and religious identities written onto bodies *do* matter.

However, the contours of the secular at stake here are not simply along the fault lines of Hindu-Muslim. A teacher was appointed to investigate the incident, and a meeting was held with Saiju and Hasar. Saiju, standing in front of the teacher's desk, explained his version of what happened. He stated that his attackers, before pummeling him, asked him why he, from a Namboodiri Brahman family, should be best friends with a Muslim. They told him that he should know better.

Notwithstanding his height, what is revealed here is that Saiju was an appropriate choice to play Vamana/Vishnu not only because he is a Hindu but also because he is a high-caste Brahman, whose father, incidentally, still performs priestly religious rituals. Who could be more appropriate from the perspective of Hindu nationalism? Saiju becomes problematic when he transgresses the boundaries of religious community to fraternize with a Muslim, whom he "allows" to play the role of a Hindu king.

The politics of caste and religion initiated by the ABVP students was condemned vigorously by the teacher. However, the way in which he reacted revealed secularism's own ambivalent politics of caste. On hearing what Saiju had to say, the teacher became irate, shouting, "Tell him this is SN College! No caste [jati], no separate religions [madam], one God! We are all humans first, remember this is SN!" Furious, he went on to say that in the next meeting, he was going to ask Saiju's attacker his last name and then ask him his caste. He derisively snorted that the student must be an "SC/ST"—referring to the category of Scheduled Caste and Scheduled Tribe, the lowest category of caste within the language of the state—because they were the ones who were zealous about *Hindutva*, or Hindu nationalism.

The teacher's narrative reveals the slippages between caste, religion, and community within a putatively secular public place, the college. In the first instance, this incident reveals the complex politics of caste that Hindu nationalism instantiates. Deploying the hierarchy of caste, and using it to berate the transgressive Saiju, the ABVP and other organizations within Kerala are working hard to attract and subsume lower-caste organizations and communities within a larger Hindu nationalist identity. The success of the ABVP within this college is testimony to that strategy. However, the secular apprehension of this "communalization" of the college, as the teacher put it, reveals the workings of caste hierarchy within the production of the secular self. The teacher quotes from the teachings of Sree Narayana to vigorously contest what he sees as the casteism of these Hindu nationalist students. In order to chastise their reference to caste, he draws on Narayana Guru's denial of caste as a reality ("no jati") and his affirmation that above and beyond separate religions (madam), the ultimate community is a universal human one under one God. However, the teacher's comment about the attacker's possible caste background reveals the ways in which his own self-understanding as secular is tied to a politics of his relative caste privilege that is far from erased. From the point of view of this adamantly secular teacher, the ABVP students must be from the lower castes. It is only they who could be drawn to the irrational, the non-modern, and the anti-secular. Drawing on the anti-caste formulations of Narayana Guru, the teacher denies caste as a valid category when reference is made to the Brahman Namboodiri caste background of the beleaguered Saiju. In the next moment, however, he draws on the bureaucratic state language of caste categories (SC/ST) in order to express the upper-caste identity that underlies his sense of himself as secular.

The incident begins as a Hindu-Muslim conflict and then gets displaced onto a caste conflict by the teacher. He has little to say to Hasar, the Muslim student. The teacher is most upset that Saiju's attackers have referenced—in fact, actually spoken—Saiju's caste name. In the putatively secular space of this community-based college, no reference to one's caste is allowed, as caste has literally become unspeakable. However, this does not mean that caste hierarchy is not asserted. When the teacher threatens to publicly ask the offending students to state their last names and reveal their caste, he is transgressing a line in order to embarrass them. This is also an attempt to reinscribe his own secular credentials by asserting his (high) caste status. In order to do this, rather than refer to these students by traditional caste names, something that his secular self finds most offensive, he switches registers and uses the modern state category of SC/ST (Scheduled Caste/Scheduled Tribe) in order to differentiate and mark his own social position. His secularism is entangled with his relatively upper-caste identity. He does not think of himself as upper caste in terms of a traditional caste hierarchy; rather, he understands a modern, secular outlook to be part and parcel of his upper-caste identity.

The secular character of the school, in which Onam was to be celebrated as a simple cultural program, is threatened by an increasingly militant Hinduism that challenges the relative inclusivity of the reformed, egalitarian, secular, and ambivalently Hindu vision of a community-based college. This secularism confronts this militancy through the logic of caste inequality, in which, in this case, the secular credentials of the teacher are rooted in his relatively upper-caste, enlightened, and secular worldview. This incident reveals the instability of the idea of "Hindu" in an equally unstable "secular" public.

CONCLUSION

In this essay, I propose that paying attention to the everyday cultural politics of caste identities—understood as relational—within the spaces of democratic secular citizenship in India would allow us to examine caste, not as a kind of substantial entity that "persists" in and through the spaces of the modern, but rather as a critical category of contestation within contemporary postcolonial India. The modern transformations of caste relations within Kerala reveal a terrain of re-imaginings of caste hierarchy—on the part of both the upper and lower castes—within the horizon of secular modernity. The specific instance of the Ezhava-based, anti-caste Sree Narayana movement reveals a reworking of Hindu tradition in dynamic relationship to the emergence of the secular modern.

Educational institutions, such as the one that I examine, embody the ambiguous complexities of definitions of community—Ezhava, Hindu, and human—within the movement. An ambiguous "Hindu secular" of both an upper-caste and a lower-caste variety seeks to displace caste while redefining religion. It is this Hindu secular that provides fertile ground for an ascendant Hindu nationalism. It also is the space of an ambiguous caste erasure, one that marks without naming. The everyday politics of sociality, college festivals, and competitions reveals the slippages and tensions between caste, religion, and the secular. Through this exploration, this essay has sought to draw attention to the everyday politics of secularism, one that critically apprehends the tensions and dynamics between public and private, tradition and modernity, religion and the secular.

ACKNOWLEDGMENTS

An earlier version of portions of this essay appeared in *Social Analysis* 50(3), Winter 2006: 38–60.

NOTES

1. While Louis Dumont's work rendered caste as a "traditional" religious system, the historical anthropology of caste has demonstrated how understandings of the caste system, by both anthropologists and the state, are linked to the administrative and knowledge practices of the colonial state (cf. Appadurai 1986b; Cohn 1987a;

Dirks 1987). In this essay, I explore how we can apprehend caste within everyday, institutional contexts.

2. Of course, the history and scope of the reservation system must be contextualized within the larger history of the politics of caste in the emergence of Indian nationalism; the tensions between Dalit leader B. R. Ambedkar and Gandhi on the question of separate electorates for untouchables, which Gandhi opposed; and the ways in which the Indian constitution has defined the right to equality (see Galantar 1984).

3. For example, the Bahujan Samaj Party and the Samajwadi Party, both of which have strengths in the state of Uttar Pradesh.

4. The term "Dalit" (literally, downtrodden or oppressed, from the Sanskrit root *dal*, meaning "broken" or "crushed"), used to refer to those understood as untouchables, expresses the politicized self-definition by various strands of the anticaste movement within India today. Rejecting the term "Harijan" (Children of God), coined by Gandhi, as condescending, the term "Dalit" seeks to draw attention to the perceived condition of oppression faced by untouchables today.

5. Here, I draw on Vivek Dareshwar's suggestive article (1993) where he outlines the ways in which caste is repressed within the secular self-understanding of the upper-caste and -class citizen in modern India. He argues that we need to understand caste as a relational identity marker within concrete institutional and ideological formations in order to move beyond the tradition-modernity dichotomy that characterizes the ways caste has been understood.

6. For some sense of this debate, see Bhargava (1998a).

7. Onam is the largest festival in the Indian state of Kerala, lasting for ten days and falling during the Malayali month of Chingam (August–September). It marks the homecoming of legendary King Mahabali, celebrates the harvest, and is a time when homes are cleaned, families gather, and gifts are exchanged.

8. For more information on the distinction between Brahmanical and non-Brahmanical gods, see Mines (this volume).

PART FOUR

Practicing Religion

The "world religions" of Hinduism, Buddhism, Islam, Jainism, and Sikhism, as well as Christianity and Judaism, have long found a home in South Asia.[1] Perhaps it is this flowering of so many religious traditions that has led many Westerners to imagine that South Asia is a very "spiritual" place. For many middle class Americans and Europeans, as well as Asians, the practice of yoga, meditation, Ayurvedic medicine, and other "Eastern" traditions has been promoted as a healthy, spiritual alternative to our harried, anxiety-filled and materially overwhelming lives. That is, South Asian religions have, since the nineteenth century, been structured by Westerners in opposition to capitalist values and economic culture. However, looking at the practical religious experiences of residents of the region, it turns out that material well-being, politics, power relations, and the violence these sometimes entail are also aspects of South Asian religious life. The intertwining of religion with politics and economics can be discerned in even the briefest outline of the histories of these religions in South Asia.

What today we refer to as "Hinduism"[2] is practiced by the majority of Indians and Nepalis as well as by a large minority of Sri Lankans. Hindus trace the roots of their religion back at least 3,500 years to a set of Sanskrit texts called the Vedas. The Vedas, which include mythology, ritual instruction, magical formulas, philosophy, and criticism, formed the basis of what is often referred to as Brahmanical Hinduism. Brahmanical Hinduism took the form of "orthodox" or "orthoprax" sacrificial rituals performed and controlled by Brahman priests, who, for the most part, were the ones who wrote, read, and studied the Vedas. These Brahmans were considered to be the highest class in a four-class (*varna*) system that some see as the beginnings of what is now commonly called "caste." Richard Davis (1995: 12–16) describes how, beginning perhaps around 500 BCE, some scholars became impatient with and critical of Brahmanical hegemony over the rituals of sacrifice. These scholars began to reflect critically upon the actual meanings of the sacrifice and the Vedas. In a set of texts called the Upanishads, they developed philosophical concepts such as *moksha* (release), *sannyāsa* (renunciation), *karma* (actions), *samsāra* (transmigration or rebirth), *yōga* (disciplined practice), and *dharma* (codes of conduct appropriate to different classes of creatures), among others. These still form the basis of much Hindu thought and action.

In fact, it wasn't until about the seventh century CE that Hinduism started to shift significantly toward a theistic imagination, where gods such as Siva, Vishnu, and Sakti, among many others, were represented in images and worshiped in temples. This marked the beginning of a new religious focus on *bhakti*, or devotion, a mode of worship that emphasized a direct (that is, unmediated by Brahman priests) emotional connection between worshipers and the gods they loved. Bhakti remains today the dominant, some would say "popular," mode of Hindu practice, and as Diana Eck (1981) has shown in an engaging introduction to popular Hindu worship, it is eyesight (*darshan*), the exchange of vision between devotee and god, that lies at the heart of bhakti worship (see also Fuller 1992, and Mines, this part). Historically, Hindu kings—who allied themselves variously to competing sects associated with certain gods, for example, Siva as opposed to Vishnu—used temple construction and patronage as one important means of asserting hegemony over a territory (see Mines, this part). In cities, towns, and villages today, the establishment and patronage of temples remains closely tied to social, political, and economic power (see, e.g., Appadurai 1981; Fuller 1992; Dirks 1987). In this way, Hinduism has been part and parcel of power struggles and historical changes since its inception. To cite another example, responses of Indian nationalists to nineteenth-century British colonial concepts of the religion and nation are part of what informs today's Hinduism (this is true for South Asian Islam, as well). And now Hinduism has become linked to the politics of the nation-state in the form of Hindu nationalism, a religious politics that has led to new political parties vying for elected positions in parliament and also to sometimes violent clashes between interest groups or "communities" defined by religious identity.

Buddhism and Jainism both developed out of the same period of reflection and the same critical reassessment of exclusionary Brahmanical control of sacrifice as did the Upanishads. Both religions stress that the path to liberation or enlightenment is one of austerity and renunciation. Both encourage monastic orders for both men (monks) and women (nuns). And both teach that enlightenment can be achieved by anyone, regardless of social class or standing. Jainism was founded by Mahavira, or "Great Hero" (599–527 BCE). Born a prince in a warrior family, Mahavira renounced attachments to the material world and defined the path that today Jains strive to follow. The basic principle of Jainism is "that all living things have an immortal soul (*jīva*) that should strive to be liberated from matter (*ajīva*)" (Levinson 1996: 101). Matter, in the form of karma (action), clings to the soul, thus tying the soul to the material world in an endless cycle of rebirth (*samsāra*). In order to be liberated from this cycle, one should follow an ascetic path that includes renunciation of sex, vices, anger, greed, ego, and even attachments formed by love, pain, and pleasure. Prominent in Jainism, too, is the practice of *ahimsa*, nonviolence to all living things. Mahatma Gandhi's influential method of resistance through "nonviolence" is based in part upon this Jain concept. Such a path is too difficult for most humans, who must do the best they can and work for a higher rebirth that will provide them the opportunity and strength to renounce the world, to become a nun or monk, and then, finally, achieve liberation. Most of the world's Jains, numbering about five million, live in India.

Buddha was born as Siddartha Gautama (566–486 BCE). Like Mahavira, he was born a prince in a kingly family whose company and values he renounced. After years of ascetic wandering, Buddha achieved nirvana while meditating under a fig tree. Out of compassion, Buddha devoted his life to teaching others how to follow his example and break the cycle of death and rebirth—a cycle that causes only suffering—and attain nirvana, or enlightenment. The path to nirvana resembles in many ways the Jain path: practice self-discipline, meditation, and wisdom (Carrithers 1983: 71). Buddhism was a proselytizing religion, and as a consequence it spread very quickly all over Asia, where it is still widely practiced in many places (Sri Lanka, Nepal, Southeast Asia, Japan, China, Tibet, and Korea). Though it is no longer widespread in India, Buddha's message that enlightenment is available to all, and not just to the higher classes of society, is one reason that beginning in the 1950s, the social reformer Ambedkar encouraged India's so-called Untouchables to convert to Buddhism. Islam and Christianity, too, are often attractive to the lowest castes for their emphasis on human equality (parity, more accurately) in relation to God (though socially caste has persisted to some extent in all of these religious groups).

Islam is the religion of the majority populations of Pakistan and Bangladesh, with minority populations throughout South Asia. Islam was founded in 610 CE in Arabia when Muhammad began receiving the revelations now collected in the Qur'an. The Qur'an is considered by Muslims to be the word of Allah as revealed to Muhammad. Along with the Hadith (books recording Muhammad's own words and actions in life), the Qur'an is the authoritative text of Islam. The religion spread very quickly, moving west throughout the Middle East, across North Africa, and into Spain; and moving east into what are now Iraq, Iran, Afghanistan, and parts of Pakistan. Islam did not establish itself firmly in the rest of South Asia, particularly India and beyond, until 1206, when Qutb al-Din declared himself the sultan of Delhi after defeating the Hindu ruler. In 1526, this sultanate was supplanted by the Mughal Empire when the Emperor Babar entered India from Central Asia and established wide hegemony over much of what is now north India and Pakistan (Davis 1995: 32). Just as Hindu kings established their territories in part by building and patronizing temples, so, too, did many Muslim rulers establish territories in part by constructing and patronizing mosques (Muslim rulers also continued to establish Hindu temples in many cases, to uphold strong relations with Hindu subjects). It is important to note here that the vast majority of South Asian Muslims today did not migrate to India from elsewhere, but rather are the descendants of indigenous South Asians who converted to Islam as many as seven hundred years ago. Such conversions continue today, though not in large numbers.

Islam in South Asia takes various forms, with followers distinguishing among several different sects and movements. One of the principal distinctions in South Asian Islam occurs between those who pursue a more orthodox Islam that sticks closely to textual traditions and those who pursue a more mystical or devotional path, Sufism, which often includes the recognition and worship of saints. Both orthodox Muslims and followers of Sufism rely upon Islamic texts and codes of action such as the "five pillars of Islam."[3] But while orthodox Muslims adhere strictly to textually prescribed behaviors and laws and "submit" to the authority and power of Allah (God) as revealed in the texts, many Sufi movements emphasize less the textual and more the personal and mystical relation between humans and Allah (Davis 1995: 35). Some Sufi sects believe that certain persons—saints—are specially endowed with God's power and can channel and dispense that power to other people, places, and things. Because these sects emphasize the presence of God's power in persons and places, they have often resulted in syncretic movements attracting Hindus, who also see divine energy enlivening objects and humans and places on earth (see Flueckiger, this volume). Many orthodox Muslims—usually urban and educated—challenge the validity of Sufi sects because they regard Sufi saint veneration as somewhere between ignorant folk practice and heresy. "Islamization" refers to the religio-political process whereby orthodox Muslims work to get all Muslims to adhere to a more orthodox understanding of Islam. Some of the conflicts between different ways of being Muslim can be seen in Marsden's chapter in this part.

Sikhism was founded by Guru Nanak (1469–1539), the first of Sikhism's ten gurus. Guru Nanak was born to Hindu parents, and as an adult renounced his settled life and wandered South Asia in search of truth. The religion he founded is often described as a syncretic blend of Hindu and Muslim traditions, though today Sikhs see their religion as independent and true, not derivative. Sikhs believe that a person can unite with God (Sat Nam, literally "True Name") through discipline and purification, which help one overcome the five vices of greed, anger, self-centered pride, lust, and attachment to material things. By acting, instead, with contentment, honesty, compassion, and patience, a person can attain a higher rebirth, and eventually, through many rebirths, can attain union with God (Levinson 1996: 217–19). Meditation is a primary form of worship for Sikhs, and the primary Sikh text is called the Granth, a compilation of verses by many authors that is used as an authoritative guide to beliefs and attitudes. Sikhs worship in a temple called a *gudwara*, the most famous of which is the Golden Temple in Amritsar, India, in the state of Punjab, a site with its own history of political violence. Observant Sikhs are recognizable by their adherence to the "five k's": *kesh* (uncut hair, including beards—men usually tie their head hair in a turban), *kangha* (a small comb worn in the hair), *kara* (a steel bracelet), *kachhahera* (knee-length "britches" usually worn under other clothes), and *kirpan* (a ceremonial sword).

Unlike Buddhism, Jainism, and some forms of Hinduism where renunciation is the key to release from samsara, in Sikhism it is believed that a person can obtain union with god while living everyday life as a married, family person, what South Asians sometimes refer to as a "householder." Furthermore, Sikhs do not find it necessary to follow a path of "nonviolence"—they may eat meat, fight in the military, and kill in good cause. Most of the world's twenty million Sikhs live in northwest India, in the Punjab, but many have migrated to Europe and North America as well (see Hall in part 6).

Christianity, practiced by only about 3 percent of South Asians, also has a surprisingly long history in the region. Myth has it that St. Thomas came to Kerala in 42 CE and established a Syrian Christian community there. Whether or not this is true, it is certain that by 600 CE there existed in Kerala a flourishing Syrian Christian community (Fuller 1976). Jesuit missionaries brought Roman Catholicism to South Asia beginning in the early sixteenth century, when the Portuguese Jesuit St. Xavier arrived in Goa, on the west coast of India, and as other Jesuits arrived in Sri Lanka. In Sri Lanka, Dutch colonizers brought Calvinist Protestantism in the seventeenth century, when the British, too, brought Protestantism to India. More recently, evangelical Protestant Christianity has spread in South Asia with foreign, and now native, missionaries "spreading the word." Judaism, too, is practiced in India, though by only a few remaining souls concentrated in Mumbai, Kolkata, and Cochin. Most Indian Jews have now migrated to Israel, and those living in India number only a few thousand. There are records of Jews living in what is now the state of Kerala as early as the tenth century CE, though the earliest (and still active) synagogue there dates from the sixteenth century, in Kochi. Parsis, or Zoroastrians, who follow an ancient religion that originated in Persia, also live in India and Pakistan in very small numbers (up to 100,000), mostly in Mumbai.

Many studies of South Asian religions focus primarily on their textual traditions (the so-called great traditions). The chapters collected in this part demonstrate a long-standing anthropological concern with how people practice or "do" religion in their lives. The religious "doctrines" of the great traditions outlined above only sometimes, and only partly, inform the way that people today practice religion. Practice, some of the chapters show, may sometimes even contradict doctrine to the point of being considered heterodox by religious elites.

* * *

People often speak of "the Hindu Pantheon" as if it were a closed set of gods related in definite patterns of which all Hindus are aware. It is true that most Hindus will have no difficulty talking about major gods such as Siva, Vishnu, and Krishna, and forms of the Goddess such as Kali, Durga, and Parvati, as well as some of the relations among them. However, every place—be it a village, urban neighborhood, or town—has its own distinctive set of gods. This set may include the pan-Hindu gods mentioned above, but also includes local gods whose identities are unique and tied to the history of the people and events of that particular place. Mines's chapter describes the gods who inhabit one village in south India, and explains some of the ways in which gods and humans are considered alike and different.

McKim Marriott's famous essay revels in a north Indian Hindu festival called Holi, a riotous spring festival that celebrates the god Krishna in all his youthful exuberance. In Holi festivals all over north India, revelers spray each other with colored powders and waters in a wild carnivalesque party. In Marriott's depiction, we see how villagers use Holi to critique the everyday forms of gender and caste relations, making their Holi into a "ritual of rebellion," that is, a ritual that exposes and critiques the power structures of everyday life.

Kim Gutschow's chapter takes on squarely the differences that often exist between "doctrine"—the texts and rules, both written and spoken ideals of a religion—and "practice," the religious life that persons enact in their everyday lives. Here we see that while Buddhist doctrine states that gender is no more a hindrance to enlightenment than caste or class, the reality of the situation is very different for Buddhist nuns in Kashmir. Gender does make a difference.

One of the pressing issues in the Islamic world in the twenty-first century is the spread of fundamentalist movements through a process of "Islamization," and the sometimes violent tactics that some fundamentalist groups take in promoting their radical form of Islamic law. Pakistan, home to millions of moderate Muslims, is one area of the world where this issue is particularly relevant. Magnus Marsden's chapter analyzes and complicates simplistic views of this Islamization process as it works in Chitral, a region in northern Pakistan that has been affected a great deal by many different Islamic movements, including the Taliban. He finds that Muslims in that area find many creative ways to negotiate their differences and to live a rich and varied Muslim life, a life that is also a mindful life in which different people work to live together in peace.

Naveeda Khan's chapter also looks at Muslim life in Pakistan. She focuses on a devout family living in the city of Lahore and their surprising, to her, relation with a jinn—a powerful supernatural being—who lived with them in their house for several years. This jinn would make its presence and thoughts known through a young daughter in the family. Khan's chapter is a reflection on family, childhood, and friendship, a reflection made possible through the presence of this jinn.

The final chapter in this part demonstrates an important aspect of religious life all over South Asia, namely the ways in which religions are not closed containers that separate people into warring communities but are rather syncretic. That is, much religious practice in South Asia blends aspects and elements of different religious ideas and practices. In this case, Joyce Flueckiger relates how Amma, a female Muslim religious healer in the south Indian city of Hyderabad, brings together, as at a crossroads, not only people of all different religions, but also ideas, stories, and symbols from different religions into her own Muslim healing practice.

NOTES

1. Statistics posted in 2009 by the U.S. Department of State (www.state.gov/www/background_notes/index.html) indicate the following religious populations: INDIA: Hindu 81.4%; Muslim 12.4%; Christian 2.3%; Sikh 1.9%. Other groups including Buddhist, Jain, Parsi, are under 1% of the total population. PAKISTAN: Muslim 97% with small minorities of Christians, Hindus, and others. BANGLADESH: Muslim 88.3%; Hindu 10.5%; Christian, Buddhist, and others under 1%. NEPAL: Hindu 81%; Buddhist 11%; Muslim 4%; and others 4%. SRI LANKA: Theravada Buddhist 70%;, Hindu 15%; Muslim 7.5%; Christian 7.5%. Statistics for Sri Lanka are from the 2001 Census of Sri Lanka, accessed 5-18-09 at http://en.wikipedia.org/wiki/Religion_in_Sri_Lanka#cite_note-DCS-0.

2. We put the term "Hinduism" in quotation marks because the term was not in use throughout the history of the religion. "Hindu" derives from "Indu," a term used by Muslim migrants to mean something like "all those people over there who are not Muslim and who live on the other side of the Indus River." It was not until the nineteenth and twentieth centuries that the term became consistently applied to a religious community. Throughout the long history of "Hinduism," there has not ever been a unified community, text, or set of universal beliefs, though today's Hindu nationalist movements would argue otherwise.

3. These five pillars are (1) *Shahadah,* the declaration that "there is no god but God and Muhammad is his messenger"; (2) *Salat,* or prayer, which is ideally conducted five times a day, facing Mecca—and all over South Asia, one can hear the call to prayer coming from the mosques five times daily; (3) *Zakat,* a tax levied on all Muslims that is used to support members of the Muslim community who are in need; (4) fasting during Ramadan, the month during which Muhammad is said to have received the Qur'an; and (5) *Hajj,* or pilgrimage to Mecca—all Muslims who are able to do this at least once in their life should do so.

17

The Hindu Gods in a South Indian Village

Diane P. Mines

In Yanaimangalam, a village in Tamil Nadu, south India, residents compare both castes and gods along several dimensions. They describe castes as relatively high (*ocanta*) versus relatively low (*talnta*), as big (*periya*) versus little (*cinna*), as pure (*cuttam*) versus impure (*acuttam*), the latter correlating roughly with vegetarian on the one hand and meat-eating on the other. They describe gods in similar terms, as high to low, big to little, vegetarian to meat-eating, and also as soft (*metuvāka*) to fierce (*ukkiramāka*). Both humans and gods may be further distinguished residentially. Higher and "bigger" (powerful, landowning) castes live in a central residential cluster, while the lower and "little" (landless, service-providing) castes live on the peripheries of the village and in small hamlets out across the fields. It is the same with gods. The higher, more "pure" gods live in the interiors of the central village: in temples on village streets and in alcoves and framed posters on the walls of residents' houses. Low-ranking, "impure," meat-eating gods live outside: out in the fields or the wastelands beyond, outside the house in back courtyards facing away from the house. Given these parallel associations between humans on the one hand and gods on the other, it is certainly easy to see why many scholars have presented analyses where the pantheon of ranked gods "symbolizes" ranks among humans (e.g., Fuller 1987: 33; Dumont 1986 [1957]: 460; cf. Mines 1997a).

In this essay, I wish to introduce some of the gods of Yanaimangalam by briefly describing some of the stories and histories of temples and gods in that village. In every Hindu village and neighborhood in South Asia reside many gods, but in no two places does the very same set of gods live. Some gods, such as the universally recognized gods Siva, Vishnu, Krishna (an avatar, or incarnation, of Vishnu), and the goddess Kali, can be found all over South Asia, in villages, towns, and cities both north and south. Others, such as Yanaimangalam's Vellalakantan, are unique to one place. Scholars have sometimes described the distinction between universally recognized gods and strictly local ones as a distinction between a "great tradition" and a "little tradition" of Hinduism. But residents of Yanaimangalam have their own set of distinctions, too.

Residents of Yanaimangalam distinguish among three kinds of gods, what I will gloss here as Brahmanical ("great tradition") gods, village goddesses (*ūr ammaṇ*), and fierce gods (*māṭaṇ* or *pēy*, lit. "ghost"). As noted above, residents compare these gods along several dimensions of contrast—high to low, pure to impure, vegetarian to meat-eating. But the dimension of contrast they stress the most is that of soft to fierce. For example, when I asked a neighbor, Ramayya Thevar, why the village goddess went on procession through the village streets while the fierce god Cutalaimatan ("Fierce God of the Cremation Ground") did not, he spoke not of relative rank but of relative benevolence. The goddess is mother (*tāy*), he said. She protects people and the village. Fierce gods like Cutalaimatan, he said, are dangerous to people in the village. Similarly, one day when I was hiking across the burning dry summer fields from the fierce Cutalaimatan's temple with two young priests, Subramaniam and Venki, I asked these young Brahmans why the Brahmanical god Murukan, son of Parvati and Siva and brother of elephant-headed Ganesh, lived in the village's central residential area, nestled among houses and freely gazing down residential streets, while Cutalaimatan lived so far out across the fields in the wastelands around the cremation ground. They replied that Murukan, like the rest of his *type* (using the English word and meaning Brahmanical gods such as Siva, Krishna, and Ganesh), is soft (*metuvāka*) while fierce gods are cruel or fearsome (*payaṅkaramāṇatu*).

From one end of the spectrum to the other, soft gods (of which the Brahmanical are the softest) are those who are generally calm, stable, and beneficent. Fierce gods on the other hand are wild, unstable, and unpredictable. The fierce gods may prove protective and beneficent at one time, then cruel at another. They may unpredictably attack a person if they feel the slightest insult or if they simply feel overheated by, for example, seeing a beautiful young woman walking by. The village goddess belongs in between, as befits her well-known dual or "ambivalent" nature (Doniger 1980; Ramanujan 1986: 55–61; Kinsley 1986), where sometimes she is identified with the Brahmanical and benign, the cool goddess Parvati, devout wife of Siva, while at other times she is identified with the fearsome Durga or Kali—unmarried forms of the goddess who, in a not really very motherlike manner at all, wield weapons, ride lions, crack skulls, and drink blood to match their hot nature.

BRAHMANICAL TEMPLES

On the day of my first visit to Yanaimangalam, well before I had moved in, I was invited to "see" the gods in the Siva temple at the end of the Agraharam street, the traditional Brahman community of the village. Officious elders sent a boy to fetch the temple's priest. The priest arrived. He was blue-eyed blind with cataracts, a bit plump, and he wore his white hair in the manner of Brahman priests, shaved in front and with the long hairs in back tied behind his head in a knot. I followed him down the street and a dozen or more children followed behind me like an eager wagging tail. At the end of the street loomed the temple—the largest structure in the village. Weeds grew from fissures in the weathered stone walls, long ago painted in red and white vertical stripes. In front of the temple, a square tank choked with lotuses gave way to the flooded rice fields beyond. The priest unlocked the thick, castle-like wooden doors with a prodigious skeleton key. They creaked open and we, along with the sun's light, entered the temple's dank interior. The light startled temple bats, and as we ducked through the ever lower doorways that led further into the temple toward the interior "womb-rooms" (*garbha-graha*) that housed the images of gods (see fig. 17.1), surely hundreds of bats shot past us out of those same doorways in through which we had ducked. The blind priest walked smoothly through their parting rapids and I, *knowing* bats to be good at avoiding even moving objects, tried to follow smoothly in his wake. My failure in this endeavor to "look cool" worked much to the amusement of the giggly tail of children who squirmed so close behind me. Once we had all traded places with the bats and approached the shrines (there were several in the many-halled temple, to different forms of Siva and to his consort goddess Parvati), the priest lit camphor to show us the deities one by one. A bronze image of Nataraja, the "Dancing Siva" (fig. 17.2), was clothed in leopard-skin cotton and draped in wilting flowers from the morning's *puja*, or worship. The flame sparkled off his chiseled features and off the bronze flames that framed him. As the priest circled the camphor flame, we looked at the god, obtaining darshan, a visual exchange. Then the priest, with batlike radar, passed a tray of purifying ash (*vipūti*) out to the few worshipers present. I placed two rupees on the tray as an offering, took a pinch of ash to smear my forehead, then headed outside, now shielding my eyes from the open sunlight.

After visiting the Siva temple, I was beckoned down a wide earthen path leading between the rice fields to the river that flowed on the north side of the village. There, another priest, who specialized in serving Vishnu, conducted me through another large temple. There I received not ash (ash is Siva's special substance) but some red powder (*kumkumam*) to dot my forehead and some leaves from Vishnu's favorite plant, *tulsi*. This temple, I later learned, was much older than the three-hundred-year-old Siva temple. The Vishnu temple was six hundred years old. This village, I realized, had a long history.

The stone walls of both the Siva and Vishnu temples are adorned with inscriptions that bear witness to regional and village history. The inscriptions are chiseled in several languages, including Telugu, Malayalam, and old Tamil interspersed with Granta script, all unreadable to average mod-

Figure 17.1. Darshan. Worshipers look into the "womb-room" while a
Brahman priest bathes the Murukan, son of Siva, in cooling milk.

ern Tamil readers. The inscriptions are, however, clear signs—indexes—of
the kingly past of temple and village patronage. The inscriptions tell of the
founding of the temples, name the kings who founded them, and record important transactions, gifts, patrons, and hereditary servants of the temples.
Smaller village temples to Krishna (an avatar, or incarnation, of Vishnu) and
Ganesh (the elephant-headed son of Siva) also bear such inscriptions.

Yanaimangalam's red-and-white-striped temples to Siva, Vishnu, Krishna, and Ganesh put Yanaimangalam on the map of history. They link the
village both to the administrative present and to official histories, to Sanskrit myth, to high art and architecture, and to literary languages. These
are temples that—along with Krishna, Pillaiyar (Ganesh), and Murukan
temples and shrines—make Yanaimangalam part of the "great" tradition of
Indian Civilization (the Classical, Sanskritic, Male, Universal, etc., to borrow
from Ramanujan's 1973 description of great traditions). These temples are
nothing less than historical data, data recorded in stone and then recorded
again in colonial and Indian government documents that detail the bronze
sculptured images, the dates of temple construction, the kings who commissioned them. All of this information is based on the inscriptions etched
into temple walls, translated into English (the language of the great bureau-

Figure 17.2. Waving a camphor flame around Nataraja, the "Dancing Siva."

cratic tradition) in epigraphical records that may be found in libraries at the University of Chicago, at Harvard, and at Berkeley, too. When I lived in the village, government officials would come to Yanaimangalam in their jeeps to record again an inscription, or to show the new district collector the glory of the region's past inscribed in the *paṭṭikāṭus* (the "rustic," "hick" villages) of the region. Village residents are aware of the historical interest outsiders have in these temples, and are eager to show them off to visiting officials and, it seems, anthropologists. Today these old Brahmanical temples are administered centrally from Ambasamuttiram, a large temple town about twenty-five kilometers west of Yanaimangalam.

VILLAGE GODDESSES

Despite the historical and artistic significance of the Brahmanical temples, very few villagers spend much of their time or many of their economic resources worshiping in those temples. Occasionally a Brahman family from Mumbai or Delhi, or Chennai or Tirunelveli Town, or, in one case, from Monterey, California—strangers to Yanaimangalam's current population—would come to visit one of these gods whom they claimed as their lineage (*kula*) god (usually it was Vishnu by the riverbank they came to visit and claimed as their own). But everyone in the village worships the village goddess. To her is attributed the power of fertility—fertility of soil, of humans, and of animals. There is no one in the village unaffected by her power (*cakti*) to assure good crops of rice and to help the living bear healthy children.

Eleven goddess temples and shrines dot the map of Yanaimangalam. Each of the five residential areas that Yanaimangalam comprises has its own goddess temple. In addition, several lineages sponsor their own temple to the village goddess. Though the goddesses have different names (Yanaiyamman, Uccimakakkali, Muppatatiyamman, Mariyamman, among others) as well as independent temples on different sites, all eleven are said to be the same power (*orē cakti*). As the Tamil saying goes, "The life is one, the forms are two [many]" (*uyir oṇṟu, uruvam iraṇṭu*). There are some other goddesses, such as the "fierce goddess" named Issakkiyamman, who are said to be a "different power" (*vēṟu cakti*).

Puzzling over the many forms of the one life that is the village goddess, I asked a respected older man in the village, Virapandi Muppanar, to relate the "birth story" of the goddess named Muppatatiyamman, who lives in a small alcove built into the wall of a house compound. I noticed her one day as I was passing by. He denied any knowledge of her "birth story" and suggested I ask someone else. Obviously I had asked the wrong question, so I rephrased it. This time I asked how it was that the same goddess could be in so many places at once. He then started to tell me the story I had been hoping for. It wasn't the story of her birth, but the story of how she came to be in Yanaimangalam, in this place and that.

He started out by relating a little about how in the old days, long before there were people in the village, the goddess had come down from the north and passed through the area, wandering about, pausing to rest here and there. As she walked, small traces of her powerful substance, her *sakti* (*cakti* in Tamil), were left behind in the places she traversed. In the places she paused or stopped to rest, her sakti soaked into the soil, and there it remains to this day. Sometimes her presence in the earth is discovered by people. Other times her image might appear on its own, as they say about the main village goddess, Yanaiyamman. Virapandi Muppanar continued by telling me how her presence on the spot by the wall was discovered.

> It was a long time ago, about five generations ago, about the time of the white man, and about the time of the Vikkayamarattin Kottai story. There was an unmarried boy, about eighteen years old, one of four children in his family. The goddess was always possessing him. She would possess him and he would dance from village to village. His family picked a fight with him over this strange behavior, so he ran away. But a few days later he came back. He said to his mother: "I'll show you the truth." He took a clay pot full of burning rags and danced with it all night around the village. A lot of people figured he was just pretending to be possessed, and they spoke disparagingly about him. He went all around the village and early the next morning

he came back. He went straight into the shed under the tamarind tree in his family courtyard, and there he put down the burning fire pot, came out, and locked the door behind him. A few days later, he returned. It was a Tuesday. He took up the pot again and went around the village. Even though several days had passed, the pot was still aflame! It was still burning, just like that! Seeing this, the people changed their mind and thought that there must be a goddess in that place [in the shed by the wall].

As far as the human residents of Yanaimangalam are concerned, goddesses have "always already" been in the village. Marking the earth with her wanderings, she is rooted in the soil, and her image might spring up anywhere, like a tree's root might throw up shoots far from its trunk. Her power is a quality that shapes the village's topography: it create zones of greater and lesser energy (sakti), and discovering those places links human beings to that power.

FIERCE GODS

In Yanaimangalam, there are at least sixteen temples and shrines to fierce gods and goddesses. Most of these gods live on the margins of the village territory, outside of the residential areas, out in the fields or beyond in the wasteland (*kāṭu*) (fig. 17.3). Even those that live within the residential village are nonetheless talked about as living outside. "Outside" is, after all, a relative term: outside the house in the courtyard (fig. 17.4), or outside the courtyard on the street. Unlike the village goddesses and unlike Brahmanical deities, fierce gods are not paraded through the streets in processions, nor are they generally brought inside the house for worship. If a fierce god residing in a house courtyard proves too violent or touchy for peaceful daily life, families have been known to remove them as they brought them—in a handful of earth—taking them out into the wasteland, further away from settled areas.

As unpredictable and unstable as anger itself, these gods may protect or attack. Residents of Yanaimangalam give them wide berth in many daily contexts, choosing their paths of movement to avoid directly passing by or standing in front of the hot gaze of a fierce god. In myth and ritual, these gods are often subordinated to the village goddesses as guardians who live near but outside her temple, much like the humans who live outside the central village residential area are thought by many higher-caste residents to be subordinate and unruly as well.

While kings and, more recently, wealthy upper-caste residents established and patronized Brahmanical temples, and while the goddess traveled to what is now Yanaimangalam independently of humans, leaving powerful traces in the places she moved and rested (hence "self-appearing"), village

Figure 17.3. Vellalakantan, a fierce god out in the fields.

residents see fierce gods as having come to Yanaimangalam in two other ways. More rarely, fierce gods are created in the village itself: as gods or goddesses born from men or women who have met violent deaths. All over Tamil Nadu, fierce gods are born in violence and injustice. Their stories of origin are sometimes local stories of humans murdered and then reborn as violent deities (Blackburn 1988; Trawick 1991; Mines 2005). Or, their origins may be linked to Brahmanical mythologies (*purānas*) where fierce gods are the offspring of anger, intrigue, and violence or injustice among those gods thought more benign (Knipe 1989; Hiltebeitel 1989). Either way, the violence of their origins and vengeful natures is often reflected in their murderous depictions as sword-wielding mustachioed heroes ready to fight (fig. 17.3) or as fanged, terrifying women who look ready to bite. The following case illustrates the ferocity of these gods. Here is what I learned in 1990 when I asked Picchaiya, an "untouchable" resident of an area of Yanaimangalam called Middle Hamlet, about a small, faceless clay image in a palmyra tree grove at the edge of the village. (This is my retelling of his explication.)

Figure 17.4. Cooking rice for "Backyard Matan." This fierce god is present in the small white-washed earthen image on the lower left.

One day, about forty years ago, a Thevar youth—unmarried and about eighteen years old—was walking up the road to the main village. He walked past a temple festival that Middle Hamlet S.C. [so-called untouchables] were conducting to their god Panaiyatiyan ["He at the foot of the palmyra tree"]. The higher-caste Thevar youth threw out some derogatory remarks as he walked past the festival, angering the fierce god. A few yards further up the road, just before entering the first residential street, the youth suddenly fell to the ground vomiting blood. He died as suddenly as he fell, and everyone attributed his death to the fierce god's anger. In 1990, the youth's lineage members conducted a puja for their ancestor. At this time the identity of this Thevar youth [whom they referred to as "grandfather"], was becoming conflated with Panaiyatiyan himself. The victim was becoming a lesser form of the god who had killed him.

Second, and more often, fierce gods come into Yanaimangalam from elsewhere, often through the agency of village residents who, often unwittingly, transfer these gods—or spread them, rather—to the village. They bring gods bodily and they bring them in substances, such as trees and, commonly, "handfuls of earth" (*piṭimaṇ*) (see also Inglis 1985), as the following story, summarized from the stories told to me by several village residents, illustrates.

Many years ago, a group of men from Yanaimangalam went up into the forest near Cabarimalai [a nearby mountain that starts in Tamil Nadu and peaks in Kerala] to cut a tree for the flagpole in front of the Siva temple. In the tree-cutting party was a Carpenter to do the cutting, a Thevarmar man, and two Pillaimar men [these are caste names]. They ascended the mountain and searched the forest for a tall tree. They found it. They cut it down. They brought it back to the village and set it up in front of the Siva temple. Then, all at once, the four men were struck violently ill. A specialist determined that ghosts and other fierce beings inhabited the tree they had brought down from the mountain. Being deprived of their home, these evil beings had grabbed hold of [piṭiccatu] the culprits, that is, possessed them. One remedy was available. The families of each of the men were instructed to go back to the place where they found the tree, take a handful of earth from that spot, and bring it back to the village. There they should deposit the earth near their houses and on those spots build permanent shrines to these fierce beings, adopting those gods into their lineage as lineage gods (kulatēvaṅkaḷ). This way the gods would leave the men alone. And that is how the temples for Kalamatasami, Talavaymatasami, Cappanimatasami, and Cutalaimatan-by-the-Carpenter's-House were established.

A similar story, first told to me by a woman from the Thevar neighborhood and retold here, reveals how the god Sivalaperi Cutalaimatan came to Yanaimangalam.

One day, a Thevar man went all the way to a village called Sivalaperi about thirty miles from Yanaimangalam in order to swear an oath to the god Cutalaimatan, who lived in that village. The man had been accused of theft in the village, and the accuser agreed that it the suspect swore his innocence in front of this fearsome god, he would let the matter drop. So, the accused went to Sivalaperi, and there he apparently lied to the god, judging from the subsequent events. A black goat followed the man all the way home from the temple. Once home, the man tried to kill the goat (for curry), but the goat grew huge and attacked both him and his kinsmen with disastrous and deadly consequences—a pregnant woman in the family was killed. To quell the god's righteous anger, only one recourse was available: the accused had to not only admit his guilt, but also establish a shrine to the god in his backyard. He did this by returning to Sivalaperi with surviving family members. From there he took a handful of earth from the earthen temple floor, and brought it back to Yanaimangalam, where he "planted" it, and thereby the god's power, in the courtyard outside his house.

Just as the goddess's sakti resides in the soil, so too does the power of fierce gods. Even the images of these fierce gods themselves are most often formed from earth (fig. 17.4). These may be simple temporary mounds of earth formed by devotees for worship, mounds that then erode back into earth with wind and rain, only to be re-formed for the next puja, or they may be terra-cotta images sculpted by Potters (Inglis 1985).

* * *

In Yanaimangalam, there are thirty-five temples to the three kinds of gods described above. Most days, the temples are quiet places. Priests go there daily, or maybe only twice a week in some cases, to feed and bathe and care for the gods. Passersby may drop in to receive darshan, to offer a prayer, or to make a request. On their way home from morning baths in the river, many drop by the Vishnu temple or the goddess temple to see the gods and obtain some red powder or white ash to smear on their clean foreheads, a final cleansing ritual to begin the day. For most of these temples, there are also occasional festivals—in some cases there are several festivals a year, others are annual, and some are even less frequent. Some festivals are relatively small, limited to just one lineage in the village. Others are multi-caste affairs in which most village residents participate.

I wish to end this descriptive essay with one more story. This story was told to me by Andi, a low-ranking man of the Dhobi, or Washerman, caste. Though low-ranking, he is a powerful man in the Cutalaimatan temple because of his ancestor's link to that god. This story is about how gods can alter human relations, including relations of rank between caste groups in the village. This story hints at how temples serve as venues where caste rankings can be undermined, challenged, and sometimes even reversed.

> One day, about a hundred years ago, a man of the powerful, landowning-dominating Muppanar caste was out working in his field by the riverbank. He saw something floating down the river toward him. He fished it out, and found it was a banana shoot. He planted it on the edge of his field.
>
> It just so happened that his field lay in the line of sight of the fierce god Cutalaimatan, whose stone, power-filled image stood nearby, positioned to look across this field. Cutalaimatan is the god of the cremation ground, and he has a propensity to attack—sometimes quite violently—passersby who displease him or who make him jealous. So, people tend to avoid him, to tiptoe around him. But this fellow's field lay right in the god's line of sight, and there wasn't much he could do about that. His best recourse was to defer to the god, to soften him up, and to hope for the best.
>
> The Muppanar farmer's strategy was simple. He tried to win over the god by making a vow. He promised Cutalaimatan that he would give him the first stalk of bananas that his new tree produced, in return for the god's protecting the plant and field.
>
> A year passed and the banana plant flourished and produced a big stalk of bananas. The owner came out and cut the stalk and took it home, forgetting his vow to Cutalaimatan. He took one banana from the stalk, peeled it, and took a big bite. Immediately he choked, spat out the banana, and could eat nothing from then on.

He realized that the fault was his for forgetting his vow, and so this higher-caste man went to see a local man favored by Cutalaimatan, a lower-ranking Dhobi (Washerman) named Mukkan, to enlist his aid and find a solution. He went to Mukkan because he and his entire lineage were the special devotees of Cutalaimatan. They took care of him and he took care of them. Mukkan was the one whose connection to the god was closest: Cutalaimatan regularly possessed him and communicated his needs through this human god-dancer/host (*cāmiyāṭi*). The solution that the Dhobi and the god offered was that the Muppanar man and his whole lineage should adopt Cutalaimatan's younger brother, Mundacami, as their own special god. They should construct a shrine to Mundacami opposite Cutalaimatan's shrine, and worship there from now on, side by side with the low-ranking Dhobis, *as equals*. So, to this day the Muppanar and the Dhobis are equal (*cammam*) in that temple.

A chance event (a banana shoot floating down the river) led to a vow made, and then a vow broken. A vow broken established a permanent relation between a low-ranking, peripheral god and a relatively high-ranking, central caste. This relation between the god Mundacami and the Muppanar lineage is understood as an enduring, substantial, bodily relation between the god and lineage members, and it cannot be attenuated at will. The Muppanar lineage (which corresponds roughly to the local Muppanar caste grouping) in Yanaimangalam is forevermore substantially connected with their new god. The god inhabits their houses, bodies, and lives. The god eats what they eat, the god possesses them, the god fills them with energy and can also cause them illness if displeased. The new relation of "equality" established between Muppanars and Dhobis takes on a social, publicly enacted reality in temple festivals that take place three times a year at the cremation-ground temple that houses both lineage gods. South Indian temple rituals, as is widely reported, are venues where ranks among participants, as well as community inclusions and exclusions, are established through multiple ranked transactions from the god to the devotees in an idiom of "honor" (*mariyātai*) (see, e.g., Appadurai and Breckenridge 1976; Appadurai 1981; Dirks 1987; and Dumont 1986 [1957]). During the festival at the Cutalaimatan/Mundacami temple, one of many ways that ranks are established is through ordered transactions in which the Dhobis receive first honors and the Muppanars receive second honors (and others in order afterward). That is, the Dhobis receive their shares (*paṅku*) of the temple leftovers first, and have authority over the distribution of remaining shares. Moreover, when devotees make their rounds, visiting the gods at the shrine, they pay homage first to Cutalaimatan and his Dhobi god-dancer and only second to the Muppanars' lineage god and god-dancer. The Dhobi, being connected to the older brother god, is, it turns out, first among equals.

18

The Feast of Love

McKim Marriott

I shall try here to interpret Krishna and his cult as I met them in a rural village of northern India while I was conducting my first field venture as a social anthropologist. The village was Kishan Garhi,[1] located across the Jumnā from Mathurā and Vrindaban, a day's walk from the youthful Krishna's fabled land of Vraja.

As it happened, I had entered Kishan Garhi for the first time in early March, not long before what most villagers said was going to be their greatest religious celebration of the year, the festival of Holī. Preparations were already under way. I learned that the festival was to begin with a bonfire celebrating the cremation of the demoness Holikā. Holikā, supposedly fireproofed by devotion to her demon father, King Harnākas, had been burned alive in the fiery destruction plotted by her to punish her brother Prahlāda for his stubborn devotion to the true god, Rāma.[2] I observed two priests and a large crowd of women reconstructing Holikā's pyre with ritual and song: the Brahman master of the village site with a domestic chaplain consecrated the ground of the demoness's reserved plot; the women added wafers and trinkets of dried cow-dung fuel,[3] stood tall straws in a circle around the pile, and finally circumambulated the whole, winding about it protective threads of homespun cotton. Gangs of young boys were collecting other combustibles—if possible in the form of donations, otherwise by stealth—quoting what they said were village rules, that everyone must contribute something and that anything once placed on the Holī pyre could not afterward be removed. I barely forestalled the contribution of one of my new cots; other householders in my lane complained of having lost brooms, parts of doors and carts, bundles of straw thatch, and an undetermined number of fuel cakes from their drying places in the sun.

The adobe houses of the village were being repaired or whitewashed for the great day. As I was mapping the streets and houses for a preliminary survey, ladies of the village everywhere pressed invitations upon me to attend the festival. The form of their invitations was usually the oscillation of a fistful of wet cow-dung plaster in my direction, and the words, "Saheb will play Holī with us?" I asked how it was to be played, but could get no coherent answer. "You must be here to see and to play!" the men insisted.

I felt somewhat apprehensive as the day approached. An educated landlord told me that Holī is the festival most favored by the castes of the fourth estate, the Śūdras. Europeans at the district town advised me to stay indoors, and certainly to keep out of all villages on the festival day. But my village friends said, "Don't worry. Probably no one will hurt you. In any case, no one is to get angry, no matter what happens. All quarrels come to an end. It is a *līlā*—a divine sport of Lord Krishna!" I had read the sacred *Bhāgavata Purāna*'s story about Prahlāda and had heard many of its legends of Krishna's miraculous and amorous boyhood.[4] These books seemed harmless enough. Then, too, Radcliffe-Brown had written in an authoritative anthropological text that one must observe the action of rituals in order to understand the meaning of any myth.[5] I had been instructed by my reading of B. Malinowski, as well as by all my anthropological preceptors and elders that one best observes another culture by participating in it as directly as possible.[6] My duty clearly was to join in the festival as far as I might be permitted.

The celebration began auspiciously, I thought, in the middle of the night as the full moon rose. The great pile of blessed and pilfered fuel at once took flame, ignited by the village fool, for the master of the village site had failed to rouse with sufficient speed from his slumbers. "Victory to Mother Holikā!" the shout went up, wishing her the achievement of final spiritual liberation rather than any earthly conquest, it seemed. A hundred men of all twenty-four castes in the village, both Muslim and Hindu, now crowded about the fire, roasting ears of the new, still-green barley crop in her embers. They marched around the fire in opposite directions and exchanged roasted grains with each other as they passed, embracing or greeting one another with "Rām Rām!"—blind in many cases to distinctions of caste. Household fires throughout the village had been extinguished, and as the assembled men returned to their homes, they carried coals from the collective fire to rekindle their domestic hearths. Many household courtyards stood open with decorated firepits awaiting the new year's blaze. Joyful celebrants ran from door to door handing bits of the new crop to waking residents of all quarters or tossing a few grains over walls when doors were closed. As I entered a shadowy lane, I was struck twice from behind by what I thought might be barley, but found in fact to be ashes and sand. Apart from this perhaps deviant note, the villagers seemed to me to have expressed through their unified celebration of Holikā's demise their total dependence on each other as a moral community. Impressed with the vigor of these communal rites and inwardly warmed, I returned to my house and to bed in the courtyard.

It was a disturbing night, however. As the moon rose high, I became aware of the sound of racing feet: gangs of young people were howling

"Holī!" and pursuing each other down the lanes. At intervals I felt the thud of large mud bricks thrown over my courtyard wall. Hoping still to salvage a few hours of sleep, I retreated with cot to the security of my storeroom. I was awakened for the last time just before dawn by the crash of the old year's pots breaking against my outer door. Furious fusillades of sand poured from the sky. Pandemonium now reigned: a shouting mob of boys called on me by name from the street and demanded that I come out. I perceived through a crack, however, that anyone who emerged was being pelted with bucketfuls of mud and cow-dung water. Boys of all ages were heaving dust into the air, hurling old shoes at each other, laughing and cavorting "like Krishna's cowherd companions"—and of course, cowherds they were. They had captured one older victim and were making him ride a donkey, seated backward, head to stern. Household walls were being scaled, loose doors broken open, and the inhabitants routed out to join these ceremonial proceedings. Relatively safe in a new building with strong doors and high walls, I escaped an immediate lynching.

I was not sure just what I could find in anthropological theory to assist my understanding of these events. I felt at least that I was sharing E. Durkheim's sense (when he studied Australian tribal rites) of confronting some of the more elementary forms of the religious life. I reflected briefly on the classic functional dictum of Radcliffe-Brown, who had written that the "rites of savages persist because they are part of the mechanism by which an orderly society maintains itself in existence, serving as they do to establish certain fundamental social values."[7] I pondered the Dionysian values that seemed here to have been expressed, and wondered what equalitarian social order, if any, might maintain itself by such values.

But I had not long to reflect, for no sooner had the mob passed by my house than I was summoned by a messenger from a family at the other end of the village to give first aid to an injured woman. A thrown water pot had broken over her head as she opened her door that morning. Protected by an improvised helmet, I ventured forth. As I stepped into the lane, the wife of the barber in the house opposite, a lady who had hitherto been most quiet and deferential, also stepped forth, grinning under her veil, and doused me with a pail of urine from her buffalo. Hurrying through the streets, I glimpsed dances by parties of men and boys impersonating Krishna and company as musicians, fiddling and blowing in pantomime on wooden sticks, leaping about wearing garlands of dried cow-dung and necklaces of bullock bells. Again, as I returned from attending to the lacerated scalp, there was an intermittent hail of trash and dust on my shoulders, this time evidently thrown from the rooftops by women and children in hiding behind the eaves.

At noontime, a state of truce descended. Now was the time to bathe, the neighbors shouted, and to put on fine, fresh clothes. The dirt was finished. Now there would be solemn oblations to the god Fire. "Every cult,"

Durkheim had written, "presents a double aspect, one negative, the other positive."[8] Had we then been preparing ourselves all morning by torture and purgation for other rites of purer intent? "What is it all going to be about this afternoon?" I asked my neighbor, the barber. "Holī," he said with a beatific sigh, "is the Festival of Love!"

Trusting that there would soon begin performances more in the spirit of the *Gītagovinda* or of Krishna's *rāsa* dances in the *Bhāgavata Purāna*, I happily bathed and changed, for my eyes were smarting with the morning's dust and the day was growing hot. My constant benefactor, the village landlord, now sent his son to present me with a tall glass of a cool, thick green liquid. This was the festival drink, he said; he wanted me to have it at its best, as it came from his own parlour. I tasted it, and found it sweet and mild. "You must drink it all!" my host declared. I inquired about the ingredients—almonds, sugar, curds of milk, anise, and "only half a cup" of another item whose name I did not recognize. I finished off the whole delicious glass, and, in discussion with my cook, soon inferred that the unknown ingredient—*bhāng*—had been four ounces of juice from the hemp leaf known in the West as hashish or marijuana.

Because of this indiscretion, I am now unable to report with much accuracy exactly what other religious ceremonies were observed in the four villages through which I floated that afternoon, towed by my careening hosts. They told me that we were going on a journey of condolence to each house whose members had been bereaved during the past year. My many photographs corroborate the visual impressions that I had of this journey: the world was a brilliant smear. The stained and crumpled pages of my notebooks are blank, save for a few declining diagonals and undulating scrawls. Certain steaming scenes remain in memory, nevertheless. There was one great throng of villagers watching an uplifted male dancer with padded crotch writhe in solitary states of fevered passion and then onanism; then join in a remote *pas de deux* with a veiled female impersonator in a parody of pederasty, and finally in telepathic copulation—all this to a frenzied accompaniment of many drums. I know that I witnessed several hysterical battles, women rushing out of their houses in squads to attack me and other men with stout canes, while each man defended himself only by pivoting about his own staff, planted on the ground, or, like me, by running for cover. The rest was all hymn singing, every street resounding with choral song in an archaic Sakta style. The state of the clothes in which I ultimately fell asleep told me the next morning that I had been sprayed and soaked repeatedly with libations of liquid dye, red and yellow. My face in the morning was still a brilliant vermilion, and my hair was orange from repeated embraces and scourings with colored powders by the bereaved, and probably by many others. I learned on inquiry what I thought I had heard before, that in Kishan Garhi a kitchen had been profaned with dog's dung by masked raiders, and that two housewives had been detected in adultery with neighboring men.

As an effect of the festivities in one nearby village, there had occurred an armed fight between factional groups. In a third, an adjacent village, where there had previously been protracted litigation between castes, the festival had not been observed at all.

"A festival of *love*?" I asked my neighbors again in the morning.

"Yes! All greet each other with affection and feeling. Lord Krishna taught us the way of love, and so we celebrate Holī in this manner."

"What about my aching shins—and your bruises? Why were the women beating us men?"

"Just as the milkmaids loved Lord Krishna, so our wives show their love for us, and for you, too, Saheb!"

Unable at once to stretch my mind so far as to include both "love" and these performances in one conception, I returned to the methodological maxim of Radcliffe-Brown: the meaning of a ritual element is to be found by observing what it shares with all the contexts of its occurrence.[9] Clearly, I would need to know much more about village religion and about the place of each feature of Holī in its other social contexts throughout the year. Then perhaps I could begin to grasp the meanings of Krishna and his festival, and to determine the nature of the values they might serve to maintain.

There were, I learned by observing throughout the following twelve months in the village, three main kinds of ritual performances—festivals, individual sacraments, and optional devotions. Among sacraments, the family-controlled rites of marriage were a major preoccupation of all villagers. In marriage, young girls were uprooted from their privileged situations in the patrilineally extended families of their birth and childhood. They were wedded always out of the village, often many miles away, to child husbands in families that were complete strangers. A tight-lipped young groom would be brought by his uncles in military procession, and after three days of receiving tribute ceremoniously, he would be carried off with his screaming, wailing little bride to a home where she would occupy the lowest status of all. Hard work for the mother-in-law, strict obedience to the husband, and a veiled, silent face to all males senior to herself in the entire village—these were the lot of the young married woman. Members of the husband's family, having the upper hand over the captive wife, could demand and receive service, gifts, hospitality, and deference from their "low" affines on all future occasions of ceremony. Briefly, sometimes, there would be little outbreaks of "Holī playing" at weddings, especially between the invading groom's men and the women of the bride's village: in these games, the men would be dared to enter the women's courtyards in the bride's village and would then be beaten with rolling pins or soaked with colored water for their boldness. Otherwise, all ceremonies of marriage stressed the strict formal dominance of men over women, of groom's people over bride's. When married women returned to their original homes each rainy season for a relaxed month of reunion with their "village sisters" and "village brothers," the whole village sang sentimental songs of the *gopīs'* never-fulfilled longing for their idyllic childhood companionship with Krishna and with each other. Sexual relations between adults of humankind were conventionally verbalized in metaphors of "war," "theft," and rape, while the marital connection between any particular husband and his wife could be mentioned without insult only by employing generalized circumlocutions such as "house" and "children," and so on. The idiom of Holī thus differed from that of ordinary life both in giving explicit dramatization to specific sexual relationships that otherwise would not be expressed at all and in reversing the differences of power conventionally prevailing between husbands and wives.

Aside from the Holī festival, each of the other thirteen major festivals of the year seemed to me to express and support the proper structures of patriarchy and gerontocracy in the family, of elaborately stratified relations among the castes, and of dominance by landowners in the village generally. At Divālī, ancestral spirits were to be fed and the goddess of wealth worshiped by the head of the family, acting on behalf of all members. The rites of Gobardhan Divālī, another Krishna-related festival, stressed the unity of the family's agnates through their common interest in the family herds of cattle. On the fourth day of the lunar fortnight which ends at Divālī[10]—indeed, on certain fixed dates in every month—the wives fasted for the sake of their husbands. On other dates they fasted for the sake of their children. The brother-sister relation of helpfulness, a vital one for the out-married women, had two further festivals and many fasts giving it ritual support; and the Holī bonfire itself dramatized the divine punishment of the wicked sister Holikā for her unthinkable betrayal of her brother Prahlada. At each other festival of the year and also at wedding feasts, the separation of the lower from the higher castes and their strict order of ranking were reiterated both through the services of pollution-removal provided by them, and through the lowering gifts and payments of food made to them in return. Since the economy of the village was steeply stratified, with one third of the families controlling nearly all the land, every kind of ritual observance, sacramental or festival, tended through ritual patronage and obeisance to give expression to the same order of economic dominance and subordination. Optional, individual ritual observances could also be understood as expressing the secular organization of power, I thought. Rival leaders would compete for the allegiance of others through ceremonies. A wealthy farmer, official, or successful litigant was expected to sponsor special ceremonies and give feasts for lesser folk "to remove the sins" he had no doubt committed in gaining his high position; he who ignored this expectation might overhear stories of the jocular harassment of misers at Holī, or of their robbery on other, darker nights. Once each year, a day for simultaneous worship of all the local deities required a minimal sort of communal action by women, and smaller singing parties of women were many, but comradeship among men across the lines of kinship and caste was generally regarded with suspicion. In sum, the routine ritual and social forms of the village seemed almost perfect parallels of each other: both maintained a tightly ranked and compartmentalized order. In this order, there was little room for behavior of the kinds attributed to Krishna's roisterous personality.

"Why do you say that it was Lord Krishna who taught you how to celebrate the festival of Holī?" I inquired of the many villagers who asserted that this was so. Answers, when they could be had at all, stressed that it was he who first played Holī with the cowherd boys and with Rādhā and the other *gopīs*. But my searches in the *Bhāgavata*'s tenth book, and even in that book's recent and locally most popular adaptation, the *Ocean of Love,*[11] could discover no mention of Holī or any of the local festival's traditional activities, from the bonfire to the game of colors. "Just see how they play Holī in Mathurā district, in Lord Krishna's own village of Nandgaon, and in Rādhā's village of Barsana!" said the landlord. There, I was assured by the barber, who had also seen them, that the women train all year long, drinking milk and eating ghee like wrestlers, and there they beat the men *en masse*, before a huge audience of visitors, to the music of two hundred drums.

"I do not really believe that Lord Krishna grew up in just that village of Nandgaon," the landlord confided in me, "for Nanda, Krishna's foster father, must have lived on this side of the Jumnā River, near Gokula, as is written in the Purāṇa. But there in Nandgaon and Barsana they keep the old customs best."

The landlord's doubts were well placed, but not extensive enough, for, as I learned from a gazetteer of the district, the connection of Krishna, Rādhā, and the cowgirls with the rising of the women at Holī in those villages of Mathurā could not have originated before the early seventeenth-century efforts of certain immigrant Bengali Gosvāmin priests. The Gosvāmīs themselves—Rūpa, Sanātana, and their associates—were missionaries of the Krishnaite devotional movement led by Caitanya[12] in sixteenth-century Bengal, and that movement in turn had depended on the elaboration of the new notion of Rādhā as Krishna's favorite by the Telugu philosopher Nimbarka, possibly in the thirteenth century, and by other, somewhat earlier sectarians of Bengal and southern India.[13] The village names "Nandgaon" (village of Nanda) and "Barsana" (to make rain—an allusion to the "dark-as-a-cloud" epithet of Krishna) were probably seventeenth-century inventions, like the formal choreography of the battles of the sexes in those villages, that were contrived to attract pilgrims to the summer circuit of Krishna's rediscovered and refurbished holy land of Vraja.[14] Of course, privileged attacks by women upon men must have existed in village custom long before the promotional work of the Gosvāmīs—of this I was convinced by published studies of villages elsewhere, even in the farthest corners of the Hindī-speaking area, where such attacks were part of Holī, but not understood as conveying the message of Lord Krishna.[15] But once the great flow of devotees to Mathurā had begun from Bengal, Gujarat, and the South, the direction of cultural influence must have been reversed: what had been incorporated of peasant practice and local geography into the *Brahmavaivarta Purāṇa* and other new sectarian texts must have begun then to reshape peasant conceptions of peasant practice. At least the Krishna-ite theology of the "love battles" in Kishan Garhi, and possibly some refinements of their rustic hydrology and stickwork, seemed to have been remodeled according to the famous and widely imitated public performances that had been visible in villages of the neighboring district for the past three centuries or so. The Mathurā pilgrimage and its literature appeared also to have worked similar effects upon two other festivals of Krishna in Kishan Garhi, in addition to Holī.[16]

To postulate the relative recency of the association of Rādhā and Krishna with the battles of canes and colors in Kishan Garhi was not to assert that the entire Holī festival could have had no connection with legends of Krishna before the seventeenth century. Reports on the mythology of Holī from many other localities described the bonfire, not as the burning of Holikā, but as the cremation of another demoness, Pūtanā.[17] Pūtanā was a demoness sent by King Kamsa of Mathurā to kill the infant Krishna by giving him to suck of her poisonous mother's milk. The Pūtanā story could no doubt claim a respectable antiquity, occurring as it did in the *Viṣṇu Purāṇa* and the *Harivaṃśa;* it was known in Kishan Garhi, although not applied currently to the rationalization of the Holī fire, and represented an acquaintance with a Krishna senior in type to the more erotic Krishna of the *Bhāgavata Purāṇa* and the later works. Even if I peeled away all explicit references to Krishna, both older and more recent, I would still have confronted other layers of Vaiṣṇavism in the Holī references to Rāma, whose cult centered in the middle Gangetic plain and in the South. And then there was the further Vaiṣṇava figure Prahlāda, another of ancient origin. Finally, I had to consider the proximity of Kishan Garhi to Mathurā, which was more than merely generically Vaiṣṇavite in its ancient religious orientations: Mathurā was thought to have been the original source of the legends of the child Krishna and his brother Balarāma, as suggested by Greek evidence from the fourth century BCE as well as by the Purāṇic traditions.[18] Assuming that urban cults may always have been influential in villages and that such cults often carried forward what was already present in rural religious practice,[19] I thought it probable that the ancestors of the people of Kishan Garhi might well have celebrated the pranks of some divine ancestor of the Purāṇic Krishna even before their less complete adherence to the cults of Rāma and other gods later known as avatars of Viṣṇu. If these historical evidences and interpretations were generally sound, if Krishna had indeed waxed and waned before, then what both I and the villagers had taken to be their timeless living within a primordial local myth of Krishna appeared instead to represent rather the latest in a lengthy series of revivals and reinterpretations mingling local, regional, and even some quite remote movements of religious fashion.

Beneath the level of mythological enactment or rationalization, with its many shifts of contents through time, however, I felt that one might find certain more essential, underlying connections between the moral constitution of villages like Kishan Garhi and the general social form of the Holī festival—so the functional assumption of Radcliffe-Brown had led me to hope. Superficially, in various regions and eras, the festival might concern witches or demonesses (Holikā or Holākā, Pūtanā, Ḍhoṇḍhā), Viṣṇu triumphant (as Rāma, Narasiṃha, or Krishna), Śiva as an ascetic in conflict with gods of lust (Kāma, Madana, or the nonscriptural Nathurām), or others.[20] Festival practices might also vary greatly. Were there enduring, widespread features, I wondered? From a distributional and documentary study by N. K. Bose, I learned that spring festivals featuring bonfires, a degree of sexual license, and generally saturnalian carousing had probably existed in villages of many parts of India for at least the better part of the past two thousand years.[21] Spring festivals of this one general character evidently had remained consistently associated with many of India's complex, caste-bound communities. Even if only some of such festivals had had the puckish, ambiguous Krishna as their presiding deity, and these only in recent centuries, many seemed since the beginning of our knowledge to have enshrined divinities who sanctioned, however briefly, some of the same riotous sorts of social behavior.

Now a full year had passed in my investigations, and the Festival of Love was again approaching. Again I was apprehensive for my physical person, but was forewarned with social structural knowledge that might yield better understanding of the events to come. This time, without the draft of marijuana, I began to see the pandemonium of Holī falling into an extraordinarily regular social ordering. But this was an order precisely inverse to the social and ritual principles of routine life. Each riotous act at Holī implied some opposite, positive rule or fact of everyday social organization in the village.

Who were those smiling men whose shins were being most mercilessly beaten by the women? They were the wealthier Brahman and Jāṭ farmers of the village, and the beaters were those ardent local Rādhās, the "wives of the village," figuring by both the real and the fictional intercaste system of kinship. The wife of an "elder brother" was properly a man's joking mate, while the wife of a "younger brother" was properly removed from him by rules of extreme respect, but both were merged here with a man's mother-surrogates, the wives of his "father's younger brothers," in one revolutionary cabal of "wives" that cut across all lesser lines and links. The boldest beaters in this veiled battalion were often in fact the wives of the farmers' low-caste field laborers, artisans, or menials—the concubines and kitchen help of the victims. "Go and bake bread!" teased one farmer, egging his assailant on. "Do you want some seed from me?" shouted another flattered victim, smarting under the blows, but standing his ground. Six Brahman men in their fifties, pillars of village society, limped past in panting flight from the quarterstaff wielded by a massive young Bhaṅgin, sweeper of their latrines. From this carnage suffered by their village brothers, all daughters of the village stood apart, yet held themselves in readiness to attack any potential husband who might wander in from another, marriageable village to pay a holiday call.

Who was that "King of the Holī" riding backward on the donkey? It was an older boy of high caste, a famous bully, put there by his organized victims (but seeming to relish the prominence of his disgrace).

Who was in that chorus singing so lustily in the potters' lane? Not just the resident caste fellows, but six washermen, a tailor, and three Brahmans, joined each year for this day only in an idealistic musical company patterned on the friendships of the gods.

Who were those transfigured "cowherds" heaping mud and dust on all the leading citizens? They were the water carrier, two young Brahman priests, and a barber's son, avid experts in the daily routines of purification.

Whose household temple was festooned with goat's bones by unknown merrymakers? It was the temple of that Brahman widow who had constantly harassed neighbors and kinsmen with actions at law.

In front of whose house was a burlesque dirge being sung by a professional ascetic of the village? It was the house of a very much alive moneylender, notorious for his punctual collections and his insufficient charities.

Who was it who had his head fondly anointed, not only with handfuls of the sublime red powders, but also with a gallon of diesel oil? It was the village landlord, and the anointer was his cousin and archrival, the police headman of Kishan Garhi.

Who was it who was made to dance in the streets, fluting like Lord Krishna, with a garland of old shoes around his neck? It was I, the visiting anthropologist, who had asked far too many questions, and had always to receive respectful answers.

Here indeed were the many village kinds of love confounded—respectful regard for parents and patrons; the idealized affection for brothers, sisters, and comrades; the longing of man for union with the divine; and the rugged lust of sexual mates—all broken suddenly out of their usual, narrow channels by a simultaneous increase of intensity. Boundless, unilateral love of every kind flooded over the usual compartmentalization and indifference among separated castes and families. Insubordinate libido inundated all established hierarchies of age, sex, caste, wealth, and power.

The social meaning of Krishna's doctrine in its rural North Indian recension is not unlike one conservative social implication of Jesus' Sermon on the Mount. The Sermon admonishes severely, but at the same time postpones the destruction of the secular social order until a distant future. Krishna does not postpone the reckoning of the mighty until an ultimate Judgment Day, but schedules it regularly as a masque at the full moon of every March. And the Holī of Krishna is no mere doctrine of love: rather it is the script for a drama that must be acted out by each devotee passionately, joyfully.

The dramatic balancing of Holī—the world destruction and world renewal, the world pollution followed by world purification—occurs not only on the abstract level of structural principles, but also in the person of each participant. Under the tutelage of Krishna, each person plays and for the moment may experience the role of his opposite: the servile wife acts the domineering husband, and vice versa; the ravisher acts the ravished; the menial acts the master; the enemy acts the friend; the strictured youths act the rulers of the republic. The observing anthropologist, inquiring and reflecting on the forces that move men in their orbits, finds himself pressed to act the witless bumpkin. Each actor playfully takes the role of others in relation to his own usual self. Each may thereby learn to play his own routine roles afresh, surely with renewed understanding, possibly with greater grace, perhaps with a reciprocating love.

NOTES

1. "Kishan Garhi," a pseudonymous village in Aligarh district, Uttar Pradesh, was studied by me from March 1951 to April 1952, with the assistance of an Area Research Training Fellowship grant from the Social Science Research Council. For his comments on this paper, I am indebted to David E. Orlinsky.

2. In this local version of the Prahlāda story, King Harnākas will readily be recognized as Hiraṇya Kaśipu of the Purāṇas, e.g., *Viṣṇu Purāṇa* 1.17 (p. 108 in the translation by Horace Hayman Wilson [Calcutta: Punthi Pustak, 1961]). Holā or Holākā, in the oldest texts a name for the bonfire or festival and unconnected with the story of Prahlāda or other scriptural gods (see the sources cited by Pandurang Vaman Kane, *History of Dharmaśāstra* [Poona, 1958], Vol. V, pp. 237–239), appears only in recent popular stories as a female, and as a relative of Prahlāda. For Holī stories of the Hindi region generally, see William Crooke, *The Popular Religion and Folk-Lore of Northern India* (London: Archibald Constable & Co., 1896), Vol. II, p. 313; for similar tales from Delhi State, see Oscar Lewis, with the assistance of Victor Barnouw, *Village Life in Northern India* (Urbana: University of Illinois, 1958), p. 232; and for versions from the Alwar district of Rajasthan, see Hilda Wernher, *The Land and the Well* (New York: John Day Co., 1946), pp. 199–200.

3. Some of the cow-dung objects for the Holī fire are prepared after the Gobardhan Divālī festival in autumn, with the materials of Gobardhan Bābā's (= Krishna's ?) body. See McKim Marriott, "Little Communities in an Indigenous Civilization," in McKim Marriott, ed., *Village India* (Chicago: University of Chicago Press, 1955), pp. 199–200. Other objects are prepared on the second or fifth days of the bright fortnight of the month of Phagun, whose last day is the day of the Holī fire.

4. Books VII and X, as in *The Śrīmad-Bhagbātam of Krishna-Dwaipāyana-Vyāsa*, J. M. Sanyal, trans. (Calcutta, n.d.), Vols. IV and V.

5. Alfred Reginald Radcliffe-Brown, "Religion and Society," in *Structure and Function in Primitive Society* (London: Cohen & West, 1952), pp. 155, 177.

6. Bronislaw Malinowski, *Argonauts of the Western Pacific* (London, 1932), pp. 6–8.

7. "Taboo," in Radcliffe-Brown, *Structure and Function*, p. 152.

8. Émile Durkheim, *The Elementary Forms of the Religious Life*, Joseph Ward Swain, trans. (Glencoe, Ill.: Free Press, 1947), p. 299.

9. *The Andaman Islanders* (Glencoe, Ill.: Free Press, 1948), p. 235.

10. Details of some of these festivals are given in Marriott, ed., *Village India*, pp. 192–206. The social organization of Kishan Garhi is described more fully in McKim Marriott, "Social Structure and Change in a U.P. Village," in M. N. Srinivas, ed., *India's Villages* (London, 1960), pp. 106–121.

11. Lallu Lal, *Premasāgara*, Frederic Pincott, trans. (London, 1897).

12. Frederic Salmon Growse, *Mathurā: A District Memoir* (2nd ed., 1880), pp. 72, 93, 183–184.

13. Ibid., pp. 178–221; John Nicol Farquhar, *An Outline of the Religious Literature of India* (London: Oxford University Press, 1920), pp. 238–240.

14. Growse, *Mathurā: A District Memoir*, pp. 71–94.

15. Women beat men at or near the time of Holī among the Gonds of Mandla district, according to Verrier Elwin, *Leaves from the Jungle* (London: J. Murray, 1936), p. 135; in Nimar, according to Stephen Fuchs, *The Children of Hari* (New York: Praeger, 1950), pp. 300–301; and elsewhere in Madhya Pradesh, according to Robert Vane Russell and Hira Lal, *The Tribes and Castes of the Central Provinces of India* (London, 1916), Vol. II, p. 126, and Vol. III, p. 117. The usage is reported also from Alwar in Rajasthan by Hilda Wernher, *The Land and the Well*, p. 208, and from Delhi by O. Lewis and V. Barnouw, *Village Life in Northern India*, p. 232.

16. At Krishna's birthday anniversary, biographies of his life by poets of Mathurā are read. At the Gobardhan Divali, the circumambulation of the hill by the pilgrims is duplicated in model; see McKim Marriott, "Little Communities," in McKim Marriot, ed., *Village India*, pp. 199–200.

17. See W. Crooke, *Popular Religion and Folk-Lore*, Vol. II, pp. 313–314; and Ṛgvedi (pseud.), *Āryāncā Saṇāncā Prācīna va Arvācīna Itihāsa* (in Marathi) (Bombay, n.d.), p. 399.

18. F. S. Growse, *Mathurā: A District Memoir*, p. 103.

19. R. Redfield and M. Singer, "The Cultural Role of Cities," *Economic Development and Cultural Change*, III (1954), pp. 53–74.

20. W. Crooke, *Popular Religion and Folk-Lore*, Vol. II, pp. 313–314, 319–320; P. V. Kane, *History of Dharmaśāstra*, Vol. V, pp. 237–240; Ṛgvedi (pseud.), *Āryāncā Saṇāncā Prācīna va Arvācīna Itihāsu* (in Marathi), pp. 399–400, 405.

21. Nirmal Kumar Bose, "The Spring Festival of India," in *Cultural Anthropology and Other Essays* (Calcutta, 1953), pp. 73–102.

19

The Delusion of Gender and Renunciation in Buddhist Kashmir

Kim Gutschow

In the enlightened mind, there is no male or female.
In the Buddha's speech, there is no near or far.

Byang chub sems la pho mo med;
rgyal ba' bka' la nye ring med.

This Buddhist proverb from Kashmir illustrates the ideal doctrinal view that gender is supposed to be an illusion and not an obstacle on the path to enlightenment. In practice, however, gender appears to be a considerable obstacle on the monastic path. The manner in which the Buddha first founded the nuns' and monks' orders enshrined the dialectic of power between those orders. By making nuns subordinate to monks, the Buddha enabled the latter to amass considerable social, symbolic, and economic capital at the expense of nuns, their female counterparts in the Buddhist order. Despite recent challenges from feminists and international Buddhist reformers, nuns in Buddhist Kashmir have faced a glass ceiling in terms of ritual knowledges and practices. As a result, nuns were assumed to count less than monks and were also "left out of the count" in literature on Buddhism in Kashmir.

My method of emphasizing nuns over monks, as well as practice over doctrine, diverges from earlier scholarly approaches to Tibetan Buddhism. It pursues a heuristic laid out by Michelle Rosaldo (1980) and Sherry Ortner (1996), who have argued that one should not study women in isolation from men, nor should one isolate gender from other axes of social asymmetry.[1] While previous studies of Buddhist nuns (Barnes 1987, 1994; Tsomo 1988, 1996) have attempted to reconstruct the history of nuns, they have overlooked the dynamics of power between monks and nuns by which nuns have come to be second-class citizens in the monastic realm. Lopez (1995b, 1998) has shown how the field of Buddhist studies has long privileged the text and doctrine over the informant and her practices, while offering an essentialized and timeless Shangri-La image of Tibetan Buddhism. I follow Lopez's call to deconstruct the myths about Tibetan Buddhism, by looking at the tropes that have been used to describe Buddhist nuns in literature on Buddhism in Kashmir.[2]

Until recently, much of the scholarship on Buddhism in Kashmir either ignored or misrecognized nuns due to a narrow doctrinal image of what a nun should look like. The absence of nuns in much of the literature on Buddhist monasticism in Kashmir is especially disconcerting given that nuns make up nearly two-fifths of the resident monastic population in the Kashmiri subdistrict of Zangskar.[3] This ratio, which may be one of the highest in the entire Himalayan realm, is twice as high as the ratio of nuns to monks in the Indo-Tibetan borderlands before 1959 and eight times as high as the ratio in Tibetan refugee monasteries by the late 1980s.[4] Zangskar, which comprises the southern and safer half of Kargil district—the site of recent military clashes between India and Pakistan in the summer of 1999—has been Buddhist since at least the tenth century, although it is also home to a minority of Sunni Muslims. Although it covers an area roughly twice the size of Rhode Island, Zangskar's meager population of 12,000 makes it one of least populated regions in India.[5] The inhabitants, who live in over a hundred hamlets and villages at elevations between 3,000 and 4,200 meters, sustain a resident monastic population that makes up nearly 4 percent of the total population.

Although most of the monastic population of Zangskar lives in its seven monasteries and nine nunneries, nuns have more unorthodox residential arrangements. While most ordained nuns reside at a nunnery in monastic cells, some nuns live temporarily in the village caring for their aged parents. Regardless of where they reside, all nuns must work daily in the village in exchange for their daily bread. Some nunneries also house elderly women who are not ordained but take on five precepts—not to kill, steal, lie, commit sexual misconduct, or take intoxicants. This state of affairs was so confusing for many scholars that they often lumped ordained novices together with such elderly precept holders who had never been ordained and had no religious function in village life. While both these women are called "nuns" (jo mo) in the local vernacular, lay precept holders are also known as "village nuns" (grong pa'i jo mo) and never as ordained novices (dge tshul ma).[6] While the association between ordained nuns and elderly spinsters has contributed to a degraded image of Tibetan Buddhist nuns, past scholars failed to ask several critical questions: Why do ordained nuns work on village farms? Why don't they have the same institutional support that monks do? Why have nunneries become retreat centers for merit-making, while monasteries have served as centers for art, education, politics, business, and philosophy? To answer these questions, let us consider how nuns came to be second-class citizens within the Buddhist monastic order.

THE LAW OF THE BUDDHA

According to canonical texts, the Buddha allegedly accepted women into his monastic order on one condition: that they adopt the so-called Eight Chief Rules (*Garudhamma*). These rules specified that nuns may neither censure nor admonish monks and that nuns must take their ordinations, bimonthly confessions, rainy season retreats, and penances in the presence of monks. The Buddha's aunt objected to only one of the eight rules—the one specifying that even a senior nun who has been ordained one hundred years must bow down to a youthful novice who has been ordained but a day—but her objection was overruled by the Buddha himself. While scholars have suggested that these baneful rules may never have been spoken by the Buddha, their lasting legacy is undeniable (Falk 1980; Gross 1993; Horner 1930; Paul 1985; Sponberg 1992; J. Willis 1985). The cumulative effect of the Eight Chief Rules was to give monks the pastoral rights to discipline and punish nuns. Monks came to regulate the traffic in nuns, by controlling women's admission to and exclusion from the nuns' order at all stages of the process. In Kashmir today, monks still officiate most rites of passage that nuns must undergo, including first tonsure, novice ordination, entrance into the monastic assembly, absolution, penances, expulsion, and final cremation (Gutschow 1998, 2000).

When the Buddha subordinated nuns to monks, the nunneries were never able to gain the same power and wealth that monasteries could, and eventually the nuns' order died out in many parts of South and Southeast Asia. As popular and devotional forms of Hinduism grew in the first millennium, the newly formed Buddhist orders had to compete for a shrinking base of donors. During this period, Buddhist nuns could not command the same educational and ritual prestige that monks could. Due to decreasing patronage, lineages of fully ordained nuns died out one by one across the subcontinent, as region after region lost the ability to form the requisite quorum of ten nuns to ordain the next generation of nuns. The monks' order also suffered, and was nearly wiped out in medieval Sri Lanka and Tibet, for instance. Yet by importing monks from elsewhere, often at great expense, the royal patrons in these places managed to perpetuate the lineage of fully ordained monks even in times of considerable social and political turmoil.[7] In contrast, little effort was made to revive the nuns' order when and where it collapsed.

By the twelfth century, women could no longer seek full ordination in much of South and Southeast Asia. While Tibetan Buddhist orders allowed women to ordain as novices, they never supported a lineage of fully ordained nuns. In Sri Lanka, Burma, Thailand, Laos, and Cambodia, women have the option of holding between eight and ten precepts as de facto rather than de jure nuns.[8] By 1988, of the 60,000 women worldwide who held some form of

Buddhist precepts or monastic vows, only one-fourth were fully ordained nuns, who lived mostly in China, Taiwan, Korea, Vietnam, and the West.[9] The recent efforts to reinstate a full ordination lineage in the Tibetan tradition and in Sri Lanka with the assistance of East Asian nuns from Taiwan or Korea has not had much impact in Kashmir.[10] Although the Dalai Lama has given his support, many monastics and some feminists remain opposed, albeit for different reasons. Senior monks argue that formal teaching structures are not yet in place, while feminists hold that female renunciants are better off outside this disciplinary gaze of monks.

In Buddhist Kashmir, the lack of full ordination left novice nuns at the mercy of fully ordained monks who amassed enormous amounts of symbolic and economic capital. Monks became virtuoso ritualists, philosophers, and bureaucrats, while nunneries devolved into impoverished and politically irrelevant retreat centers.[11] While renowned religious women such as Machig Labdron, Yeshe Tsogyal, and Nangsa Obum taught unconventional Tantric teachings outside the monastic framework, nuns rarely had the chance to transmit esoteric teachings to their own disciples. Each generation of nuns had to go to the monks for further teachings and advanced ritual training. The exclusion of women from philosophical dialectics and esoteric ritual practices was maintained in each of the four schools of Tibetan Buddhism (Gelug, Kagyud, Sakya, and Nyingma). Until recently, nuns were ineligible to attend the highest monastic and ritual colleges of the Dalai Lama's own Gelug school of Tibetan Buddhism. Western feminists have asked the Dalai Lama to accept nuns at his exclusive philosophical academy in Dharmsala, the Namgyal Institute of Dialectics. Other initiatives have led the avant-garde nunneries in Kathmandu, Kyirong, and Kopan to teach nuns sacred arts like the construction of sand mandalas (*dkyil 'khor*), burnt offerings (*sbyin sreg*), and meditative dances (*'chams*).[12] Significantly, these are the ritual practices that have earned Tibetan monks fame and cash in their travels abroad.

While the Buddha clearly disavowed the role of the priest in purifying others, Buddhist monks in Zangskar have monopolized many ritual practices, including the expiatory and purificatory rites that are so essential to the maintenance of village and household space. In Zangskar as elsewhere in India, the female body exemplifies an innate impurity that the male does not.[13] Due to menstruation and childbirth, women's bodies are conceptualized as inherently impure and thus offensive to the deities of place and space who guarantee household, village, and monastic prosperity. Even though nuns are never mothers, and if elderly, have ceased to menstruate, they remain excluded from many places and rituals of power where Tantric deities, local guardian deities, or underworld spirits are worshiped. Monks have preserved the sole authority to officiate the expiatory and propitiatory rites (*gtor rgyab, brgya bzhi, mdos, glud*), ritual ablutions (*khrus*), and agrarian circumambulations (*'bum khor*) that cleanse monastic, village, and household spaces from ritual pollution. At routine life-cycle events to which both assemblies of nuns and monks are invited, such as funerals and weddings, the ritual roles for nuns and monks are carefully segregated. Only monks may officiate the cremation rite (*sbying sregs*) and the transfer of the corpse's consciousness (*cho ga*), and only monks conduct the ritual transference (*g.yang 'gugs, zor*) of the bride from her natal to her husband's household and clan deity. Despite their textual and ritual literacy, nuns are called to perform basic household rites only as substitutes when monks are unavailable.

THE ECONOMY OF MERIT IN KASHMIR

Because the monks' order is still considered to be a higher "field of merit" than the nuns' order in Kashmir today, villagers channel their donations and alms to the monastery. Historically, giving to monasteries offered donors both political prestige and private merit. The historical record for Zangskar and Tibet offers many examples of kings and nobles who gave land grants to charismatic monks during times of political or social crisis in order to demonstrate their piety.[14] By the time of the Permanent Settlement in 1908, local monasteries held one-tenth of all cultivated land in Zangskar. By 1994, Zangskar's largest monastery still owned ninety times the average private holding of 2.8 acres per household.[15] Even today, one out of four households in Zangskar still sharecrop one or more fields from a monastery, and some sharecroppers own no land whatsoever. Monasteries command enormous rents, as well as customary donations of corvee labor, grain, butter, firewood, dung, and other services. In contrast to the monasteries, most nunneries collect neither rents nor other tithes. At present, five of nine nunneries in Zangskar have no fields at all, and the other four own a handful of fields from which they harvest a pittance. The monastery in Karsha annually earns one hundred times as much grain as the nunnery, although there are only four times as many monks as nuns.[16] Because nunneries have so little endowment, they cannot afford to feed their members on a daily basis. Karsha nunnery's rites are sponsored on a rotational basis by nun stewards who solicit donations of butter, flour, and other staples.

Institutional poverty forces Zangskari nuns to toil selflessly on their parents' farms in exchange for their daily bread. Even as their shorn heads and sexless maroon robes signal a lofty intent to renounce the worldly life, nuns are pulled back into productive roles by households unwilling to lose an able-bodied servant. According to a common Tibetan proverb, "If you want to serve, make your son a monk, if you want a servant, make your daughter a nun." The dutiful daughters and sisters who toil on their father's or brother's estate years after taking monastic vows ensure the agrarian prosperity of lay households as well as monasteries. Classical Buddhist injunctions against nuns performing chores for monks are overlooked by monks who recruit nuns to wash, sew, and cook for their private benefit. Moreover, the monastic community has no compunction about recruiting nuns to perform the most menial and labor-intensive tasks on the monastic estates, such as weeding the monastery's fields; tending huge flocks of monastic cattle and yaks at the high pastures for half the year; washing, drying, and roasting thousands of kilos of grain that the monastery collects from its sharecroppers; and baking thousands of loaves of bread for two annual festivals—around winter solstice and before spring plowing. In theory, compassion is supposed to be applied universally; in practice, it is exacted along lines dictated by custom and kinship.

While renunciation is a full-time occupation for monks, it is an unpaid but meritorious vocation for nuns. Sending a daughter to the nunnery is like placing her in a state school without a scholarship. She may have access to peers, knowledge, and travel that take her far beyond the provincial village life, but she must pay her own way. On the other hand, sending a son to the monastery is like enrolling him in an Ivy League or Oxbridge college with a full fellowship. Not only is he guaranteed a handsome stipend for his studies, but his elite education and status will provide him with ample opportunities for privilege and private profit for the rest of his life. The senior monks and reincarnate[17] priests graduate into more obscure offices for which the duties are less and less understood but the remuneration in cash and kind ever more handsome. In recent decades, increasing opportunities for employment in the civil and military sectors of the state economy have left monasteries struggling to attract young members. Monasteries are rapidly losing monks to the pull of the secular and consumer world, while some nunneries are gaining members and others are being founded in villages where there have not been nuns for centuries. How can this be?

WHO BECOMES A NUN IN ZANGSKAR?

Given the patriarchal nature of Buddhist monasticism, why would an able-bodied woman in the flower of her youth still wish to join the nunnery? Why do young women continue to pursue the Buddha's discipline of detachment in a region where the economy of merit is giving way to an economy of consumption? Let us look at the narratives told by a few nuns at the largest nunnery in Zangskar, Karsha.

Tsering was raised by her mother, who had never been married to Tsering's father. Although customary law gives the father custody of his child after she is weaned, Tsering's mother simply refused when her father came to collect her at age four. She pointed out to her former lover that while he had a wife and children, she was single and would need Tsering's help on her fields. Tsering and her mother lived together until she was sixteen, when she got the shock of her life. One day, she came upon her father telling her mother that a neighbor had sent the "asking beer" (*'dri chang*), the first of many negotiations necessary to arrange Tsering's marriage. Tsering spun on her heels and took to the hills behind the house, climbing up and up the cliff until she was dizzy, only stopping when the village and her house were no more than a speck far below. While her father and mother called her all afternoon, she remained hidden in the safety of the red rocks. She sat and thought about how to avoid the indignities under which her mother had chafed. Her mother's first liaison, with Tsering's father, had been disastrous. As the youngest and most spoiled of five sisters, her mother had inherited a parcel of land and some livestock from Tsering's grandfather. With the security that property brings in a land where most women are disenfranchised by virtue of their sex, her proud mother was unwilling to submit to Tsering's father's illicit affairs. Her mother's next affair was with an abusive drunk. As Tsering sat and recounted these relationships, she decided she would never marry. She waited until night fell, when she heard the jingle of her father saddling his horse and the familiar clop of the hooves fading in the distance. As she came down, her mother teased her about getting married but agreed to let her become a nun, as she asked. She realized how helpful it would be to have a daughter close by for daily chores.

Palmo told me about the misfortunes that brought her to the nunnery. Because Palmo's mother was only a mistress and never a wife, she was forced by custom to relinquish her rights to raise her daughter. Her mother's role as clandestine mistress of several brothers in the same household gave her little respect and no authority over the children she bore. Palmo's paternity was decided by lottery among the three brothers who had shared Palmo's mother's bed. Following customary law, Palmo was taken away from her mother to be raised by her father, who would have the rights to her labor until she was married. Palmo's father came to take his daughter away from her mother when he moved to a distant village, where he married his brother's widow. Palmo was an outsider twice over in her new stepmother's house. Her father was a powerless second husband who would never fill his deceased brother's shoes, while Palmo was a sign of his past infidelities. Palmo was only fed the leftover scraps after others had eaten and given clothes that her stepsister had neglected. Palmo lost count of how many times she ran away to her mother's village, before her father came to beat her and take her back home. Palmo vowed never to wind up a spurned mistress like her mother, and asked her father's permission to join the nunnery. When her father and stepmother stalled in hopes of keeping Palmo at home to do chores, she threatened to kill herself. After years of private study and a steady resolve to join the nunnery, Palmo convinced her father to take her to the nunnery, although he has barely supported her since that day.

Chosnyid had to struggle to renounce for she was an eldest daughter who flagrantly disobeyed both her parents and society. Shortly before she and her best friend were to be married, they went to hear the Kalachakra teachings given by a famous monk. They were so moved, they offered their hair and jewels to the monk, begging him to shave their heads and allow them to take up five precepts. When her parents heard that their daughter had shaved her head and given away her jewelry, they were livid with rage. Her father came to fetch her at the nunnery, telling her that he'd been negotiating her wedding for five years, with considerable expense. Thrashing her soundly, he tied her onto the horse in front of him like a child and took her home. When his daughter outwitted him and fled back to the nunnery, her father came to fetch her once again. For a year, Chosnyid and her father were engaged in this tedious game of hide-and-seek until she could bear it no longer. When the snows melted, she fled over the passes to Dharmsala, where she became a nun and settled near the Dalai Lama's personal monastery. She has never returned to Zangskar, although twenty-five years have passed.

THE STRUGGLES AND MOTIVATIONS FOR RENUNCIATION

What do these stories tell us about the struggle for renunciation in Zangskar? A propensity for religious study or devotion, the words of a charismatic teacher, and childhood hardship or abuse all influence the choice to renounce lay life. Yet one cannot leap to facile generalizations. While domestic abuse, jealous stepmothers, and illegitimacy crop up in the lives of many Zangskari women, only a few will reach the nunnery gates. There is no single factor that determines who becomes a nun, yet a few patterns emerge. Over half the nuns at Karsha come from homes where there is only one parent due to parental death, divorce, or illegitimacy. Nearly two-thirds of the Karsha nuns were sent to live with relatives as au pair girls during their childhood. During this period away from home, many of them may have learned the self-abnegation and stoicism essential to the celibate life. Oldest daughters from unbroken homes, who would ordinarily be destined for marriage, almost never become nuns.[18] While there is no bar against wealthy or aristocratic daughters joining the nunnery, most nuns come from households at the middle-to-lower end of the income spectrum.

Caste, rather than class, presents one of the more salient obstacles to the religious life in Zangskar. Women who belong to the lowest stratum (*rigs ngan*), which is made up of three named clans, Gara, Beda, and Mon, are ineligible to join the nunnery, without exception. Although Zangskar does not have a caste system of hierarchically ranked jati, the members of these three clans are treated like outcasts and denied intermarriage and commensality with the rest of the population. They cannot join a monastic assembly because, as one nun put it quite pithily, "If the blacksmith becomes chantmaster and must sit at the head of the seating row, where shall we sit?" In other words, she could not imagine a reversal of the traditional seating hierarchy (*gral*), in which the members of these lower strata must always sit at the end of the row, nearest the door.

While the women in these stories share a determined desire to escape the inevitable hardship of their lot, joining the nunnery does not happen overnight. Even those young women who flee to the nunnery somewhat abruptly must dedicate themselves to a lengthy period of tutelage. While many young women dream of becoming nuns or later regret that they didn't, the educated elite who actually become nuns must persevere through a lengthy apprenticeship and training period. In these changing times, when Urdu and English literacy are critical to desirable government jobs or military service, young girls are taught Tibetan even more rarely than young boys. Those who make it into the ranks of the nunnery or the monastery are few and far between. Young women who become nuns must show extraordinary aptitude in order to grasp the archaic syntax of classical Tibetan while memorizing abstruse philosophical texts of which little is understood or explicated. Women do not arrive at the nunnery gate "by accident" as much as by sustained efforts. Those women who join a monastic assembly are not unwanted spinsters, widows, and divorcees with no other options in life but to get themselves to a nunnery. None lack the endurance necessary to stick to the straight and narrow path while avoiding the seductive lure of mundane desires and affairs in which they must learn to play no part.

> Everything by your own will is blessed happiness,
> Everything by another's will is suffering.
>
> (*Rang dbang thams cad dge ba yin
> Gzhan dbang thams cad sdug bsngal yin.*)

Several nuns recited this popular Zangskari proverb when asked to explain why they became nuns. What they meant was that the freedom to make merit rather than babies or more housework was one of the most important reasons for joining the nunnery. The two most common reasons given for joining the nunnery were (1) to earn merit to avoid a female rebirth the next time around and (2) to avoid the suffering of marriage and maternity. Merit is seen as the vehicle that takes one out of suffering and transports one into a better rebirth. In fact, many nuns explain that they are at the nunnery not so much out of choice but because of their destiny or karma. In other words, the merit they have accumulated in their previous lifetimes is far more important than any choices they may have made or failed to make. Yet seeing one's position as a karmic boon does not deny agency or prevent nuns from surmounting considerable obstacles, as the stories above suggest. Adversity forges determination as much as endurance for those who are truly dedicated to the renunciant lifestyle.

Many nuns told me quite explicitly that they became nuns to avoid the pain of abusive marriages, miscarriages, and infant deaths that they have seen their sisters and girlfriends experience. These fears are not exaggerated in a region where one in three children dies under the age of five. The local prevalence of alcoholism, domestic abuse, and rape results in unhappy marriages and a fairly high rate of divorce, while fears of rape are a constraint on women's freedoms and vocational opportunities.[19] The nunnery still serves as a haven for those women who aspired to freedom from domestic drudgery, despite the recent increases in educational and vocational opportunities. While a small percentage of students actually complete ten years of education at shoddy government schools in Zangskar, nearly 99 percent fail the secondary leaving exam and are thus ineligible to obtain most higher government posts. In recent decades, some of the rare women who have passed the exam have become nurses, teachers, and medical orderlies, but many still lack the wealth and prestige to secure a job in the lucrative government sector, for which there are always far more applicants than positions. Yet women may still choose the nunnery over a secular career, which does not free a woman from her husband's or brother's authority. Nuns, in contrast, gain a "room of their own" at the nunnery, which leaves them relatively free to pursue meditations, studies, and merit.

Why would parents want to send a daughter to the nunnery? Yalman (1962) has argued that poor families in Sri Lanka benefit by sending their children to the monastery. This rational choice framework does not apply in Zangskar for several reasons. Firstly, Zangskari families who give up their daughters to a nunnery still have a mouth to feed, because of the institutional poverty of nunneries. Secondly, a more important motivation from the parents' perspective is gaining an adult worker who will help on the family estate. Unlike elsewhere in South Asia, Zangskari households face shortages of labor rather than food. The recent migration of young men out of Zangskar for education or jobs in the military and civil sectors has reduced the pool of available adult labor and made it even more desirable to have a daughter become a nun and servant. Poor households who cannot afford the costly ritual sponsorship required of nuns who join the monastic assembly may choose to keep their daughters at home as spinsters rather than letting them become nuns. Lastly, prospective nuns face significant emotional and psychological obstacles, not the least of which may include their families. One cannot treat monasticism as a solution to the problem of rural poverty. If poverty were the main reason that children joined the nunnery or monastery, these institutions would be overflowing with members. The spiritual gains of monasticism are tempered by the obstacles and difficulties of maintaining lifelong vows. Sometimes these include the families themselves. While some parents welcome the prospect of a daughter at the nunnery because they gain both merit and a lifelong servant, others are hesitant to commit their children to such a path. The risk of being forced to leave the monastic life for breaking one of the root vows hinders many prospective applicants from even joining.

MODERNITY AND MONASTICISM IN KASHMIR

In recent years, local and foreign feminists have made attempts to revolutionize the education of nuns in the Kashmiri regions of Zangskar and Ladakh. The Ladakhi Nuns Association has been founded by a charismatic local nun, Ani Palmo, to benefit some two dozen nunneries in eastern Kashmir, while harnessing the more recent flood of foreign sponsorship. Kashmir's Buddhist nunneries came onto the map of global feminism after the Fourth International Conference on Women and Buddhism was held in Leh, Ladakh, to promote Buddhist women's education, ordination, and religious training (Gutschow 1995). The entwined flows of capitalism and feminism have resulted in a flurry of expansion and building at over a dozen Ladakhi nunneries, several of which were founded in the last decade. Many of these nunneries face severe shortages of housing, land, and educational resources. In an effort to educate nuns about the value of the monastic discipline, Ani Palmo organized a series of innovative monastic conferences in the late 1990s. Learned Ladakhi monks holding doctorates of theology explained the meaning and importance of the novice precepts to nuns, using explanatory texts such as *The Essential Ocean of Vinaya*. The instructors explained that every monastic bears a karmic burden, not only for him- or herself, but as an example for laypeople. Ani Palmo concluded the conference with a memorable speech about how a nun's virtue is like a white cloth: once stained, it can never be clean or pure again. It is far too early to tell if these efforts will lift the glass ceiling on the nuns' vocation or simply reinforce yet again the subordination of undereducated nuns to monks.

Whether the Buddha intended it or not, the monastic order was adapted to prevailing social hierarchies from the moment of its inception. Impoverished and undereducated communities of nuns have had little opportunity to learn the ritual practices or acquire the knowledge controlled by monks. While Buddhist doctrine has attempted to transcend gender by arguing that it has no bearing on the potential for enlightenment, Buddhist practice maintains disparity at every turn. When parents send their daughters to the nunnery in exchange for merit, they also earn a share of her labor henceforth. Although Buddhism is often portrayed as having a politically correct ideology on many issues, including the environment, its stance on gender has been not as enlightened as it could have been.

ACKNOWLEDGMENTS

Tibetan terms are written following the standard Wylie system of transliteration although Kashmiri spellings may vary from Lhasa Tibetan. I thank the nuns, monks, and individual families who have hosted me in Zangskar for their boundless patience, compassion, and generosity. The Jacob Javits Foundation, the Mellon Foundation, and the Harvard Department of Anthropology funded my research between 1991 and 1997. Thanks to Michael Aris, Hanna Havnevik, Arthur Kleinman, Sarah Lamb, Sarah Levine, Diane Mines, Jan Willis, and Nur Yalman for helpful comments and conversations.

NOTES

1. Ortner (1996) follows Rosaldo (1980) in arguing that the issue of male dominance is less interesting than the study of how that dominance is framed differently according to the relations between the sexes and the interrelationship of other asymmetrical relations in any given society.

2. Lopez's (1998: 211) critical deconstruction of Tibetan Buddhism repeats the common tropes about nuns when it notes, "Unmarried daughters often became nuns (sometimes remaining at home). Other women became nuns to escape a bad marriage, to avoid pregnancy, or after the death of a spouse." Such images do not represent the current reality in Kashmir, where not one of the 115 resident nuns I have interviewed in the last decade was a divorcee and only one was a widow.

3. Scholars who have described Zangskar's seven monasteries while ignoring its nine nunneries include Crook and Osmaston (1994), Dendaletche (1985), Dargyay and Dargyay (1980), Dargyay (1987, 1988), Petech (1977, 1998), Schuh (1976, 1983), and Snellgrove and Skorupski (1980).

4. Shakabpa (1967) reports the ratio of one nun for every nine monks in Tibet before 1959. Havnevik (1990: 85) reports 653 nuns and 6,337 monks in India, Nepal, Sikkim, and Bhutan before 1959; and 340 nuns and 6,278 monks in Tibetan refugee monasteries by the late 1980s. Gutschow (1998: 97) reports that Zangskar's nine nunneries housed 116 nuns while its seven monasteries housed 297 monks in 1997.

5. Aridity and altitude allow for the cultivation of three subsistence crops—barley, wheat, and peas—as well as extensive flocks of sheep, goats, cows, yaks, and crossbreeds (mdzo). Most villages have between 50 and 500 inhabitants, who are bound by a patrilineal kinship system, which permits a medley of patrilocal and matrilocal polyandry, polygamy, monogamy, and monastic celibacy.

6. Scholars who describe the pathetic status of "village nuns" in Kashmir but largely ignore monastic nuns include Crook and Osmaston (1994) and Dollfus (1989). Compare Klein's (1985) description of unordained and unmarried women in eastern Tibet, known as ka ma, who dressed like Buddhist nuns and could join the circle of monks' tents in order to concentrate on religious practices. Ortner (1989, 1996: 119) also describes unordained women (khor ba) or "peripheral ones," who are affiliated with Sherpa nunneries in Nepal.

7. Falk (1980) and Barnes (1994) describe the devolution of the nuns' order in India. Gombrich (1971; Gombrich and Obeyesekere 1988) notes that each time the monks' order was in danger of collapse in Sri Lanka—in 1065, 1596, 1697, and 1753—a quorum of either Burmese or Thai monks came to revive the monks' ordination lineages.

8. Tsering and Russell (1996) indicate that between the twelfth and the sixteenth century, several Tibetan women may have been ordained as nuns by monks alone, without the benefit of quorum of fully ordained nuns.

9. Tsomo (1988) notes that 60,000 women hold Buddhist precepts throughout the world: 15,000 are fully ordained nuns, 5,000 are novices or probationers, and 40,000 hold a varying number of precepts (five, eight, or ten).

10. The debate about reestablishing the nuns' full ordination tradition is discussed in Bartholomeusz (1992), Gombrich and Obeyesekere (1988), Li (2000), and Tsomo (1988, 1996).

11. Although Buddhist discipline actually forbids monastics from handling money, most Zangskari monastics accept payment for their ritual services, and some serve the monastic treasury that loans cash to local villagers in addition to managing other endowments. Gutschow (1997, 1998) describes the historical origins of the economy of merit that enfolds the monastery, nunnery, and village households in Zangskari society.

12. Kerin (2000) describes the Kyirong Thukche Choling nunnery in Nepal, which has begun to teach sacred arts with the support of the Dalai Lama.

13. Gutschow (1998) summarizes the exclusion of women from sacred space in Zangskar, while Ortner (1973) and Daniels (1994) describe the role of women in the purity-and-pollution dynamic of Tibetan culture.

14. In the sixteenth century, for instance, an abbot paid the ransom fee for the king of Zangskar during a war with the Kashgar chieftain, Mirza Haidar. In return, his monastery was rewarded handsomely with huge estates throughout western Zangskar and in the neighboring kingdom of Ladakh.

15. Gutschow (1998) and Riaboff (1997) have discussed the statistics on land ownership in Zangskar.

16. If the membership were proportional with its sharecropping income, the monastery should have 2,000 monks. Karsha nuns receive 8 kilograms of grain every three years, while Karsha monks receive roughly 60 kilograms of grain per year. Compare the nunnery in Nepal, which provided each of its twenty-three members with 84 kilograms of grain per year, as Fürer-Haimendorf (1976) and Aziz (1976) noted.

17. A reincarnate priest or monk is one for whom a rebirth is actively sought out and identified after his death. Although there are thousands of recognized reincarnate monks in Tibetan society, the most famous example is the lineage of Dalai Lamas, who served as spiritual and political leaders of Tibet from the mid seventeenth century until 1959.

18. Out of more than one hundred nuns I interviewed in Zangskar, not a single one was an oldest daughter. Chosnyid, who was an exception to this rule, had to flee Zangskar in order to evade the marriage her parents had arranged and desperately sought to consummate.

19. In one Zangskari village of more than four hundred persons, there was one rape per year between 1993 and 1997, which is was more than thirty times the all-India rate between 1985 and 1995 according to one estimate (Chaturvedi 1995). Zangskar's estimated infant mortality rate of 250 per thousand was over three times the all-India rate (75 per 1,000) for 1996.

20

Muslim Village Intellectuals: The Life of the Mind in Northern Pakistan

Magnus Marsden

Today more than ever before, there is a need for sophisticated anthropological insight into the forms of individual and collective self-transformation for which the problematic term "Islamization" has come to be widely used. Among both academics and popular commentators, the "Islamizing" process is often represented as a matter of irresistible pressures to embrace a single, all-powerful model of moral and spiritual perfection based on behavioral codes derived either from Qur'anic texts or from the teachings of Islamic jurists and other authorities. So-called village Muslims are often said to be either straightforwardly resistant or meekly submissive and uncritical in their responses to the calls of self-styled Islamic purists and reformers. I present a very different account of the processes of Islamization in Chitral, a region of northern Pakistan that has been profoundly affected by movements of both local and global Islamic activism, including the rise and fall of the Taliban regime in nearby Afghanistan, and the effects of regional conflict involving the region's majority Sunni and Shia Ismaili sectarian communities.[1]

For the last seven years my fieldwork among the Khowar-speaking people of this remote and beautiful mountain area has taken me to exuberant week-long polo tournaments played out on dusty poplar-lined polo grounds, and to night-time male-only public musical programs at which delighted crowds have cheered touring performers combining exquisite Persianate verse with penetrating contemporary satire. Above all, on the road in crowded minibuses with long-distance travelers, and in local homes and teashops, I have taken part in endless hours of conversation with my Chitrali friends, all of whom spend their days and nights in continual exploration of the arts of conversation, interpersonal debate, and public verbal exposition.

From *Anthropology Today* 21(1), February 2005, pp. 10–15. Reproduced with permission of Blackwell Publishing Ltd.

Figure 20.1. View of Markaz, the administrative center of Chitral District.

They are people who value verbal skill and emotional refinement to a very high degree. They are also people who think, react, and question when they are called upon to change their ways or conform to new standards of spirituality and behavior. Their reactions to the demands of so-called Islamizers are not necessarily dismissive or hostile. What they do believe is that an individual wishing to live well and in tune with divine will must cultivate his or her mental faculties, exercising critical thought and what an anthropologist would call emotional intelligence on an everyday basis.

Everything I saw and experienced in Chitral made me realize that the best recent studies of life and thought in the Muslim world have been right to insist on the complexity and diversity of what it means to live a Muslim life. Anthropological work on, for instance, veiling practices (Brenner 1996) and the impact of new media on Muslim thought and identity (e.g., Eickelman and Anderson 1999) has furnished insights into Muslim life that contest models which seek to explain the homogenization and "perfection" of Muslim thought and identity in the contemporary world. What is scarce in specialist academic writing, however, is rich ethnographic insight into the ways in which Islamizing messages are received by village Muslims. So when I attended musical programs in Chitral at which the most requested performance entailed a local poet imitating one of the region's most powerful pro-Taliban mullahs, did this mean that the Chitral region was simply an eccentric holdout in an otherwise Islamized world, or could the daily lives of Chitral people furnish broader insights into the thought and experience of Muslims living in rural regions of the contemporary Muslim world?

FLYING COACHES: CHITRAL AND THE FRONTIER

Chitral is Pakistan's northernmost administrative district, and a part of the North West Frontier province. It is a poor and relatively remote region; in winter all roads to the region are blocked by snow. Chitral is different in many ways from other regions of the Frontier. The Frontier is dominated politically and numerically by Pashto-speaking Pukhtuns, who have been the focus of sustained research in anthropology.[2] Yet most if not all Chitral people, who call themselves Chitrali or Kho, are proud to assert that they are different in profoundly important ways from their Pashtun neighbors.[3] The main language spoken in Chitral, Khowar, is an Indo-Aryan language unintelligible to both Pashto- and Urdu-speakers.[4] Moreover, unlike in other districts of the Frontier province, there is a substantial population of Shia Ismailis, who are also Chitrali Khowar speakers, in the region. Many Sunni Muslims in Chitral and elsewhere in Pakistan hold that the Ismaili Islamic tradition is a deviation from pure Islam.[5] There have, indeed, been episodes of violent conflict between Sunni and Ismaili Muslims in Chitral, yet they continue to live together largely peacefully in many of the region's villages.

While Chitral is different in important ways from other regions of the Frontier, Chitral people are conscious and informed about what they call "down Pakistan" and the "outside world." One topic of discussion for many Chitral people is the nature and impact on their own lives of religious education as currently taught in Pakistan's Islamic seminaries (*madrasas*). Madrasas are an important dimension of life for many Chitral people: attending religious seminaries has been a major form of education for people in the region for at least the last fifty years, yet since the mid-1980s, the number of young Chitrali boys studying in ethnically diverse but largely Pukhtun-dominated Deobandi madrasas has increased considerably.[6]

The impact of messages emerging from radical Islamic religious seminaries (madrasas), both in Pakistan's Frontier province and elsewhere, on the thought processes of Muslims is now a focus of attention among many academic and popular commentators. Yet much of this work takes as self-evident that these messages are homogeneous and that their reception is uncontested, especially in poor and geographically remote regions of the Muslim world, where madrasas are often assumed by outsiders to be a focus of enthusiastic allegiance and even armed militancy. There are, however, few detailed ethnographic studies of this process of reception. More general models tend to represent the village Muslims' reception of "reformist Islam" either as a reflection of ignorance of normative Islamic doctrines in rural

Figure 20.2. A Chitrali village elder.

settings or as straightforward resistance or meek submission to forms of religious authority originating from sophisticated urban centers.[7]

However, I found such approaches unhelpful in coming to an appreciation of the complexity of the ways in which Chitral people tackle the task
of being Muslim in a world where both madrasas and an array of religious-
political movements connected to them (including the Taliban) are powerful
and influential. This is not to say that Chitral is untouched by radical Muslim
teachings about contentious issues such as the veiling of the women and the
supposedly un-Islamic nature of both local customs and the Western media:
both of these concerns are the topic of addresses made from the pulpits of
the region's mosques, and small explosive devices have been used to destroy
the satellite dishes that beam both Indian and Western television channels
into the region's relatively wealthier houses and tea shops. Yet there was a
very wide range of responses to such messages. This range included Muslims who professed ardent allegiance to the most vigorous kinds of Islamist
positions, others who were critical but appreciative of Islamizing messages,
and yet others who were publicly outspoken in their opposition and criticism. In a region in which two contrasting Islamic doctrinal traditions co-
exist, this diversity makes living a Muslim life in Chitral even more complex
and fraught, and the relationship between Chitral people who respond in diverse ways to radical Islamizing messages is the source of much discussion
in the region's villages and small towns. Yet what is striking is that while in
some cases such relations result in moments of open and even aggressive
conflict, in other situations the debate is heated but nevertheless considered
intellectually stimulating and of inherent value to those involved.

Chitrali religious students (*talib-e ilm*) bring back to the region the teachings they have learned in madrasas elsewhere in Pakistan: when they return to their villages for their summer holidays, wearing "down country"–style prayer caps, they often try to persuade their Sunni friends and family members that their Ismaili neighbors are non-Muslim infidels; they may attempt to stop their brothers from playing music with friends in the village, and throw away the bottles of home-brewed red wine they find hidden beneath their fathers' beds. Yet Chitral people do not unthinkingly defer to the pronouncements of their "little brothers" (*phuk brargini*) who have studied in the madrasas of "down Pakistan." One place where the vibrant nature of the engagement between the talib-e ilm and Chitral people less inclined toward the puritanical Islamic lifestyle they preach is most clearly evident is in the convoys of minibuses that make the fourteen-hour journey between the headquarters of the Frontier, Peshawar city, and Markaz, the region's administrative center. The journey for all passengers—for the most part Chitral people, with the occasional group of Punjabi tourists, Afghan refugees, and religious preachers from "down Pakistan"—is uncomfortable, hot, and tiring. Yet it can also be full of laughter and joking: Chitrali students put much energy into persuading the Pukhtun bus drivers to play cassettes of their favorite Chitrali love songs, and they click their fingers to the sound of the drivers' favorite Indian music hits. Since October 2002, when a coalition of religious parties was elected to government in the Frontier's Provincial Assembly, the police have also been instructed to ensure that music is not played in public transport on the region's roads. Most drivers claim, however, that the mullahs have no power to prevent them deciding what to listen to in the confines of their minibuses. "What power do the mullahs have to beat my backside? If I want music, I play music," was the response of many Chitral drivers I spoke to.

More worrying than the holders of authority and morality outside the bus, however, are their less influential but equally fervent supporters within. Playing music in the confined space of the minibus is a great source of irritation to the young madrasa students who, fingering their rosary beads and stroking their newly sprouting beards, plead with the driver (*ustaz*, literally "teacher") to turn off the music and play a Qur'anic recitation cassette instead. Such disputes are rarely completely resolved, but the drivers, mostly Chitrali and Pashtun men, leaning over the wheel of their vehicle, smoking cigarettes and hashish out of the window, and periodically stuffing chewing tobacco (*naswar*) into their mouths, often tell the aspiring mullahs that if the music is turned off they will crash into the deep ravine below. These young religious men are, then, seen as having the capacity to silence Chitral people, stop them from engaging in free and intelligent discussion, and, critically, transform their emotional states by preventing them from experiencing "open" (*kulao*) and "happy" (*khoshan*) moods, making them, instead, "frightened" and "bored." In spite of these pressures, however, many Chitral people are prepared to engage volubly and critically both in their presence and with the young scholars themselves; acting against the "little Taliban's" religious injunctions also offers Chitral men a chance to display masculine bravado.

POLITE GATHERINGS

Despite the severe difficulties of life in their homeland (*watan*), most Chitral people breathe a sigh of relief when they disembark from the minibuses that have carried them home from Peshawar and other down country Pakistani cities. Many say that there is greater peace (*scoon*) in the villages of Chitral, and that they are saved from the speed (*tezie*) of city life. Yet at the same time, they also speak of their lives as being full of tension (*tensien*) and anxiety (*pereshani*): unemployment, loans, and the unfriendly behavior of neighbors who should ideally be affectionate and loving are all enough to send most sensitive (*ihsaz korak*) Chitral people into periods of *tensien*. In this setting of sadness and anxiety one way in which many Chitral people seek enjoyment in their daily lives is through the shared experience of music and dance. During my stay in Chitral a great deal of my time was spent attending musical programs at which local musicians, poets, and comedians perform. Indeed, the sound of music was an ever-present feature of life in the region: cassettes of local Khowar music were constantly playing in the region's houses, jeeps, and shops, and my friends and I often traveled along dark mountain roads in search of musical entertainment for the evening.

There is a diverse tradition of musical performance in Chitral—the musical programs I explore here are known as gatherings, or the *mahfil*, and are characterized by their almost tea-party-like politeness. We would gather in the early evening for a meal of roast meats and rice in a friend's house; importantly, the hosts as well as the guests included both Ismaili and Sunni Muslims.[8] In the host's house my friends and I would always have to be on best behavior: we would stand when someone entered or left the room, deferentially offer glasses of water, and address our friends as the "veins of our heart" (*hardio batin*). Depending on the company we were in, sometimes before we ate or started to listen to the musicians perform we would share a bottle of home-brewed mulberry spirit, and on other occasions in more pious company prayers were offered before the entertainments began. Wine (*sharab*), my more "free" friends would often tell me, is supposed to "clean the heart" and stimulate engaging and meaningful conversation, unlike hashish (*bong*), which has the capacity to make clean minds dirty and generate sexual and immoral thoughts. When my friends did drink, however, they did so looking over their shoulder, and mostly behind locked doors: the region's religious authorities were not averse to naming "drunkards" from the villages, declaring them infidels, and shaming them in their addresses in the region's mosques.

The expert musicians who attended these musical programs were amateur performers: they did not accept payment for their music, but played, rather, for the sake of interest (*shauq*) and a love of music. When not playing in the houses of their friends, the musicians worked as shopkeepers, medical assistants, forestry officers, telephone exchange operators, and members of the police force, but they were also local celebrities in the region. Like those in attendance, the members of the musical group were also a mix of Ismailis and Sunnis—indeed, their lead singer was an Ismaili man in his mid-twenties. The instruments they played included the local four-stringed Chitral sitar, the *jeer can* (an empty petrol can used as a drum), a large *daff* (tambourine), and twin kettledrums, or *damama*. The musicians would accompany the voice of the lead singer of the group, and he would sing, mostly, modern Khowar love songs written by local poets. One popular song composed by a Sunni man in his mid-thirties and often recited was "If the heart is not troubled, then who will write the love song? If there is no dew on the green mountain pasture then who will write the love song?"

The songs performed, while recently composed by Chitral poets, drew upon older traditions of Persianate Sufi poetry: many of them described the pain of the heart (*hardio dard*) caused by separation from a lover, compared the broken heart to the shards of glass from a smashed bottle of wine, and described how love had made the "intellect astonished, but the heart compelled" (*'aql hairan magam hardi majboor*). These love songs, then, were reflections on the possibility of losing control of the intellect through the experience of heightened emotional states induced by love. Indeed, many of the musicians and poets told me that their work was deeply influenced by the real-life experience of love relationships. The emphasis on losing control of the conventions of daily polite behavior increased as the evenings progressed: the melancholic music speeded up, men who liked to dance stood and performed, and they were given encouragement by clapping and whoops of laughter and hisses of joy. Dancing with their arms outstretched, feet gently moving to the beat of their drum, men threw their heads back, looked skyward, and spun to the rhythm of the music. Many of the mahfil goers also commented that only someone with a deep knowledge of the music could ever experience its effects to their full extent. These Chitral people made clear connections about the interconnectedness of emotional and intellectual processes, and emphasized the desirability of these for their daily lives.

These programs are loved for more than just their music and dance, however. During the middle stage of a musical program of this type, men in the room who were known to be excellent impersonators would stand up and imitate people: one of the favorite impersonations during my stay in the region was of a religious scholar from the region who was a known supporter of the Taliban. The man who performed this impersonation, Mufti, was a well-known love poet, though he also claimed to be a supporter of the Islamist Jama'at-e Islami party—an important Islamist political party power-ful in Pakistan and known for supporting the introduction of a strict *shari'a* legal code.[9] Yet in the setting of the mahfil Mufti sat with his legs crossed, pointed his finger in the air, and gave comic *fatwas* (religious edicts) concerning what was and was not permissible for Muslims. Men would "lose" their "senses" laughing as they saw Mufti reincarnated as a well-known Chitrali religious scholar telling the audience that so long as there was no woman in the room then, for Muslims, anything was permissible. However, Mufti had also caught the attention of the region's religious authorities: they told him that he had committed blasphemy in his love songs, and was acting in an un-Islamic way by imitating one of the region's most famous and respected "bearded ones." And there were even some followers of the musical group itself who claimed that Mufti overstepped the mark in his imitations of the mullah, and was on the verge of apostasy.

The diversity of opinions and attitudes among Muslims in Chitral does not reflect any simple division between those in the region who are unaware of Islamic doctrinal norms and those who have been informed about such standards and have subsequently altered their behavior in order to become "true Muslims." Neither can these performers be categorized simply as tra-ditionalists resisting reform-minded Muslims—many of them are them-selves supporters of parties and movements promoting Islamic reform and purification. Rather, what is visible in Mufti's imitation of the mullah is that Chitral Muslims not only have diverse opinions about living a Muslim life, but also actively handle this diversity by continually exploring and discuss-ing it; they are involved in relations founded upon dynamic and sometimes argumentative engagement about issues of great importance for them. The enjoyment of the mahfil, then, is not only about the experience of altered emotional states: a significant component of its fun (*mazah*) is the display of critical and creative intellectual prowess.

LOCAL PHILOSOPHERS

It is not, however, only in the ecstatic moments of shared joy in music and dance that Chitral people act in ways that challenge both the pronounce-ments of the region's *ulama* and dominant Western stereotypes about the state of Muslim thought and identity in the contemporary world. There is also a tradition of critical debate and discussion that is an active, valued, and ongoing feature of everyday life in the villages of Chitral. In the village in which I mostly stayed, the most significant way of passing the time was discussion and sometimes acrimonious debate with one's fellow-villagers. Moreover, where we might expect the discussions of village Muslims in a remote region of Pakistan to be narrowly confined either to the discussion of Islamic doctrine and practice or to concerns of family honor and reputation, the intellectual life of the village Muslims with whom I lived broached sensi-

Figure 20.3. Chitrali village schoolgirls picnicking on a
day out in the mountain pastures in spring.

tive issues that are important in the present day, and they see the village as
both having and needing to sustain an intellectual life.

Chitral people distinguish between mindless gossip (*faltu mashkulgik*)
and mindful discussion and debate (*bhas korik*): the former is often viewed
as being bad for both individual health and village morality, the latter as an
important way of relieving the boredom of village life and improving the
standards of failing village morality. Furthermore, it is not only the village's
male, educated, and wealthy few who engage in such discussions: while
some of the people engaged in it were men who were well-educated by local
standards, less well-educated men and, strikingly, women also often played
an important part in these discussions. Moreover, even illiterate folk in the
region were recognized as having the ability to contribute in thoughtful and
critical ways to conversations about an array of interconnecting themes important for the villagers: they are known by their fellow villagers as "local
philosophers" (*watani falsafa*).

My friends were, they often told me, eager to discuss complex and abstract ideas, and we would spend long afternoons sitting on metal garden
chairs in the orchard of a friend, drinking tea, eating mulberries, apricots,
and apples, and enjoying conversation and debate. In these discussions one
theme of great importance for my friends was the nature of the act and experience of thought. I was often told that "true" thought flies high and free,
is the sign of a good and intelligent person, and that free thinkers appear
happy and fat. Yet many villagers also had great anxieties about thought. I
was often told that those who became lost in thought soon became thin and
weak: thinking too much alone, unlike thought allowed to pour out in a
sociable exchange of ideas, was dangerous and to be avoided at all cost. Chitral villagers, then, see thought as something that has positive and negative

dimensions, and understand it as being intimately connected to both bodily and mental well-being.

One of my friends, Aftab, a Sunni man in his early thirties, had master's degrees in both international relations and political science. His father and mother were both uneducated, and he was unemployed: despite his high levels of educational achievement he had found it impossible to realize his dream, which was to work in Pakistan's prestigious civil service. As a beneficiary of a master's-level education, Aftab was not in any sense an atypical villager: most of his friends in the village had studied for master's degrees in subjects such as Urdu literature, sociology, and political science. According to many analyses of contemporary Islam this is exactly the type of Muslim whom we would expect to become a supporter of one of the many Islamist parties now powerful in Pakistan—full with the passion of education, schooled in the teachings of Islam, and angered by his inability to enter a lucrative position in the state of Pakistan, Aftab could easily be assumed to have turned to anti-state, anti-Western, and *jihad*-oriented forms of Islamism.[10] Indeed, Aftab was a one-time supporter of Pakistan's Islamist Jama'at-e Islami party, and many of his friends told me that while at college he was very religious: he had prayed regularly and made friends with religious scholars and teachers. Yet Aftab had now cultivated a reputation for being something of a thinker (*soorch korak*) in his village—this was something of which he was proud, especially when his friends and neighbors called him *kabil* (intelligent), a philosopher (*falsafa*), and, perhaps most importantly of all, "a man with an open mind" (*kulao dimargho mosh*).

Aftab loved nothing more than voicing provocative statements before gatherings of the village's youth (*juanan*) and sometimes, even, the respected elders (*lilotan*). On one occasion, while sitting in the orchard of a Sunni friend who had married that day, he said loudly to a gathering of about ten young Sunni and Ismaili men that if they wanted to live a truly Islamic life of purity and honesty then instead of kissing their girlfriends in secret behind the darkened bushes by the river, they should embrace them openly in the village's alleys and lanes: "honesty and openness," he declared, "should be even more important for Muslims than shari'a" (the Islamic legal code). Aftab went on to tell one of his friends sitting with him, Majid, a Sunni man of about thirty who had a master's degree in sociology and who claimed to support the Taliban, that his dream of a utopian Islamic government was a false one: such a form of government, Aftab declared, would simply push more things under the surface and make the system and people's minds more hypocritical even than now. For Aftab, it was openness that Pakistan and its people needed, not secrecy (*koashteik*). Some of the boys listening to the conversation were now giggling into their handkerchiefs, and some of Aftab's more Islamist-inclined friends did say they thought he had gone mad (*gaderi*). Aftab himself once told me that one of the village elders had told him that it "had reached his ears" that Aftab's once impeccable Islamic standards had slipped, and he was reported to be saying things against Islam and the "bearded ones." Aftab was clearly upset by this gossip, yet he was also proud of the reputation he had earned as "open-minded," and was considered by most if not all villagers to be a greatly valued feature of village life.

Gaining a reputation for being a "local intellectual" or "open-minded," then, is not easy; nor does such a reputation come without its fair share of stress and anxiety. For not only are the standards that villagers set for "open-minded" thought and behavior complex and subtle, so too there are many forces in the village that work to constrain the degree to which people can think and behave "freely." What is critical, however, is that the constant struggle to demonstrate the possibility of generating independent intellectual ideas and standards, and taking an individual stand on matters of great personal significance, is one that is recognized as having the potential of unleashing unsettling anxieties—yet despite these dangers, is considered good, valuable, and worthy of personal sacrifice.

CONCLUSION

The diversity of opinion about how to live a Muslim life in Chitral is not merely the product of competition between divergent Islamic doctrinal traditions. Nor should it be understood as a manifestation of "ethnicized" religious and cultural values in the region. What I have sought to show in this article is that in both village and urban settings, Chitral people have found creative and distinctive ways of living together. They do not always do so peaceably or even sociably, and they are certainly not immune to the sectarian differences and other sources of tension that generate violent conflict in their own and other Muslim societies. Nevertheless, in almost everything they do both within and beyond the private spaces of the household and hamlet, the Chitralis I know manifest a continual recognition that the life of a good Muslim is a mindful life, in which the play of refined and emotionally sensitive thought processes is and should be a critical element of everyday human interaction. These are convictions that both the women and men I know bring to bear on their engagement with authority and their sense of their own individuality, and they are enacted above all in their reflective and energetic engagement in a world of often painful and disturbing change and unpredictability.

NOTES

1. I first lived Chitral as a school-leaver in 1995 and made three subsequent visits before conducting a 20-month period of "formal" anthropological fieldwork in the region between April 2000 and October 2001. This period of fieldwork was followed up by three further shorter stays.

2. The most detailed studies of Pukhtun society are Barth 1959, Ahmed 1983, Lindholm 1982, and Banerjee 2000.

3. There are a number of colonial accounts by British soldier-scholars of Chitral: see, especially, Robertson 1899 and O'Brien 1895. On the region's history, see Parkes 2001.

4. Many Chitral people do, however, understand and speak Urdu; those educated beyond the age of 16 are often also competent in English, and Chitral people who have lived in other regions of the Frontier are often fluent Pashto-speakers.

5. On sectarian conflict in Pakistan, see Nasr 2000.

6. The number of religious seminaries in Pakistan's Frontier Province has increased greatly over the last 20 years; most of these are affiliated to the reformist Deobandi school, and Chitral is a major center for the recruitment of students for these seminaries (see Malik 1996). On the history and development of Pakistan's *madrasa* network, see Zaman 2002.

7. In both academic and popular literature, reform-minded Muslims of many different doctrinal traditions are widely referred to as fundamentalists and Islamists. While it is important not to oversimplify, I will employ the term "reformist" to describe the wide range of "bearded ones" (*rigisweni*) whom Chitrali villagers and townsfolk see as adherents of strict, reform-minded Qur'anic forms of Islam. Such folk are also referred to as "hardened" (*saht*), "preachers" (*tablighi*), and "extremists" (*imtihai pasand*).

8. Women never attended this mahfil type of musical program. While women and girls did enjoy listening to local Khowar-language music in the privacy of their own homes, they also often told me that they preferred the more "modern" and lively Hindi film cassettes their male relatives bought in the bazaar for them.

9. On the Jama'at-e Islami, see Nasr 1994.

10. See Kepel 2002.

21

In Friendship: A Father, a Daughter and a *Jinn*

Naveeda Khan

ONE SUMMER'S DAY

What is it to encounter a human-like nonhuman form of life? How does one make a life with it? What resources are provided by one's religious tradition and everyday life to assimilate such an experience? A Muslim family with whom I am very close in Lahore, Pakistan, came to have *jinns*, supernatural beings, in their household. In the face of forceful disapproval from their co-religionists, who felt that such extended exposures to supernatural beings were bad for piety, this family found a way for their relationship to a specific jinn to work to enhance their efforts at improving themselves as pious Muslims. In the process of understanding how this family constructed their relationship to the jinn, we are also given insight into the fragility built into family life in Pakistan.

For two years prior to 2001, I had been in and out of Lahore doing dissertation research on the urban spatial manifestations of sectarianism (see Khan 2003). It was summer, and my days of spending time in mosques, religious seminaries, and shrines were cut short by the intensity of the heat and by the sudden sandstorms that made it difficult for Farooq sahib, my Urdu teacher and co-researcher, to navigate his scooter and for me to hold on to my seat on the pillion behind him. Instead, we would duck into a bank to pay a bill or linger at a bookstore to catch the cool waves from the air conditioner. Most afternoons I spent in Sandha, one of the many densely populated but unauthorized urban settlements around the Mall in Lahore. At Farooq sahib's house, which always seemed to be in a state of perpetual vertical expansion, I would trail his wife and daughters in their movements up and down stairs and on their rare trips outside. On occasion I would accompany the women to the local ice cream parlor to seek refreshment with a

Figure 21.1. Farooq sahib.

falooda (a drink of milk, ice cream, and vermicelli). When I would go to speak to the men of the house, I would find them in a small, sparse room, decorated solely with a poster of the Prophet's mosque in Medina, where they worked on the two computers owned by the family. In addition to teaching *Islami-yat* (the fundamentals of Islam and Islamic history) at a local school, Farooq sahib ran a small compositing business, which they referred to as composing, in which handwritten Urdu texts, mostly religious, were typed into the computer and then sent out for printing to the numerous small publishers crowding the Urdu bazaar in Anarkali. As will become clearer in the course of this article, the nature of this work resonates with Farooq sahib's mode of self-fashioning.

Our days were punctuated by the call to prayer, the men leaving for the mosque for each prayer and the women snatching time out of their schedules to go off to a quiet corner of the house to pray. I was, in a manner of speaking, in a powerhouse of religious rectitude: everyone in the household was a declared Deobandi (followers of a path [*maslaq*] affiliated with the Sunni reformist movement dating from nineteenth-century colonial India, see Metcalf 1982), and the sons of the household were active members of the Tablighi

Jamaat, the missionary arm of the Deobandi (see Metcalf 1993; Masud 2000; Reetz 2002). They traveled regularly through mosques in and around the city preaching to Muslims to return to the right path by expunging from their religious practices the accretions of customs in the form of innovations (*bida*) or the idolatrous association of objects or persons with God (*shirk*) (Metcalf 1997). Often when I sat in a horse and buggy or a rickshaw with Adeeb, one of Farooq sahib's two sons, while en route to an interview, he would strike up a conversation with the driver that would end with Adeeb urging him to go to his local mosque. "You will find solace there from your daily life," Adeeb would say quietly.

Imagine my surprise one afternoon when Farooq sahib and Rahima baji, his wife, walked into the room in which I lay dozing, speaking between themselves about the ants they had seen on the steps of the house. I wasn't paying attention. "Ants?" I asked, half asleep. Farooq sahib, putting on that voice of his that always indicated to me that I ought to be taking notes, declared:

> Naveeda, did we ever tell you that we had jinn living with us? We got them from an acquaintance who had inherited a group of jinn from his father, a famous *amil* [magician/healer]. But he has no use for these jinn so he gives them to whomever he thinks will benefit from them. But the recipients have to be good Muslims. Each of the men in this family was given a jinni. Hostile jinn once attacked our house posing as ants. We knew they could not be just ants because they would bleed when we killed them, whereas ants do not bleed. Thankfully, our jinn helped us to get rid of them.

By this time I was sitting up. At my look of shock at what I was hearing he assured me that the jinn had since returned to their original guardian.[1] He had made no efforts to bring them back as he felt that the family had ceased to make entreaties directly to Allah through their growing reliance upon the jinn. "Our faith [*aqida*] had become weak, and our obligatory worship [*ibadat*] was suffering." However, he continued exasperatedly: "For a while we were the most harangued house in this neighborhood, with the women dropping by all the time to ask us to locate lost keys, secure marriages, get their husbands jobs, like we were *amils* (magician/healers) or something. If the women could, they would have the jinn undertake worship on their behalf." Mildly intrigued by my interest, Farooq sahib's family related story after story to me about the jinn who had shared their home with them. "Oh, we hadn't told you about them," they said. However, after a day or two of this, their interest began to wane. "Naveeda, better get back to your research," Farooq sahib declared. In what follows I provide a short account of the jinn from the perspective of the Islamic tradition, as I do later for what it is to be a child or to follow the Prophet's *sunna* (lit., trodden path) or to even have a friend.

JINN IN CONTEXT

The most important verification of jinn is to be found in *The Holy Quran* in Sura 72, titled Al-Jinn, which opens thus:

> Say: It has been
> Revealed to me that
> A company of Jinn
> Listened (to the Qur'an).
> They said, "We have
> Really heard a wonderful Recital."

And, further on,

> There were some foolish ones
> Among us, who used
> To utter extravagant lies
> Against Allah;
> But we think
> That no man or jinn
> Should say aught that is
> Untrue against Allah (1993: 1830–31)

The most cited prophetic tradition (*hadis*, pl. *ahadis*) in support of jinn is the one in which the Prophet asked his assembled companions who among them would come with him to a gathering of jinn. When none volunteered, he pressed one of them into service. The two walked until they had left human settlement far behind and found themselves in a desolate area. In an open field stood tall figures that struck fear in the heart of the Prophet's companion. The Prophet recited the Qur'an to this silent receptive crowd, after which he turned back. When he was a little way away from the figures, he picked up a piece of bone and dung from the ground and flung it at them. He told his companion that he had asked God that the jinn be able to get sustenance from this during their travels. In other words, he had interceded on their behalf to God (El-Zein 1996: 332).

These two passages provide the strongest textual verification of the existence of jinn within Islam. Belief in the existence of jinn is considered equivalent to belief in the existence of angels, one of the primary articles of faith in Islam, and consequently, to disbelieve in them would be heretical.[2] The majority of Muslims believe jinn to be a species of spiritual beings created by God out of smokeless fire long before he created humans out of mud. God gave jinn the earth to inhabit. They are drawn to both good and evil. In this regard they are different from angels, who were created out of pure light and are incapable of evil and are, therefore, given the heavens to inhabit (Hughes 1988 [1885]; entry under *Djinn* in *Encyclopedia of Islam* 2003). In many ways jinn are the equivalent of humans in that they are endowed with passions, rational faculties, and responsibility for their own actions (El-Zein 1996). Biologically, they eat, grow, procreate, and die much like humans. Socially, they organize themselves as humans do (Westermarck 1926). However, jinn are capable of shape shifting, fast movement, great acts of strength, and long lives. They are also known to eavesdrop upon the angels in the lower reaches of heaven to acquire limited knowledge of the future (Hughes 1988 [1885]; Westermarck 1926; El-Zein 1996; *Encyclopedia of Islam* 2003). Humans and jinn co-inhabit the earth; however jinni haunts are primarily desolate places such as forests, ruins, and graveyards. The relations between the two may vary from mutual indifference to warfare in the distant past, to relations of love and guardianship between members of both species. For humans, such a relationship may disrupt their lives through spirit possession (see Crapanzano 1980; Boddy 1989; Bowen 1993; El-Zein 1996; Rothenberg 1998; Pandolfo 2000; Siegel 2003). Humans have long struggled to bring jinn within their possession to harness their powers. However, as we shall see, these relations between humans and jinn are constantly evolving. My account of the jinn in Farooq sahib's family can, therefore, be read as a recent installment in this long history of relations between humans and jinn.

The word of Islam was sent to jinn as it was to humans, through the Prophet Muhammad. In other words, jinn pre-exist Islam. After the introduction of Islam, jinn became divided between those who became Muslims and those who did not. However, in the shift to Islam, the jinn began to be more associated with evil, whereas previously both good and bad had been equally ascribed to them. An early theological debate, which remains unresolved, was whether Iblis (the devil) originates from this species (Hughes 1988 [1885]; El-Zein 1996; *Encyclopedia of Islam* 2003). Some claim that he was allowed among the ranks of angels because of his immense devotion to God and was later banished from the heavens after his refusal to kneel before Adam. This association with Iblis hints at the anxiety that currently accompanies a belief in the existence and disruptive tendencies of jinn. Another classical theological debate that continues into the present deliberates whether jinn are indeed a different category of being from humans or whether they are forces of nature or projections of human interiority, in the Muslim sense, as are the little mischievous spirits (*nafs*) that make up a self (Bowen 1993; El-Zein 1996; see Metcalf 1997 on nafs).

In South Asia, I have found a general acceptance of the anthropomorphic existence of jinn and their disruptive, possibly evil, tendencies, intermixed with a wariness that this acknowledgement of alternative worlds not be seen as yet another marker of Muslim irrationality. My intent in this article is not to address this sense of insecurity that arises from an almost quotidian acceptance of jinn, nor do I do justice to the rich anthropological and psychological literature that interprets the belief in jinn as complex arrangements of cultural memory, political strategy, mental illness, and individual subjectivity (see Crapanzano 1980; Boddy 1989; Bowen 1993; El-Zein 1996;

Rothenberg 1998; Pandolfo 2000; Siegel 2003). In my argument, the appearance of the jinn within a family provides insight into the manner in which Islam is inhabited by its worshippers while bringing to the fore tensions that undergird everyday life.

MARYAM THE MEDIUM

When the jinn first came to them some seven years prior to my arrival in 1999, Farooq sahib's immediate family included his wife and their two sons and three daughters (born in that order). Their conduit to the jinn was Maryam, the second of Farooq sahib's daughters, who was then an eight-year-old girl. When I first met Maryam, she was fifteen and had finished her education at a private school for girls after passing her metric examinations. Her elder sister, who was sixteen, was to be married shortly, so Maryam had assumed many of the household duties she once shared with her sister. Her family continued to view Maryam as the most spiritual of the girls, while her eldest brother Adeeb also had a reputation for piety from an early age.

Although I did not observe Maryam's transition from childhood to adulthood, I imagined how it must have been for her by observing the family's treatment of their youngest daughter, Farah, who was eight when I first met her. At that age, Farah did not as yet observe the veil (*purdah*) but frisked around in frocks and high heels and occasionally dabbed some lipstick on her mouth. She was frequently indulged by being held and kissed and asked to recite *nat* (a form of poetry in praise of the Prophet). However, by the end of my stay, when she was almost ten, she was already being pulled protesting out of her sleep to say her prayers with the family since she would soon be of an age when she would be accountable.

According to Islamic beliefs, children are born free of sin and have the ability to communicate with divine beings (Das 1989); however, they are considered beings without reason (*aql*) and therefore carry the threat of being easily led astray (Lapidus 1976; Aijaz 1989; Devji 1994). Consequently Islamic and Qur'anic instruction has to begin as early as four years of age to ensure that children are provided guidance from early in their lives. By the time their children are ten years old and are considered to have reached the age of sexual maturation, Muslim parents are urged by religious scholars (*ulama*, sing. *alim*) to hold them responsible for any missed religious duties, notably the reading of the Qur'an, prayers, and fasting. According to a hadis quoted in a child-rearing manual, "the Prophet (S.A.W.) has said that we should call upon our children to offer prayers when they are seven years old and when they are ten years they should be punished for missing prayer and should have separate beds" (Aijaz 1989: 32). By this time, parental entreaties may be replaced by punishment if children have not formed the habit of prayer and fasting (Aijaz 1989: 30).[3] Farooq sahib would himself espouse this normative position on childrearing before and after Maryam's encounter with the

· Figure 21.2. Maryam the medium, as an adult.

jinn; however, during her period of encounter, Maryam embodied the dutiful child in a different way.

As an eight-year-old, Maryam had a window into the spirit world, channeling communications between the jinn and her family. At times she would look into the palms of her hands to see what the jinn would have her see; at other times, the stories about her relationship to the jinn suggest her ability to see how this world was intertwined with the jinni world, a mirror of this one. She saw the jinn interspersed among her family members. She relayed the requests of the human world to the jinn to seek their advice, instructions, and sometimes expressions of their desire. For instance, one day she told her father that one of the jinn wanted to taste human food, and with her father's permission, she instructed the jinn that he could enter her father's body. That day, as Farooq sahib related to me, he had an appetite that frightened him with its enormity. He felt that he would have stayed rooted to his seat on the floor and would have eaten throughout the night, if he had not run out of food.

When the jinn first came to Farooq sahib's house, the family's curiosity would compel them to spend long hours conversing with the jinn about their lives in the jinn world. In the course of these initial introductions, one of them revealed himself as a *sahaba* jinni. The title "sahaba" refers to a close companion of the Prophet, or at least one who was alive at the time of the Prophet, thus having the opportunity to see him at first hand and to relay his teachings directly from the Prophet himself. Moreover, certain ahadis (prophetic traditions) attest to Muhammad's conversion of tribes of both people and jinn to Islam. Given the long lives attributed to jinn, it was conceivable to have a sahaba jinni alive today.[4] And given the importance acceded to the pious actions of the sahaba, it was thus no surprise that Farooq sahib would be interested in this particular jinn upon whom to model his behavior as a pious Muslim upholding the Prophet's example.

PIOUS IMITATION

I understood Farooq sahib's preoccupation with the Prophet's example. From the beginning of my research Farooq sahib had been integral to the picture of religious differences I was putting together. It was he amongst my various Urdu teachers who had taken it upon himself to teach me the nuances of the theological aspects of religious conflict. He would not let me slip into a comfortable modernist pose of dismissing these differences as the political expressions of the *petit bourgeoisie,* as identity politics. It was through his very confident articulations and his heated conversations with others that I understood how ontological these differences were, that is, how they expressed different lived relations to the time and personality of the Prophet, to nature, and to creation.

Farooq sahib was by no means a religious scholar, but he took such scholarship seriously. He was *sayyid* (noble-born, those who claim descent from the Prophet). He was a calligrapher by training, a teacher of Urdu and Islamiyat by vocation, and a composer of computer-generated religious texts by profession. For him calligraphy in the Islamic tradition was the textual expression of that which is enjoined upon every Muslim, to "imitate Muhammad." Just as the calligrapher, now composer, seeks to make the most perfect copy of a text without introducing any novelty into it, so too did Farooq sahib and his sons struggle to make themselves the perfect imitation of the Prophet, to uphold his *sunnah* (his manner of life) without introducing any innovation into it.

By the time I met Farooq sahib he had already tried out another mode of imitating the Prophet, different from the Deobandi path and yet still within Sunni Islam in Pakistan, through passionate love for and ecstatic identification with the Prophet. This was the Barelwi path (see Sanyal 1996; Buehler 1998), into which he was born, which is generally recognized as infused with Sufism. In this path the Prophet was immanent in the world, present everywhere, of course, with the permission of God, so as not to grant God's powers to another even if it were the Prophet himself, the most beloved of God. Farooq sahib's own family, that is, his parents and sisters and brothers, who had stayed behind in Delhi, India, at the time of the Partition of 1947, had remained Barelwi. Farooq sahib moved to Lahore in part so that his wife could be closer to her own family and in part so that he could ply his profession as calligrapher and, later, composer, in a place where Urdu would be the *lingua franca* of the nation. However, through his ceaseless copying of religious texts, old and new, authentic and inauthentic, in the new nation of Pakistan, in which flourished much experimentation with Muslim identities, Farooq sahib had come to realize that this was not the correct path through which to experience the Prophet.

So the sahaba jinni was the one with whom the family was most taken. In fact Maryam would spend most of her time describing Sulayman.[5] He was tall, I was told.[6] He had a long beard that he kept well groomed. He was always dressed in spotlessly clean clothes. He kept his face arranged in a serious expression and was careful not to indulge in loud outbursts of laughter. Although he looked stern, he smiled easily. He would sit down to eat or drink. He was also very gentle with Maryam. She said she never felt frightened in his presence and claimed him as a friend. The family was captivated by these details about Sulayman's comportment, much more so than the descriptions of the physical landscape and social structure of the jinn world also related by Maryam. In fact, her father and brothers would listen carefully to her descriptions of Sulayman as examples of the correct way to imitate the Prophet's example.

THE JINN IN THE WEAVE OF DOMESTICITY

While the jinn introduced a new model of piety for the family, how did his introduction into the family bring the dynamics of the family to the fore? Although Farooq sahib's immediate family was not living in a joint family arrangement, the exact number of inhabitants remained in flux. Relatives came and went as the family retained close ties with its extended kin, who would visit from as far away as Multan, Karachi, and even Delhi. Furthermore, there was an expectation of future growth, as the adult sons would soon have their families within this household.

Over the time I was in Lahore, the unproductiveness of the sons was a continual source of tension within the family. While Farooq sahib toiled at numerous paying jobs, Adeeb spent much of his time undertaking work that was pious but unremunerated, such as taking private lessons with a well-known alim; doing the beat of the neighborhood to invite male members of households to pray in the mosque; preparing lessons with his Tablighi companions in their center in Lahore; going on retreats to convert errant Muslims in other parts of the country and abroad; and even on occasion retreating to the mosque for prayer and contemplation for Ramzan, the Islamic month of fasting. Although the family, Rahima baji in particular, was very proud of him, they also felt very keenly the meagerness of his contributions to the family coffers. Of late, Adeeb had gained a lot of weight and, together with his beard, head cap, and loose, flowing tunic, he looked much older than his twenty years. People had started to refer to him as a *mulla*, once a title of respect but now a derogatory term for a religious personage who is seen to spend most of his time sitting around the mosque (see Ewing 1999; Khan 2003).

His younger brother Ali was not doing much better. At the beginning of our acquaintance, he was ambivalent about being openly pious, preferring to spend his free time hanging out with his friends, watching pirated Hindi films, and generally exploring opportunities to leave Pakistan. By the end of my stay, he had been drawn to the more strident aspects of the Deobandi path, seeking to correct members of other Sunni paths for their misuse of Islamic law. Fashioning themselves on the militant group Sipah-e Sahaba, Ali's group called themselves Sipah-e Hanafiya (warriors of *Hanafiya*). One time, disgusted by the failure of Adeeb and Ali to provide more financial support to the family, Farooq sahib spat out at them, "why don't you call up ghosts [jinn *bhoots*] to make some money." If they considered themselves too superior to take up regular jobs, then why didn't they simply resort to being amils (healers/magicians) to make some money? By this time, the jinn had already come and gone from the family, and, from what I could make out, the family had seen it beneath themselves to profit monetarily from them. Although Adeeb had shown some talent in the profession, for him to turn to *amaliyyat* (the practices associated with being an amil) now would be a considerable step down for these well-born boys.

Meanwhile, in 2001 Rahima baji's sister died quite unexpectedly in nearby Multan, leaving behind two young children who came to live with Farooq sahib and Rahima baji shortly after. Farooq sahib agreed to keep them and even adopt them if necessary, but the children pined for their father. At the same time there was some concern about how Farooq sahib would manage financially if they were to live with him permanently. No one dared approach the children's father about this matter. Instead they sat around speculating whether he planned to remarry and abandon his children altogether.

By this time, the jinn had returned to the amil, and in any case, Maryam was no longer a child and could not serve as a medium. Nonetheless, the family decided to have Farooq sahib's youngest daughter, Farah, speak to Sulayman the jinni about what lay ahead for the young children. However, Farah did not fare as well as Maryam. She was alternatively frightened of the jinni and upset at him for not taking her to Mecca as he had promised. The family then sent the children of the deceased woman to transmigrate to Multan with Sulayman to see what was in their absent father's mind. When they returned to their bodies, they described how they had seen their father at home packing his bag. This offered hope that he was coming to pick them up, as he did indeed shortly afterward, but then just as quickly sent them back. Throughout the time I was there, the children remained in limbo, moving among several households.

Keeping in mind this unresolved tension of the children's fate and the straitened state of finances within the family, I turn briefly to a third story, that of the withholding of forgiveness. Rahima's mother had become the de facto guardian of the motherless children. A beautiful old woman untouched by the ravages of time, she had returned to mothering, she said, when she ought to be knitting sweaters. Her domestic arrangements were themselves a continuing source of tension within Farooq sahib's household. She had been estranged from her husband for almost a decade and lived in Lahore with her eldest son, while her husband, whom she never referred to by name but always as "he," lived with Farooq sahib and Rahima baji. He would only emerge from his dark corner downstairs to go to the mosque to pray. Having developed a cough that racked his body, he feared that he might die soon and wished to reconcile with his wife. He had sought her out on several of her visits to Farooq sahib's house, but as she told me, although she wanted to do the right thing by him, his presence made her sick. Spurred on by Rahima baji, Farooq sahib attempted to reconcile the two. When all the stories of the jinn were being told to me, Rahima's mother came up and said almost ruefully, "Naveeda, I too was offered a jinni once. Now what is a jinni but a man? And I don't want to have a relationship with a man ever again."

The stories related above of the disappointment of parental expectations, the abandonment of children, and a wife's estrangement from her dying husband hint at the tensions that tear at families, even one as closely knitted as this one. A final story suggests how familial relations figured in the threat of a nonhuman other within the domestic sphere in the shape of a malevolent witch.

During the time when Maryam still served as the family's medium and long before I came into the picture, Farooq sahib had traveled to India to spend time with the Barelwi (a different sect of Islam) side of his family. Maryam remained restless the entire time he was away, scared that he might never come back. She asked her mother to take her to their amil friend almost every day so that she might speak with Sulayman the jinni. Every day she would whisper something to him. Meanwhile, Farooq sahib tried to get his Indian visa extended to allow him to spend more time with his family in Delhi. However, it seemed to him, particularly in retrospect, that his every attempt failed. Dejected, he had to return on the very day that his original visa expired. Maryam rushed to greet him at the door of the house, but then she fell back screaming. Apparently a thirty-foot witch (*churail*)[7] had followed Farooq sahib back from India. Farooq sahib immediately dropped his bags at the door and rushed to the mosque to say his prayers. When he returned home, Maryam assured him that the witch had left. If Maryam had still been frightened, he said, he would have had to tear up the city looking for someone to rid him of the witch, but thankfully prayers had done the trick. When I asked Maryam why she did not want her father to stay in India, she replied that his family there was not going to let him go and that

they had literally bewitched him because they were jealous he was returning to his other family. When I asked Farooq sahib what he thought of this
suggestion, he shrugged and thought it genuinely possible that his Barelwi
family would pull such a prank because they did not take his being a Deobandi seriously enough. I pushed him on this statement. After all, it was a
grave accusation to make against one's own brothers and sisters. "Jealousy
is a strong force. Sometimes those who are jealous do not even know how
they bind others up," he replied. Although the witch may well have been the
projection of Maryam's sense of loss at her father's absence, jealousy of his
other family, or even fear that he was in alien country hostile to her own, for
Farooq sahib, the witch was to be located squarely within the Barelwi affiliation of his family.

CONCLUSION

Thus far we have mulled on ways in which the relations to a jinn and familial
relations stand next to each other. Family stories about their time with the
jinn have allowed me to tease out key dimensions of everyday life in this
family. Let us mull over friendship as one more element in this milieu that
constitutes everyday life. Unquestionably, friendship has a place of privilege
within the Islamic tradition. One cannot control the family into which one is
born or the family one begets, and there even exists an injunction in which
the author claimed that it is best to disown one's children if they continue to
resist parental authority to mold them into pious Muslims (Aijaz 1989). However, good friends aid one another in the pursuit of piety. "A trusted friend
is a safe treasure in the world and his companionship is to be greatly valued.
This is possible only in good fellowship for good and pious works" (Karim
1989: 549). Certainly, friendship nourished Adeeb, providing a resolution to
a standing tension within his family over his unproductiveness. It opened
up a future for him to continue to be pious in the way he desired. After I left
in 2001, in his travels with his Tablighi companions he met and befriended
a young industrialist who recently gave him a job as the prayer leader of a
mosque on his industrial estate in the fringes of Lahore. There Adeeb finally
accepted his talents as an amil and began to dispense cures and spells to the
workers in the estate. He married the younger sister of the industrialist and
secured a marriage for Maryam with another of his Tablighi companions.
Maryam now has a child, and the two often return home to stay with her
parents for extended periods of time while her husband travels to spread the
word of Islam.

    What of the friendship that Maryam once shared with Sulayman the jin-
ni? Maryam did not seem to remember much. She had been busy assuming
the role of the only grown daughter in her parents' home by the time I left
Lahore in 2001, and she was now busy in her new role as a wife and mother.

Yet here too something had changed. When I last spoke with her about her experiences in the winter of 2004, she readily claimed a friendship with Sulayman, grateful that he never frightened her in their many interactions. She had missed him after he left them. Farooq sahib and Rahima baji recalled that she had cried herself to sleep for weeks after. She claimed to have had dreams, such dreams, but she cannot recall them now. She just recalled the sense of those dreams with a shiver, while busy making us tea. Even now her sister-in-law, Adeeb's wife, teased her lightly about Sulayman.

Did Sulayman simply aid in the family's pursuit of piety? In place of her words, I imagine a certain friendship, derived in part from my own readings of *Tales of the Arabian Nights* and from the insight that perhaps Maryam too was not unfamiliar with these stories. As in the famous tale of Aladdin and the magic lamp, now caricatured through the Walt Disney production, a child finds a genie and can be literally pulled out of a certain existence to soar the skies. Maryam had shared in Sulayman's joy of discovering human food. She whispered her secrets into his ears to engage him in her projects. She traveled to places with him (although Sulayman refused to go to the United States). She was able to help out her family and her neighbors and she was able to take leave of her body, which was already changing beyond her control. Soon the time would come when she would not be able to access this world any longer, and I imagine her father was not averse to the jinni leaving before she was faced with a sense of loss. Is Sulayman then the arc of a certain line of flight for Maryam? I am not saying that hers was a miserable existence from which Sulayman, or even the idea of Sulayman, provided her certain escape. Instead, I am suggesting that a rich friendship between a human and a nonhuman is possible, even allowed, within the rubric of the Islamic tradition.

NOTES

1. I was not surprised at the claimed existence of jinn, as I had been told of alternative worlds to the human one and of the material and spiritual negotiations that humans enter into with the inhabitants of these worlds. What shocked me was that I had understood Farooq sahib's family to accept only obligatory worship (*ibadat*) as the legitimate way to approach God, having heard only their derision of other intercessionary modes in the two years I had known them. Yet here, in the last leg of my research, I was learning that they had once had jinn in their possession. This raises an interesting question about the temporality of memory (or even of fieldwork itself): Why did it take this family almost two years to remember to tell me this experience? Or was it a question of trust?

2. Even the Mutazilates, early Muslim materialists, dared not discount the existence of jinn, although on the few occasions they spoke of them they referred to jinn as uncivilized tribes inhabiting the world (El-Zein 1996).

3. The importance of the child for the Muslim family cannot be emphasized enough. "In the Middle East, the child is seen as the crucial generational link in the family unit, the key to its continuation, the living person that ties the present to the past and to the future" (Fernea 1995: 4). The burden of raising them as good Muslims rests heavily upon parents not only in the interests of grounding Islamic society but also in ensuring their standing before God. As a child, I was often urged to attend to my Arabic lessons and prayers with seriousness so that my parents might meet their maker without shame or fear of retribution on the Day of Judgment.

4. In the following story, we have reference to a sahaba jinn:

> Some people left for Mecca. They lost their way and felt that they were about to die, so they put on their shrouds and lay down waiting for death to come. Then a jinni came from the trees and said: "I am one of the jinn who listened to the Prophet. I heard him saying: 'The believer is like a brother to the believer. He is his eye and his guide and never forsake him.' This is the water and this is the way." Then he guided them to the water and showed them the way. [El-Zein 1996: 313]

5. While I have changed the names of all my subjects in this article, I have left the original name of the favored jinn. This is because I want to draw attention to the significance of the name Sulayman to the history of jinn. In the Qur'an, Sulayman is mentioned as the prophet and the king to whom God gave the power to discourse with animals and jinn, whose powers Sulayman in turn harnessed to construct the temple named after him. In Surat Saba, it is elaborated that the jinn continued to build the temple after Sulayman died and only realized that he was dead when the staff upon which his body had been leaned crumbled, having being eaten by termites, and the body fell over. Stetkevych writes that the mythopoetic registers of the Qur'an and of the Arabic-Islamic culture have been neglected within the field of Islamic studies (1996: 2). One could make a similar argument for the mythopoetic registers of everyday life within Muslim societies. Sulayman the jinn introduces perhaps a mythic moment in the Islamic tradition in which men, beasts, and jinn lived in close communication and cooperation in opposition to the present context, in which prophets, kings, and caliphs are invoked to express difference and dissonance among men. Furthermore, Das has made the interesting argument that children take "frequent recourse to the mythic" in making sense of their often violently changing social reality (1989: 288). This leads me to speculate further upon the (unintended?) agency of Maryam in mediating King Sulayman's claim upon this violent present as a different modality of being with difference.

6. Jinn are creatures of smokeless fire; that is, they do not have a fixed form. However, if they show themselves in one particular form to humans, they remain in that form as long as they remain in sight. The only way they can change forms is if they can trick the humans into looking at a copy of them, which then frees them to take another form or to escape into formlessness (El-Zein 1996). This suggests something of the coercive force humans may exert upon jinn, fixing them to a form when they may wish to be other. In this instance, however, the jinn left the family after the men were forced into dancing the traditional *bhangra* dance at a cousin's wedding. The jinn condemned this as immoral behavior that they did not wish to condone through their continued existence as part of this family. See Rothenberg 1998 for another instance of how jinn provide a barometer of everyday morality.

Interestingly, Farooq sahib said that he was very embarrassed to face his neighbors after the jinn left his family. Although he did not provide any explanation for his embarrassment, one can guess that it looked bad for the family to be so judged by a jinn and to suffer a loss of power and status. However, he quickly got over the loss.

7. More specifically, this is the ghost of a woman who has died during childbirth, a very inauspicious and very likely a vengeful figure.

22

Vernacular Islam at a Healing Crossroads in Hyderabad

Joyce Burkhalter Flueckiger

I was quite literally called to Amma, the Muslim female healer who is the focus of this essay, by the green flag that flies atop her courtyard. I was in the south Indian city of Hyderabad in 1989 to co-direct a folklore fieldwork workshop, the focus of which was to be Muslim women's life histories. From the Osmania University Guesthouse, perched up on a rocky hill overlooking a neighborhood of university housing for nonacademic employees (janitors, clerks, watchmen, etc.), I noticed a green flag flying in the middle of the neighborhood. I knew that under such a flag, we would find some kind of Islamic ritual activity, and hoped it would be a place from which to begin to find women with whom to work. Somewhat nervously, I walked with two Hindu workshop participants across the road and into the cluster of homes to see who or what was beneath the green flag.

There, in a shaded courtyard under the green flag sat several Muslim women in their black *burqās* (the long cloak/veil worn by many Muslim women in South Asia), Hindu women in brightly colored saris, and a handful of men. Others were crowded around a small doorway, straining to catch a glimpse of someone inside or hear a voice from within. We stood at the periphery of that group and asked what was happening. When Amma heard chatter of "some women from the outside," she called us into the healing room. She was seated on the floor in front of a small wooden writing desk covered with slips of paper held down by paperweights. Ten to twelve people were seated on the ground around her. She asked them to move over to make space for the three of us, invited us to sit down, and soon called for tea.

Amma was a middle-aged woman who briefly identified herself as a *pirānimā* (wife of a *pīr*, a Sufi teacher/master) who meets patients here in the healing room and writes *tāvīz* (amulets upon which are written Qur'anic verses, numbers, and names of God). Her healing practice, she continued, was based on the Qur'an, and its success was guaranteed for illness caused by spiritual forces (which she later named as including infertility, failure-to-

Figure 22.1. Patients waiting in the courtyard of Amma's healing room, 1989.

thrive babies, runaway or disobedient children, abusive marriages, chronic pain, stolen gold, runaway goats, interfering neighbors, failing businesses, and restlessness). She was curious how we had found her. I explained that we were living across the street in the guesthouse for three weeks, but that we were restless staying inside and studying all day; we wanted to meet our neighbors. After all, I continued, "What's the use of staying only in the guesthouse and classrooms?" The patients sitting around Amma laughed and confirmed our intuitions: "*Correct*; *correct*."[1]

SPIRITUAL HEALING AS VERNACULAR PRACTICE

Amma's healing room represents a level of non-institutionally-based Islamic practice that I have identified as "vernacular Islam." Vernacular Islam is shaped and voiced by individuals in specific contexts and in specific relationships, individuals who change over time, in social, economic, and political contexts that also shift. To study vernacular Islam—in this case, through the lens of a specific female healer in South India—is to identify sites of potential fluidity, flexibility, and innovation in a religious tradition that self-identifies as universal and is often perceived to be ideologically monolithic. Ethnographic research for this chapter was conducted in the 1990s.[2]

Amma sits in a healing room built off her living quarters, where she meets as many as forty to fifty patients a day—Hindus, Muslims, and Christians—writing amulets of various kinds, battling what she calls illnesses of *śaitān* (literally, the devil): physical, social, and mental illnesses caused by spiritual disruption. Amma's prescriptions externalize and ritually manipulate *śaitāni* (negative forces), distancing or destroying them. However, Amma continually reminded me that her deep spiritual wisdom and authority were needed to make any of the ritual prescriptions effective. And patients are more concerned with what she says—her performatives such as, "Your son *will* return home," her storytelling and practical advice—than they are in the specifics of what she writes on amulets. Spiritual illnesses, Amma asserts, can be countered only by spiritual healing, and purely physical illnesses can be healed only through allopathic (physical) treatments. While for the latter, she readily recommends specific doctors (from obstetricians to optometrists), her referrals are not reciprocated by allopathic doctors.

Numerous spiritual healing alternatives are found within a mile radius of Amma's healing room. In one direction is a Hindu goddess shrine where, in hopes of gaining fertility, Hindu petitioners tie coconuts in the limbs of the trees that surround it, and many Muslim petitioners offer *tāzziyā* (bamboo representations of the tomb of the Prophet's martyred grandson Hussein) at that same site. Down the road the other direction is a *dargāh* outside of which sits a Muslim Baba selling rings of precious stones that are said to protect the body and restore the balance of its elements. Further into the neighborhood adjacent to the university one finds Saint Anthony Cathedral, where a diverse array of patients lines up on Thursday mornings to receive the blessing of healing from the saint. Across the entrance of a charismatic Christian church in the same neighborhood hangs a banner that reads "Jesus Heals" (rather than the perhaps more familiar evangelical Christian mantra "Jesus Saves"), and the church identifies itself as a "healing church." Many patients participate in more than one of the healing systems represented by these sites, sometimes sequentially and sometimes at the same time.

While spiritual healing characterizes many vernacular religious traditions in India, each healing site is uniquely created by those who "sit" in it and the means through which they claim authority to be there. In the case of Amma's healing room, it is her gender that most uniquely characterizes her practice; she sits in a traditionally male ritual role, that of the Sufi pir, who is a spiritual teacher and healer. Amma's husband, Abba, is such a pir, but he is not literate in Arabic writing, upon which the healing practice depends.[3] When Amma became a disciple of a healing pir and showed an interest in learning the healing system, Abba gave her permission to do so. Upon completion of her training and sitting *cillā* (a forty-day spiritual retreat), she slowly began to meet the *public,* meaning both men and women, and Hindus, Muslims, and Christians. This contrasts Amma with other Muslim women who may practice some kind of domestic healing (also distinguished

Figure 22.2. Amma blessing a patient with *duā* prayer
at the end of a healing session, 1991.

from Amma's practice in that these women do not use written treatments)
within their own families or for female friends and neighbors. Amma and
Abba share a symbiotic relationship, dividing between them the traditional
roles of the pir; Amma is the healer and Abba the teacher. Amma has received authority to heal from Abba, and most of Abba's disciples come to
him through Amma's healing practice.

RELIGIOUS IDENTITIES IN THE HEALING ROOM

During the course of my first meeting with Amma, perhaps in an effort to
make me and my two Hindu colleagues feel at ease—although I later heard
similar statements in several other contexts—Amma asserted, "There are
only two castes [*jāti*, species, true distinctions]: men and women. Muslims,
Christians, Hindus—they're all the same." "Jati" literally means "birth" and
is the Indian-language term for regional, endogamous caste groups into
which one is born. It is also the word for species, so that in Indian language
translations of the story of Noah and the ark—for example, when the animals go up into the ark two-by-two, according to species—they are said to
go up "jati by jati." Here, Amma asserts that gender crosscuts and super-

sedes superficial boundaries of religious difference, and that gender is the ultimate boundary of distinction between human beings.

Amma's assertion about gender and religious identities directs us to two significant features of vernacular Islam as performed in her healing room: (1) the articulation of an Islamic cosmology and ritual practice that is encompassing of difference and (2) the potential flexibility of gender roles in domestic and ritual contexts of Islam in practice. Concerns about gender and religious identities carry differential weight in the healing room itself, however. Amma and her patients often talk about their gendered experience and negotiations of gendered roles and authority; and many patients say they come to Amma *because* she is a woman, whom they experience to be more loving, patient, and understanding than male pirs. However, the shared religious cosmologies and rituals that permit religious healing across religious difference were assumed by Amma's patients and rarely articulated or debated.

Amma's patients often asked me what I was writing down in my little notebook, as I was sitting at the healing table. I told them that I wrote down the name of each patient; whether s/he was Hindu, Christian, or Muslim; the presenting problem; the diagnosis; and the prescription. Amma often shook her head at my response, disappointed that I hadn't learned that, as she said, "Jo-ice, there is no Hindu or Muslim here," at *this* place. This is not to say that Amma and her patients don't know who is a Hindu and who is a Muslim when they meet and speak with each other in the healing room. Visually, Hindu and Muslim identities in Amma's healing room and courtyard are marked in several ways. The most obvious marker for women is whether or not they are veiled (which, for Muslims, may range from covering one's head with the end of a sari to wearing the full, black burqa). But not all Muslim women veil. Among unveiled women, Hindus can be identified by the vermillion powder forehead mark. Further, sari styles and colors and types of jewelry may also differ according to caste and religious identities. For the majority of men who come into the healing room, it is more difficult to visually determine whether they are Muslim or Hindu unless they have just attended a Hindu ritual and have the forehead marking on, or if they are highly observant and committed disciples of a Muslim pir. Male disciples' commitment to both their pir and Islamic identity is marked by their shoulder-length hair, beards, *surmā* (eye liner), and embroidered or white crocheted skullcaps/head coverings. Even were there to be any question of religious identity visually, as soon as a patient gives his/her name to Amma to begin the diagnostic process, the name itself indicates his/her religious affiliation.

But *at this place*, in the healing room, religious distinctions and identities are not those that matter most to either Amma or her patients. The patients who come to Amma for healing, whether they are Muslim, Christian, or Hindu, recognize in her a charismatic woman who controls spiritual forces that cross religious boundaries and have impinged upon their lives in negative ways. This much they share, although their identification and interpretation of these forces and their understanding of the means through which Amma controls them may vary significantly.

THE HEALING ROOM AS A CROSSROADS

I have identified Amma's healing room as a *caurāstā*, a crossroads (literally, four roads) where the importance of religious identity collapses. A caurasta in Indian contexts is conceptualized as a center: one of many such centers in a network of multiple roads with numerous crossings. In traditional Indian cities, towns, and neighborhoods, caurastas are meeting places, where roads and people are experienced primarily as coming together rather than going out. They are public gathering places and social spaces; their corners bustling with tea stalls, bus stands, and movie theaters; filled with crowds and conversation. It is with these connotations that Amma's healing room serves as a crossroads, a caurasta: a public social space uniquely created by the particular roads and travelers who travel through it.

Amma's healing room is a physical locale where patients of many different religious identities share the crisis of illness, and their search for healing has brought them into the presence of a charismatic Muslim healer, with whom they enter both short-term and lifelong relationships. But the healing room is not a space where they dwell; it is a caurasta. When they go home and arrange the marriages of their children or conduct death rituals for their parents, it matters very much whether or not they are Muslim or Hindu. Once axes of difference cross through the caurasta, where they may be said to collapse or be overlooked in favor of the common "task" or performance at hand, they reassert themselves in different contexts (at the far ends of the axes), such as endogamous marriage requirements, death rituals, family law (such as divorce), attitudes toward image worship, political voting blocs, and reserved seats in universities and government employment. The further the axes move out from the caurasta, the more it "matters" who is Hindu and Muslim.[4] In other contexts of self-representation, textually educated members of religious communities may identify textual traditions as the crucial identity markers, and identify vernacular practices that are not described or proscribed in the texts to be extraneous to the tradition—not "real" Hinduism, Islam, or Christianity.

Patients who come to Amma's healing room share more than simply human affliction and attraction to a charismatic healer. Religious healing across religious boundaries is possible, in part, because patients share (and Amma reinforces and performs) features of a unifying cosmology, a spiritual plane that crosses boundaries of difference at the crossroads. Patients assume the possibility of spiritual forces negatively impinging on physical, social, and

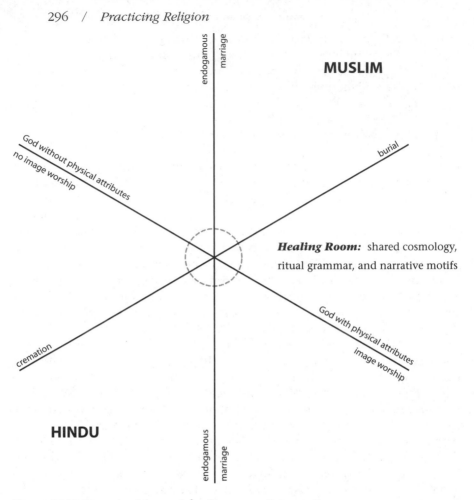

Figure 22.3. *Caurāstā* of Amma's healing room. Intersecting axes of identity and context.

spiritual bodies, resulting in illness. Amma often teaches that such spiritually caused illnesses can be countered only through spiritual healing. Patients are also familiar with and accept the ritual grammar of the healing room, the performance of which impacts the spiritual, social, and physical worlds. Exactly *how* healing is effected is less of a concern to patients than their perception and experience that it *does* take place. Finally, Amma herself helps to create the inclusive nature of her healing room, the caurasta where there is no "Hindu and Muslim," through narrative performances that draw on motifs that cross boundaries of Hindu and Muslim narrative repertoires.

AN ENCOMPASSING COSMOLOGY

The supernatural world. As one might expect, Amma and Abba emphasize through rhetorical performance cosmological features that are shared, rather than those that may create division between their Hindu and Muslim patients and disciples. They often articulate an encompassing, flexible cosmology that accommodates elements of both Hindu and Muslim worldviews. Part of this encompassing framework is the acceptance of a continuum of power and permeable boundaries between human and nonhuman worlds, as well as what kinds of beings populate the nonhuman world: deities, ghosts, angels, *jinn*, and saints and "devils." In the cosmology performed in the healing room, Allah stands alone and unique as the creator of all things and beings; in this way "unity of God" (*tawhīd*) is affirmed. But, after the important affirmation of Allah's distinct quality, Amma and Abba do not deny the existence and power of Hindu deities. They imagine a religious landscape in ways similar to that of other South Asian religious traditions (including Indian Christianity)—a landscape populated by a wide variety of spiritual beings who are not necessarily or inherently good or evil, but simply powerful—and it is at the level of these classes of beings that healing is often effected. Some of these spiritual beings have distinct identities and personalities and can be said to "belong" to one or another religious tradition, although they themselves cross the boundaries of those traditions; others are identified by terms that are translations between Telugu and Urdu for the same classes of spiritual powers that exist in both traditions.

Because of the fluidity of language usage in the healing room, between Telugu and Urdu (Amma speaks Telugu to her Hindu patients and Urdu to her Muslim patients),[5] and the differences between each language's range of meanings and usages of some classificatory words, such as *avatār* (incarnation) and *śakti* (spiritual power), what exactly is meant by their usage in a given context can be ambiguous. For example, when I asked Amma once to tell me about a Hindu goddess festival being celebrated in neighborhoods all over Hyderabad at the time, she immediately responded by acknowledging the power of the goddess and then introduced the expansive category of *avatār* (incarnation, specifically the ten incarnations of the Hindu deity Vishnu).

> This [festival] is to remind Hindus in the same way that our *ālam* [flags/standards paraded at Muharram] remind us of the suffering of Hussein.[6] Of course she has sakti [spiritual power]. Theirs are saktis [goddesses, female] and ours are *bābās* [male]. [After a long pause she continued.] You know, we, too, have an avatar; ours is the seventh. [I asked who that was]. Muhammad. He's the seventh. You know, there are Ram and Krishna. Who were the others? [I listed a few, but she was less concerned with names and numbers than

the quality of God that the avatar implied]. Yes. Isn't it sweet that God came down in human form?

In this case, Amma is equating first saktis and babas and then prophets and avatars as classes (one could even say jatis/species) of beings. Babas are human saints who have accrued spiritual power and who perform miracles, particularly after their deaths. They are not deities, and by equating saktis with babas, Amma would seem to be acknowledging their spiritual power without granting them the status of "goddess" or deity. Similarly, Muslims do *not* consider prophets to be deities; but, like the Hindu avatars, they are sent by God to teach God's revelation, to correct incorrect belief and practice of humans. A Hindu may hear Amma's equation of avatar and prophet as implying prophets are gods, since Hindus consider Vishnu's avatars to be gods. However, a Muslim may make just the opposite inference about the relationship—equating avatars to prophets, rather than the other way around. Amma is amazed at the compassionate nature of God, that he would show his nature to humans through human form. She does not necessarily mean here incarnation in a Christian or Hindu sense—God in human form—but God's love being revealed through humans who are extraordinary, filled with God's love and light: prophets and avatars.

Just as Muhammad is placed in the seemingly infinite expansive avatar system, Amma and Abba also contextualize the avatars in a specifically Muslim, but similarly expansive, category of prophets. The Qur'an mentions twenty-five prophets by name; however, Muhammad is reported to have said that there were 124,000 prophets and 315 messengers, creating the possibility of an expandable system of unnamed prophets (Hughes 1988 [1885]: 475). In one teaching, Abba described a historical line of prophets in which he included the Hindu deity and avatar of Vishnu, Ram.[7]

Like avatar (incarnation) and *nābi/pegambar* (prophet), *maukīl* (messenger) is another expansive category that may encompass powerful beings from across traditions, although the term itself is a Muslim category. Most of the amulets upon which Amma writes call upon one or more maukils—including the four archangels and various jin—to carry out her orders: to protect a patient from evil eye, remove fevers, close the mouth of an antagonist, and so forth. The Hindu deity Hanuman, known for his powers to fly through space and cover wide distances, is also considered such a messenger. One of Amma's disciples calls upon Hanuman in his ritual practice of *hazrat* (finding lost objects or persons) which Amma has given him permission to exercise in her healing room. He first calls upon Hanuman to find and call upon the saint Sulayman Baba, who is beseeched to reveal the location of lost objects. Amma's spiritual, disciplined practice has given her power to order a wide range of maukils to carry out her commands. She told me, "I can even make Kali [a Hindu goddess] sit. Kali will come and fold her hands in front of me."

Scholars and practitioners of Hinduism are used to hearing a Hindu perspective of an expansive worldview that accommodates the "other"—where

Figure 22.4. Abba giving a teaching to his disciples, 1995.

boundaries of difference become internal, and in which one may find room for religious figures or spiritual agents of "other" traditions in an expanding pantheon of deities, a flexible system of avatars, and the mantra "there is one truth and the paths are many." However, a similar inclusivity or encompassment is not commonly associated with Islam.[8] Yet Amma narrativizes and performs just such an encompassing cosmology of powerful beings, one in which Allah is distinguished as the creator under whom is an expansive hierarchy of differentiated powerful beings. In contrast to Amma and Abba who articulate this inclusive cosmology, most of the patients who come to Amma's healing table have a much more generalized worldview—they share common problems and illnesses, and they acknowledge that these may be caused by a range of spiritual forces that impinge on the physical world (specifically onto/into the physical, social, and spiritual body). But as laypersons, patients are less concerned with the specific names or classification of the spiritual beings upon whom Amma calls or with articulating a cosmology that crosses religious traditions.

The human world. Under the authority of Allah exists a continuum of spiritual powers that includes prophets, avatars, jinn, maukils, gurus, and deified dead and ghosts; ordinary humans (patients) are situated on a far end of that continuum. Here in the human realm, Amma asserts that any difference other than sexual difference is "manmade," socially constructed, not created by God, and hence insignificant on the broad scale of what "matters," that is, faith and devotion to God:

> You shouldn't doubt Allah, whether you be Hindu or Muslim, or anyone else. Even if someone's a Hindu, but he has *bhakti* [devotion], you shouldn't dismiss him; a Muslim, too, if he has bhakti, you shouldn't dismiss him either. One has it and so, too, does the other. One says "Ram Ram" and the other "Rahim Rahim." There's only that much difference, isn't there? One has the call to prayer [*azān*] and the other the bell [*pūjā* bell, puja being a Hindu ritual of making offerings to the physical image of a deity].[9] There's only that much difference. There's puja and there's *sajda* [one of the physical positions of Muslim prayer, *namāz*]. But there's little difference between them. Allah likes all this play. Look, in the end he liked this [Islam]; and having preferred this play, all this happened. Isn't that right?
>
> . . . It's not a matter of caste [jati, distinctions between humans]. It's all our doing, this caste business [she proceeds to name various castes, as follows]. No one came made from god as a Komati. The Brahman wasn't created separately; the Reddy didn't come separately; the Rajput didn't come separately; the Harijan [former untouchable castes] didn't come separately. They were all one mother's son, one father's son. . . . Now I say that the blood is all the same. What are the [true] castes [jati]? A man and a woman. *We're* the ones who have divided [humans] into all these [other] castes.

NARRATIVE MOTIFS AND PERFORMANCE

One of the ways in which the shared cosmological plane is created and articulated at the healing crossroads is through Amma and Abba's narrative performances. While Muslims cannot, and do not, explicitly participate in worship of the physical images of Hindu deities, they may and do participate in an expansive imaginative narrative world that crosses easily across religious boundaries, one that includes traditionally "Hindu" narratives. One way in which Amma and Abba employ common Indian narrative motifs is to localize, expand, and make familiar Qur'anic narratives, such as the story of Miriam, mother of Issa/Jesus, below. In the course of explaining to a patient that treatments such as those she prescribes probably do not exist in the United States, where there are no poor people, Amma nevertheless asserted that spiritual healing would still be necessary for spiritually caused problems. Her son reminded her that most people in the United States were Christians; still, he continued, "Sometimes, even among Christians there are some important [i.e., spiritually powerful] people who pray with folded hands and there is a cure. But there's a little difference." Amma interrupted him, "No, no, this healing power is available to all humans. If they have devotion, why wouldn't this be the case?" Then she launched into the story of Miriam:

Even in our Qur'an there's mention of Miriam and everything that Issa [Jesus] told us. . . . He was a prophet. As many prophets have come and gone on earth, they have all died. But he didn't die. He went up; he became a star and disappeared. So they call him god, but we call him a prophet.

Bibi Miriam was young. She had neither mother nor father, so she was living with her brother and sister-in-law after her parents died. So Bibi Miriam was living with her brother. She was taking a bath when above her in the sky, Jibrail [the angel Gabriel] passed. Jibrail's shadow struck the water. It also hit her and she became pregnant. And what did her sister-in-law say? "She's done bad things." Then her brother said, "No, my sister's not like that. My sister is honest." [But] the sister-in-law gave her a lot of trouble. She gave a lot of trouble to Bibi Miriam. When I read this in her book, I read it and cried a lot at her fate.

Then the sister-in-law told her husband to leave her in the jungle. Her brother took her to the woods and left her there, crying as he left. She [Bibi Miriam] said, "Brother, go now. Why are you taking blame for me? I made no mistake [did no wrong]." Then she stayed in the jungle. Her nine months passed there, living on roots and leaves in the jungle. She made a hut with leaves. Her nine months passed, and she started having [labor] pains. She held on to some rocks, a rock and then a vine. . . . She was in such pain she passed out. Angels came to help her. They came to help her with the delivery. They cleaned and bathed the baby. They washed his hands, and a stream formed; they washed his legs and another stream formed. This all happened when Issa was born. The stream from his hands is called *zamzam*, and the water from his feet is called *kosar*. When people drink the water of zamzam, they gain good health. The water of zamzam is still available, but not the water of kosar.

The narrative weaves together both Muslim and Hindu motifs and references. The spring/well of zamzam is a contemporary sacred site in Mecca said to be the spring from which Hagar and Ishmael drank when they were banished to the wilderness by Ibrahim (Abraham); the spring appeared to them as a miracle in the desert. Pilgrims to Mecca drink from the well and take bottles of its water home with them, in much the same way Ganga river water is taken home by Hindu pilgrims for ritual uses and to distribute to those at home some of the blessings of the pilgrimage itself. The water of kosar is a river or pool in Paradise. While Hindu patients/audience members listening to this narrative may not recognize the specific references to zamzam and kosar, they are intimately familiar with the idea of sacred waters and their healing powers. And, in fact, waters are sacralized right in Amma's own healing room, when she blows prayers over bottles of water brought to her by patients, thus empowering those waters to protect and heal those who drink them.

This narrative draws on another common motif shared with several Hindu narratives: that of the shadow of a celestial compromising the chastity of a woman. Even more striking is the similarity between the description of Miriam giving birth in the jungle and that of Sita at the end of certain versions of the Ramayana. In some Ramayana narrative variants, the pregnant Sita is abandoned by her brother-in-law Lakshman (on the order given by Ram) in the jungle, where she gives birth to her twin sons, with only nature coming to her aid. Like Miriam, she hangs onto vines and branches to aid her in her delivery.

Many narratives performed by Amma and Abba share more than motifs across traditions; they frequently tell full narratives that are drawn from traditional "Hindu" mythological stories. When I asked Abba how he understood the elephant-headed deity Ganesh, whose festival was being celebrated at the time with the installation of images at neighborhood crossroads all over the city, including a clearing right behind Amma's healing room, he did not answer with a theological pronouncement about the deity and his existence, but simply responded with a story, the story of Ganesh's creation. He did not preface his performance with an identification of the narrative as "Hindu," or "this is what Hindus say," but his telling implied that this is, quite simply, the way it is:

> Shankar [Shiva] had gone to meditate in the forest. When he was gone, Parvati took dirty bath water [water in which she had bathed] and formed Ganesh.
> [Amma interjects]: She made a doll.
> Shankar came back from the forest and asked, "Who is this standing outside of Parvati's bath?"
> He was born in water and he's thrown back into water [i.e., at the end of the festival, his clay images are immersed in water]. Parvati wanted to get married, but every man [she wanted to get married to] said, "But you're my mother." At last Shankar came. He said he would marry her if she became a little girl; so she became a little girl. . . . Then Shankar went back to the forest [to meditate].

In this short performance, Abba actually conflates two distinct narratives, shifting from that of Ganesh's creation by his mother, Parvati, to one of Adipara Shakti, the primordial goddess who had herself created the gods and so none of them wanted to have sex with her, since as their creator she was like a mother. Abba identifies Adipara Shakti here as Parvati, whom Shiva (Shankar) agrees to marry if she becomes a girl again.

I found the question, "how do you understand" (*kaise samajte hain*) a particular Hindu deity or festival to be more open-ended and productive than asking whether or not Amma and Abba "believed in" that particular deity. Here, Abba's answer through narrative is as ambiguous as my question; narrative provides him a space within which to acknowledge the existence of the deity in an imaginative world without declaring him to be a god or not. To share a narrative repertoire is not necessarily to imply a shared interpretation of those narratives in the different contexts in which they are performed. Abba does not worship Ganesh like a Hindu might before undertaking a new venture, but Ganesh is fully present in his imaginative world. I might add here that this particular performance was a much-abbreviated version of the story as it exists in many other contexts, leaving out many details; but it answered my question in a more imaginative, expansive way than it had been asked.

A SHARED RITUAL GRAMMAR

Like the narrative motifs and contours of the stories told in Amma's healing room, the basic grammar of her healing rituals is understood by most of her patients, even if the specifics may not be familiar to her Hindu (or Muslim, for that matter) patients. It is rare that a patient questions Amma's ritual prescriptions (such as wearing or burning a written amulet or carrying to a crossroads a clay pot filled with ingredients to attract a negative spiritual being or evil eye away from the patient's body) as being something beyond their understanding or experience. New patients are often confused as to what to do, at what time of day, and with which kind of paper amulet, their repeated questions often causing gales of laughter among returning patients and disciples around the healing table. But they *do* understand the power of a particularly powerful healer to call upon spiritual forces to come to her aid through the power of the word. I often heard returning patients explain to new Hindu patients that Amma's written amulets were the same as Hindu *mantram* (oral incantation), only one is written and the other spoken.

Amma's prescribes the ritual of *utāra* (literally, to take off) for forms of what she calls "heavy" evil eye. The ritual involves circling a clay pot filled with cooked rice, flowers, and 100 grams of uncut, raw (goat) liver around the head and down the length of the body of a patient in order to draw away the evil eye; the pot should then be carried away and left at a crossroads. The ritual of circling an attractive physical object (often cash) around a person to deflect or absorb evil eye is commonly practiced in numerous ritual contexts in South Asia—Hindu, Muslim, Christian. For example, a similar ritual action is frequently performed at various times during wedding celebrations, when cash is circled three times over the head of the bride and/or of the new couple to deflect any evil eye that may be drawn to the beautiful and auspicious couple, or a black mark of kohl is drawn on the bride's cheek for a similar protective purpose. This much of the ritual is readily accessible and understandable to anyone coming to the healing table, although the specific object/s that are prescribed in Amma's prescribed utara may feel unfamiliar (and in the case of the raw liver, for some upper-caste, vegetarian Hindus even repugnant). From among the many rituals in Amma's healing repertoire, utara is the ritual that is identified most often by some middle-class, educated Muslims as "Hindu"—perhaps because it does not involve the written word, specifically that of the Qur'an.

Amma employs two other non-written prescriptions that are also shared by healers of other religious traditions. One of these is called *davā* (literally, medicine). The prescription is given when Amma has diagnosed (by comparing the lines in a patient's hands) that someone has put "something" in the patient's food to influence the patient's actions. Both Hindus and Muslims who come to Amma's healing table accept the possibility that social and physical illnesses can be transferred through material substance; in this case it is intentionally (and secretly) transferred via food. An herbal prescription of twigs and leaves from the jungle (to be ingested, causing the patient to throw up the illness-causing substance, or to be burned to rid a room or home of negative influence) is another example of ritual substances and action shared across religious boundaries. When I asked Amma about the rationale of using herbs (as opposed to the oral or written word, upon which she had almost exclusively relied, except for utara), she told me, "There's great sakti [spiritual power] in these jungle herbs," and proceeded to tell a short version of the story of Hanuman (from the Ramayana), who flew to a specific mountain to find such healing herbs to bring the dying hero Lakshman back to life. Like Abba, who told the story of Ganesh earlier, she did not tell this as a *Hindu* story, but as a narrative that is part of her own repertoire—one that contextualizes and makes space for what was for Amma an innovative practice of using jungle herbs, leaves, and sticks as part of her prescriptive repertoire.

While ritual grammar may be shared, interpretation of that ritual may differ, particularly the interpretation of the relative hierarchy of spiritual beings and who/what it is who actually effects healing. But most patients do not consciously interpret the ritual at all—they have put their faith in a charismatic, successful healer, and usually simply carry out her prescriptions. If patients do not fulfill the ritual prescriptions, it is rarely because they do not believe in the possibility of their efficacy, but usually because there are too many details in the prescription to remember, the patient improves without the prescription, the patient and his/her family do not have the financial resources to comply with the prescription, or they are simply too busy or overwhelmed to fulfill their part in what can be time-consuming prescriptions.

RETURN TO VERNACULAR ISLAM

The vernacular healing practices and worldview that enable spiritual healing across religious boundaries, described in this essay, are not accepted as legitimate by all South Asian Muslims. Many reformists have criticized vernacular practices such as these—as well as honoring saints, and worshipping at their tombs (dargahs)—as being infiltrations of Hindu practice and ideology into Muslim communities (Ewing, 1997; Van der Veer, 1992; Liebeskind, 1998). Spiritual healing like that practiced by Amma, one that calls upon angels and other powerful messengers (through written amulets) to intervene in the physical and social world, is, according to the critical Muslim voices that I heard (including many South Asian Muslims living in the United States who have heard me present conference papers on Amma's healing practice), only a small distance from what is perceived to be "heretical" saint veneration that belies the crucial Muslim concept of tawhīd (the unity of God).

Internalizing this critique, my first working title for the book I published on Amma's healing practice was *Healing at the Boundaries*. Even as I argued that my purpose in writing the book was to analyze vernacular Islam as *practiced* and not to be prescriptive about what was "true" or "false" Islam, I had unconsciously internalized the critique that Amma's practice was on the periphery of some "true (monolithic) Islam." After a year's fieldwork in Amma's healing room in 1994–1995, I returned to Hyderabad to sit at Amma's table for a month in 1996 with an uneasy question of how to frame my book in such a way as to protect her (and myself) from the incessant critique that "this isn't Islam." Perhaps, I thought, this kind of healing practice really *was* peripheral to Hyderabadi Muslim culture, a perspective I may have missed by centering my work with a single individual and physically situating my fieldwork primarily in her healing room and contexts related to it.

However, returning to Amma's healing table with this question of marginality (and, therefore, legitimacy with relationship to Islam) troubling me, I was immediately struck by the fact that Amma herself (and her patients and disciples) did not see her practice or this healing space as marginal at all. During the month I lived in Hyderabad on this visit, I asked most everyone with whom I spoke outside of the healing room—Hindu, Muslim or Christian—whether they or anyone in their family had been to a spiritual healer like Amma. I only came across a handful of people, regardless of educational level or religious background, who had not had any experience with religious healing. Some of the Muslim respondents were the same individuals who had earlier voiced objection to my research; but now, when asked specifically about their own experiences, they admitted that when, for example, a child had been chronically or critically ill, or a woman in the extended family had had problems of infertility, someone in their families had visited a pir or dargah for healing.

Amma is surely aware of the critiques of the kinds of practices in which she engages, but this debate only entered her healing room on one occasion during all the months that I worked with her. One of Amma's closest disciples and his three brothers were absent from the healing room when I returned to Hyderabad in 1999. This disciple had been a regular at Amma's healing table, and we had become friends, so I asked where he was. Another disciple told me the four brothers had found a new guru/pir who had told them that "all these things" that Amma did were wrong; he said the disciple had "become a Wahabbi" (member of a reformist sect that originated in Arabia). Amma did not engage in this conversation except to mutter under her breath, "Let him go." Amma sees herself and her practices not as peripheral, but at the very center, a center through which multiple axes of religious identities meet and cross at what I have called a "crossroads." As an ethnographer of religion, I take seriously Amma's self-identification as "Muslim" and have sought to understand how and when this identity is shaped, enacted, and articulated at this site of vernacular Islam.

POSTSCRIPT: INTO THE NEXT GENERATIONS

Abba died in January 1998, on the auspicious twenty-seventh day of Ramadan, the day that marks the Qur'an's first revelation. After Abba's death, the issue of male spiritual and worldly inheritance became contentious between his son, Khalid, and Amma. Khalid had technically inherited spiritual succession through having received Abba's *khilāfat* (permission to make disciples, implying succession) many years earlier. Without Abba's physical presence, Abba and Amma's interdependence was dramatically disrupted; Amma's authority was sidelined, and her healing room became relatively empty. Her son boldly took over family, financial, and spiritual authority. By Abba's second death anniversary, when I returned to Hyderabad, the rift between Amma and her son and other disciples seemed to be on the mend, but her clientele never grew back to its high numbers of the mid-1990s. It is difficult to say whether this was because of the power struggle, her increasingly poor eyesight and arthritic pain, and/or the demoralizing experience for Amma of Abba's death and the shifts in family and disciple relationships.

Amma died in 2001 of heart failure, and perhaps of a broken heart. She was buried alongside Abba at his gravesite near the Old City, at the base of the hill on which sits the Falaknuma Palace, in an open rocky field of thorn bushes. By Abba's second death anniversary, the gravesite had already become a small dargah: a raised cement platform on which his grave was enclosed by metallic screening, topped by a small metal cupola. The site has continued to grow, and when I returned in 2007, I did not recognize it as I passed through what was now a growing neighborhood of new homes and shops. Next to a new mosque, the dargah is now fully walled in, with a large green-painted dome; Amma's and Abba's graves have been raised and enclosed by a silver-metallic awning.

On the other side of the city on Osmania University campus, Amma's son, Khalid, sits at her healing table in the evenings and weekends, after he returns from his day-job at the university; and when he is at work, his wife, Lateefa, serves the few patients who come by. They are both assisted by their

Figure 22.5. Abba and Amma's *dargāh* during *sandal* celebrations
of Abba's ninth death anniversary, 2007.

son Akbar, who in 2007 was in his early twenties and studying for an M.A.
in English. He, more than his parents, calls on Amma's authority, telling stories of learning the gift of healing by sitting by her side. Khalid plans to give
Akbar his khilafat (the official recognition of inheritance) when he becomes
a little older and is married, but he has already inherited Amma's gentleness,
spiritual intuitions, and charisma.

ACKNOWLEDGMENTS

This essay is drawn from selected portions of my book *In Amma's Healing Room: Gender and Vernacular Islam in South India*. Copyright © 2006 by Indiana University Press.

NOTES

1. Words in asterisks indicate that the English word has been used in an otherwise Urdu or Telugu conversation or narrative. While Amma does not "know" Eng-

lish, English words pepper her speech and that of others who come to the healing room. This is a common phenomenon among non-English speakers in urban India, whose speech patterns are heavily influenced by television and movies.

2. To convey the immediacy of the healing room, I use the ethnographic present in this essay to describe Amma's healing practice as it existed in the 1990s, although she died in 2001. I visited Amma nearly every year between 1990 and 2001, spending a full year sitting in her healing room nearly daily in 1994–1995.

3. The healer asks the name of the patient and that of his/her mother, writing them out in Arabic script; each letter has a particular numerical value, and the healer adds these numerical values together along with the numerical value of the lunar date. The sum is then divided by three or four, and the quotient determines the diagnosis of the patient's problem.

4. Healing sites are only one of several kinds of crossroads where Hindu and Muslim traditions have traditionally—and still do—intersect and/or share space. Other similar caurastas include shared genres of music, classical dance genres such as Bharata Natyam performed by both Hindu and Muslim dancers, festivals in which members of different religious traditions invite each other to their homes, shared linguistic and literary traditions, certain marriage and other life cycle ritual customs (including turmeric "baths" for brides and application of henna on their hands), shrines of Muslim saints where both Hindus and Muslims come to worship, and the relationships between living gurus and disciples from different religious traditions.

5. Most Hyderabadis understand at some minimal level, but many with much greater fluency, both Urdu and Telugu.

6. Notice here that Amma is identifying with a Shii ritual tradition of Muharram processions, although she herself is not Shii nor does she personally participate in these processions. Her usage of "our" is broadly inclusive of all Muslims; internal differences are not marked in this context when she is speaking about the relationship of Hindu and Muslim categories of spiritual beings.

7. While this correlation between Muhammad and Vishnu's avatars is not a common expression, Richard Eaton cites a similar cosmology and specific association between prophet and avatar in Saiyid Sultan's Nabi-Bamsa (16th century Bengal), in which the author classifies "the major deities of the Hindu pantheon, including Brahma, Vishnu, Shiva, Ram, and Krishna, as successive prophets of God, followed in turn by Adam, Noah, Abraham, Moses, Jesus, and Muhammad (1994: 286).

8. Richard Eaton has identified these kinds of processes as the accretion aspect of conversion, in which people add "new deities or superhuman agencies to their existing cosmological stock, or . . . [identify] new deities or agencies with existing entities in their cosmology (1985: 113). He, however, is looking at the process from the Hindu perspective that finds room for Muslim powers, rather than from a Muslim perspective. Further, I am suggesting that these processes may take place without conversion.

9. It's interesting that Amma includes puja as an example of Hindu ritual that is no different than Muslim prayer, since worship of images is a line of difference that Muslims do not, cannot, cross. This practice stands at the far end of the axes of religious identity that cross at the caurasta of the healing room.

PART FIVE

Nation-Making

Colonialism had a profound effect on the structure of all South Asian societies, and for these as for many other "post-colonies" in the world today, the move from being a colony to being independent nation-states has been accompanied by struggles to define anew national identities and boundaries. Both violence and peace-making processes have played a role in this process of nation-making.

By about 1800, the British had effectively colonized most of South Asia. British presence in mainland South Asia started in the 1600s with the British East India Company. The British colonized Sri Lanka a little later, in 1796, when they took over territories held there by the Dutch, who had colonized the island from 1658 to 1796. (The Dutch themselves had taken over from the Portuguese, who controlled the island from 1505 to 1658.) In India (which included what is now Pakistan and Bangladesh), to protect company interests in the face of an attempted mutiny by Indian soldiers in 1857, the British established direct colonial rule, and they let go of it only in the middle of the twentieth century. India and Pakistan (including what is now Bangladesh) achieved independence in 1947. Sri Lanka (previously Ceylon) followed shortly thereafter in 1948. Nepal, while never directly colonized, nonetheless was politically structured in part by British policy, having entered into enduring treaties with the British in the nineteenth century. The struggles of many colonized peoples to redefine territories and national languages, histories, and ideologies began, in most places, well before independence and continue today in these post-colonies. The chapters in this part all address some of these ongoing struggles.

If we can think of the "state" as the political and legislative apparatus of a country, then what is the nation? According to Benedict Anderson (1991), the nation is an "imagined community." That is, the nation is in large measure formed upon an idea of belonging that is based on the construction of a common culture through such things as speaking the same language, reading the same newspapers, constructing a shared history and sense of the past, and practicing a common ideology (such as equality or democracy) or religion or heritage (see Bate, this part). Importantly, none of these shared cultural features are a priori; that is, none of them pre-exist the human beings who create them. Because of this, it is also important to understand that imagining a nation also involves some persons or groups having the power to influence and define what those common ideas, languages, ideologies, and pasts will be. Whose version of the past will become the defining concept of nation? Whose language will become "official"? Whose life practices will become the "norm"? Who will be excluded, or granted second-class status in a nation not of their own making?

In British India, the very moment of independence was already a startling challenge to the struggle to define independent nations. Outgoing British and incoming Indian leaders came to an uneasy agreement to bifurcate India into two nations, India and Pakistan, a trauma known as Partition. Partition was the result of contentious and difficult agreements reached by three parties: the British, led by Lord Mountbatten; the Indian Congress Party, led by Jawarhalal Nehru (Mahatma Gandhi was against Partition); and the Muslim League, led by Muhammed Ali Jinnah. While the historical causes leading to Partition are complex (for accessible historical overviews see Lapierre and Collins 1975; Metcalf and Metcalf 2006), among those causes was a fear on the part of Muslims that they would be a loathed minority in a majority Hindu state, and the fear on the part of all parties that violence and even civil war might erupt. Partition was no peaceful solution, however: no less than a million people on both sides of the new border lost their lives in the mass migrations that followed, as Muslims whose homes were now in "India" fled to Pakistan, and Hindus who found themselves in what was now Pakistan fled to India (see Butalia, this part). The aftermath of Partition continues to be felt today in the conflicts over Kashmir as well as in other parts of India. Kakar (1995), for example, demonstrates how Partition remains a motif in current Hindu-Muslim violence in India, and three chapters in this part point to some of the ramifications of Partition for the everyday lives of both Muslims and Hindus in India today (Butalia, Menon, Ring).

Pakistan itself was further divided in 1971, when Bangladesh (previously East Pakistan) declared independence from West Pakistan (see Sisson and Rose 1990). Among the causes for this declaration was the fact that East Pakistan was culturally and linguistically distinct from West Pakistan (not to mention over a thousand miles distant!), despite their shared religion. East Pakistanis "imagined" themselves to be a distinct people (*Bengali* Muslims), and they resented West Pakistan's hegemony.

Even within a nation, certain groups might feel excluded or threatened and thus wish to break off and form their own nation. In the 1920s, Tamil nationalists in south India called for a separate Tamil nation. Their argument was that the linguistic and cultural heritage of the Tamils was different from numerically and politically more powerful northern Indians and was therefore endangered by the hegemony of the Hindi language and north Indian cultural values, which the Tamil nationalists constructed as Other. (Such conflict marks other nations, too, including the United States, where the Civil War has become a symbol that continues to contribute to the construction of "Northern" and "Southern" identities.)

These conflicts over national belonging are not remnants of the past. Today in India, for example, one leading political party is the Hindu nationalist BJP, or Bharata Janata Party, which from 1998 to 2004 came to power on a platform of religious and caste identity politics. In their efforts to build a constituency, they constructed a revisionist history of India as an originally Hindu nation—glorious, peaceful, and beneficent—that was destroyed by Muslim invaders. They assert that their hopes for the "recovery" of this Hindu nation are still threatened, now by affirmative-action-type programs and legislation that favors so-called minorities. Among these "minorities" are Muslims whom Hindu nationalists defined as outsiders, despite the fact that Indian Muslims are *Indian* and are not immigrants. In order to proclaim a "nation," in other words, they created a nationalized past that would help create an imagined community who would vote to regain their "lost" community (see, e.g., McKean 1996; van der Veer 1994; Menon, this part).

Today, literally as we write this section in May 2009, news from the small island nation of Sri Lanka is that the twenty-five-year civil war there is at an end, though not by any peaceful means. Since at least 1983 that nation has been torn by violence resulting from national redefinitions of linguistic, ethnic, and territorial boundaries in the wake of colonial rule. For historically complex reasons (see, e.g., S. Tambiah 1991 [1986]; Daniel 1996), Sri Lanka's population has come to see itself as divided between two linguistic/ethnic groups: Tamils and Sinhalese. The Tamils are a numerical minority, though in previous decades they were seen by some as economically privileged, in part due to the position that many Tamils held in the British colonial government. Some segments of the Tamil population, reacting to governmental policies that disadvantaged them in the new democratic nation of Sri Lanka, with its Sinhala majority, sought to establish an independent or at least semi-autonomous Tamil enclave on the northeast portion of this small island nation. The warfare and violence that resulted from these and other factors left at least 70,000 people dead, and left Sri Lanka a maze of checkpoints and military outposts, and a place where violence has become a part of everyday life for many (see Lynch and Trawick in this part, and Daniel in part 6).

* * *

The chapters in this part all address how constructing political communities—nations as well as other political groups—of shared language, history, and/or heritage impacts the everyday lives of citizens. As noted above, one of the defining moments of national inclusion and exclusion in South Asia came in 1947 with the Partition of India and Pakistan. Urvashi Butalia traverses the spaces of Partition in her personal essay that addresses the impact of Partition on her own family, as on many families on both sides of the India/Pakistan border. She takes us from India to Lahore, Pakistan, to visit an uncle she had never met, and in so doing releases the stories and longings of the past into the present, where Partition still resides in so many ways. She relates Partition as much more than a political divide. It is, she writes, a "division of hearts."

Laura Ring's chapter takes place in Karachi, Pakistan, a town also historically altered by the 1947 Partition when the large Hindu population left Pakistan for India and made room for a large influx of Muhajirs, that is, Indian Muslims who fled India for Pakistan and now see themselves as inheritors of the Pakistani nation. Ring's essay focuses on the way that women living in a new, modern, and multiethnic apartment building play a role in creating a civic, modern nation. In this building—a kind of nation writ small—women's everyday work includes not only cooking, cleaning, and caring for children, but also maintaining an edgy, intricate peace in a city and nation often divided, sometimes violently, by ethnic and religious conflict.

Crossing back into India, Kalyani Menon's chapter shows how Partition affects contemporary politics in India, where Hindu nationalist politicians use the image of Partition as part of their rhetoric for ousting Islam and returning India to a glorified Hindu past. Menon's article details the important role that female Hindu nationalist religious renouncers (religious persons who have removed themselves from worldly affairs) play in propagating Hindu nationalist ideologies. They do so by creatively redefining the concept of renouncer as someone who is both ideally religious and also legitimately worldly in this nationalist context.

Bernard Bate's chapter turns away from Partition and from Hindu nationalism to focus on the qualities of democracy in Tamil Nadu, a state in south India. He details how the everyday activity of "reading the newspaper" creates political identities and emotional ties to state-level political leaders in Tamil Nadu. Politicians take out newspaper ads featuring poems that praise the chief minister of Tamil Nadu, and in so doing create for themselves a political identity. Bate argues that these ads—as well as posters and arches that mark the city of Madurai—are effective in rendering power precisely because in both form and content the ads evoke emotional responses in those who view them (including the politicians themselves). The "state" becomes then not only "imagined" but also "felt" as a wondrous object, objectified in glorifying poetic and print images of its leader.

Writing on female factory workers in Sri Lanka, a country torn not only by civil war but also in recent decades by political movements protesting economic disparity, Caitrin Lynch describes how young rural women trying to make a living by working in textile factories find themselves held up as national symbols. The Sri Lankan (Sinhala Buddhist) nation—through a certain rhetoric of economic development—refigures women as essential for asserting the continuity of "tradition" in the face of the increasing modernization and westernization of both economy and culture.

Finally, Margaret Trawick takes us from young Sinhala factory workers to a rural area in northern Sri Lanka, home to a substantial Tamil population and also home territory for the Tamil Tigers (LTTE), the dominant revolutionary insurrectionist group which fought for an autonomous Tamil region. Trawick interviews schoolchildren about the impact that the civil war in Sri Lanka has had upon their lives. In an area decimated by war since before they were born, these children have grown up with violence, death, and fear as a part of their daily lives. How, Trawick wonders, can children who live so close to death every day still have the courage to continue to think of their futures and work to build lives of peace?

23

Voices from the Partition

Urvashi Butalia

The political partition of India caused one of the great human convulsions of history. Never before or since have so many people exchanged their homes and countries so quickly. In the space of a few months, about twelve million people moved between the new, truncated India and the two wings, East and West, of the newly created Pakistan. By far the largest proportion of these refugees—more than ten million of them—crossed the western border which divided the historic state of Punjab: Muslims travelling west to Pakistan, Hindus and Sikhs east to India. Slaughter sometimes accompanied and sometimes prompted their movement; many others died from malnutrition and contagious disease. Estimates of the dead vary from 200,000 (the contemporary British figure) to two million (a later Indian estimate), but that somewhere around a million people died is now widely accepted. As always, there was widespread sexual savagery: about 75,000 women are thought to have been abducted and raped by men of religions different from their own (and indeed, sometimes by men of their own religion). Thousands of families were divided, homes were destroyed, crops left to rot, villages abandoned. Astonishingly, and despite many warnings, the new governments of India and Pakistan were unprepared for the convulsion: they had not anticipated that the fear and uncertainty created by the drawing of borders based on headcounts of religious identity—so many Hindus versus so many Muslims—would force people to flee to what they considered "safer" places, where they would be surrounded by their own kind. People travelled in buses, in cars, by train—but mostly on foot, in great columns called kafilas, which could stretch for dozens of miles. The longest of them, said to comprise nearly 400,000 refugees travelling east to India from western Punjab, took as many as eight days to pass any given spot on its route.

This is the generality of Partition: it exists publicly in history books. The particular is harder to discover; it exists "privately"—in the stories told and retold inside so many households in India and Pakistan. I grew up with them: like many Punjabis of my generation, I am from a family of Partition refugees. Memories of Partition, the horror and brutality of the time, the harking back to an often mythical past where Hindus and Muslims and Sikhs lived together in relative peace and harmony, have formed the staple of stories I have lived with. My mother and father come from Lahore, a city loved and sentimentalized by its inhabitants, which lies only twenty miles inside the Pakistan border. My mother tells of the dangerous journeys she twice made back there to bring her younger brothers and sister to India. My father remembers fleeing Lahore to the sound of guns and crackling fire. I would listen to these stories with my brothers and sister and hardly take them in. We were middle-class Indians who had grown up in a period of relative calm and prosperity, when tolerance and "secularism" seemed to be winning the argument. These stories—of loot, arson, rape, murder—came out of a different time. They meant little to me.

Then, in October 1984, the prime minister, Indira Gandhi, was assassinated by her security guards, both Sikhs. For days afterward Sikhs all over India were attacked in an orgy of violence and revenge. Many homes were destroyed and thousands died. In the outlying suburbs of Delhi more than three thousand were killed, often by being doused in kerosene and then set alight. They died horrible, macabre deaths. Black burn marks on the ground showed where their bodies had lain. The government—now headed by Mrs. Gandhi's son Rajiv—remained indifferent, but several citizens' groups came together to provide relief, food, and shelter. I was among the hundreds of people who worked in these groups. Every day, while we were distributing food and blankets, compiling lists of the dead and missing, and helping with compensation claims, we listened to the stories of the people who had suffered. Often older people, who had come to Delhi as refugees in 1947, would remember that they had been through a similar terror before. "We didn't think it could happen to us in our own country," they would say. "This is like Partition again."

Here, across the River Jamuna, just a few miles from where I lived, ordinary, peaceable people had driven their neighbors from their homes and murdered them for no readily apparent reason other than that they were of a different religious community. The stories of Partition no longer seemed quite so remote: people from the same country, the same town, the same village, could still be divided by the politics of their religious difference, and, once divided, could do terrible things to each other. Two years later, working on a film about Partition for a British television channel, I began to collect stories from its survivors. Many were horrific and of a kind that, when I was younger and heard them second or third hand, I had found hard to believe: women jumping into wells to drown themselves so as to avoid rape or forced religious conversion; fathers beheading their own children so they would avoid the same dishonorable fate. Now I was hearing them from witnesses whose bitterness, rage, and hatred—which, once uncovered, could be frightening—told me they were speaking the truth.

Their stories affected me deeply. Nothing as cruel and bloody had happened in my own family so far as I knew, but I began to realize that Partition was not, even in my family, a closed chapter of history—that its simple, brutal political geography infused and divided us still. The divisions were there in everyday life, as were their contradictions: How many times have I heard my parents, my grandmother, speak with affection and longing of their Muslim friends in Lahore, and how many times with irrational prejudice about "those Muslims"? How many times had I heard my mother speak with a sense of betrayal of her brother who had married a Muslim? It took 1984 to make me understand how ever-present Partition was in our lives too, to recognize that it could not be so easily put away inside the covers of history books. I could no longer pretend that this was a history that belonged to another time, to someone else.

RANAMAMA

This story begins, as all stories inevitably do, with myself. For many years while this story has lived with me, I have thought and debated about how to tell it, indeed whether to tell it at all. At first it was painful and, I thought, too private to be told. Even though my uncle had said, time and again, that he did not mind my telling it, even though my mother knew I wanted to tell it, I still couldn't get rid of a sense of betrayal. I was convinced they didn't realize the implications of what they were saying. Perhaps then the simple thing to do would have been to show the story to them before I let it go. But when I thought of doing this I realized I did not want to. Because if I am to be honest, I had already decided the story had to be told. In many ways, as I began to see it, the telling unfolded not only my story, not only that of my family, but also, through their lives, many other stories, all of which were somewhere woven into a narrative of this strange thing we call a nation. This may sound very grandiose, and in the telling of this story—and all the others that follow—I don't mean to theorize about grand things. But I do want to ask questions: difficult, disturbing questions that have dogged me ever since I embarked on this journey.

For long, too, I have debated about how I would begin this story once the task of telling was upon me. There are so many beginnings, it was difficult to choose. Was it, for example, the stories of the trauma and pain of Partition, the violence that it brought, that I had heard all my life, that started me on this search? Was it the film I worked on for some friends which brought me in touch with Partition survivors that began this trajectory for me? Or was it 1984, the year that brought the aftermath of Indira Gandhi's assassination:

the killing and maiming of thousands of Sikhs in Delhi, the violent upheaval and dislocation of their lives, which recalled Partition with such clarity? Or was it all of these? I don't really know. Here, at any rate, is one beginning. Others, too, will surface somewhere in this narrative.

It was around 10 o'clock on a warm summer night in 1987 that I found myself standing in the veranda of a rather decrepit old house in a suburb of Lahore. A dusty bulb, hanging from a single plaited wire, cast a pale light on the cracked, pistachio green walls. I was nervous, somewhat frightened, and also curious. The enormity of what I was about to do had only just begun to dawn on me. And predictably, I was tempted to turn around and run. But there was nowhere to run to. This was Lahore, it was night, women did not walk out into deserted streets—or indeed crowded ones—alone in search of nonexistent transport.

So I did what I had come to do. I rang the bell. A short while later, three women came to the barred window. I asked if this was the house of the person I was in search of. Yes, they said, but he wasn't there. He was away "on tour" and expected home later that night. This was something I had not bargained for: had he been there I had somehow foolishly imagined he would know me instantly—despite the fact that he had never seen me before and was probably totally unaware of my existence. Vaguely I remember looking at the floor for inspiration, and noticing that engraved in it was the game of *chopar* that my mother had told us about—it was something, she said, that my grandfather had especially made for his wife, my grandmother. Gathering together my courage I said to the three assembled women: "I'm looking for him because I am his niece, his sister's daughter, come from Delhi."

Door bolts were drawn and I was invited in. The women were Rana's wife—my aunt—and her daughters—my cousins. To this day I am not sure if it was my imagination or if they were actually quite friendly. I remember being surprised because they seemed to know who I was—you must be Subhadra's daughter, they said, you look a bit like her. Look like her? But they had never even *seen* my mother. At the time, though, I was too nervous to ask. I was led into a large, luridly furnished living room: for an hour we made careful conversation and drank Coca Cola. Then my friend Firhana came to collect me: I knew her sister, Ferida, and was staying at their house.

This could well have been the end of the story. In a sense, not finding my uncle at home was almost a relief. I went away thinking, "Well, this is it, I've done it. Now I can go home and forget about all of this." But that was easier said than done. History does not give you leave to forget so easily.

* * *

Crossing the border into Pakistan had been easier than I thought. Getting a visa was difficult, though ironically the visa office at the Pakistan High Commission ran two separate counters, one for people they called "foreigners" and the other for Indians. At the latter, crowds of people jostled and pushed, trying to get together all the necessary paperwork, while outside an old man, balding and half-bent at the waist, offered to take instant photos, using a small bucket of developer to get them ready. Once over the border at the airport, however, everything looked familiar—the same chaos, the same language, the same smells, the same clothes. What I was not prepared for was the strong emotional pull that came with the crossing. I felt—there is no other word for it—a sense of having come home. And I kept asking myself why. I was born five years after Partition. What did I know of the history of pain and anguish that had dogged the lives of my parents and grandparents? Why should this place, which I had never seen before, seem more like home than Delhi, where I had lived practically all my life?

What was this strange trajectory of histories and stories that had made it seem so important for me to come here? Standing there, in the veranda of my uncle's house, I remember thinking, perhaps for the first time, that this was something unexpected. When I had begun my search, I wasn't sure what I would find. But I wasn't prepared for what I did find. This was something no history lesson had prepared me for: these people, strangers that I had met practically that instant, were treating me like family. But actually the frontier that divided us went so deep that everywhere you looked—in religion, in politics, in geography and history—it reared its ugly head and mocked these little attempts at overcoming the divide.

Ranamama, outside whose house I stood that night, is my mother's youngest brother. Like many north Indian families, ours too was divided at Partition. My mother, who was still single at the time, found herself on the Indian side of the border. Ranamama, her brother, chose to stay behind. According to my mother and her other siblings, his choice was a motivated one. He wanted access to the property my grandfather—who was no longer alive—owned. With all other family contenders out of the way, he could be sole owner of it. Because of this, and because of the near impossibility of keeping in touch after Partition, the family "lost" contact with Ranamama. For forty years, no one communicated with him, heard from him, or saw anything of him. Until, that is, I went to see him.

* * *

Ever since I can remember we had heard stories of Partition—from my grandmother (my father's mother) who lived with us, and from my parents who had both lived through it very differently. In the way that I had vaguely registered several of these stories, I had also registered Rana's. Not only had he stayed back but worse—and I suspect this was what made him a persona non grata in our family—he had become a Muslim. My mother made two difficult and dangerous journeys, amidst the worst communal violence, to Lahore, to fetch her family to India. The first time she brought her younger brother, Billo, and a sister, Savita. The second time she went to fetch her mother and Rana, the youngest (her father had long since died). But, she said, Rana refused to come, and he wasn't willing to let my grandmother go either. He denied that he wanted to hold on to her for the sake of my grandfather's property, which was in her name, and he promised to bring her to India soon. This never happened. Once the country was divided, it became virtually impossible for people of different communities to move freely in the "other" country. Except for a few who were privileged and had access to people in power—a circumstance that ensured relatively smooth passage—most people were unable to go back to their homes, which had often been left behind in a hurry. There was deep suspicion on both sides, and any cross-border movement was watched and monitored by the police and intelligence. Rana and his family kept contact for some time, but found themselves constantly under surveillance, with their letters being opened, and questions being asked. After a while, they simply gave up trying to communicate. And for forty years it remained that way. Although Rana remained in my grandfather's house, no one spoke or wrote to him, no one heard from him in all these years. Sometime during this time, closer to 1947 than not, my family heard unconfirmed reports that my grandmother had died. But no one really knew. The sense of deep loss—of family, mother, home—gave way to bitterness and resentment, and finally to indifference. Perhaps it was this last that communicated itself to us when, as children, we listened to stories of Partition and the family's history.

* * *

At midnight, the phone rang in my friend Ferida's house. We were deep in conversation and gossip over cups of coffee and the salt/sweet tea the Pakistanis call *kehwa*. She listened somewhat distractedly to the phone for a minute—who could be calling at this time?—and handed it to me, suddenly excited, saying, "It's your uncle." As Ferida had answered the phone, a male voice at the other end had said, apparently without preamble, "I believe my daughter is staying with you. Please call my daughter, I would like to speak to her."

"Beti," he said to me as I tentatively greeted him, "what are you doing there? This is your home. You must come home at once and you must stay here. Give me your address and I'll come and pick you up." No preamble, no greeting, just a direct, no-nonsense picking up of family ties. I was both touched and taken aback.

We talked, and argued. Finally I managed to dissuade him. It was late, he was tired. Why didn't we just meet in the morning? I'd get my friend to bring me over. "I'll not settle for just meeting," he told me, "don't think you can get away from here. This is your home and this is where you must stay—with your family."

Home? Family? I remember thinking these were strange words between two people who hardly knew each other. Ought I to go and stay with him? I was tempted, but I was also uncertain. How could I pack my bags and go off to stay with someone I didn't know, even if there was a family connection?

The next morning I went, minus bags. He remarked on it instantly—where is your luggage? Later that evening he came with me to Ferida's house. I picked up my bags, and we went back together to his home.

I stayed with my uncle for a week. All the time I was aware of an underlying sense of betrayal: my mother had had no wish to re-open contact with her brother, whom she suspected of being mercenary and scheming. Why else, she asked, had he stayed back, held on to the property, and to the one person to whom it belonged: my grandmother? Over the years, her bitterness and resentment had only increased. But, given my own political trajectory, this visit meant too much to me to abandon. And once I had seen my uncle, and been addressed by him as "daughter," it became even more difficult to opt out. So I stayed, in that big, rambling *haveli*,[1] and for a week we talked. It was an intense and emotionally draining week. For a long time afterward I found it difficult to talk about that parenthetical time in my life. I remember registering various presences—my aunt, my younger and older cousins, food, sleep—all somewhat vaguely. The only recollection that remains sharp and crystal clear is of the many conversations my uncle and I had.

Why had he not left with his brother and sisters at Partition, I asked him. "Why *did* you stay back?" He replied that, like a lot of other people, he had never expected Partition to happen the way it had. "Many of us thought, yes, there'll be change, but why should we have to move?" He hadn't thought political decisions could affect his life, and by the time he realized otherwise, it was too late, the point of no return had actually been reached. "I was barely twenty. I'd had little education. What would I have done in India? I had no qualifications, no job, nothing to recommend me." But he had family in India, surely one of them would have looked after him? "No one really made an offer to take me on except your mother. But she was single, and had already taken on the responsibility of two other siblings."

And my grandmother? Why did he insist on her staying on, I asked, anxious to believe that there was a genuine, "excusable" reason. He offered an explanation; I did not believe it. "I was worried about your mother having to take on the burden of an old mother, just like I was worried when she offered to take me with her. So I thought I'd do my share and look after her."

My grandmother, Dayawanti, died in 1956. The first time anyone in our family learnt of this was when I visited Ranamama in 1987 and he told me. For years, we'd heard that she had been left behind in Pakistan, and we were dimly aware that rumor put her date of death variously at 1949, 1952, 1953, sometimes earlier. But she had lived till 1956. Nine years after Partition. At the time, seven of her eight children lived across the border in India, most of them in Delhi. Delhi is half an hour away from Lahore by air. None of them knew. Some things, I found, are difficult to forgive.

The way Ranamama described it, the choice to stay on was not really a choice at all. In fact, like many people, he thought he wasn't choosing, but was actually waiting to do so when things were decided for him. But what about the choice to convert? Was he now a believer? Had he been one then?

What did religion mean to him—after all, the entire rationale for the creation of two countries out of one was said to have been religion. And, it was widely believed—with some truth—that large numbers of people were forced to convert to the "other" religion. But Rana?

"No one forced me to do anything. But in a sense there wasn't really a choice. The only way I could have stayed on was by converting. And so, well, I did. I married a Muslim girl, changed my religion, and took a Muslim name."

But did he really believe? Was the change born out of conviction as much as it was of convenience? It is difficult for me to put down Rana's response to this question truthfully. When I asked him if I could write what he had said, he said, "Of course, write what you like. My life cannot get any worse." But my own feeling is that he wasn't really aware of the kinds of implications this could have. So I did what I thought I had to: I silenced those parts that needed to be kept silent. I make no excuses for this except that I could not, in the name of a myth called intellectual honesty, bring myself to expose Ranamama or make him so vulnerable.

"One thing I'll tell you," said Rana in answer to my question, "I have not slept one night in these forty years without regretting my decision. Not one night." I was chilled to the bone. How could he say this? What did he mean? How had he lived through these forty years, indeed how would he live through the next forty, if this was what he felt? "You see, my child," he said, repeating something that was to become a sort of refrain in the days we spent together, "somehow a convert is never forgiven. Your past follows you, it hounds you. For me, it's worse because I've continued to live in the same place. Even today, when I walk out to the market, I often hear people whispering, 'Hindu, Hindu.' No, you don't know what it is like. They never forgive you for being a convert."

I was curious about why Ranamama had never tried to come to India to seek out his family. If he felt, so profoundly, the loss of a family, why did he not, like many others, try to locate his? Admittedly, in the beginning, it was difficult for people to cross the two borders, but there were times when things had eased, if only marginally. But he had an answer to that too: "How could I? Where would I have gone? My family, my sisters knew where I was. I had no idea where they were. And then, who in India would have trusted an ex-Hindu turned Muslim who now wanted to seek out his Hindu relatives? And this is the only home I have known."

And yet, home for him was defined in many different ways. Ever since television had made its appearance, Ranamama made sure he listened to the Indian news every day. When cricket was played between the two countries, he watched and secretly rooted for India. Often, when it was India playing another country, he sided with India. More recently, he sometimes watched Indian soaps on the small screen. And, although he had told me that his home in Lahore was the only home he had ever known, it was to India that he turned for a sense of home. There is a word in Punjabi that is enormously

evocative and emotive for most Punjabis: *watan*. It's a difficult word to translate: it can mean home, country, land—all and any of them. When a Punjabi
speaks of his or her watan, you know they are referring to something inex-
pressible—some longing for a sense of place, of belonging, of rootedness.
For most Punjabis who were displaced as a result of Partition, their watan
lay in the home they had left behind. For Ranamama, in a curious travesty of
this, while he continued to live on in the family home in Pakistan, his watan
became India, a country he had visited once, only briefly.

His children and family found this bizarre. They could not understand
these secret yearnings, these things that went on inside his head. They
thought the stories he told were strange, as were the people he spoke about:
his family—Hindus—from across the border. The two younger girls told me
once, "Apa, you are all right, you're just like us, but we thought, you know,
that *they* were really awful."

And who could blame them? The only Hindus they had met were a couple of distant relatives who had once managed to visit, and who had behaved
as orthodox Hindus often do, practicing the "untouchability" that Hindus
customarily use with Muslims. They would insist on cooking their own
food, not eating anything prepared by the family, and somehow making
their hosts feel "inferior." Bir Bahadur Singh, one of the people I interviewed
later in the course of my work on Partition, told me what he thought of the
way Hindus and Sikhs treated Muslims:

> Such good relations we had that if there was any function that we had, then
> we used to call *Musalmaans* (Muslims) to our homes, they would eat in our
> houses, but we would not eat in theirs and this is a bad thing, which I realize
> now. If they would come to our houses we would have two utensils in one
> corner of the house, and we would tell them, pick these up and eat in them;
> they would then wash them and keep them aside and this was such a terrible
> thing. This was the reason Pakistan was created. If we went to their houses
> and took part in their weddings and ceremonies, they used to really respect
> and honor us. They would give us uncooked food, *ghee, atta, dal,* whatever
> *sabzis* they had, chicken, and even mutton, all raw. And our dealings with
> them were so low that I am even ashamed to say it. A guest comes to our
> house and we say to him, bring those utensils and wash them, and if my
> mother or sister have to give him food, they will more or less throw the roti
> from such a distance, fearing that they may touch the dish and become pol-
> luted. . . . We don't have such low dealings with our lower castes as Hindus
> and Sikhs did with Musalmaans.

*   *   *

As the years went by, Ranamama began to live an internal life, mostly in
his head, that no one quite knew about, but everyone, particularly his family,
was suspicious of. His children—especially his daughters and daughters-in-

law—cared for him, but they all feared what went on inside his head. For all the love his daughters gave him, it seemed to me there was very little that came from his sons. Their real interest was in the property he owned. Perhaps the one person who, in some sense, understood the dilemmas in his head was my *mami*, his wife. She decided quite early on, and sensibly I thought, that she would not allow her children to have the same kind of crisis of identity that Rana had had.

They were brought up as good Muslims, the girls remained in *purdah*, they studied at home from the *mullah*, they learnt to read the Koran. For the younger ones especially, who had no memory of or reference to Partition, Rana, with his many stories of his family, his friends, his home, remained their father, and yet a stranger. In some ways, this distanced him further from the family and served to isolate him even more. In other ways, in a curious kind of paradox, his patriarchal authority was undermined, making him a much more humane father than one might normally find in a middle-class Punjabi household. But for several of his family members, he was only the inconvenient owner of the property, to be dispatched as soon as possible.

I could not understand how he could have lived like this: was there anyone he could have spoken to? He told me no. How could he talk about what was so deep, so tortured? And to whom? There was no one, no one who could even begin to understand. Some things, he told me, are better left unsaid. But why then was he saying them to me? Who was I? One day, as we talked deep into the evening, stopping only for the odd bit of food, or a cup of tea, as he told me about his life since Partition, I began to feel oppressed by him. "Why," I asked him, "why are you talking to me like this? You don't even know me. If you'd met me in the marketplace, I would have just been another stranger. Yes, we speak the same language, we wear similar clothes, but apart from that . . ." He looked at me for a long moment and said, "My child, this is the first time I am speaking to my own blood."

I was shocked. I protested. "What about your family? They are your blood, not me."

"No," he said, "for them I remain a stranger. You, you understand what it is I'm talking about. That is why you are here on this search. You know. Even if nothing else ever happens, I know that you have been sent here to lighten my load."

And, in some ways I suppose this was true. I did understand, and I began to wonder. About how many people had been torn apart like this by the event we call Partition, by what is known as history. How many had had to live with their silences, how many had been able to talk, and why it was that we, who had studied modern Indian history in school, who knew there was something called the Partition of India that came simultaneously with Independence, had never learnt about this side of it? Why had these stories remained hidden? Was there no place for them in history?

* * *

That first time I returned to India from Pakistan, I brought back messages and letters and gifts from the entire family to various members on this side of the border. Ranamama sent a long letter, addressed to all his sisters (his one remaining brother was dead by then). Initially, my mother found it difficult to get over her bitterness and resentment, and to face the letter I had brought. Her sisters, all five of them, who had gathered in our house, sat in a row, curious, but also somewhat resentful. Then someone picked up the letter and began reading, and soon it was being passed from hand to hand, with memories being exchanged, tears being shed and peals of laughter ringing out as stories were recounted and shared.

Tell us, they demanded, tell us what the house looks like. Is the guava tree still there? What's happened to the game of chopar? Who lives at the back now? . . . Hundreds of questions. I tried to answer them all—unsuccessfully. How could I tell them who was in which room or how the house had changed, when I hadn't seen the original house myself? Rana's letter was read and reread, touched, smelt, laughed and wept over. Suddenly my mother and my aunts had acquired a family across the border. We kept in touch after that; occasional letters did manage to arrive. I went back to Lahore several times and met him again. Once he wrote to my mother: "I wish I could lock up Urvashi in a cage and keep her here." And she told me I had made a real difference in his life. As he had, I think, to mine, for he set me on a path from which it has been difficult to withdraw.

But old resentments die hard. And there are many things that lie beneath the surface that we cannot even apprehend. Once, when I was going to visit him, my mother said to me: "Ask him . . . ask him if he buried or cremated my mother." I looked at her in shock. Religion has never meant much to her—she isn't an atheist but she has little patience with the trappings of religion.

"Why does it matter to you?" I said to her.

"Just ask him," she said, implacable.

I asked him.

"How could she have stayed on here and kept her original name? I had to make her a convert. She was called Ayesha Bibi," he said. "I buried her."

* * *

For some years the border between Pakistan and India seemed to have become more permeable. As a result I was able to make several visits and to cement my relationship with Ranamama. Once, when his second youngest daughter was getting married, I took my mother and her elder sister with me to visit him. There was a great deal of excitement as we planned the visit, for it was really like a visit to the unknown. They didn't know what their brother would look like, how he would react to them, what their home would look like, what their beloved city would have to offer them. . . . At Lahore airport Rana came to fetch his sisters. The last time my mother and aunt had seen their brother was forty-one years ago, when he had been a young twenty-year-old: slim, tall and smart. The man who met them now was in his sixties, balding and graying. He wore an *awami* suit, the loose *salvar* and shirt made popular by Bhutto. I tried to imagine what he must have seen: two white-haired women: my aunt, in her seventies, and my mother, in her mid-sixties. The reunion was a tentative, difficult one, with everyone struggling to hold back tears. I stood aside, an outsider now. My friend, Lala, who came to the airport as well, tells me that she has never forgotten the look on their faces—she has no words to describe it. Everyone made small talk in the car until we reached home. Home—this was the house in which my mother and her brothers and sisters had grown up. They knew every stone, every nook and cranny of this place. But now, much of it was occupied by people they did not know. So they were forced to treat it politely, like any other house. My aunt was welcoming, warm, but also suspicious. What, she must have wondered, were these relatives from the other side doing here at the time of a family wedding? How she must have hoped that they would not embarrass her in front of her guests!

For the first two days Rana and his sisters skirted each other. They talked, but polite, strained, talk. On the third day somehow the floodgates opened, and soon the three of them were locked in a room, crying, laughing, talking, remembering. Rana took his sisters on a proper tour of the house: they were able to go back into their old rooms, to find their favorite trees, to remember their parents and other siblings. I, who was the catalyst at the airport meeting, was now redundant. Earlier, I had told them that I would stay with Lala, and that's what I had done. But not without a sense of guilt. Now, I was glad I'd done that—they can talk now, I thought, without having me around.

But what I didn't reckon on was that while one family bonded, the other grew more distant. For Rana's own family, the arrival of the two sisters was, quite naturally, something to be concerned about. A girl was being married. What if the potential in-laws objected to Hindus in the family? What if the Hindus were there to reclaim their land? What if the Hindus did something to embarrass the family at the wedding? And, a further complication: my mother and my aunt are the older sisters. Custom demanded that they be given respect. This meant making space for them in the wedding rituals. Yet how could this be done? So, small silences began to build up between "this" side of the family and "that," and I was struck by how easy it was to recreate the borders we thought we'd just crossed.

* * *

Contact with Rana was maintained for some years. I managed, somehow, to go to Pakistan again and see him. But it wasn't easy. He began to worry that he was being watched by the police, and he gradually stopped writing. For a while my mother continued to send him letters and gifts, but slowly even that petered out. Several times, I sent him letters and messages with my friends until one brought back a message—try not to keep in touch, it makes things very difficult. This wasn't just something official, but also within the family, for his sons put pressure on him to break contact with his Indian family. And then, in any case, it became more and more difficult to travel from one country to the other.

It's been many years now since I have seen Rana. I no longer know if he is alive or dead. I *think* he is alive, I *want* him to be alive—no one has told me he isn't—so I shall have to go on believing that he is. And I keep telling myself, if something happened to him, surely someone would tell us. But I'm not even sure I believe myself when I say that. Years ago, when Rana answered my mother's question about whether he had buried or cremated my grandmother, I asked if he would take me to her grave. I still remember standing with him by his gate in the fading light of the evening, looking out onto the road and saying to him, "Ranamama, I want to see my grandmother's grave. Please take me to see it." It was the first time he answered me without looking at me: he scuffed the dust under his feet and said, "No my child, not yet. I'm not ready yet."

* * *

On the night of August 14, 1996, about a hundred Indians visited the India-Pakistan border at Wagah in the Punjab. They went there to fulfill a long-cherished objective by groups in the two countries. Indians and Pakistanis would stand, in roughly equal numbers, on each side of the border and sing songs for peace. They imagined that the border would be symbolized by a sentry post and that they would be able to see their counterparts on the other side. But they came back disappointed. The border was more complicated than they thought—there is middle ground—and also grander. The Indian side has an arch lit with neon lights and, in large letters, the inscription MERA BHARAT MAHAAN—"India, my country, is great." The Pakistan side has a similar neon—lit arch with the words PAKISTAN ZINDABAD—"Long Live Pakistan." People bring picnics here and eat and drink and enjoy themselves. Every evening, a ritual takes place which repeats, lest anyone forget, the aggression the two countries practice toward each other. As the flags are lowered, border security personnel of India and Pakistan rush toward each other, thrusting their faces at each other, then turn smartly and step away. The whole ritual is carried out with such precision that you wonder at how much they must have had to work together to establish their lines of difference. Farther down at Attari, during the day as people arrive at the border, coolies dressed in different colors—blue and red to differentiate them as "ours" and "theirs"—meet at the twelve-inch line that forms the boundary, passing heavy bags and sacks across from one head to another; the boundary is crossed as their heads touch, while their feet stay on either side.

The suffering and grief of Partition are not memorialized at the border, nor, publicly, anywhere else in India, Pakistan, and Bangladesh. A million people may have died but they have no monuments. Stories are all that people have, stories that rarely breach the frontiers of family and religious community: people talking to their own blood.

NOTES

1. Editors' note: Derived from the Persian, meaning "an enclosed place," *haveli* refers to a private mansion or large household in north India and Pakistan.

24

A Day in the Life

Laura Ring

Editors' note: Laura Ring argues in her 2006 book, Zenana: Everyday Peace in a Karachi Apartment Building *(zenana means "the women's quarters"), that women living in the new modern civic space of an urban apartment building in Karachi, Pakistan, construct—through their everyday lives—a tense peace in a city and nation frequently torn by ethnic conflict. When Pakistan was created in 1947 at the Partition of British India, it was envisioned as a unified Muslim nation, a homeland for South Asian Muslims who would otherwise be left as a minority in a dominantly Hindu India. But the groups that make up Pakistan are themselves culturally diverse, thus giving rise to a violent contest between universalizing, assimilative narratives of national identity and narratives of ethnic difference. The dominant ethnic groups Ring writes about are Sindhis, from the southeast province of Sindh, Punjabis from the northeast province of Punjab, Baluchis from the southwest province of Baluchistan, Pathans from the northwest frontier provinces, and Muhajirs, not so much an ethnic group but an identity based on migration at Partition from what is now India. Muhajirs, though a minority of Pakistan's population, regard themselves as the natural inheritors of the nation, ideal-typical Pakistani nationals: Urdu-speaking Islamic citizens. While Muhajirs speak Urdu (the national language of Pakistan) as a first language, the others all have their own language, history, ethnic dress, food, and other practices. In addition, certain religious practices distinguish these different groups, with some emphasizing more orthodox Islam, and others emphasizing devotional practices often seen as heretical by more conservative Muslims.*

Ring argues that in this multiethnic building—a kind of nation writ small—women's work includes not only cooking, cleaning, and caring for children, but also maintaining an edgy, intricate peace. For the women, such peace enables their own daily lives and their desires for neighborly intimacy with other women in a setting where they do not have much freedom to move about the city at will. But despite these immediate desires for friendship, they are in fact— through gossip, sharing chores, borrowing cups of flour, and the like—also participating directly in nation-making activities. They are creating a space and mode of public interaction that holds in suspense the tension between ethnic identities on the one hand, and civic/national identities on the other. They speak with one another not in their vernacular languages (Sindhi, Punjabi, Pushto, etc.), but rather in the national language, Urdu. They downplay ethnic differences by playing up crosscutting ties and similarities. They even downplay class differences in order to erase any hierarchies in their building in favor of the kind of equal citizenship idealized by the Pakistani nation.

In this portion of her book, Ring outlines the daily routine for women in the "Shipyard," the apartment complex in Karachi where she lived with her husband (who had grown up in Karachi) and son for more than a year while conducting fieldwork. Ring uses the metaphor of the open versus closed door to signify the national or civic "open" space that women enable in everyday life even as they also participate in and perpetuate their ethnic identities.

* * *

Any Karachiite living near tree life—almond or walnut groves, guava trees, coconut or date palm—will almost certainly be awakened each morning by the singing of birds. Whenever we stayed at my in-laws' flat in Old Clifton, the ravens and koels nesting in the *chiku* tree outside our bedroom window would awaken us just before sunrise with chatter, shrieks, and song. But in the Shipyard, which is surrounded only by sand and desert scrub, residents awaken to the sound of the *azan*, or call to prayer. The Sunni mosque three blocks south of the Shipyard employed an exceptional *muezzin*, whose dulcet and ardent call to prayer was marred only by the intermittent crackle of the loudspeaker.

With the azan, women rise for ritual ablutions and prayer while the men make their way to the nearby mosque to pray in company. Many men say their *fajr* (sunrise) prayers at home, and of course not every Muslim man or woman prays the prescribed five times a day; some do not pray at all. But nearly every woman I knew in the building purported to relish these serene moments of devotion and tried to sell me on the purely pragmatic benefits of prayer (a feeling of peace, limber muscles from the obligatory prostrations, etc.) as well as the spiritual ones. But life with a small child had made me a jealous guardian of sleep, and I usually managed to doze through the morning azan and its hauntingly sung pronouncement that "it is better to pray than to slumber."

Even for those women who do not rise to pray, the day must begin early, for there is breakfast to be made. It was the rare family that would breakfast on cornflakes and Weetabix; most of my neighbors were frying flatbread and omelets or preparing stew for the morning meal, all washed down with several cups of strong, sugary tea.

After breakfast, the men would make a hasty departure, most of them taking buses to their place of work in the city center or beyond, which meant a half-mile walk to the nearest bus stop in ovenlike heat (except for the winter months). A smaller number would hop on their motorcycles—the second sleep-shattering sound that met my comparatively lazy mornings—and still fewer sped away in tiny economy cars.

With the men gone, women would turn their attention to getting children ready for school. Children bathed every morning, and as far as I was able to gather, adults did the same (this in addition to the ritual washing, or *wuzu*, that precedes each of the five daily prayer sessions). Bathing in the Shipyard generally entailed heating a large pot of water and mixing it with cold water in a bucket (*balti*); the bather would then stand or crouch down, pouring cups full of water over his or her head and body. While many Shipyard bathrooms had showerheads affixed to the walls, most were not connected to water tanks, and thus would function only at water delivery time. Moreover, the showers offered no temperature control; if one's water heater (which few people owned) was on, the water was scalding; if off, frigid. Balti-bathing was not surprisingly a preferred option (and incidentally, one that made far more efficient use of water in situations of habitual scarcity).

Clean and dressed, children were sent off to school. If they were old enough, they walked with a group of kids. If they were young, they were walked to school by their mothers. This was an ambivalent experience for women. Aliya complained that it was a tiring task, interfering with the multitude of household chores that occupied her mornings. Zubaida complained that she felt self-conscious walking along the wide streets and fearful of strange men, wild dogs, and potential kidnappers.

Meeting male neighbors along the way was even more awkward. Zubaida told me how one day, returning from taking her children to school, she met Ilahi Sahib on the path. She kept her head down and quickly walked past him without a word. Later, in a huff, he complained to his daughter-in-law, Ruhi, that Zubaida had failed to greet him when they passed on the street. "But where I come from, women never call out to men," Zubaida told me. "We only greet in reply, and sometimes not even then. What will people think if I'm calling out to men on the street?"

When one woman was sick or busy with houseguests, another mother would walk her children to school. For a while, Aliya and Zubaida talked about hiring a van to collect their children, but in the end their husbands could not be persuaded. Parveen, who taught Urdu and Islamiyat at an English-medium school not within walking distance, would ride to school with her children (who attended the school for free) in taxis and rickshaws. I usually left the building a little before nine to drop Faizan at his Montessori school several miles away, and if Parveen was running late, she and her daughters would catch a ride with me. After the summer, when Ruhi got a job teaching Urdu and Islamiyat at a school some distance away, her husband began driving her and their daughter to school. Although he worked in the real estate office on the ground floor of the Shipyard and thus had no need of the car, there was no question of Ruhi driving herself to work; like nearly every other woman I knew in the building, she had never learned to drive.

On returning from dropping the children, women would begin their array of morning chores. Garbage had to be gathered together for the building's sweeper, Bashir, and handed to him at the door. After sweeping the halls and stairwells and collecting each resident's garbage, Bashir would lug the trash to a dumpsite a quarter of a mile away. Frequently, before Bashir's arrival, residents would already have been visited by Afghani children from the adjacent squatter camp, asking for *kachra* (trash), which they would take back to their tents to rifle through for any usable or edible items. On days when the *batliwala* came, women would call him to come and take away their bottles, newspapers, old sandals, and other recyclables in exchange for small tidbits or practically worthless coins. Sometimes the barter was more creative, featuring "*chusas* for *chapals*" (chicks for sandals) and other unlikely trades.

On various days in the month, women could expect a morning visit from the *chowkidar,* delivering gas bills, electric bills, and a request for the building fees. Each flat paid three hundred rupees or so a month to cover the building sweeper's salary, water delivery, the chowkidar's salary, and the cost of lighting the hallways. Gas and electric bills were invariably paid by the men in the family, who would go and stand in interminable lines at local pay windows in shopping plazas. I, however, always paid because women were never expected to wait in line at such places, and men always graciously stepped aside to let me or other women (who were few) go first.

Every morning shortly after sunrise, the newspaper deliveryman would silently slide the newspaper under one's door. But once a month, he would ring the doorbell, requesting payment. He had the annoying habit of doing this right after *fajr* prayers—as as early as 6 AM. For many households, this was not inconvenient; husbands or brothers-in-law, finished with their prayers, would answer the door and handle the matter. My household, however, would be deep in sleep. My husband or I would open one eye in disbelief, look at the clock, and fall back asleep. Eager to collect payment, the newspaper seller would try the next day, and the next, until finally, bleary-eyed, my husband would make it to the door before the seller had given up in disgust. This pattern so confused my body that for months I would wake

up at 6 AM and insist that the doorbell had rung. Furious, my husband Sheheryar would jump out of bed and run to the door, only to find no one there.
I suspected that the newspaper seller—a surly man who hadn't appreciated
Sheheryar's request that he refrain from ringing the doorbell before 9 AM—
was playing tricks on us. It wasn't until our trip to Kalaam some months
later that I realized the power of my imagination, for that first morning in
a guest house in the frosty hills, I awoke at 6 AM as always to the imagined
sound of a doorbell.

Nearly every household in the building employed a woman sweeper,
always referred to as *masi* (mother's sister), to do some of the dirtier and
more taxing of the household chores. Bashir's wife, Sharifa, and his sister-
in-law, Iqbal, each cleaned four or five flats in the building. While the masi
swept and mopped the floors and cleaned the bathrooms from top to bottom, women residents would dust furniture, finish washing the breakfast
dishes, and sort laundry. Some households sent their dirty clothes to the
dhobi (washerman), who also collected and delivered in the morning, or, like
Parveen, did the washing themselves. Most, however, paid the masi to help
with the washing at home.

Clothing was always washed in the morning to give it plenty of time
to dry on the line before sunset. The morning water delivery happened at
around 9 AM, and those households that lacked storage tanks almost always
did their laundry at this time. It is, in flats, a system bereft of labor-saving
aids; there is no washboard, no wringer, no Latin American–style *pila* (although a handful of lucky souls had washing machines that, while incapable
of agitating, would spin the clothes dry—wringing out wet clothes being by
far the most physically draining part of doing laundry). Clothes are worn
once and washed daily, due to the dusty, humid, and sweaty living conditions and a significant concern for cleanliness (for one thing, clothes must be
unstained for ritual purity in prayer).

In most of the households that I visited, this was a cheerful time of day.
While some women had little interest in chatting with the masi and took
little pleasure in their daily chores (as was the case, according to Iqbal, with
Kulsoom and the Baluch woman who lived above us), most women seemed
to enjoy their work and had friendly, teasing relationships with the masi.
When she helped clean my flat, Iqbal and I talked nonstop about our children, other families in the building, and life in Karachi in general. When
cleaning in Zubaida's flat, Iqbal was forever laughing and fending off Zubaida's teasing chatter: "Look, my masi is so 'smart' (meaning trim and attractive—and she was, in fact, stunningly beautiful); that's why she has so many
children. Her husband can't keep his hands off her!"

In some households, the sweeper was left to do the work without help,
which Iqbal resented. In Zubaida's flat (as in mine and Parveen's), the work
was done together. Aliya said that she always closely supervised her masi,
Sharifa (the phrase she used means to "keep standing on her head"), because

it ensured that the work was done correctly. But even this supervision was filled with laughter and friendly teasing.

The relationship women had with their sweepers was also one of patronage; most women—who were themselves struggling financially—would save bits of food, medicine, or used clothing for their masi and, whenever possible, undertake to hire her for "extra" jobs (like acid-cleaning the bathrooms or, in Iqbal's case, leg waxing). Of course, however pleasant the atmosphere or warm the relationship with her employer, a sweeper still holds a low-status occupation with dreadful insecurity and backbreaking labor, undertaken in the best and the worst of health, from respiratory infection to late pregnancy. And for women residents, she is still a servant, who will quite likely try to cheat one by overcharging or doing shabby work.

From the time men left in the morning until their return for lunch, it was not at all uncommon to see all the outer doors of the flats on one's floor slung open, with just the screen door separating the private space of individual residences from the semipublic space of the hallway. In fact, I quickly came to view a closed door as a signal that men were home and that I (or other visitors) should take care before entering. It was at these times, when doors lay open, that the connection and exchange between women neighbors was at its height.

Alongside the scuff of the broom on the cool tiled floors and the hum of the generator as it pumped tanker-purchased water up to the roof, one would invariably hear loud staccato knocks on the doorjamb and the squeak of screen doors opening as neighbors visited neighbors. Requests for kitchen items were manifold: a cup of flour, a teaspoon of cumin seeds, boiled water. Information was at a premium: Has Iqbal come yet? Did you receive your gas bill? Did you hear what happened to so-and-so? Help with chores was petitioned: My brother's wife is coming for lunch. Will you help me make flatbread? My mattresses need airing. Can you help me turn them?

At any given time in the morning, someone was visiting someone somewhere. It was rare that I spent a morning in someone's flat without being joined by at least one other neighbor. When dashing over to Parveen's flat to borrow coriander, I found Zubaida there, showing Parveen how to make *suji ka halwa* (semolina pudding). When I was drinking tea at Zubaida's, Seema stopped by to commission some embroidery work from Zubaida's relatives in the village. When I was giving Ruhi English lessons in her drawing room, Mahvish stopped by just to chat. When I was visiting Mrs. Habib in her corner flat, Qazi Sahib's wife dropped in and joined us for tea. When returning a plate to Kulsoom's flat, I found Sakina, Seema's *bhabi* (brother's wife), chatting with Kulsoom in the doorway.

The informality of visits like these was marked by the manner in which visitors (or borrowers or petitioners) would dress. Without exception, women in the Shipyard wore *shalwar kameez* on a daily basis.[1] The national dress of Pakistan, the shalwar kameez—often referred to by women simply as a suit, or *jora*—features a long-sleeved, knee-to-calf-length tunic over baggy, pleat-ed, and tapered pajama-type pants. The *dupatta,* or scarf, is a long strip of cloth worn either draped over the shoulders or on the head. When stepping into the hallway en route to another flat, women will most likely be wear-ing their simple everyday suits; throwing a dupatta over their shoulder and slipping on chapals, cheap flip-flops, women make their visits. In contrast, when walking their children to school, women don proper, dressier sandals and cover themselves more carefully—usually over their heads—with their dupattas. Thus the variability between bare feet, flip-flops, and shoes—and the absence or degree of presence of dupatta—enacts a continuum of privacy and publicity, informality and formality, ease and discomfort, that the flat, the hallway, and the street represent.

As the morning drew to a close, women turned their attention to the midday meal. Vegetables purchased from the *thailawala* (vendor) outside one's window that morning were pared and chopped; sometimes chicken or meat was marinated and fried; curry dishes or lentils were prepared, *chapa-tis* (thin, unleavened bread) were kneaded and rolled, or rice was rinsed and soaked. It was at these times that I got some of my best cooking tutorials: how to make *shami* kebabs that don't crumble, how to make the ultrathin *phulka chapati,* and what in the world to do with the gag-inducing *karela* (bit-ter gourd).

Around 1 PM, the children were collected or they made their way home from school, and the final lunch preparations were begun: chapattis dry-fried on the *tawa* (concave cast iron frying pan) or rice set to boil. Fresh-faced and changed out of their school clothes, children were often deputized to distribute tasty samples of their mother's cooking—from pumpkin kebabs to *dal gosht* (lentils cooked with meat)—to select flats in the building. Husbands arrived home, doors would close, and lunch was served.

Lunch was generally a private affair during the work week. The few times Sheheryar and I ate lunch at neighbors' flats, it was on Saturdays, with neither school, nor office, nor the lengthy Friday afternoon prayers on the schedule. While Sheheryar, Faizan, and I would eat a comparatively pathet-ic meal of fast food or makeshift sandwiches on weekdays, my neighbors would enjoy a leisurely, heavy lunch. Those residents who owned a dining table would set the food and plates there, with or without silverware, and parents and children would take their seats around it. A greater number of residents would spread a *dastarkhan* (tablecloth) out on the floor and lay their food and plates on top of it. The family would then sit, cross-legged or loosely kneeling, around the dastarkhan and eat, using bite-sized pieces of chapati to break off bits of meat and soak up rich and spicy gravy.

Food and the manner in which it was eaten were understood by Shipyard residents—and city dwellers as a whole—to be linked with class status. That some people owned dining tables and others did not was no small matter. Middle-class status hinged, to some degree, on the possession of such items as drawing room sofas, armchairs, and coffee tables, dining room tables and chairs, and beds complete with headboards and mattresses. There was also the ideal—unattainable for most Shipyard residents—that children have their own bedroom, separate from their parents (although even in those households, like Aliya's and Parveen's, where the children did have their own bedrooms, they nevertheless slept each night in their parents' room).

But more specifically, women often spoke as if food encoded some social hierarchy in which they came out far from on top or in the know. In one of my first meetings with Zubaida, as we stood in my dining room talking about the long day she had spent cooking in preparation for her in-laws' impending visit, she exclaimed, with perplexed amusement: "Women in this city are going to restaurants, and look at me!" On another occasion, Zubaida told me that her brother, upon graduating from Sindh University, was invited to a Chinese restaurant by his professor: "When they asked that the chef make them his most special dish, he brought out onions! Onions!" Zubaida laughed in amazement. "Eh, we also have onions, and we don't think they're something special." To Zubaida and other Shipyard residents, restaurants and hotels constituted an unknown, incomprehensible world of secret modes of judgment—an intimidating world in which women fear they may be judged lacking.

It was not simply a matter of financial limitations that kept Zubaida and other similarly positioned families from such places (although it was unquestionably a prohibiting factor). When my Urdu tutor was invited to dinner by a British client, he balked: "What will they serve? How will I know how to eat it?" he worried. Speaking of expensive hotels and restaurants, Ruhi said, "We don't like to go to such places. See, we are afraid. What if we have to go to the bathroom and we can't find our way and we have to ask the clerks for help? When our men can't speak to them in English, they'll look down at us, as if to ask, 'Oh, why are you here?'" In another context, Ruhi was deeply offended when her employers at an English-medium grammar school requested that she learn English so she could better communicate with students' parents. "It makes me feel very strange," she said, "that in my own country, I'm made to feel that speaking my own language is not good."

Women rarely spoke directly about perceived class or status differences in the building. If the topic of so-and-so's car or this or that person's new sofa came up, a woman might shrug and say, "We are not rich people" (*ham amir log nahin*). Disapproval of income disparities might emerge through criticisms about so-and-so's "ultramodern" behavior, but for the most part, such differences (beyond the extremes of rich [*amir*] and poor [*gharib*]) were denied, explained away as misperceptions (e.g., "They spend all their money on furniture; we're saving ours to buy a flat," or "He may earn a lot, but he has two households to support," and so on). Perhaps it is more accurate to say that women were reluctant to *concede* higher status, income, or class to others; at the same time, an ethos of egalitarianism—preached in Islam, and

evident in ordinary discourse—inhibited, or rendered suspect, direct assertions of status superiority.

After lunch, when the men had returned to work, the tempo of the building slowed. It was common practice, after the dishes were washed and
dastarkhans or tables wiped down, for women to take a nap. Considering
their late-to-bed and early-to-rise schedule, this extra rest was much needed.
Children would often nap, too. Or they would sit or stretch out on the floor
doing homework or quietly playing, occasionally making subdued forays
into the hall in search of playmates. Sometimes naps were rejected in favor
of slightly more formal visits. A neighbor might send a daughter to a friend's
flat to reconnoiter: Is Auntie sleeping? Would she like a visitor? The anticipated pleasure of such visits (and the dictates of hospitality) would rouse
any woman from her bed. Tea would be made, and hostess and guest would
settle comfortably in the drawing room for leisurely conversation.

These were the kinds of visits I received from those neighbors with
whom I had fewer dealings, and it was my sense that this was generally the
case. Kulsoom, Mrs. Habib, and Hina's mother were most likely to call on me
in this manner, as were Seema (Hina's mother's *devrani,* or husband's younger brother's wife) and Batool (Kulsoom's daughter), who often came to see
me when they were visiting their families in the Shipyard. Unlike morning
visits, during which cleaning, tailoring, cooking, or other household duties
were rarely halted, these visits required the host to set aside other business
and give full attention to the guest—to the extent that appointments were
often missed and other engagements, duties, or plans unquestioningly were
postponed.

By late afternoon, most children were busily engaged with "tuitions"—
after-school lessons in a variety of subjects, from English, to Urdu, to Sindhi,
to math, and so on. Whether this widely felt need to hire home tutors was
due, as some suggested, to the outrageously rigorous curriculum of British-
influenced grammar schools or, as others suggested, to the efforts on the
part of underpaid teachers to earn extra money tutoring on the side, I cannot
say. In the Shipyard, much of the tutoring was done by barter: for example,
Zubaida would tutor twelve-year-old Beenish in Sindhi, and Beenish in turn
would tutor Zubaida's children in English.

By early evening, men would begin returning home from work. The
family would often take tea together—complete with biscuits, store-bought
bread, snacks, or sweet dishes—and the pace of life in the building would
once again increase. Men would head to the nearby mosque for *maghrib* (sunset) prayers, while children raced into the hallway with shouts of laughter accompanied by the endless crack of screen doors slamming. Indeed, it seemed
to me that this time of day was dominated by the comings and goings—the
kind of roving antics—of Shipyard children.

Because men were in residence once again, women's casual traffic between flats was inhibited. Children, at these moments, became a useful pre-
text, or opportunity, for sociality. Women were forever wandering up and

down the halls, stopping at various doorways and inquiring after their children. This is how I first met Zubaida and Ruhi. Zubaida had come in search of Meher and Zain and found them happily doing puzzles on my living room floor. Ruhi had come asking after her daughter Sana, but neither Sana nor Faizan were with me. After a long stroll up and down the hallways chatting and asking after our children, we found them in Aliya's flat, sneaking chocolates from a candy jar in her drawing room.

Children thus enabled women's continued sociality even after men came home from work, largely because keeping track of children was an expected part of women's duties, and husbands could hardly expect their wives to return home without chatting with the mothers of their children's playmates; that would be unthinkably rude.

On the other hand, children could also be handy if one wished to avoid social interaction. If a woman was busy with housework or guests, children could be sent out to hunt down siblings, return something borrowed or borrow something else, or conduct reconnaissance. In my first few weeks in the Shipyard, children would appear frequently at my door in search of information: Where was I from? What was my son's name? and most important: Were we Muslim or "Christmas"? But children also came to our door on reconnaissance missions when I was out of town in Islamabad; while it might not "look nice" (*acha nahin lagta*) for a woman to seek out my husband and ask after me, it was perfectly acceptable for her daughters (e.g., Hina, Nazu, Anam, or Meher) to do so. "When is Auntie coming back?" they would ask. "How is her health?" "Who is that auntie who keeps coming in the evenings?" (Nothing improper: it was my sister-in-law Fauzia.)

Aside from its utility in enabling the continued socializing of their mothers, children's play had its own relatively autonomous character. Children made their own visits, played in one another's flats (at times they were sent to play in the hall when they became too disruptive, although the tolerance level for this was very high), and raced up and down the hallways on bicycles or roller skates, with balls and boxes and a multitude of props found and imagined. Children had no fear that their play would disturb the adults and bring about criticism or scoldings. "Why would we scold?" Ruhi asked me. "They are all our children."

Indeed, children were treated extremely well by adults strange and familiar. Older children were teased and plied with sweets, while younger ones were fed, petted, and picked up. Parents had little fear for their children—as young as two—wandering in the hallways, for all adults looked out for and seemed to share a stake in the fate of any child. When Faizan fell down the stairs on his bike with loud cries and clamor, innumerable doors were flung open and concerned neighbors rushed to help and comfort.

As children were such an integral part of local social life, women who were childless were the object of great pity. Aliya often talked with me of her great joy in her children, Anam and Shan, for they were born, in quick succession, after eight years of unexplained, heart-wrenching infertility. Ruhi, who had a six-year-old daughter, Sana, lamented that she was thus far unable to conceive a second time. "I pray and pray, but it's not happening. *Allah malik hai* [God is sovereign]. What can I do?" My women neighbors (as well as my cousins and other in-laws) were always asking me when the next child was coming, reminding me that it is not good for children to be alone and that I needed a girl. When I did find myself pregnant with my second child several months before my fieldwork ended, my neighbors became ever more solicitous, sending me plate after plate of food, lending me looser clothing, and advising me not to wear heels or work in the heat.

As all these stories suggest, children in the building were genuinely cherished, moving in and out of adult life all day and usually sleeping in their parents' bedroom at night. But because children were always present, they were also less focal; adult schedules were not molded around children's bedtimes or set naptimes. Moreover, I discerned no strongly expressed desire on the part of women for peace and quiet, for time away from children, or for privacy.

While children go about their socializing and men entertain themselves, women prepare the evening meal in much the same manner as they do midday. Unless relatives or a husband's friends are visiting, dinner is a family affair. This was equally true for my household, which habitually piled into the car at 8:30 PM and drove northeast two miles to eat dinner with my in-laws. That my husband's family remained such a central referent in my life (despite our nuclear, neolocal residence) served as a reminder to me that, while women pass their everyday lives in buildings like the Shipyard, much of what they consider permanent, relevant, and determinant of their actions, desires, and decisions rests in their ongoing relations with their extended family, natal and affinal. Women talked together often about the alternately baneful and salutary influence of sisters and mothers-in-law, and they reminisced about warm relationships with siblings and parents. Aliya was regularly visited by her elder brother, bearing gifts from Dubai, where he lived and worked; Zubaida spoke on the phone daily with her favorite bhabi; and Ruhi told me of the conflicted desires she felt to return to her father in the village and yet to stay here with her husband: "A woman has so much love [*pyar*] and concern [*pareshan*]—for father, husband, child—that the heart fills [*dil bhar jata hai*]."

Not everyone in the Shipyard was living in a nuclear, neolocal household. Some flats housed three generations, and many others housed the joint families of two or more brothers. In one case, two separate flats in the building were occupied by the same extended family: parents and a grown son with his wife and children on one floor, and three brothers (one married with children) on another (and they were also related by marriage to another household in the building).

But even for those households where the extended family is not in residence, the influence of in-laws in particular is ever apparent. Like me, Shipyard women were routinely welcoming in-laws or—accompanied by their husbands—heading to affines' houses or villages for religious holidays and ceremonies, weddings, circumcisions, or funerals. And by reputation, mothers-in-law have a more nefarious influence, controlling, even from afar, things like their daughter-in-law's visiting habits and other aspects of her—and the conjugal couple's—life.

In contrast, I could hardly have survived, much less conducted fieldwork, without the influence (and at times interference) of my mother-in-law. Because I knew so little about the pragmatics of life in Karachi, her advice was welcome, and because my anticipated stay in Karachi was finite, the control that her advice and involvement implied was (generally) tolerable. In fact, it was thanks to my mother-in-law's involvement and her contacts that we ended up taking a flat in the Shipyard, and it was with her that we had our first encounter with the building president, Ilahi Sahib.

We had just finished unloading the last of our belongings from my sister-in-law's trunk when Sheheryar's mother, doubling back, brought Ilahi Sahib to our door. "Here, you must meet the building president," she said. "He's a very responsible man. I've met him now, and he'll give you help if you need it."

Sheheryar shook Ilahi Sahib's hand, and I smiled and nodded, taking a few steps backward as he lumbered into the room. "Before I met your mother," he said to Sheheryar, "I thought all Aga Khanis were *kafirs* [infidels]. *Kafirs!*"[2] My mother-in-law smiled benignly, and they left us to our unpacking, which we undertook after a good, rip-roaring laugh.

[. . . There exists a] broad discomfort with announcing ethnic difference in the building. Like class or status distinctions, the expression of ethnic and sectarian differences is, in many ways, suppressed in everyday contexts. Some weeks after moving in, I related Ilahi Sahib's amusing (I assumed) comments to my new friends Aliya and Zubaida, and they reacted with vitriol rather than laughter. Such comments were "beyond belief," "nonsensical," and "rubbish," they told me. In a city where people were killing and dying in the name of such differences, his comments were truly seen as no laughing matter.

But just a few weeks later, Zubaida told me, in her customarily ebullient tone, that when we first moved in, she said to herself, "Oh, I think he's Sindhi. I *hope* they're Sindhi!" When I asked her what difference it made, she shrugged and said, with a sheepish grin, "*Hamari biradari hai* [It's our clan]." The line between a kind of pleasurable play with difference or different degrees of belonging, and the more threatening *ranking* or excluding that such differences implied, rendered talk about ethnicity awkward and even out of place between neighbors.

This was similar to residents' efforts to imagine the building as a kind of unified community, with norms of neighborly assistance, affection, and togetherness, but at the same time incontrovertibly divided into units of private property, interests, and priorities. When Hina's family moved out of the Shipyard and another moved in, our new neighbor asked if he could place one end of a split unit air conditioner on our balcony, so that it would not ventilate into the hallway. We agreed, but my mother-in-law disapproved and phoned the building president to put a stop to the proceedings. Later I complained to Ruhi about my mother-in-law's interference, but Ruhi, to my surprise, took her side. "She did the right thing. People here, they grab things [*qabza karte hain*]; first, you let them keep the AC on your balcony, and soon they'll be saying, 'This is our flat' [*yeh hammra flat hai*]." The contradictory pulls to invoke or deny ethnic bonds and to open up and close off one's space came together and were fascinatingly upended when an electrical fire shook the building.

Sometime after dinner, and most often between 11 PM and 1 AM, Shipyard residents prepared for sleep. Those children who had fallen asleep on floor cushions or sofas were carried to the bedroom, and their parents retired for the night after completing their individualized grooming routines (involving such bathroom shelf staples as Dr. Forhan's dental powder, face and body creams, hair tonics, and moustache combs). Outer apartment doors generally remained closed, and the building was bathed in silence and darkness until dawn. But one night in late summer, this silence was broken by frantic shouts from the chowkidar, and the darkness was illuminated by a riot of sparks flying from the building's entryway. The electrical boxes were on fire. Male residents who rushed to the scene immediately noted the alarming proximity of the fire to a gas line, and fearing an explosion, they ran up the stairs and down hallways to knock on each door and warn the residents to evacuate.

We evacuated in two lines: the men went out the north entrance, which meant passing the scene of the (pretty much self-limiting) fire in the entryway; the women and children went down the south stairs and out the south exit, which was ordinarily locked and barred, so that the chowkidar need keep watch over only one entrance. Despite their assertions about the possibility of an explosion, the men remained in the gully, no more than ten or fifteen feet from the fire; the women and children gathered at the portico facing the sea, many of them barefoot and bereft of dupatta—a sure sign of the frame-breaking nature of the situation (Goffman 1974).

Despite the inconvenience—the bare feet, the sleeping children in arms—the atmosphere on the portico was festive. Women chatted breathlessly about the evacuation and speculated about the dangers. Hina's brother Imran would periodically race over from his watch in the gully and provide updates on the fire and the efforts to extinguish it. But from the midst of these excited murmurs, an angry voice was raised: "It's your fault," an old woman blurted, gesturing at me. "You have such a big AC."

I glanced around at the suddenly discomfited crowd, and Zubaida leapt to my defense: "What rubbish! Everyone runs an AC," she retorted, adding, under her breath, "Crazy old woman."

Our rented flat did, indeed, have a large air conditioner installed on the northside bedroom wall, though, like many other families in the building, we rarely ran it, for the electric bills were prohibitively steep. But there were other ways—besides the obvious cachet of my American passport—in which our comparatively elite economic and social status must have been marked. We owned a car, we spoke English, and we occupied a northern corner flat (the only three-bedroom flats in the building). That this economic disparity would create some resentment was not surprising. But it is significant that any such feelings—or their expression—were inhibited in everyday interaction. Something about the context of crisis—the spatial reorderings, the unaccustomed proximity and visibility of all one's (women) neighbors at once, outside of the context of everyday exchange—enabled the direct expression and criticism of perceived status inequality—or, from another perspective, it allowed the *suspension* of everyday civility that is such a central part of neighborly coexistence.

Meanwhile, as my husband told me later, the men were hard at work trying to get the bureaucrats at the electric company, KESC, to shut off power to the Shipyard so the fire could be put out. This necessitated numerous drives to the KESC building and heated arguments with the technicians over what it would cost (in bribes). Far from festive, the mood in the gully was one of frustration, with the men watching helplessly as electrical boxes burned beyond repair.

The roving boys, however, seemed exhilarated, sharing in the festive mood of the portico, while at the same time sampling the adventure and danger of the gully. As Sheheryar stood watching sparks fly from the entryway, a Sindhi boy between ten and twelve years old sidled up to him and asked gleefully, "So you're Sindhi?"

Nonplussed, Sheheryar answered, "Yes. Well, my mother is Sindhi, and my father's Muhajir."

"So you're half Sindhi," the boy prompted.

"Yes," Sheheryar nodded, his attention caught between the more immediate drama of the fire and the—what seemed to him—rather incongruous conversation.

"But you speak Sindhi."

"No."

"Oh well, then, you're one-third Sindhi!" the boy announced with a laugh and ran off toward the portico.

Clearly, the same set of disordered circumstances that allowed a neighbor to publicly criticize my socioeconomic advantage was at play in the above interaction. The Sindhi boy was empowered by the intensity and simultaneous presence of neighbors—separate from the privacy and restricted access of flats—to directly approach Sheheryar (his senior both generationally and in terms of social status). Significantly, at this moment of extreme (universalizing) identification, when building people are united physically in unprecedented ways, bonds of ethnic affinity—normally suppressed—become articulable (if only by a child and, even then, still read by the adult interlocutor as incongruous). There was even space for playing with this affinity, probing the degree to which this (vaguely illicit, particularizing) identification (Sindhi? One-half? One-third?) could be imagined . . .

NOTES

1. On special occasions like weddings, women would often wear *saris* or other wedding attire like *shararas* or *ghararas*. Very few women other than Hindus or Parsis would wear saris on a daily basis. Those who did were almost invariably Muhajir or even more recent immigrants from India. Women's dress marked many things: adulthood vs. childhood, respectable vs. shameless, and modern vs. retrograde (not to mention Hindu vs. Muslim or Pakistani vs. Indian). That little girls could wear dresses and pants served to further demarcate the significance of their abandonment at puberty. Women were risking their reputations if they donned pants, skirts, or even sleeveless shalwar kameezes or dupatta-less ensembles. At the same time, women who wore *hijab* (headscarf) or *burqa* (full body covering) risked being viewed as relics in the city, even while their attire could be deemed proper from a small town or village perspective.

2. Sheheryar's mother is Aga Khani; his father's family, and Sheheryar himself, are straight Shia.

25

Living and Dying for Mother India: Hindu Nationalist Female Renouncers and Sacred Duty

Kalyani Devaki Menon

To live in the face of death? To live in the world and yet be free from the world? Have we ever fulfilled our duty by sitting in the forest? This is why even renouncers have to help society while staying free of human affairs. We have to fulfil our duty/responsibility not run away from it. We should not run away from problems. Today it is very important for India to understand the message of the Gita.
—Sadhvi Rithambara 22.8.1999

Sadhvi Rithambara is a female renouncer belonging to the Sadhvi Sakti Parishad, a branch of the Hindu nationalist movement in India whose membership is limited to Hindu female renouncers (*sadhvis*). She was speaking to a rapt audience of men and women in Ramakrishna Puram in Delhi in 1999 during the Sri Mad Bhagavad Gita Gyan Yagya. This three-day event had been organized by the Vishwa Hindu Parishad to spread the message of the Bhagavad Gita, an important Hindu scripture. Rithambara used the Gita to argue that the principles of worldly involvement and renunciation are not opposed to each other. According to her, renouncers must fulfill their duty to society while also maintaining their detachment from the everyday involvements of human beings.

Classical theories of renunciation suggest that the renouncer must remove him/herself from the world of attachments, desires, luxuries, and pos-

An earlier version of portions of this essay appeared in *Women's Renunciation in South Asia: Nuns, Yoginis, Saints, and Sinners,* edited by Meena Khandelwal, Sondra L. Hausner, and Ann Grodzins Gold. Copyright © 2006 by Palgrave Macmillan.

sessions in order to attain liberation from *saṃsāra* (the cycle of birth, death, and rebirth). Yet, how should we understand the deep involvement of female renouncers in Hindu nationalist politics? Hindu nationalist sadhvis use the Gita to suggest that it is imperative for them to engage in righteous action that upholds *dharma*, the moral order of the world.[1] They also argue that it is the sacred duty of Hindus to participate in this struggle for dharma, identified as the struggle to establish India as a Hindu nation. Indeed, for Hindus already familiar with a long tradition of modern renunciation that includes serving the world, sadhvis' discussions of politics are not necessarily aberrant.

Here I examine how Hindu nationalist sadhvis (female renouncers) use Hindu texts and ideology to disseminate the movement's politics and to justify their own worldly involvements. Examining speeches and conversations with Hindu nationalist sadhvis in Delhi, I analyze how they interweave religious ideas with Hindu nationalist ideology. Their efforts imbue political action with a sacred injunction and suggest that their calling is not to remove themselves from the world but rather to shape that world and infuse it with the values, ideology, and politics of Hindu nationalism. Their dual status as renouncers and as women makes them particularly effective vehicles for the movement's politics. By linking religion and politics, sadhvis frame Hindu nationalism as a religious movement, and suggest that it is the sacred duty of Hindus to participate in its politics. Indeed they are vital to the expansionary power of Hindu nationalism because of their ability to appeal to Hindus within and beyond the movement, and to produce a nationalist Hinduism in which the movement's politics are inextricably intertwined with religious ideas and imagery.

RENUNCIATION AND VIOLENCE IN CONTEMPORARY INDIA

Hindu nationalism, a violent political movement consisting of multiple organizations that share the goal of making India a Hindu nation, has become increasingly dominant in India. The Bharatiya Janata Party (BJP), the electoral wing of the movement, formed the national government, albeit in coalition with other political parties, from 1998 until 2004. The BJP's political ascendance was aided by the Vishwa Hindu Parishad (VHP), a Hindu nationalist organization with which the renouncers discussed here affiliate, and which was at the forefront of the movement to build the Ramjanmabhumi Temple at the site of the Babri Masjid, destroyed by Hindu nationalists in 1992.[2]

In rallies and events leading up to the destruction of the mosque, Hindu nationalist renouncers used religious ideas and their renunciant authority to rouse Hindus to destroy the mosque and build a temple in its place. Sadhvis belonging to the VHP's Sadhvi Sakti Parishad became quite prominent during the Ramjanmabhumi agitation. In particular, two female renouncers, Sadhvi Rithambara and Uma Bharati, escalated to fame as they stood in front of crowds of Hindus exhorting them to defend Hinduism, destroy the mosque, and kill Muslims, who were constructed as the paramount threat to Hindu India (see Sarkar 2001: 269). Scholars have noted the highly sexual and gendered imagery employed by these sadhvis (A. Basu 1995; Ghosh 2002) in their condemnations of Muslim men. In their speeches they suggest that Muslim men committed atrocities against Hindu women and figuratively violated the honor of India, conceived as the goddess Bharat Mata. The power of women (albeit renouncers) calling on men to avenge the honor of Hindu womanhood is central to the successful mobilization of men to engage in acts of violence against Muslims. While most Hindu nationalist ideologues are men, it is important to understand how the agency of sadhvis is critical to constructing the affective power of Hindu nationalism in the minds of ordinary people. Their acts interlace religion and politics, imbuing Hindu nationalism with a sacred injunction and recruiting their audience as subjects of a Hindu nation under siege.

The events discussed here occurred in the context of the Kargil War between India and Pakistan in 1999, an occasion that charged these injunctions with a particular urgency. The war broke out in May 1999 after the Indian army discovered that Pakistanis had breached the line of control and occupied several Indian army positions in Kargil district in the state of Jammu and Kashmir (S. Ganguly 2001: 116, 124–25). Facing criticism for their failure to act on intelligence regarding these incursions, and concerned about upcoming elections, the BJP-led government focused on the creation of national affect through screening television clips about soldiers dying in Kargil. Meanwhile, Hindu nationalist organizations such as the VHP organized events to honor the soldiers who had died in the battle and framed the breach of the line of control as a violation of the sacred body of goddess Bharat Mata. Much of the material examined here is derived from speeches given by sadhvis at these events. Alluding to an emerging national narrative on the war, sadhvis used religious imagery to interpret the violent conflagration between India and Pakistan and mobilize Hindus to engage in Hindu nationalist politics.

AWAKENING *SADHVI SAKTI*

Sadhvi Kamlesh Bharati, the head of the Sadhvi Sakti Parishad, asserted in her speech at the Sri Mad Bhagavad Gita Gyan Yagya, that in addition to attacks on "mothers and sisters" and on Hindu values, in recent years, "two *lakh* Hindu girls are converted by Christians and Muslims every year. Our temples are being converted into mosques. If our *sadhvi sakti* (strength) is awakened then these attacks on our dharma (religion) will stop." According to her, the Sadhvi Sakti Parishad organized programs like this one to promote Hindu values, culture, and rituals, and to teach people to "consider Bharat Mata as a mother and seat her on the throne of the universe."

The vision of India as Bharat Mata has deep implications for Hindu nationalism. A relatively new form of the goddess, Bharat Mata was first conceived in Bankimchandra Chattopadhyaya's novel *Anandamath* in 1882 (McKean 1996: 44). In the novel, Chattopadhyaya clearly links Bharat Mata to ancient forms of the goddess—Kali and Durga. For most Hindus, Kali and Durga, like other goddesses, are understood to be different manifestations of the great goddess, Devi. Consequently, the relatively recent provenance of Bharat Mata is not an issue for most Hindus, who can easily incorporate her into a constellation of goddesses who are part of their daily rituals of worship.

Building on a common Hindu nationalist construction of a Hindu nation under siege, Sadhvi Kamlesh Bharati argues that the dishonor of Hindu women and girls must be fought against alongside the greater dishonor of Bharat Mata and the Hindu values that both represent. The image of women's honor that must be protected from violation is one that is central to Hindu nationalism and to nationalist movements all over the world.[3] Yet, instead of simply portraying women/goddesses as victims of violence, she asserts that "sadhvi sakti" can stop attacks on dharma. "Sakti" can be translated as strength, but it also specifically refers to the female creative principle that women are thought to embody. Although sadhvis are supposed to be neither male nor female, they often continue to be viewed as women and to play roles that are consistent with those of female householders (Khandelwal 2004). Given that women bear the unequal burden in Hindu nationalism of both embodying and transmitting Hindu cultural traditions, values, and morals, it is perhaps the femaleness of sadhvis that uniquely positions them to prevent attacks on dharma and to organize events to promote Hindu ideas. Thus, it is not surprising that sadhvis play a prominent role in the cultural politics of Hindu nationalism. Indeed, Hindu nationalist sadhvis may be visible precisely because they are female and are able to deploy their gendered identities to produce, disseminate, and recruit Hindus into a uniquely Hindu nationalist construction of religion.

The image of India as Bharat Mata also suggests that it is both the patriotic and the religious duty of Hindus to defend this goddess/nation. As Tanika Sarkar (2001: 278) has argued, defending the integrity of India's borders becomes a religious necessity because an attack on territory constitutes a violation of the sacred body of the goddess. This was powerfully invoked by Hindu nationalist sadhvis when speaking about the Kargil War. At a speech delivered to Hindu nationalists gathered to honor soldiers who had died in Kargil, Sadhvi Rithambara evoked the image of soldiers sacrificing their lives for this goddess/nation:

Our greatest respects at the feet of those who gave their lives at the feet of
Bharat Mata. We salute that mother's womb, that mother's lap, that mother's
love, her affection, in whose shadow our country's brave soldiers learnt to
sacrifice for their motherland. We salute those widows who laid their *sindhuri*
(married) nights, their happy days, at the feet of Bharat Mata.[4]

In this passage, both men and women must sacrifice for Bharat Mata, yet
these sacrifices are clearly defined according to Hindu nationalist constructions of gender. Here violence is glorified and men are asked to embrace
death in defense of Bharat Mata. Women are applauded for their ability to
sacrifice the pleasures of motherhood and sex (codified in sindhuri nights)
and for teaching their sons to be brave and patriotic. Images of mothers sacrificing sons or wives sacrificing husbands resonate with a broader cultural
glorification of female sacrifice[5] and are powerful ways to recruit women
into the movement.

Sadhvi Rithambara is one of the most skillful orators in the movement.
Bishnupriya Ghosh argues that Rithambara is one of the key Hindu nationalist women who engage in public performances as "instigators of affect
and emotion, and as progenitors of non-rational collective identifications"
(Ghosh 2002: 259). That Rithambara is a woman is not incidental to her centrality. Amrita Basu has argued that in Hindu nationalist imagery women
are closely associated with "emotion rather than reason" (1995: 164). I believe
this is crucial to understanding why sadhvis play such a prominent role
in the movement. Although female renouncers are supposed to have transcended gender, it is because they are identified as women that they are able
to forge the patriotic ardor that drives Hindu nationalism. As a renouncer,
Sadhvi Rithambara is supposed to be detached from passions. However, as
a woman she is expected to be emotional. Arguably, Sadhvi Rithambara's
prominence in the movement is related to the ambiguity of her own subject
position as a passionate renouncer.

This production of affect and emotion was central to Rithambara's performance at the Kargil event. The large auditorium of the Constitutional
Club on Rafi Marg in New Delhi was filled to capacity, and yet the room
was quiet as Rithambara's voice trembled with emotion, and tears streamed
down her face. Several in the room wept along with her, caught in the spell
of her powerful oratory. As she continued her speech her voice became more
angry and passionate until she was almost screaming the words to a silent
auditorium; "On Islamabad's chest will rest India's flag, up till Rawalpindi
and Karachi . . . up to the Indus river it will all become India.[6] Then for eons
and eons there will not be a devil like Jinnah.[7] There will be a Kashmir but
there will not be a Pakistan."[8] As the audience cheered in response to these
statements, it became clear that Sadhvi Rithambara's passionate anger inflected the imaginations of those present and perhaps recruited them into

the discursive constructions of Hindu nationalism. As a woman, Rithambara can be a passionate renouncer who generates the affect necessary to recruit individuals into the movement's embrace.

The image of Bharat Mata torn asunder by Partition whose sacred body will be reintegrated in an undivided, and Hindu, India is important in Rithambara's speech. The idea of *akhand Bharat* (undivided India) is central to Hindu nationalists and is an image that is called upon repeatedly in speeches given by sadhvis, including Rithambara. She refers to this at the Gita event as well, suggesting that it is the sacred duty of Hindus to fight for an akhand Bharat. At this event she skillfully integrates Hindu nationalist politics into her exegesis of the Gita to suggest that the struggle for an akhand Bharat is a struggle for the very moral order of the world—for dharma. She begins by saying, "The martyrs of Kargil, according to the guidance of the Gita, sacrificed themselves for their country. They gave their bodies for their country. What will we give? We will listen to the *pravachan* [lecture] and then go home and live surrounded by comforts."

In Rithambara's speech, the Kargil War is compared to the War of Kurukshetra, the fratricidal battle between the Pandavas and Kauravas in the Mahabharata, the ancient epic that contains the Gita. In the Gita, Krishna asserts that it is Arjuna's sacred duty to fight the Kauravas, and, revealing his cosmic form, he shows Arjuna that the relatives and teachers he is so reluctant to fight are already dead. He tells Arjuna that they will die regardless of Arjuna's actions because their death is necessary to uphold dharma. Krishna tells Arjuna to act as Krishna's "instrument" so that he may "win glory" (Bhagavad Gita 11. 32–33, trans. Miller 1986). Referencing this, Rithambara says:

> Bhagvan Krishna says, Arjun, the Kauravas standing in front of you are evil. They endanger dharma. If you do not kill them Arjun then I will. If the enemy does not understand friendship then it is necessary to give them a strong reply. This is the goal of the Sadhvi Sakti Parishad. I want to make a request to Atalji [then the Prime Minister of India] that you had gone there taking a bus with the message of friendship. But that rogue called Sharif [then the Prime Minister of Pakistan] did not understand your friendship. Now it is necessary, instead of taking a bus to take a tank and go. In Pakistan go up to Rawalpindi, Lahore, and Karachi. . . . Because we know that those who don't make mistakes we call god. Those who make mistakes and repent we call humans. And those who make mistakes and don't repent we call the devil. But those who make mistakes again and again without repenting we call Pakistan.

The audience began to cheer and clap, delighted by Rithambara's indictment of Pakistan. By juxtaposing the Gita and the Kargil War, Rithambara suggests that both are dharmic wars. Alluding to Vajpayee's visit to Pakistan in February 1999 on the newly established bus service between New Delhi and Lahore, Rithambara argues that Pakistan responded to this overture of friendship with an act of aggression—crossing the line of control in Kashmir—resulting in the Kargil War. Rithambara sees this as reason not only to defend territory but also to fight to regain the dharmic order that, from her perspective, requires an akhand Bharat, an undivided India. Related to this notion of akhand Bharat is a sense of injustice that this land, firmly linked to the nation as imagined, has been taken away from its rightful claimants. Rithambara asserts that it is only with creation of akhand Bharat that the "river of peace will flow" and that the "sacrifice" of the soldiers will be honored. Until then the intrusions will continue, the violence will continue, and such violence, on the part of Hindus fighting for a moral order, will continue to be justified.

For Rithambara it is the sacred duty of Hindus to engage in violence in defense of Bharat Mata. She ended her speech at the Gita event saying: "My request to you is when the time is right to play the *bansuri* [flute] then do so. Now it is the time of conflict. It is the time for the *sudarshan chakra* [Krishna's sacred weapon]. Join the war. Learn about the circumstances all around you and fulfill your duty." Krishna of Jayadeva's twelfth-century poem Gitagovinda is the cowherd who sits in the secret grove playing his bansuri and awaiting his lover, Radha. This powerful metaphor for devotion to god, where the worshipper is cast as the lover longing for union with his/her beloved (god), is all right, says Rithambara, at certain moments. However, she argues, a time when India and Pakistan are at war is not the moment to sing devotional songs. Rithambara tells the audience that this is the time to pick up weapons and participate in the battle. She continues a few sentences later, "Lord Krishna says: Arjun, those who have to die, they will surely die. . . . Death is simply a change of clothes, a few moments of rest. To live is the greatest art. But this is also the truth. Those who are scared of death have no right to live."

Rithambara ended her speech with these words as the audience burst into enthusiastic applause. She suggests that it is the duty of Hindus to pick up their weapons and fight in the battle without fearing death. These words, which combine vigilante heroism with religious imagery, clearly animated the audience. Alluding to Krishna's counsel in the Gita, she argues that the sacred duty of Hindus is not to live in the jungle and contemplate detachment, to sing devotional songs, or to "to listen to the pravachan (religious lecture) and then go home and live surrounded by comforts." Rather, she crafts a new nationalist Hinduism wherein it is the religious duty of Hindus to act—even violently—in defense of Bharat Mata.

During these events, the affective oratory of Hindu nationalist sadhvis such as Rithambara becomes central to the movement's ability to frame Hindu nationalist politics within a religious lexicon. This lexicon invokes images of cosmic war (Juergensmeyer 2000), suggesting that violence is necessary to rid the world of immorality. While some might argue that these sadhvis are simply using religion to further their political agenda, I suggest instead that their construction of religion is inextricably linked with their politics. Following Talal Asad (1983), religious belief and practice are inseparable from the world of power and politics, and it is analytically problematic to imagine a pure religious space untainted by politics. Indeed, religion was inseparable from politics in the words and deeds of the Hindu nationalist women I worked with and is central to understanding their engagement in the movement.

WHAT'S IN A SPEECH?

Using ancient Hindu texts and deities, sadhvis construct a nationalist Hinduism in which the movement's politics are ineluctably linked to religious duty. As religious renouncers whose task it is to make esoteric religious ideas speak to the intricacies of life in the contemporary world, these sadhvis are uniquely positioned to inscribe Hindu nationalism with a sacred injunction. By infusing their religious lectures with the political aspirations of the movement, sadhvis become charismatic leaders who bridge the gap between the sacred and the mundane. Yet, how does the audience view these powerful acts of oratory? Below I examine how members of the movement responded to the sadhvis' speeches, and show how sadhvis themselves construe their involvement as exclusively dharmic rather than political.

The speech given by Sadhvi Rithambara at the Kargil event was an eloquent lesson to me about the impact of the words of religious renouncers. While most in the audience were either members of the movement or people involved in Hindu nationalist grassroots campaigns based at their schools or vocational training classes, a few individuals I met were attending because of personal relationships with members of the movement. Priya Trivedi, a young woman sitting next to me in the auditorium, although not a member of the movement, had begun attending events at the invitation of Jamuna Sinha, a leader of the Delhi VHP's women's wing. She told me with awe in her voice that she heard Atal Behari Vajpayee speak at one such event the previous week. Clearly, her association with Jamuna was giving her access to powerful people, which she may not have had before. In this example, Jamuna's befriending of Priya and her gradual introduction to the movement illustrates a strategy commonly used by Hindu nationalists as well as right-wing movements in other parts of the world (A. Basu 1998: 179–80; Blee 2002: 133). Although relatively new to Hindu nationalism, Priya was deeply moved by Rithambara's speech. Friendly and vivacious as we conversed before the event, her mood was transformed during Rithambara's speech. As Rithambara spoke of the women who had lost their husbands and sons in Kargil, Priya sobbed in the seat next to me. As widows and mothers walked across the stage to receive awards recognizing their loss, Priya continued to cry, empathizing with their pain. Rithambara's words resonated deeply and evoked in her the emotional power of national belonging and national loss.

Despite references to war and violence, members of the audience viewed the sadhvis' speeches as religious events. At both the events, members of the audience crowded around the sadhvis after the speeches to touch their feet and be blessed by them. At the Gita event, we were all given *prasad* after the prayer led by the sadhvis was performed at the end of each day. Prasad is blessed food that is traditionally given to devotees at a temple, a religious ritual, or other religious function. To give prasad to those gathered in the audience clearly marks the event as a religious occasion. I had taped all the speeches, and after each of these events, Hindu nationalist women asked me for copies so that they could listen to, in their words, the "pravachan" again. The choice of language is significant here. A pravachan is a religious lecture usually delivered by a Hindu renouncer. By calling these speeches pravachans, women were clearly coding these events as religious occasions. In fact, most of the women I worked with were deeply religious, and it was clear from their language and their actions that they viewed these women as spiritual authorities.

Another example illustrates the attitude that those attending these events had toward Hindu nationalist female renouncers. At the Gita event, the audience was seated on the ground facing the stage where the sadhvis were sitting. Having never been able to sit cross-legged for any length of time, my knee began to cramp and I tried to stretch my leg to relieve the pain. I had barely stretched it out when an older woman seated near me smacked my leg and told me crossly that one does not point one's feet at sadhvis. Suitably reprimanded, I sat upright, swallowed my pain, and digested the reverence with which the woman viewed the sadhvis. This incident clearly revealed that while many secular Indians might view Hindu nationalist sadhvis as charlatans who fabricate religious meaning to further their political aspirations, for those attending these events they are religious figures whose words possess sacred authority and who are understood to have penetrated the illusions of the world.[9] Indeed this is why sadhvis are so effective at constructing Hindu nationalism as a religious movement and weaving its political ideals into the religious imaginary of those present.

The sadhvis themselves seem to construct their actions as dharmic and as distinct from politics. One elderly renouncer, Sadhvi Kiran Bharati,[10] told me that she decided to join the movement because she was angered by what she believed was incontrovertible evidence that the Babri Masjid stood at the site of the Ramjanmabhumi Temple. In her narrative, it was not the compulsions of electoral politics but rather the anger provoked by a sense of injustice to Hindus that motivated her to become a part of the movement. Of course, such narratives are not innocent of political agendas, even if sadhvis and their supporters suggest that they are. In her analysis of women's life narratives, Sarah Lamb contends that narrative, even if inaccurate, must be viewed as "a mode of social action, a creative act of self making and culture making, through the telling of words" (Lamb 2001: 20). Kiran Bharati's narrative on this point is instructive in the portrait it presents of a renouncer moved by the passion of perceived religious persecution rather than by the seamier world of electoral politics. Her articulation of Hindu nationalist politics as a defense of dharma illustrates how religious symbols are given meaning through their complex interactions with politics in the world (Asad 1983).

I do not want to suggest that all members of the movement seamlessly reproduce this image of Hindu nationalist sadhvis. Like any cultural system, Hindu nationalism is not a bounded totality but contains within it diverging tendencies, ambiguities, and inconsistencies. Consequently, we must also analyze the perspectives of those who do not reproduce norms, and the alternative visions and challenges that they may contain (see Raheja and Gold 1994). One such challenge came from Vimla when she questioned renunciant authority by irreverently gossiping about the romantic involvements of renouncers in a conversation that implied that at least some of them were frauds. Vimla told me with a laugh that there is nothing difficult in being a renouncer. She said, "You just have to look spiritual and then people will give you Mercedes cars and you will live in luxury." Here Vimla transgresses the movement's norms and thereby challenges us to move beyond a vision of Hindu nationalism as a bounded and coherent discursive totality. Yet, Vimla's critique was not the view that I commonly encountered in my conversations with Hindu nationalists.

CONCLUSION

Skillfully intertwining the political and the sacred, sadhvis play a critical role in disseminating Hindu nationalist ideology to those within and beyond the movement. They strategically employ their dual subjectivity as women and as renouncers to mobilize Hindus to participate in Hindu nationalism. Using Hindu images, texts, and their renunciant authority, sadhvis imbue Hindu nationalism with a sacred injunction, and suggest that it is the dharmic duty of Hindus to participate in its violent politics. Imbued with sacred power, the words of Hindu nationalist sadhvis are central to the processes through which the Hindu nationalist movement disseminates its politics and recruits support at the grassroots level. It is through these women renouncers that the movement is able to construct a nationalist Hinduism that is not only ineluctably linked to Hindu nationalist politics, but also provides a vehicle to disseminate Hindu nationalist images of nation and subject that further its violent, xenophobic, and exclusionary agenda.

NOTES

1. The sadhvis used "dharma" to refer variously to the moral order of the world, duty, and Hinduism.

2. Hindu nationalists claimed that a temple to the Hindu God/King Rama had existed at the site of the Babri Masjid, a mosque built in the sixteenth century by the Mughal Emperor Babur in Ayodhya. Throughout the eighties Hindu nationalists, particularly those affiliated with the VHP, mobilized Hindus to participate in the movement to destroy the mosque and build a temple in its place. The mosque was destroyed on December 6th, 1992.

3. See Yuval-Davis 1997.

4. *Sindhur* is a red powder that married women wear on their heads. Here Rithambara is referring to nights shared with their husbands as married women.

5. See Mankekar 1999: 259–88.

6. These are cities in Pakistan. Islamabad is the capital of Pakistan.

7. Mohammad Ali Jinnah was the leader of the Muslim League and the Pakistan movement in colonial India.

8. Rithambara is referring to the conflict between India and Pakistan over Kashmir.

9. See also A. Basu 1995; Rajagopal 2001; Sarkar 2001.

10. This is a pseudonym.

26

Political Praise in Tamil Newspapers: The Poetry and Iconography of Democratic Power

Bernard Bate

O, Auspicious Leader
Who has ushered in
   a Golden Era of Rule!
O, Revolutionary Leader
Whom we worship daily
    turning evil-doing wastrels
    into question-marks . . .
Every movement of your tongue
Results in beneficial development schemes!
Even wastelands flourish
If your foot steps there!
I bow my head
    at the coming of your golden feet
I put my hands together
    and it cools my intellect
to welcome you
bowing down to worship your feet.
       —Advertisement placed by Sathur K. Sundarapandian,
                Kamarajar District Secretary,
          AIADMK (*Malai Murasu* 22.VIII.94: II)

The poem above, entitled "I Worshiped Your Golden Feet," exemplifies the kind of poetry that dominates the pages of Tamil newspapers when a major politician comes to town. This one is different from others only insofar as it is somewhat more original. Most of the poems I take up in this paper are far more formulaic: they frequently slap together stock phrases of adulation to weave a new poem that says nothing different from a hundred others in the newspaper that day. But they all attribute to J. Jayalalitha, the chief minister of the state of Tamil Nadu, India (1992–96), a certain divinity worthy of worship, even of the most physical forms of worship such as prostrating at one's leader's feet or self-mutilation; they all attribute to her sole agency of the state ("every movement of your tongue [*nāvacaippellām*][1] results in beneficial development schemes [*nalattiṭṭam*]"); they all assert that her mere presence in a particular place will bring forth abundance and fertility, growth and greenness ("Even wastelands flourish if your foot steps there!"); they all claim she is the very embodiment of such qualities as love, compassion, intelligence, the Tamil language, and history itself; and finally, they all address her in very familiar terms such as "family deity," or "deity of my heart," and most significantly, as "Mother"—as an intimate, powerful being.

This essay outlines two interrelated projects. In the first project I examine some of these poems in order to describe an aspect of the imaginings of power in the political practice of Tamil Nadu. In the case of the chief minister, the notion that her bodily presence in a wasteland will produce abundance or that her tongue is the source of all development projects suggests that the image of Jayalalitha in these poems is an aestheticized image (Daniel 1996) of an abstraction, that is, the state (Abrams 1988). I evoke the concept of the "aesthetic" to suggest the "fixing" or "objectification" (Cohn 1987a) of otherwise fluid sociocultural categories in discursive interaction. I also use the term to suggest that the discursively constructed object is imbued with emotional charge, plus or minus, attraction or repulsion. The realm of the aesthetic might be characterized as occupying one end of a continuum of possible takes on the world, from an embodied, emotional, "gut" reaction to a more "rational"—perhaps (better) rationalized—"ideology" of human action, products of action, and institutions. Both aesthetic and ideology are in constant interaction in people's everyday practical engagement with the world. And both, in turn, are the templates for that engagement. The "state" (or other aestheticizations of power), in no matter what form it may be imagined, probably partakes more of the embodied aesthetic end of the continuum than of the conscious rationalizations of ideology. The "state" is never a neutral imagining but always an image to which we either tie ourselves in devotion or patriotic love or defy with parricidal hatred.

But these imaginings do not merely follow some logic peculiar to the nation-state, whatever that may be (cf. Chatterjee 1993; B. Anderson 1991 [1983]). Rather, imaginings of the state are informed by common potentialities peculiar to Tamil society that are produced and reproduced in the practices of everyday life. Praise, what we will call *bhakti*, or "devotional love," appears to be a master aesthetic of the practices discussed in this essay.[2] Praise, I argue here, is an ancient Indian cultural logic (Appadurai 1990; Ali 1996) that informs the discursive practices whereby one aestheticizes power as an intimate being, such as a family deity or mother, who will grant us the benefits of her presence and respond to our appeals. Appadurai describes the praise of superiors in Hindu India, especially kings, as anchored in the logic of worship. Praise is, above all, a ritual activity, which produces a "hierarchical intimacy" (Babb 1986, quoted in Appadurai 1990)[3] between the worshiper and the worshiped, which is, often enough, a deity. The ritual practice, though intimate, is performed for others to see; it is meant to be observed and evaluated by onlookers. As such, it is an aesthetic practice both as one that can be evaluated positively or negatively and also as one that has emotional content—in the case of the praise poetry the content of devotional love, bhakti. As I will discuss below, contemporary political praise poetry draws on, and is structurally similar to, at least three other genres of praise in Tamil Nadu: the contemporary practice of greeting a leader who has graced a public meeting with his or her presence, the ancient praise of kings in inscriptions of their accomplishments, and medieval bhakti poetry.

The second project looks at the medium of this discourse, the newspaper, as an object of inquiry in ethnographic research: what importance does the newspaper have for the ethnography of a place, a practice, or a people? The newspaper as an object of ethnographic inquiry violates traditional categories of anthropological research (Herzfeld 1992: 120–21, n. 5): an anthropologist of a nonliterate society spends time "in the field," whereas scholars of literate civilizations work in archives or libraries. And as Akhil Gupta remarks, the newspaper also appears incompatible with traditional notions of ethnographic time and practice in the anthropology of the present:

> Treated with benign neglect by students of contemporary life, [newspapers] mysteriously metamorphize into invaluable "field data" once they have yellowed around the edges and fallen apart at the creases. And yet it is not entirely clear by what alchemy time turns the "secondary" data of the anthropologist into the "primary" data of the historian. (1995: 385)

The newspaper, though, is a textual artifact that is an integral part of daily life among vast numbers of people, even among those who may read nothing else. An ethnographer "in the field" of an Indian city would be missing much if s/he ignored the newspaper not only as a cultural text but as the focal object of a wide range of practices. It is also a medium accessible to a wide range of people, a means to advertise one's business, marriageable son or daughter, or political patronage. The newspaper, in other words, has a social life far livelier than most ethnographic research has so far given it credit for. My second concern, then, is to explore how the newspaper, as a widely accessible mode of mass media, can be a space, like other spaces in the society—the street or the political stage—where people announce their allegiance to their political leaders through praise, tie their names to them, and, in so doing, make themselves great.

I will begin with a discussion of the Tamil newspaper as a focal object in daily practice and as a medium of political patronage. After briefly outlining some of the major themes of the poetry I will then discuss its layout on the page and its iconography. The newspaper image or text does not exist in a vacuum, though, either in terms of its placement on a page or section of the newspaper or in its wider resonance with the world around it. In the end, I will explore how these textual and visual images fit into the wider world in which the newspaper is produced and read by examining some of the textual, visual, and architectural images of praise found (almost) every day on the streets of Madurai.

Newspapers, those daily, sometimes twice-daily, mediations of the social world beyond our immediate face-to-face interactions, are time-bound textual objects. While Benedict Anderson called them "one-day bestsellers" (1991: 35) they are quite different from books, bureaucratic documents, or other textual artifacts that are produced to stand the test of time, to "record," to transcend the ephemerality of the spoken word, to endure.

They do resemble at least some books, though, such as the Bible, the Qur'an, or other such texts, insofar as they occupy a central place in many people's daily rituals, often in the mornings, but at other specific times of day as well.[4] In the city of Madurai, Tamil Nadu, men (particularly men) gather at tea stalls early to smoke, drink tea or coffee, and read the newspaper or listen to a reading of it. The tea stall owners keep a few papers around that are taken apart page by page, each leaf passed around so one paper can be read simultaneously by a number of people. Frequently, someone will read an article out loud, his recitation sharply marked as the written form of the language—indeed, his language is even marked as "journalese," that form of written Tamil massively influenced by the grammar of English newspapers. The ritual of early morning reading is often repeated, somewhat more diffusely, after six when the evening papers are delivered. In this way, newspapers are part of the daily rhythm of life in Madurai, like meals, prayers, going to work or temple, or taking an afternoon siesta—activities that vast numbers of people regard as integral, essential aspects of their days.[5]

But unlike a book, a particular edition of a newspaper is an artifact of and for the moment, a punctual object whose value (under ordinary circumstances) is limited to a few hours. In a city like Madurai, with three main morning papers and two main evening papers, the value of the morning paper is at its greatest at sunrise, far less at midday, and by dusk it is worth only its weight as scrap.[6] A half-day bestseller, at best. At the same time, the fact that someone took out a political ad or published an article or poem in a particular newspaper can point to that particular moment, those particular people in those particular relations. Similarly with articles that concern an individual: these become objects the individual might keep folded up in the back of his or her bureau, mementos of a moment in which his or her name transcended everyday life and became a part of history.

Finally, as Anderson has famously argued, the newspaper allows the imagining of a community far beyond the face-to-face world in which it is read (1991: 32–36, 61–65), that is, the "imagined community" of the nation-state. But these imaginings are closely tied to the particular discourses or events occurring at that particular moment in time. And the community imagined is internally differentiated, politically contested, hierarchized, and bounded off from others in particular ways. Each newspaper in Tamil Nadu has very definite political party affiliations or sympathies, so the multiple imaginings of community will have differing evaluations from paper to paper. The "community" imagined on any given morning by *Thikkathir* (Ray of Fire), an organ of the Communist Party of India (Marxist), will be very different from that imagined by *Thina Thandhi* (The Daily Wire), Tamil Nadu's most popular daily, which was originally modeled on the British tabloid *The Daily Mirror* (Jeffrey 1997: 254). What Anderson calls the "fictive reality" of an imagined collectivity generated through the daily reading of the Tamil newspaper, then, is a highly political reality, and that politics is constantly changing.

The advertisements I examine here were taken out by local politicians on days of their leader's arrival in their towns or districts.[7] The hundreds of ads that dominate the pages on those days spill over the regular sections into special sections (*ciṛuppumalar*) issued by the newspapers in order to hold them all. The sudden appearance of the very excess of Jayalalitha images and the sudden storm of praise—O, Amazon Warrior; O, Protector Deity; O, Doctor Revolutionary Leader—never effaces the fact that these ads are taken out by locally well-known people who direct their messages not only to their leaders but to their constituents, their colleagues and competitors within the party, and their political enemies. The larger and more extravagant the ads, the greater one's presence in that town's political organization, and certainly the greater one's image in the sight—in the literal, early morning gaze—of the visiting leader thumbing through the local newspaper. Invariably, a politician's welcome contains a large image of "The Big Person," the leader's name or appellation in the boldest print, and a poem addressed to her. The local politician's photograph placed prominently at the bottom of the page, his or her name always in the second boldest print, ensures that this "enchanted forest of adulation" (Mbembe 1992) never entirely bewitches us as some "authorless" text expressing timeless truth.

The overall structure and main motifs of these poems have a number of antecedents that reveal the overall logic of praise. Of many possible, I mention here three: the welcome address of stage speaking; medieval bhakti poetry; and the praise of kings found in *prasasti* and *meykkīrti* poems of kingly praise. The "welcome address" (*varavērpurai*), a performance genre of *mēṭaittamiḻ*, or "oratory," ends with the phrase *varuka! varuka! enru varavērkirōm:* "We welcome you with (shouts of) 'Welcome! Welcome!'" The most common vocatives—what we might call *hailing utterances*—printed boldly in the advertisements also resonate with the moment of welcoming a

Figure 26.1. Jayalalitha as Andal. "O, Reincarnation of Mother Andal!/ O Excellence whom All the World Praises!/Welcome!/ Shower Riches Upon Us! Placed by P.B. Selvasubramaniyaraja of the Revolutionary Leader Frong, Rajapalayaiyam, Kamaraj District." Quarter-page ad, *Malai Murasu*, August 28, 1994: 1.

leader to a speaking event. The event organizer at the microphone shouts out "O, Doctor Revolutionary Leader"—and the crowd responds, "Long Live!"; he shouts: "O, Amazon Warrior Who Protects Social Justice"—they respond, "Long Live!"; "O, Family Deity"—"Long Live! Long Live! Long Live!" The event becomes marked by the rhythm of the chant-and-response (which may last for five minutes or more), the passion of the party cadres as they throng the stage, and the frenzy that frequently erupts as the faithful struggle with organizers and bodyguards to garland their leader or give her a gift with no regard to the proper time and place for such things. The welcoming of the big person and the vocative chanting is always a moment of intense energy and enthusiasm, one of the aspects of political meetings that mark them as sites of intense desire and longing.

Looking at these vocatives we get a sense of the range of appellations Jayalalitha's supporters generate for her as well as of the variety of images that are deployed in the aestheticization of the state. She is hailed, firstly, as a leader of specific groups such as "the poor," the "common people," or the "the Tamil lands"; she is a "Golden Leader," a "Leader equal to a Lion," a "Leader whom all the world praises." Secondly, she is characterized as a re-incarnation of famous historical figures: kings (e.g., Pari, a Sangam-age king known for his philanthropy), queens (e.g., Jansi Rani, a Rajasthani queen who is said to have strapped her newborn crown prince on her back and fought off the Muslim invaders of her kingdom), and literary figures (e.g., Andal, the famous author of bhakti poetry; see fig. 26.1). Thirdly, she is hailed as a deity: "O, God of Our Heart," "O, Goddess of Dharma," "O, Protector Deity of Social Justice," "Family Deity," and "God of Our Hearts." The remainder of the vocative appellations can be broken down into such categories as history/literature/language (O, Tamil; O, Golden Book of History); light/ lamps (O, Sacred Lamp of the Southlands); the heart (O, Vital Heartbeat of the Poor); land or architecture (O, Land That Sprouted Heroism); intimate beings (O, Mother); and a series of abstractions such as bravery, love, statecraft, sacredness, and motherhood. It is precisely the combination of all of these qualities and identities that are woven together in this aestheticized image of Jayalalitha as the sole agency of the state, indeed, as the state itself. Her appearance at opening ceremonies for multimillion-rupee state development projects—which are the impetus for the praise poetry—become celebrations of her personal largesse; her movement across the landscape of Tamil Nadu is praised as the movement of state power itself. Most of these themes are represented in the following two poems.

Poem 2

O, Jansi Rani of the Tamil lands
   who has come to bestow
   the Anna medal on police officers!
O, Land that sprouts victory!
O, Doctor Revolutionary Leader,
   esteemed Premier of the Tamil Lands,
Welcome! Welcome!

O, Amazon Warrior who protects social justice
   who has won
   69% caste reservation
   which will bring well-being
   for tomorrow's society
   and will make the dispossessed prosper!
Welcome! Welcome!

By your arrival
Madurai achieves excellence!
I welcome you
in praise and worship

   Your true servant
   T. K. Rathakrishnan, B.E., M.L.A.
   Thirmangalam Assembly District
   Madurai District
   (*Malai Malar* 19.IX.94: V)

Poem 3

O, Mother
Who has given us life
Our God of personal grace
The very embodiment of
 Intelligence, Ability, Refinement, Discrimination, Love, Compassion,
 Achievement, History, Epoch, Honesty,
 Ability, Strong Will, Political Strategy
Welcome! Welcome!

We touch your feet and worship you.
 C. Singam, Asst. Secretary, Madurai District AIADMK, Madurai
 Sellur K. Raji, Secretary, 16th Ward, AIADMK, Madurai
 (*Malai Malar* 19.IX.94: XI)

The second most obvious antecedent for the praise poem, as suggested at the outset of this chapter, is bhakti poetry, or the poetry of devotion to a personal deity. Newspaper poems seem to particularly resemble the poetry of the medieval devotional text of Tamil Saivism, *Tēvāram*. The fact that one reads the same basic structure in the newspaper poems over and over again is similar to a reading of the *Tēvāram*, which is organized in thematic cycles of praise to Lord Siva. One example taken from the *Appar Tēvāram*, composed as early as the seventh century, might suffice to indicate the obvious connection between the two poetic traditions:

. . .
bright flame, celestial being
who stands as the pure path,
bull among the immortals,

honey who dwells in Tiruvaiyaru!
I wander as your servant,
worshipping and singing your feet.
(*Appar Tēvāram* IV.39; trans. Peterson [1989: 286])

Compare the above with the poem below placed in the *Malai Muracu* by a minister of the Tamil Nadu Legislative Assembly from Kamarajar District, Mr. J. Balagangatharan:

Poem 4

O, sacred lamp of the Southlands!
O, light of the Dravidian family!
O, burning torch of poor people!
O, Athiparasakti
vital ruler of this earthly world!
O, esteemed Doctor Revolutionary Leader

who transforms these Tamil lands into a Golden Realm!
I welcome you
I touch your golden feet and worship you!
  J. Balagangatharan, B.Sc., B.L., M.L.A.
  District Secretary
  Revolutionary Leader Front
  Kamarajar District
  (*Malai Muracu* 22.VIII.94: III)

Obviously, a number of motifs have been borrowed directly from medieval bhakti poetry, not least of which being the evocation of lamps, lights, and fire: elements of worship and icons of power. The mode of worship is hyperbolic (at least from some points of view), intensely emotional, and aesthetically crafted. Today, these same poems are recited in the evenings at major Saivite temples throughout Tamil Nadu.

Thirdly, the contemporary praise poem appears to partake of the same logic of the pan-Indic Sanskrit *prasasti* inscriptions dating in Tamil Nadu from the same period as the first bhakti movements (Appadurai 1990: 110, n. 1). Prasasti were inscriptional "praise prefaces" that identified the king as a divine descendant of a deity and bestowed titles (*virutu*), "emblems," or "honors" upon the king from a subordinate. The Tamil counterpart of the prasasti prefaces, which developed during the Chola period (ninth to twelfth centuries CE), are *meykkīrtti*. Meykkirtti differ from prasasti prefaces by their far more standardized formats and their attention to the achievements of the king and not to his genealogy (Davis 1985: 5). For a variety of reasons, genealogical claims were absent. Rather, the Chola king was praised for his conquests on the hot battlefield and the protection of his home landscape, cool and green under his all-encompassing royal parasol. In other words, the king's actions and accomplishments are more important than any authorial claims of legitimate pedigree. Meykkirttis praise the king's works by which the land is transformed, made lush and fertile ("even wastelands flourish if your foot steps there").

In each case, the welcome address, the bhakti poem, and the prasasti/meykkirtti inscription, the leader is praised publicly, emotionally, and hyperbolically. The following poem, sponsored to celebrate the inauguration of a number of state-run development schemes, appears to touch on all of the above categories:

O, Sacredness! O Sacred Lamp!
O, Great Light of Dravida!
O, Encyclopedia of History
  who achieved (a policy of) 69% caste reservation!
O, Fantasy who brought the Kaveri River
  to fatten this golden fertile country for all of history!
O, Lamp of the Lighthouse!

O, Golden Light of the Lion Throne
   which is the cradle of the Child who came to show
   the world the Grammar of Motherhood!

O, Our Goddess of Love
   who has placed her foot
   in Anna District!

O, Leader equal to the Lion!
Mother, May you $(n\bar{\imath})^8$ come! O, Welcome!

   Forever Your Faithful Servant,
   P. Kumaraswamy, B.Sc., B.L., M.P.
   Palani Parliamentary District
   (*Malai Malar* 23.IX.94: V)

The member of parliament's poem contains aspects of all three of the antecedents mentioned above. It is firstly organized as a complex vocative phrase directed toward Jayalalitha. Secondly, its characterization of the leader by the use of motifs such as lamps, lights, and majestic creatures such as lions, as well as its overall mood of praise, resonates clearly with medieval bhakti poetic practice. Thirdly, Kumaraswamy publicly praises the chief minister's achievements, such as her political struggle to ensure that 69 percent of state government appointments will be filled by members of Scheduled Castes and Tribes and the Backward and Most Backward Classes. And despite the fact that Tamil Nadu's ongoing dispute with neighboring Karnataka over the free flow of the Kaveri River had not been resolved at that time, the poem attributes to Jayalalitha not only the successful settlement of the problem but the very flow of the river itself and the unending fertility of the Tamil lands! The invocation of such images of lamps and lights—common among all the Dravidian parties—suggests that her presence casts a light in the darkness (of opposition rule), brings cool greenness to the lands that were parched; the imagery appears to parallel the old meykkirti opposition of arid battlefields and the cool, fertile lands of the landscape under the royal parasol.

The layout and iconography, too, like the poetic description of Jayalalitha as a deity, king, or queen, suggests the imagining of both hierarchical and intimate relationships to the leader. Her image is literally framed in borders and boxes that confirm her royal-cum-divine identity. In addition to rather standard borders of the red, white, and black colors of her party, the AIAD-MK, Jayalalitha stands framed by temple pillars or in a *maṇṭapam* (a pillared hall frequently in a temple); she is shown shaded by the royal parasol; she is seated in the Lion Throne reviewing her all-women police brigades—which she has just instituted—marching by. The lion, so frequently mentioned, has numerous resonances in contemporary Tamil culture. The lion, as in Europe, is the sign of royalty par excellence; it is also said to be Jayalalitha's zodiac

Figure 26.2. Multiple JJ. Ad placed by P. Balasubramanian, Madras. Full-page ad, *Malai Malar*, September 24, 1994: XXXV (Special Section).

sign. One woman examining a page featuring a number of lions—which had been arrayed around Jayalalitha in an ad placed for a ceremony to decorate police officers—suggested to me that the lions were policemen standing guard around the chief minister. Finally, just as each deity has a vehicle, so too does Jayalalitha have the lion—the same vehicle, by the way, of the pan-Indian goddess Durga and the local Tamil deity Mariyamman.

The hierarchical distancing of the leader as god or king is fused with a sense of intimacy. Hierarchy is expressed in top/bottom oppositions, and intimacy in the choice of portraits as well as their orientation vis-à-vis each other. One P. Balasubramanian, head of the Tamil Nadu Produce Sales Board, placed a full-page, full-color ad in the *Malai Malar*, an evening paper (fig. 26.2). Other than a small picture of himself with some text at the bottom of the page, the ad features a large central photograph of the chief minister, dressed in a white sari, smiling pleasantly and gazing down and off page. The central photograph is surrounded by sixty smaller images of exactly the same image, the larger one and most of the smaller ones appearing to gaze warmly at Bala himself! Orienting the chief minister's picture such that it smiles at the ad's sponsor is a frequent technique in these ads.

Hierarchical relationships are equally transparent. Numerous ads feature the hierarchical ordering of Jayalalitha just below figures such as the

Figure 26.3. Mural at "The Space of JJ." (*JJ tital* near Cimmakkal, North Veli Street junction.) Commissioned by "Coconut Shop" R. Mariyappan (pictured lower right). The two standing figures are Ariñar Annadurai (left) and M. G. Ramachandran. The two leaves are the official voting sign of the AIADMK. The image in the circle at center is Periyar E. V. Ramaswamy. The mural reads, "O, Lioness who appears as a burning lamp to light the Tamil lands which have been cast into darkness! O, Goddess of Revolution! O, Mother! O, Tamil!" The writing at the bottom of the mural notes that this painting was sponsored by the "Madurai City Self-Protection Force."

founder of the Dravidian movement, Thandai Periyar E. V. Ramaswamy, and the DMK and AIADMK founders Ariñar ("The Scholar") Annadurai and "Doctor Revolutionary Leader" M. G. Ramachandran (MGR), respectively (see note 8). In such a position she mediates the relationship between those late, great political figures and the local politician pictured at the bottom of the page. This same logic is repeated by lower-level political workers inserting their district-level leaders in between themselves and Jayalalitha; or to foreground their local patronage to an even greater degree, the local leader's picture is placed by his or her subordinates in the same line as the former leaders.

These ads constitute but one of a series of activities local politicos undertake to welcome their leader and, importantly, to tie their names to hers. The placement of the praise poem is, thus, a practice that shares a contexture—"the texture that surrounds and the texture that constitutes" (Daniel and Peck 1996: 1)—with a wide range of related practices. The most notable of

Figure 26.4. Mural at Workshop Road. The mural was sponsored by
Pon. Arumugam, R. T. Paramasivam, and M. G. Pandikumar, subordinates of "Coconut Shop" R. Mariyappan, whose name is prominently featured in the picture itself. Above the image of Jayalalitha and Coconut
Shop are portraits of M. G. Ramachandran (left) and Ariñar C. N. Annadurai. The heading reads: "34th Ward Revolutionary Leader Front."

these practices include street-level activities that are structurally similar to
the newspaper poems. Ceremonial arches are inscribed with the same vocative salutations, especially "Revolutionary Leader," "Mother Tamil," "Family Deity," and so on, and during the caste reservation agitations, "Amazon
Warrior Who Protects Social Justice." The very same phrases taken out in
newspaper ads appear on posters, banners, and wall paintings such as the
mural sponsored by one of Madurai's most prominent supporters and (therefore) benefactors of Jayalalitha, "Coconut Shop" R. Mariyappan, at a place he
dubbed "*JJ tiṭal*," or "The Space of J. Jayalalitha" (fig. 26.3):

> O, Lioness
>> who appears as a burning lamp to light the Tamil lands
>> which have been cast in darkness!
> O, Goddess of Revolution!
> O, Mother!
> O, Tamil!

Figure 26.5. Mural at the Ganesh Temple, Cimmakkal.

This painting, along with several others in Madurai commissioned by Mariyappan's supporters, has the same structural properties as many of the ads examined above as well as other poetic and iconographic representations of praise. Mariyappan's supporters commissioned a number of painted images on structures throughout Madurai in 1994 and '95. There appears in this and other paintings a crisscrossing of gazes and postures, from Mariyappan in the lower-right-hand corner worshiping Jayalalitha; to Jayalalitha on the left worshiping MGR and Annadurai (who appear to float like ghosts); and back again to Periyar, framed not unlike a revered ancestor's portrait hanging in the hall of someone's home.

This spatial logic is equally evident in the painting on Workshop Road (fig. 26.4). Also commissioned by political workers of Mariyappan's camp, this brightly painted mural depicts Mariyappan reverently saluting Jayalalitha, who lights a lamp over a sun-drenched Madurai, a landscape dominated by the Meenakshiyamman Temple's towering gateways (*kōpuram*). The portraits of their political forebears above (MGR and Annadurai) appear here, too, to balance off the names of the mural sponsors below. Again, as in bhakti poetry, praising the servants (e.g., Mariyappan) of the servants (Jayalalitha) of the lord (Meenakshiyamman) is a long and fruitful strategy in Tamil practices of the production of political power. But not merely this: Mariyappan and the chief minister appear framed in a tableau, a domestic scene of husband and auspicious wife of childbearing years (*cumaṅkali*) reverently worshiping God. Taking in this image in one glance, our minds shift back and forth from an image of hierarchical salutation to a fantastic Holy Family wherein our local leader—himself a source of great benefit—dwells married to the our Mother/Goddess. What fruits, what benefits, such a union produces!

It is exactly this contexture of the newspaper image with different discursive practices taken from a wide range of different domains—from the public meeting and wall murals and posters that saturate Madurai's landscape to the practices within domestic spaces and temples—that demonstrates the power of the image of praise. I've begun to show here how the newspaper page resonates with other spaces, and how the very placement of the praise poem is but one of a series of related practices. We praise our leader, and weave together as many images of power as we have available to us, creating something very new in the deployment of material very old. In this, the praise of Jayalalitha is like so many other practices of nation-building: the elements strike us as very old, but their deployment in contemporary practice is quite new.

This personification and aestheticization of the state, and the decorating of her with images that span both history and the domains of royal-cum-devotional practice, is a product of the production of power. And, as an aesthetic practice, the omnipresence of Jayalalitha in textual, visual, and architectural images does invoke a wide range of emotional responses. I have dealt here only with the positive emotions expressed by her loyal servants. As this is a political practice, you can be sure that negative responses to these images are also expressed, and just as vehemently (e.g., Geetha and Rajadurai 1995: 201–203).

ACKNOWLEDGMENTS

This essay is based on research conducted between 1992 and 1995 in Madurai, Tamil Nadu, India, as an aspect of my inquiries into Tamil oratory and democratic practice. Research and writing were funded through a Junior Research Fellowship of the American Institute of Indian Studies, a U.S. Department of Education Fulbright-Hays Dissertation Fellowship, a Charlotte W. Newcombe Fellowship offered by the Woodrow Wilson Foundation, and by two years of generous support by the Committee on Southern Asian Studies at the University of Chicago. A previous version of this paper was delivered in "The Hidden Manifest: Newspapers in Ethnographic Research," a session of the 96th annual meetings of the American Anthropological Association, San Francisco, 22 November 1997. Thanks to Akhil Gupta, John Kelly, McKim Marriott, Sarah Lamb, Diane Mines, Mary Scoggin, and Gregory Starrett, who offered substantive comments on earlier drafts.

NOTES

1. I use standard English spellings for the names of places (e.g., Madurai), persons (e.g., Mariyappan), or institutions (e.g., newspapers such as *Malai Murasu*). All other Tamil terms are transcribed according to the method outlined in the Madras University Tamil Lexicon.

2. Usually translated as devotional love, bhakti has characterized many moments of South Asian devotional practice over the centuries and among certain sects (Ali 1996; Cutler 1987; Davis 1991; Peterson 1989; Ramanujan 1992 [1981]; Singer 1972). But the logic of bhakti—not strictly a religious logic per se—informs not only the devotional practices associated with deities, but relationships to powerful entities in general. Richard Davis's tripartite definition of bhakti, "recognition of the god's superiority, devoted attentiveness, and desire to participate in his exalted domain" (Davis 1991: 7, as quoted in Ali 1996: 144), serves equally well to describe the practices of local politicians vis-à-vis their sponsors and political leaders. As the poems and images that saturate city spaces on walls, over streets, and on the pages of newspapers described below demonstrate, these three characteristics—praise of superiority, devotedness, and participation—are integral aspects of Tamil political practice.

3. The concept of a "hierarchical intimacy" was first mentioned to me by A. K. Ramanujan in 1992. McKim Marriott also notes that the concept was discussed widely in seminars and classes during the 1970s at the University of Chicago (personal communication, 15 November 1999). Such a mode of intimacy is common between parents and children, between beloved teachers and students, and, of course, between a devotee and his or her deity. In contemporary American Christianity, for instance, the relationship between Jesus and those who call him "my friend" certainly qualifies as "hierarchical intimacy."

4. This is not the case, however, with Tamil devotional literature, in which the textual artifact bears the same relation to the "text" as a musical score bears to the music, i.e., the traditional Tamil text has its reality in performance, not necessarily in its artifactual form. For a discussion of the Tamil text as a performative practice, see Kersenboom 1995.

5. Contrast the image of the tea-stall newspaper reading with Anderson's description of it, following Hegel, as a prayerlike activity that takes place individually "in the lair of the skull" (1991 [1983]: 35).

6. During my research I examined five newspapers daily (along with a variety of weekly and monthly magazines): the three morning papers, *Thina Thandhi, Thina Malar,* and *Thina Karan,* and two evening papers, *Malai Murasu* and *Malai Malar.*

7. Given limitations of space, I cannot even begin to do justice here to the rather baroque political situation in Tamil Nadu today. I therefore have limited my discussion to advertisements taken out by only one of the Tamil nationalist, or Dravidian, parties—the ruling party during my inquiries in 1992–95—the All India Annadurai Dravida Munnetra Kazhagam (AIADMK). The AIADMK was formed as a breakaway party from the Dravida Munnetra Kaghagam (the Dravidian Progress Association, or DMK) in 1972 by the great cinema idol, M. G. Ramachandran (MGR). His lover and frequent leading lady, Dr. J. Jayalalitha, succeeded MGR as leader of the AIADMK after his death in 1988. Much to the chagrin of the DMK—which was founded by Ariñar C. N. Annadurai—MGR named his new party in memory of

Aṇṇā, "Elder Brother," Annadurai. Both the DMK and the AIADMK look to Thandai Periyar, "The Great One," E. V. Ramaswamy, as the philosophical founder of the Dravidian movement.

8. The second person singular pronoun, *nī* (the equivalent of the French *tu*, German *Du*, etc.), would not be used in face-to-face interaction with such a high-status person as the chief minister; one would rather use the second person plural *nīṅkaḷ* (French *vous*, German *Sie*, etc.), or, better yet, the third person plural (rational) *tāṅkaḷ*, literally "they," in addressing Jayalalitha or other supernal beings. *Nī* is used to address children, intimate friends or family members, and—most significantly for our purposes here—*one's deity.*

27

Mala's Dream: Economic Policies, National Debates, and Sri Lankan Garment Workers

Caitrin Lynch

The Truth about Women Workers at Garment Factories
By Mala, a Sri Lankan garment worker (written in 1996)

It is a known fact that the garment industry's contribution toward the Sri Lankan economy and industrial development is enormous. However, if you consider development from the correct perspective, the story is quite different. What you see is a group of intelligent, hardworking, and educated people who work until the last bead of sweat drops to achieve a production target set by the management. The majority of these workers are women.

Most of these young women come from very conservative, respectable, ordinary families. Most of them were brought up under the guidance of their parents preserving traditional Sinhala customs.

Though these women are well educated, intelligent, and talented, their chances of obtaining a government job are limited. When they feel the economic burden their parents go through, they cannot stay home doing nothing. So a woman has to decide to leave the nest she was living in with her parents and siblings, give away the love and security she had under her parents' roof, and join the workforce in the garment industry located in the city. She does this with a lot of hopes, ambitions, and determination to achieve economic independence for her and her family. Though the public opinion about women in the garment industry is not that favorable, women who join the workforce are often surprised to realize that they are joining a set of very able, capable, efficient, and hardworking young men and women. These workers are not a group of stupid people as they have been labeled by the outside world. With our young woman's fears about the garment industry fading, she willingly joins the young men and women who sweat to match the speed of the machines at which they work, in order to achieve the targets. She was determined to give her best to achieve what the others were achieving to match the production targets. The labor she does to provide the production target for one day is priceless.

Unless she meets the efficiency of the machines she is working with, it is certain that she will be subjected to bitter verbal abuse from superiors. While trying to match the production target, workers have to maintain the quality of the product. After eight hours of hard labor, most often they are forced to work extra hours. At the end of the workday, most of these women are too tired even to talk with their family or friends. She walks back toward her hut tiredly like an innocent doe coming to a heavenly abode at sunset. Some of the workers have to live in boarding houses specially put up for them by the neighbors who live around these factories. There is nobody to love them, comfort them, or to listen to them, neither at those factories nor in the boarding houses. The love, compassion, comfort, and peace of life they enjoyed while growing up with their parents and siblings are long gone.

It is very unfortunate to note that some people exploit the innocence of these girls for their sexual needs. The loneliness, frustration, and newfound freedom lead them to look for comfort in strangers and opportunistic people. Sometimes girls themselves are to blame for this as they invite trouble by inappropriate behavior. Though this is not the story of most of the women working in the garment industry, it has certainly led to tarnish the image of them in Sri Lanka. Sadly, it is a common practice in our society to blame factory workers for all the vices happening in the society. This sort of unwanted publicity helps to bring the self-confidence and morale down. The obvious result of this is that the majority of innocent girls who value ethics, moral and cultural values, dignity, and pride are also being treated as dirt. This is an added stress and a cause for depression for the girls who have undergone enough agony at work. The society has not tried to understand the real people who work behind those machines nor their natural talents.

Even though the mass media has done nothing much to change the image of "the garment girl," we have to be thankful to them for at least taking some effort to restore it.

By means of short stories, novels, dramas, songs, and essays some media are trying to establish the fact that "garment factory girls" are normal human beings like all other people who are employed in other industries.

However, the mass media should take more aggressive efforts to bring out the truth about the lives of innocent, educated, talented, hardworking garment factory girls and the value they bring to the Sri Lankan economy and to the family. If people could appreciate the women who add value to the Sri Lankan economy the same way they appreciate the money those women bring in, Sri Lanka will be a much better place for everybody. I hope one day people will treat them as equals.

The day it happens will be a dream come true.

Mala penned these words for me in 1996, when she was four years into a job at a Sri Lankan garment factory.[1] I had first met Mala when I began ethnographic research at her factory two years prior. In this narrative and in our many conversations, Mala articulated concerns she shared with her coworkers who struggled over how families, neighbors, and others throughout Sri Lankan society perceived garment workers. She and her coworkers occupied highly visible and publicly stigmatized jobs, and yet these were important jobs for the national economy, not to mention for personal fulfillment and family financial support. Mala paints a picture of stigma and scorn, but she dreams of recognition of the important role that women garment workers play in the nation's economy and future.

Women's labor has been an important cornerstone of economic development in Sri Lanka's liberalized economy. The nation's largest source of foreign exchange is the export-oriented garment industry, which employs 83 percent women, most of whom, like Mala, are Sinhala Buddhists, the majority population on the island nation (Tilakaratne 2006: 2–5; Arai 2006: 35). Seventy-four percent of Sri Lankans are Sinhala, most of whom are Buddhist (a small minority are Christian). Tamils (mostly Hindu, some Christian) are the primary ethnic minority. Since 1983, the majority Sinhala government has been at war with a rebel group known as the Liberation Tigers of Tamil Eelam—the LTTE is fighting for independence in regions of the country where Tamils form the majority.[2] In the context of a nation at war, the economy has taken on paramount importance. And yet, women who work in such a critical economic role are commonly known by derogatory and sexually connotative nicknames, such as "Juki girls," "Juki pieces," or "garment pieces." The word "Juki" in these nicknames is derived from a Japanese industrial sewing-machine brand commonly used in Sri Lankan factories.[3] The Juki-girl stigma had emerged by 1979, two years after Sri Lanka liberalized its economy. As I write in 2009, this stigma still stands as a powerful critique leveled at the hundreds of thousands of women employed in the garment industry.

The terms "Juki pieces" and "garment pieces" objectify women by making them seem like nothing more than things or pieces of dry goods. As one Sri Lankan newspaper editorial notes, the term "Juki pieces" indicates that these women "are treated like some expendable commodity" (*Daily Mirror* 2005: n.p.; cf. Hewamanne 2002: 7–8). The Sinhala term for "pieces," *baḍuwa*, has powerful sexual connotations, and all these nicknames connote sexual promiscuity. The stigma of being a garment worker is so damaging and widespread that Sinhala newspaper marriage proposals sometimes disqualify garment workers with the phrase "no garment girls" or "no Juki girls" (Y. Tambiah 1997).

But *why* are garment workers so stigmatized? In the face of globalized economic and cultural processes, concerns about how women should behave are central to how Sri Lankans understand the effects of economic liberalization on their society. Furthermore, as other scholars have shown, in many times and places women have become symbols of the nation (Mayer 1999; McClintock 1995; Parker et al. 1992). In association with the symbolic elevation of women, daily practices have emerged to monitor and control female modesty and respectability as a measure of national status and prestige. An intense concern with women's moral purity pervades war-torn Sri Lanka. While men are encouraged to be aggressive and fight for the country, women are valorized both as mothers, who heroically sacrifice their sons for the nation without complaint, and as traditional women, who maintain ethnic purity through their heightened morality, even as the nation around them falls into disarray.[4] During this post-liberalization era of war and global engagement, women's behavior has been the locus of considerable anxiety about how much foreign influence is detrimental to the nation. This anxiety in part stems from the historical convergence of social and economic changes with the escalation of the LTTE campaign for independence. Because the implementation of the new, open economy coincided with the escalation of ethnic conflict into a separatist civil war between the government and the LTTE, the assumed moral perils of economic liberalization and globalization have been interpreted against the specter of the nation's disintegration. The Juki-girl stigma and Mala's dream of recognition must be understood in this national context.

ECONOMIC LIBERALIZATION AND NATIONAL IDENTITY

Sri Lanka is one of many postcolonial and third-world societies that adopted economic liberalization policies in the mid to late twentieth century as they participated in World Bank and International Monetary Fund structural adjustment programs. Sri Lanka liberalized its economy in 1977, and the following year a predominantly female workforce was hired in the nation's first free trade zone.[5] As other scholars have argued, in postcolonial nations the dominant response to economic and cultural globalization is often cultural fundamentalism: people conceive of the entry into their nation of foreign goods, people, ideas, and commodities as a threat to revered cultural traditions. Sri Lanka is no exception. Since the economic reforms, there has emerged in Sri Lanka a deep-seated fear of neocolonialism in response to a huge increase in the amount of foreign trade the country participates in, and the speed and volume of movement of people, things, and ideas into and away from the island. Sri Lankans perceive the world as getting smaller—many have relatives abroad and speak about the world as being readily at hand to those given the right opportunities. Borders are permeable, both in terms of the movement of people and finances (tourists, development workers, foreign investors, and funding to the LTTE flow in; refugees, housemaids, elite college-aged students, and the rapper M.I.A. flow out) and in terms of the entry of goods and images that did not exist in Sri Lanka prior to the economic reforms (e.g., Pepsi, Kentucky Fried Chicken, U.S. and Australian television programs).

The demarcation of women's appropriate behavior has been central to how Sri Lankans make sense of the economic and social changes accompanying the recent economic reforms.[6] The contemporary period has been characterized by intense debate about how much foreign and Western influence is suitable for the country, and how women are situated within these changing social relations. Women's labor has been the basis of two leading sources of foreign exchange in the liberalized Sri Lankan economy: women's factory employment within Sri Lanka and women's employment as housemaids or factory laborers abroad (especially in the Middle East). With large numbers of village women migrating to Colombo and abroad for employment since the late 1970s, the morality of female migrant laborers has emerged as a primary target of nationalist discourse about the moral integrity of the nation (de Alwis 1998, 197–98; Gamburd 2000; and this volume).

In this context of the idealization of women's moral appearance and behavior, imagine how people might read the presence of thousands of unmarried, primarily Sinhala Buddhist factory women in the nation's free trade zones, living in boarding houses without their families. I now turn to demonstrate how national politics, economic critiques, and cultural concerns all converge in the figure of the Juki girl—the very women about whom Mala so eloquently writes.

JUKI GIRLS

The centerpiece of the government's economic liberalization package was the establishment in 1978 of the Katunayake Free Trade Zone (FTZ) in an urban area on the outskirts of Colombo, the nation's capital. Situated near the international airport, the Katunayake FTZ is by far the largest of Sri Lanka's eight FTZs today. Of the thousands of factory workers in Colombo, by far the most work in the garment industry. Soon after its establishment, there emerged considerable societal concern about good village girls going bad in Katunayake—and the particular locus of concern has been the sexuality of these young women. Among the several derogatory nicknames for the town and the FTZ are *premakalāpaya* (the zone of love) and *vēsakalāpaya* (the zone of prostitutes), both based on the real name *nidahas velenda kalāpaya* (the zone of free trade).[7]

A concerted moral campaign against FTZ garment workers has focused on reports of prostitution, premarital sex, rape, sexually transmitted disease, abortion, and sexual harassment in the FTZs. In the 1990s and 2000s, repeated newspaper features as well as popular teledramas and feature films focused on women FTZ workers. Between 2001 and 2003 alone, four popular Sinhala-language feature films focused on women garment workers (Abeysekera 2005; cf. Hewamanne 2008). These visual media often focus on women's sexuality through a dichotomy of city and village, the latter symbolizing the nation's purity and traditions (Abeysekera 1997: 5; 2005). The clear message in these media is that the suitable role for women is as wives and mothers, that the village is a haven where women fulfill their expected roles, and that garment factories are contributing to the rapid erosion of national traditions.

The "Juki" nickname is part of common parlance today, and women and men of various backgrounds throughout the island use the term to connote sexual promiscuity. I have identified three interrelated social dimensions to the Juki-girl stigma. Underlying all three are concerns about the agency being exhibited by young women in their encounters with economic globalization.

First, critics of Juki girls seem to read the public visibility of these women as indicative of their lack of adherence to what are understood as traditional roles for village women. These roles involve a seamless transition from daughter to wife and, soon thereafter, mother (Bandarage 1988). Within these traditional expectations, someone must always be controlling women (first the parents, then the husband; brothers can substitute for either). There is no stage of life at which it is considered appropriate for single, unmarried women to live away from their parents and communities.[8] Meanwhile, most of the Katunayake garment workers live in boarding houses away from their parents, so they enjoy more freedom in their social lives than other single women of their age. For instance, they usually walk home from work in groups or with boyfriends, and some go with men to films or to watch airplanes at the nearby airport. Criticisms of these women often articulate a concern that young women who are not controlled by parents will not be controllable at work: they will not behave correctly in their expected roles in a disciplined industrial labor force.

Second, there is an important class dimension to the Juki stigma, a point also noted by the sociologist S. T. Hettige (2000, 190–91). Class mobility exhibited by poor village women (as manifested in their new fashions, consumption patterns, and ways of speaking, and their participation in various forms of entertainment) is perceived as a threat to the status quo by middle- and upper-class Sri Lankans, in the cities as well as the villages. In this regard, during my extended field research in the mid 1990s, middle-class Sri Lankans in Kandy and Colombo sometimes told me that they could not distinguish between factory workers and office workers on their commute. They also told me they could no longer find good domestic servants because garment factories now employed many people who would have previously become servants.

Third, there may also be present an element of male anxiety about female employment, especially given the fact of widespread male unemployment. Masculinity in Sri Lanka is measured in part by men's abilities to take care of women—their mothers, sisters, wives, and daughters. For this reason, men in all classes of Sri Lankan society are generally expected to tell their wives to quit their jobs as soon as they marry. Because the garment industry employs only a small percentage of men, many unemployed men have seen women receive jobs that they wish were open to them. The sociologist Asoka

Bandarage (1988: 69, 72) argues that these women, like Sri Lankan women who work as domestic servants in the Middle East, are condemned because they are away from the patriarchal control of husbands or fathers, and their economic and social independence threatens male authority (cf. Gamburd, this volume).

Taken together, these three points reveal that, in short, these urban women garment workers are violating social norms that hold urban poor and rural women "as the sole upholders of the manners, customs and traditions of a glorious Sinhala past" (de Alwis 1998: 193–94). Despite an expansion of women's involvement in paid work since the economy was liberalized in 1977, the Juki stigma has held on with remarkable tenacity and has even reached beyond the urban areas to affect women like Mala, who works in a village garment factory. Mala and her coworkers worked in or near their villages, and lived with their parents or husbands (if married). And yet they fought this stigma daily to demonstrate that they were good village girls who also happened to work in garment factories.

MALA'S AMBIVALENCE

When I first met her, Mala stood on the forefront of a new economic and social project in Sri Lanka. She was a villager who had found industrial employment without migrating to the capital city Colombo or its outskirts. When a factory opened near her village in 1992, Mala had been trying for several years to find a job that suited her educational qualifications and allowed her to stay with her family until she married. Mala had taken her exams at the end of high school and received high marks. But, in a country offering too few openings for qualified students, she was not admitted into university. Just a few years earlier a youth revolt had paralyzed her village, surrounding towns, and much of the southern part of Sri Lanka. Mala and her family survived the revolt, but fellow villagers were killed or disappeared; during the revolt and the ensuing government crackdown everyone she knew lived in fear. Among other concerns, the rebels argued that the government paid insufficient attention to generating jobs for educated youth and that liberal economic strategies adopted since the late 1970s had benefited the urban, English-educated elite to the detriment of most others in Sri Lankan society. Mala did not speak English, hailed from a poor family that did not have access to powerful people, and despite her good exam results was still unable to find a job several years after completing high school.

I had many hours of conversations with Mala. Here I would like to illustrate an imagined, but probable, scenario dating to when Mala first had the chance to seek a garment factory job. Mala, like the many Sri Lankans who read newspapers and watched television regularly, would have been well acquainted with a state project begun in early 1992 that founded garment factories throughout the country in response to the revolt and its cry for rural jobs. The 200 Garment Factories Program was a decidedly new economic strategy that reversed previous patterns of industrialization by bringing factories to villages. Mala would have heard that a factory was slated to open in her district, just a few villages away. But she would have been ambivalent about seeking employment there. While some newspapers touted this new industrialization program as a panacea for rural unemployment and poverty, she had been reading reports for many years about how employment of young women in garment factories led to the disintegration of Sri Lankan society. Articles with titles such as "First to the Free Trade Zone, Second to Party Culture" exposed the ways in which young women not only were overworked, underpaid, and subjected to abuse at these factories but also began to adopt new modes of dressing, speaking, and socializing that defied Sri Lankan expectations for women's behavior. Mala did not want to be exploited inside or outside the workplace and did not want to associate with women who did not share her moral values. She addresses these very issues in her words included at the start of this essay.

Even so, working in a factory in a nearby village was attractive to Mala. She would not need to leave her family, and the well-paid jobs offered benefits such as free breakfast and overtime pay. In factory-opening-ceremony speeches that were widely publicized on television and radio and in newspapers, the president, industrialists, Buddhist monks, and ordinary people praised the program and asserted that it would bring important benefits to the nation. The program's champions explicitly articulated a vision in which economic development would be accompanied by cultural preservation. Indeed, speakers even noted that by continuing to live at home, garment workers would be able to stay under the moral protection of their families. This vision would have comforted Mala, who was concerned about what she had heard about free trade zones—about men who would take advantage of urban garment factory women and about women who seemed to forget their values on becoming garment workers.

Thus, although she supported the opposition political party, Mala would have been tempted by some of the president's arguments about this program. Employment in these factories held the promise of a job and respect. These benefits could be attained in her village, where parents and fellow villagers ensured that morality prevailed. She would have read text from President Ranasinghe Premadasa's factory speeches such as this, quoted in a national newspaper:

> I thought I should first bring about a situation where the latent talents and skills of our poor village youth could be brought up to the surface for due recognition. That is why I planned to start factories in villages first. Now the high quality of work of our village youth has won acceptance even of foreign investors. Our village youth were treated with disdain for [a long time]. They were called good-for-nothing "Kalakanniyas" (miserables). I wanted to rid

the social psyche of this long-held [misconception]. And I have succeeded in achieving this through the Two Hundred Garment Factories Program. . . . For our village youth, who had developed the moral and physicl [sic] strength to stand strain or stress and who are used to hardwork, garment manufacture is mere child's play. . . . We are discovering the richness of our poor and holding it out to the gaze of the entire world. You can feel proud that the government you braved terror to elect is doing this, for the first time. (A. S. Fernando 1993: n.p.)

Mala would have noted favorably how the president linked moral and physical discipline, activity, and work. It was obvious from this and other speeches that the president aimed to provide opportunities to villagers and involve them in the development process so they would not attempt another revolt. He tried to do this while also emphasizing the importance of moral and physical discipline for the nation. He argued that villagers' inherent knack for hard work was not only good for the nation but also conveniently aligned with capitalist discipline. As it turns out, the youth for whom "garment manufacture is mere child's play" were mostly women; employing women was consistent with nationalist and capitalist expectations about women's inherent discipline.

Twenty-two-year-old Mala was the perfect candidate for one of these jobs. She cared about the nation's future, her excellent high school performance meant she had the requisite skills and discipline, she was ready to work hard, and she was poor. By the end of 1992 she had obtained a job as a sewing-machine operator in the nearby factory, where she was poised to achieve her, and the president's, goals—or so she thought. Her 1996 written narrative that opens this essay shows that four years later she still had not quite achieved all her goals. Her real "dream" she presents in her closing paragraphs: "If people could appreciate the women who add value to the Sri Lankan economy the same way they appreciate the money those women bring in, Sri Lanka will be a much better place for everybody. I hope one day people will treat them as equals. The day it happens will be a dream come true."

MALA AND SOCIETY'S "CROSS-EYED LOOKS"

I first began to appreciate the complexities of being a garment worker from Mala, when she had written a plea for respect on a questionnaire I distributed a few weeks into my factory research. In a space where I asked for "additional information for me to know about you or the factory," Mala foreshadowed the longer narrative (printed above) that she would later write for me:

A lot of people in society think garment factories are places without any culture. . . . When we come to work amidst society we are subjected to the insults of young people just like us. It would be a great resource if there arose in the world a movement that would be able to properly direct the cross-eyed way society looks at the valuable services of valuable male and female workers. Can a person's character be concluded from a job?

Of course her final query was rhetorical. Mala adamantly wanted me and others to understand that garment workers are not, by default, loose and immoral women. In the face of the Juki stigma, Mala, like many workers, was trying to get another job when I knew her—what she described as a "good" job. To this end she was learning English at the factory, taking courses in sewing and bridal dressing, and sitting for government teaching exams. In a letter to me six months after I had returned to the United States, Mala told me she wanted to quit her job because she couldn't bear the "mental and physical pain" of the work. Physical pain may have referred to any number of problems such as back pain, headaches and dizziness, weight loss, respiratory problems from inhaling cotton dust, or other ailments. Factories were often stifling hot, and women often complained to me of feeling faint. On several occasions I saw women carrying a collapsed colleague to the first-aid room.

When Mala referred to "mental pain," it could have been in regard to at least two different issues, which we had discussed on many occasions: the crude manner in which some of the managers treated workers and the lack of respect garment workers received in their village and wider communities.

Mala told me that although managers had never scolded her harshly, she often witnessed rough treatment directed at others. One day when we ran into each other in a shop in the nearby town, I had an animated conversation with Mala and a co-worker. Jayanthi worked in the finishing section, folding men's dress shirts and inserting pins to hold them in shape. That day in the shop, Jayanthi told me she found it painful to hear the production manager speak to workers as if they were children, saying things to them like, "Where did you go to school? In a toilet?" When she heard that, she knew that the women in question must have felt *läjjay* (ashamed, embarrassed) to be scolded so in front of their coworkers, and especially among fellow villagers.

Mala felt the lack of respect for garment workers in many ways. Fellow travelers on the daily commute sometimes insulted her, and villagers sometimes scorned her. Although many people in the area wanted to work at the factories, Mala told me that when she first got the job, neighbors insulted her mother by saying: "You say that your daughter got good exam results. Could she find a better job? Why did she have to go to a factory?" Indeed, Mala had done quite well in her A-Level exams and just missed getting the marks that would have gained her admittance to a university. She had been stymied in her efforts to get a government job, a rejection she attributed to her family's support of the opposition political party. As she wrote in the same questionnaire, "I tried very hard to get a job according to my educational qualifications. . . . As my financial problems were increasing, with a sad heart I accepted this job because I could not get any other job."

In a January 2000 letter, Mala told me she was still working as a machine operator at her factory—it had been seven years since she had started there, but she could not find another job. She told me that she had recently taken quality-control courses in Colombo on Sundays with the hopes of getting promoted to a staff quality-control position. At the same time, Mala continued her self-employment courses. She had completed weekend courses in every aspect of wedding preparation—making and decorating cakes, dressing brides, styling hair, making jewelry, sewing bridal saris—and so was qualified to be employed as a wedding coordinator. She hoped to plan weddings while she continued working in a garment factory and perhaps after she married, if her husband wanted her to stop working at the factory. I learned in a letter in 2003 that Mala had wed through an arranged marriage and stopped working altogether at the insistence of her new husband.

NATIONAL DEBATES, INDIVIDUAL EXPERIENCES

In Sri Lanka, post-independence political discourse, but especially post-liberalization discourse, has focused on how to reconcile modernity and morality, or economic gain and social obligation. In effect, Sri Lankans have been asking: "How can our country be economically strong and competitive but still follow its age-old traditions?" This common postcolonial question comes with a distinctly nationalistic edge for many contemporary Sinhala Buddhists in light of the two perceived threats to the nation noted above: the separatist movement by the LTTE has threatened the integrity of the nation-state's borders since the early 1980s, and Westernization threatens the integrity of the Sinhala nation's culture. In the face of these twin threats, many Sinhala Buddhists consider women to be the agents who will hold the nation together. Women have been invested with such a responsibility because—as is the case in many societies throughout the world—they are imagined to be at the core of Sri Lanka's moral identity.

The state's attempts to reconcile economic development and cultural preservation are important for understanding the experiences and dreams of Mala and her fellow workers. At the same time that these economic and cultural issues were being skillfully negotiated by the state, most Sri Lankans also tried to negotiate them in various ways. Premadasa's discourses had a direct effect on Mala and her coworkers as well as on their factory managers and owners. Some of the managers took Premadasa's imperatives to heart and tried to model their factories on values like "the spirit of caring and sharing" that he invoked in his speeches. Furthermore, the discourses also affected how the workers made sense of their factory experiences, because they often embraced Premadasa's vision. His promises and dreams affected many of their own daily movements, their decisions, and, as we can see with Mala, their dreams.

While I do not find it a stretch to move from Mala and her coworkers to the Sri Lankan nation, my move does require some explanation. I am relying on certain anthropological conceptions of "the everyday" and power, or of agency and structure. The hallmark of the anthropological method—participant observation—yields minute details on individual experience, behavior, and meaning. However, the best anthropological analyses do not stop at the minutiae of daily life. The next step is to move from the individual (and her experiences and values) to the contexts within which individuals live and make sense of their lives. Anthropologists strive to situate particular people in historical and political context while also focusing on individual choices and feelings. With my short analysis here of Mala's writings, experiences, and her dream, I have only begun to strike that balance.

ACKNOWLEDGMENTS

Adapted from my book *Juki Girls, Good Girls: Gender and Cultural Politics in Sri Lanka's Global Garment Industry* (2007). Thanks are due to the numerous people who helped me with that book, and to Sarah Lamb and Diane Mines, for inviting me to contribute to this volume and for providing valuable feedback on this essay.

NOTES

1. Mala's name is a pseudonym, to protect her identity. Deepani Ambalangodage translated Mala's essay from Sinhala.

2. The two main ethnic groups in Sri Lanka are Tamils and Sinhalas (also known as "Sinhalese"). The minority ethnic groups in Sri Lanka include Tamils (18%—mostly Hindu, some Christian), Muslims (7%), and small populations of other groups. (The U.S. Library of Congress cites these 1981 census figures at http://countrystudies.us/sri-lanka/38.htm. There was no census in 1991. For results of the incomplete 2001 census see www.statistics.gov.lk.) The terms "Sinahala" and "Tamil" also refer to the languages spoken by Sinhala and Tamil people; the first language of Muslims is generally Tamil.

3. The Juki Corporation, a Japanese company, is the world's largest manufacturer of industrial sewing machines, and it has been selling sewing machines in Sri Lanka since 1976 (V. Perera 1998).

4. See de Alwis 1998; de Mel 1998 and 2001; Jayawardena 1992; S. Perera 1996; Tennekoon 1986.

5. A free trade zone (FTZ) is an area of a country where a government eliminates or reduces trade barriers (e.g., tariffs and quotas) in order to attract foreign investment.

6. Women have also been the center of debates about earlier economic and social change, such as under colonialism. See Lynch 2007: ch. 3.

7. The usage of the term *vēsakalāpaya* is noted in Weerasinghe 1989: 319; and *premakalāpaya* is a term I frequently heard during field research.

8. One obvious exception would be university residence halls, but the "wardens" who run these single-sex halls act very much as parental figures.

28

Interviews with High School Students in Eastern Sri Lanka

Margaret Trawick

The school at Anilaaddam is one of the largest in the hinterlands of eastern Sri Lanka, with over eight hundred students in the elementary and high school sections.[1] Its catchment area consists of several villages on the edge of territory held by the Liberation Tigers of Tamil Eelam (LTTE), just across a narrow lagoon from territory controlled by the Sri Lankan Army. For more than eighteen years, the LTTE have been fighting the Sri Lankan government for an independent Tamil-majority state, which would include the area in which Anilaaddam is situated. All the members of the LTTE are Tamils, and many of them come from the eastern hinterlands, including villages in the vicinity of Anilaaddam. The government army consists mainly of Sinhala-speaking men from the southern part of Sri Lanka. The government army is assisted in its war against the LTTE by Tamil paramilitary groups, with names such as EPRLF (Eelam People's Revolutionary Front), TELO (Tamil Eelam Liberation Organization), and PLOTE (People's Liberation Organization of Tamil Eelam). These groups once fought for an independent Tamil Eelam, but now they have joined the Sri Lankan government. Their main job is to find and identify members or suspected members of the LTTE, and to capture and kill them if possible. The paramilitary organizations consist of boys recruited from the local Tamil populace. The paramilitaries as well as the LTTE include teenagers in their ranks. Also assisting the army is the STF (Special Task Force of the police). From 1987 to 1989, the IPKF (Indian Peace Keeping Forces) also occupied the area. People who were adults around Anilaaddam during that time report that the IPKF were more brutal even than the Sinhalese in their treatment of Tamils.

The ferocity of the war in Sri Lanka is intense, and Tamil civilians are its principal victims. Habitations close to the border between territories controlled by hostile groups are most vulnerable to being "caught in the crossfire"—a euphemism for direct and intentional attacks by armed organizations and raiding parties on civilians, their homes, stores, and cattle. The people who live in such places are small farmers and agricultural laborers. Many of them are so poor that feeding themselves and their families from day to day is their greatest concern. Malnourishment and its attendant diseases are visible everywhere. The problem of getting food is greatly exacerbated by the war. Such is the situation in Anilaaddam.

I visited the Anilaaddam school in January and February of 1998 to interview students about their experiences of the war. The ultimate goal of the interviews was to learn not just how these young people had been affected by the war, but what choices they had made in the face of this war, and why. What options did they perceive to be available to them? What motivated them to choose one option over another? In particular, what motivated them to join, or not to join, the LTTE?

The year 1987 was a crisis point for people here: the year of the prawn project massacre. During that year, on one day, more than eighty civilian men were captured and summarily executed, because the owner of the prawn farm (a foreign entrepreneur) was suspected of selling kerosene to the local branch of the LTTE. The foreign entrepreneur sued the Sri Lankan government, and the families of the victims received some monetary compensation for their loss. But the memory of the massacre—men being shot in the head, one by one, before one another's eyes on a junction at Anilaaddam, their bodies being hauled off, burnt somewhere, and never recovered—remains vivid in the minds of people who live here.

Again in 1991, the rice mill massacre brought the war home to the people of Anilaaddam in the most horrible way. As a tractor full of Sinhala soldiers was entering the area, it tripped a land mine laid as a trap by the Tigers, and several of the soldiers were killed. The remaining soldiers went on a rampage, killing all the civilians in sight. Some were shot, their bodies thrown in a pit and burned on the spot. Others sought refuge in a rice mill. They burned to death when the soldiers set the mill on fire. In all, over 160 civilians from in and around Anilaaddam died on that one day.

In between such major disasters, intermittent aerial attacks, shelling, ground attacks, disappearances, and abductions have kept civilians in a state of constant fear. What was always most surprising to me was the way they were able to live their lives, between attacks, in a more or less normal, even celebratory fashion. Anyone born in this area after around 1980 could not clearly remember a time without war. Most of the students in the Anilaaddam school were of this category. A generation was coming of age who could only imagine what peace might be like. Peace for them meant two kinds of freedom: freedom from fear and freedom to move, or to stay where they were, according to their own will. All of them were restricted in their movements by army checkpoints throughout the cleared area across the lagoon, where they had to travel to get medical care if they needed it, or to sell produce in the towns, or to visit relatives, or to get job training, or any of countless other things.

In the midst of all this, some gave up on schooling, but remarkably many—probably the majority—kept faith and continued to attend the impoverished school available to them. When I asked them what the most im-

portant experience in their life had been, almost all of them answered either
school or the incident of 1987 or of 1991, depending perhaps on how they
interpreted the question. Several of the students had developed a contin-
gency plan: if the army attacked their area again, they would join the LTTE;
if not, they would finish their schooling and live as civilians—or as one boy
put it simply, he would join the LTTE or he would live. In fact, the students
took it for granted that if they joined the LTTE they would die. They knew
this from experience: the siblings and friends they knew who had joined the
LTTE had mostly died. They had seen the bodies of those killed in combat.
They had no illusions concerning what they were in for if they joined the
Tigers. The ones who actually joined were not much different from ordinary
teenagers, and were no less realistic in their view of the movement than
those who chose not to join—which is to say, who chose not to die at this particular time. Although the students who did not join the Tigers sometimes
expressed incomprehension as to why their friends and siblings had joined,
they also expressed almost unanimous strong sympathy for the Tigers. The
Tigers were people they knew, people of the area; they had no cause to fear
them. Moreover, the Tigers did not arbitrarily attack and kill civilians, as
the army did. It was clear from what the students said that they had learned
and accepted the revolutionary ideology of the LTTE: their analysis of what
the war was about and what had to be done for the Tamil people to achieve
their freedom. But the students also reported that the Tigers encouraged
them, even urged them, to stay in school and finish their degrees. This was
a remarkable assertion, given the fact that at that time the local Tigers were
engaged in an intensive recruitment campaign, and were openly announcing their serious shortage of manpower. Just three months after these interviews, at a big public performance, an important leader of the military
section of the Tigers came onstage and virtually pleaded with parents to
let their children join the movement, and with young people not to excuse
themselves from service for any but the most serious reasons. Meanwhile,
the students reported that about six people from the class ahead of them in
school had joined the Tigers the previous year. In other words, even from
this school which one might expect to be a strong recruitment base for the
Tigers, only a small minority of those eligible had actually joined. Perhaps
the students were hiding the truth concerning the number of recruits. But
the large number of able-bodied young men and women living in the village
who were manifestly not members of the LTTE seemed to bear out the students' claims. There was no evidence at all of forcible recruitment. I think the
Tigers knew that forcible recruitment would lead to an ill-disciplined and ineffective fighting force, at best. They already had problems with people they
had armed and trained who had used their positions for personal gain and
then fled to become informers for the army. The students, too, were all too
aware of this problem. It was a problem for them, as well. They knew some of
the turncoats personally. They knew some of the members of the anti-LTTE

paramilitary groups who roamed the region. They had suffered beatings at checkpoints from these individuals, whom they knew, and who knew them.

The students were in the terrible position of being able to identify members of the enemy groups to the LTTE, and members of the LTTE to the enemy. Whenever a young civilian traveled from the Tiger-held side of the lagoon to the army-held side, he or she could be captured and forced to become an informant. Moreover, if any civilian bore a grudge against another, he or she could falsely report to the army that the other was a Tiger. That the civilian community maintained its integrity under these conditions is a fact worthy of note. We must ask ourselves why Anilaaddam has not become another Pine Ridge or Buffalo Creek.[2]

Historians of a certain bent have often argued, or even assumed, that warfare strengthens a society, by giving people a common cause, toughening them through adversity, and so forth. The Spencerian view of survival of the fittest prevailed throughout the colonial British Empire. The "fittest" in this view were those individuals most capable of fighting and winning—or, on a larger scale, those nations most able to wage war against other nations and conquer them militarily. Colonial historians and indeed anthropologists admired "warlike" peoples, from Maori to Masai, respecting those who put up a good fight against the colonizers. After conquest these people were recruited into the colonizers' own militaries. Tamils were traditionally not among those people. Those modern Tamils who take pride in the military prowess of the LTTE are (in my view) seeking prestige according to the old Spencerian model. But times have changed, and spokesmen for postcolonial world powers represent themselves as despising ethnic warfare.

Moreover, Tamil society in Sri Lanka has been decimated by the war. Thus, anyone who imagines that civilian society in a place like Anilaaddam derives strength from the war itself need only visit the place to be divested of that illusion. Civilian culture in eastern Sri Lanka, including Anilaaddam, is not militant and does not condone violence. For this reason, many civilians express profound ambivalence toward the LTTE. Whether Saiva (worshiping Siva) or Christian, they believe that killing is deeply sinful, and the Tigers, however righteous their cause, however evil their enemy, take this sin upon themselves whenever they take a life. Even some Tigers themselves believe this: to take on this sin is part of their sacrifice. Perhaps this is why they do not talk about an afterlife. They do not expect God to reward them for what they have done. A girl who joins the LTTE perceives herself as having no future. This is not to say she has lost her sense of individual personhood. She has lost hope of personal fulfillment, but for what she finds in the movement, and she has lost hope of personal continuation, but for the hope of being remembered. For her, love is all—love in present living hearts, love out of time. Civilian young people are much the same. Many of the students at Anilaaddam expected that they would never see an end to the war. For as long as they lived, they would live in this hell. Some said peace would come when the Tigers won, but no one ventured a guess as to when this would happen. None of these students believed that peace was possible under Sinhala rule. Certainly there could be no peace under army occupation: from these students' point of view, the army was the war. Army weapons killed their fathers, army soldiers raped their sisters and tortured their brothers. Army advances were what they feared. Army checkpoints were what restricted their freedom. They never said but perhaps they knew what the Tiger leaders also knew, that a military victory by the LTTE was impossible, that long-term army occupation of Tamil areas was a distinct likelihood. Only a deus ex machina might possibly save them, some foreign intervention, some helping hand reaching out from the sky. Some better-off students at privately run schools in town expressed exactly this desire. But the students of Anilaaddam had seen no helping hands reaching down from the sky, and they entertained no dreams that any outsider would save them. This dreamlessness was implicit, I think, in the students' predictions that the war would never end.

Total despair, the lack of a future, is often cited as a cause for disaffection among youth, for their displays of cynicism, reckless short-term selfishness, and acts of aimless violence. The students at Anilaaddam faced a grim future indeed. But among these students, despite severe poverty, despite exposure to chronic violence, danger, and displacement, despite the destruction of families, despite the urging of people they admired in the LTTE to join in the armed conflict, interpersonal fighting was disdained. Some stated that there was no fighting among students at all, that all were in accord. Some stated that only little kids got into fights. One stated that he had been in fights, but when I asked him, "Who wins?" he answered that both win. I should have asked him, "What kind of fighting is this, where both sides win?" In my presence, no child over the age of five displayed the slightest antagonism toward any other child. Among high school students, almost all said they enjoyed sports such as cricket and football, and some were avid players. It may be old-fashioned, but I think it is not unreasonable to surmise that physical aggression was channeled and disciplined in this way. The sports contests I watched in March 1998 showed that students took strong pride in being students, that they had what can only be called intense school spirit, and that athletic and academic accomplishment were the arenas in which their pride was asserted. The point here is not to claim that students in these schools never fought among themselves, but that they wanted me to perceive them as above spontaneous fighting. This held true even of those who stated their intention to join the Tigers.

Is there a way to explain such courage? It might be plausibly argued that the children I saw were special: they were the survivors. Of course there were ones who had dropped out of school, succumbed to cynicism. In the Tiger-controlled area, there were one or two wandering bands of little boys.

On the army side, I was told by many sources, there were no street children, and indeed I never saw any. The reason was that it was too dangerous to be out on that side after nightfall. Students and adults living on the army side told me that boys who became cynical and dropped out of school early joined one of the movements, for money, for safety, for getting a gun. They got to be the abusers, rather than the abused, but in fact they were not all that safe. On the Tiger side, only Tigers had guns. There were no drugs but alcohol and tobacco, and these were strongly discouraged. Alcohol was confiscated when it was found by Tigers, who poured it on the ground. Thus two sources of violence among civilians were taken away. Plus, as students said, the Tigers themselves encouraged the students to study. Perhaps, then, the Tigers may be awarded partial credit for students' walking the line. But even if we gave Tigers full credit, we would be begging the question of where the people as a people, Tigers and civilians, got their strength.

Supporting them all, bearing them up under all conditions, was the earth beneath their feet, which gave their lives beauty, meaning, and sustenance. The culture of regeneration was strong in Anilaaddam, where all the families were farming families. The students of Anilaaddam were proud of what one boy called the tradition of all the people here of cultivation. These embattled and impoverished students loved their family homes and loved growing things. They aspired to be teachers of children if they were fortunate enough to pass their exams.

It seemed to me that they had determined to want only this: to farm the land, even someone else's land, so that they could feed others; and to acquire knowledge, even though they might never use it for their own purposes, so that they could pass it on to others. When I asked them what they wanted to be when they became adults, they never said things like doctor or engineer—the usual answers one would expect from (for instance) middle-class Jaffna Tamils or Indian Tamils. Even when such answers were urged upon them by adults watching the interviews, the young respondents would not pretend to set for themselves more ambitious goals.

Humility of this kind should not be mistaken for absence of self-esteem. If military and political prosecutors of the war in Sri Lanka read this report, they will only learn what they have already been told by other sources: attacks on Tamil civilians by the army or its supporting paramilitary groups only encourage young people to join the LTTE. Some join because of revolutionary ideals or because of admiration for the members of the LTTE or because of a burning desire to fight back against the military that has abused and humiliated them or, in some cases, because they have decided to die. But others join explicitly because they feel safer as members of the LTTE than as unprotected civilians. This is not so much because the LTTE have the weaponry and the training to fight back, as because the LTTE know in advance of impending army attacks, and they get most of their members to safe places in the jungle before the attacks begin, while they leave civilians to fend for themselves. The Tigers may leave civilians unprotected for the purpose of getting young people to leave civilian life and join them, but more likely it is because they cannot safely convey to the general populace the intelligence reports they have received. Moreover, they have no means of protecting civilians; indeed, fighting back against an army offensive is almost certain to intensify the siege. Especially when the ranks of the LTTE are depleted, they will act with extra caution to preserve the lives of their own members. Their greatest asset is a trained and experienced fighting force, and this takes years to raise. Thus engaging the Tigers in massive bloody battles is not the way to destroy them, as they will avoid such battles if they need to preserve manpower. Terrorizing Tamil civilians is also clearly counterproductive. In the midst of terror a young person will think, "If I stay as I am I may die now; if I join the movement I will probably die later." And they will join the movement now. Such a choice is not made impulsively, nor, it would seem in most cases, out of anger. In general, acting in anger is discouraged. Anger is attributed by Tamil people to those who act violently against them, such as the army or the paramilitaries. Anger is not attributed to people one perceives as one's friends. Young people and adults, Tigers and civilians, have no difficulty confessing that they have experienced anger, but no one brags about actions they may have taken in anger, any more than they brag about beating other kids in schoolyard brawls. Hence, even people who have been beaten by the army, or who have seen kin killed by the army, do not necessarily respond by joining the Tigers. It is an interesting case of cultural misunderstanding, perhaps, that ordinary Sinhala soldiers assume that someone who has been beaten will join the Tigers for revenge, so that any young Tamil man or woman who bears the scars of beating or torture is almost automatically assumed to be a Tiger. It is as though the Sinhalese cannot conceive of any other response to the brutality of their own comrades. Unbridled anger is, after all, their own response to real or perceived harm done to them. And yet they continue to batter unarmed Tamil civilians, as though inviting retaliation. Human beings can adapt to anything, and the young people of Anilaaddam have adapted to terror. They are prepared to live with terror for the rest of their lives, and to make rational choices in the moments of terror's intensity. They are also prepared to live with peace, and peace is of course what they want most: no more fighting and no more army. They cannot end the fighting and they cannot make the army go away. But in the intervals between moments of terror, the lives they build for themselves are lives of peace.

*   *   *

I interviewed twelve students in the school on three separate days. The students included six boys and six girls, with their ages ranging between 13 and 22. The median age was 16.5 and the average age was 17. Some students were chosen by the teachers and some came and asked to be interviewed while I was there. The interviews were not private; teachers and other students were present. I had a list of questions that I asked each student. Sometimes I would follow up on a statement that a student made; with one or two students certain questions were omitted because they were redundant. I told the students that what they told me would be used in a book I was writing about their experiences of the war, and that I would keep their identities confidential. Nevertheless, under the circumstances it was impossible for me to keep information given by particular students from spreading throughout the school, and thence possibly to the army. The students must have edited what they said to me, not only for this reason, but for the equally serious reason that I was a foreigner intending to represent them to the outside world. The content of the interviews given below will immediately demonstrate to the reader how inadequate formal, tape-recorded interviews can be as a means of trying to learn what people think. At the same time there is no substitute for recording and preserving the exact words of the people whom you are trying to know. Otherwise, as an ethnographer, you have nothing to write down but your own perceptions and memories, and these can be very faulty indeed. Using the words of the students as building blocks, I have attempted to construct a kind of miniature oral history of the war as it has happened in this place, as these young people remember it. In the text below, each paragraph is a string of short sentences, each of which was the response to some question of mine. Here, I have omitted the questions, so that the answers appear as a continuous narrative. I have not changed the words of the respondents, except where necessary for clarity, to fill in what a one-word response was in answer to. In the original interview, the brevity of most responses is even more apparent than it is with my questions deleted. For all these reasons, the text below is not smooth or easy to read. It is raw and rough. But it is exactly the truth of what happened, exactly the words that were said on these days by these people. Among other things, the brief answers reflect the stark quality of the respondents' experiences. They do not speak about the smell of burning flesh, the sight of spattered blood and brains, the screams of men pleading for their lives. And yet from their terse words, we know they have experienced these things. They respond as in a court of law. And we know they do not lie because the Sri Lankan military has confessed to the killings of 1987 and 1991, to the beatings of countless suspected terrorists, and to the bombing of places where terrorists are suspected to be. Though we may trust these students not to lie, we will know that their memories also are imperfect. Some of the events they describe happened when they were very young, and recollections will therefore be hazy. The dates they give for certain events do not always match the dates given by adults for the same events. Discussion of the events with others

over the years will also have shaped their memories. And the brevity of responses suggests also that some students were reluctant to say any more to
me than they had to. Some probable reasons for such reluctance have already
been stated above. Finally, the reader will understand that the topics discussed and the memories evoked are of the most painful kind. Forgetting
can be healing, and the last thing I wanted was to unheal these children, to
put them in pain again. Hence I did not push them, but tried to let them lead
me wherever they wanted to go. For the most part, they did not take the lead.
Sometimes they led me to unexpected places.

In total, I asked all the students about a dozen main questions. Space
does not allow me to include all the answers to all the questions here. These
are the answers I got when I asked my first question: "How have you been
affected by the war?"

Student no. 1

... My uncle died due to the violence [*vanseyal*] problems. The army shot him.
He was running because of some problems in town. They shot him while he
was running away. I was thirteen years old then. He was my mother's own
brother. He was twenty-two years old. He was not married.

... In the land-mine incident in 1991, forty-one civilians in this school
were shot dead. They were people from this village. People we knew.

... I have been displaced twice in my life, to Arayampathy and to town.
Due to the war the army bombed us and we had to move.

Student no. 2

... I have no father. Mother is at home. Father was affected by the violence at
Pillaiyaaradi [a village adjacent to Anilaaddam] in 1991. I was ten years old
then. A land mine exploded and the army got angry and shot him. We were
afraid. They were waiting nearby with knives to cut us. They took my father
away. They came into our house before and after the bomb blast. When they
came into the house, we did nothing. We were afraid. They came into the
house, started to cut us and shoot us. But then they left.

Student no. 3

... Near our house at the junction, we had a shop. The army destroyed it and
the STF [Special Task Force of the Sri Lankan police] looted it earlier. That
was in 1987. We lost two and a half lakhs [rupees 250,000]. Now we have built
another house on that same land and are living in it. In 1987, I was five years
old. I remember that time. At that time, we had prawn farming here. Suddenly they came and shot some people and took my father to the jail. They
beat him up there and released him. Then they took all our things and gathered them up and threw them to civilians. We did not see the people who

were being shot. They took them away in tractors. My mother cried. Three days after the shooting they took my father to jail. He is living now. He is doing farm work. Because of the STF beating, he was blinded. After that he was operated on in Batticaloa Hospital and now he can see a little. My brothers do the farm work with him.

. . . I am the youngest in my family. I had four older sisters. One died. Due to a small problem, my mother hit her for doing wrong. So she drank oil and died. Oil used for farming. It was a small problem. But she got angry and did it. That was in 1976. I was not born then.

. . . When we speak with the army or the STF, they ask whether we support the LTTE. We say no. Otherwise they will beat us. My older brother was beaten. The Indians [IPKF] beat him. The EPRLF informed on him. They beat him and gave him electrical shocks and everything. Now he is well. He farms. He does not get angry. He is married and has children and all. He can't join the movement.

. . . The last time the army came here was in 1996. They were moving around here. We were hiding. Then they gathered the people and had a meeting at the school. They did not do anything to anyone. They came because the LTTE had hit a camp and took artillery shells from there. The army came to recover those shells. They left immediately. They stayed for only one day. When they were leaving, the LTTE attacked them. A Black Tiger[3] blew himself up. That happened in Kilimalai.

. . . Our family has not been badly affected by the war. The house was lost. No lives were lost. There has been only material loss.

Student no. 4

. . . We have been affected by the war. I have gotten a beating by the army. When there is fighting, when people travel, they capture and beat them. I was fourteen years old then. It was in 1995. When there was fighting, the army came and stayed here. They beat me with sticks. They beat me here, in Anilaaddam, when I was going by bicycle from home, on the road. They caught me and took me alone and beat me. There were fifty or a hundred of them, but only one of them beat me. They said that I supported the LTTE. They released me after the beating. When I came home, my stomach was upset. I went to the hospital. I did not say I was beaten, I said I fell off my bicycle. They believed me. There were no serious wounds. I don't know if they beat people now. Only if you go to the other side of the lagoon [*turai*] will they beat you. We don't go there anymore.

. . . Previously we were living in the fields in Unnichai. Because of the army's arrival there, we moved here to Anilaaddam. Our house and belongings were destroyed, so we came here. . . .

. . . I don't know about land mines. I have heard. It exploded in Pillai-yaaradi. A land mine. In that, the army took eighteen or twenty Tamils and put them in a pit and burnt them alive. The father of one of our friends also died then. He was forty-five or fifty years old. We knew him well. We did not go and see because the army was standing next to the pit.

. . . My mother died due to the violence. She was displaced and shot dead by the army. It happened when I was small, so I can't tell the details.

Student no. 5

. . . I am not more affected than anyone else, but all Tamil people have been affected by the war. At the checkpoints they check our ID cards, they check our clothes and parcels and so forth. They ask if we are Tigers. They beat us. I was beaten in 1997, only last year. They accused me of being a Tiger. They beat me with a baton. They asked me to turn around and they beat me. It lasted for five minutes, then they released me. The army has been to our house. They looked around and asked if there was a Tiger. Then they left. They take us to the camp and make us do work such as loading soil, loading clay. After we do the work, they release us. The army captures people and beats them. If they take about five or six people, they will release one or two. The rest are shot. My mother's younger brother was taken away, he did not come back. The army shot and killed him. I was small then, I don't know what year it happened.

. . . When the army came to our house, it was 1995. They were doing a roundup. They looked around and asked if there was a Tiger and left. My mother, father, older sister, and younger sister were there. They are afraid that there are Tigers, so they come and search. If they capture someone and beat them, they will tell the truth. When they did the roundup, they captured my mother's elder sister's son. They beat him and released him. He did not talk about it. He was wounded on his knee. They tied him upside down and beat him. He was eighteen. Now he is at home, doing agricultural work.

Student no. 6

. . . My age is thirteen. I was born in 1985. My mother is alive. My father is not. The army shot him in 1987. I do not know why they shot him.

Student no. 7

. . . My mother and father are both alive. Father left. I have two older brothers and three older sisters. I am the youngest. My brothers are in the village. They do not work. Two of my sisters are married. No one in my family has died or been wounded during my lifetime. I live in my mother's house. I have never stayed in any other house. The most important experience in my life is studying. What makes me happy is playing. I go to the movies. That makes me happy. What makes sickness come to me is fever. Grief does not come to me. What makes anger come to me is fighting. I fight with other children when they scold me. When we fight, both win. The most important person in my life is mother. The most important problem in my life is food.

Ordinarily what we eat is rice. We get vegetables. We get chicken. We eat one meal a day. My mother goes to work. She sells rice. That work brings our only income. I do not know my father. I do not know why he left. I do not know when he left. I remember him. He was good. He will not come back. When I finish my studies I will work. I have not been affected by the war.

Student no. 8

. . . Mother's mother died of disease. Mother's uncle [*ammaavuda maamaa*] died because of the war. When he was in the paddy fields the army came and shot him. It was five years ago. When the army came to the LTTE base and did a roundup, he too ran away and they shot him. While we were here, they shot him there. The army chased Father's younger brother too into the fields and shot him, at the same time they shot Mother's uncle.

. . . People we know have been taken by the army. They lifted them onto trees and beat them. They threw stones at them. They gave them no food, they made them work, they crushed them, it is said.

. . . Now they [the army] won't come. The LTTE are here, after all. And if they come, there is a river in between. They [army operatives] would dress in white shirts like common people and come and shoot and run. It happened like that in 1997. Now it doesn't. It happened twice. They would just wear a sarong and come. They would wear a sarong and hide the rifle and shoot and run. Now it doesn't happen that way. The LTTE stand at the junction. Therefore they [army] can't come. The LTTE examine people they suspect. They stand also at the ferry launch, to confiscate liquor and pour it out. The LTTE are there, therefore the army doesn't come.

. . . I am not affected by the war, but the people I told you about before were all affected. With that, all the Tamil people have been affected.

Student no. 9

. . . My father died in 1983, when I was a small child. It happened when he tried to settle a street fight. My mother told me about it. She said that when two people were fighting each other, he went in between and was accidentally hurt by a knife and died in the hospital. He was a bus driver for CTB [Ceylon Transporting Board, a government public transport service].

. . . Apart from my father, my three older brothers have died. They joined the LTTE and were shot by the army.

. . . I live now in Anilaaddam, at my sister's house, but this is not my home village. We moved here because the army burned our house. That was in 1987. I was five years old. My mother told me about these things. She said that EP [EPRLF] burned our house because they were angry at my brothers. 1987 was the first year I realized a war was happening in this country, the year they killed the people at the prawn-raising project.

. . . The most important event in my life was the bomb explosion in Pillaiyaaradi. The army came and beat all the people and took some people and put them into the pit made by the bomb explosion and killed them. We ran away to the other side of the lagoon, to Aayirampaaddu. We stayed in a refugee camp. I was about ten years old at the time. I was afraid. We ran away because of fear. It frightened me very much, when they took those people with them. They closed the door of this school and lifted their guns and fired them. We were refugees for ten days, then we returned home. This event changed my thinking. This event was the first one that happened here. There was an incident that happened before at the prawn-raising project, where the army shot and killed several people. But this incident made us refugees. In 1987, although I was very small, I remember what happened. Several of our village people were hurt but none of my relations. The small children were afraid and stayed with their mothers. I am afraid of the army.

. . . I am affected by the war. I do not see any great differences between affected and unaffected people. There are small differences. Those who are unaffected are a little bit richer. The others are poor. The reason for this difference is that there are no brothers or fathers in the families of the affected. If there are brothers and fathers, they can earn money and build a house.

Student no. 10

. . . The bomb blast in Pillaiyaaradi was the most important event of my life. We were in Munaikkaadu when the incident happened. We didn't know much about it immediately. We came to know about the incident later. We didn't run away. My father's brother was shot dead during that incident. After this incident, I came to know about war. Before that, I didn't understand what war was. At that time I was eight years old.

. . . Before 1990, people were talking about the war but I didn't understand well. After the horrible killing of 1990, I came to know about the war.

. . . What causes me fear is this. We are staying on this side [of the lagoon]. The Razeek group [a Tamil paramilitary group working for the army] comes to the bank of the lagoon and sometimes they come into the village and kidnap people. Not on the other side but on this side. Because of this we have no peace at night. They have taken people from this place—not relatives, but people we knew. After they take them, sometimes they release them, but sometimes nobody knows what happens to them. They enter the village of Anilaaddam, in the corner, on this side of the lagoon. They come by small boat. They don't come every day, but occasionally. The LTTE know about this, but how long can they keep watch for them? If they [the Razeek group] came every day, they [LTTE] could keep watch. But if they come only occasionally, then it is difficult. They [LTTE] don't go every day to the harbor where people travel through, but they go there whenever people travel to the other side through the harbor at night. The Razeek group came last year. December 1997 they came. [This would have been less than two months prior to the date of the interview.] They took one person and released him. Nobody knows what happened to the people taken by them earlier.

Student no. 11

. . . They came to the school and closed the window and seized us and beat us. They fired their rifles. We were very afraid and we threw down our books and ran away. They also beat two teachers and took some people from here and put them in the pit. When they came, we threw down our books and didn't go to our house but ran to the other side and stayed somewhere there and came back to our home the next day.

. . . Now we are staying in our own house in this village. During the first problem we moved and came back when it was over. When the army came and shot and captured people, we went and hid in the paddy fields. Two weeks we stayed there. I was twelve years old at the time. Our whole family went there. It was so hard to get food and water. We slept on the ground. We were afraid.

Student no. 12

. . . The army shot my father's brother's family, in 1992, in a paddy field. When they were all in the paddy field, the army came to round them up. Then they all started to run. At that time the army shot them. We were afraid and we thought our lives were also going to end. Because in that incident, a whole family—father, mother, and a boy were shot dead. It was a great shock. We wept.

. . . Apart from this, in 1987, in the trouble that happened here, about twelve of our relatives were killed, of whom six were our close relatives. I remember it. It was a real shock. Because at that time I was fourteen years old and was able to understand what was happening. I did not know what war was before this incident. It was the first incident here.

. . . We live in Pillaiyaaradi. When the bomb exploded here in 1991, we were displaced to Aayirampaaddu. We faced difficulties there, too, then we moved from there to a paddy field, and from there we came back home. We were refugees for three weeks, because there in Pillaiyaaradi about sixty-five people were killed. They burned our houses. There were no places to stay. Therefore, we too experienced hardship, and for about a month we survived however we could, fleeing from one place to another. The shooting incident in 1987 and the bomb explosion in 1991 were the most important events in my life. They changed my thinking. In this nerve-wracking situation, I thought, what is the point of studying? That feeling arose in my mind. I left my studies for two years and started again after I returned to the village. For the two years that I was out of school I stayed with my parents. But after people said, "You should study," a somewhat better mental state arose in my mind, and I came back to study.

. . . When the land mine exploded in 1991, we were frightened. When classes were going on, we all ran to this very town, to Munaikkaadu, away from our school in Pillaiyaaradi to this school. Here, they took everyone and locked them in this very room [in the school, where I am conducting the interview]. They lifted their rifles and fired them and at that same time and place, they beat the teachers. All of the boys, many people, ran away. Many girls were hurt; they were inside the school. After they took everyone and locked them up, two or three of those [soldiers] who came took many common people and made them raise their hands, and put them in the pit and shot them. They were afraid that a bomb might be here. But a bomb was not here. It exploded over there in the neighboring village. That is why we ran over here, thinking we would be safer.

In the future, if I have the convenience to stay at home, I will stay. If I have to run away, I will have to run away with everyone else.

NOTES

1. The names of all places mentioned in this account have been changed to fictional names by the author. This article was written prior to the defeat of the Tigers in 2009.

2. These are two communities in North America that have been so badly damaged by human-inflicted and natural disasters that the people who live in them have all but given up hope of dignified survival. Pine Ridge is an Oglala Lakota Sioux reservation in South Dakota where alcoholism, unemployment, violence, and poverty are rife. The current situation of the Oglala Sioux at Pine Ridge is a consequence of many years of abuse by the U.S. government. Buffalo Creek is a hollow in West Virginia that contained a number of towns and villages roughly the size of Anilaaddam and its neighbors. In 1972, a large dam burst, due to negligent strip-mining practices that had been carried out over decades by the Pittston Coal Co. In a matter of minutes, 118 were dead and over 4,000 people were left homeless. The community never recovered. (See Kai T. Erikson, *Everything in Its Path: Destruction of Community in the Buffalo Creek Flood* [New York: Simon and Schuster, 1976].)

Although the chain of disasters that have afflicted the people of Buffalo Creek and Pine Ridge are monstrous, what has happened to the people in and around Anilaaddam is no less horrible. The question of how the Anilaaddam people have managed to hold out through all these horrors is therefore not a trivial one.

3. Black Tigers are specially trained suicide bombers of the LTTE.

PART SIX

Globalization, Public Culture, and the South Asian Diaspora

South Asian social-cultural life is not bound within the specific locales or regions that constitute geographically what we know as South Asia. Rather, it is in essential respects flowing, mobile, and public. People, ideas, values, commodities, media images, and popular cultural forms flow into, out of, and around South Asia to create what can be considered a "public culture." This public culture is very much a part of South Asians' everyday lives, both for those in the diaspora and for those who live in the villages and cities of South Asia while partaking in localized public or global cultural forms.

Arjun Appadurai and Carol Breckenridge coined the term "public culture" in their 1988 article "Why Public Culture?" in *Public Culture*. They use it to refer to a "zone of cultural debate" (6) within which persons engaging in many areas of study (including history, literature, anthropology, media studies, the arts, and folklore) discuss the relationship between a local culture (Indian culture or Tamil culture, for example) and the apparently uniform, global, or transnational culture that seems increasingly to define a homogeneous cosmopolitan elite culture—the world's urban middle and upper classes who share many of the same tastes and values.[1] Before Appadurai and Breckenridge, Milton Singer called attention to the kinds of public cultural performances so important to understanding South Asia in *When a Great Tradition Modernizes* (1972). Singer defined cultural performances as the particular instances of cultural organization—such as plays, musical concerts, public lectures, dance performances, weddings, temple festivals—through which Indians, and perhaps all people, think of their culture (70–72). Through the study of such performances, Singer argued, scholars can piece together understandings about the culture and values of the society in which these performances are produced and consumed.

While Singer was primarily interested in how localized cultural performances could be connected to the study of *Indian* civilization as a whole (that is, how the performances were about, derived from, and creative of that whole), the public culture project situates itself more globally. It looks at the ways nations such as India or Sri Lanka have developed forms of public culture that derive from and draw them into the cosmopolitanism of the rest of the world, at the same time that the global cosmopolitan culture is changed according to (i.e., appropriated by) local cultural forms (Appadurai and Breckenridge 1988: 5). A main thrust of the work of those participating in the public culture debate is to demonstrate that processes of modernity and globalization—in South Asia as elsewhere—do not mean simply global homogenization at the expense of the local culture. Their work, rather, explores the ways in which modernity in, for example, India, is *Indian*, and how the meanings and uses of global cultural forms are altered as they are locally (and culturally) consumed and appropriated.

For example, it is now commonplace all over Tamil Nadu, India—in cities, towns, and villages—to watch the Olympics, to wear blue jeans, to buy and eat prepackaged snack foods, and, at least in the larger towns, to eat in fast-food restaurants. Chennai (Madras), the capital city of Tamil Nadu—like Mumbai (Bombay) or New Delhi or Karachi—looks more and more like any city anywhere. Yet at the same time, the consumption of cosmopolitan cultural items may take on culturally unique forms, their Tamil "stamps." For instance, the TV on which people watch sports may be outdoors and common to a community, the gift perhaps of a local politician or other leader; blue jeans may signify a particular form of worldly connection to the "West"; McDonald's joints may sport lamb burgers as well as different aesthetics, meal times, seating arrangements, condiments, and so on. As another example, take going to the movies in Tamil Nadu: The audience often throws flowers and other gifts to heroes and deity-characters on the screen; they garland the posters of the stars much as they do the images of gods and politicians. They may even perform rituals for them, and they incorporate film showings into other kinds of rituals (weddings, temple festivals, etc.). The Tamil cinema is a Tamilized cinema. In West Bengal, old-age homes are not merely globally ubiquitous institutions for making families and societies modern, but rather unique local institutions creatively forged and interpreted, critiqued and expanded, by local actors. There is a widespread perception among Bengali residents of old-age homes, for instance, that these homes—commonly referred to as "ashrams" (or *bṛiddhāśrams*, "[spiritual] shelters for the old")—are a contemporary version of the classical Hindu forest-dweller life stage, in which persons purposefully leave their households of reproduction on a path of late-life spiritual cultivation; and they are also appreciated sites of *sevā*, respectful service toward elders—a key component of perceived Hindu modes of aging (Lamb 2009; and part 1 of this volume).

Studies of public culture and globalization in South Asia have explored such phenomena as people's relationships to the Indian cinema—now the largest movie-making industry in the world (e.g., Pandian this part; Dickey 1993; Derné 2000); Indian television viewing (e.g., Mankekar 1999); the ways international tourism intersects with the lives and imaginations of Mt. Everest Sherpas (e.g., Adams 1996; Ortner 1999); the production of advertising in India (Mazzarella 2003); middle-class Nepali youth's experiences of modernity, mass media, and consumer culture (see Liechty, part 1 of this volume, and 2002); and how an international gerontology, and the dynamics of Indian cinema, news media, and popular medicine are linked to the imagining of aging (Cohen 1998; Lamb 2009). These works scrutinize equally how public (or global or cosmopolitan or "Western") forms of culture impact upon South Asian people's lives and how various people in South Asia produce, fashion, and reinterpret these forms. Vincanne Adams (1996: 12) writes of "the culture that floats between the two groups of participants"—Westerners and Sherpas—as each produces and uses representations of the other in their lives.

One force that has had a profound impact on the nature of public culture and globalization in South Asia over the past decades is the series of reforms collectively known as economic liberalization. In 1991 the Indian Congress government of Prime Minister P. V. Narasimha Rao inaugurated a comprehensive program of economic deregulation, which lowered the formerly stringent barriers to foreign trade (similar processes were initiated in Sri Lanka in the late 1970s). As William Mazzarella notes, one of the most significant results of this reform was "the sudden presence of hundreds of foreign brands on Indian shelves, television screens, and billboards" (2002: 397, n. 2). Within five years, imports doubled, exports tripled, and foreign capital investment quintupled (Derné 2005: 178). Opportunities for both consumption and employment became increasingly shaped by global markets (see, e.g., Kapur, part 1 of this volume; Lynch, part 5; Mankekar and Radhakrishnan, this part). Transnational satellite broadcasting made its Indian debut in January 1991—cable television offerings were suddenly competing with state-run television, at the same time that the slackening of foreign-exchange restrictions allowed Hollywood films to vie with Bollywood productions. Steve Derné notes the radical transformation of India's media: "Fueled by advertisers trying to reach the new Indian market, the number of television channels grew from one state-run channel in 1991 to seventy cable channels in 1999. Access to television increased from less than 10 percent of the urban population in 1990 to nearly 75 percent by 1999. In 1991, cable television reached 300,000 homes; by 1999 it reached 24 million homes. With the easing of foreign-exchange restrictions, previously unavailable Hollywood films were dubbed into Hindi and screened widely" (2005: 178). Such an environment of economic liberalization and media globalization fostered a powerful climate of social-cultural change and heady intermingling of local and global images and ideologies.

The diasporic flows of South Asian people to and from various parts of the world are also an important part of the making and experiencing of public or transnational cultural forms. As people move—whether by choice, or by necessity as a refugee (Daniel, this part)—they creatively combine and rework the ideas, values, images, and lifeways that constitute what they perceive to be their new site (such as America or Britain or the Middle East) and their homeland (such as India or Sri Lanka).

South Asians have moved in significant numbers at particular historical moments to various locales, including Africa, Fiji, Trinidad, Great Britain, the United States, Canada, and the Middle East. They arrived in East and South Africa mostly as indentured laborers under British colonial rule after 1860. Later, some came as free immigrants. Mahatma Gandhi himself spent several important formative years in South Africa in his mid-twenties, working as a (British-trained) barrister for the civil rights of local Indians. South Asians still make up a significant ethnic group in the region today (see, e.g., du Toit 1990). In fact, the British used South Asians as indentured laborers in many of their sugar-producing colonies, such as British Guiana, Mauritius, Fiji, and Trinidad. John Kelly (1991) investigates the Fiji Indian community under the British in the early 1900s and its efforts to mount an anticolonial Hindu reform society.

South Asians in Britain come from a wide range of class, regional, and religious backgrounds. As members of the British Commonwealth, South Asians—from the subcontinent as well as from East and South Africa—were earlier entitled to stay and work in the United Kingdom for as long as they wished, and many settled there, particularly during the postwar years when Britain was badly in need of extra labor. In the 1960s and '70s, however, amid public concern over the "race problem" in Britain, the United Kingdom tightened its immigration laws, making it very difficult for South Asians to migrate to the country unless they had close family ties there (Gardner 1995: 35–50; Kathleen Hall 2002). Ethnic census data were collected for the first time in Britain in 1991. According to these figures, people of Indian ethnicity make up the United Kingdom's largest ethnic group, followed by Black Caribbeans and then Pakistanis (Kathleen Hall 2002). Kathleen Hall in this part explores the complex forging of class, racial, and ethnic identities among second-generation British Sikhs. Paula Richman examines a feminist group of mixed-ethnic South Asian and African Caribbean women in Southall, Greater London, as they work on a creative, progressive performance of the Hindu Ramayana. Bhangra music emerged among British-born South Asian youth in the mid-1980s—with its roots in the persistent beat of the traditional north Indian folk dance known as *bhangra* in Punjab—and since then it has flowed between New York, Delhi, Mumbai, Port-au-Prince, Toronto, and other scenes of the South Asian diaspora as a vibrant form of transnational popular culture (Gopinath 1995; Maira 1999).

Prior to 1965, few South Asians were admitted to the United States, although Punjabi men migrated to rural northern California at the turn of the century (from about 1850 to 1930) to help develop California's agriculture as cheap Asian labor (Leonard 1992). Since 1965, when the United States vastly opened up immigration opportunities for people from Asia, the South Asian American community has grown significantly, and in the 2000 U.S. Census "Asian Indians" reached the status of the fastest-growing Asian American group. Until recently, the majority of South Asians entered the United States as graduate students and highly educated professionals. Now the class backgrounds of South Asian Americans are becoming somewhat more varied, as less professional kin come to join U.S.-settled families, or as laborers are brought over to work in places like the computer sweatshops of California's Silicon Valley. The South Asian American population is still quite "young," and the scholarly work on South Asian Americans has tended to focus on youth and the ambiguities of second-generation identity (e.g., Narayan, this part; Maira 2002). Over the past decade, however, more and more older South Asians have come to the United States, seeking to join their U.S.-settled children in their old age, striving to sustain their visions of family intimacy across generations and now nations (Lamb 2009).

Since the 1970s, when oil prices boomed and created a host of new job opportunities in the Middle East, many South Asians from Bangladesh, Sri Lanka, and India have migrated also to countries such as Saudi Arabia and Kuwait in search of employment. Men have ended up primarily in low-level oil industry jobs (see Gardner 1995), while women from Sri Lanka have sought work as domestic housemaids (Gamburd 2000; and part 2). Refugees from war-torn Sri Lanka have also desperately fled to Canada, England, Germany, and the United States—although they are sometimes bluntly expelled from these destinations and returned back to almost certain torture and death, as Daniel's piece here searingly portrays.

Although people have emigrated from India for centuries, it has been only over the past few decades that it has become almost *expected* for young adults of India's cosmopolitan middle classes to migrate abroad for higher education and professional opportunities, and then very frequently to end up settling permanently overseas. The Government of India recognizes the cultural and economic significance of expatriate Indians, and in 2002 launched a Persons of Indian Origin card scheme, allowing holders visa-free entry and rights to buy property and invest in the nation, aiming as well to "reinforce their emotional bonds . . . to their original country."[2] The comings and goings of nonresident Indians (NRIs) play a significant role in India's cosmopolitan public culture.

The people who make up the South Asian diaspora come, it is clear, from strikingly diverse national, ethnic, and class backgrounds, and move for very different reasons. Some remain in their new places, and others continue to travel regularly back and forth between South Asia and their diasporic homes. Most, whether or not they travel themselves, continue to creatively combine and rework the images, values, goods, and lifeways from what they see as their multiple cultural worlds, transforming each system, and themselves, in the process, and in so doing creating rich, novel forms of public culture.

* * *

Although scholarship on public culture and globalization in South Asia has dwelt on the urban middle classes, public culture is also very much a part of rural life. Anand Pandian's piece examines the intimate intersection between Tamil commercial film and everyday life in the Tamil countryside today. He explores how rural citizens of the Cumbum Valley draw from films in order to navigate the ethical trials of their daily lives, as the villagers find both that their everyday lives are somehow cinematic in their very nature, and that in turn cinema is an appropriate medium for the narration of their trials. Pandian argues that "cinema has emerged as one of the most powerful and supple means by which rural people in south India grapple with the challenges and imperatives of modernity."

Purnima Mankekar analyzes the eroticization of two domains of public culture in India that represent contemporary manifestations of globalization: the discourses and desires surrounding commodities, and television programs telecast on transnational television. Focusing on lower-middle-class and upwardly mobile working-class families in New Delhi in the late 1990s, Mankekar explores how many women are coming to express their erotic longings via yearnings for commodities, many of which are simultaneously intensely desired but also out of reach, as is unrequited love. Mankekar's piece probes as well the anxieties surrounding new consumerist desires, as some (parents, husbands, mothers-in-law) find the new "extravagant" habits of especially younger women to be "dangerous" both economically and in terms of the potential erosion of "tradition." At stake in these desires and anxieties, Mankekar finds, is "not only the reconfiguration of hierarchies of gender, caste, and class within India, but the very definition of Indian culture."

Paula Richman asks what happens when the ancient Hindu epic Ramayana travels abroad. In a London community, a feminist group of South Asian and African Caribbean women staged a Ramayana performance, reflecting a precise moment in the history of South Asian immigration to the United Kingdom. Their innovative performance was meant both to critique the racism, labor conditions, electoral politics, and sexism of their local British society and to connect them and their viewers to South Asian cultural traditions. Through her chapter, Richman reflects that diaspora is perhaps "less about 'being in exile from home' and more about being tied to two places."

Kathleen Hall's work is also situated in the United Kingdom. She explores the complex ways second-generation British Sikh youth—born in Britain to upwardly mobile families who grew up in the villages of Punjab or the racially divided cities of East Africa—live their lives "in translation," as they negotiate the conflicting cultural worlds of being both "British" and "Sikh."

Smitha Radhakrishnan examines how the phenomenal growth of India's information technology (IT) industry has produced a transnational class of professionals who are actively engaged in constructing a notion of a new India that is global in scope, yet Indian in essence. Drawing from interviews with female software engineers in Silicon Valley and Bangalore, the chapter argues that a new discourse of belonging to India is a fundamentally gendered one that relies on the ability of professional women to make delicate balances between an "Indian" home life and a "global" professional life.

Kirin Narayan turns to second-generation South Asian American lives through their stories. Concepts of diaspora and displacement often go together, Narayan reflects, but what she is interested in exploring here are the ways second-generation South Asian Americans forge their own "emplacement"—strategies of coming to belong somewhere—through telling stories about themselves, family folklore, and reworked cultural mythology.

Finally, E. Valentine Daniel's piece powerfully, disturbingly, conveys some of what it can be like when the "everyday" dimensions of life are suddenly—poof—gone—because you're a refugee; when you move from homeland not out of choice but in desperation to stay alive; and when you come to a land you have heard and dreamed of as a place of "freedom" but are faced with forces seemingly as brutal and impervious as those you escaped from—such as gang rape in a detention center and the cold bureaucracy of a U.S. judicial and immigration system.

NOTES

1. See also Appadurai 1996; Breckenridge 1995; and the journal *Public Culture*.

2. See the Indian Embassy site: www.indianembassy.org/policy/PIO/Introduction_PIO.html, and Dhooleka Raj's chapter 7 of *Where Are You From? Middle-Class Migrants in the Modern World*, "Being British, Becoming a Person of Indian Origin" (2003: 165–83).

29

Cinema in the Countryside: Popular Tamil Film and the Remaking of Rural Life

Anand Pandian

Any man today can lay claim to being filmed.

—Walter Benjamin (1968: 231)

On a hot March morning in 2002, I set off by foot for the southernmost orchards of the Cumbum Valley, a triangular vale tucked between the mountains of the Western Ghats and the plains of Tamil Nadu in southern India. Farmers throughout the valley were preparing to plant another crop of onions, and many laborers were at work that day raising orchard soils into the small divided beds most suitable for planting and irrigating onion bulbs. I came across my friend Pandian, a young wage laborer who had managed to save up enough money to take a half-acre plot of orchard land on mortgage three years back. He was working alongside the Dalit laborers he had hired to heap the loose red soil of the field into small rows of rectangular beds. Leaning over at one point to scrape a bit of dry soil into a low-lying hollow on the field, Pandian broke out suddenly into a few lines of song, drawn from the 1987 film *Velaikaran*—"Making beds in the orchard, I'm looking, looking. . . ." "This is the work," he told me when I looked on with bemused surprise. His wife Ayyammal later told me that her husband often sang this song as he worked on the orchard tract: "Isn't that the work he does? He sings of that."

This was by no means the first time that I found cinema bent to suit the needs of daily life in rural Tamil Nadu. Throughout my fieldwork on the subject of agrarian social reform in the southern Tamil countryside, I was struck by the extent to which film had crept into the intimate texture of rural experience. Scenes and songs from commercial Tamil film streamed endlessly from tea-stall televisions, speakers mounted on street corners and rooftops to signal special occasions, and living rooms tuned nightly to the same popular channels. Many of my interlocutors turned most often to didactic lyrics and dialogues drawn from such films in order to navigate the ethical trials of everyday life. Young men and women professed a close identification with—or even a love for—one or another popular actor or actress. Older men and women spoke in turn to blame cinema for the moral depravity of contemporary youth. A surprising number of families could point to relatives who had sought a place in the distant film industry of Chennai, several hundred kilometers to the north. Each of these phenomena testifies to one of the most prominent ways in which the rural citizens of the Cumbum Valley identify the very nature of the present: as a *cinema kaalam*, or an "age of cinema."

The identification of the rural present as an especially cinematic time is greatly indebted to a significant development in Tamil commercial film production that began in the 1970s: the emergence of a genre of cinema dedicated to the realistic depiction of rural life onscreen. These "nativity" films—as they have been termed by moviemaking professionals—are shot extensively in rural locales: depicting peasant protagonists, staging dialogues in regional dialects and idioms, and introducing folk rhythms and instruments into cinematic soundtracks. Many among the hundreds of these films have been staged in the Cumbum Valley and the surrounding countryside, often by filmmakers hailing from the region itself. I was startled to find certain elder villagers reacting with cynicism to my own first earnest attempts to record their field and folk songs, voicing a suspicion that I intended only to sell their oral traditions to moviemakers for a handsome profit! That the Tamil film industry has been extraordinarily concerned in recent decades with depicting rural custom and culture onscreen is widely obvious.

What I seek to do in this essay is to chart some of the most significant points of intersection between Tamil commercial film and everyday life in the Tamil countryside today. I am less concerned here with what these films *mean* and more with what they *do:* that is, the myriad ways in which Tamil celluloid has interposed itself as the language and landscape of daily life.[1] Rather than addressing the narrative unity of particular cinematic texts, in other words, I attend to the multiple and dissonant ways in which fragments of cinema come to work as incitements to *live* in a particular fashion. Cinema has emerged as one of the most powerful and supple means by which rural people in south India grapple with the challenges and imperatives of modernity.

Each portion of this essay calls attention to one of four aspects of such popular engagement with film in the countryside: cinema as an arena of spectatorial pleasure and desire; as an instrument of everyday moral practice; as a way of articulating the character of quotidian rural experience; and as a field of active rural participation in production. I rely on evidence culled from over a year of ethnographic fieldwork concerning modern agrarian developments in the Cumbum Valley, a fertile and well-irrigated agricultural region west of Madurai in southern Tamil Nadu.[2] The tales that follow focus in particular on the village of KG Patti near the head of the valley, a settlement of over one thousand households populated primarily by Kallar, Gounder, and Dalit castefolk. By anchoring this essay in a series of encounters and anecdotes, I seek to convey how filmic residues have worked themselves so closely into the fine grain of Tamil rural experience.

* * *

On a June evening in 2002, I snuck off to the Yuvaraja theater in the town of Cumbum with my young friends Bose and Malai. We were on our way to see *Thulluvathoo Ilamai*, or "Youth Leaps About," a new film about the trials and pleasures of adolescence, directed by Kasturi Raja. As we bumped along on my motorbike down the gravelly road from KG Patti, Malai said that this was their own *thulli thiriyum kaalam*, or "time to leap about and wander"—refusing to heed their parents, resisting the pressure to wed, indulging in whatever mischief suited them. Both of these young men, just a few years younger than myself, easily related to the story and especially its closing statement that youth should be allowed by their parents, teachers, and other wards to enjoy themselves freely. Throughout the film, Bose and Malai pointed out nearby locations that they recognized onscreen: a bus stand, a college campus, another regional movie theater. Relishing the tales of a young man's first exposure to razors, cigarettes, beer, and pornography, they remarked again and again about the "reality" of the film. Although they were rural electrical workers and the story narrated the exploits of educated urban kids, the film invited wider masculine identification with its visual and aural pleasures.

The Yuvaraja theater was packed with hundreds of people that night, a rare event as far as I had seen. Forms of cinematic spectatorship have changed a great deal since the first tin-roofed movie sheds were put up in the larger towns of the Cumbum Valley several decades ago. Nearly every village in this relatively prosperous region now has at least one satellite cable television network running lines to individual houses and making cinema broadcasts available on a daily basis. By no means does every home have a television, but with at least a couple present on even the poorest streets of each village—not to mention most of the tea stalls and even some of the grocery stores—films are far more easily accessible to rural residents today than in the scattered halls that once monopolized their presentation.

Figure 29.1. Young men act out a scene from the 1999 film *Sethu* in the midst of a temple festival.

One consequence of these proliferating screens is that the viewing or reception of cinema has assumed a far more fragmentary form than in earlier years. Rural viewers are much more likely to catch a few minutes of a film onscreen in a moment of rest after an afternoon meal, on the occasion of a visit with a friend or relation, or in the midst of a lull in a tea-stall conversation, than by means of a trip to a cinema-hall screening. This is even more the case with respect to popular Tamil film songs, which are not only screened independently on televised programs but also mixed together and loudly replayed on the occasion of most domestic festivities. As I will argue in what follows, this fragmentation of transmission greatly shapes the nature of its rural reception.

The attractions of the cinema leave their many marks on the lived spaces of the countryside in other ways as well. Here as elsewhere throughout the state, fan clubs are a ubiquitous means of both social affiliation and distinction, among young men in particular (Dickey 1993). In 2001 and 2002, when I conducted fieldwork in the Cumbum Valley, clubs devoted to younger stars such as Vijay and Ajit, as well as older stalwarts such as Rajni Kanth, Vijay Kanth, and Satyaraj, were common. Groups of young men would celebrate the weddings of their friends by plastering public walls with printed posters of congratulation, usually distinguished by the image of a favored star.

A rival crowd of youths might retaliate in turn by identifying their own congratulatory posters with a notable villain or antagonist to this particular actor. Glossy color portraits of cinema stars are also circulated among friends as framed gifts on such occasions. Although barber shops and roadside stalls are also plastered with posters for Hollywood pictures and pornographic "blue films," the prevalence of these Tamil film idols testifies to the continued appeal of commercial Tamil cinema among contemporary rural youth.

Much of what is attractive in these films to young men and women alike is the image of a romantic love cast in an inevitable tension with social and familial expectation (Inden 1999). Although almost all of these rural youths would ultimately bend to the convention of an arranged marriage, I met hardly any who had not nurtured the fantasy of a romantic attraction pursued to public recognition, if not clandestine consummation. The latter prospect bedeviled most of the parents and grandparents of adolescent boys and girls that I knew, who often blamed the obvious evidence of bus-stop flirtations, riverside glances, and furtive love notes circulated by pint-sized messengers on the tempting spectacles of film itself.

This silhouette of love had grown so threatening that many parents admitted to arranging marriages for their children at ever younger ages, seeking to bypass the dangers of adolescence altogether. An elderly wage laborer named Karupayi amma had married her own daughter off at the age of fifteen for this reason—in this "age of cinema," she told me, the desires of young boys and girls could no longer be restrained. For her and for many of her peers, cinema was a recurrent lesson in corrupted wants, one that displaced what they saw as the more virtuous traditions of the past. When I accompanied her and a small group of women laborers on a weeding expedition one morning, for example, Karupayi amma complained that the pair of teenage girls in the group neither knew nor enjoyed the folk *kaattu paattu*, or "field songs," that the older women were singing: "Our songs aren't fit for them," she observed. And indeed, while these older women playfully sang and repeated their folk verses for me with an exaggerated and comical gusto, I noticed the two young girls singing a few recent film lyrics to each other in a quieter riposte, each teaching words that the other did not yet know.

As a young and unmarried man conducting fieldwork in south India, I rarely had the chance to speak directly with younger women concerning these controversial themes. It was clear to me, however, that these girls were not alone in taking cinema as an arena of pedagogy. Other elder men and women that I knew turned to cinema for a language of ethical instruction and moral critique, rather than for an exemplar of modern moral degradation. It is to this latter possibility that I turn now.

* * *

I knew Manivannan as a massive middle-aged man with a heart of equally generous proportions. Unlettered and mostly unschooled, he had spent most of his life felling hardwood trunks from the mountain forests surrounding the village, until the strain of this illicit enterprise led him to buy a small herd of goats instead. I tagged along with him one July morning as he drove these animals into the fallow stubble to the south of his village, women harvesting sesame on scattered expanses in the distance. As we ambled along, we began to speak of the rash of recently unveiled adulteries in the village. "A man should not behave just like cattle," Manivannan observed. "He should not feel desire for the things of another." These were lines from a film song whose name he had forgotten. But he went on then to muse on another animal in verse—

The heart is a monkey,
man's heart is a monkey—
Let it leap, let it escape and run,
and it will land us in sin,
it will shove us into attachment.

These were lines I often heard repeated in the village. A monkey could be coached even to ask men for money, Manivannan went on to explain, arguing instead that "it must be habituated." But those who failed to train their own monkey natures should be tossed aside, he suggested, like one rotten fruit among a basket of tomatoes.

"The heart is a monkey," or *manam oru kurangu*, was the most popular song from the 1966 Tamil film of the same name, scripted by Tamil playwright and critic Cho. Ramaswamy as a loose adaptation of *Pygmalion*. This was only one of the many film songs and dialogues from numerous periods and genres that the men and women of the Cumbum Valley regularly invoked as guides to proper self-conduct. A plowman, for example, once noted to me that although one could reform the habits of an unruly bull, men would change only as a result of their own volition, citing lyrics to this effect sung by MGR in the 1961 hit *Thirudaathee*, or "Don't Steal."[3] In the midst of a heated debate about the difference between sincere and "thievish" love among youths, a teenage grape orchard laborer brought up the narrative of Thangar Bachan's 2002 *Azhagi* in order to insist on the virtues of an amorous devotion even in the face of its impossibility. And Manivannan's own brother Mohan paused to carefully recite the lines I had overheard him singing as we worked together on his orchard one October morning: "Man desires the soil, the soil desires man—the soil wins in the end but the heart hides this from us," a truth proclaimed by Rajni Kanth in the 1995 *Muthu*.

The "social" films of mid-twentieth century India were clearly marked by their overt concern for moral redemption, presenting a hero who must navigate—as Vasudevan (2000) has observed—between rival spaces of virtue, villainy, and respectability. The explicit moral pedagogy of films such as *Thirudaathee* continues to resound in everyday discourse in the Cumbum Valley, brought into the present by the replay of popular lyrics over public

loudspeakers, by regular televised retrospectives, and through other channels of transmission. But the appearance of Tamil film as an element of moral
instruction in everyday life has another broader yet hazier horizon intimat-
ed by the brief examples I have just presented. The narrative unity of individual films as emblems of moral propriety is of less concern here than the
exemplary value of particular scenes, lyrics, or dialogues to the pursuit of a
desirable way of acting, feeling, or thinking. It is these cinematic fragments,
drawn as pieces from the archive of available film, that come to matter most
in the imagination and exercise of an ethical life.

My woodcutter friend Manichamy, for example, reciting yet another line
from an unknown film in the midst of another conversation on his small
doorstep one afternoon, told me that filmic lyrics whose philosophies he ap-
preciates are "recorded" in his heart, while the remainder are simply forgotten. Although references to such lines were an inseparable part of his
discourse on the necessary resistance of a "good man" to the temptations
of "crooked paths," he could rarely identify the films that he had drawn
them from, the actors who had spoken them, or the scenes that they had
punctuated. Rather than calling my attention to particular films, he would
preface each quotation with a more general invocation: "as they have sung
in that time" or "as that poet has said." These lines appeared in the space
of everyday conversation as anonymous reverberations. The repetition and
recirculation of older moral themes by means of cinema—the visage and dic-
tion of a roaming poet and devotional saint that actor Muthuraman assumed
in 1966, for example, when singing of the heart as a monkey—draws moral
tradition forward into the present as a tumbling cascade of fragments.

Rural men and women in south India today find their ideas of virtue
among many different arenas of moral pedagogy: cautionary tales printed
in vernacular newspapers; lessons on character from schoolbook texts; rhetorical claims of public leaders; religious discourses broadcast through temple loudspeakers and personal cassettes; popular proverbs, jokes, and folk
verses shared in tea stalls, on courtyard stoops, and in working fields; and
indeed, didactic lyrics and dialogues from popular cinema and teleserials.
Tamil film emerges here as one among the many archives of elements with
which one may assemble the image of a well-lived life: one that is significant,
I might stress, for the lettered and unlettered alike. But more particularly, in
recent years Tamil cinema has come to provide for rural citizens an image of
the very life they are already living in the present. I turn now to the closure
of the gap between cinema and countryside in commercial Tamil film, and
its consequences for the texture of rural experience.

* * *

Every now and then in the Cumbum Valley, a quiet morning or afternoon
would be interrupted by the sudden bursting of firecrackers and the loud
broadcast of a single song from the 1993 Tamil film *Kizhakku Chimaiyilee,* or

Figure 29.2. A marching band plays a song from the 1993 *Kizhakku Chimaiyilee* as a party of maternal uncles arrives at a ritual ceremony.

"In the Eastern Country." As its horns and drums rose to a stirring crescendo, some of the first lines of this song would proclaim a moment of arrival: "Your maternal uncle comes carrying gifts for you, he is bringing golden anklets to give to you. . . ." These lyrics and the particular scene that they ornament celebrate the generosity and concern with which a brother fulfills the social expectation for his care of his sister's children. The film itself is a cinematic ode to the customs and traditions of the Piramalai Kallar caste, a community to which its director, Bharatiraja, belongs. Among Kallar households as well as those of many other castes in the region today, this one song serves as the ordinary means of marking the moment in family rituals and ceremonies when a maternal uncle arrives to discharge his obligations. Film has come to provide a language for the social life of kinship and attachment.

This was only one of the many ways in which I found cinematic references and likenesses flashing up repeatedly among the foundations of everyday rural life. A young man and I were picking our way down a riverbank when he expressed a desire to wait for a few minutes and wave his legs in the water—"like cinema." Another youth described how he had eloped across this very river with his lover several years ago, averring that "it happened just like cinema." An elder man described how he had come to this village on his own as a youth, in the same way that Sivaji Ganesan had once been abandoned as a baby in the forest of a particular film. Another elder man showed me his outstretched hands when I ran into him working on his orchard tract. "See the toiling hands," he said, gesturing toward a 1976 film of the same title—"like MGR." And I was sitting one afternoon under the shade of a tamarind tree with my friends Bose and Malai, chatting about certain cultural practices in the region, when one chided the other for his many references to Tamil films. "You shouldn't speak about cinema," Malai said— likely with the integrity of my anthropological interview on his mind—to which Bose retorted sharply: "*Dey,* they're making cinema about nothing but our culture!"

There is no question that the close resemblance today between village life in the Tamil country and the universe of Tamil cinema has much to do with the turn of many south Indian filmmakers toward the quotidian trials of rural life itself. The "nativity," or folk quality, of their films can be traced back to the genre of commercial moviemaking that emerged in the mid-1970s with the aim of conveying the countryside in a realistic idiom. The *man vaasanai,* or "scent of the soil," often attributed by critics to this cinema, derives from its wide use of rural locales for shooting, regional dialects for scripting, and folk elements in its soundtracks. Three of the most important exponents of the genre—director Bharatiraja, music director Ilaiyaraja, and lyricist Vairamuthu—hail from the Cumbum Valley and the surrounding countryside. In his many interviews Bharatiraja has consistently represented himself as a "villager" at heart, keen on evoking in his films the everyday savor and affective resonance of forgotten modes of rural conduct: a markedly ethnographic *verité* (Shanmugasundaram 1997). The "soil" stands in this cinematic imagination as a metonym for the village itself in all its purity and difference from the norms of urban civility. Vairamuthu himself described *man vaasanai* to me—in an interview at his office in 2002—as "an idiomatic expression of our culture."

Sundar Kaali (2000: 174) has called attention to the way in which Tamil nativity films from the mid-1970s onward shifted narrative agency from the hero to the village itself as a "collective actant." What I find most striking is the way in which individual rural actors today seize upon these representations of the village environment as a means of articulating the significance of their own deeds within it. In other words, what is at stake in the reception of such cinema by rural Tamils is the character of their own lives and practices rather than the narrative meaning of the cinema to which they turn. Suffused by their auteurs with the resonance of the rural landscape, these films are taken by rural subjects as a way of expressing the quality of their own struggles with the substance of the countryside. The soil itself is laden with a cinematic texture. This is clearest when farmers rely on filmic residues to speak of their own agrarian experience.

On a March morning just one week after cultivator Pandian had sung of making crop beds—the incident with which I began this essay—I ran into cultivator Logandurai tending to his own small plot of onions in a nearby tract. A middle-aged farmer from a well-respected family in KG Patti, Logandurai had spent most of the previous night drawing water to irrigate bed after bed of onion shoots. The electric current powering the motor in the well that he relied on had suddenly cut off before this task was complete. He had returned this morning to water the soil that remained dry. The field was far from the well, and the stream of water flowing into its channels was thin and sluggish. I squatted on a bund to chat with Logandurai as he waited for the flow to slowly fill each rectangular bed. And then he too began to sing. "In desire I raised a bed and planted a single shoot," he said with a smile as he crouched down to loosen a wall of soil dividing a dry bed from the running stream. I laughed in surprise and asked if he knew which film this song had come from. "Isn't it Ramaraj?" he asked, naming a Tamil actor once noted for his rustic films. I learned later that it had come from *Enga Ooru Kavalkaran*, or "Our Village Watchman," a 1988 Tamil film starring this man indeed.

Enga Ooru Kavalkaran depicts a romance between an honest and diligent village watchman and a young woman named Puvayi, who belongs to an agrarian household of a different caste. An invocation to the goddess Meenakshi at the very beginning and references to the Vaigai River's floodwaters make it clear that the film is set in the Madurai countryside of southern Tamil Nadu. The song sequence that Logandurai quoted from follows one of the first scenes of the film, when Puvayi leads other women of the village in the transplanting of paddy seedlings from a nursery bed into a wet field. She gives voice to its lyrics as she dances through these fields with the other women, chasing after goats and other animals through a lush green terrain. The song is a paean of amorous and religious devotion, set to orchestral melodies and the gentle rhythm of a folk beat. Puvayi sings of herself as the earnest lover of a distant male god, beseeching him to come and protect the crop so that it ripens fully. Delivered in a local dialect, the lines of the song suggest that she is concerned about the fruition of much more than the plants that she is dancing among. The soil bed raised "in desire" here lies within the landscape of her own heart, which will ripen only with the fulfillment of her love for him.[4]

These qualities of the song might appear to present a certain puzzle. Why would a middle-aged cultivator in the midst of his agrarian labors assume the voice of a young woman in devoted love? But when I asked Logandurai why this song had come to mind at that particular moment, he mentioned none of these features of its cinematic setting. The lyrics had instead provided a language with which to convey the nature of his own work the previous night and that morning. "With how much desire, irrigating water the whole night. Wasn't able to irrigate four sets of beds—then how would it be?" he asked. He described the hopes and desires with which he had struggled to

Figure 29.3. "Making beds in the orchard, I'm looking, looking . . ." Pandian liked to sing as he and Ayyammal worked on the tract that they had carefully cultivated.

raise these shoots: clearing the residues of the previous crop, plowing the soil countless times, making a sleepless journey by truck to purchase these onion bulbs, losing even more sleep watering the crop. A line had been wrested from a filmic love song to convey the affective resonance of an altogether different kind of embodied experience. But this seizure of a filmic fragment was prompted by a specific likeness between film and rural life. The image of a raised soil bed brokered a recursive relation between cinema and the everyday: each had come to rely on the other for its depth and texture.

Closely sutured into the fabric of rural existence, Tamil "nativity" films aid in what Appadurai (1996) has described as the "production of locality." Cinema not only generates persuasive representations of the countryside, but also infiltrates these places and their inhabitants themselves as an instrument of imagination and interpretation. With these relations in mind, I want to turn briefly to the means by which everyday experience is recomposed as filmic artifact in the universe of Tamil rural cinema.

* * *

In the 1980 film *Kallukkul Iiram*—"Moisture within the Stone"—Bharatiraja portrayed himself directing a film shoot in a Tamil village, and the trail of desire, threat, fascination, and ultimately destruction that shadowed the divisive enterprise.[5] His films have consistently set the village milieu against the larger world in a relation of hostile tension, V. Chakravarthy (1986) has observed. But the very movement toward the rural that Bharatiraja and his colleagues propelled has now thoroughly caught much of the Tamil countryside within the machinery of cinematic production itself. The village, in other words, must be understood as a locus of filmmaking as well as of public reception. Take the Cumbum Valley, for example. Bharatiraja himself was born here in the small town of Alli Nagaram, some forty kilometers north of KG Patti. Music director Ilaiyaraja maintains a waterside bungalow just a few kilometers upstream from the village, along the same river. Rising director Bala hails from the village of NT Patti, no more than a few kilometers to the north of KG Patti. Many in the region have tapped these and other kin relations to seek a foothold in the Tamil film industry as artistes, technicians, and crew. But more to the point perhaps, numerous films have been shot in the area itself.

Tamil filmmakers rely on a dispersed network of location managers in order to identify apt places for shooting their features. There are certain areas, such as the Pollachi countryside of western Tamil Nadu, that have hosted the making of literally hundreds of commercial films and televised serials.[6] In the pursuit of novelty and diversity of visual spectacle, location managers continuously seek to identify new sites suitable for film: increasingly, of course, in exotic locations beyond the boundaries of India itself. But as nativity continues to maintain a certain niche in the Tamil commercial film market, camera crews are drawn on a regular basis to regions such as the Cumbum Valley as well. In my first few weeks in the area I was surprised to discover that one film—the 1985 *Rasathi Rosakili*—was shot almost exclusively in the village of KG Patti itself. Some of my closest interlocutors here had themselves landed bit parts in the narrative. I turn now to this experience of theirs in order to broach one more question concerning the intimacy between cinema and rural life: how does it feel to find oneself onscreen?

Directed by S. Devaraj, *Rasathi Rosakili* is a tale of terrestrial moral failure and cosmic revenge. Kuda Thevan secretly poisons his own widowed uncle in order to enjoy the latter's abundant wealth and possessions. He and his wife raise the widower's only son, Surattai, as a guileless farm boy, planning to wed him to their own daughter in order to secure their claim to the dead man's lands. Surattai falls instead for his own poor cousin Rasathi, and the two become lovers. The unscrupulous Kuda Thevan kills Surattai and stages the murder as a suicide. But the young man returns to walk the earth as a furious and vengeful *pey*, or demon, terrorizing his antagonists until they stumble into and drown within the same well where his body had been dumped. Rasathi inherits Surattai's possessions on behalf of their unborn child, and a satisfied demon ascends a white beam of light into the heavens.

Close to two decades later, many men and women in KG Patti had stories to tell concerning the making of the film. The artistes and crew had settled into "Boatman" Raju's large house within the village itself for several weeks of shooting. Comedian Goundamani would sit on a porch asking old women to gather around him, I was told, while his diminutive sidekick Senthil searched the village lanes for iced lime sherbet. Cultivator Logandurai himself spoke of teaching the actress Sulochana how to carry bundles of threshed paddy on her head. Another man described how he and his friends had lingered then as children on the outskirts of the working crew—"we would wander around only with them," he said. When I tracked down a cassette copy of the film in Chennai and arranged to have it screened on the village's closed-circuit cable service, those who watched it with me could point out familiar locations onscreen: the threshing mill, the Ganapathi temple, the road to Suruli Falls, and so on. Certain things had even remained the same in the intervening years, I was told: Devarasu, for example, still poured tea at the same grocery store of his that he had tended as an extra in the film.

At the same time, however, I was surprised to discover that *Rasathi Rosakili* was not the most popular of movies in the very village where it was shot. Many simply found it boring, deriding it as an "old-style" production and a tedious "saw," or *rambam*—as painful as the experience of serrating one's own neck with a dull blade. Others argued that it had failed to closely represent the character of life in the village: the nuances of regional dialect, or the way in which women sat together outside in the evenings to talk and share gossip. It was suggested by some that such criticisms of the film stemmed from the jealousy and disappointment of those who had been left out of its scenes. But even those who had won a small place within it seemed less than enthusiastic about their role in its making. When I asked Logandurai if this was a good film, he laughed and said that it was "rustic" and solely about agriculture. Meanwhile, Devarasu complained of being represented as a "supply-master" or servant in the film. Yelled at and disrespected by a customer onscreen, his place in the story was a reason for regret rather than pride.

A more particular problem lay with the manifest intent of the film, which begins with an image of producer and writer Rama Pandian standing behind a podium to inform his viewers that the scenes to follow were based on a "real event." Born in an adjacent Cumbum Valley village himself, Rama Pandian studied sociology at Madras University before embarking on a lucrative career in shipping. The presentation of rural culture in Tamil film serves a specific purpose, he told me as we spoke on the porch of his Chennai home: "it reveals the heart." He had scripted *Rasathi Rosakili* as an allegory for the story of his own uncle Chinnasamy Chettiar, who had clashed with a powerful landlord named Kottaichamy Thevar in the 1950s. Kottaichamy's henchmen had reportedly murdered Chinnasamy in the mountains above the Cumbum Valley, disguising the deed as an elephant attack. When a stray buffalo forced Kottaichamy's car to veer off the road into a tamarind tree soon thereafter, killing him too, it was widely suggested that Chinnasamy himself had assumed the form of this animal as a vengeful demon. Rama Pandian had seized upon this incident to produce a cinematic censure of the "rowdyism" of his native milieu, the "atrocity" perpetrated by a caste different from his own. That the film was a "scolding" of the Kallar community that dominated KG Patti village was well known.

Caste clashes are an undeniable feature of public life in the southern Tamil countryside today, and they have been tackled quite successfully in numerous Tamil films. The failure of *Rasathi Rosakili* to win appreciation from its own subjects lies perhaps in the paradoxical character of its claim to realism: because it was too real and at the same time not real enough—because, in a sense, it insisted too crudely on the shame of rural society itself. Those who seek to cast the quotidian life of the countryside in the register of collective fantasy always run the risk of lingering on forms of experience that their own subjects find increasingly undesirable. Rama Pandian's film dwelt on aspects of life in the Cumbum Valley that many here identify as the relics of a less civil age. Tamil rural cinema captures and preserves for posterity what its makers themselves find appealing and unappealing in this milieu. But pleasure in such representations depends on the vitality of a popular desire for what they represent. Few may love a village film whose very subjects begin to appear as unlovable themselves.

* * *

I did not come to the Cumbum Valley to study cinema. Yet its traces were inescapable at every turn. I asked people of the region to speak about their own lives, and found them speaking their own experience instead by means of film—

"My story is like a cinema story."

"The history of my life deserves a cinema."

"My story could make four pictures, that's how much I've suffered."

"I could even sell the tale of my hardship as a cinema script one day."

"Even if the tickets were 100 rupees it would pack the houses, this story would make that good a cinema."

Statements such as these, which I often heard, testify to a widespread sense among the rural people I knew that their everyday lives were somehow cinematic in their very nature. These statements imply both that these were lives appropriate for the cinema and that cinema in turn was an appropriate medium for the narration of their trials. This may also be true of course for the urban audiences of Tamil cinema, and in particular its urban spectacles;

in calling attention to these rural spirals of experience and representation, I have intended only to show what an examination of such recursivity might disclose.

In these pronouncements of a markedly cinematic life we must also recognize an element of pride in the face of hardship, a complex feeling that has been nurtured in part by Tamil cinema's close attention for nearly thirty years to the everyday trials and tribulations of rural existence. But we must also ask at the same time whether social suffering in rural Tamil Nadu today is at least partly due to a waning of public interest in the countryside itself as a realm of advancement and wellbeing. As economic rhetoric today dwells incessantly on the urban middle classes, and Tamil cinema also turns toward their exploits in localities as far-flung as London, Sydney, and Los Angeles, the image of the village begins to blur, decay, and fade from view. The future of a vital rural cinema in south India appears as uncertain as that of a vital rural life.

NOTES

1. "We will never ask what a book means, as signified or signifier," write Deleuze and Guattari (1987: 4): "We will ask what it functions with, in connection with what other things it does or does not transmit intensities, in which other multiplicities its own are inserted and metamorphosed."

2. See my recent book, *Crooked Stalks: Cultivating Virtue in South India*, which concerns the cultivation of the soil, the cultivation of an ethical life, and the colonial and post-colonial politics of collective identity.

3. For an analysis of MGR as moral paragon, see Pandian (1992).

4. The language of the song plays on the landscape poetics of Tamil devotional verse. For a discussion of this literary genre, see Cutler (1987).

5. See Kaali (2000) for a discussion of this film.

6. The region is often described as a "mini-Kodambakkam," in reference to the Chennai seat of the Tamil film industry, and I intend to closely study it in future research.

30

Dangerous Desires: Erotics, Public Culture, and Identity in Late-Twentieth-Century India

Purnima Mankekar

During the early 1990s, the Indian public sphere witnessed a proliferation of representations of erotics. Some of the erotic (re)charging of the public has been attributed to the expansion of transnational public culture, in particular the images, texts, and commodities flooding India after the liberalization of the economy. It has also been attributed to the advent of transnational satellite television—and here, I refer not only to "imported" shows such as *The Bold and the Beautiful* and *Santa Barbara* but, more importantly, to soap operas, films, and talk shows produced specifically for viewers in India and its diasporas, and beamed via transnational satellite networks such as STAR (Satellite Television for the Asian Region), Sony Entertainment Television, and Zee TV.[1] In this essay, I analyze the eroticization of two domains of public culture: the discourses and desires surrounding commodities, and television programs telecast on transnational television. My objective is to examine the place of erotics in the reconfiguration of gender, family, class, and nation occurring in metropolitan centers such as New Delhi in late-twentieth-century India.

Following up on earlier ethnographic research on mass media (Mankekar 1999), the analytic core of my data draws on interviews, oral histories, and participant observation with lower-middle-class and upwardly mobile working-class families in New Delhi between 1992 and 2000, the textual analysis of television programs and advertisements, and a careful examination of policy documents and market research data.

A study of erotics presented unique challenges to my ethnographic practice, in part because of the difficulties in talking about these topics with low-

Excerpts from "Dangerous Desires: Television and Erotics in Late Twentieth-Century India," by Purnima Mankekar, *The Journal of Asian Studies* 63(2), May 2004, pp. 403–431. Copyright © 2004 Association for Asian Studies. Reprinted with the permission of Cambridge University Press.

er-middle-class and working-class women in urban India.[2] I became acutely sensitive to the importance of respecting the silences, hesitations, and discursive detours that saturated our conversations. My informants tended to discuss erotics in the idiom of power as much as pleasure and, more importantly, would do so through metaphors, tropes, and gestures: we thus had to learn to glean each others' thoughts and feelings indirectly rather than solicit or express them directly.[3] For instance, many women I spoke with expressed their erotic longing via their yearnings for certain commodities or through their remarks about television shows. I deemed it neither ethical nor culturally appropriate to interrogate my lower-middle-class and working-class informants about their attitudes toward sex or, worse, their sexual practices: my concern was not with how the proliferation of erotics in the public sphere has affected the sex lives of people in late-twentieth-century India. Instead, my analysis of the cultural significance of erotics is based on ethnographically refracted practices of analyzing the intertextual field in which my informants lived and loved.

Rather than see erotic desire in opposition to nationalist affect (cf. Mankekar 1999), I am interested in tracing the relationship between the two. How did nationalist belonging and notions of "Indianness" shape how erotic desire was constituted? Conversely, how did new representations of the erotic mediate the reconfiguration of "Indian culture"?

GENEALOGIES OF THE EROTIC IN INDIA

This paper militates against the notion that transnational mass media swept into India to *introduce* images and discourses of the erotic. Indeed, by tracing the (re)eroticization of the public sphere in India, the ensuing discussion also serves to interrogate Eurocentric and universalistic notions of erotics.[4] Diverse genealogies of the erotic co-exist in Indian public culture(s).[5] My objective in the following partial genealogy is simply to underscore that late-twentieth-century representations of erotics did not emerge in a cultural or discursive vacuum and that, in all probability, they resonated with older, perhaps residual (Williams 1977), conventions of erotics.

While it is beyond the scope of this paper to compare recent representations of erotics with pre-modern ones, late-twentieth-century representations need to be situated vis-à-vis heterogeneous traditions of erotics in the pre-modern past such as the Kamasutra (said to have been written between the second and fourth centuries CE), Bharata's Natyashastra,[6] the work of Abhinavagupta (in the eleventh century), Kalidasa's Kumarsambhava, the twelfth-century poem Gitagovinda by Jayadeva, Tamil *akam* poetry, and medieval *bhakti* poetry dedicated to Krishna.[7] Many bhakti poems were in local languages (rather than in Sanskrit), and continue to be influential in contemporary, Hindu popular culture. Indo-Islamic *sufi* traditions incorporated the erotic into aesthetic conventions expressing the mystical union of the devout with the Divine Beloved.[8] Among Indo-Islamic and Urdu performative traditions, the most influential in contemporary popular culture is the *ghazal*.[9]

In the modern conjuncture, the most ubiquitous and influential form of popular culture in India and its diasporas is popular film. Popular music, circulated in audio cassettes or CDs, or consumed as music videos on television, draws largely on film music. Film and television have developed a symbiotic relationship, and many televisual representations of erotics— whether in MTV-style music programs or television serials—draw on the representational strategies and narrative conventions of popular film. The past few decades have also witnessed the flowering of heterogeneous print media, ranging from novels, magazines, and pamphlets in English and regional languages to "Indianized" versions of U.S.-based magazines such as *Cosmopolitan*. In general, contemporary representations of erotics in hegemonic popular culture are predominantly heterosexist in orientation, thus inscribing heterosexual erotic desire as normative, if not normal.[10] This does not, of course, preclude readings or interpretations of these representations in terms of homoerotic desire, which might sometimes lie just beneath their surfaces (Gopinath 2005).

There is no unitary or singular "Indian" discourse on erotics. At the close of the twentieth century, discourses of erotics proliferating in the Indian public sphere drew upon various pre-existing genealogies or existed in uneasy tension with them. It is also crucial to note that prior genealogies of the erotic have not survived unchanged through the ages. As part of larger discursive formations, they are as contingent and contested as other discourses and have been appropriated and reconstituted at different historical moments: for instance, contemporary conflations of middle-class respectability with the sexual modesty of women have been influenced by colonial and Victorian discourses of gender and domesticity (cf. Bannerjee 1989; Chatterjee 1993; Tharu 1989). Hence, instead of either harking back to a static tradition of "Indian erotics" or assuming that transnational media caused the Westernization or homogenization of "local" discourses of the erotic, we might consider how local cultural forms are produced in articulation with the translocal, and also how the transnational itself is reconfigured as it intersects with the local or, indeed, the national (Gupta and Ferguson 1997).

Given that there are such rich and heterogeneous genealogies of the erotic in India, what is so notable about recent representations? First, as I will argue shortly, recent representations of the erotic are imbricated with the feverish commodity consumption precipitated by the expansion of mass culture, the liberalization of the Indian economy, and the proliferation of globalized capital. Second, the production, circulation, and consumption of these representations occur in a transnational, intertextual field. Furthermore, representations of the erotic in postcolonial India frequently provoke discourses of the defense of "Indian" or national culture: notwithstanding older traditions of

erotics, contemporary representations are often associated with Westernization and are, therefore, deemed transgressive. Nowhere is this association
stronger than with reference to women's erotic desire.

DANGEROUS DESIRES

I first learned of the conjunction between erotic desire and the desire to
consume, what I term "commodity affect," through my fieldwork in India.[11]
Several observers have pointed to the eroticization of representations of
commodities; hence, there is nothing new about the argument that desire
is cathected onto objects. Commodity affect, as I define it, ranges from the
desire to consume a particular object, the desire to acquire it, to the desire to
display it. More importantly, desire in commodity affect pertains not just to
the pleasure of acquiring a commodity, but also to the pleasures of gazing
upon it—what Louisa Schein terms browsing the commodity space (1999).
But beyond gazing upon commodities, it was the *yearning* for commodities
that appeared laced with erotics. Significantly, the lower-middle-class and
working-class women I worked with could not afford to purchase most of
the commodities they so lovingly viewed in ads and in shop windows. Their
yearning for these commodities was itself a source of pleasure, a pleasure
not dissimilar to erotic yearning.

The eroticization of the commodity needs to be placed in the larger context of commodity aesthetics. Commodity aesthetics shape not only our
sense of visuality but, also, our "sensual understanding" of the material
world (Haug 1986 [1971]: 8). In addition, commodities might themselves be
cathected with libidinal desire such that "a whole range of commodities can
be seen casting flirtatious glances at the buyers, in an exact imitation of or
even surpassing the buyers' own glances, which they use in courting their
human objects of affection" (19). Thus, even though a majority of men and
women I worked with could not always afford to buy all the commodities
they so ardently desired, they were, nevertheless, interpellated by commodity aesthetics in terms of their desire to desire them, gaze upon them, and
consume them.

Let me now describe how one woman represented her daughter-in-law's
desires for commodities. This woman's discourses of commodity desire are
mediated by her relationship with her daughter-in-law and, therefore, by
their respective positions in the politics of the family. They are also mediated by their caste and class positions and, thus, need to be situated in a
broader sociohistorical context. The possibility of acquiring consumer goods
presented some lower-caste individuals and families with potential access to
a middle-class lifestyle. Although acquiring such a lifestyle did not, by any
means, enable them to transcend their caste position, to a limited extent it
enabled an apparent realignment of caste and class. For Omvati's family, and

many others like it, the consumption of commodities became an especially fraught marker of their struggles for upward mobility.

Omvati was in her mid-fifties when I first interviewed her in 1992, and her household was one of the few lower-caste ones in their neighborhood. She lived with her son Satish, daughter-in-law Radha, and their four-year-old son, Sonu. Satish worked as a clerk in a government office, and Radha was employed as a salesperson in a government-run fabric store. Omvati was extremely proud that her son was the first in their extended family to have received a college degree and, more importantly, to hold a government job. For Omvati, as much as for Radha, modernity was indexed not only by Radha's college education but, equally, by her fashionable clothes. The entire family was acutely conscious of two harsh social facts: one, that their struggles to achieve middle-class status were only just beginning and, two, that their aspirations to middle-classness were viewed with considerable resentment by their (largely) upper-caste and middle-caste neighbors.

When I first met them, Radha was in an advanced stage of pregnancy and Omvati was very happy at the prospect of having another grandchild. At the same time, it was clear to me that Omvati resented Radha's closeness to Satish. Omvati often commented sarcastically on Radha's "obsession" with adorning herself and about the couple going out together in the evenings to the movies or to the nearby bazaar.[12] She commented that Radha was "greedy," but most of the time, it wasn't clear to me if she was referring to Radha's "greed" for commodities or for her husband. Omvati frequently complained that "city girls" were "different" from girls in her village: city girls like Radha were independent, ambitious, and always hankered after "more." "They want too much," she said, "and that is dangerous." I got the distinct impression that, in Omvati's discourse, the dangers of erotic desire were conflated with women's desires for commodities. This impression was confirmed in my subsequent interactions with her and Radha.

Omvati hinted at the relation between erotic desire and desires for commodities several times. She complained: "I think these days women want too much. They want everything. It is dangerous to always want all the time. What will happen to the family if women always want more and more?" Frequently in my interactions with the family, I would get an acute sense that when Omvati complained to me about Radha's "greed," she was not merely talking about Radha's desire for commodities. This was confirmed when, on another occasion, Omvati repeated, "Girls these days, especially city girls, want everything." When I pushed her to clarify what she meant, she replied: "They want more things. They always want to have, have, have. But they also want a lot from their husbands." In Omvati's discourse, Radha was emblematic of the urban, modern Indian woman whose dangerous desires articulate the co-implication of erotic desire and the yearning for commodities.

Omvati was not the only one to suggest the mutual imbrication of erotics and the yearning for commodities. Sunita, another young, lower-middle-class woman, compared her "feelings" for commodities with love. Sunita, who was unmarried, rarely went shopping. But she enjoyed watching ads on TV and going to the nearby market to window-shop. One day, I asked how she felt about looking at ads and shop windows even when she knew she couldn't afford to buy the commodities being advertised. She responded that her longing for these goods was like unrequited love. Using language that reminded me of a dialogue from a Hindi film, she said:

> It's like when you love someone [*jab kissise mohabbat ho jati hai*] and they don't love you back. You don't stop loving that person. You get happiness from looking at them, and from knowing they are there. It is like that. It's nice to look at these new things that have come into the market. We can't afford them. We may never be able to afford them. But who knows. And in any case, what is wrong in wondering?

According to Slavoj Žižek, fantasy provides the coordinates or frame for desire: "Through fantasy we learn to desire" (1989: 118). Through wondering or (in my terms) fantasizing, Sunita learned to desire. The fantasies of women like Sunita were engendered not just by the desires to acquire commodities, but also by their experiences of longing and deprivation. At the same time, women like Radha and Sunita seemed to obtain a bittersweet pleasure from their desire for commodities, from what Schein has termed the desire to desire (1999: 366, 369). The desires evoked by commodities were at once real and phantasmic, desires which were impossible to fulfill "within the parameters of sociality [the 'symbolic' in Lacanian terminology, capitalism in Marxian]" (Allison 1996: 27) There seemed to be a pleasure in imagining, in fantasizing about, the kinds of lives that might be possible if one owned these commodities. This pleasure was like the bittersweet pleasure of falling in love even when one knew that it was unrequited.

While most of the other examples in this paper are about women, it is essential that we do not attribute consumerist desires solely to them: the most casual observations of households and markets in urban India will attest to the fact that men shared equally, if not more, in these longings for commodities. Almost all the men that I met in the course of my fieldwork aspired to own at least some of the commodities advertised on television, such as color television sets, VCRs, automobiles and, especially in the case of younger men, fashionable clothes. Yet, significantly, apart from some concerns about how consumerism was preventing families from saving money, there did not seem to be a moralistic discourse about how *men's* consumer habits might be undermining "Indian culture" or "tradition." In contrast, women's desires for commodities were more likely to be perceived as a threat to the moral (and not just financial) welfare of the family, or as indicative of an attrition of "traditional" values under the onslaught of transnational mass media. Even those men who coveted the latest VCR or scooter would complain to me, without the least irony or self-consciousness, of how the extravagant habits of their wives and daughters were not only driving them to bankruptcy but, more pertinent to my argument here, also encouraging them to adopt "Western" or "foreign" lifestyles and aspirations and therefore threatening to erode their "tradition."

Also, let us not forget that the yearning for commodities implicated women in more ways than one. In some cases, the febrile consumerism of the middle and lower-middle classes led to a rise in demands for increasingly ostentatious dowries. Consequently, young brides were especially vulnerable to being harassed for dowries. Almost all of the lower-middle-class men and women whom I interviewed, in particular those with daughters of marriageable age, expressed intense anxieties about the kinds of dowries that they would be expected to provide, and many young women were terrified about the kind of treatment that they would receive if their in-laws were dissatisfied with the dowries that they brought with them when they got married. As noted by V. Geetha, "It is not accidental that dowry demands are never simply that: they inscribe themselves literally and metaphorically on the wifely body. They constitute this body as a thing, which may be discarded if it cannot yield its essential 'use' value" (1998: 314). For many of the women with whom I did fieldwork, on the other side of the pleasures of yearning for commodities lay a sinister nexus between consumerist desire, avarice, and the gendered body.

TRANSNATIONALISM, COMMODITY EROTICS, AND THE INTERTEXTUAL FIELD

At the time when I did the fieldwork for this project, the markets and streets of urban and semi-urban Indian centers presented many examples of the visual density of transnational public culture, exemplifying what Appadurai and Breckenridge have described as, an "interocular field . . . structured so that each site or setting for the socializing or regulating of the public gaze is to some degree affected by the experience of the other sites" (1995: 12). This interocular field is also inter*textual*, and was constituted by texts ranging from advertisements and billboards dominating cityscapes and the novels and magazines conspicuously displayed in kiosks and newspaper stands in markets, railway stations, and bus stands; to the proliferation of television channels now available for people to watch in the privacy of their homes; and, of course, the ubiquitous persistence of popular cinema.

As Haug points out, in its widest sense, the aesthetics of a commodity frequently become detached from the object itself (1986: 17). In late-twentieth-century India, representations of commodities were everywhere. In addition, after the 1990s, the intertextual field constituted by transnational media was simultaneously saturated with representations of erotics. This intertextual field was refracted by the heightened presence of globalized capital and transnational media. The 1980s were dominated by a significant shift in the government's economic policy from capital goods investment to a consumer economy. This shift in investment was accompanied by the imposition of structural adjustment policies by the International Monetary Fund, which emphasized decreased social spending by the state and a relaxation of curbs on imports. The expansion of the middle classes and the rise in consumer spending correlated with (and accelerated after) the advent of transnational television in 1991.[13] The spectral presence of "the West" shaped many of the conflicts and debates that arose at this time about the definition of "Indianness" and the boundaries between the "East" and the "West."

EROTICIZING THE INTIMATE

If the introduction of transnational satellite television in 1991 led to far-reaching quantifiable changes in terms of the numbers of channels now available to viewers, it also precipitated a marked qualitative and discursive shift in television programming from an earlier emphasis on nationalist themes and "social messages" (the mainstay of state-owned TV from the mid-1980s to the early 1990s; cf. Mankekar 1999) to an explicit focus on the intimate. Many of the serials shown on transnational networks contained extremely conservative representations of gender and family, with many extolling the virtues of "traditional" (that is, extended) families. At the same time, the new preoccupation with the intimate entailed diverse representations of the erotic unprecedented on Indian television (see also John 1998: 368). The programs of the early 1990s displayed a new fascination with erotic relationships, particularly marital, premarital, and extramarital relationships, and contained new and varied representations of erotics. These programs included serials (for instance, *Tara* [Zee TV], *Shanti* [Star], and *Hasratein* [Zee TV]), sitcoms, talk shows (such as *Purush Kshetra* and *The Priya Tendulkar Show* [both El TV]), made-for-TV films and miniseries, music programs (many of which were based on songs from Indian films), Indianized versions of MTV, and television advertisements telecast on transnational networks but produced specifically for audiences in South Asia and its diasporas.

But for years now, popular films have provided opportunities for the public expression of erotics. Since the Indian film industry is so large and heterogeneous, let me focus on popular Hindi or Bollywood films. How were televisual representations of erotics different from those prevalent in popular Hindi film? As Rachel Dwyer points out, in Hindi films, erotic longing is frequently portrayed in terms of romance, and expressed through the use of song, fetishization, and metaphor (2000). Representations of erotics in Bollywood films have shifted over time. As one viewer pointed out to me, while in older Hindi films sexual desire tended to be portrayed rather elliptically (which, she claimed, accentuated rather than diffused their erotic power), more recent Hindi films, with songs like *Jumma Chumma de de* ("Give me, give me a kiss"; *Hum,* music director Laxmikant Pyarelal; lyrics Anand Bakshi) or *Choli ke Peeche kya hai* ("What lies beneath my blouse?" *Khalnayak;* music director Laxmikant Pyarelal, lyrics Anand Bakshi) were fairly explicit in their representation of erotic desire. Yet, despite the sometimes explicit display of erotics in song sequences, in terms of narrative focus, erotics in early 1990s Hindi films tended to be subordinated to and subsumed under romance (cf. Dwyer 2000).[14] In contrast, television programs in the early 1990s represented erotic desire in a relatively open-ended manner. Furthermore, the erotic constituted a *central* and *explicit* focus of many television programs.

For instance, Indi-pop music videos in the 1990s frequently focused on women's erotic desires. One popular Indi-pop music video, *Deewane deewane to deewane hain* (Shweta Shetty; Magnasound), has the heroine complaining about the number of men who wish to have sexual relationships with her. In a husky voice, pulsating with erotic desire, she humorously describes how, despite her turning them away, these "mad men" persist in their desire for her (*deewane deewane hi rahenge*). There is nothing coy or virginal about her—her clothing, her demeanor, and her voice are all strident with erotic desire; she turns down her lovers' amorous advances not to protect her virtue but because she is weary of their pursuit. The movements of her body, as she gyrates sensuously to the music, and her expressions, as she alternately arches her eyebrows in mock scorn or shrugs her shoulders as if to dismiss their ardor, emphasize that she wants to control when (not if) she will have sex with them. The video contains several close-ups of the men pursuing her, with the camera lingering voyeuristically (but also parodically) on their bare, buffed upper bodies. A series of frames focus on one of the men vainly flexing his muscles for our consumption. These shots target not just women in the audience but, through their evocation of homoerotic desire, men as well.

The closing frames of this video are particularly significant. Tired of turning away the "mad" men who are trying desperately to woo her, our heroine stands outside her boudoir inviting each of them in. As soon as the last man has entered the room, she locks the door from outside. The camera immediately takes us inside: we see the men bump into each other and discover they have been conned into believing that they will be able to make love with her. But they do not stay disappointed for too long for they discover an erotic interest in *each other.* We next see them enter into a collective, unmistakably sexual, embrace. The video ends with our heroine standing outside the room, smiling smugly, knowingly. She has been able to shake them off and deflect their erotic interest in her onto each other. While most televisual representations reinscribe erotics in heteronormative terms, music videos like *Deewane deewane to deewane hain* also contain an explicit homoerotic content, and a few others portray men and women cross-dressing and/or displaying homoerotic desire.

Some of the television programs produced after the advent of transnational satellite networks reveal a complicated discursive terrain in which erotic desire was, at once, foregrounded and held in tension with familial obligation. Erotic desire was variably positioned vis-à-vis conjugality and these representations, in turn, had consequences for how the family was portrayed. As in Hindi films, most television serials kept alive the tension between the purportedly sacrosanct nature of the (extended) family and the conjugal unit (cf. John 1998 and Niranjana 1995). However, while the conflict between conjugal desire and duties toward the extended family is hardly new (it is, in fact, the subject of innumerable folk tales, songs, and novels; see, for instance, Raheja and Gold 1994), television programs of the 1990s exhibited an increased visibility of conjugality. As I learned from my fieldwork, this heightened visibility of conjugality articulated with the tension many of my informants experienced between conjugal desire and obligations and duties toward the extended family (cf. John 1998): several of my informants spoke explicitly of how the "new" emphasis on the married couple threatened to tear the "traditional" joint family asunder.

However, erotic desire on television was not confined to the conjugal relationship. In a hegemonic context where erotic desire was presumably contained within the confines of heterosexual marriage, what did televisual representations of erotic desire outside or before marriage signify? In many serials and talk shows in the early 1990s, women were portrayed engaging in premarital and extramarital affairs, bearing illegitimate children, seducing younger men, and defying parental restrictions by pursuing erotic desire and—unlike cinematic representations of erotically assertive women—these women were represented not as hyper-Westernized vamps but as "modern Indian women."[15] For instance, Savitri, the heroine of a popular television serial *Hasratein* (Zee TV), was portrayed as a modern woman who is a partner in a public relations company. The serial's central story line focuses on Savitri's fifteen-year relationship with a man who is married and has another family. Savitri, or Savi as she is known in the serial, and her lover live together and have a child. A successful, upper-middle-class professional, she is supremely self-confident as she advances in her career. Most of my lower-middle-class and working-class informants disapprove of Savi. But, as several of them insisted, she remained quintessentially "Indian" in her devotion to her children and in her loyalty to her husband and his parents.[16] *Hasratein* ends on a highly ambivalent note. Savi's lover is injured in a car accident and loses his memory. His wife and parents take care of him and convince him that they are his (primary) family. He remembers only fragments of his life with Savi, and cannot recognize their daughter. When he fails to regain his health and memory, his wife decides to take him abroad for treatment. In the end, Savi and her daughter are left alone. Savi is clearly punished for pursuing erotic desire, that too for a married man. Yet, she is represented with tremendous sympathy. She is always portrayed as elegantly yet modestly dressed (she is frequently portrayed in "traditional" Indian clothes); she is soft-spoken and performs all the conventional duties of a wife and mother; she is dignified and respectful but doesn't hesitate to fight for her rights.

Savi's portrayal is noteworthy for several reasons. Although her pursuit of erotic desire in this serial is not represented without ambivalence (she does suffer for her transgressions), she is represented as a mature and dignified woman (rather than as immature or promiscuous). Second, in narratives like *Hasratein,* the pursuit of erotic pleasure becomes the hallmark of a particular kind of woman: upper-class, usually professional—but still "Indian" in her loyalty to her family and to other "traditional" customs and conventions. While *Hasratein* was, by no means, the norm, this serial, along with others such as *Tara, Shanti,* and *Swabhimaan,* revealed ambivalent and shifting discourses of Indian Womanhood in which women struggled to juggle their responsibilities and duties to their families vis-à-vis their pursuit of erotic pleasure.

Women viewers' reactions to these representations spoke volumes—not of their own erotic desires per se, but about the changing configurations of gender and nation that occurred in late-twentieth-century India. In most cases, these reconfigurations were refracted by class. Many of the lower-middle-class and working-class women I worked with were quick to point out that most of the women pursuing erotic pleasure on television were upper-middle-class or upper-class, with successful careers and financial independence. At the same time, several of the women I interviewed argued that these women's stories revealed how "Indian culture" was changing. While some hastened to add that these were not changes that they wanted to institute in their own lives, they believed nonetheless that "Indian culture" was being transformed, and these TV heroines were harbingers of other changes that would follow, such as the break-up of families, teen pregnancies, and so on. As one lower-middle-class woman pointed out to me, the sexual freedom recent heroines like Tara and Svetlana enjoyed was enabled by their financial independence. She insisted that it fell to the middle classes to "protect" their culture and their values (*apni sabhyata, apne sanskar ki raksha madhya varg ke logon ko hi karni hai*). Like several other informants, this woman claimed that most "rich people," the upper classes, had been "contaminated" by Westernization, in particular, by their access to Western education and, in some cases, their ability to travel abroad. In general, for many of my Hindu informants (of different castes), one way to retain ties with "Indian culture" was by watching the televising of Hindu epics (see Gillespie 1995; Mankekar 1999; Rajagopal 2001).

Several others, who were highly critical of representations of erotics on television, responded to them with anger and defensiveness. They often reacted by appropriating Hindu nationalist discourses of national purity in which Indian culture was conflated with a pristine Hindu culture. For instance, one upper-caste and lower-middle-class woman said that she felt that

"when the winds of change blow" it is important to "return to our roots."
When pushed to clarify how one might return to one's "roots" and what
these "roots" were, she explained it in terms of a pristine Hindu culture (see
also, Oza 2001 and Rajagopal 2001). These discourses about roots and Indian
culture were aligned with Hindu nationalist discourses about the recupera-
tion of a "glorious Hindu" culture as national culture that were predicated
on excluding, sometimes eliminating, Other (Islamic, Christian, and lower-
caste) cultures.

CONCLUSION

The mass consumption of texts and commodities made possible by the advent of transnational television in the 1990s had consequences not only for
viewers' imagination of erotics and intimacy but, perhaps, also for their perspectives on upward mobility, and affiliations to community. Unlike what
Schein found in China (1999), where the desire to desire may be interpreted
as a critique of the state, in India the desire to desire was incited and en-
dorsed by uneasy alliances between the state, domestic industry, and multinational capital. Arvind Rajagopal has pointed out that "through the genre
of advertising, television promotes a libidinal economy that helps secure and
reproduce the physical economy and is interwoven with it" (1999: 58). Transnational television played a crucial role in the yoking of erotic and commodity desire not only through the advertisements it telecast but, equally
importantly, through a range of other programs, such as talk shows, serials,
and MTV-inspired music programs.

It is important to note that not all my informants derived pleasure from
or were even comfortable with televisual representations of women as erotic
subjects.[17] Many responded by increasing their surveillance of family members and neighbors; still others, by aligning themselves with Hindu-nation-
alist and exclusionary discourses of cultural purity and national culture. In
some instances, representations of erotics in public culture resulted in the
reification of the boundaries between Indian and "Western" culture. When
perceived as foreign or Western in orientation or origin, representations
of erotics were deemed extremely threatening to the purported purity of
national culture—as indicated by the controversies surrounding the Miss
World pageant in Bangalore in December 1996 (see Oza 2001), and the protests against the portrayal of a lesbian relationship between the heroines of
Deepa Mehta's film Fire (Gopinath 2005 and Patel 2004). In the public protests
surrounding both these controversies, transnational television, multinational capital, and the globalization of the Indian economy were all conceived
as threats to the purity of Indian culture. In these protests, Indian culture
was reified, and its difference from "Western" culture essentialized and fe-

tishized. Erotics became the terrain on which these reifications of Indianness took place.

While it has *not* been my intent to describe "the sexual lives of [urban] Indians," I have examined how the construction and evocation of erotic pleasure provides us with a lens to trace the contours of a sociohistorical conjuncture. I was witness to the twinning of desire and deprivation for many of the men and women whom I got to know during my fieldwork. This combination of desire and deprivation was built into the very structure of commodity capitalism and the specific forms it acquired in late-twentieth-century India.[18] The erotic was deeply enmeshed in psychic and structural configurations of longing, pleasure, and power, and was part of the constitution of subjectivity along axes of caste, class, gender, and family position. Erotics constituted a force-field of power, pleasure, and danger through its articulation of desires and anxieties pertaining to upward mobility, class, modernity, and tradition. At stake in these desires and anxieties was not only the reconfiguration of hierarchies of gender, caste, and class within India, but the very definition of Indian culture.

ACKNOWLEDGMENTS

This paper is a drastically redacted version of my article "Dangerous Desires: Television and Erotics in Late-Twentieth Century India," *Journal of Asian Studies* 63, no. 2 (May 2004): 403–31. I thank Anne Allison, Tom Boellstorff, Steve Caton, Lawrence Cohen, Vasudha Dalmia, Akhil Gupta, Charu Gupta, Sarah Jain, Sudipta Kaviraj, Arthur Kleinman, Matthew Korhman, Francesca Orsini, Renato Rosaldo, Kumkum Sangari, Louisa Schein, Mary Steedly, Stanley Tambiah, Barbara Voss, Ann Waltner, and Woody Watson for their comments, not all of which I have been able to adopt. I would like to thank Aditya Behl for his generous and patient assistance regarding representations of the erotic in sufi and Urdu literature. Rozita Dimova, Manishita Dass, and Robert Rollings provided insightful suggestions and excellent research assistance. Last but not least, I remain indebted to the men and women with whom I conduct my fieldwork for their invaluable insights and generosity.

NOTES

1. Although representations of erotics continue to be enormously popular, the late 1990s and early 2000s (coinciding, not surprisingly, with the consolidation of the stronghold of the Hindu nationalist Bharatiya Janata Party over both the state and civil society) have also seen a profusion of television serials that valorize "family values," in particular, the virtues of the Hindu joint family. However, far from replacing or displacing the earlier emphasis on erotics, these new serials may be interpreted, in part, as a backlash against them and, more importantly, as articulations of ongoing debates about the cultural implications of transnational media.

2. Perhaps my experience would have been different had I chosen to interview rural women on sex and erotics; cf. Raheja and Gold 1994.

3. Compare to V. Geetha's discussion of the covert and indirect expression of women's erotic desires (and frustrations) (1998).

4. As Manderson and Jolly posit with respect to cross-cultural studies of sexuality, erotic desire is most fruitfully analyzed in terms of cultural encounters and "confluences" (1997).

5. The scholarship on erotics in Indian literature, myth, and popular culture is voluminous. See, for instance, Bannerjee 1989; Bhattacharya 1975; Doniger 1996; Kakar 1989; Nandy 1980; and Rege 1996. On the politics of sexuality in colonial and nationalist contexts, see Das 1996; Sinha 1997; Srinivasan 1985; Thapan 1997; Uberoi 1996.

6. It appears to be difficult to date the Natyashastra. Dimock et al. date it to before the sixth or seventh centuries CE (1974).

7. For more information on erotics within Sanskritic rasa theory, see Dimock et al. 1974 and L. Siegel 1978. On the elaborate classification of love in the Gitagovinda, see L. Siegel 1978, especially pages 42–57. On Tamil akam poetry, in which "the central relationship is that of man and woman," see Dimock et al. 1974: 172 and Ramanujan 1973: 170–81. On the erotic components of bhakti poetry, see Lele 1981.

8. See Schimmel 1975, especially pages 287–89.

9. See Dwyer 2000 and Manuel 1993.

10. The relationship between same-sex erotics and the formation of gay and lesbian identities in modern India has been a site of controversy among analysts of popular culture, queer theorists, and gay and lesbian activists in India. Scholars such as Dwyer have argued that "[i]n India, some people enjoy same-sex sexual activity without wishing to claim a gay or lesbian or even bisexual identity; it is simply that they have sex with someone of the same sex but they expect to marry and live in a heterosexual relationship" (2000: 51–52), thus drawing a distinction between same-sex desire and the formation of gay and lesbian identities. Another perspective is offered by Giti Thadani, who points to the ways in which "heteropatriarchal" discourses have rendered gay and lesbian desire so invisible as to have foreclosed the articulation (until very recently) of gay and lesbian identities (1996). The formation of gay and lesbian identities is, therefore, mediated by a politics of (in)visibility and (il)legibility. In this regard, the heteronormativity of the representations I analyze in this paper may serve to reinforce the hegemonic invisibility and illegibility of gay and lesbian identities.

Nevertheless, there is a burgeoning gay and lesbian movement in India. See Reddy in this volume, Cohen 1995, G. Patel 1998, and Thadani 1996 on same-sex and gay and lesbian erotics in contemporary India.

11. See Deleuze and Guattari 1983 on affect.

12. Omvati's discomfort with the relationship between her son and daughter-in-law is not unusual in the context of the politics of extended families in North India (see, for instance, Raheja and Gold's discussion of the tensions surrounding conjugality in rural North India [1994]). However, it also articulated with the new visibility of conjugality in the public sphere: I will return to this theme later in the paper.

13. See Mankekar 2004 on discourses surrounding consumer spending in the early 1990s.

14. In most Hindi films erotic desire continues to be subsumed within discourses of romance, and premarital and extramarital erotic relations continue to be depicted as transgressive. Some notable examples of such films are *Salaam Namaste, Corporate* (V One Entertainment, 2006), *Hum Tum,* and *Kabhi Alvida Naa Kehna* (Dharma Productions, 2006).

15. In some Hindi films, for instance, *Drishti* (1991; directed by Govind Nihalani) or *Paroma* (1985; directed by Aparna Sen), which narrate the erotic awakening of married women through extramarital relationships, women are severely punished for pursuing erotic pleasure. It is also important to note that these films are not conventional Bollywood films, but are "crossover" films made by directors who have established their reputations in "middle cinema."

16. This is corroborated by researchers Page and Crawley, who report that middle-class students in Ahmedabad did not find Savi to be "bold." According to Page and Crawley, asked whether *Hasratein* was bold, one student replied: "It is bold, but Savitri does not act bold. She is like a traditional wife"; another responded: "She respects everyone and teaches me to respect everyone" (2001: 166).

17. Cf. Giddens's reminder that sexuality might also be "worrying, disturbing, fraught with tensions" (1992: 177).

18. I wish to thank Sudipta Kaviraj and Kumkum Sangari for their help with clarifying the ideas presented in this paragraph.

31

A Diaspora Ramayana in Southall

Paula Richman

Editor's note: The Ramayana is one of Hinduism's oldest and best-loved epic stories. It probably began even as early as 500 BCE as an oral story, but over the centuries has been retold, rewritten, televised, and acted out (theatrical versions are called Ramlila) in many different languages in many different versions. Richman's article presents us with one such version, what might be called a "postcolonial" version. The story, in briefest synopsis, goes something like this: The king of Ayodhya is childless, but makes a sacrifice from which are born three sons, each to a different wife. Rama is the eldest. Because of jealousy and strife in the palace, Rama's brother Bharata is named king upon their father's death, and Rama—the rightful heir to the throne—is sent into a fourteen-year exile. With him go his wife, Sita, and his loyal youngest brother, Lakshmana. While in exile, Rama defeats and banishes many evil creatures. Finally, with the aid of his monkey friend Hanuman, Rama vanquishes even the evil Ravana, a many-headed demon king who would wreak havoc in the universe and who has lusted after and finally kidnapped Sita. Having saved the kingdom and Sita from the demons, and having lived out his exile, Rama returns triumphantly to Ayodhya, where he reigns as a just and dharmic king. In a controversial episode, not part of all versions, Rama fears that Sita's chastity and purity may have been sullied by Ravana. Doubting Sita, unjustly, he allows her to jump into a fire. But she emerges unscathed—so pure is she—and they rule together as king and queen.

A longer version of this essay originally appeared in the *Journal of the American Academy of Religion* 67, no. 1 (Winter 1999). Reprinted with permission.

What happens when the Ramlila travels abroad? On 19 October 1979, a feminist group of South Asian and African Caribbean women in Southall, Greater London, staged a Ramlila that reflects a precise moment in the history of South Asian immigration to the United Kingdom. The women who produced the play, members of the Southall Black Sisters (SBS),[1] did so to help defray legal costs of friends arrested when they participated in a protest against the neo-Nazi National Front Party. SBS incorporated into their rendition of the Ramlila humorous commentary with a topical slant. In doing so, they linked events portrayed in the performance to the racism, labor conditions, electoral politics, and sexism they encountered in everyday life.

Like traditional Ramlilas, the performance ended with the death of Ravana, king of the Demons, but the SBS Ravana was unique. He sported a huge mask composed of ten heads, upon each of which was drawn a person or symbol that represented an aspect of immigrant life in Britain. Some heads bore pictures of conservative political leaders, while others carried symbols of racism, such as the insignia of the British riot police. The Ramlila performance culminated with fireworks to celebrate the destruction of Ravana, to the accompaniment of cheers from the audience. The Ramlila's dramatic structure, casting practices, and interpretation of Ravana tell us a great deal about the historical moment of its performance.

They also reveal some broader insights about how a religious text can migrate from South Asia to Britain, retain its formal contours, express diverse aspects of the diaspora experience, and continue to be part of the multifaceted Ramayana tradition. SBS produced a Ramlila of great creativity, reflecting in unique ways the specific experiences of those onstage and many of those in the audience, but it also contains elements that are in consonance with what recent scholarship has revealed about the Ramayana tradition in South Asia. In SBS's incorporation of women's perspectives, it echoes aspects of women's folk-song traditions in South Asia (Narayana Rao 1991; Nilsson 2000). Its inclusion of topical humor is part of a long tradition of linking improvisatory commentary to local events (e.g., Blackburn 1996; GoldbergBelle 1989). Its skillful use of multiple frames enables characters to provide metanarrative about themselves and the story (Hess 1993, 2000; Shulman 2000). In short, the SBS created a Ramlila in keeping with long-established trends within Ramayana tradition.

In the past, Western and Indian scholars have paid most attention to authoritative tellings of Ramkatha (Rama's story), especially the one attributed to Valmiki (Goldman 1984: 1, 6; Pollock 1993: 263). More recently, however, scholars have increasingly turned their attention to oral renditions (Blackburn 1996), commentarial concerns (Hess 2000), and transformations shaped by print culture (Narayana Rao 2000). Such studies have demonstrated the range, diversity, and vitality of nondominant tellings of Ramkatha. A close examination of the SBS Ramlila reveals a great deal about the capaciousness of the Ramayana tradition: the SBS has recounted and recast the story in re-lation to their locality, its social structures of dominance, and their concerns about gender.

Recent research has highlighted how many tellings of Rama's story ques-tion hierarchies of power (e.g., Freeman 2000; Lutgendorf 2000; Richman 1991; R. Lamb 1991). Interrogation of gendered representation proves par-ticularly salient in the SBS Ramlila. Unique in its casting practices, its mix of Punjabi and English, and its vision of Ravana, the SBS Ramlila lies squarely in the midst of a Ramayana tradition that is diverse, inventive, and open to questions.

MIGRATION AND SBS

Most early South Asian immigrants to Southall left the subcontinent soon after Partition (1947), arriving in Greater London in the late 1950s. Primarily Sikhs or Hindus and mainly Punjabi speakers, many came from the peas-ant proprietor class whose members had lost land, savings, and security through the dislocation that accompanied Partition. Upon arrival most were able to obtain jobs only at factories in or near Southall, at low pay, with long hours and few benefits (Brah 1996; Fryer 1984; Visram 1986; Dhanjal 1976; Lee 1972). In the late 1960s and early 1970s, a new group of South Asians from East Africa arrived in Southall, bringing with them their middle-class urban experience as well as skills as owners of small businesses, enriching the Southall community in many ways (Bhachu 1985; Brah 1996; Institute of Race Relations 1981). Soon after their arrival, however, immigration came under explicit attack by the National Front (NF), a party that presented itself as protecting the "racial purity" of England (Taylor 1978; Hanna 1974; Nu-gent 1976).

The NF's announcement that it would hold an election meeting on 23 April 1979, in Southall, was the first in a set of events leading to the SBS Ramlila. Just two days before the planned meeting, an NF leader called upon members to emulate the heroes of H. G. Wells's *The Time Machine* and de-feat "dark-skinned, hook-nosed dwarfs" (Dummett 1980: 190). Not surpris-ingly, a large group of protesters from Southall and elsewhere in the country showed up to contest the views of the NF. The presence of the police that day was large as well, with highly visible representation from the Special Patrol Group police, a corps of crack riot police. In the violence that ensued during the meeting and protest, hundreds of protesters were injured, one man died, and about seven hundred were arrested. While "mainstream" English-language newspapers such as the *Daily Telegraph* reported the event with the headline "Asian Fury at Election Meeting" and the subheading "40 Police Hurt in Protest over National Front" (24 May 1979), a local newspaper, *Punjab Times*, argued that people of Southall had been reduced to "the status of a British Imperial Colony from that of a town of free citizens" (1 May 1979).

In the aftermath of the event, SBS met to discuss how they should respond. The group contained women of South Asian descent born in Britain, women with South Asian parents who had grown up in East Africa, and women of African Caribbean descent born in Britain or the Caribbean. The Asian community in Southall was larger than the African Caribbean one at that time, and the groups had different pre-immigration histories. Yet SBS women found that their roots in colonized countries and their current experience of racism and sexism in Britain gave them many shared experiences, issues, and hopes.[2] The founding members of SBS ranged from teenage schoolgirls to young postgraduates and working women.

Earlier, SBS had undertaken a series of community projects to improve the lives of girls and women in Southall and had worked with other organizations to combat racism in Greater London. They also staffed an advice center on Saturdays at the Southall Rights Building, volunteering their time to give information about legal issues and immigration laws, as well as providing support to women experiencing difficulties in their families or relationships. Heretofore, male elders and community leaders within the South Asian community had counseled wives to use strategies of avoidance and compliance when dealing with domestic violence and other gender-related issues. SBS felt that women needed advice from other women, especially ones without a vested interest in maintaining the status quo within families.

Some male members of the Southall community greeted the formation of SBS with suspicion. A few saw SBS as troublemakers who threatened the stability of the family structure, especially because they helped women who fled their homes because of domestic violence. Other men felt that the South Asian community should speak as a single group, and SBS would undermine that. Some worried this new group might later siphon funds away from established social service organizations or draw support away from such groups as the Southall Youth Movement, founded in 1976 to combat racist attacks. Nonetheless, SBS-initiated projects such as picketing the "Miss Southall" beauty contest won them support in the larger community. Feminist goals in this case had paralleled those of some male-dominated groups who had earlier been suspicious of SBS. After the events on 23 April in Southall, SBS chose a Ramlila as their means to express their solidarity with those arrested and with the larger Southall community.

CONCEPTUALIZING A RAMLILA

Among the stories that hold a special place in South Asian culture, SBS chose Ramkatha because its narrative resources helped them to dramatize their ideal relationship to their community and to express their defiance of British racism. Rama and Sita show their deep commitment to virtue when they save the reputation of Rama's father for truthfulness by going into forest exile. During their stay there, the demon Ravana tricks Rama into leaving Sita alone and then abducts her. After an extended search Rama finds Sita, defeats Ravana in battle, and rescues his wife. This narrative has long been dramatized in South Asia.

Several factors shaped the SBS decision to perform a Ramlila in response to the incidents of 23 April 1979. First, as an anti-racist group, they sought some form of symbolic action that would make visible their outrage about police brutality against the black population of Southall. A benefit performance whose proceeds would be donated to the Southall Legal Defense Fund, an organization helping to defray the legal costs of those charged in the 23 April conflict, seemed an appropriate project. Although the SBS realized that the performance might not raise a large amount of money, they viewed the benefit both as a material contribution and as an expression of solidarity.

Second, they wanted to undertake a project that would demonstrate publicly their connection to the cultural traditions of their community, as understood by their elders. Such an event would show that criticisms of SBS as divisive to the community were unwarranted. SBS chose a Ramlila because of its link with Divali, a major South Asian festival of lights long popular in north India, in which Hindus commemorated the destruction of a demon.[3] Before communalism in India became as pronounced as it did later, lighting lamps and sharing sweets with one's Hindu and non-Hindu neighbors was common at Divali in many parts of the subcontinent. SBS chose a Ramlila at Divali because of its traditional connections with unity, celebration, and good fortune.

Third, the story of Ravana's destruction resonated strongly with recent events. Ramlila celebrates the victory of good over evil, dramatizing a tale of oppressive rule destroyed by the perseverance of those committed to virtue. At a symbolic level, it could be seen as paralleling Southall resistance to abuse from the British state, and might comfort those recovering from the physical and psychological wounds of policy brutality in April.

Finally, the shared feminist convictions of members of SBS challenged them to find an appropriate way to depict the relationship between Rama and his utterly devoted wife Sita. In most well-known tellings of the story, the portrayal of Sita could be seen as reinforcing patriarchal views of gender. SBS members did not want to stage a play that could be seen as contradicting the feminist tenets of SBS. On the other hand, if they found an appropriate way to incorporate their critical views into the play, it could provide them with an opportunity to share their political convictions with members of their community. At that time, they were the only inside group that could mount a critique of sexist attitudes to improve it, rather than attack it from the outside to disparage South Asian culture, as some racist groups had done.

Therefore, the SBS chose to stage a unique Ramlila that would combine cultural appreciation with cultural critique. Many South Asian members of SBS had participated in Ramlilas during their school years. The SBS decided to produce a Ramlila similar to such plays in general, but differing in ideological goals. This drama would question patriarchal attitudes in the community, but do so in a spirit of affection and celebration.

Immediately complex issues surfaced. Several Marxist SBS members felt that supporting the project would affirm religious ideals (and according to classical Marxist thought, religion is the opiate of the masses, as well as epiphenomenal). Second, as one member asked, "What's the contribution of this play to the African Caribbean community?" The Ramayana was linked primarily with South Asian Hindu culture, so why should African Caribbeans or, indeed, other South Asian religious groups such as Sikhs and Muslims, see it as a meaningful drama for them?[4] In response, the group sought to mount a Ramlila that would strengthen and celebrate the entire Southall black community, and contest patriarchal ideologies at the same time. But this, pointed out another member of the group, might offend orthodox members of the community who would attend expecting a pious reiteration of the story. Would such a performance defeat the goal of bringing the community together? SBS wanted to create a thought-provoking Ramlila that would take into account these multiple concerns (Brah 1988).

Financial and temporal limitations contributed to the improvisational nature of the production. The SBS had virtually no funding and exactly three weeks to prepare the drama to be staged on Friday, 19 October 1979. SBS received help from many people, including the Indian Workers Association, which loaned them a venue; an Indian classical music teacher who volunteered to provide musical accompaniment to enhance the mood of the scenes; and an Indian restaurant in Southall that provided free sweets to distribute to members of the audience. Samosas, fried dumplings stuffed with spicy potato filling, were donated for sale at the performance as a fundraiser. Several women donated old saris to be sewn into a stage curtain, while others lent jewelry and other props. Many women who were not SBS members helped set up the stage, put out chairs, distribute sweets, and sell tickets. The performance was publicized in local shops and by community groups, as well as some nationally based anti-racist groups. A small notice appeared in the *Southall Gazette* (19 October 1979).

The collaborative manner in which SBS wrote the script, in keeping with its principle of coalitional practices, led to a play whose emphases were intensely debated, critiqued, and revised before the performance. Perminder Dhillon, to whom primary responsibility fell for synthesizing the many ideas for the script, recounted in an interview with me the intensity and excitement of working through and with the many views taken into account in conceptualizing the play (1994 interview). The collaborative manner in which the play developed also meant that the SBS Ramlila represented the views of the group in a way that no performance put together by a single director could.

PERFORMING THE SBS RAMLILA

SBS told Rama's story in ways that would encourage members of the audience to question some widely accepted cultural assumptions about women, but would still contain elements that made the drama clearly recognizable as a Ramlila. The play included the familiar events in the story: Rama's birth, the exile to the forest, the abduction of Sita, and Rama's victory over Ravana. Although the narrative remained fairly standard, certain decisions about casting and framing devices introduced multiple perspectives into the drama.

In contrast to some Indian dramatic traditions where men play both female and male roles (because acting is considered disreputable for women),[5] in the SBS Ramlila women played all the parts. In addition, casting choices deliberately thwarted traditional expectations. For example, Sita was played by a tall Asian woman, while Rama was played by a short African Caribbean woman. This casting undercut notions that the story "belongs" to a single ethnic group. It also subverted a widely held belief that a "proper" wife must be shorter than her husband.

In a manner crucial to its critical edge, the SBS production included a storyteller and two jesters, who mediated between the events depicted and the audience: The storyteller would come onstage, give background for the upcoming scene, and begin to comment on its significance. As she did so, the two jesters would interrupt her, drawing the audience's attention to traditional sayings, pointing out topical parallels, or interrogating certain assumptions about women reflected in the scene. One jester, a South Asian woman fluent in both English and Punjabi, included well-known Punjabi expressions in her speeches. The other jester, an African Caribbean woman, found ways to translate those Punjabi phrases in her comments, mediating for audience members who did not know Punjabi. Both functioned to disrupt the familiar, easy flow of the Ramayana narrative and question stereotypical gender roles in the play.

For an example of how this structure worked, consider how SBS dealt with the birth of Rama and his brothers. After many childless years, Dasaratha performed a special sacrificial rite, as a result of which his three wives conceived and gave birth to male children. What a great celebration the king sponsored! At this moment the first jester said:

> Yes, it was like that when my brother was born—a great celebration and my family passed out *laddhus* [a round sweet made of brown sugar and butter]. But when I was born, they didn't celebrate. My mother said, *"Hi Veh Raba, soota mundiyan dha thaba."*

Immediately following the first jester's comments, the second one responded by paraphrasing the Punjabi comment in English, and adding her own economic analysis of the situation:

> She said to God, "Why don't you just throw me a bunch of boys?" Why such jubilation when the son is born, but not the daughter? She must have been worrying about the dowry to be paid for the marriage of a daughter.

The interchange between jesters directs the listeners' attention to the socioeconomic forces that immediately begin to shape parents' attitudes toward their children: It was not a daughter per se that was disagreeable; instead it was the custom of giving dowry for a bride, and thus commodifying her, that allowed such fears about and responses to the birth of daughters to continue.

One performer recalled that her mother brought to the play a grandmother and some elderly aunts who spoke Punjabi and knew little English. They were used to sitting through community meetings conducted in English without understanding them, coming anyway in order to meet friends and feel part of their community. Until the first jester's comment, they had viewed the drama primarily as a pious reiteration of Lord Rama's greatness, enjoying the event in their own terms, as a religious holiday and a chance to socialize. Their perception of the Ramlila received confirmation as they entered the theater and received special Divali sweets. They responded to the first jester's idiomatic Punjabi comments with laughs of recognition; the play called attention to the greater value placed on male babies than female babies, a fact of life with which they were all too familiar. That women outnumbered men in the audience meant many of them had personal experience with the differing ways in which the birth of a girl or a boy was greeted.

The majority of those of South Asian descent who attended the SBS Ramlila spoke English. For example, one member of the cast recalled that her mother brought along not only pious older womenfolk but younger sisters, brothers, and cousins who were fluent in English as a result of their schooling. Thus the second jester's translation of the Punjabi phrase and the dialogue between the two jesters enhanced the process of questioning certain gender assumptions that might otherwise have been received without further reflection.

The jesters included pointedly topical comparisons to show that the relationships in the story were not only ones enacted in some mythic past, but echoed events in the daily life of the audience. In one scene, for example, Sita begged her husband to take her along on his forest exile, but he refused, claiming to her that life would be too harsh for her: her tender lotus-feet might get cut by thorns and bruised by rocks. Sita hit him in the shoulder with a thump and said, "I'm good enough to wear myself out doing all the housework in our home, but not good enough to go to the forest with you?" Submissively, Rama replied, "Whatever you say, my dear." His response parodied the way a "proper" wife is "supposed" to answer her husband's commands.

At another point, when the narrator enumerated the heavy duties that fall to a wife, a jester interrupted, saying, "Yeh, it's a bit like how hard the women at T'walls Factory work, isn't it?" Many South Asian women worked long hours at local factories, and then returned home to cook and clean house. The jester asked why women have to work a shift outside the home, and a shift inside the home as well. The scene also undermined the gender construct of a wife as a weak creature.

The Ramlila presented these topical comments humorously, in a non-threatening way, linking them to daily life by referring to familiar places. Among the actors and audience members whom I interviewed, it is this topical humor that has remained most sharply etched in people's memories of the Ramlila. Almost everyone remembered the funny asides of the jesters, a few repeating the Punjabi line quoted above. Several others recited word for word, as a high point of the performance, the line about Sita's tender lotus-feet and its irony; these women had to deal on an everyday basis with multiple pressures and dangerous work environments in factories, laundries, their homes, and during their journeys to and from work. They had little time to worry about their tender lotus-feet.

Members of the cast raised questions about notions of masculinity as well. In a scene set in the forest, for example, Rama's brother Lakshmana heard the calls of wild animals, cowered in fear, and then ran to hide behind Sita, who reassured him, "Don't worry, I'm here." This line would be particularly comic for regular Ramlila-goers because Lakshmana is usually portrayed as a fearless warrior, ready to attack anyone who poses the slightest threat to Rama, Sita, or the kingly lineage.

Toward the end of the Ramlila where Rama battles Ravana, the objects of critique shift from gender relations to the current electoral situation in Southall. As the brief program notes say, "Ravana is killed by Rama. Good wins over evil" (Southall Black Sisters 1979: 1). The interpretation of Ravana as Evil Incarnate determined the appearance of Ravana's mask, composed of ten different visual images. Several of the heads were enlarged photographs of specific people, including Enoch Powell, major figures in the NF, a local member of the Ealing council, and even Prime Minister Margaret Thatcher. Other heads represented oppression in more abstract form. For example, the hat worn by riot police was drawn on one head to stand for police brutality. A bobby's black hat over a drawing of a pig symbolized the policing to which the community was subject on a regular basis (Dhillon 1979). Another drawing represented the increasingly restrictive immigration laws that threatened to tear apart families and penalize those whose parents were not born in Britain. The symbolism of Ravana, therefore, encompassed crucial concerns not just of South Asian immigrant communities but of African Caribbean ones as well.

The practice of culminating the Ramlila by burning Ravana in effigy, accompanied by celebratory fireworks, is an ancient and venerable one, symbolizing the conquest of good over evil. In the SBS production, after Rama defeated Ravana, the storyteller told the audience, "I'll see you in the carpark, where we'll finish Ravana off." There SBS set off fireworks, much to the delight of the spectators. In this Ramlila, the destruction of Ravana's effigy symbolized the desire to end racism in Britain. This final message brought together the concerns of the varied members of the audience: Punjabi and English speakers, South Asians and African Caribbeans, people from Southall and anti-Nazi activists that came from afar. The fireworks were a celebratory moment, and they gestured toward a future when all people in Southall could live without fear, humiliation, or deprivation of their rights.

HERE AND THERE

Several of the original SBS members, speaking in the 1990s in interviews with me, look back on the 1979 Ramlila as a moment of singular unity. In the more than two decades since the performance, pan-minority unity has been harder to achieve. Increasing competition for council funding and housing, as well as tensions caused by the financial constraints of the Thatcher and Major years, have tended to put one community in competition with another at times (Baumann 1996: 60–71). Among children of South Asian descent who identify with the cultural heritage of their parents but have grown up in England, some community boundaries have become more clearly marked, at least partially due to political events in India, Pakistan, and Bangladesh. Indira Gandhi's decision to bring troops into the Sikh Golden Temple in Amritsar (1984), the subsequent assassination of Mrs. Gandhi, and the rioting that took the lives of hundreds of Sikhs split Hindus and Sikhs more strongly than ever before. The destruction of the Ramjanmabhumi/Babri Mosque in Ayodhya and the riots that developed in response to it in Pakistan and Bangladesh, as well as in India, tend to make it harder and harder for Hindus and Muslims to carry on coalitional politics. Events surrounding the publication of Salman Rushdie's *Satanic Verses* also took their toll (Asad 1993). Thus, current reflection on the SBS as a moment of unity raises intriguing questions about the notion of diaspora. How is unity in Britain tied to or separate from conceptions of unity in South Asia? Is diaspora less about "being in exile from home" and more about being tied to two places?

Finally, the SBS Ramlila raises intriguing questions about the nature of representation in the context of South Asian immigration. For example, one might ask whose "culture" does the SBS Ramlila represent? It cannot be equated purely with Hindu identity, since key members of the production were African Caribbeans and/or Marxists. Among the South Asians, both Sikhs and Hindus were involved. Nor could it be said to be an exact reflection of the entire Southall South Asian community, since the audience was made up primarily of women. Furthermore, it is possible that some orthodox Hindus might even find the performance "inauthentic" because the play did not linger on auspicious scenes for *darshan* of Lord Rama, as most pious Ramlilas do. Finally, one could not label it a pristine transportation of a particular Indian regional performance to Britain, since its performers used an eclectic style of script development and borrowed from a number of dramatic forms.

Rather than arguing that the SBS performance was not a "real" one, one must question the notion of a homogeneous Indian tradition transplanted to England. The Ramayana tradition has long encompassed both authoritative and oppositional tellings (Richman 2000). Authoritative tellings of Ramkatha such as those by Valmiki and Tulsidas tend to reaffirm the power of the king, the priest, and the male patriarchy. In contrast, the SBS self-consciously sought to avoid reaffirming such patriarchal norms. Their oppositional Ramlila suggests ways of overcoming sexism within their own community and racism within the wider British community. The SBS Ramlila represented the diversity of the nonwhite population in Southall. Its combination of cultural appreciation and cultural critique may mirror the ambiguities and contradictions of other South Asian diaspora communities as well.

ACKNOWLEDGMENTS

I thank Avtar Brah, Perminder Dhillon, Parita Mukta, and several other members of the original Southall Black Sisters, who graciously shared their time and memories with me and gave me suggestions for improving an earlier version of this paper. Leela Fernandez, Michael H. Fisher, and Lakshmi Holmstrom also made helpful comments. I alone am responsible for any errors.

A longer version of this essay, with extensive comparison between this and other women's Ramayanas, first appeared in the *Journal of the American Academy of Religion* 67, no. 1 (Winter 1999): 33–57, and was reprinted in a somewhat different form in *Questioning Ramayanas, A South Asian Tradition* (New Delhi: Oxford University Press, and Berkeley: University of California Press, 2000).

NOTES

1. Recently a group whose membership does not overlap with the original group of "Southall Black Sisters" (formed in 1978–79) also adopted the name "Southall Black Sisters." Throughout this article, I refer only to the original Southall Black Sisters.

2. Some comments on the "Black" in "Southall Black Sisters" are also in order here. A number of South Asians and African Caribbeans in Southall viewed themselves as part of a larger black identity, because of their shared history of colonialism

and the racist assumptions upon which it rested. The sense of black identity as a unifying force developed in the later 1970s and remained strong in the 1980s; many used the term "black" (and, in some British circles, continue to use it) self-consciously as a political term to indicate unity among various nonwhite minority groups fighting racism. The term "Asian" had been used to describe Asian immigrants in Kenya and Uganda. Although "Asian," when used to describe people of the Indian subcontinent, is more limited than "black," it still involves unity across boundaries, since it includes people of different nationalities (Indians, Pakistanis), religions (Hindus, Muslims, and Sikhs primarily), and classes (mostly lower and middle class).

3. Divali lasts for four or five days, depending upon the lunar calendar, and falls sometime in October or November each year. Until fairly recently Sikhs shared the celebration of Divali with Hindus, since Guru Amar Das had approved of it for Sikh congregations. In the years of South Asian immigration under discussion in this paper, Sikhs and Hindus in Southall did celebrate Divali together. After Mrs. Gandhi ordered the destruction of the Golden Temple in Amritsar, and then was assassinated by two Sikh bodyguards, the situation changed in Southall and elsewhere. Today, Hindus celebrate Divali and Sikhs celebrate the holiday as the day of Guru Hargobind's release from the Gwalior jail. See Nesbitt 1955.

4. Many Indians in the Caribbean did, however, celebrate Divali and perform Ramlilas. For ethnography and photographs of Ramlila performances in Trinidad, see Niehoff and Niehoff 1960.

5. Examples include *terukuttu* performances in Tamil Nadu, Kathakali plays in Kerala, and the *svarup*s of the Ramnagar Ramlila performance of Varanasi.

32

British Sikh Lives, Lived in Translation

Kathleen Hall

[I]f . . . the act of cultural translation (both as representation and as reproduction) denies the essentialism of a prior given originary culture, then we see that all forms of culture are continually in a process of hybridity. But for me the importance of hybridity is not to be able to trace two original moments from which the third emerges, rather hybridity to me is the "third space" which enables other positions to emerge.

—Bhabha 1990: 211

Migrant people live their lives within a cultural "third space," a site of social encounters and cultural articulations that engender processes of cultural change characterized by hybridity, fragmentation, and displacement. Within this cultural "third space," cultural orientations and identities are made rather than merely given (Bhabha 1990: 211; Stuart Hall 1996: 629). The everyday lives of migrant people are lived through acts of translation; practices of representation, reproduction, and contestation through which they negotiate what are often contradictory cultural influences in their lives. In these acts of translation, "tradition" becomes an object of reflection and re-invention, just as new lifestyles, cultural practices, and identities come to be created.

The article is drawn from my work with second-generation British Sikhs, children of migrants who are forging life paths through everyday acts of cultural translation.[1] These young people often say they feel pulled between "two cultures," pressured to conform to two very different ways of life, one viewed as "Sikh," the other "English." They express their dilemmas in dichotomous terms, while in practice they engage a broad range of cultural influences interwoven in the taken-for-granted fabric of their daily lives. Their tastes in clothing and food, in the television programs they watch, and the activities they engage in, all reflect cultural mixing. Yet, if the cultural influences within their lives are multiple and varied, what leads them to feel torn between two distinct and separate cultures?

British Sikhs perceive the cultural influences in their lives in dichotomous terms, I argue, because they encounter in their lives two dominant socializing forces. These socializing forces, within Sikh communities and in British society more generally, work against cultural mixing as they define and reinforce cultural boundaries. They attempt to mold the next generation into particular types of Sikhs and British nationals in order to reproduce the status quo within, as well as mark the boundaries between, "Sikh" and "British" communities. Acts of translation, then, engage British Sikhs in negotiating two contradictory cultural processes: cultural reproduction, or pressures to maintain the status quo, as well as cultural production, or processes through which individuals negotiate these normative pressures as they create new or reinvent "traditional" identities and lifestyles.

In the section that follows, I describe tensions between forces of cultural reproduction and cultural production in the lives of British Sikhs. I then move on to consider how tensions between these two processes are experienced and negotiated by Sikhs themselves. I portray the experiences of some of the Sikhs I grew to know in Leeds, providing brief portraits of the very different lives they are creating as British Sikhs in England.

BECOMING BRITISH SIKHS

Sikhs as a people are associated historically with Sikhism, a modern religion tracing its origin to the birth of the first Sikh guru, Guru Nanak, in 1469. Their homeland is the Punjab, a state in northern India. Most of their historic shrines are found in the territory on either side of the border separating India from Pakistan, an area that was, prior to Partition, considered part of Punjab. Over the past century, their travels and relocations have created a global Sikh diaspora that stretches from Punjab to Kenya, England to the United States, and Fiji to Singapore.[2]

Many among the first generation of Sikhs to grow up in Britain were born to upwardly mobile families, to parents who came to adulthood in the villages of Punjab or the racially divided cities of colonial East Africa. The life paths of these young people bridge the boundaries of race, ethnicity, and class. In their everyday lives they move through social worlds separated by these boundaries and learn to inhabit the "third space" in between. As they reach adulthood, they fashion lifestyles that reflect a vast range of cultural orientations, from those that celebrate the aesthetic sensibilities of the urban cosmopolitan to others that reassert the value of "tradition" and seek to maintain aspects of Sikh religious and Punjabi cultural heritage.

Growing up in England, British Sikhs imagine their futures in relation to numerous possible identities, potential communal ties, and alternative life paths.[3] Their sense of self is molded by contradictory cultural influences in contrasting social settings and transmitted through multiple forms of media. In their homes, at the Sikh temple (or *gurdwara*), as well as in religious education classes in British schools, "their culture," "their heritage," and "their religion" are represented in distinctive ways. As members of the South Asian diaspora their sense of what it means to be "Asian," "Indian," or "Sikh" is shaped by ideas and images, film narratives and artistic forms circulating across networks linking Leeds, Vancouver, New York, and Amritsar (Appadurai 1991; Gillespie 1995; Gopinath 1995).[4] As teenagers in a capitalist culture, British Sikhs also consume youth culture commodities that provide myriad cultural styles and subcultural orientations to use in creating adolescent identities (Sharma, Hutnyk, and Sharma 1996; Maira 1999).

Analyses that simply celebrate the creative potential within processes of cultural production and identity formation, however, ignore the cultural constraints as well as the social barriers that they, as the children of immigrants and as racial minorities, frequently face.[5] Social actors, particularly those defined as different, do not produce new cultural forms or make identity choices freely, independently, and in isolation. Identity and lifestyle choices have social consequences in terms of how the dominant society, family members, neighbors, teachers, peers, and co-workers evaluate one another's everyday conduct in relation to particular cultural distinctions, moral codes, and normative standards. To choose to be traditional or cosmopolitan can have significant social and personal consequences, in terms of one's status in British society and within British Asian communities.

These constraints are evident in the way young people consistently feel caught between two cultures. To make sense of the disjuncture between the choices in their lives and the way they perceive these choices, their "choices" need to be considered in relation to the normative pressures that inform them. Many accounts of second-generation South Asians in Britain and in the United States have noted the powerful influence that familial demands for loyalty to traditional cultural ideals can have in young people's lives. Yet, this, I argue, is only part of the picture.

As the first generation to grow up in Britain, second-generation British Sikhs are subject to two explicit projects of social reproduction. They are the focus of attempts on the part of the dominant British national community and the caste-status communities within the Sikh population to socialize the next generation. Relations of power and inequality in these status communities are legitimated by normative values and beliefs inscribed within two contrasting ideologies.[6]

An ideology of family honor (or *izzat*) provides the basis for determining a family's position within the status hierarchies that exist within each Sikh caste community. The ideology of family honor gives expression to normative expectations concerning gender relations, modesty among young women, and moral behavior among Sikhs more generally. A family's honor, its status in the caste community, is most influential, perhaps, in determining the family's ability to arrange good marriages for their children, particularly their daughters.

A second ideology, what I call the ideology of British national purity, supports a belief in a pure and homogeneous British nationality (Gilroy 1987). This ideology represents British identity as primordial or given, an identity that cannot be chosen or achieved and must, to survive, be protected and preserved. This construction of Britishness as rooted in time and territory excludes Britain's citizens of color and serves to legitimate racialized boundaries of national belonging. The ideology of British national purity supports a form of "cultural racism" specific to Europe in the era of decolonization, one that has arisen in response to the postcolonial reversal of migratory movements in which ex-colonial peoples from the old colonies have settled in the old metropoles. Articulated within notions of nationalism or national purity, the dominant theme of this form of racism "is not biological heredity but the insurmountability of cultural differences" and "the incompatibility of life-styles and traditions" (Balibar 1991: 21). This construction of social difference in terms of incommensurable racialized cultural essences informs ongoing processes of cultural reification and corresponding acts of social exclusion that continue to divide the dominant white population from Britain's newest citizens of color.

Each of these ideologies represents communities that are more idealized than real, more imagined than enacted. Each reflects a commonly shared desire for social wholeness, a desire to impose order in a world of cultural flow and flux, to protect boundaries of belonging perceived to be under threat. As conservative forces, they attempt to halt the forward march of social and cultural change. The conflicting demands in these young people's lives are not conflicts between two distinctive bounded cultures. They derive from dominant ideologies that do not reflect the complex and heterogeneous cultural orientations found within Sikh communities and in British society. While not all those identified as "Sikhs" or as "British" may subscribe to these ideological constructs, these ideologies continue to support dominant relations of power, privilege, and authority within Sikh caste communities and in British society. Hence, for many, particularly young people still under the normalizing gaze of family and school authorities, these ideologies police the boundaries of group belonging.

As British Sikhs negotiate the boundaries, social expectations, and constraints supported by the ideologies of British nationalism and of family honor, they develop a sense that they live between two worlds, worlds they frequently refer to as "English" and as "Indian." They associate things "Indian" with being "traditional," and things "English" with being "modern." Yet, in their everyday lives these young people enact a much broader range of lifestyles. Their lives embody a creative tension that engages the dialectics of power and inequality as well as the dynamics of cultural improvisation and transformation. They negotiate these fields of power and meaning through acts of translation. From this interstitial perspective, this "third space," British Sikhs observe and reflect upon different cultural influences, forms of oppression as well as future opportunities; and, in everyday practice, they produce hybrid identities and lifestyles, "traditional," cosmopolitan, and often a mixture of both.

I turn now to the stories of individuals I grew to know in Leeds, England, descriptions that illustrate the range of lifestyles British Sikhs are creating, as well as the consequences these young people have encountered in relation to choices they have made. These stories capture their struggles to create new ways of being black and British, Sikh and middle class, in England.

BECOMING MODERN TRADITIONAL SIKHS

Kulwant and Amarjit are Ramgarhia Sikhs. Kulwant's family is from Punjab, Amarjit's from Kenya. Both came to Britain before they were five. Their families are middle class. Amarjit's family brought economic and cultural capital from East Africa; Kulwant's has become economically successful since arriving in England. Kulwant is a successful solicitor, Amarjit a radiologist.

Kulwant and Amarjit fell in love as their marriage was being arranged. The couple and their families are very religious and quite active in their respective gurdwaras. Amarjit's family attends the Ramgarhia gurdwara frequented nearly exclusively by East African Sikhs, while Kulwant's family has been active in another temple whose members are largely from Punjab. Neither Kulwant nor Amarjit has taken *amrit pahul* ("nectar of immortality") or, in other words, undergone baptism for initiation into the Khalsa (the order of baptized Sikhs established by the tenth and final Sikh guru, Gobind Singh, in 1699).[7] Yet, they are both Kesdhari Sikhs (Sikhs who retain the *kes*, or uncut hair), and both, for the most part, keep the five symbols (the Five Ks) of the Sikh faith: kes, *kanga* (a comb worn in the hair), *kara* (a silver bracelet), *kachh* (a pair of underwear traditionally worn by soldiers), and *kirpan* (a sword or dagger worn on the side of the body in a holster that wraps diagonally around one shoulder). Kulwant wears a turban, except on Saturdays when he plays cricket.

Kulwant worries a great deal about the survival of the Sikh religion in Britain. He reads widely on the subject of Sikh history and religion and has taught "Sunday school" classes for teenagers at the temple in an attempt to pass on this knowledge to the next generation. Kulwant is concerned that the essential principles of Sikhism are at risk. The young have little knowledge of the faith and, in his view, show little interest in learning. More profoundly, perhaps, he fears that certain practices among the first generation threaten to "Hinduize" Sikhism (a fear, of course, that is hardly new within Sikhism or unique to Sikhs in Britain). Sikh women, in particular, he feels, grant supernatural power to ritual acts, to sounds, to scents, and, most critically, perhaps, to particular holy people. In contrast, the essence of Sikhism, for Kulwant, is in its textual base, in the teachings of the original ten Sikh gurus contained in the Sikh holy book, the Guru Granth Sahib. A Sikh's faith, he believes, should be grounded in a rational, literate, and informed understanding of Sikh religious teachings. Kulwant dedicates his free time to reading, teaching, and taking a leadership role at the gurdwara in order to protect the purity of his religious tradition.

Amarjit's everyday life revolves around her family. While she is tremendously close to her own family, she and Kulwant live with his parents. This, for Amarjit, is a source of great ambivalence. She feels fondness and respect for her in-laws and values living in an extended family unit, in which her children are learning Punjabi. Yet, having grown up in Britain, she is frustrated that the elderly people she lives with and cares for are not her relations. While she enjoys the communal nature of family life—the constant flow of relatives and friends through the doors of her in-laws' home—she wishes they would phone before coming and, on arriving, would not expect her to prepare a full Indian meal. Amarjit's ambivalence fuels her fantasies of moving out on their own, of enjoying the kind of domestic privacy that she imagines exists within a British nuclear family.

When I visit Amarjit, our days are spent in perpetual motion, preparing meals and traveling from house to house, gurdwara to gurdwara, children in hand, to be with relatives or to join in the festivities at yet another wedding. Between my visits, her letters tell of new babies born, siblings who have wed, and the deaths of elderly loved ones.

BECOMING COSMOPOLITAN

Devinder was born in Britain. Her parents too are quite religious and active in the Sikh temple. Devinder's parents came to England during the early sixties from a village in Punjab where, as members of the Jat caste, their families were landowning farmers. When her father first arrived, he stopped wearing the turban; but following the storming of the Golden Temple in Amritsar in 1984, he began once again to keep the symbols of the faith.[8] Devinder's family is upwardly mobile. Her father started his own small business and, as the eldest family member, worked to put his brothers (though not his sisters) through university while his own children were young.

During my first stay in Britain, Devinder, the eldest among her siblings, was studying dentistry at Leeds University while living at home. She was a successful student and remains a dutiful daughter. Her appearance at the time reflected her respect for the cultural ideals of her family; her hair was long and plaited, her face was free of makeup, and her dress modestly covered her body, usually in a jumper (sweater) and jeans. She never wore a skirt or a dress. Though strongly devoted to her family, she is not religious.

Outside of family events and weddings, she avoids the gurdwara and other Asian-specific spaces, where she says she feels awkward and out of place.

Devinder possesses a double consciousness. She is quite aware of differences between how she views herself and how she and her family are seen through the eyes of the dominant British population. This awareness was deepened by a sense of "release" she felt during a visit to India, where, for the first time, she felt English and did not feel marginalized racially.

> *Devinder:* [W]hen I went to India for my holiday it was really funny because I thought that I'd been released. I could walk in the streets and I felt a part of it. Everybody looked like me and behaved like me. It's funny because I never thought I was conscious of it, but I felt suddenly as if I was home. It's silly, isn't it? I've lived here all my life so this should be the place. I mean I was really happy to come back. It was really, really nice to have been there, but I think I was happier just coming back home. But while I was there I had this feeling, you can't imagine.
> *K. H.:* Did you feel different in any way from the people that were there?
> *Devinder:* Well, yes, I did feel different. . . . I could see by the way I was dressed they knew that I'd come from England. . . . That wasn't the difference— that I could speak English and they couldn't. That's not the point. It's just that if I wore an Indian suit, I suppose, and went somewhere, they wouldn't know where I was from. What's the difference?

Devinder comes from a lower-middle-class family; her academic success has taken her across racial and class boundaries, deepening and refining, in many ways, her understanding of how power relations are legitimated by the signification of social difference. In spite of her academic success at university, she had a profound sense that she did not belong in the white middle-class world of her classmates. Her family and her background did not "fit," did not correspond to the taken-for-granted British norm. The pressures of otherness, of living two lives, at that time permeated her everyday experiences.

> *Devinder:* I've never had a really close English friend like you because nobody else would understand. They can't understand the two different—the fact that I can cope with the way my parents are and still be happy at university. And not totally living the way students are supposed to live. . . . [I'm] two different people. I get into the car to come home, I'm somebody else.
> *K. H.:* Is that hard?
> *Devinder:* It depends which side of me dominates. Because there are times when the university side dominates and that interferes with home life. But when I'm at home like I have been for the last four weeks it's going to be harder getting used to going back there. Not consciously, but I suppose I'm just aware of it because you asked me. I wouldn't normally think of it. I mean I'll be successful here, but I want a home in India.

When Devinder finished her course at university, her parents informally initiated the process of arranging or assisting her marriage. A number of frustrating meetings with potential partners ensued. At the point when her patience was about to give out, her father happened to meet a very interesting young Sikh man at a wedding and invited him home to tea. Raj and Devinder met, were very attracted to one another, discovered they had a great deal in common, dated, fell in love, and married. Like Kulwant and Amarjit, Raj and Devinder are of the same caste. Both their families came from villages in Punjab, and both their fathers have established businesses in England. Raj's father, in particular, has made a great deal of money in manufacturing and export. Raj attended public school (the British equivalent of U.S. "private" school), graduated from university, and is employed by the government. He also is not religious and has never kept a turban—though Devinder's younger sisters were quite taken with the romantic image of Raj on his wedding day, standing tall, handsome, and heroic in his turban.

The couple lived for a short time at Raj's parents' estate in an upper-class village in the country outside London, but they soon decided they preferred the city and purchased their own flat in central London. Marriage has transformed Devinder. A few months after the wedding, I went to visit. When she met me at the train, I didn't recognize her. Her hair was short, her eyes enveloped in a lovely shade of blue, and she was dressed in a knee-length navy skirt, white blouse, tailored jacket, navy tights and heels. Devinder tells me that except for subtle middle-class forms of racism she senses periodically, she now feels that she somehow "fits in." She and Raj have driven through France and across Ireland. They subscribe to the opera, eat out regularly, and catch all the latest art films. And, in between, they visit their families.

BRIDGING THE BORDERLAND

Jas is from a middle-class family. His father, a Ramgarhia Sikh from Punjab, has a university degree. They are quite religious and very active in the Sikh temple. During his high school and university years, Jas blended into a very middle-class English world. He never wore a turban or attended the gurdwara. Recently, Jas decided to grow his hair and begin to wear a turban. This reconnection to his faith came at the same time as his engagement to his white English girlfriend.

These seemingly contradictory developments in Jas's life reflect, in part, the political transformation he has undergone in the last few years. While completing his M.A., Jas became involved in local politics and community organizing, work that he says has "politicized him." While passionate about politics, he remains concerned about the ramifications of his choices. His unease is evident, as he characterizes "getting tunneled" into race work and getting married as "significant crises."

Jas: I'm getting tunneled into another kind of area called race work. That I find unhappy because it's not what I want to do. Being here has been very very useful because it's politicized me, it's given me information about how the system works and how individuals in the system work, etc., etc. But now I'm personally getting labeled into that. And now there's another significant crisis. I'll probably get, not probably, I am getting married to a white woman. . . .

K. H.: Are your dad and mom okay with the marriage?

Jas: Yes, now they are, yeah. But you know there's all kinds of dilemmas on both sides. You know, it's not just my mom and dad. I think it's . . . it's probably worse for my parents in the sense that in Sikh society marriage brings more friends, gives them more relations.

Imagining raising children with his soon-to-be wife has prompted Jas to think about being a Sikh in a new light. Marrying a non-Sikh, a non-Asian, has given him a heightened sense of why his "tradition" is important to him.

Jas: I've just been on a holiday with my so-called girlfriend at the moment, and one of the questions was, what are we going to do with our kids? Are they going to wear a turban? And I in the ostrich situation say yes. No questions asked, yes. I want my kids . . . I will have no choice for them being black or white, they'll have to be both, they'll have to go into both kind of cultures. . . . [T]he minority culture is the culture which I think they will question the most because they will be like this more, they will question that more, because the majority culture is there anyway. . . . I want to keep the identity going. I want them to be, find out about the faith, where they belong. I want to give them this sense of belonging. They belong here, you know, their granddad, their grandparents are in Leeds and Manchester, one happens to be Sikh, one happens to be white. They will both love them, they will.

As he identifies what his children will have to confront in relation to racial, cultural, and religious differences, Jas speaks from the perspective of his own experience. Growing up in Britain, he too developed a double consciousness, a consciousness that his cultural background would be questioned and could not be taken for granted or simply "lived." He has been forced to think critically about his identity, and he has continued to question, to identify with as well as to challenge, the ways of his parents' generation. His words reflect an objective distance, a space of self-awareness about his choice to marry outside his "race" and culture, while simultaneously proclaiming, visibly, his identity as Sikh. Proud, he still wonders where it will lead.

I still, until we get married she can't get involved with the gurdwara, really, we can't go hand and hand, boyfriend and girlfriend. But I think, you know,

I think she would take it on. She's the kind of person who would say, well look, I may not become a Sikh, but I will come to the gurdwara. I'll have to dress up and do something. But she's brilliant. I don't personally recognize that sometimes, because I do this ostrich thing. So, yes I think, I feel more powerful, you know, in having a turban. . . . It makes you do certain things. So like here, dressing up, putting the turban on, makes you take care of how you present yourself. It makes you think all the time who you are. There are certain things you wouldn't do in public that you might do otherwise.

Forced when growing up to "think all the time about who you are," Jas has learned to think about who he is in a thoughtful, reflective manner. Becoming politicized and thinking about his tradition through the eyes of his future children have brought Jas back to his community, to an identification with being Sikh, to political activism, and to work with British Sikh youth.

BATTLING RACISM

I grew to know Jaspir quite well during the course of my first stay in Leeds. She was the daughter of a very religious Punjabi Ramgarhia family. Her father has achieved a fair degree of economic mobility, having built a successful business. He was also quite active in both gurdwara and local city politics. Jaspir was a serious, thoughtful, and outspoken college student. We spent hours talking about the dilemmas faced by the second generation, dilemmas about which she was passionately concerned.

After I left Leeds, Jaspir's life-path took a painful turn. She had just taken a "race" job with a local authority in Yorkshire. She was acting on the political principles that her father, as well as her life experiences, had instilled in her: she was engaged in the fight against racism. Jaspir fell in love with a man she met at her job. This would have been difficult enough for her "traditional" family. But the man she chose to love is Afro-Caribbean, and she chose to love him openly, publicly, against her family's wishes. This choice profoundly wounded Jaspir's family and had serious consequences for their standing in the Sikh community. Reacting in pain to their feelings of betrayal, her family disowned Jaspir. When her favorite aunt died, she was not invited to the funeral. Jaspir's act challenged the principles of Sikh family honor, and she is no longer a member of her family.

Jaspir's story brings to light the contradictions in her father's world and the consequences that can result from challenging the status system. In loving a black man, she acted in accordance with the anti-racist ideals for which her father fervently fought, but against the principles of Sikh family honor that he felt were fundamental to his faith. She bravely chose to follow her heart and her politics along a path of resistance, but without her family, she must find the path a lonely one.

BECOMING BRITISH (AND EVENTUALLY AMERICAN)

I remember the first time I saw Ravi. I was sitting in a car with her sister and brother-in-law waiting for her to appear from her medical school lab at Leeds University. We were heading out on the motorway to visit Ravi's sister's family in Cardiff, Wales. "There she is. Finally!" her brother-in-law announced in frustration. I looked up to see a strikingly beautiful young woman with lush black hair in a spotted fake-fur coat, short blue skirt, black lace tights, and funky black and white loafers. She hopped in back with me and we talked all the way to Wales. She complained about school, said she disliked medicine on the whole, and quietly mentioned her white English boyfriend, Ben. They were living together, planned to marry, maybe, but her family had not quite adjusted to the idea just yet.

Ravi, while herself not at all religious, is from a very religious Ramgarhia Sikh family who came to Britain from Kenya. Ravi's parents were both educated within the British colonial educational system and had professional careers both in Kenya and in England. During the days we spent with her sister, Ravi and I continued to talk incessantly as we decompressed—her from university, me from fieldwork—over wine, samosas, and crisps (potato chips). We shared our personal tales of the trials of student life, and she taught me all about Leeds—which clubs were "in," and where I could find the best bargains on clothes and Chinese food to die for. She was and remains totally "hip." Her interests and obsessions, activities and travels, seldom take her into purely Asian social worlds. She thinks of herself as British and, when "race" is marked, as a black woman. She has been forced to confront racism and sexism often during her medical schooling and in the initial stages of her career. She takes these irritations in stride, avoids incidents when she can, and continues to frame her life, individualistically, around pleasures and accomplishments.

We met a few times at O'Hare airport in Chicago when she was flying through to her residency in Barbados or to see relatives in California. One summer I received an invitation to her wedding at a Unitarian church in New York City, where Ravi and Ben now reside. I was in Britain at the time and could not attend. All of Ravi's relatives, her parents, sisters and brothers, nieces and nephews, and aunts and uncles, flew to New York from Britain and California for the wedding, which, her sister reported, the couple forgot to have videotaped. Ravi and Ben have settled in Manhattan, where they are both practicing medicine.

In forging her life path, Ravi has found ways to subvert the dominant pressures of family honor and of British racism, partially, perhaps, by removing herself completely from the Sikh community in Leeds as well as from Britain itself. Her family has adjusted to her choices, and they have accepted Ben into the fold. Ravi's two older sisters, in contrast, chose to marry

Sikh men whom they were introduced to through more "traditional" arrangements. One husband wears a turban while the other does not. Cultural change is taking distinctive forms between, as well as within, British Sikh families.

CONCLUSION

British Sikhs are paving life paths through everyday acts of translation. They are producing new identities and fashioning novel lifestyles, from the overtly "cosmopolitan" to the decidedly more "traditional." Their stories highlight what many postmodern analyses of hybrid identity formation too often seem to ignore, the constraints and the personal costs associated with cultural mixing, with making choices that directly challenge boundaries of belonging. Through their struggles, old boundaries are slowly becoming blurred, just as new relations of inequality are continuing to emerge, particularly in the form of class differences that increasingly divide the British Asian population. As they raise their children and enjoy their grandchildren, second-generation British Sikhs will continue to reflect on the nature of their culture and their identity in England and will make choices, at each new life stage, that reconfigure their relationship to both. Identities, like culture, are constantly remade in ongoing processes of becoming, processes experienced, in the moment, as everyday acts of being.

ACKNOWLEDGMENTS

The material presented here is drawn from a longitudinal field research project that I began in 1986 and is ongoing. The project has been supported by a Fulbright Fellowship, a Spencer Doctoral Fellowship, a Spencer/National Academy Post Doctoral Fellowship, and a University of Pennsylvania Research Foundation Grant. I would like to take the opportunity to express deep gratitude and warm appreciation to my mentor, Bernard Cohn, whose creative inspiration first set me off on this particular path many years ago.

NOTES

1. This piece is taken from a broader study of the social mobility experiences of British Sikhs growing up in Leeds, England (see K. Hall 1995 and 2002).

2. More in-depth analyses of the history of Sikhs in Punjab can be found in McLeod (1997) and Oberoi (1994). For studies of Sikh migrant populations, see Singh and Barrier (1996 and 1999) and Barrier and Dusenbery (1989). My work builds upon the earlier research with first-generation Sikhs in Leeds carried out by Roger Ballard and Catherine Ballard (see Ballard 1989; Ballard and Ballard 1977).

3. In this account, I use the term "South Asian" to refer to people who have migrated from the South Asian subcontinent to various parts of the world and "Asian" or "British Asian" to refer more specifically to South Asians in Britain. "Asian" is the term used in Britain to refer to citizens of South Asian origin, regardless of whether they originally migrated from Pakistan, India, Bangladesh, or East Africa (the homelands of the majority of South Asians in Britain). I also refer to second-generation Sikhs as "British Sikhs" to emphasize their citizenship and cultural identification as British.

4. See Vertovec (1997) for a useful analysis of the concept of "diaspora."

5. Visweswaran (1997), making a distinctive yet related point, has called upon researchers to consider more closely the relevance of class differences to particular South Asian migration histories and settlement experiences.

6. My use of the concept of ideology is similar to what Comaroff and Comaroff, following Raymond Williams (1977: 109), have defined as "an articulated system of meanings, values, and beliefs of a kind that can be abstracted as [the] 'worldview' of any social grouping. Borne in explicit manifestos and everyday practices . . . this worldview may be more or less internally systematic, more or less assertively coherent in its outward forms. But, as long as it exists, it provides an organizing scheme for collective symbolic production" (Comaroff and Comaroff 1991: 24).

7. Men and women keep the Five Ks, but among Punjabi Sikhs, only men wear turbans. Amritdhari Sikhs are those who have undergone baptism by the double-edged sword (*khande-da-amrit*) into the Khalsa (brotherhood). Amritdhari Sikhs are required to adhere to a code of conduct, the Rahit Maryada, which includes keeping the Five Ks. Amritdhari Sikhs have traditionally been distinguished from Sahajdhari Sikhs, who have not been baptized. This distinction was instituted after the tenth guru, Gobind Singh, first elected a segment of the Sikhs to undergo baptism into the Khalsa. Kesdhari Sikhs (those who keep kes) are Sahajdhari Sikhs who keep the five symbols of the faith. Other Sahajdhari Sikhs choose to cut their hair and to practice Sikhism without keeping the symbols. According to McLeod, only about 15 percent of Sikhs are Amritdhari and another 70% "heed the principal requirements of the rahit" (McLeod 1999: 64; see also Lal 1999 and Oberoi 1994).

8. It is not possible to provide an adequate account here of the tragic history of "Operation Bluestar" and the assassination of Prime Minister Indira Gandhi. For an analysis of these events and the Khalistani movement more generally, see Tatla (1999) and Axel (2000).

33

Examining the "Global" Indian Middle Class: Gender and Culture in the Silicon Valley/Bangalore Circuit

Smitha Radhakrishnan

In June 2006, the cover of *Time* magazine featured the face of a beautiful Indian woman, clothed in the finery of a traditional Indian dancer. Amidst the jewels, distinctly Indian features, and the *bindi*[1] was a prominently displayed headset, the icon of India's booming call center industry. The woman is smiling demurely, but gazing directly into the camera, apparently at ease among seemingly contrasting paraphernalia. Her face is superimposed on top of a golden halo of elaborately embroidered silk, converting the image of a face into something as iconic as a flag. "India Inc.," reads the headline. "Why the world's biggest democracy is the world's next economic superpower and what it means for America." A few days later, a follow-up article on *Time*'s website introduced the woman on the cover, who was not acknowledged in the print version—a professional Indian woman living in California. Gunjan Thiagarajan, age twenty-nine, was invited by a friend to be photographed by a stock photographer, and was asked to interact with various kinds of technological gadgets in her dance costume in exchange for one hundred dollars. She was not a model or an actress, but a marketing professional who grew up in Nigeria, moved to the United States in the 1980s, and is now married to a U.S.-based Sri Lankan. The article suggests that Thiagarajan's personal history makes her an appropriate model for a globalizing India. Thiagarajan was told by her friends, the article says, that she was a good choice for the cover, as she "represented the best of a progressive global Indian woman" (Myers 2006).

While several magazines have focused on India's economic boom in recent years, often featuring Indian women, *Time*'s cover inadvertently drew in

From "Examining the 'Global' Indian Middle Class: Gender and Culture in the Silicon Valley/Bangalore Circuit" by Smitha Radhakrishnan, *Journal of Intercultural Studies*, Volume 29(1), pp. 7–20, 2008. Reprinted by permission of the publisher (Taylor & Francis Ltd, http://www.informaworld.com).

a diasporic woman to represent India's success. Her Indianness was marked not through her location in India, but through bindi, jewelry, headset, and, implicitly, her Indian-but-global femininity. The follow-up article online underscores the appropriateness of Thiagarajan's face for projecting a new India. Not only did the image of Thiagarajan's photo deliver the message that *Time* intended, but Thiagarajan's story, the person behind the photo, became one more symbol of a global India: a nation rooted in an exotic, classical culture, which is nonetheless able to integrate seamlessly into a technology-driven global political economy. Implicit in the success of this image in communicating these messages are two interrelated trends: the centrality of the diaspora in articulating an ideology of "global Indianness" and the importance of a particular brand of femininity to convey the progress of the nation.

My examination of "global Indianness" stems from the notion put forth by my informants that "being global"—associated with participation in the global economy, professional success, and a cosmopolitan outlook—could be readily reconciled with "being Indian," associated especially with strong family values and a sense of belonging to the nation and cultural traditions of India. The reconciliation of the "global" and the "Indian" is a fundamentally gendered negotiation, resting upon an explicitly gendered articulation of "balance" between individual professional success and the maintenance of the family. Professional Indian women, in both India and the diaspora, must ensure the continuity of the Hindu family.[2] This balance is articulated vividly in the narratives of professional IT women in Bangalore and Silicon Valley.

"GLOBAL INDIANNESS" AT HOME AND IN THE WORLD

In the last ten years, a sense of India as a global nation has come to maturity alongside India's booming information technology (IT) industry. Economic liberalization beginning in the 1990s opened up India's economy by lowering tariff barriers, encouraging foreign investments, and investing in infrastructure to support high-end service industries, especially in the area of high-tech. These economic shifts fueled India's development into a hub for outsourced IT work, creating an upwardly mobile class of educated professionals in urban India whose numbers have been close to doubling every year (NASSCOM 2005). In a previous generation, young technical talent sought opportunities outside India, but today, many Indian engineers seek their fortunes within the country, and IT professionals who had previously moved to the United States are increasingly seeking opportunities "back home," indicating a shift from "brain drain" to "brain circulation" (Saxenian 2000). At the same time, it has become increasingly commonplace for Indian engineers to go "onsite" to a U.S. firm for training, support, or product development for a few months or a year (Aneesh 2006). These trends have brought an affluent transnational Indian middle class of IT profession-als to the center of a new nation-building project. As urban India experiences the optimism of an economic upswing, and the members of the diaspora in-creasingly engage in it, an ideology of "global Indianness" has crystallized—a set of beliefs and practices that are tied at once to a global lifestyle and to a deep sense of belonging to the Indian nation. Where previously middle-class Indians tended to view Indianness and Westernness as opposed to one an-other, the ideology of global Indianness makes the two compatible; a sense of "Indianness" sets the moral and personal boundaries for the material suc-cesses available in the West.[3]

Increasingly, nonresident Indians (NRIs), especially returning IT pro-fessionals, are deeply engaged in the project of building a "global India," defined simultaneously through an exclusive cultural identification, a con-structed set of "core values" (surrounding especially commitment to fam-ily), and a consumer-oriented lifestyle. The "new middle class" of India has been noted to exhibit this peculiar combination of values, where religious nationalism becomes reconciled with the liberalization of public culture and rising levels of consumption, especially of goods with a "foreign" character (Mankekar 1999; Mazzarella 2005; Rajagopal 1999). New opportunities for diasporic Indians to return to India fuel the further convergence of values, ideologies, and attitudes between India's new middle class and their newly returned diasporic counterparts. For NRIs, India continues to represent the source of an authentic culture, and return to India offers the opportunity for the renewal of cultural and family values liable to be degraded outside India.

Images such as *Time*'s cover, however, hint at the idea that the production of "global Indianness" is also importantly mediated through gender and that diasporic women have an important role to play. Indian national and cultural history has historically been articulated in deeply gendered terms. Partha Chatterjee has argued that during the anti-colonial Indian national-ist movement in the nineteenth and early twentieth centuries, middle-class Bengali women served to mark the spiritual essence of the nation, thought to be located in the domestic sphere (1990). Even in the diaspora, Indian women mark an essential Indianness, and are held to constructed standards of Indi-an womanhood, with varying impacts on their lives and communities (Bha-chu 1995; Bhattacharjee 1999; Das Gupta 1997; Mukhi 1998). Since the 1990s, the visibility of Indian women in the public sphere, ranging from right-wing Hindu politics to international beauty pageants, has reflected shifting, and often competing, representations of Indianness to the nation and the world. These representations have also engaged the diaspora in important ways (S. Kumar 2004; Oza 2001; Rai 1995; Sarkar 1995).

Global Indianness is importantly articulated through the bodies and rep-resentations of iconized "global Indian women," of which *Time*'s Thiagarajan is perhaps only the most recent instance. The success of Indian women in international beauty pageants since 1994, coinciding with India's economic boom, launched Indian women onto a global stage as paragons of both Indian virtue and cosmopolitan style, no longer weighed down by the shackles of tradition (Ahmed-Ghosh 2003; Parameswaran 2004). Professional IT women have become a similar kind of icon, as media representations of India's booming IT industry have often carried a woman's face (Baker and Kriplani 2004; Friedman 2004; Pink 2004). At a national level, the success of the Indian beauty queen and the professional Indian IT woman helped to bring women to the center—both as producers and as beneficiaries—of India's global economic success.

Drawing from fifteen months of ethnographic research and over a hundred interviews with professional Indian women working in IT on two continents, here I argue that a gendered vision of "global Indianness" circulates through IT professionals between Silicon Valley and Bangalore. I demonstrate the ways in which the gendered ideology of global Indianness is embodied and upheld by professional Indian IT women, both in India and in the Silicon Valley. I suggest that the notion of finding a "balance," fundamental to the notion of global Indian identity, is one that is achieved through the everyday practices of professional Indian women, and is expressed through a language of progress and sacrifice.

GENDERED "BALANCE" AND GLOBAL INDIAN CULTURAL FLOWS

The importance of "balance" between individual and family responsibilities was a recurring theme in the narratives of professional IT women I interviewed. Although these women expressed a diversity of viewpoints on how they achieve—or fail to achieve—that most desired balance in their own lives, they frequently referenced a common set of values and morals that they defined as "Indian." While there were a wide range of attitudes, practices, and values considered Indian amongst my informants, a value and commitment to the family and to elders almost always came up explicitly. Identification as Hindu and a sense of belonging to India were often implicit, arising as taken-for-granted associations rather than explicit values to be actively pursued and inculcated.[4] For most women, "Indian" values were incorporated into what they understood to be "global" values with little or no conflict, and were even understood as being complementary.

The Global, but "Not-Too-Ambitious," Individual

Professional IT women, whether or not they love their work, associate their ability to work with a sense of the development of an individual self, whether in Bangalore or in Silicon Valley. This individual self is often understood to be a part of their global or cosmopolitan identity, while Indianness is associated more with collectivity and family solidarity. These aspects are sometimes seen as being in conflict, but they are just as often reconciled with one another through an understanding that for Indian women, individuality must be circumscribed by the family. The idea of a limited individuality was most clearly articulated with regard to work, where even the most driven of professional women claim that they are not ambitious at the expense of their families.

For women working in the United States, or those in Bangalore who had returned from the United States, working and living outside of India offered them the opportunity to develop a strong sense of individuality, which they understood to be in contrast with the constraints of living in India. Shreya, a manager working at a multinational tech firm in the Silicon Valley, explained that her time in the United States, where she was removed from the complacence of her upper-class life in India, gave her the time and personal space to develop a strong sense of self. She says,

> I was never that kind of an ambitious person who had ever set goals for myself. . . . What I was lacking was some time to align my career to think about myself. So, this country offered me that. . . . In India, it's not how you view yourself as a person, [but] it's how the rest of the world views you [that makes up] what you consider yourself to be.

In Shreya's narrative, India is a place of collectivity, and the United States is a space of individuality. While Shreya sees herself as individualistic, she also says that the Indian side of her is deeply tied to her family and that she is driven by the prospect of making her family proud of her. Similarly, Priya, a twenty-six-year-old software consultant in California, boldly states, "I am a global Indian." She explains that she has developed a strong sense of independence since she left India, because of the increased freedom she gained through her profession, to travel alone and interact with a range of people. Ultimately, however, Priya believes that her individual development makes her more capable of passing on a rich and equitable sense of belonging to India to her children, such that family serves as the primary anchor for the individual.

In India, professional women regard the workplace in itself as an opportunity to develop the individual self, but these women are careful to point out the dangers of too much individual drive. Usha, a thirty-three-year-old optics engineer in Bangalore who pursued graduate work in the United States, works in a highly specialized area for a large American multinational firm. She enjoys the intellectual stimulation and independence she receives from her job, and sees the ways in which other professional women around her are gaining independence and autonomy from conventional expectations. Despite this, Usha feels that working women who are educated suffer from the problem of too much "headweight." She explains,

> You do it for your own independence and happiness . . . [but] a working woman should really balance things. She should never make her husband feel that I'm prioritizing something in life and not him. It's difficult. But in a generation's time, things will change. It will take time.

During her time in the United States, she found Americans to lack that balance and be too individualistic. In contrast to Usha's case, Meena, a thirty-year-old mechanical engineer in Bangalore, had been a dedicated career woman from the beginning, working much more for the intellectual stimulation than the money, especially in her previous firm. Despite having a child, she continued to work long hours. At some stage, though, she started to think that she had gone too far, and was missing out on her daughter's life. She accepted a less stimulating job with better hours in another multinational. Meena explained how she had to place her family ahead of her love for the job:

> In [my previous firm], the money was just 20 percent of the reason. Eighty percent of the reason was the job. Okay? The work. In this company, I would say that 45 percent would be the salary, and the rest would be the job. . . . In fact, my previous manager could not believe I was leaving because he knew how much I loved it. And then I told him—no way, boss, I'm leaving. I'm just too bad a mother.

In Meena's narrative, she explains her past tendency to prioritize her job over her daughter as a mistake that she now had to compensate for. She does not wish to give up her career altogether, but she wishes to slow down for the sake of her family. Meena recognizes that she made this choice as a woman with a husband in a well-paid job. Her decision, then, was represented in a language of an individualized "choice," but that choice was at the outset framed by considerations of gender and class.

In each of these cases, Indianness is understood as a set of family-oriented values that enriches and sometimes constrains the opportunities for individualization that the IT industry brings, whether in Bangalore or the Silicon Valley. The interplay between the individualizing forces of the United States or the workplace and the perceived "constant" of Indian culture is a dynamic one that works in different ways for different individuals, such that women are constructing individualism in a particular way; rather than becoming atomized individuals typical of Western models of individualism, the brand of individualism they develop supports and reinforces a sense of belonging to the family.

Family Comes First

Commitment to the Indian family is critical for women not only for the development of an individual self, but also for conceptualizing a career trajectory. The dilemma of choosing between a career and family is a culturally loaded issue for most respondents, who deal with the matter through a wide range of strategies. Despite this variation, however, women in both Bangalore and Silicon Valley understand that a decision to place their career before their family would be one that would violate a set of "Indian" values, and the benefits derived from working would become less desirable.

Gautami, a twenty-six-year-old graphics specialist in India, has been working for five years, and uses her substantial income to back her parents and siblings financially. Gautami's plans for her future, however, hang importantly on her parents' expectations that it is now high time that she married. Despite the stimulation she gets from her job, Gautami is very clear that from the moment she marries, her priorities will change. She says that she would love to be a housewife, care for her in-laws and look after her kids. If her husband allows her, she will continue to work until she has kids, but not afterward. Later, she says:

> Around thirty-five, forty, when you're rising up the ladder, I think I'd prefer to settle down with my family and my husband. . . . Because ultimately, it's your family for whom you're doing it. And if they're not happy, it really doesn't make any difference, so it's better that you spend time with them and make them happy rather than earning money and money and money and nothing else.

Here, Gautami indicates clearly that the stimulation she enjoys from work is ultimately linked to her support of a family—her parents and siblings for now, and her own family in the future. As such, when climbing the ladder becomes a purely material pursuit that does not benefit the inner well-being of the family, it is no longer necessary. Out of the twenty-two interviewees in India who were within this age and experience bracket, half spoke with conviction that they planned to prioritize their families over their jobs in the long haul. Only one of these twenty-two interviewees was sure that she would continue working and climb the corporate ladder, come what may. The remainder were ambivalent, hinging their plans on the wishes of future husbands and in-laws.

Silicon Valley women faced with the decision of whether or not to move back to India find that decision deeply entangled with career sacrifices they are already making as Indian mothers in the United States. Lakshmi, a thirty-four-year-old engineer working in Silicon Valley, expressed the difficulties she faces balancing her professional and family life, and how the move back to India, which her husband has already decided is best for the family, further challenges these difficulties to a point that she may no longer be able to bear. For Lakshmi, her work is a part of her—something that gives her meaning and motivation. Despite this, she has put boundaries on her career climb since she had children, declining offers for managerial positions and keeping her hours to a minimum. Her decision to continue working, however, has faced vocal opposition from her mother-in-law, who feels it is not right for her to be going to work with children at home. Lakshmi's own mother, who lives in the Bay Area, has supported Lakshmi's career, filling in with childcare when needed. Although Lakshmi's husband has already accepted a position in Bangalore, she finds herself pulled in opposite directions. While she feels that the imperatives of Indian motherhood require her to move to India for the sake of keeping the family together, Lakshmi is hesitant. Her predicament is overloaded with cultural meanings. If she decides not to join her husband in India, choosing to pursue her career and life in the United States instead, her status as an Indian mother is in jeopardy. If she agrees to go, she has sacrificed her present career for an uncertain future in which she may or may not find a job. Yet, she feels compelled to choose the latter option in order to uphold her Indianness by being a good mother, a dilemma she expressed pointedly in her interview. She explains:

> I'm now caught in this conflict. . . . One side of me says that I should put aside my wants and preferences and make it work for the family. But the other side of me says, if I'm not okay with this, how efficient am I going to be as a person? [. . .] How am I going to make it work for my kids?

Gautami and Lakshmi exemplify the ways in which professional women feel compelled to define what is Indian narrowly, where the true core of Indianness lies in a heterosexual and often patriarchal family. In such a family, the career of the mother is something that supplements a family life, but cannot overtake it. Implicit in this setup is the presumption of affluence, where a husband's income provides the basis for the well-bring of the family, and the wife, as the protector of the middle-class domestic realm, must continue to protect the sanctity of that space, echoing the gendered division of labor in the rhetoric of Indian nationalism during the colonial period.

The Progress and Respectability of the New Indian Woman

Previously existing ideals of domesticity and nationhood, however, have fused with contemporary notions of a global Indian nation to shift gendered ideals of middle-class respectability. Whether in India or the diaspora, professional IT women feel their professional achievements to be indicative of the progress of India, and also experience the benefit of an added respect for their professional lives, even compared to middle-class housewives, who were the embodiment of respectability for a previous generation. Despite the checks on their career that women may negotiate, involvement in a professional career with a global scope often improves the position of women in their families, and prompts them to feel included in the optimism of a globalizing India.

Sunita, a twenty-eight-year-old software engineer in India, says, "If you work, then everyone respects you. Even your husband unconsciously, he will respect you more. . . . It's not that we need the money. There's property, a husband who is earning. . . . But I feel respect in this job." For Sunita, her educational credentials, her earning capacity, and her high-status job earn her concrete advantages in her personal life. She is regarded as an important decision maker in the family, and is sought out for advice in all major family decisions. Sunita is not alone. Most of the women I interviewed in

India commented specifically on these benefits of working in IT. Usha, the thirty-three-year-old optics engineer in Bangalore who had pursued graduate work in the United States, had explained that it was women who were mainly responsible for making sure that work, which was strictly for one's own development, would not overtake the duties that come with being a wife. At the same time, however, Usha was clear that earning a high salary gained her more respect from her husband than she would otherwise have, and allowed her to support her parents financially. She explained that the integration of women into highly paid jobs made parents more proud to have a working daughter, who can often support them just as well as a working son. These important symbolic and material benefits, however, do not necessarily accrue to all working women or all women working in global industries. Women working in call centers, for example, are considered less respectable in the urban-middle-class imagination. Call center workers are consistently perceived as less educated, less family-oriented, and thus, unable to uphold the ideals of Indian middle-class womanhood. The perceived contrast between the call center industry and the IT industry suggests that professional IT women possess a cultural capital that has become increasingly valuable in a changing urban India.

In the United States, Indian women working in IT experience a similar respectability in their families and communities, and constantly relate their positions in the United States to the progress of women in India. Vidya, an engineer working in Silicon Valley, has returned to the university for further education so that she can occupy a better IT job than she had before. The time that she took off to have her children made her feel left behind. For Vidya, her work identity makes her feel as if she is a better mother, more equipped to give her children things to make their lives more comfortable. Compared to other Indian mothers who do not work, she feels more respected, and feels that she is improving herself. Neera, a high-level manager at a top Silicon Valley firm, while expressing sentiments very similar to Vidya and others about the respectability of IT for women, added that her excellent technical education in India, which has led her to her current position, indicates the advanced approach of Indian culture to the idea of women in science and engineering. While she finds negative stereotypes of women in engineering prevailing in the United States, Neera believes that the widespread acceptance and respect for professional IT women in India will lead India to great heights in the global economy. She views herself as part of that process.

In these ways, Indian professional IT women, whether in India or the United States, view their own progress in a global technical industry as tied to India's progress in the global cultural economy. Their own heightened respectability within their families and communities serves to underscore the prevailing conviction that Indian society is undergoing a fundamental change. In the voices of these professionals, these changes are for the better, as they adopt the value of the individual at work from what they understand to be "global" culture, while still maintaining what they see to be the "core values" of the nation, namely, allegiance to the Indian form of family. When understood in the context of a shared sense of global nation-building among the Indian diaspora, these gendered symbolic meanings become all the more salient as they traverse back and forth between Bangalore and Silicon Valley.

By coming to understand the complex ways in which professional IT women relate to a global vision of India, and the ways in which that relationship plays into their personal and professional lives, we begin to see the continued importance of gender as a lens through which the Indian nation is constructed and concretized. Media portrayals of Indian women working in IT present the shift to a global economy in India as one that also has brought a shift in gender relations. Such a portrayal, however, veils the complex ways in which conventional values of womanhood and the Indian family underpin the decisions of professional women in the new global economy. The interplay between a progressive India, predicated on global success and a global image; and a cultural India constructed as traditional, Hindu, and family-based, is one that is made real not only through the lives of women living in India, but also in the voices of Indian women abroad, whose dilemmas circulate between Silicon Valley and Bangalore as a critical part of the symbolic exchange between India and its diaspora.

CONCLUSION

India's new middle class of tech workers and an affluent Indian diaspora are together engaged in a contemporary nation-building project. Supported by the strength of a common position in an information-driven global economy, this transnational group of professionals actively constructs an ideology of belonging to the nation that reconciles the individualism and consumerism of a "global" culture with the intimate family values of "India." Professional IT women provide a key insight into the production of this new language of belonging to the nation. Their narratives of commitment to the Indian family, which their individual aspirations may only supplement or enrich, expose the ways in which gendered assumptions are built into an ideology of "global Indian" belonging. In this project, women become critical in defining the practices and beliefs that can legitimately support an exclusive Indian cultural identification.

In examining the gendered face of global cultural flows, I suggest that the ways in which Indian women negotiate their positions as individuals, as mothers, and as icons of a new nation are connected in important ways to changing representations of woman-as-nation icons in India, past and present. Their middle-class status lends them the authority to legitimize large-scale cultural and economic changes, but to do this, they continue to anchor themselves in the construct of the Indian family. Although the Indian family is often narrowly defined as heterosexual and often patriarchal, its ability to be relevant to women in a range of cultural milieus makes it accessible to Indian women in Bangalore and California alike. As the examples here demonstrate, Indian women in these two locations do not necessarily operate under identical circumstances. Indeed, while the family might be seen as motivation for a more ambitious career, as in the case of Shreya in Silicon Valley, that same family can be understood as a reason to shorten a seemingly successful career trajectory, as in the case of Gautami in India. Thus, "global Indianness" is still a dynamic ideology—one that draws attention to gender and class, while continuing to retain an important fluidity across contexts and personal histories.

NOTES

1. Derived from the Sanskrit word *hindu,* meaning "a drop, small particle, dot," a bindi is a round mark or dot worn on the center of the forehead.

2. Although of course not all professional Indian women are Hindu, the professional IT women in Bangalore and Silicon Valley whom I researched largely identified as Hindu and saw themselves as espousing Hindu values especially within the family.

3. The transnational resonance of "global Indianness" has also drawn significantly from the strength of a Hindu nationalist movement that has been strongly supported by the upwardly mobile diaspora (Rajagopal 2001; van der Veer 2004). While I do not focus on the centrality of Hindu identification here, the ways in which IT professionals articulate a Hindu identification alongside a "global" one also constitute an important part of the "global Indian" ideology I describe.

4. Note that the assumption among informants that "Indian" is implicitly also "Hindu" fits with Lukose's definition of the "Hindu secular" in her chapter in part 3, that is a concept of citizenship that at once eschews religion even as it assumes it.

34

**Placing Lives through Stories:
Second-Generation South
Asian Americans**

Kirin Narayan

"Displacement" and "diaspora" are two terms that often move together, hand in hand. Wandering through the terrain of anthropological discourse, diaspora and displacement measure the ways in which the last two decades of theory have complicated the relations between culture and place (Appadurai 1996; Bammer 1994; Gupta and Ferguson 1997; Lavie and Swedenburg 1996). Global flows, ethnoscapes, traveling cultures, and hybridity loomed large in the theoretical landscapes of the 1990s, and form a backdrop for anthropology in the new century, too. In this essay, I will explore a third term that seems to me to skip at the heels of "displacement" and "diaspora," but has not yet been sufficiently recognized at their side: "emplacement." By emplacement, I mean the strategies of coming to belong somewhere, as when people in diaspora who have left old homes struggle to make new ones. Emplacement occurs in concrete geographical space, in settling into homes, in the establishment of community resources such as specialized grocery stores, and in arenas for gathering, such as mosques, gurdwaras, or temples. Also, emplacement is an imaginative process, the orienting of self within multiple frameworks of meaning. Drawing on life stories from second-generation South Asian Americans, I argue here that telling one's own stories, staking out a space for one's own meaning, is a powerful discursive means of emplacement.

RESEARCH BACKGROUND

There is a long history of people of South Asian origin leaving South Asia for different parts of the world, whether on account of trade, movement within the British colonial labor force, indentured labor contracts, or the seeking of new opportunities (Clarke, Peach, and Vertovec 1990; Tinker 1974). In the

United States, a noteworthy South Asian presence can be traced to the early part of the twentieth century, particularly after 1905, and centered on the west coast (R. Daniels 1989: 11–25). Many of these settlers were Sikhs, who often met strong racial prejudice. After the passing in 1917 and 1924 of immigration bills that excluded most people of Asian origin, the numbers who entered dwindled, and those who were in the United States encountered difficulties in obtaining citizenship and owning land. In 1946, naturalization for those of South Asian background became possible, and also small quotas of immigrants were allowed each year. It was not until 1965, though, that the immigration law was changed, allowing for twenty thousand people each year from each country in South Asia, and showing preferences for educated professionals as well as close relatives of citizens and permanent residents (Helweg and Helweg 1990: 58–60). Since then, the flow of immigrants has continued to be tied to the vagaries in immigration laws: the middle-class professional bias of the first flood of immigrants later came to include working-class relatives, and more recently, skilled technological workers on temporary visas have added to the South Asian presence in the United States (Leonard 1997).

Migration and the changed imaginative relationship to countries of origin as well as countries of settlement have been noted as creative forces in modern fiction (cf. Rushdie 1991). In 1994, I published a novel that featured Indians living in the United States (Narayan 1994). What I knew about the South Asian Americans around me was rooted in the randomness of my own experience or the experiences of friends. To my discomfort, though, I found that people seemed to assume that my expertise as an anthropologist of South Asia somehow extended to the materials of my fiction. In a hurry, I set about trying to gain some scholarly credentials in order to be able to answer wider questions about South Asian American experiences. Apart from exploring the scholarly literature, I also began to interview people.

I was particularly intrigued by second-generation South Asian Americans, mostly the children of the post-1965 immigrants. As someone of mixed cultural background myself—I grew up in India with a Gujarati father and German-American mother—I saw these second-generation individuals as potential mirrored selves, as twinned others. They looked more "authentically" Indian than I did, yet I also sensed that they were far more American than I. How, I wondered, did they perceive themselves?

Between 1995 and 2000, I periodically taped, wrote down, or simply listened to personal narratives from second-generation Indian and Pakistani Americans who were willing to give me their time. All the young men and women I approached knew they were helping me out on two scores: first, to instruct me as an anthropologist, and second, to give me insight into the character of Indian American Nikhil/Nick, for a second novel that was taking shape on my computer screen. Somehow, asking for help with the character of Nick became an unanticipated, rich method for eliciting life stories:

Nick served as a catalyst with some (though not all) of the people I interviewed, inspiring the telling of powerful personal stories that could potentially become part of his experience, too.

The twenty people I spoke with at length were all connected in one way or another to the Midwest, and to university life, whether as students, faculty, or the children of faculty: it would be safe to say they were all of middle-class background. All of them had grown up in the United States from at least the age of five onward, and most were born here. They ranged in age from eighteen to forty at the time of the first interview, and had lived before in places as varied as Libya, Palo Alto, Cincinnati, and Ahmedabad. For all these people, I have used pseudonyms and have tried to suppress other identifying markers. I have also, as much as possible, attempted to maintain a dialogue through drafts of writing.

In undertaking these interviews, I have been uncomfortably aware of my own inadequacies in trying to reciprocate for the gift of stories through tea, meals, my own stories, or even advice on subjects ranging from graduate-school applications to romantic dilemmas. The reward has been many new friendships as well as a wealth of new research materials. A disadvantage of remaining in contact with people through time, though, is that life stories are an unstable and contingent genre, subject to change. Whether on account of personal changes, such as marriage or graduation, or political shifts, such as the post-Kargil era of strained relations between India and Pakistan, several people I contacted in 2000 said that their perceptions of their own pasts had changed and were we to redo the interviews, I would be likely to learn different stories. One person no longer identified with the term "South Asian American." This essay, then, should be viewed as provisional, representing a period in the late 1990s, among some South Asian Americans based in the Midwest.

Though often mockingly termed "American Born Confused Desis," these young people did not appear to be confused or floundering; rather, they were masters of code-switching, showing different sides and combinations of themselves in different cultural contexts (cf. Ballard 1994: 29–33; Brah 1996: 41–42). Working with an immensely articulate and reflective set of individuals has also made it difficult to muster up the ethnographic authority to transform the delights of the spoken word into written publications. After all, everyone in this group could certainly write to represent themselves and their own story if they wished. I take heart from what twenty-year-old Najma reflected: "See, what's interesting for us is how our own stories might relate to the others of us who grew up here; this is what you can do for us."

NESTED STORIES

Since the 1920s, anthropologists have been interested in life stories as a way to locate cultural generalities and historical forces within the experiences and narrated perceptions of actual people (Langness and Frank 1981). While the term "life history" is often used by anthropologists recording such narratives, I prefer to use "life story" in order to draw attention to the fragmentary, constructed, varied, and contextually evoked nature of the stories people tell about themselves (cf. Peacock and Holland 1993: 368). The kinds of stories that people narrate about themselves are not only retrospective, organizing memories, but also prospective, laying down frameworks of meaning that may guide actions in the future (Bruner 1987). Also, as I argue here, the telling of stories is a form of imaginative emplacement.

The life stories of second-generation South Asian Americans located at the confluence of different cultural influences suggests that it may be useful to think of life stories as conglomerates of different sorts of narratives, some personal, some collective. In this essay, I examine three classes of stories that emerged from my transcripts: (1) stories told about oneself; (2) the reframing of pre-existing family folklore, for example, tales a parent might have told about him- or herself, or prior ancestors; (3) the retelling of larger cultural stories, such as myths or folktales, as part of one's own experience.

Personal Experience

Personal narrative formed the largest frame for the tales I elicited, with occasional family stories or oral traditions nested inside. The life stories I heard resonated strongly with other research on second-generation South Asian American lives (e.g., Agarwal 1991; Bacon 1996; Maira 1998). The content of the stories was shaped by several important vectors: South Asian region of parents' origin, United States region of upbringing and the South Asian presence there, era of upbringing (for example, the 1960s versus the 1980s), gender, and sexual orientation, all of which were differentially experienced depending on the other shaping forces.

Despite all the diversity in particulars, many stories had a similar shape. Conflict between the South Asian and the American sides of self through childhood tended to reach a miserable pitch of anger, depression, denial, or repression in middle-school years. In college, there was usually self-discovery, with the developing of new strategies for being South Asian and American, too. Yet even as this resulted in a greater sense of personal integration, manifest in the telling of the stories, almost everyone I talked to also referred to an ongoing compartmentalization between the self they were creating of their own and the self that was more oriented toward family. (The one marked exemption was Najma, of Pakistani background, whose parents were so open-minded and tolerant that she felt she could confide to them about any struggle.) Many of the people I spoke to, then, felt duplicitous with their parents. As Sudam said, reflecting on how he couldn't tell his parents about his girlfriend, who, though also Indian American, was from a different caste and region, "I'm one person with family, another person with friends. I lead totally different lives. It's too complicated to explain to each side, so I don't bother." Note, however, that in frankly narrating the tensions he faced between his parents and friends, Sudam used the space of a story to bring the two sides of his life together.

Humor was often emphasized in these accounts, though the humor could verge on the bitter. Reflecting on what India represented to her as a Gujarati child in Indiana, Medha stated,

> *Medha:* I really hated it. I really hated being Indian. I wanted to shed any-thing that was Indian about myself—other than clothes, because Indian clothes are cool!
>
> *K.N.:* Did you wear the clothes to school?
>
> *M:* I would. I would wear the *pyjāma*. But I would wear a different blouse. Yeah. I would wear the Indian clothes to school. But I wanted to shed anything that was Indian, because I always got the constant "Girls in India don't do that, and it doesn't matter what people here do. You're Indian and that's your culture. And this is what you do, and as long as you're in this house you're going to abide by the Indian culture." And everything was so Indian culture, American culture, there was no pos-sibility of merging.

Like many young women I talked to, Medha felt her brother had not been as conflicted and depressed by the gulf between gender expectations com-ing from the Indian parents and American peers. Similarly, Asha, who grew up in a Gujarati family in Milwaukee, reflected that her own brother was more comfortable in his Indianness than she was: "You know, like, he *can* be Indian because he doesn't face a lot of the same things that I do as a woman in being more Indian. You know, for me to be more Indian would be to give up things. For him to be more Indian is actually to get—to earn some privi-lege, and I don't think he sees that."

Young men were usually aware that things were harder for their sisters. The men too spoke of their own sense of being suspended between Indi-anness or Pakistaniness and Americanness, represented as polarities. Vas-ant, who grew up in Santa Clara, California, in the 1960s, described how he sought to cover up his difference, to "do everything to fit in and not rock the boat in any way"—excelling in sports, he found, was one way of finding acceptance as an American male. Arjun talked of growing up in Cleveland fascinated by American history, "even the esoteric details and stuff, and that I think was part of country-loving, you know. Like in some ways, I felt like if I learned this stuff, maybe, you know, then they would accept me or some-thing like that."

For men as well, parents could be a repressive force, guiding their deci-sions from what to major in to social interaction. Though girls were super-vised more, and more haunted by middle-class, upper-caste nationalized images of chaste Indian women (cf. Maira 1998), for men, too, issues of dat-ing and sexuality were a recurring node of inner confusion as well as overt conflict with parents.

One of Dinesh's favorite stories, "a classic," in his own words, was a suspenseful and dramatic account of how, when he was visiting home from college, his parents had discovered something subversive in his room and were so upset that they telephoned him at the party he was at with his non–South Asian friends, asking him to return home. He imagined that they had found his stash of dope, but it turned out that they had unearthed an unopened and signed condom given to him as a joke gift from a girl at graduation. "Do you use condoms?" his father asked. Though relatively sexually inexperienced, Dinesh responded with bravado, saying, "All the time!" which led to his parents' lamentations over the possibility of arranging his marriage.

Manjeet described his confrontations with his parents in terms of their being Indian, and him, challenging their authority, as American.

> I couldn't date. It would seem strange for me to date somebody, you know. Go out on a date with some—some girl, or go out with a girl? Or even, like, stay out late . . . my mom would say that in our culture we don't go out with girls. Or we don't, you know, we don't—we don't kiss girls. . . . You know basically, just, "No, you can't do that!" [laughing]
> And I would be, like, "wнy?"
> She's like, "You can't do it."
> And I would be like, I would be like, being an American, wanting to know the reason why I can't do this, you know?
> And my dad's like, "There's no reason why. Just deal with it."
> It's like, I realized—I probably came to accept arbitrary rules, you know, by my parents over me, and the fact that me doing this, like, hurt my mom so much that she can't even tell why it hurts her, you know? She doesn't really know why. It's just like, it's bad. And so I have to realize that if I want to do it, I'm gonna have to hurt her in order to do it.

America, then, represented a challenging of pre-existing traditions, and was set up in opposition to "our culture" as perceived by parents. The issue of parents' construction of the homeland, a different kind of nostalgic emplacement, would be the subject of a different essay (cf. K. Ganguly 1992; Prashad 1996). Indeed, one could view the tension between South Asian-born parents and their America-raised children as being partly the result of their different placements within imaginative landscapes of meaning in terms of what "India," "Pakistan," or "the United States" might represent.

Yet such placements, of course, were not fixed, but could change with time, and be evoked differently in different contexts. Asha, for example, responded to my question of what India meant to her by saying, "Well, mainly family. . . . I mean until I was old enough to understand geography, I always thought that India was one of the states in the United States." After all, she said, they went to what her mother called India-na to visit her mother's brothers in what Asha and her brother imitated as "Indian-apolice." It was only as she grew older that the family network of meaning stretched, and she realized that India was a faraway place.

All the life stories I heard featured powerful moments of revelation, when the speaker saw a new way of placing himself or herself in a semiotic or contextual field that balanced allegiances toward both peers and parents. For Kavi, who grew up in a Jain family in New Jersey, self-understanding came through observing a recent immigrant from India at her high school in the 1980s.

> There was this one kid who for some reason I always think of. He was a freshman, I guess I was a junior. He could not speak English at all, and he was very very small. He looked like he was eleven. He was very small, a very very thin child. He had this huge book bag.
>
> Anyway, I just remember seeing him, and he always sat completely by himself, and no one talked to him. One day I remember seeing him—like I said it didn't erupt in violence most of the time—but I saw him mostly being pushed and sort of shoved out of the way.
>
> I said something like "Why don't you just leave him alone." I guess the epithet then was "Gandhi." I don't understand why that became a curse word. I remember them saying that and saying about him dressing badly. Or something. And I said, "Why don't you just leave him alone!" Because this child, this kid really, he was really just sad, he was always alone and he was so tiny, really, so vulnerable. And I remember these kids turning to me and saying, "This is nothing to do with you," because I don't have any kind of accent.
>
> And I remember that for me—and I could be rewriting the past—I remember that being for me a pivotal time that I stopped trying so hard to, like, hide away being Indian, and starting to realize that these were the kinds of people, that was what was making me angry, and not my family. Because I did spend time being ashamed of my family. The fact that my parents had accents, that they didn't really eat at American restaurants, they didn't know how to do that. You know, dinner somewhere, they didn't exactly know how to go about things. The whole money issue was always hard. But anyway, this was when I stopped feeling so bad about myself and just realizing that there were a certain kind of people I just really didn't like.

Such moments of revelation often emerged in a series, as the speaker discovered different ways of bridging and mingling multiple cultures rather than experiencing them as an opposition framed by parents. For some, this meant learning more about South Asia, whether by taking classes in college, or by joining a Hindu student group, like Parvati, or by traveling alone rather than with parents to India or Pakistan, like Dinesh, Arjun, and several other men. For others, this meant becoming knowledgeable and active in larger U.S. minority issues, or becoming involved in political action (cf. Matthew and Prashad 1999/2000). Shankar, for example, had grown up in a Milwaukee suburb, feeling "very white." During his second semester at the University of Wisconsin, though he was pressured by a prestigious accelerated pre-med program, he also began taking classes "that expanded how I looked at where I was, and the stories that I heard, and who I talked to." Among the classes he took was one on race and ethnicity that sensitized him to subtle racism around him as well as educating him on historical inequalities.

In a good-natured parody, Jyoti, who grew up in Cleveland in a family with south Indian roots, outlined two strategies of finding a new balance—becoming more Indian, or becoming more knowledgeable as a United States minority—as "two kinds of stories."

> There are the kids who love their culture and do *bhangra* dance and say *"chalo, chalo"* [let's go] to each other on the street. They talk to each other in Hindi. There are tons of kids like this in Berkeley. Like I was by the Xerox machine in Berkeley, and this girl came up to me, and she said something to me in Gujarati. I said, "I don't know what you're saying." She said, "Why don't you speak your language?" I said, "Because I'm not Gujarati." But she was born here! So there are those kinds of South Asian second-generation kids. When they tell stories, they tell stories of like, going to the Indian parties, and how Mom does *puja* [worship] in the house, and this and that, about their Indian-ness, you see what I mean? And then there's MY kind of South Asian.

To illustrate what she meant about her kind of South Asian, Jyoti told me a story about she and her friend Sumitra swapping stories about the first time that their mothers cut their hair and wore Western clothes in their professional lives. She also humorously recounted being mistaken as an "Indian from India" by fellow Americans when she was traveling in Varanasi (resulting in a quip from her mother, who, alluding to the pervasive presence of doctors of Indian origin in the United States, said: "You should have asked them who their doctor is!"). Jyoti reflected:

> I think our stories are all about how we negotiated being Indian and being American, and finding a DIFFERENT balance. I think of my balance as sort of—I'm loath to say it—more assimilationist. See, our stories aren't just about being more Indian in America, they're about being American AND Indian.

Family Stories

As Stuart Hall has noted: "[I]dentities are the names we give to the different ways we are positioned by, and position ourselves within, the narratives of the past" (1990: 225). One of the main sites that the past is transported within diasporas is in family stories. Jean Bacon has explored what she terms the "family idiom" in her account of Indian American assimilation within the United States: that is, orientations shared within families that surfaced in the themes or styles through which parents and children told of their lives in interviews (Bacon 1996: 78). While I ideally would have interviewed the parents of the people I spoke with to gain a sense of how family stories and orientations are transmitted, even without the input of parents, it was clear that the identity of most individuals drew ballast from family stories.

The form of family story most often told involved tracing the routes of arrival: how it happened that the parents emigrated and the person was born here. Given the class background of most of the people I talked to, the story of immigration was also often one of parental accomplishment, often resulting in pressure for children to do well, too. As Sudam said, "Yeah, for me, I feel I am a total overachiever. That's my middle name." Later he commented, "I want to be a little bit more relaxed, but I'm really driven to make my mark on history." When I countered by asking, "Where does that come from?" Sudam responded, "I don't know. My dad was very ambitious. He did lots of activities, he was a student leader. It died off as he grew older. But I think he made a solid impact on this." He then went on to tell the story of how his father arrived in the Chicago area in 1972 as a trained physician.

Bina, a graduate student who grew up in the Chicago area, described how she thought of herself in terms of her family, starting with a tale that was often repeated to her when she visited India and sat on an outdoor swing with her maternal grandmother, mother, and aunts.

> I have wonderful stories that have been passed on to me. I'll start with my grandmother because that's really the one I know well. . . . My grandmother, when she was about four, I guess, her father died, leaving her mother widowed with two daughters. As you probably know, her mother had to shave her head and wear a red sari and that kind of thing, and it was just really, really—she couldn't leave the house, so they were basically penniless and they didn't have any money. So my grandmother, who by the time she was six was in school, because of her good grades, she was able to get a scholarship, and with that money they started saving. And eventually that was the money that would put her sister through a wedding. So my grandmother really used her intelligence and scholarship and all that to bring the family together, and there's a lot more to that story, but basically she worked really hard. . . . She became a lawyer, so she was able to claim land. . . . She was able to use that land—sold it, and then with that money they were able to survive. My grandmother, then, really is brilliant and has used her intelligence all her life to survive. So a lot of her stories are really about using what you can in your life, given your station in life, but completely restrictive because she was a woman. And this was something that I've been told so many times as a child.

These stories about accomplishments on Bina's mother's side were offset by negative examples from her father's side, where his sisters all appeared to be trapped in unsupportive marriages. These diverging legacies have made Bina determined to excel in her education, and to support herself.

Sometimes the lineage evoked through stories could go back several centuries. Manjeet, for example, told me of his grandfather who migrated from the Punjab, living apart and sending back remittances for fifty years. In an almost offhand way, he also revealed his Sikh family's lineage of healing:

My dad would tell us stories about Guru Gobind Singh coming to Gobind-pur, that's why the village is named after him, you know? The crippled—crippled man being on the ground. And him taking the knife they use to cut the wheat with and it going back and forth between him and the man. And it's called *bāgbi*, I think, I'm not sure. Then—then him getting up. And being able to walk. And now any—everybody—every male from the village . . . can do this. Any male. . . . So people come from all over the country to our house for us to do this to them . . . —the healing of Sikhs.

Manjeet went on to tell me of how a Sikh taxi driver from New York came all the way to Cincinnati so Manjeet's father could exchange a steak knife back and forth, and so heal the man's back.

Sometimes, though, family stories could also be repressive, particular-ly when they involved comparison with other South Asian kids. Everyone seemed to grow up hearing about the successes of cousins, or even of South Asian American peers. Medha spoke with disdain of the stories her mother told of her cousin back in Gujarat. She'd talk, said Medha,

[a]bout how my cousin could cook a meal for eighty people when she was eight years old, or something like that. Things like that. Or how she had this beautiful long dark thick hair. It was just like "all Indian girls are supposed to have long luscious hair." And I came to really detest that. I hated all the comparison. I couldn't understand. To me it was very clear, "I'm living in America, OF COURSE I'm not going to be like my cousin." But it seemed like they just couldn't get that!

Retelling her mother's story, Medha reframed it with her own punch line. This reading of new meanings into older stories is common to any trans-mission of folklore, but perhaps in an immigrant context the frames change faster. Kavi, for example, now a graduate student in a humanities discipline, noted the conventionality in her middle-class family: no art, no books. "Can we be an extended family who don't do anything different?" she asked. Scanning family stories for resonances to her own restless desire to break free, live alone, and pursue a higher degree in a non-science-related field, she could at first find only minor rebellion, like a cousin in Uttar Pradesh eating Chinese food. Then she found kinship with her grandmother.

My grandmother was nineteen. After my father had been born, she tried to commit suicide, and she threw herself off the roof, and she ended up hurting her hip and her leg, and she's been crippled ever since. That's some spark of acting out that hasn't reappeared in my generation! What I'm doing is totally incomprehensible to the majority of my family.

In this retelling, then, Kavi took a skeleton out the family closet, reappropri-ating it as a courageous protest.

Mythology and Folktales

Given the rich profusion of oral traditions in South Asia, it is no surprise that folktales and mythology surfaced in family contexts in the United States, too. Zeynab, for example, recalled how her Pakistani mother would tell assorted family stories as well as folktales as she drove the children to appointments across the city where they lived.

> *Zeynab:* I guess I've heard some of the stories over and over. I think I remember them differently as a child than I did when I was older. A lot of them were about a mother's devotion to her child. There was one that used to make me cry *every* time I heard it, and then, there were . . .
>
> *K.N.:* What was that?
>
> *Z:* That one was about . . . a mother whose husband had died in the war. Independence. Fighting for Independence. And she had to raise the son. Alone. You know, working in other people's houses. She used to clean their clothes, scrub their floors, a very hard life. And she did it just because she wanted to give her son a good life with all the things that he would need.
>
>   So the son grows up with everything he wants and he falls in love with a woman. And the woman is very *chālāki*, very. . . .
>
> *K.N.:* Sly, clever.
>
> *Z:* Very sly. And also very selfish. She was very resentful of her mother-in-law's love for the son. He had fallen head over heels in love with her. I mean, he was, you know, *dīvāna* [crazily in love], right? So he wanted to marry her. . . . So the woman says I'll marry you only if you kill your mother and bring me her heart. And so the young boy *eventually* succumbs. He became so overwhelmed with his passion for this woman that one night he goes and kills his mother and he takes out the heart. And then he's walking to his lover's home and he trips over a rock and he falls. And then, a voice, his mother's voice comes from the heart and says, "Son, are you okay?"

Zeynab's mother's voice, speaking Urdu, had left powerful traces on the texture of this poignant story. Zeynab said, "Oh! I used to cry and cry and cry when I heard that. . . . I think that in a lot of ways, you know, I did see my mother in that role because she had really made a lot of sacrifices for all of us. I mean, she had literally given her life to us." The use of folktales like this, then, could serve as a powerful link between generations, inspiring reflection not just on larger meanings but also on relationships between parents and their children.

It was at the level of religious folklore that the most difference between backgrounds was apparent, with second-generation South Asian Americans being differentially exposed to different bodies of mythology by parents or even grandparents. While parents' hope often appears to have been inculcating a firm sense of nationalized religious identity, second-generation individuals appeared to sometimes adapt such stories in creative, even resistant, ways. Medha, for example, found a new strength and confidence after going off to college, and began challenging her parents on a variety of subjects, including Hindu mythology.

> There are stories about Prahlad, who had this awful father who was against God and wanted to proclaim himself as God, and Prahlad would have none of that and he was disobeying his father because he knew there was something better. I want to say to my parents, "So when I disobey you it's because I *know* that there's something better, it's not because I want to throw it in your face." And that's not something they want me to see in that story! What they want me to see in that story was "Oh, he was so devoted to God that even though his father was doing all this to him, he was still devoted to God." We definitely have different interpretations of things and they are very rigid. That doesn't work well with the lifestyle that I have made for myself here.

Another strategy was to bring together imagined characters from different cultural settings. Shankar confessed that he identified with the god Shiva, whose name he carried. As he reported, "They said, well, this god has a cobra around his neck. I always had a fascination with snakes. I used to in first grade watch as many snake shows and documentaries as I could." At the same time, he also had admired Superman, and at one point had identified with Superman so strongly that he adopted blue contact lenses, like Christopher Reeve. "Not because I wanted to be white-like but because of the contrast, dark skin, blue eyes."

The *Amar Chitra Katha* mythological comic books were pressed upon most Hindu children by their parents. Arjun, who grew up in Ohio, learned his Indian stories from these comic books, or from his mother reading aloud Hindu myths. He drew on these story characters to illustrate his own sense of dislocation. For example, he identified strongly with the tragic, unacknowledged brother Karna in the Mahabharata epic "because of his kind of outcast . . . birth . . . his outcast background." While Shankar had Hindu gods and comic-book superheroes coexisting in his imagination as a child, Arjun actually mingled them together, inventing a hybrid mythology, "like Batman and Bheem [a strong brother in the Mahabharata]."

> [S]uperheroes were a part of my imagination. My mythology if you want to call it. So I was thinking to myself, "Yeah, I have this secret society, a secret association, a secret identity that nobody here understands or can figure out." And it's kind of—in a way, like the alter ego of a Batman. Like when he goes into the bat cave, you know, nobody . . . knows about his secret life. . . .
>
> So it was that sort of thing, for me. And that was my way—I think—at the time, of understanding my religion, my difference, my ethnicity. Because at the time, of course, you have no vocabulary. You have no concepts. So this is the way I thought of it. At that moment, I think it was a positive valuation of my situation.

THE USES OF STORIES

Too often, anthropologists fixate on the particular life-story texts they have gathered and neglect to inquire what other situations these stories are used in, and what forms of cultural politics manifest in narrations (cf. Rosenwald and Ochberg 1992). After the interviews, I tried to get back to different people I had talked to in an attempt to better understand the wider life of their stories. Here are a few of their responses:

Najma wrote on email that she tells stories about her experience to "just about anyone who I feel can relate. Mostly, I feel, because I want someone to help me through this experience where I feel few can truly understand and give me meaningful advice." Similarly, Vina stated, "To me, intimacy is about sharing secrets. I don't tell these stories much, just sometimes to close friends. And, also to my therapist." Zeynab also felt that her memories were precious and personal. Since she had told her stories as gifts to me, my challenge has been to incorporate her articulate voice in my writings for a larger audience in a way that will hopefully not make her feel too exposed.

The women, then, mostly seemed to concur on storytelling as relating to the creation of intimacy or the assumption of pre-existing intimacy. Jyoti, though, one of the most hilarious of all the storytellers, wrote that she loved telling stories "because I like to entertain people, I use them to explain myself, I use them to fill in open spaces in conversation."

The men whom I was able to get answers from also had varying views. At one extreme was Dinesh, an exuberant performer of his own tales, who said on the phone, "I tell stories for shock value. Like my condom story is a classic, I tell it to Americans [meaning white Americans] if they ever say their parents are too strict. With Indian kids I love to tell stories about my drug use. Like, you know, it's all about subverting expectations."

Shankar, though, who is younger and more cautious, reported that he did not tell his stories much to others: mostly his strategy was to ask questions, and listen. He said that he wished that he knew "more Indian kids" to share these stories of growing up with, so they could support each other.

Vasant, who grew up in the 1960s with virtually no South Asian American peers to identify with, most poignantly articulates how telling stories functions as emplacement within a changing social landscape. I first spoke to him in 1997 as South Asian American undergraduates were a growing presence on campus, *chai* appeared in coffee shops, *bindis* showed up on rock stars' foreheads, and *mehndi* (henna) became available in temporary tattooing kits at Walgreens. Looking back in 1999, he said, "I never told anyone those stories about growing up before. When I told you these stories it was a form of catharsis, I guess. But it raised questions, too: what intersections had made it possible to say now what wasn't possible to say before?"

CONCLUSIONS

Using the term "emplacement," I want to call attention to the *process* of staking out space rather than to *any single moment of fixed arrival*. After all, there are multiple spaces and multiple strategies by which people make space in the world for their distinctive experience. In a brilliant article critiquing the invention of authenticity in the South Asian diaspora, Radhakrishnan points out that the mutation of an "Indian" identity into an "ethnic" or hyphenated American one reminds us to question whether "identities and ethnicities are not a matter of fixed and stable selves but rather the results and products of fortuitous travels and recontextualizations" (1994: 222).

Life stories among second-generation South Asian Americans worked as emplacement in two ways. First, the very act of making narrative coherence appeared to be a way of integrating conflicting identities. If elements did not fit together anywhere else, they were made to do so in the stories. Telling stories that bridge different arenas of diasporic experience becomes a powerful way of placing the self, and finding new ground for being a culturally mixed but not necessarily mixed-up person.

Second, by telling these stories, inserting distinctive experience into a wider social arena, life stories, like ethnic literature more generally, can be a powerful vehicle of asserting "I'm Here" (cf. Ling 1991). Whether the stories are told to friends, therapists, or nosy anthropologists, the act of telling is also a way of taking others along on the journey that one has lived, with emotional, social, and political consequences. I believe that the same narrative impulse that underlies oral storytelling about lives also permeates the vibrant short story, memoir, and essay collections addressing South Asian American experience that burgeoned in the 1990s (Dasgupta 1998; S. Gupta 1999; Ratti 1993; Rustomji-Kerns 1994; Srikanth and Maira 1996; Women of South Asian Descent Collective 1993).

When I share drafts of this essay with those I interviewed, the concept of emplacement appears to resonate with their experience. Dinesh rephrased my central argument, saying, "See, this emplacement is all about accepting that you don't belong anywhere but the space that you make." In an email, Vasant emphasized the psychological importance of emplacement by reflecting that his need to tell the stories rose from a boiling over of "the feelings of fatigue from a constantly floating state of UNplacement (a condition of feeling like I belong nowhere, so it's not even 'displacement' because that assumes one felt emplaced at some point in the past)."

These comments underscore the importance of stories in this era of multiple identifications, multiple locations, multiple possible sites of return. For those of us who span so many selves and spaces that it seems we can never rest from the work of building bridges back and forth and back again, perhaps the only momentary home is in stories. Making and remaking stories, we frame our own shelters to house the divergent meanings we carry around. Sharing, spreading, claiming distinctiveness, or making alliances with stories, we stake out new spaces in the power-laden, shifting contours of multicultural landscapes.

ACKNOWLEDGMENTS

I am grateful for support from the University of Wisconsin Graduate School, particularly in the form of a Vilas Associateship Faculty Award, an H. I. Romnes fellowship, and a faculty development grant that have enabled me to explore new directions in my research. I am deeply indebted to every kind person who gifted me with time, stories, and critical readings. In honoring confidentiality, I cannot thank you all by name here. Audiences at the Wisconsin South Asia Meetings, the American Folklore Society, the University of Wisconsin, Cornell University, and the University of California at Riverside have all helped in shaping this essay. Special thanks to Regina Bendix, Veena Dwivedi, Sarah Lamb, Maria Lepowsky, Diane Mines, Seema Rao, Hemant Shah, Deepak Sharma, and Nina Tayyib for sustained insights and editorial suggestions.

35

Unexpected Destinations

E. Valentine Daniel

Editors' note: E. Valentine Daniel, in his book Charred Lullabies, *attempts to understand some of the causes and effects of the civil war in Sri Lanka, in particular some of the toll that the war has taken upon Sri Lanka's Tamil population, as well as upon the nation itself. In this excerpt from chapter 6, Daniel discusses some of the kinds of experiences that Tamil refugees from Sri Lanka (see part 5) have when they flee their nation in search of refuge elsewhere. We enter his book at a point where Daniel has been discussing three "phases" of Sri Lankan Tamil migration to Britain. The first phase, Phase 1 immigrants, are "the elite." They were upper-class Sri Lankans who migrated well before the civil war, either during or in the wake of colonial rule, often to obtain advanced professional and graduate degrees. By staying in England, this group severed their ties to Sri Lanka and became British citizens. Phase 2 immigrants are those who came not as elites, but as students from a variety of class backgrounds in the 1960s and 1970s. Facing unemployment at home and locked out of universities, which had imposed a quota system that worked to the disadvantage of many Tamil students, they found England to be a viable alternative for pursuing education as well as employment. Many were disappointed to find that the jobs which were available to them, and for which they were often overqualified, were frequently limited to the service sector, such as in gas stations or convenience stores. Phase 3, the phase that this selection focuses upon, consists of "refugees," those who beginning in the 1980s fled Sri Lanka in order to stay alive.*

The early arrivals of Phase 3 had still been those with at least some means: the means to leave before Britain began tightening her laws, before the Immigration Carrier's Liability Act was passed,[1] before racketeers got into the act of facilitating the asylum-seeker's escape with false papers at high cost, before the price for getting to Heathrow went from under four hundred British pounds to more than five thousand. The "success stories" with petrol stations and retail stores that one is likely to hear from asylum-seekers apply mainly to those early arrivals who came to Britain before 1985. For the very poor—increasingly the profile of the average Tamil arriving at Heathrow during the latter part of the 1980s—the new exorbitant passage was bought for only one family member through his or her family's going deeply into debt, in some instances after selling house and possessions. No longer could the one who entered Britain raise enough money to pay back his or her own debt, let alone raise enough to pay the going price for chancy "illegal" exits and entries of other members of the family. And even if and when this was possible, the pits and snares were too many and far too hazardous. There are cases known to the London-based Joint Council for the Welfare of Immigrants in which middlemen—also Tamils—have abandoned groups of Tamils at "transit points" in such faraway places as Bangkok and Nairobi, after these same middlemen absconded with the five thousand plus pounds' "setup money" they received from their charges. Such a middleman takes them to an apartment or a room and tells them to stay put—lest they be caught by the authorities—until he makes arrangements for the next leg of the journey to London or some other Western capital. The room or apartment in question is locked from the outside to ensure double protection. The anxious and frightened group waits, at times for days, until hunger and/or suspicion gets the better of them and they break loose or start screaming for help. Some such desperate and penniless escapees are then offered, by yet another set of racketeers, the opportunity to become drug couriers as a means of buying their way back onto the road to asylum. A refugee who gave me the above account concluded it by saying:

> You ask me about Tamil nationalism. There is only Tamil internationalism. No Tamil nationals. Never was. Never will be. This is Tamil internationalism. Being stuck in a windowless room in Thailand, or a jail in Nairobi or Accra or Lagos or Cairo or America. Or being a domestic servant in Singapore or Malaysia for a rich Tamil relative. Being part of a credit card racket in London. Crossing Niagara Falls into Canada. I am told there is even a Tamil fisherman on a Norwegian island near the North Pole. All internationals. And don't forget the briefless barrister at Charing Cross who tries to hawk his specialty as an immigration lawyer to anyone who is gullible enough to believe him. He is a Tamil too.

The African destinations were explained to me as follows by yet another informant:

No one plans on ending up in Africa. This happens because of drug-pushing middlemen. Customs in African airports are not that strict. And most of the airport officials are bribed by other agents.

Q. Who are these agents? Tamils?

A. They are. Mainly members of PLOTE.[2] They are caught and deported from European ports back to their last stop, usually Nigeria.

The African connection was widely explained in the following manner: Middlemen in Thailand or Pakistan buy desperate Tamils tickets to African destinations, giving them a package of drugs and a promise of a final European or Canadian destination. The Tamils' only obligation is to hand over the package to an African courier in Africa. Unlike Tamils, Africans are willing to carry their drugs in a form undetectable by European customs: stuffed in a condom that is then swallowed. Because of this method, Africans passed through customs with ease until recently, when a swallowed condom burst in a courier's stomach. The courier was rushed to the hospital where he died, and an autopsy exposed the game. Even though the Tamil role in the Africans' trafficking of drugs has achieved widely held folkloric truth, I have been able neither to confirm nor to disconfirm this story with any Tamil who has directly participated in this dangerous activity. It is known, however, that the use of drugs is strictly prohibited not only by the general Tamil cultural strictures and the opprobrium it could bring upon those who violate them, but also by the moral policing of the LTTE. Drugs are meant for Europeans. The money that is believed to result from the sale of drugs is meant for the war effort in Eelam.

The story of Tamil asylum-seekers ending up in the United States is a curious one. The number of asylum-seekers who have been granted asylum in the United States over the past decade is around a dozen, more than half of whom are Sinhalas who fled the government's crackdown on dissidents in the south of the island. It is widely known in the Tamil community that it is virtually impossible to get asylum in the United States. Almost none who sought asylum in the United States had intended to do so in the first place, but had been trapped in transit on their way to Canada, where they had hoped to find refuge. The story of Shanmugam is both unique and typical and is worth recalling in some detail.

Shanmugam was a twenty-eight-year-old Tamil whom I came to know in 1989 through a human rights attorney in Seattle, who asked me if I would serve as an expert witness at his hearing before an immigration judge. According to Shanmugam and affidavits sent on his behalf by justices of the peace and other prominent citizens of Jaffna, he was the son of a farmer. He had an older sister and a younger brother. He was unconnected with any of the several Tamil militant groups operating in Jaffna. But he was persecuted by two Tamil militant groups, members of the Indian Peace-Keeping Forces, and the Sri Lankan army. He had bullet marks on his foot and shoulder where he had been shot by an EPRLF[3] guard. He finally fled Sri Lanka in fear of his life. Now let me continue the narrative based on his account to his attorney and me, and to the court.

From 1980 until the riots of 1983 he lived with his married sister in a suburb of Colombo. He had moved from Jaffna to Colombo because he wanted to prepare himself for the G.C.E. (Advanced Level) exams by attending a private "tutory" in Colombo. In 1983, Sinhala mobs attacked his brother-in-law's home by setting fire to it. His sister had left for Jaffna, to deliver, as is customary, her first child in her mother's home. His brother-in-law, who tried to face the mob and dissuade them from attacking his house, was killed. Shanmugam jumped out of a back window and over the garden wall and fled the scene. After spending several weeks in refugee camps in Colombo, he joined an exodus of Tamil refugees and went to Jaffna by boat.

Back in Jaffna, he and his younger brother tried their best to hide from recruiters from the various Tamil militant groups combing Jaffna for volunteers who would be trained to fight the Sri Lankan state. In 1985, his seventeen-year-old brother disappeared, leaving behind a note informing his parents that he was joining the liberation struggle. In 1986, Shanmugam was taken in for questioning by members of the Sri Lankan army. After two weeks of considerable beating and torture, and interventions by the then government agent and his pleading mother, he was released to his parents. Then came the Indo–Sri Lankan Peace Accord by the terms of which the Indian army occupied northern and eastern Sri Lanka so as to restore peace between the Tamils and the Sri Lankan state. A few months after the LTTE had declared its battle against the Indian army, members of the Indian army took him in for questioning. The solitary confinement and beatings lasted for a week. Again, he was released. Again, Shanmugam attributes his release to his mother's indefatigable pleadings with the Indian commander. No sooner was he released than he was captured by the LTTE and taken in for questioning. This time the questions were about what he had told the Indians and what he knew about the whereabouts of his brother. In response to the first question he told them all that he remembered. As for his brother's whereabouts, he said that he knew nothing, not even which militant group he had joined. During the first week of his confinement, he was relentlessly tortured. During the second week, even though the questions continued, he was treated well by the Tigers.

The very day he was released by the Tigers, he was recaptured by the Eelam People's Revolutionary Liberation Front. The EPRLF was a Tamil militant group that came under the good graces of the Indian forces and was given a certain measure of civil and military authority over the citizens of Jaffna. But members of this group also abused their authority, had alienated many Tamils of the north, and came to be seen as the lackeys of the occupying Indians. According to Shanmugam, the torture under the EPRLF was the most severe. First, they were convinced that he had gone voluntarily to the LTTE to divulge details of the interrogation by the Indians, and wanted to know what he had told them. Second, convinced that his younger brother was with the Tigers, they were keen on capturing him for the Indians, who were by now at war with the Tigers. After several weeks of incarceration, torture, and interrogation, Shanmugam managed to escape. He fled Jaffna and after several days of walking through the jungle, he reached Mannar. From there he bought his passage on a speedboat and reached India. From India he informed his parents of his safety and his whereabouts. He knew that it would be only a matter of time before one of the militant groups, if not the Indian authorities, would catch up with him. While in Madras, he learned that he could get a forged passport and a ticket to Canada. Through labyrinthine means he informed his parents of his plans to buy a passport and leave for Canada. A month later, his mother and sister sold all their jewelry, and his father sold most of their land; through equally labyrinthine means they sent him $5,000. With this money he was able to buy a forged passport at a discounted price and to pay a travel agent, who supplied an air ticket, arranged the route of his flight, and provided him with a contact who knew someone in Vancouver, B.C.; the contact would help him learn the ropes for applying for and obtaining asylum in Canada. The only thing he was told he needed to remember was to destroy his passport and flush it down the toilet of the airplane just before landing in Vancouver. His passport was red in color, Malaysian, and was quite worn from considerable use. It seemed as if it had belonged to a Malaysian businessman.

Shanmugam was routed through Hong Kong and, unlike his compatriots who were stranded in Bangkok, did not have to leave any of the airports en route until he reached Seattle. All that he had seen of the countries through which his flight pattern took him were the airports' transit lounges. In Seattle, all passengers had to disembark and go through U.S. customs before continuing on their flight to Vancouver. No one had warned him of this wrinkle in his itinerary. Even before he got to the long line in front of the customs officer's high table with his tin trunk in hand, he was apprehended by another officer and taken in for questioning. He told them his story. He told them that he had no intention of remaining in the United States but wanted to reach Canada. When given the choice of either being sent back by the next available flight or being incarcerated until he received a hearing, where the odds of his repatriation to Sri Lanka were almost assured, Shanmugam chose the latter. This is a short and sweet version of the more detailed, horrendous tale he had told his lawyer and me, and later, a court over which a judge by the name of Kahn presided.

A particular episode of the court hearing merits retelling because it illustrates yet another aspect of refugees' predicament that goes unreported: Shanmugam spoke no English and understood almost none. To assist him, the court had hired a South Asian living in Seattle who had been certified by Berlitz as qualified to translate English into Tamil and vice versa. Under cross-examination, Shanmugam had just finished describing the burning of his sister's house in Colombo and the murder of his brother-in-law.

> Defendant: And then I ran through the side streets, to avoid the mobs.
> Prosecutor: Who were these mobs made up of?
> Translator: (Renders an intelligible translation in a form of Tamil heavily accented by Malayalam.)
> Defendant: Sinhalas.
> Translator: Sinhalas.
> Judge: Were there policemen on the street?
> Translator: (Translates the question correctly into Malayalam. The defendant strains to follow him and then answers.)
> Defendant: Police and army.
> Translator: Yes.
> Judge: Did they help you?
> Translator: (Translates question into Malayalamized Tamil, but the defendant seems to follow the drift of the question, and responds.)
> Defendant: No. They hit me with their rifles. And when I fell down, they kicked me with their boots and said, "Run, Tamil, run."
> Translator: Yes.

At this point I told the defense attorney that the translation was incorrect, and he conveyed this to the judge.

> Judge (to defense attorney): Your expert witness is an expert on Sri Lanka. But the translator is an expert in the language spoken and accordingly has been certified by Berlitz. Is your expert witness certified by Berlitz as an expert in . . . Tamil?
> Defense attorney (after seeing me shake my head): No, Your Honor.

Almost immediately after asking the prosecutor to continue, the judge interrupted the prosecutor, asking the court recorder to stop recording the proceedings and turn off the tape recorder. Off the record, the judge asked me to render what I thought was the correct translation of the defendant's response to his question.

> Expert witness: He said that the police and soldiers did not help him but hit him with the butts of their rifles and, when he fell down, kicked him with their boots and said, "Run, Tamil, run."
> Judge (to Berlitz translator): Is that correct?
> Translator (now realizing that there is a native speaker of Tamil in the courtroom): Yes, Your Honor.

At another point in the hearing:

Prosecutor: Are you a Malaysian?
Translator: (Renders an intelligible translation.)
Defendant: No.
Prosecutor: What is your nationality?
Translator: Tamil or Sinhala?
Defendant: Tamil.
Translator: Tamil.
Prosecutor: So you believe in a separate Tamil nation in Sri Lanka?
Translator: Do you want a Tamil nation (*tēśam*)?
Defendant: No. I don't even have a country (translatable as "a place to which
     I belong").
Translator: No.

Malayalam is a language spoken in southwest India. Linguists estimate that its breakaway from early Tamil occurred around the thirteenth century. The mutual intelligibility between modern Malayalam and modern Tamil is akin to that between Italian and Spanish. Imagine a monolingual Italian-speaker certified by Berlitz as one who speaks and understands Spanish, and appointed to serve as translator in a court of law between English-speaking attorneys and judge and a monolingual Spanish-speaking defendant. Such was Shanmugam's predicament.

As a postscript to this memorable trial I might add that Judge Kahn rendered his judgment against the defendant. In his judgment he thanked me for my testimony and for educating the court on the recent history of the ethnic tensions in Sri Lanka. But he declared that in the final analysis, he was compelled to take the word of his State Department in meting out his judgment. According to the State Department, "there was no fear of persecution in Sri Lanka."

After two years we learned that Judge Kahn's judgment had been upheld by higher courts. Shanmugam was sent back to Sri Lanka. His family came to meet him at the Colombo airport. They claim to have seen him arrive at customs and then to have waited for him to emerge. But he never came out. After several hours of waiting and inquiries and receiving different kinds of answers, they tried to console themselves by saying that their having seen him briefly must have been only an illusion. Other inquiries pointed toward Sri Lanka's Special Defense Forces, who, it was said, had whisked him off to the notorious Fourth Floor for interrogation. Whatever the case may be, Shanmugam has been neither seen nor heard from since that day.

While waiting for his appeal, Shanmugam had learned Spanish from co-detainees who had come from countries such as El Salvador, Guatemala, and Nicaragua. The detention center was a small international community of card-playing, Ping-Pong batting, story-swapping, language-learning males. Far fewer women were apprehended at the border, and when they were, most of them chose to return to Sri Lanka or managed to get themselves bailed out by relatives in the United States and then found their way to Canada. But there were children who were arrested and detained and whose story needs to be told, if only because of the uniquely dangerous situation into which they are thrown by a well-meaning legal system. Two such cases merit our attention.

AND CHILDREN

Karunaharan was sixteen years old. He too, like Shanmugam, had his asylum-seeking trip to Canada cut short at the U.S. customs in Seattle. He came from a middle-class family in Jaffna and had, until his escape, attended the prestigious secondary school of Jaffna College along with his older sister. One day when he and his sister were walking back home from school, they were stopped by a Sikh soldier of the Indian Peace-Keeping Forces. He was told to wait on the road while his sister was taken into a house occupied by some Indian army officers. Within minutes of her disappearance behind the closed door of the house, he heard his sister's screams. He ran to the side window of the house, and through a crack he saw his sister "being shamed."[4] Then he ran to the front door, which was being guarded by two grinning Indian soldiers, and tried to get access. He was kicked by one of them, and he fell to the ground unable to breathe. Then he heard his sister's screams become muffled, and grow fainter and fainter, and then he heard her no more. He thought that he was dying. Then he thought that his sister was dead. He sat up and wiped his mouth. There was blood. The place of the two soldiers who were guarding the door had been taken over by two others. And finding them engrossed in their own conversation, he crept back to the window just in time to see his sister being shot in the back. He sneaked back to the main road, and when he reached it, he heard a second shot. He ran home sobbing and screaming. After that incident, his parents managed to get him on a flight to Canada, which brought him into Seattle's detention center instead.

Karunaharan was not an adult and therefore was put in a detention center for children, where his co-detainees were streetwise American teenagers who were incarcerated for crimes that ranged from selling drugs to aggravated assault, to robbery, and even rape. Bright as he was and as much as he tried to adjust to the ethos of the place, his middle-class village background in conservative Jaffna had not prepared him for this. He was gang-raped the very first night and beaten up the next. His attorney succeeded in persuading the judge to release him to the custody of a Tamil citizen in the Seattle area in whose charge he was to be kept until his next hearing. He eventually crossed the border into Canada and was granted asylum there.

Shoba was ten years old when the Indian troops came to Jaffna to keep the peace. When I interviewed her with her attorney in Seattle, she was thirteen. According to her, the Indian soldiers whom the citizens of Jaffna had welcomed with garlands had, within a few months, become enemies of all the people, excepting those who joined the "EP" or supported them. (People in her neighborhood secretly called the EPRLF "EP" and rhymed it with *nāi pī,* "dog shit.") The EPRLF ranked foremost among organizations conceiving of a state based on socialist principles of equality: equality for all castes, both sexes, the Tamils of the various regions, and the Sinhalas. But when given the power of the gun and command by their Indian superiors, low-ranking cadres in particular became drunk with power and patrolled the streets intimidating the citizens. When an EPRLF officer rode in his car, other vehicles had to pull over to the edge of the road; when an EPRLF cadre walked along a street, ordinary citizens had to step to the side, even into a ditch if that was the only side left to the road. Those who refused to grant the respect due were taken in and punished or even beaten on the spot. Schoolchildren whose parents were not open supporters of the EP were especially afraid of running into uniformed members of the movement. They usually rode their bikes and chose side lanes and byways to make their way between home and school. One day Shoba and her friends were returning from school on their bikes laughing over a joke that her friend had cracked, when they suddenly ran into an EP commander with his assistants. They all quickly got off their bikes. The girl who had cracked the joke was her best friend, the class comic and very smart. She was so taken aback by the armed "soldiers" that she just got off her seat, did not have time to wheel the bike to the side of the road, and so stood astride her bike as if in shock—but still had a smile on her face because of her joke. One of the EP men jerked her off her bike. While the other threw the bike to the side of the road and smashed it, the commander ordered the man who had hold of her to take her to the field and made her kneel down. While Shoba and her schoolmates looked on in terror, the commander gave them a lecture about respect and the EPRLF, and then turned toward her kneeling friend and shot her in the head. Then he put his gun in his holster saying, "Let this be a lesson to you." The children pushed their bikes home, sobbing in silence for fear of being heard by the "soldiers," who continued on their promenade.

When she reached home, she broke into hysterical sobs. Her mother and father shook her to make her speak, tell them what had happened. Finally, her father, who had never spanked her, slapped her in order to calm her down. Then she told them what had happened. Her father warned them to expect trouble. "An old woman has shot an Indian officer," he told her. The Indian army had ordered the residents of a neighborhood to vacate their houses, so that they, in response to a tip-off, could carry out a search for Tigers and their weapons. The old woman had refused to leave; she merely huddled in a corner and whimpered in terror. Since the North Indian soldiers did not know Tamil, a compassionate South Indian officer—a Malayalee—went into the woman's low-doored hut and bent down to assure her in the little Tamil he knew that she would be safe under his protection, and pleaded with her to leave with him. The woman pulled out a machine gun that had been concealed by the drape of her sari and shot the officer to death. She in turn was riddled with bullets by the two Indian *jawāns* who had been waiting outside.

Even though the killing of the officer had taken place in another area of the peninsula, it was widely known that whenever a soldier was killed, the army would go on a rampage. This was truer of the Sri Lankan army during their earlier occupation, but it happened with the Indians as well. Shoba's father also had heard that those neighborhoods which "stole electricity" by jerry-rigging connections to the main line were thought to be LTTE sympathizers who were rewarded with LTTE expertise. Shoba maintained that this was not true, that ever since the onset of fuel and electricity rationing, citizens all over Jaffna had resorted to devices for beating the restrictions. As predicted by her father, that afternoon around four o'clock, soldiers came to the neighborhood. Most men had been tipped off to the Indians' arrival and had fled. The soldiers ordered everybody to step out of their homes, and the homes were searched. After the search was finished, the residents, all of them women, were told to go back in. Then a soldier came out of a house dragging a woman and her infant son. Shoba ran into the backyard to peek through the palm-frond fence and see what was happening. The senior officer asked the woman where the man of the house was. She said she did not know. He shot her dead. She fell backwards still holding onto her infant. When her hands let loose of her child and fell to her side, the child, still seated on her stomach, started to scream. The soldiers first left the child and his dead mother on the ground and walked out the front gate. A few moments later, one of the soldiers returned and shot the infant with one bullet. Suddenly there was not a sound to be heard.

That was the night her parents decided to send her out of the country. She had a cousin in Canada, and that would be her destination. But she had no passport. They managed to get her a forged passport, in which her age was recorded as eighteen rather than thirteen. She was too young to travel alone. So they found a naturalized Canadian relative and changed her name to read as if she were his wife; they then traveled to Canada as husband and wife. When they were apprehended in Seattle, it was clear that she was younger than eighteen and much too young to be married. Confessions were wrung out of them with ease. She and her partner were arrested. The partner posted bail and left for Canada. Fortunately for Shoba, there was a guard who, sensing the danger she faced in juvenile detention, pleaded with the judge to release her to the custody of someone—she herself was willing—who would take care of the young girl until her hearing. (In several instances, guards who have seen the danger that these children are in have volunteered to take them into their own homes.) The attorney assigned to defend Shoba got in touch with a Tamil family he knew and asked them if he might request that the judge release her to their custody. The male head of the family said that they would have been only too glad to help but feared to get drawn into anything that could signal their presence to the LTTE members who were operating in Europe and Canada, and who were very aggressive fund-raisers for the cause of Eelam. They did not want their name to appear on any LTTE list for fear that this would instigate the Sri Lankan government to harass and persecute family members who still remained on the island. Next, the lawyer contacted an Estate Tamil family that had intermarried with the Sinhalas. This family willingly and gladly took in Shoba, saying that Estate Tamils were still Indian Tamils and therefore had nothing to fear from a Sri Lankan movement such as the LTTE. After two weeks, they flew with her to Ithaca, where she was handed over to a Sri Lankan Tamil Catholic priest who took her across the Niagara bridge into Canada; there she applied for asylum and was met by her cousin. Before she crossed over, the priest asked her what she planned to do in Canada. Her answer: "Keep away from anyone who talks about Eelam or Sri Lanka or motherland."

Children much younger than Karunaharan and Shoba, as young as five years old, have been put onto planes unaccompanied by any adult and sent to Germany and Switzerland. The German and Swiss news media featured these arrivals in their headline stories. While some kind German and Swiss citizens rushed to adopt them, others described this as a new "wave" and called the children economic refugees. I expressed my puzzlement to a German woman at these children's being called "economic refugees." She saw what was happening as being quite straightforward, based on "confessions" by the children themselves. Most of the children who arrived at one of these country's airports, when asked where their parents were, would say, "Mommy said for me to go and that she will come soon and join me." That was the evidence: a mother's ruse to claim the right to emigrate to the country as a parent, once the child was naturalized! That the child would have to grow up to adulthood before being able to sponsor his or her parent, which would take as many as thirteen more years, did not seem like much of an issue. What this woman told me in an interview in Heidelberg was of course repeated more than once over the German and Swiss media. Many of the kind souls who offered to adopt these children, on the one hand, could not believe the cruelty of their parents, on the other: that they could lie to their children when they knew that they had neither plans nor possibility of following their children. The second group is no closer to the truth than the first.

Unfortunately or otherwise, most South Asian parents choose to hide the truth when the truth, they opine, is likely to cause immediate pain, sorrow, and sadness. This is so with terminally ill patients from whom the nature of their illness is concealed as long as possible by both physician and relatives. This is especially true of parents and children. A mother who is about to administer her child some bitter medicine will not hesitate to lie about its bitterness. The mother who sent off her unaccompanied child to Switzerland or Germany most probably did not have the luxury of reflecting on the long-range psychological trauma that such deceptions would wreak on her child. The story of one woman who had dispatched her child in such a manner and whom I had the opportunity to interview in Sri Lanka is likely to have been a typical variant of the accounts of other mothers (and, in a few instances, fathers) who resorted to such desperate actions.

Punitham lost her father, both brothers, and two of her four children. Left with only a son and a daughter, she decided to somehow or other get at least her son to safety. She knew that it would be only a matter of time before the next shell would fall or the next bullet would hit. She was determined to send her child to any country and have fate take over. Her choice for him was between certain death in Sri Lanka and a chancy life somewhere else. The only country that would not return her child, she had heard, was Germany. So she sold all her possessions and got her son a ticket. She could not get herself to tell her son the truth. How could she be so cruel? How could she tell him that he was never going to see her again, that she would most probably be killed, and that he most likely would be able to live? If she had told him that, how could he have left her behind and gone with the stranger whom he called "uncle," who took him to the airport? The only gift she thought that she could give him was the gift of life. And she is glad that she gave that to him. But otherwise, she says, "there isn't a day that goes by that I don't pray for him, and weep for him. He was my only son. He is my only son. I am glad he did not die for Sri Lanka or for Eelam. Maybe he will remember Tamil. That is enough. He will be a German-Tamil. That is enough." Economic refugee, indeed!

The Disaggregation of Identity

Many of the men who, having left their wives and children, came to Great Britain after 1985, came to escape death. Now they hold little hope of seeing their families again. They live in a state of heightened anxiety bounded by a seven-year limit: by the end of the seventh year they must, by law, be notified as to whether their application for asylum has been accepted. Many, unable to bear the strain, have returned home regardless of the consequences awaiting them, some to meet their death there. Others have gone back to Sri Lanka after learning that the reason for their having left that country in the first place no longer exists: their families have been wiped out by one armed group or another. The intransigence of British authorities and the scale of British xenophobia and racism vis-à-vis refugees (as evidenced by the frequent headlines of London's tabloids) are astounding when one realizes that between 1979 and 1989 Great Britain, with a population of almost 58,000,000, admitted only 54,935 refugees, a mere 0.09 percent of the total population. Of these only 7,910 were Sri Lankans (Turner 1996). If white Britain's reluctance to give refuge to asylum-seekers is astounding, Phase 1 Tamils' willingness to share in this sentiment is ironic, but also understandable. They, like the white Britons, believed in a nation and a nationalized past. In the case of Phase 3 refugees, the more urgently they needed a nation or a national past, the more authentically they encountered its unavailableness. The more obtrusively this unavailableness pressed itself upon the lives of these refugees, the more the nation and a national past revealed itself as something just occurrent and nothing more. The national past had been loosened from its hitherto unexpressed inclusion in the background practices of these Tamils. The nationalized past became an isolated property, a cipher.

By the beginning of the 1990s, further changes were observed in the composition of the more recent asylum-seeking cohort. Now, not only did young men and women who had escaped the Sri Lankan and Indian armies seek asylum in Britain, but war-hardened and disenchanted militants, escaping tyrannous militant groups of their own, were arriving in London. This group introduced a climate of suspicion on the one hand and a pervasive cynicism on the other. The most prominent target of this cynicism was the nation. I have witnessed arguments between these Tamils and their fellow Tamils, who had embarked upon the project of finding and establishing their national past, in which the former thought that the distant past, which obsessed their fellow nationalists, was irrelevant at best and a sign of derangement at worst. The only past they knew and cared enough not to want to be caught in was the recent past of war, rape, torture, and death that they had just escaped. Phase 3 Tamils have also begun to establish new alliances and to adopt new attitudes toward identity and difference that are now marking them off from Phase 1 Tamils in unprecedented ways. A series of examples will illustrate my point.

A number of Phase 3 Tamils who began at the petrol pump moved up to managing the petrol station and the attached "mini-markets," and then on to acquiring small grocery stores run by Ugandan Indians whose children now have no interest in inheriting their parents' businesses. Along with entailing late hours and hard work, the running of these shops presents a unique problem in customer relations. In Sivapalan's case, for instance, one of his customers is an older English woman who comes to his shop every day to ask him why he sells these nasty-smelling and strange-looking things, and why he does not take it all and go back to where he came from. Sivapalan smiles and checks out the items she buys—because they are inexpensive in his shop—and wishes her a good day. I asked him what he felt. He said, "Hate!" and then added, "But I also know we will win and they will lose." I did not press him to unpack that statement but let it bask in its polyvalence. Sivapalan, and other Tamil shop owners like him, have another interesting customer in the young Afro-Caribbean British male. Some of these young men—"at least one per night"—walk into his shop and pick up a pack or two of beer, presenting, however, only a packet of chewing gum at the cash register. When asked about the beer, the young man boldly declares, knowing full well that everyone knows otherwise, that he brought the beer from outside and owes money only for the gum he bought at this store. Sivapalan takes the money for the chewing gum and lets him go. This practice is so well known that it even piques the sympathetic ire of Phase 1 Tamils, who wonder why the Tamil shopkeeper does not inform the police. Phase 3 Tamils consider this kind of advice a sign of the utter ignorance of Phase 1 Tamils, and of the distance that separates the two groups. For one thing, the policeman is their foremost enemy. In support of these sentiments Phase 3 Tamils supplied me with stories of police racism, injustice, and violence too numerous to recount here. As one Tamil put it, "The policemen of the world should have a country of their own." For another, the shopkeepers find the rage of their "law-abiding" Phase 1 counterparts amusing and out of place. Even I was impressed by the equanimity with which these shopkeepers reacted to these blatant acts of shoplifting. Even though these Tamils did not extend alliances of interpersonal relations to the Afro-Caribbean Britons, they extended them alliances of understanding. They did not see them as breaking the law but as having broken with the law. To this extent their experience was a common one.

Tamils have little to do with the Afro-Caribbean community, a group whose "urban ways" they cannot relate to; people who, in their view, "give the family low priority." However, they find African immigrants much more compatible allies. Not only do many of the latter share Phase 3 Tamils' asylum-seeking status; they also have "rural values." That these new links of affect materialize may be illustrated by the following incident.

Sahitharan was a twenty-nine-year-old asylum-seeker from Sri Lanka. He was waylaid by a group of young whites and bashed to death in London's Eastham. Several of the London-based organizations working for refugees organized a protest march. Over 4,000 people of all ethnic groups joined the march. But there were only 150 Tamils, all from Phase 3. The largest non-Tamil representation at the rally was made up of black Africans. It is of interest that the trustees—all Phase 1 Tamils—of the Wimbledon Hindu temple denied the organizers of the march the right to hang posters on the temple premises. Their reason? "We do not want to antagonize the white community."

Other alliances have been forged among Phase 3 Tamils that have become more vital than any they ever had with their fellow Tamils of the other phases or the separatists/nationalists at home. Most of these alliances span across national boundaries to fellow asylum-seekers in other European countries who have fled both the nationalist Sri Lankan army and the equally nationalist Tamil militant groups. To the immigrant Tamils, the nationalized past that each of these groups is frantically trying to construct is something they have broken away from in the same manner that they feel they have broken with the law. Alliances have also extended to other refugees fleeing other national pasts, and a keen interest is shown in organizations such as Amnesty International whose scrutiny transcends national boundaries.

NOTES

1. This act made it the responsibility of air and sea carriers to ensure that their passengers carried valid papers. Failure to do so made the carrier liable to heavy fines.

2. The People's Liberation Organization of Tamil Eelam is one of the several Tamil liberation movements that were born in the mid-1980s. This group never did engage in combat either with the Indian or with the Sri Lankan state. But it became quite wealthy through investments made in Bombay and the running of a passport-forging shop in that same city. The drug-pushing charge is quite widely leveled against this group, but I have been able neither to confirm nor to dis-confirm it. Its leader, Uma Maheswaran, was killed by a member of the LTTE in 1989, after which the liberation-of-Eelam activists of this group have become extinct for all intents and purposes. The fragmented financial empire, I understand, continues to flourish.

3. The Eelam People's Revolutionary Liberation Front, a militant separatist group that, since the 1987 pact between India and Sri Lanka, has given up its demand for a separate state and has participated in government-arranged elections.

4. *Kēvaluppaṭuttinārkaḷ,* a euphemism for rape.

REFERENCES

Abeysekera, Sunila. 1997. Penalising Women's Sexual Autonomy: A Look at Contemporary Sinhala Cinema. *Options* 9: 3–7.

———. 2005. Garment Girls and Army Boys: Foretelling the Future. *Cinesith* 4: 23–29.

Abraham, Taisha, and Malashri Lal. 1995. *Female Empowerment: Impact of Literacy in Jaipur District, Rajasthan*. New Delhi: Har-Anand Publications.

Abrams, Philip. 1985. Chola Meykkirttis as Literary Texts. *Tamil Civilization* 3, no. 2–3: 1–5.

———. 1988. Notes on the Difficulty of Studying the State (1977). *Journal of Historical Sociology* 1, no. 1: 58–89.

Abu-Lughod, Lila. 1993. *Writing Women's Worlds: Bedouin Stories*. Berkeley and Los Angeles: University of California Press.

Adams, Kathleen M., and Sara Dickey, eds. 2000. *Home and Hegemony: Domestic Service and Identity Politics in South and Southeast Asia*. Ann Arbor: University of Michigan Press.

Adams, Vincanne. 1996. *Tigers of the Snow and Other Virtual Sherpas: An Ethnography of Himalayan Encounters*. Princeton, N.J.: Princeton University Press.

Afsar, Rita. 2000. *Rural–Urban Migration in Bangladesh: Causes, Consequences and Challenges*. Dhaka: University Press.

Agarwal, Bina. 1994. *A Field of One's Own: Gender and Land Rights in South Asia*. Cambridge: Cambridge University Press.

Agarwal, Priya. 1991. *Passage from India: Post-1965 Indian Immigrants and Their Children*. Palo Verdes, Calif.: Yuvati Publications.

Ahearn, Laura. 2001. *Invitations to Love: Literacy, Love Letters and Social Change in Nepal*. Berkeley and Los Angeles: University of California Press.

Ahmed, Akbar S. 1980. *Pukhtun Economy and Society: Traditional Structure and Economic Development in a Tribal Society*. Boston: Routledge and Kegan Paul.

———. 1983. *Religion and Politics in Muslim Society: Order and Conflict in Pakistan*. London: Routledge and Kegan Paul.

Ahmed-Ghosh, Huma. 2003. Writing the Nation on the Beauty Queen's Body: Implications for a Hindu Nation. *Meridians: Feminism, Race, Transnationalism* 4, no. 1: 205–27.

Aijaz, S. Zakir, trans. 1989. *Muslim Children: How to Bring Up?* Karachi, Pakistan: International Islamic Publishers.

Ali, Daud. 1996. Regime of Pleasure in Early India: A Genealogy of Practices at the Cola Court. Unpublished diss., Department of History, University of Chicago.

———. 2004. *Courtly Culture and Political Life in Early Medieval India.* Cambridge: Cambridge University Press.

Allison, Anne. 1996. *Permitted and Prohibited Desires.* Boulder, Colo.: Westview Press.

Alter, Joseph S. 1992. The Sannyasi and the Indian Wrestler: The Anatomy of a Relationship. *American Ethnologist* 19, no. 2: 317–36.

———. 1995. The Celibate Wrestler: Sexual Chaos, Embodied Balance, and Competitive Politics in North India. *Contributions to Indian Sociology* 29, nos. 1 and 2: 109–31.

Altman, Dennis. 1997. Global Gaze/Global Gays. *GLQ* 3: 417–36.

———. 2001. *Global Sex.* Chicago: University of Chicago Press.

Americans for Divorce Reform. www.divorcemag.com/statistics/statsWorld.shtml.

Amin, Shahid. 1988. Gandhi as Mahatma: Gorakhpur District, Eastern UP, 1921–22. In *Selected Subaltern Studies,* ed. Ranajit Guha and Gayatri Chakravorty Spivak, pp. 288–348. London: Oxford University Press.

———. 1995. *Event, Metaphor, and Memory: Chauri Chaura 1922–1992.* Berkeley and Los Angeles: University of California Press.

Anand, Mulk Raj. 1990 [1935]. *Untouchable.* New York: Penguin.

Anderson, Benedict. 1991 [1983]. *Imagined Communities.* New York: Verso.

Anderson, Jon W. 1982. Cousin Marriage in Context: Constructing Social Relations in Afghanistan. *Folk* 24: 7–28.

Aneesh, Aneesh. 2006. *Virtual Migration: The Programming of Globalization.* Durham, N.C.: Duke University Press.

Appadurai, Arjun. 1981. *Worship and Conflict under Colonial Rule: A South Indian Case.* Cambridge: Cambridge University Press.

———. 1986a. Center and Periphery in Anthropological Theory. *Comparative Studies in Society and History* 28, no. 2: 356–61.

———. 1986b. Is Homo Hierarchicus? *American Ethnologist* 13, no. 4: 745–61.

———. 1990. Topographies of the Self: Praise and Emotion in Hindu India. In *Language and the Politics of Emotion,* ed. Catherine A. Lutz and Lila Abu-Lughod, pp. 92–112. Cambridge: Cambridge University Press.

———. 1991. Global Ethnoscapes: Notes and Queries for a Transnational Anthropology. In *Recapturing Anthropology,* ed. Richard G. Fox, 191–210. Santa Fe, N.M.: School of American Research Press.

———. 1993. Caste Representation and the Representation of Caste. Unpublished manuscript.

————. 1996. *Modernity at Large: Cultural Dimensions of Globalization.* Minneapolis: University of Minnesota Press.

Appadurai, Arjun, and Carol Breckenridge. 1976. The South Indian Temple: Authority, Honor, and Redistribution. *Contributions to Indian Sociology,* n.s. 10, no. 2: 187–211.

————. 1988. Why Public Culture? *Public Culture* 1, no. 1: 5–9.

————. 1995. Public Modernity in India. In *Consuming Modernity: Public Culture in a South Asian World,* ed. Carol A. Breckenridge, pp. 1–22. Minneapolis: University of Minnesota Press.

Arai, Etsuyo. 2006. Readymade Garment workers in Sri Lanka: Strategy to Survive in Competition. In *Employment in Readymade Garment Industry in Post-MFA ERA: The Cases of India, Bangladesh and Sri Lanka,* ed. Mayumi Murayama. Institute of Developing Economies, Japan External Trade Organization, Joint Research Program Series, no. 140 (March 2006). www.ide.go.jp/English/Publish/Jrp/.

Arifeen, S. E., and Sangeeta Mookherjee. 1995. *The Urban MCH-FP Initiative (a Partnership for Urban Health and Family Planning in Bangladesh): An Assessment of Programme Needs in Zone 3 of Dhaka City.* Dhaka: International Centre for Diarrhoeal Disease Research, Bangladesh.

Arnold, Fred, Sunita Kishor, and T. K. Roy. 2002. Sex-Selective Abortions in India. *Population and Development Review* 28, no. 4 (Dec.): 759–85.

Arunima, G. 2003. *There Comes Papa: Colonialism and the Transformations of Matriliny in Kerala, Malabar c. 1850–1940.* New Delhi: Orient Longman.

Asad, Talal. 1983. Anthropological Conceptions of Religion: Reflections on Geertz. *Man* 18, no. 2: 237–59.

————. 1993. *Genealogies of Religion: Discipline and Reasons of Power in Christianity and Islam.* Baltimore, Md.: Johns Hopkins University Press.

————. 2003. *Formations of the Secular: Christianity, Islam, Modernity.* Stanford, Calif.: Stanford University Press.

Axel, Brian K. 2000. *The Nation's Tortured Body: Violence, Representation, and the Formation of a Sikh "Diaspora."* Durham, N.C.: Duke University Press.

Aziz, Barbara. 1976. Views from the Monastery Kitchen. *Kailash* 4, no. 2: 155–67.

Babb, Lawrence A. 1975. *The Divine Hierarchy: Popular Hinduism in Central India.* New York: Columbia University Press.

————. 1986. *Redemptive Encounters: Three Modern Styles in the Hindu Tradition.* Berkeley and Los Angeles: University of California Press.

Bacon, Jean. 1996. *Life Lines: Community, Family, and Assimilation among Asian Indian Immigrants.* New York: Oxford University Press.

Baer, Hans A., Merrill Singer, and Ida Susser. 1997. *Medical Anthropology and the World System: A Critical Perspective.* Westport, Conn.: Bergin and Garvey.

Baker, Stephen, and Manjeet Kriplani. 2004. India Rising: Programming Jobs are Heading Overseas by the Thousands. Is there a Way for the US to Stay on Top? *Business Week,* 1 March: 84–92.

Bakhtin, Mikhail M. 1981. *The Dialogical Imagination: Four Chapters by Bakhtin.* Ed. Michael Holquist. Austin: University of Texas Press.

Balibar, Etienne. 1991. Is There a "Neo-Racism"? In *Race, Nation, Class: Ambiguous Identities,* ed. Etienne Balibar and Immanuel Wallerstein, pp. 42–58. London: Verso.

Ballard, Roger. 1989. Differentiation and Disjunction amongst the Sikhs in Britain. In *The Sikh Diaspora: Migration and the Experience beyond Punjab,* ed. N. Gerald Barrier and Verne A. Dusenbery, pp. 200–232. Columbia, Mo.: South Asia Publications.

———. 1994. Introduction: The Emergence of Desh Pardesh. In *Desh Pardesh: The South Asian Presence in Britain,* ed. Roger Ballard, pp. 1–34. London: Hurst.

Ballard, Roger, and Catherine Ballard. 1977. The Sikhs: The Development of South Asian Settlements in Britain. In *Between Two Cultures: Migrants and Minorities in Britain,* ed. James L. Watson, pp. 21–56. Oxford: Basil Blackwell.

Bammer, Angelika, ed. 1994. *Displacements: Cultural Identities in Question.* Bloomington: Indiana University Press.

Bandarage, Asoka. 1988. Women and Capitalist Development in Sri Lanka, 1977–87. *Bulletin of Concerned Asian Scholars* 20, no. 2: 57–81.

Banerjee, M. 2000. *The Pathan Unarmed: Opposition and Memory in the North West Frontier.* Oxford: James Currey.

Bang, R., and A. Bang. 1994. Women's Perceptions of White Vaginal Discharge: Ethnographic Data from Maharashtra. In *Listening to Women Talk about Their Health: Issues and Evidence from India,* ed. Joel Gittelsohn, Margaret E. Bentley, Pertti J. Pelto, Moni Nag, Saroj Pachauri, Abigail D. Harrison, and Laura T. Landman, pp. 79–85. New Delhi: Ford Foundation and Har Anand Publications.

Bangladesh Bureau of Statistics. 1997. *Health and Demographic Survey: Population, Health, Social and Household Environment Statistics 1996.* Dhaka: Ministry of Planning.

Bangladesh Country Brief. 2006. Bangladesh Country Brief, World Bank Group. http://web.worldbank.org/WEBSITE/EXTERNAL/COUNTRIES/ SOUTHASIAEXT/ BANGLADESHEXTN/0.

Bangladesh Institute of Planners (BIP) and Centre for Urban Studies (CUS). 2005. *Millennium Development Goals and the City. Bangladesh Institute of Planners and Centre for Urban Studies.* Dhaka: CUS.

Bannerjee, Sumanta. 1989. Marginalisation of Women's Popular Culture. In *Recasting Women: Essays in Colonial History,* ed. Kumkum Sangari and Sudesh Vaid, pp. 127–79. New Delhi: Kali.

Bardhan, Kalpana, ed. and trans. 1990. *Of Women, Outcastes, Peasants, and Rebels: A Selection of Bengali Short Stories.* Berkeley and Los Angeles: University of California Press.

Barnes, Nancy. 1987. Buddhism. In *Women in World Religions,* ed. Arvind Sharma, pp. 105–33. Albany: State University of New York Press.

————. 1994. Women in Buddhism. In *Today's Women in World Religions,* ed. Arvind Sharma, pp. 137–70. Albany: State University of New York Press.

Barrier, N. Gerald, and Verne A. Dusenbery, eds. 1989. *The Sikh Diaspora.* Columbia, Mo.: South Asia Books.

Barth, Fredrik. 1959. *Political Leadership among Swat Pathans.* London: Athlone Press.

————. 1981. *Features of Person and Society in Swat: Collected Essays.* London: Routledge and Kegan Paul.

Bartholomeusz, Theresa. 1992. The Female Mendicant in Buddhist Sri Lanka. In *Buddhism, Sexuality, and Gender,* ed. Jose Cabezon, pp. 37–64. Albany: State University of New York Press.

Basu, Amrita. 1995. Feminism Inverted: The Gendered Imagery and Real Women of Hindu Nationalism. In *Women and the Hindu Right: A Collection of Essays,* ed. Tanika Sarkar and Urvashi Butalia, pp. 158–80. New Delhi: Kali for Women.

————. 1998. Hindu Women's Activism in India and the Questions It Raises. In *Appropriating Gender: Women's Activism and Politicized Religion in South Asia,* ed. Patricia Jeffery and Amrita Basu, pp. 1–14. New York: Routledge.

Basu, Nirban. 1994. *The Working Class Movement: A Study of Jute Mills of Bengal, 1937–47.* Calcutta: K. P. Bagchi and Company, Booksellers and Publishers.

Bauman, Richard, and Charles L. Briggs. 1990. Poetics and Performance as Critical Perspectives on Language and Social Life. *Annual Review of Anthropology* 19: 59–88.

Baumann, Gerd. 1996. *Contesting Culture: Discourses of Identity in Multi-Ethnic London.* Cambridge: Cambridge University Press.

Bayly, Susan. 1999. *Caste, Society, and Politics in India from the Eighteenth Century to the Modern Age.* Cambridge: Cambridge University Press.

Beidelman, Thomas O. 1959. A Comparative Analysis of the Jajmani System. *Monographs of the Association for Asian Studies* 8.

Benedict, Ruth. 1934. *Patterns of Culture.* Boston: Houghton Mifflin.

Benjamin, Walter. 1968. The Work of Art in the Age of Mechanical Reproduction. In *Illuminations: Essays and Reflections,* ed. Hannah Arendt, trans. Harry Zohn, pp. 217–51. New York: Schocken Books.

Berreman, Gerald D. 1979. *Caste and Other Inequities: Essays on Inequality.* New Delhi: Manohar.

Béteille, André. 1965. *Caste, Class, and Power: Changing Patterns of Stratification in a Tanjore Village.* Berkeley and Los Angeles: University of California Press.

————. 1991. The Reproduction of Inequality: Occupation, Caste, and Family. *Contributions to Indian Sociology,* n.s. 25, no. 1: 3–28.

Bhabha, Homi. 1990. The Third Space. In *Identity,* ed. Jonathan Rutherford, pp. 207–21. London: Lawrence and Wishart.

————. 1994. *The Location of Culture.* New York: Routledge.

Bhachu, Parminder. 1985. *Twice Migrants: East African Sikh Settlers in Britain.* London: Tavistock Publications.

————. 1995. New Cultural Forms and Transnational South Asian Women: Culture, Class and Consumption among British South Asian Women in the Diaspora. In *Nation and Migration: The Politics of Space in the South Asian Diaspora* ,ed. Peter van der Veer, pp. 222–24. Philadelphia: University of Pennsylvania Press.

The Bhagavad Gita: Krishna's Counsel in Time of War. 1986. Trans. Barbara Stoler Miller. New York: Columbia University Press.

Bhargava, Rajeev, ed. 1998a. *Secularism and its Critics.* New Delhi: Oxford University Press.

————. 1998b. What Is Secularism For? In *Secularism and Its Critics,* ed. Rajeev Bhargava, pp. 486–542. New Delhi: Oxford University Press.

Bhattacharjee, Anannya. 1997. The Public/Private Mirage: Mapping Homes and Undomesticating Violence Work in the South Asian Immigrant Community. In *Feminist Genealogies, Colonial Legacies, and Democratic Futures,* ed. M. Jacqui Alexander and Chandra Mohanty, pp. 308–29. New York: Routledge.

————. 1999. The Habit of Ex-nomination: Nation, Woman and the Indian Immigrant Bourgeoisie. In *Emerging Voices: South Asian Women Redefine Self, Family and Community,* ed. Sangeeta Gupta, pp. 229-52. New Delhi: Sage.

Bhattacharya, Narendra Nath. 1975. *History of Erotic Indian Literature.* Delhi: Munshiram Manohar Publishers.

Bilgrami, Akeel. 1998. Secularism, Nationalism, and Modernity. In *Secularism and Its Critics,* ed. Rajeev Bhargava, pp. 380–417. New Delhi: Oxford University Press.

Blackburn, Stuart. 1988. *Singing of Birth and Death: Texts in Performance.* Philadelphia: University of Pennsylvania Press.

————. 1996. *Inside the Drama-House: Rama Stories and Shadow Puppets in South India.* Berkeley and Los Angeles: University of California Press.

Blee, Kathleen M. 2002. *Inside Organized Racism: Women in the Hate Movement.* Berkeley, Los Angeles, London: University of California Press.

Boddy, Janice. 1989. *Wombs and Alien Spirits: Women, Men and the Zar Cult in Northern Sudan.* Madison: University of Wisconsin Press.

Boellstroff, Tom. 2005. *The Gay Archipelago: Sexuality and Nation in Indonesia.* Princeton, N.J.: Princeton University Press.

Bourdieu, Pierre. 1977. *Outline of a Theory of Practice.* Trans. Richard Nice. Cambridge: Cambridge University Press.

————. 1984. *Distinction.* Trans. Richard Nice. Cambridge, Mass.: Harvard University Press.

————. 1986. The Forms of Capital. In *Handbook of Theory and Research for the Sociology of Education,* ed. John G. Richardson, pp. 241–58. Westport, Conn.: Greenwood.

Bowen, Donna Lee, and Evelyn A. Early. 2002. *Everyday Life in the Muslim Middle East: Second Edition.* Bloomington: Indiana University Press.

Bowen, John R. 1993. *Muslims through Discourse: Religion and Ritual in Gayo Society.* Princeton, N.J.: Princeton University Press.

Brah, Avtar. 1988. A Journey to Nairobi. In *Charting the Journey: Writings by Black and Third World Women,* ed. Shabnam Grewal et al., pp. 74–88. London: Sheba Feminist Publishers.

———. 1996. *Cartographies of Diaspora: Contesting Identities.* London: Routledge.

Breckenridge, Carol A., ed. 1995. *Consuming Modernity: Public Culture in a South Asian World.* Minneapolis: University of Minnesota Press.

Breman, Jan, Arvind N. Das, and Ravi Agarwal. 2001. *Down and Out: Labouring under Global Capitalism.* Delhi: Oxford University Press.

Brenner, S. 1996. Reconstructing Self and Society: Javanese Muslim Women and "the Veil." *American Ethnologist* 23, no. 4: 673–97.

Bruner, Jerome. 1987. Life as Narrative. *Social Research* 54: 11–32.

Buehler, Arthur F. 1998. *Sufi Heirs of the Prophet: The Indian Naqshbandiya and the Rise of the Mediating Sufi Shaykh.* Columbia: University of South Carolina Press.

Butalia, Urvashi. 1993. Community, State, and Gender: On Women's Agency during Partition. *Economic and Political Weekly* 28 (17 April): 1634–47.

Butler, Judith. 1993. *Bodies That Matter: On the Discursive Limits of "Sex."* New York: Routledge.

Caplan, Lionel. 1984. Bridegroom Price in Urban India: Class, Caste, and "Dowry Evil" among Christians in Madras. *Man,* n.s. 19: 216–33.

———. 1987. *Class and Culture in Urban India: Fundamentalism in a Christian Community.* Oxford: Clarendon Press.

Carrithers, Michael. 1983. *The Buddha.* Oxford: Oxford University Press.

Central Bureau of Statistics. 1994. *Statistical Pocketbook.* Kathmandu: CBS.

Chakrabarty, Dipesh. 2000. *Rethinking Working-Class History: Bengal, 1890–1940.* Princeton, N.J.: Princeton University Press.

Chakravarthy, V. 1986. Bharatirajavin Cinema. *Ini,* October: 3–9.

Chatterjee, Partha. 1989. Colonialism, Nationalism, and Colonialized Women: The Contest in India. *American Ethnologist* 16: 622–33.

———. 1990. The Nationalist Resolution of the Women's Question. In *Recasting Women: Essays in Indian Colonial History,* ed. Kumkum Sangari and Sudesh Vaid, pp. 233–53. New Brunswick, N.J.: Rutgers University Press.

———. 1993. *The Nation and Its Fragments: Colonial and Post-Colonial Histories.* Princeton, N.J.: Princeton University Press.

———. 1998. Secularism and Tolerance. In *Secularism and Its Critics,* ed. Rajeev Bhargava, pp. 354–79. New Delhi: Oxford University Press.

Chaturvedi, Subhadra. 1995. Whether Inheritance to Women Is a Viable Solution to the Dowry Problem in India. *Journal of South Asia Women Studies* 1, no. 1: 17–23.

Chaturvedi, S., P. Chandra, C. Sudarshan, and M. K. Isaac. 1995. A Popular Hidden Illness among Women Related to Vaginal Discharge. *Indian Journal of Social Psychiatry* 11: 69–72.

Chen, Martha A. 2000. *Perpetual Mourning: Widowhood in Rural India*. New York: Oxford University Press.

———, ed. 1998. *Widows in India: Social Neglect and Public Action*. New Delhi: Sage.

Chen, Martha A., and Jean Drèze. 1992. Widows and Health in Rural North India. *Economic and Political Weekly* 27: WS-81–WS-92.

———. 1995a. Recent Research on Widows in India: Workshop and Conference Report. *Economic and Political Weekly* 30: 2435–50.

———. 1995b. Widowhood and Well-Being in Rural North India. In *Women's Health in India: Risk and Vulnerability*, ed. Monica Das Gupta, Lincoln C. Chen, and T. N. Krishnan, pp. 245–88. Bombay: Oxford University Press.

Chowdhry, Prem. 1994. *The Veiled Women: Shifting Gender Equations in Rural Haryana 1880–1990*. Delhi: Oxford University Press.

Clarke, Colin, Ceri Peach, and Steven Vertovec, eds. 1990. *South Asians Overseas: Migration and Ethnicity*. Cambridge: Cambridge University Press.

Clifford, James. 1997. Spatial Practices: Fieldwork, Travel, and the Disciplining of Anthropology. In *Anthropological Locations*, ed. Akhil Gupta and James Ferguson, pp. 185–222. Berkeley and Los Angeles: University of California Press.

Cohen, Lawrence. 1995. The Pleasures of Castration: The Postoperative Status of Hijras, Jankhas, and Academics. In *Sexual Nature/Sexual Culture*, ed. Paul R. Abramson and Steven D. Pinkerton, pp. 276–304. Chicago: University of Chicago Press.

———. 1998. *No Aging in India: Alzheimers, the Bad Family, and Other Modern Things*. Berkeley and Los Angeles: University of California Press.

———. 2006. The Kothi Wars: AIDS, Cosmopolitanism, and the Morality of Classification. In *Sex and Development*, ed. Vincanne Adams and Stacey Leigh Pigg, pp. 269–303. Durham, N.C.: Duke University Press.

Cohn, Bernard S. 1984. The Census, Social Structure, and Objectification in South Asia. *Folk* 26: 25–49.

———. 1985. The Command of Language and the Language of Command. In *Subaltern Studies IV: Writings on South Asian History and Society*, ed. Ranajit Guha, pp. 276–329. Delhi: Oxford University Press.

———. 1987a. *An Anthropologist among the Historians and Other Essays*. New Delhi: Oxford University Press.

———. 1987b. The Census, Social Structure, and Objectification. In *An Anthropologist among the Historians and Other Essays*. New Delhi: Oxford University Press.

Collins, Jane. 2003. *Threads: Gender, Labor, and Power in the Global Apparel Industry*. Chicago: University of Chicago Press.

Comaroff, Jean, and John Comaroff. 1991. *Of Revelation and Revolution*. Vol. 1. Chicago: University of Chicago Press.

Conley, Dalton. 1999. *Being Black, Living in the Red: Race, Wealth, and Social Policy in America*. Berkeley and Los Angeles: University of California Press.

Crapanzano, Vincent. 1980. *Tuhami: Portrait of a Moroccan*. Chicago: University of Chicago Press.

Cravey, Altha. 1998. *Women and Work in Mexico's Maquiladoras*. Lanham, Md.: Rowman and Littlefield.

Cre-A. 1992. *Kriyavin Tarkala Tamil Akarati* [Dictionary of contemporary Tamil]. Madras: Cre-A.

Crook, John, and Henry Osmaston. 1994. *Himalayan Buddhist Villages*. New Delhi: Motilal.

Crooke, William. 1989 [1879]. *A Glossary of North Indian Peasant Life*. Ed. Shahid Amin. Delhi: Oxford University Press.

Csordas, Thomas. 1983. The Rhetoric of Transformation in Ritual Healing. *Culture, Medicine and Psychiatry* 7: 333–76.

Cutler, Norman. 1987. *Songs of Experience: The Poetics of Tamil Devotion*. Bloomington: Indiana University Press.

Da Costa, Dia. 2008. "Spoiled Sons" and "Sincere Daughters": Schooling, Security, and Empowerment in Rural West Bengal, India. *Signs* 33, no. 2: 283–308.

Daily Mirror (Colombo). 2005. Women Victims Need More Help. Editorial. 27 May: n.p.

Daniel, E. Valentine. 1984. *Fluid Signs: Being a Person the Tamil Way*. Berkeley and Los Angeles: University of California Press.

———. 1993. Tea Talk: Violent Measures in the Discursive Practices of Sri Lanka's Estate Tamils. *Comparative Studies in Society and History* 15, no. 3: 568–600.

———. 1996. *Charred Lullabies: Chapters in an Anthropography of Violence*. Princeton, N.J.: Princeton University Press.

Daniel, E. Valentine, and J. M. Peck. 1996. *Culture and Contexture: Explorations in Anthropology and Literary Studies*. Berkeley and Los Angeles: University of California Press.

Daniels, Christine. 1994. Defilement and Purification: Tibetan Buddhist Pilgrims at Bodhnath, Nepal. D.Phil. thesis, Faculty of Anthropology and Geography, Oxford University.

Daniels, Roger. 1989. *History of Indian Immigration to the United States: An Interpretive Essay*. New York: Asia Society.

Dareshwar, Vivek. 1993. Caste and the Secular Self. *Journal of Arts and Ideas* 25/26: 115–26.

Dargyay, Eva. 1987. The Dynasty of Bzang-la (Zanskar, West Tibet) and Its Chronology: A Reconsideration. In *Silver on Lapis: Tibetan Literary Culture and History*, ed. Christopher Beckwith, pp. 13–32. Bloomington, Ind.: Tibet Society.

———. 1988. Buddhism in Adaptation: Ancestor Gods and Their Tantric Counterparts in the Religious Life of Zanskar. *History of Religions* 28, no. 2: 123–34.

Dargyay, Eva, and Lobsang Dargyay. 1980. Vorlaufiger Bericht Uber Zwei Forschungreisen Nach Zangskar (West-Tibet). *Zentralasiatische Studien* 14, no. 2: 85–114.

Das, Veena. 1989. Voices of Children. *Daedalus* 118, no. 4: 263–294.

———. 1995. National Honour and Practical Kinship: Of Unwanted Women and Children. In *Critical Events: An Anthropological Perspective on Contemporary India*, pp. 55–83. Delhi: Oxford University Press.

———. 1996. Language and the Body: Transactions in the Construction of Pain. *Daedalus* 125, no. 1: 67–91.

Das Gupta, Monisha. 1997. "What Is Indian about You?": A Gendered, Transnational Approach to Ethnicity. *Gender and Society* 11, no. 5: 572–96.

Das Gupta, Somdev. 1986. Once a Refugee, Always a Refugee. *Statesman* (Calcutta), 28 March.

Dasgupta, Shamita Das, ed. 1998. *A Patchwork Shawl: Chronicles of South Asian Women in America*. New Brunswick, N.J.: Rutgers University Press.

Davis, Richard. 1985. "*Chola Meykkirttis* as Literary Texts." *Tamil Civilization* 3, no. 2–3: 1–5.

———. 1991. *Ritual in an Oscillating Universe: Worshipping Siva in Medieval India*. Princeton, N.J.: Princeton University Press.

———. 1995. Introduction: A Brief History of Religions in India. In *Religions of India in Practice*, ed. Donald Lopez, pp. 3–54. Princeton, N.J.: Princeton University Press.

De Alwis, Malathi. 1998. Maternalist Politics in Sri Lanka: A Historical Anthropology of Its Conditions of Possibility. Ph.D. diss., University of Chicago.

de Certeau, Michel. 1984. *The Practice of Everyday Life*. Berkeley and Los Angeles: University of California Press.

Deleuze, Gilles, and Felix Guattari. 1983. *Anti-Oedipus: Capitalism and Schizophrenia*. Trans. Robert Hurley, Mark Seem, and Helen R. Lane. Minneapolis: University of Minnesota Press.

———. 1987. *A Thousand Plateaus*. Minneapolis: University of Minnesota Press.

De Mel, Neloufer. 1998. Agent or Victim? The Sri Lankan Woman Militant in the Interregnum. In *Sri Lanka: Collective Identities Revisited*, vol. 1, ed. Michael Roberts, pp. 199–220. Colombo: Marga Institute.

———. 2001. *Women and the Nation's Narrative: Gender and Nationalism in Twentieth Century Sri Lanka*. Lanham, Md.: Rowman and Littlefield.

Denny, Frederick. 1987. *Islam*. San Francisco: Harper Collins.

Dendaletche, Claude, ed. 1985. *Ladakh, Himalaya Occidental: Ethnologie, ecologie*. Pau: Acta Biologica Montana.

————. 2000. *Movies, Masculinity, and Modernity: An Ethnography of Men's Filmgoing in India*. Westport, Conn.: Greenwood Press.

Derné, Steve. 2000. *Movies, Masculinity, and Modernity: An Ethnography of Men's Filmgoing in India*. Santa Barbara, Calif. Greenwood Press.

————. 2005. Globalization and the Making of a Transnational Middle Class: Implications for Class Analysis. In *Critical Globalization Studies*, ed. Richard P. Appelbaum and William I. Robinson, pp. 177–86. New York: Routledge.

Desai, Sonalde. 2007. The Middle Class. In *The Oxford Companion to Economics in India*, ed. Kaushik Basu. New Delhi: Oxford.

Des Chene, Mary. 1991. Relics of Empire: A Cultural History of the Gurkhas, 1815–1987. Ph.D. diss., Stanford University.

Deshpande, Satish. 2003. *Contemporary India: A Sociological View*. New Delhi: Penguin.

Devji, Faisal. 1994. Gender and the Politics of Space: The Movement for Women's Reform, 1857–1900. In *Forging Identities: Gender, Communities, and the State*, ed. Zoya Hasan, pp. 22–37. New Delhi: Kali for Women Press.

Dhaka Courier. 2003. Tough Days Ahead for RMG after 2004. 16 May: 14.

Dhanjal, Beryl. 1976. Sikh Women in Southall. *New Community* 5, no. 1–2: 109–14.

Dhareshwar, Vivek. 1995a. "Our Time": History, Sovereignty, Politics. *Economic and Political Weekly* 30, no. 6: 317–24.

————. 1995b. The Postcolonial in the Postmodern: Or, the Political after Modernity. *Economic and Political Weekly* 30, no. 30: 104–12.

Dhillon, Perminder. 1979. They're Killing Us in Here. *Spare Rib*, n.p.

Dickey, Sara. 1993. *Cinema and the Urban Poor in South India*. Cambridge: Cambridge University Press.

————. 2000. Permeable Homes: Domestic Service, Household Space, and the Vulnerability of Class Boundaries in Urban India. *American Ethnologist* 27, no. 2: 462–89.

————. 2002. Anjali's Prospects: Class Mobility in Urban India. In *Everyday Life in South Asia*, 1st ed., ed. Diane P. Mines and Sarah Lamb, pp. 214–26. Bloomington: Indiana University Press.

Dimock, Edward C., Jr., Edwin Gerow, C. M. Naim, A. K. Ramanujan, Gordon Roadarmel, and J. A. B. van Buitenen. 1974. *The Literatures of India: An Introduction*. Chicago: Chicago University Press.

Dirks, Nicholas B. 1987. *The Hollow Crown: Ethnohistory of an Indian Kingdom*. Cambridge: Cambridge University Press.

————. 1990. History as a Sign of the Modern. *Public Culture* 2, no. 2: 25–32.

————. 1997. The Policing of Tradition: Colonialism and Anthropology in Southern India. *Comparative Studies in Society and History* 39, no. 1: 182–212.

————. 2001. *Castes of Mind: Colonialism and the Making of Modern India*. Princeton, N.J.: Princeton University Press.

Dollfus, Pascale. 1989. *Lieu de neige et de genévriers: Organisation sociale et religieuse de communautes bouddhistes du Ladakh.* Paris: Centre National de la Recherche Scientifique.

Donham, Donald. 1998. Freeing South Africa: The "Modernization" of Male-Male Sexuality in Soweto. *Cultural Anthropology* 13, no. 1: 3–21.

Doniger, Wendy. 1996. Sexual Masquerade in Hindu Myths: Aspects of the Transmission of Knowledge in Ancient India. In *The Transmission of Knowledge in South Asia: Religion, History, Politics,* ed. Nigel Crook, pp. 28–48. Delhi: Oxford University Press.

Doniger, Wendy O'Flaherty. 1980. *Women, Androgynes, and Other Mythical Beasts.* Chicago: University of Chicago Press.

Dooling, Richard. 1999. Diary of an Immortal Man: A Chronicle of My First 150 Years. *Esquire* (May): 80–89.

Driver, Edwin D., and Aloo E. Driver. 1987. *Social Class in Urban India: Essays on Cognitions and Structures.* Leiden: E. J. Brill.

du Toit, Brian M. 1990. *Aging and Menopause among Indian South African Women.* Albany: State University of New York Press.

Dube, Leela. 1988. On the Construction of Gender: Hindu Girls in Patrilineal India. *Economic and Political Weekly* (30 April): 11–19.

Dube, Saurabh. 1998. *Untouchable Pasts: Religion, Identity, and Power among a Central Indian Community, 1780–1950.* Albany: State University of New York Press.

Dummett, Michael, ed. 1980. *Southall 23 April 1979: The Report of the Unofficial Committee of Enquiry.* London: National Council for Civil Liberties.

Dumont, Louis. 1970. *Homo Hierarchicus: The Caste System and Its Implications.* Chicago: University of Chicago Press.

———. 1986 [1957]. *A South Indian Subcaste: Social Organization and Religion of the Pramalai Kallar.* Delhi: Oxford University Press.

Dwyer, Rachel. 2000. *All You Want Is Money, All You Need Is Love: Sex and Romance in Modern India.* London: Cassell.

Eaton, Richard. 1984. The Political and Religious Authority of the Shrine of Baba Farid. In *Moral Conduct and Authority: The Place of Adab in South Asian Islam,* ed. Barbara D. Metcalf, pp. 333–56. Berkeley and Los Angeles: University of California Press.

———. 1985. Approaches to the Study of Conversion to Islam in India. In *Approaches to Islam in Religious Studies,* ed. Richard C. Martin, pp. 106–23. Tucson: University of Arizona Press.

———. 1994. *The Rise of Islam and the Bengal Frontier, 1204–1760.* New Delhi: Oxford University Press.

Eck, Diana. 1981. *Darshan: Seeing the Divine in India.* Chambersburg, Pa.: Anima Books.

Eickelman, Dale F., and Jon W. Anderson, eds. 1999. *New Media in the Muslim World: The Emerging Public Sphere.* Bloomington: Indiana University Press.

El-Zein, Amira. 1996. The Evolution of the Concept of the Jinn from pre-Islam to Islam. Ph.D. diss., Arabic, Georgetown University.

Encyclopedia of Islam. 2003. Ed. P. J. Bearman, Bianquis, G. E. Bosworth, E. van Donzel, and W. P. Heinrichs. Leiden, The Netherlands: Brill.

Epstein, Scarlett. 1973. *South India: Yesterday, Today, and Tomorrow*. New York: Holmes and Meier Publishers.

Ewing, Katherine Pratt. 1999. The Sufi and the *Mullah*: Islam and Local Culture in Pakistan. Article presented at the American Institute of Pakistan Studies conference "Pakistan at 50," August 28–31, Wake Forest University, Winston-Salem, N.C.

Ewing, Katherine. 1997. *Arguing Sainthood: Modernity, Psychoanalysis, and Islam*. Durham, N.C.: Duke University Press.

Fabricius, Johann Philip. 1972. *Tamil and English Dictionary*. 4th ed., rev. Tranquebar, Tamil Nadu, India: Evangelical Lutheran Mission Publishing House.

Falk, Nancy. 1980. The Case of the Vanishing Nuns: The Fruits of Ambivalence in Ancient Indian Buddhism. In *Unspoken Worlds: Women's Religious Lives*, ed. Nancy Falk and Rita Gross, pp. 207–24. San Francisco: Harper and Row.

Featherman, David L., and Robert M. Hauser. 1978. *Opportunity and Change*. New York: Academic Press.

Fernandes, Leela. 1997. *Producing Workers: The Politics of Gender, Class, and Culture in the Calcutta Jute Mills*. Philadelphia: University of Pennsylvania Press.

———. 2006. *India's New Middle Class: Democratic Politics in an Era of Economic Reform*. Minneapolis: University of Minnesota Press.

Fernandes, Leela, and Patrick Heller. 2006. Hegemonic Aspirations: New Middle Class Politics and India's Democracy in Comparative Perspective *Critical Asian Studies* 38, no. 4: 495–522.

Fernandez-Kelly, Maria Patricia. 1983. *For We Are Sold, I and My People*. Albany: State University of New York Press.

Fernando, A. S. 1993. Garment Factories Only the Beginning of Industrial Revolution in Rural Sector M President. *Daily News* (Colombo), 4 February: n.p.

Fernea, Elizabeth Warnock, ed. 1995. *Children in the Muslim Middle East*. Austin: University of Texas.

Flueckiger, Joyce Burkhalter. 2006. *In Amma's Healing Room: Gender and Vernacular Islam in South India*. Bloomington: Indiana University Press.

Foucault, Michel. 1970. *The Order of Things*. New York: Vintage.

———. 1978. *The History of Sexuality: An Introduction*. Vol. 1. New York: Pantheon Books.

———. 1984. *The History of Sexuality: An Introduction*. New York: Peregrine Books.

Forbes, Geraldine. 1996. *Women in Modern India.* Cambridge: Cambridge University Press.

Freeman, Carla. 2000. *High Tech and High Heels in the Global Economy: Women, Work, and Pink Collar Identities in the Caribbean.* Durham, N.C.: Duke University Press.

———. 2001. Is Local: Global as Feminine: Masculine? Rethinking the Gender of Globalization. *Signs: Journal of Women in Culture and Society* 26, no. 4: 1007–37.

Freeman, John Richardson. 2000. Thereupon Hangs a Tail: The Deification of Vali in the Teyyam Worship of Malabar. In *Questioning Ramayanas: A South Asian Tradition,* ed. Paula Richman, pp. 187–220. Berkeley and Los Angeles: University of California Press.

Friedman, Thomas L. 2004. "The Great Indian Dream." *New York Times,* 11 March: 29.

Fryer, Peter. 1984. *Staying Power: The History of Black People in Britain.* London: Pluto Press.

Fuller, C. J. 1976. Kerala Christians and the Caste System. *Man,* n.s. 11, no. 1: 53–70.

———. 1987. The Hindu Pantheon and the Legitimation of Hierarchy. *Man,* n.s. 23: 19–39.

———. 1989. Misconceiving the Grain Heap: A Critique of the Concept of the Indian Jajmani System. In *Money and the Morality of Exchange,* ed. Jonathon Parry and Maurice Bloch, pp. 33–63. Cambridge: Cambridge University Press.

———. 1992. *The Camphor Flame: Popular Hinduism and Society in India.* Princeton, N.J.: Princeton University Press.

Fuller, C. J., and Haripriya Narasimhan. 2008. Companionate Marriage in India: The Changing Marriage System in a Middle-Class Brahman Subcaste. *Journal of the Royal Anthropological Institute* 14, no. 4: 736–54.

Fürer-Haimendorf, Christoph von. 1976. A Nunnery in Nepal. *Kailash* 4, no. 2: 121–54.

Galantar, Marc. 1984. *Competing Equalities: Law and the Backward Classes in India.* New Delhi: Oxford University Press.

Gamburd, Michele Ruth. 2000. *The Kitchen Spoon's Handle: Transnationalism and Sri Lanka's Migrant Housemaids.* Ithaca, N.Y.: Cornell University Press.

Ganguly, Keya. 1992. Migrant Identities: Personal Memory and the Construction of Selfhood. *Cultural Studies* 6: 27–50.

Ganguly, Sumit. 2001. *Conflict Unending: India-Pakistan Tensions since 1947.* New York: Columbia University Press.

Gardner, Katy. 1995. *Global Migrants, Local Lives: Travel and Transformation in Rural Bangladesh.* New York: Oxford University Press.

Gargan, Edward. 1990. Coming Out in India, with a Nod from the Press. *New York Times,* August 11.

Gazi, R., and A. M. R. Chowdhury. 1998. Perceptions of Reproductive Tract Infections among Rural Women in Bangladesh. Unpublished BRAC report. Dhaka: Research and Evaluation Division, BRAC.

Geertz, Clifford. 1973. *The Interpretation of Cultures.* New York: Basic Books.

Geetha, V. 1998. On Bodily Love and Hurt. In *A Question of Silence? The Sexual Economies of Modern India,* ed. Mary E. John and Janaki Nair, pp. 304–31. New Delhi: Kali.

Geetha, V., and S. V. Rajadurai. 1995. Eighth World Tamil Conference: Of Cardboard History and Discursive Space. *Economic and Political Weekly* 30, no. 4: 201–203.

Ghosh, Bishnupriya. 2002. Queering Hindutva: Unruly Bodies and Pleasures in Sadhavi Rithambara's Performances. In *Right Wing Women: From Conservatives to Extremists around the World,* ed. Paola Bacchetta and Margaret Powers, pp. 259–72. New York: Routledge.

Giddens, Anthony. 1992. *The Transformation of Intimacy: Sexuality, Love and Eroticism in Modern Societies.* Stanford, Calif.: Stanford University Press.

Gillespie, Marie. 1995. *Television, Ethnicity, and Cultural Change.* London: Routledge.

Gilroy, Paul. 1987. *There Ain't No Black in the Union Jack.* London: Hutchinson.

Ginsberg, Elaine, ed. 1996. *Passing and the Fictions of Identity.* Durham, N.C.: Duke University Press.

Giridharadas, Anand. 2008. With India's New Affluence Comes the Divorce Generation. *International Herald Tribune, Asia-Pacific.* February 19.

Goffman, Erving. 1974. *Frame Analysis: An Essay on the Organization of Experience.* Boston: Northeastern University Press.

Gold, Ann Grodzins. 1992. *A Carnival of Parting.* Berkeley and Los Angeles: University of California Press.

———. 1996. Khyal: Changed Yearnings in Rajasthani Women's Songs. *Manushi* 95: 13–21.

———. 2001. Counterpoint Authority in Women's Ritual Expressions: A View from the Village. In *Jewels of Authority: Women, Text, and the Hindu Tradition,* ed. Laurie L. Patton, pp. 177–201. New York: Oxford University Press.

Gold, Ann Grodzins, and Bhoju Ram Gujar. 1994. Drawing Pictures in the Dust: Rajasthani Children's Landscapes. *Childhood* 2: 73–91.

———. 2002. *In the Time of Trees and Sorrows: Nature, Power, and Memory in Rajasthan.* Durham, N.C.: Duke University Press.

GoldbergBelle, Jonathan. 1989. Clowns in Control: Performances in a Shadow Puppet Tradition in South India. In *Oral Epics in India,* ed. Stuart Blackburn et al., pp. 118–39. Berkeley and Los Angeles: University of California Press.

Goldman, Robert P. 1984. *The Ramayana of Valmiki: An Epic of Ancient India.* Vol. 1. Princeton, N.J.: Princeton University Press.

———. 1988. *Theravada Buddhism: A Social History from Ancient Benares to Modern Colombo.* New York: Routledge.

Gombrich, Richard. 1971. *Precept and Practice.* Oxford: Clarendon Press.

Gombrich, Richard, and Gananath Obeyesekere. 1988. *Buddhism Transformed: Religious Change in Sri Lanka.* Princeton, N.J.: Princeton University Press.

Good, Anthony. 1991. *The Female Bridegroom: A Comparative Study of Life-Crisis Rituals in South India and Sri Lanka.* New York: Oxford University Press.

Good, Byron J. 1994. *Medicine, Rationality, and Experience: An Anthropological Perspective.* Cambridge: Cambridge University Press.

Gopinath, Gayatri. 1995. "Bombay, U.K., Yuba City": Bhangra Music and the Engendering of Diaspora. *Diaspora* 4, no. 3: 303–21.

———. 2005. *Impossible Desires: Queer Diasporas and South Asian Public Cultures.* Durham, N.C.: Duke University Press.

Gough, Kathleen. 1989. *Rural Change in Southeast India: 1950s to 1980s.* Delhi: Oxford University Press.

Gould, Harold. 1958. The Hindu Jajmani System: A Case of Economic Particularism. *Southwestern Journal of Anthropology* 16: 434.

Government of Bangladesh (GoB). 2004. Bangladesh Economic Review, 2004. Bangladesh: Ministry of Finance.

Government of Bangladesh (GoB)–UN. 2005. Millennium Development Goals, Bangladesh Progress Report. 2005. Dhaka: Government of Bangladesh-United Nations.

Grewal, Inderpal. 2005. *Transnational Americas.* Durham, N.C.: Duke University Press.

Grima, Benedicte. 1992. *The Performance of Emotion among Paxtun Women: "The Misfortunes Which Have Befallen Me."* Austin: University of Texas Press.

Gross, Rita. 1993. *Buddhism after Patriarchy: A Feminist History, Analysis, and Reconstruction of Buddhism.* Albany: State University of New York Press.

Gupta, Akhil. 1995. Blurred Boundaries: The Discourse of Corruption, the Culture of Politics, and the Imagined State. *American Ethnologist* 22, no. 2: 375–402.

Gupta, Akhil, and James Ferguson, eds. 1997. *Culture, Power, and Place: Explorations in Critical Anthropology.* Durham, N.C.: Duke University Press.

Gupta, Ranajit Das. 1994. *Labour and Working Class in Eastern India.* Kolkata: K. P. Bagchi and Company, Booksellers and Publishers.

Gupta, Sangeeta, ed. 1999. *Emerging Voices: South Asian American Women Redefine Self, Family, and Community.* New Delhi: Sage.

Gutschow, Kim. 1995. The Power of Compassion or the Power of Rhetoric? A Report on Sakyadhita's Fourth International Conference on Buddhist Women. *Himal* 8, no. 6: 18–21.

———. 1997. Unfocussed Merit-Making in Zangskar: A Socio-Economic Account of Karsha Nunnery. *Tibet Journal* 22, no. 2: 30–58.

———. 1998. An Economy of Merit: Women and Buddhist Monasticism in Zangskar, Northwest India. Ph.D. diss., Department of Anthropology, Harvard University.

————. 2000. A Novice Ordination for Nuns: The Rhetoric and Reality of Female Monasticism in NW India. In *Women's Buddhism, Buddhism's Women: Tradition, Revision, Renewal,* ed. Ellison Findly, pp. 103–18. Boston: Wisdom Press.

Hall, Kathleen. 1995. "There's a Time to Act English and a Time to Act Indian": The Politics of Identity among British-Sikh Teenagers. In *Children and the Politics of Culture,* ed. Sharon Stephens, pp. 243–64. Princeton, N.J.: Princeton University Press.

————. 2002. *Lives in Translation: Sikh Youth and British Cultural Citizenship.* Philadelphia: University of Pennsylvania Press.

Hall, Stephen S. 2000. The Recycled Generation. *New York Times Magazine* (30 January): 30–35, 46, 74, 78–79.

Hall, Stuart. 1990. Cultural Identity and Diaspora. In *Identity: Community, Culture, Difference,* ed. J. Rutherford, pp. 222–37. London: Lawrence and Wishart.

————. 1992. New Ethnicities. In *Race, Culture and Difference,* ed. James Donald and Ali Rattansi, pp. 252–59. New York: Sage.

————. 1996. The Question of Cultural Identity. In *Modernity: An Introduction to Modern Societies,* ed. Stuart Hall, David Held, Don Hubert, and Kenneth Thompson, pp. 595–634. Oxford: Blackwell.

Halperin, David M. 1990. *One Hundred Years of Homosexuality.* New York: Columbia University Press.

Hancock, Mary. 1999. *Womanhood in the Making: Domestic Ritual and Public Culture in Urban South India.* Boulder, Colo.: Westview Press.

Hanna, Max. 1974. The National Front and Other Right-Wing Organizations. *New Community* 3: 1–2, 49–55.

Hansen, Thomas Blom. 1999. *The Saffron Wave: Democracy and Hindu Nationalism in Modern India.* Princeton, N.J.: Princeton University Press.

Harper, Edward B. 1959. Two Systems of Economic Exchange in Village India. *American Anthropologist* 61: 760–78.

Haug, Wolfgang Fritz. 1986 [1971]. *Critique of Commodity Aesthetics: Appearance, Sexuality, and Advertising in Capitalist Society.* New York: Polity Press.

Havnevik, Hanna. 1990. *Tibetan Buddhist Nuns: History, Cultural Norms, and Social Realities.* Oslo: Norwegian University Press.

Helweg, Arthur, and Usha Helweg. 1990. *An Immigrant Success Story: East Indians in America.* Philadelphia: University of Pennsylvania Press.

HelpAge India. 2002. Directory of Old Age Homes in India 2002. New Delhi: HelpAge India.

Herzfeld, M. 1992. History in the Making: National and International Politics in a Rural Cretan Community. In *Europe Observed,* ed. Joao de Pina-Cabral and John Campbell, pp. 93–122. London: Macmillan.

Hess, Linda. 1993. Staring at Frames Till They Turn into Loops: An Excursion through Some Worlds of Tulsidas. In *Living Banaras: Hindu Religion in Cultural Context,* ed. Cynthia Humes and Bradley Hertel, pp. 73–101. Albany: State University of New York Press.

———. 2000. Lovers' Doubts: Questioning the Tulsi Ramayan. In *Questioning Ramayanas: A South Asian Tradition*, ed. Paula Richman, pp. 25–48. Berkeley and Los Angeles: University of California Press.

Hettige, S. T. 2000. Globalisation and Local Culture: The Case of Sri Lanka. In *Sri Lanka at Crossroads: Dilemmas and Prospects after 50 Years of Independence*, ed. S. T. Hettige and Markus Mayer, pp. 165–205. Delhi: Macmillan India.

Hewamanne, Sandya. 2002. Stitching Identities: Work, Play, and Politics among Sri Lanka's Free Trade Zone Garment Factory Workers. Ph.D. diss., University of Texas at Austin.

———. 2008. *Stitching Identities in a Free Trade Zone: Gender and Politics in Sri Lanka*. Philadelphia: University of Pennsylvania Press.

Hiltebeitel, Alf, ed. 1989. *Criminal Gods and Demon Devotees: Essays on the Guardians of Popular Hinduism*. Albany: State University of New York Press.

Hindustan Times. 1994. Clapping Demand. November 7.

Holmstrom, Mark. 1976. *South Indian Factory Workers: Their Life and Their World*. New Delhi: Allied.

The Holy Quran. 1993. Revised and Edited by the Presidency of Islamic Researchers, IFTA. Medina, Saudi Arabia: King Fahd Holy Qur-an Printing Complex.

Horner, Isabelle. 1930. *Women under Primitive Buddhism*. London: George Routledge and Sons.

———. 1992. *The Book of the Discipline* (*Vinaya Pitaka*). Vol. 5: *Cullavagga*. Oxford: Pali Text Society.

Hospital, Clifford. 1984. *The Righteous Demon: A Study of Bali*. Vancouver: University of British Columbia Press.

Hughes, Thomas Patrick. 1988 [1885]. *Dictionary of Islam*. Calcutta: Rupa.

Hussein, Aamer. 1999. *Hoops of Fire: Fifty Years of Fiction by Pakistani Women*. London: Saqi Books.

Illaih, Kancha. 1996. Productive Labour, Consciousness and History: The Dalitbahujan Alternative. In *Subaltern Studies IX: Writings on South Asian History and Society*, ed. Shahid Amin and Dipesh Chakrabarty, pp. 165–200. Delhi: Oxford University Press.

Inden, Ron. 1999. Transnational Class, Erotic Arcadia and Commercial Utopia in Hindi Films. In *Image Itineraries: Audio-Visual Media and Cultural Change in India*, ed. Christiane Brosius and Melissa Butcher, pp. 41–68. New Delhi: Sage.

Inglis, Steven. 1985. Possession and Pottery: Serving the Divine in a South Indian Community. In *Gods of Flesh, Gods of Stone: The Embodiment of Divinity in India*, ed. Joanne Punzo Waghorne and Norman Cutler, in association with Vasudha Narayanan, pp. 89–102. Chambersburg, Pa.: Anima Books.

Institute of Race Relations. 1981. *Southall: The Birth of a Black Community*. London: Institute of Race Relations.

Irigaray, Luce. 1985. *This Sex Which Is Not One*. Ithaca, N.Y.: Cornell University Press.

Isaac, T. M. Thomas. 1985. From Caste Consciousness to Class Consciousness: Allepey Coir Workers during the Interwar Period. *Economic and Political Weekly* 20, no. 4: 5–18.

Isaac, T. M. Thomas, and P. K. Michael Tharakan. 1985. Sree Narayana Movement in Travancore, 1885–1939: Social Basis and Ideological Reproduction. Working Paper No. 214. Trivandrum: Center for Development Studies.

Jackson, Michael. 1996. *Things As They Are: New Directions in Phenomenological Anthropology*. Bloomington: Indiana University Press.

Jacobson, Doranne. 1982. Purdah and the Hindu Family in Central India. In *Separate Worlds: Studies of Purdah in South Asia*, ed. Hanna Papanek and Gail Minault, pp. 81–109. Delhi: Chanakya.

Jacobus, Mary, Evelyn Fox-Keller, and Sally Shuttleworth. 1990. *Body/Politics: Women and the Discourses of Science*. New York: Routledge.

Jaini, Padmanabh S. 1979. *The Jain Path to Purification*. Berkeley and Los Angeles: University of California Press.

Jayawardena, Kumari. 1992. Some Aspects of Religious and Cultural Identity and the Construction of Sinhala Buddhist Womanhood. In *Religion and Political Conflict in South Asia: India, Pakistan, and Sri Lanka*, ed. Douglas Allen, pp. 161–80. Westport, Conn.: Greenwood Press.

Jeffery, Patricia, and Roger Jeffery. 1996a. *Don't Marry Me to a Plowman! Women's Everyday Lives in Rural North India*. Boulder, Colo.: Westview Press, and New Delhi: Vistaar.

———. 1996b. Delayed Periods and Falling Babies: The Ethno-physiology and Politics of Pregnancy Loss in Rural North India. In *The Anthropology of Pregnancy Loss*, ed. Rosanne Cecil, pp. 17–37. Oxford: Berg Publishers.

Jeffery, Patricia, Roger Jeffery, and Andrew Lyon. 1987. Contaminating States: Midwifery, Childbearing, and the State in Rural North India. In *Women, State, and Ideology: Studies from Africa and Asia*, ed. Haleh Afshar, pp. 152–69. London: Macmillan.

———. 1989. *Labour Pains and Labour Power: Women and Childbearing in India*. London: Zed Books.

Jeffery, Roger, and Alaka M. Basu, eds. 1996. *Girls' Schooling, Women's Autonomy, and Fertility Change in South Asia*. New Delhi: Sage Publications.

———. 1997. Tamil: "Dominated by Cimema and Politics." *Economic and Political Weekly* 32 (8 February): 254–56.

Jeffery, Roger, and Patricia Jeffery. 1993. Traditional Birth Attendants in Rural North India: The Social Organization of Childbearing. In *Knowledge, Power, and Practice: The Anthropology of Medicine and Everyday Life*, ed. Shirley Lindenbaum and Margaret Lock, pp. 7–31. Berkeley and Los Angeles: University of California Press.

———. 1996. What's the Benefit of Being Educated? Girls' Schooling, Women's Autonomy, and Fertility Outcomes in Bijnor. In *Girls' Schooling, Wom-*

en's Autonomy, and Fertility Change in South Asia, ed. Roger Jeffery and Alaka M. Basu, pp. 150–83. New Delhi: Sage.

———. 1997. *Population, Gender, and Politics: Demographic Change in Rural North India.* Cambridge: Cambridge University Press.

Jeffery, Roger, Patricia Jeffery, and Andrew Lyon. 1984. Female Infanticide and Amniocentesis. *Social Science and Medicine* 19: 1207–12.

Jeffrey, Craig, Roger Jeffery, and Patricia Jeffery. 2004. Degrees without Freedom: The Impact of Formal Education on Dalit Young Men in North India. *Development and Change* 35, no. 5: 963–86.

Jeffrey, Robin. 1976. *Decline of Nayar Dominance: Society and Politics in Travancore, 1847–1908.* New Delhi: Vikas.

———. 1993. *Politics, Women and Well Being: How Kerala Became "a Model."* New Delhi: Oxford University Press.

———. 1997. Tamil: Dominated by Cinema and Politics. *Economic and Political Weekly* 32 (8 February): 254–56.

Jeganathan, Pradeep. 2002. Walking through Violence: "Everyday Life" and Anthropology. In *Everyday Life in South Asia,* 1st ed., ed. Diane P. Mines and Sarah Lamb, pp. 357–65. Bloomington: Indiana University Press.

Jesmin, Sonia, and Sarah Salway. 2000. Policy Arena. Marriage among the Urban Poor of Dhaka: Instability and Uncertainty. *Journal of International Development* 12, no. 5: 698–705.

John, Mary E. 1998. Globalisation, Sexuality, and the Visual Field: Issues and Non-issues for Cultural Critique. In *A Question of Silence? The Sexual Economies of Modern India,* ed. Mary E. John and Janaki Nair, pp. 368–96. New Delhi: Kali.

———. 2000. Alternate Modernities? Reservations and Women's Movement in 20th Century India. *Economic and Political Weekly* 35, no. 43/44: 3822–29.

Joseph, Sherry. 1996. Gay and Lesbian Movement in India. *Economic and Political Weekly* 31, no. 33: 2228–33.

Juergensmeyer, Mark. 2000. *Terror in the Mind of God: The Global Rise of Religious Violence.* New Delhi: Oxford University Press.

Kaali, Sundar. 2000. Narrating Seduction: Vicissitudes of the Sexed Subject in Tamil Nativity Film. In *Making Meaning in Indian Cinema,* ed. Ravi S. Vasudevan, pp. 168–90. New Delhi: Oxford University Press.

Kabir, A. 1998. Shocks, Vulnerability, and Coping in the Bustee Communities of Dhaka. *Discourse: A Journal of Policy Studies* 2, no. 2: 120–46.

Kakar, Sudhir. 1981. *The Inner World: A Psycho-analytic Study of Childhood and Society in India.* New Delhi: Oxford University Press.

———. 1989. *Intimate Relations: Exploring Indian Sexuality.* New Delhi: Penguin.

———. 1995. *The Colors of Violence: Cultural Identities, Religion, and Conflict.* Chicago: University of Chicago Press.

Kapadia, Karin. 1995. *Siva and Her Sisters: Gender, Caste, and Class in Rural South India.* Boulder, Colo.: Westview Press.

Kapferer, Bruce. 1997. *The Feast of the Sorcerer: Practices of Consciousness and Power.* Chicago: University of Chicago Press.

Karim, Maulana Fazlul. 1989. *Al-Hadis: An English Translation and Commentary of Mishkat-ul-Musabih.* 4 vols. Delhi: Islamic Book Service.

Kavoori, Purnendu S. 1999. *Pastoralism in Expansion: The Transhuming Herders of Western Rajasthan.* New Delhi: Oxford University Press.

Kelly, John D. 1991. *A Politics of Virtue: Hinduism, Sexuality, and Countercolonial Discourse in Fiji.* Chicago: University of Chicago Press.

Kepel, Gilles. 2002. *Jihad: The Trail of Political Islam.* London: I. B. Tauris.

Kerin, Melissa. 2000. From Periphery to Center: Tibetan Women's Journey to Sacred Artistry. In *Women's Buddhism, Buddhism's Women: Tradition, Revision, Renewal,* ed. Ellison Findly, pp. 319–38. Boston: Wisdom Press.

Kersenboom, S. 1995. *Word, Sound, Image: The Life of a Tamil Text.* Oxford: Berg Publishers.

Khan, M. E., J. W. Townsend, and S. D'Costa. 2002. Behind Closed Doors: A Qualitative Study of Sexual Behaviour of Married Women in Bangladesh. *Culture, Health and Sexuality* **4**, no. 2: 237–256.

Khan, Naveeda. 2003. Grounding Sectarianism: Islamic Ideology and Muslim Everyday Life in Lahore, Pakistan. Ph.D. diss., Anthropology, Columbia University.

Khandelwal, Meena. 2004. *Women in Ochre Robes: Gendering Hindu Renunciation.* Albany: State University of New York Press.

Kielmann, K. 2002. Gender, Well-Being and the Quality of Life. Paper presented at the "Gender, Health and Politics Workshop in South Asia, 2002," International Wissenschaftsforum, sponsored by the South Asia Institute and the Department of Tropical Hygiene and Public Health, July 18–19, University of Heidelberg, Heidelberg.

Kinsley, David. 1986. *Hindu Goddesses: Visions of the Divine Feminine in the Hindu Religious Tradition.* Berkeley and Los Angeles: University of California Press.

Klein, Anne. 1985. Primordial Purity and Everyday Life: Exalted Female Symbols and the Women of Tibet. In *Immaculate and Powerful: The Female in Sacred Image and Social Reality,* ed. Clarissa W. Atkinson, Constance H. Buchanan, and Margaret R. Miles, pp. 111–38. Boston: Beacon Press.

Knipe, David. 1989. Night of the Growing Dead: A Cult of Virabhadra in Coastal Andhra. In *Criminal Gods and Demon Devotees: Essays on the Guardians of Popular Hinduism,* ed. Alf Hiltebeitel, pp. 123–56. Albany: State University of New York Press.

Kolenda, Pauline. 1987a. Living the Levirate. In *Dimensions of Social Life,* ed. Paul Hockings, pp. 45–67. Berlin: de Gruyter.

———. 1987b. *Regional Differences in Family Structure in India.* Jaipur: Rawat Publications.

Kulick, Don. 1998. *Travesti: Sex, Gender, and Culture among Brazilian Transgendered Prostitutes.* Chicago: University of Chicago Press.

Kulkarni, V. G. 1993. The Middle-Class Bulge. *Far Eastern Economic Review* 156, no. 2 (14 January): 44–46.

Kumar, Krishna. 1991. *Political Agenda of Education: A Study of Colonialist and Nationalist Ideas*. New Delhi: Sage.

Kumar, Nita. 1988. *The Artisans of Banaras*. Princeton, N.J.: Princeton University Press.

———. 2000. *Lessons from Schools: The History of Education in Banaras*. Thousand Oaks, Calif.: Sage Publications.

Kumar, Shanti. 2004. Nationalism, and Feminism in Indian Culture. *South Asian Journal* 5: 95–105.

Kumar, Udaya. 1997. Self, Body, and Inner Sense: Some Reflections on Sree Narayana Guru and Kumaran Asan. *Studies in History* 13, no. 2: 247–70.

Lal, Bhai Harbans. 1999. Sahajdhari Sikhs: Their Origin and Current Status within the Panth. In *Sikh Identity: Continuity and Change*, ed. Pashaura Singh and N. Gerald Barrier, pp. 109–26. New Delhi: Manohar.

Lamb, Ramdas. 1991. Personalizing the Ramayan: Ramnamis and Their Use of the Ramcaritmanas. In *Many Ramayanas: The Diversity of a Narrative Tradition in South Asia*, ed. Paula Richman, pp. 235–55. Berkeley and Los Angeles: University of California Press.

Lamb, Sarah. 2000. *White Saris and Sweet Mangoes: Aging, Gender, and Body in North India*. Berkeley and Los Angeles: University of California Press.

———. 2001. Being a Widow and Other Life Stories: The Interplay between Lives and Words. *Anthropology and Humanism* 26, no. 1: 16–34.

———. 2009. *Aging and the Indian Diaspora: Cosmopolitan Families in India and Abroad*. Bloomington: Indiana University Press.

Langness, L. L., and Gelya Frank. 1981. *Lives: An Anthropological Approach to Biography*. Novato, Calif.: Chandler and Sharp.

Lapidus, Ira. 1976. Adulthood in Islam. *Daedulus* 105: 93–107.

Lapierre, Dominique, and Larry Collins. 1975. *Freedom at Midnight*. New York: Simon and Schuster.

Lavie, Smadar, and Ted Swedenburg. 1996. *Displacement, Diaspora, and Geographies of Identity*. Durham, N.C.: Duke University Press.

Lawrence, Bruce, and Carl Ernst. 2001. *Burnt Hearts: The Chishti Sufi Order in South Asia and Beyond*. Surrey, England: Curzon Press.

Lee, Trevor. 1972. Immigrants in London: Trends in Distribution and Concentration, 1961–71. *New Community* 2, no. 2: 145–58.

Lele, Jayant, ed. 1981. *Tradition and Modernity in Bhakti Movements*. Leiden: E. J. Brill.

Leonard, Karen Isaksen. 1992. *Making Ethnic Choices: California's Punjabi Mexican Americans*. Philadelphia, Pa.: Temple University Press.

———. 1997. *The South Asian Americans*. Westwood, Conn.: Greenwood Press.

Lessinger, Johanna. 1995. *From the Ganges to the Hudson: Indian Immigrants in New York City*. Boston: Allyn and Bacon.

Levinson, David. 1996. *Religion: A Cross Cultural Dictionary*. New York: Oxford University Press.

Lévi-Strauss, Claude. 1950. The Effectiveness of Symbols. In *Structural Anthropology,* pp. 167–85. New York: Basic Books.

Levy, Robert I. 1990. *Mesocosm: Hinduism and the Organization of a Traditional Hindu City.* Berkeley and Los Angeles: University of California Press.

Lewis, Oscar. 1955. Peasant Culture in India and Mexico: A Comparative Analysis. In *Village India: Studies in the Little Community.* Chicago: Midway Reprint Edition, 1986.

Lexicon. 1982. *Tamil Lexicon.* 6 vols. Madras: University of Madras.

Li, Yuchen. 2000. Ordination, Legitimacy, and Sisterhood: The International Full Ordination Ceremony in Bodhgaya. In *Innovative Buddhist Women: Swimming against the Stream,* ed. Karma Lekshe Tsomo, pp. 168–200. Richmond, Surrey, England: Curzon Press.

Liebeskind, Claudia. 1998. *Piety on Its Knees: Three Sufi Traditions in South Asia in Modern Times.* Delhi: Oxford University Press.

Liechty, Mark. 1994. Fashioning Modernity in Kathmandu: Mass Media, Consumer Culture, and the Middle Class in Nepal. Ph.D. diss., University of Pennsylvania.

———. 1995. Modernization, Media, and Markets: Youth Identities and the Experience of Modernity in Kathmandu, Nepal. In *Youth Cultures: A Cross-Cultural Perspective,* ed. Vered Amit-Talai and Helena Wulff, pp. 166–201. London: Routledge.

———. 1996. Kathmandu as Translocality: Multiple Places in a Nepali Space. In *Geography of Identity,* ed. Patricia Yaeger, pp. 98–130. Ann Arbor: University of Michigan Press.

———. 2001. Women and Pornography in Kathmandu: Negotiating the "Modern Woman" in a New Consumer Society. In *Images of the "Modern Woman" in Asia: Global Media/Local Meanings,* ed. Shoma Munshi, pp. 34–54. London: Curzon Press.

———. 2003. *Suitably Modern: Making Middle-Class Culture in a New Consumer Society.* Princeton, N.J.: Princeton.

Lindholm, Charles. 1982. *Generosity and Jealousy: The Swat Pukhtun of Northern Pakistan.* New York: Columbia University Press.

Lindholm, Charles, and Cherry Lindholm. 1979. Marriage as Warfare. *Natural History* 88, no. 8: 11–21.

Ling, Amy. 1991. I'm Here: An Asian Woman's Response. In *Feminisms: An Anthropology of Literary Theory and Criticism,* ed. Robyn R. Warhol and Diane P. Hendl, pp. 738–45. New Brunswick, N.J.: Rutgers University Press.

Lopez, Donald. 1995a. Foreigners at the Lama's Feet. In *Curators of the Buddha: The Study of Buddhism under Colonialism,* ed. Donald Lopez, pp. 251–96. Chicago: University of Chicago Press.

———, ed. 1995b. *Religions of India in Practice.* Princeton, N.J.: Princeton University Press.

———. 1998. *Prisoners of Shangri-La: Tibetan Buddhism and the West.* Chicago: University of Chicago Press.

Ludden, David, ed. 1996. *Contesting the Nation: Religion, Community, and the Politics of Democracy in India.* Philadelphia: University of Pennsylvania Press.

Lukose, Ritty. 2005. Empty Citizenship: Reconfiguring Politics in the Era of Globalization. *Cultural Anthropology* 20, no. 4: 506–33.

Lutgendorf, Philip. 2000. The Shabari Episode in Multiple Ramayanas. In *Questioning Ramayanas: A South Asian Tradition,* ed. Paula Richman, pp. 217–34. Berkeley and Los Angeles: University of California Press.

Lyall, J. B. 1874. *Report of the Land Revenue Settlement of the Kangra District.* Lahore: Central Jail Press.

Lynch, Caitrin. 2007. *Juki Girls, Good Girls: Gender and Cultural Politics in Sri Lanka's Global Garment Industry.* Ithaca, N.Y.: Cornell University Press.

Madan, T. N. 1998. Secularism in Its Place. In *Secularism and Its Critics,* ed. Rajeev Bhargava, pp. 297–320. New Delhi: Oxford University Press.

Mahbub, A., and S. M. Ahmed. 1997. Perspective of Women about Their Own Illness. Working Paper no. 16. Dhaka: BRAC–International Centre for Diarrhoeal Disease Research, Bangladesh, Research Project.

Mahmood, Saba. 2005. *Politics of Piety: The Islamic Revival and the Feminist Subject.* Princeton, N.J.: Princeton University Press.

Maira, Sunaina Marr. 1998. Chaste Identities, Ethnic Yearnings: Second-Generation Indian Americans in New York. Ph.D. diss., Graduate School of Education, Harvard University.

———. 1999. Identity Dub: The Paradoxes of an Indian American Youth Subculture (New York Mix). *Cultural Anthropology* 14, no. 1: 29–60.

———. 2002. *Desis in the House: Indian American Youth Culture in NYC.* Philadelphia: Temple University Press.

Malik, J. 1996. *Colonization of Islam: Dissolution of Traditional Institutions in Pakistan.* New Delhi: Manohar.

Malinowski, Bronislaw. 1965 [1948]. *Coral Gardens and Their Magic.* Bloomington: Indiana University Press.

Manalansan, Martin. 2003. *Global Divas: Filipino Gay Men in the Diaspora.* Durham, N.C.: Duke University Press.

Manderson, Lenore, and Margaret Jolly. 1997. Sites of Desire/Economies of Pleasure in Asia and the Pacific. In *Sites of Desire Economies of Pleasure: Sexualities in Asia and the Pacific,* ed. Lenore Manderson and Margaret Jolly, pp. 1–27. Chicago: University of Chicago Press.

Mani, Lata. 1984. The Production of an Official Discourse on Sati in Early Nineteenth-Century Bengal. In *Europe and Its Others,* ed. Francis Barker, pp. 89–127. Colchester, England: University of Essex.

———. 1989. Contentious Traditions: The Debate on Sati in Colonial India. In *Recasting Women: Essays in Colonial History,* ed. Kumkum Sangari and Sudesh Vaid, pp. 88–126. New Delhi: Kali for Women.

———. 1998. *Contentious Traditions: The Debate on "Sati" in Colonial India.* Berkeley and Los Angeles: University of California Press.

Mankekar, Purnima. 1997. To Whom Does Ameena Belong? Towards a Feminist Analysis of Childhood and Nationhood in Contemporary India. *Feminist Review* 56: 26–60.

———. 1999. *Screening Culture, Viewing Politics: An Ethnography of Television, Womanhood, and Nation in Postcolonial India.* Durham, N.C.: Duke University Press.

———. 2004. Dangerous Desires: Television and Erotics in Late Twentieth-Century India. *Journal of Asian Studies* 63, no. 2: 403–431.

Manu. 1991. *The Laws of Manu.* Trans. Wendy Doniger, with Brian K. Smith. New York: Penguin.

Manuel, Peter. 1993. *Cassette Culture: Popular Music and Technology in North India.* Chicago: University of Chicago Press.

March, Kathryn. 2002. *"If Each Comes Halfway": Meeting Tamang Women of Nepal* (with CD of original Tamang songs). Ithaca, N.Y.: Cornell University Press.

Marriott, McKim. 1976. Hindu Transactions: Diversity without Dualism. In *Transaction and Meaning: Directions in the Anthropology of Exchange and Symbolic Behavior,* ed. Bruce Kapferer, pp. 109–42. Philadelphia: Institute for the Study of Human Issues.

———. 1990. Constructing an Indian Ethnosociology. In *India through Hindu Categories,* ed. McKim Marriott, pp. 1–39. New Delhi: Sage.

Marriott, McKim, and Ronald Inden. 1977. Toward an Ethnosociology of South Asian Caste Systems. In *The New Wind,* ed. Kenneth David, pp. 227–38. The Hague: Mouton Publishers.

Marx, Karl. 1994a [1932]. The German Ideology, Part 1. In *Karl Marx: Selected Writings,* ed. Lawrence H. Simon, pp. 102–56. Indianapolis: Hackett Publishing.

———. 1994b [1859]. Preface to a Contribution to the Critique of Political Economy. In *Karl Marx: Selected Writings,* ed. Lawrence H. Simon, pp. 209–13. Indianapolis: Hackett Publishing.

Massumi, Brian. 2002. *Parables for the Virtual: Movement, Affect, Sensation.* Durham, N.C.: Duke University Press.

Masud, Mohammad Khalid, ed. 2000. *Travellers in Faith: Studies of the Tablighi Jama'at as a Transnational Islamic Movement for Faith Renewal.* Leiden: Brill.

Matthew, Biju, and Vijay Prashad, eds. 1999/2000. *Satyagraha* in America: The Political Culture of South Asian Americans. *Amerasia Journal* 25, no. 3: ix–xv.

Mayer, Tamar. 1999. *Gender Ironies of Nationalism: Sexing the Nation.* New York: Routledge.

Mazzarella, William. 2001. Citizens Have Sex, Consumers Make Love: Marketing KamaSutra Condoms in Bombay. In *Asian Media Productions,* ed. Brian Moeran, pp. 168–96. Honolulu: University of Hawai'i Press.

———. 2002. Cindy at the Taj: Cultural Enclosure and Corporate Potentateship in an Era of Globalization. In *Everyday Life in South Asia,* 1st ed., ed.

Diane P. Mines and Sarah Lamb, pp. 387–99. Bloomington: Indiana University Press.

———. 2003. "Very Bombay": Contending with the Global in an Indian Advertising Agency. *Cultural Anthropology* 18, no. 1: 33–71.

———. 2005. Middle Class. In *Keywords in South Asian Studies,* ed. Rachel Dwyer. www.soas.ac.uk/southasianstudies/keywords/24808.pdf.

Mbembe, A. 1992. Provisional Notes on the Postcolony. *Africa* 62, no. 1: 3–37.

McClintock, Anne. 1995. *Imperial Leather: Race, Gender, and Sexuality in the Colonial Contest.* New York: Routledge.

McHugh, Ernestine L. 2001. *Love and Honor in the Himalayas: Coming to Know Another Culture.* Philadelphia: University of Pennsylvania Press.

———. 2004. Moral Choices and Global Desires: Feminine Identity in a Transnational Realm. *Ethos* 32, no. 4: 575–97.

McKean, Lise. 1996. *Divine Enterprise: Gurus and the Hindu Nationalist Movement.* Chicago: University of Chicago Press.

McLeod, Hew. 1997. *Sikhism.* London: Penguin Books.

———. 1999. The Turban: Symbol of Sikh Identity. In *Sikh Identity: Continuity and Change,* ed. Pashaura Singh and N. Gerald Barrier, pp. 57–68. New Delhi: Manohar.

Mehta, Rama. 1981. *Inside the Haveli.* New Delhi: Arnold-Heinemann.

Menon, Dilip. 1994. *Caste, Nationalism and Communism in South India: Malabar 1900–1948.* Cambridge: Cambridge University Press.

———. 1997. Caste and Colonial Modernity: Reading Saraswativijayam. *Studies in History* 13, no. 2: 291–312.

———. 1999. Being a Brahmin the Marxist Way: E. M. S. Namboodiripad and the Pasts of Kerala. In *Invoking the Past: The Uses of History in South Asia,* ed. Daud Ali, pp. 55–87. New Delhi: Oxford University Press.

———. 2004. A Place Elsewhere: Lower-Caste Malayalam Novels of the 19th Century. In *India's Literary History: Essays on the 19th Century,* ed. Vashudha Dalmia and Stuart Blackburn, pp. 483–515. New Delhi: Permanent Black.

Menon, Nivedita. 2000. State, Community and the Debate on the Uniform Civil Code in India. In *Beyond Rights Talk and Culture Talk: Comparative Essays on the Politics of Rights and Culture,* ed. Mahmood Mamdani, pp. 75–95. New York: St. Martin's Press.

Menon, Ritu. 1998. *Borders and Boundaries: Women in India's Partition.* Delhi and New Brunswick, N.J.: Rutgers University Press.

Metcalf, Barbara. 1982. *Islamic Revival in British India: Deoband, 1860–1900.* Princeton, N.J.: Princeton University Press.

———. 1993. Living Hadis in the Tablighi Jamaat. *Journal of Asian Studies* 52, no. 3: 584–608.

———. 1997. *Bihisti Zewar: Perfecting Women (Maulana Ashraf Ali Thanawi's Bihisti Zewar, A Partial Translation with Commentary).* Lahore: Idara-e-Islamiat.

Metcalf, Barbara D., and Thomas R. Metcalf. 2006. *A Concise History of Modern India.* 2nd ed. Cambridge: Cambridge University Press.

Miller, Barbara D. 1981. *The Endangered Sex: Neglect of Female Children in Rural North India.* Ithaca, N.Y.: Cornell University Press.

——. 1987. Female Infanticide and Child Neglect in Rural North India. In *Child Survival,* ed. Nancy Scheper-Hughes, pp. 95–112. Dordrecht, Holland: D. Reidel Publishing.

Mills, Mary Beth. 2003. Gender and Inequality in the Global Labor Force. *Annual Review of Anthropology* 32: 41–62.

Mines, Diane P. 1990. Hindu Periods of Death "Impurity." In *India through Hindu Categories,* ed. McKim Marriott, pp. 103–30. New Delhi: Sage.

——. 1997a. From Homo Hierarchicus to Homo Faber: Breaking Convention through Semiosis. *Irish Journal of Anthropology* 2: 33–44.

——. 1997b. Making the Past Past: Objects and the Spatialization of Time in Tamilnadu. *Anthropology Quarterly* 70, no. 4: 173–86.

——. 2005. *Fierce Gods: Inequality, Ritual, and the Politics of Dignity in a South Indian Village.* Bloomington: Indiana University Press.

——. 2008. Waiting for Vellalakantan. In *Tamil Geographies: Cultural Constructions of Space and Place in South India,* ed. Martha Selby and Indira Peterson, pp. 199–220. Albany: State University of New York Press.

Ministry of Health and Family Welfare. 2001. Expanded Programme on Immunization, National Plan of Action, 2001–2005. Revised draft. Dhaka: Government of Bangladesh.

Mistry, Rohinton. 1992. *Such a Long Journey.* New York: Vintage Books.

——. 1997. *A Fine Balance.* New York: Vintage Books.

Mohanty, Chandra. 1997. Women Workers and Capitalist Scripts: Ideologies of Domination, Common Interests, and the Politics of Solidarity. In *Feminist Genealogies, Colonial Legacies, and Democratic Futures,* ed. M. Jaqui Alexander and Chandra Mohanty, pp. 3–29. New York: Routledge.

Moon, Vasant. 2001. *Growing Up Untouchable in India: A Dalit Autobiography.* Trans. Gail Omvedt. New York: Rowman and Littlefield.

Morris, Rosalind. 1995. All Made Up: Performance Theory and the New Anthropology of Sex and Gender. *Annual Review of Anthropology* 24: 567–92.

Mukhi, Sunita Sunder. 1998. "Underneath My Blouse Beats My Indian Heart": Sexuality, Nationalism, and Indian Womanhood in the United States. In *A Patchwork Shawl: Chronicles of South Asian Women in America,* ed. Shamita Das Dasgupta, pp. 186–205. New Brunswick, N.J.: Rutgers University Press.

Murthy, Anantha U. R. 1989. *Samskara: A Rite for a Dead Man.* 2nd ed. Oxford: Oxford University Press.

Myers, Rebecca. 2006. The Face of India: What It's Like to Find Yourself a TIME Cover Model. *Time* (online), posted 22 June.

Nagaraj, D. R. 1993. *The Flaming Feet: A Study of the Dalit Movement.* Bangalore: South Forum Press.

Nahar, Q., S. Amin, R. Sultan, H. Nazrul, M. Islam, T. T. Kane, Barkat-e-. Khuda, and C. Tunon. 1999. Strategies to Meet the Health Needs of Adolescents: A Review. Operations Research Project, Health and Population Extension Division. Dhaka: International Centre for Diarrhoeal Disease Research, Bangladesh.

Nanda, Serena. 1999. *Neither Man nor Woman: The Hijras of India*. Belmont, Calif.: Wadsworth.

Nandy, Ashis. 1980. Woman versus Womanliness: An Essay in Social and Political Psychology. In *At the Edge of Psychology: Essays in Politics and Culture*. Delhi: Oxford University Press.

———. 1983. *The Intimate Enemy*. New Delhi: Oxford University Press.

———. 1995. *The Savage Freud and Other Essays on Possible and Retrievable Selves*. New Delhi: Oxford University Press.

———. 1998. The Politics of Secularism and the Recovery of Religious Toleration. In *Secularism and Its Critics*, ed. Rajeev Bhargava, pp. 321–44. New Delhi: Oxford University Press.

Narayan, Kirin. 1994. *Love, Stars, and All That*. New York: Pocket Books.

———. 1997. Singing from Separation: Women's Voices in and about Kangra Folksongs. *Oral Traditions* 12: 23–53.

———. 2004. "Honor Is Honor After All": Silence and Speech in the Life Stories of Women in Kangra, North-West India. In *Telling Lives in India: Biography, Autobiography, and Life History*, ed. David Arnold and Stuart Blackburn, pp. 227–51. Bloomington: Indiana University Press.

Narayana Rao, Velcheru. 1991. A Ramayana of Their Own: Women's Oral Tradition in Telugu. In *Many Ramayanas: The Diversity of a Narrative Tradition in South Asia*, ed. Paula Richman, pp. 114–36. Berkeley and Los Angeles: University of California Press.

———. 2000. The Politics of Telugu Ramayanas: Colonialism, Print Culture, and Literary Movements. In *Questioning Ramayanas: A South Asian Tradition*, ed. Paula Richman, pp. 159–85. Berkeley and Los Angeles: University of California Press.

Nasr, S. V. R. 1994. *The Vanguard of the Islamic Revolution: The Jama'at-i Islam of Pakistan*. Berkeley: California University Press.

———. 2000. The Rise of Sunni Militancy in Pakistan: The Changing Role of Islamism and the Ulama in Society and Politics. *Modern Asian Studies* 34, no. 1: 139–80.

NASSCOM. 2005. Indian IT Industry—Fact Sheet: NASSCOM—McKinsey Report. National Family Health Survey of India, 2005–06, chapter 3. www .nfhsindia.org.

Nesbitt, Eleanor. 1955. Panjabis in Britain: Cultural History, and Cultural Choices. *South Asia Research* 15, no. 2: 221–40.

Nichter, Mark. 1981. Idioms of Distress: Alternatives in the Expression of Psycho-Social Distress: A Case Study from South India. *Culture, Medicine, and Psychiatry* 5: 379–408.

———. 1989. *Anthropology and International Health: South Asian Case Studies*. Dordrecht: Kluwer.

Nichter, Mark, and Nancy Vuckovic. 1994. Agenda for an Anthropology of Pharmaceutical Practice. *Social Science and Medicine* 39, no. 11: 1509–25.

Niehoff, Arthur, and Juanita Niehoff. 1960. *East Indians in the West Indies.* Publications in Anthropology, no. 6. Milwaukee: Milwaukee Public Museum.

Nigam, Aditya. 2000. Secularism, Modernity, Nation: An Epistemology of the Dalit Critique. *Economic and Political Weekly* (25 November): 4256–68.

Nigam, Sanjay. 1990a. Disciplining and Policing the Criminals by Birth, Part 1: The Making of a Colonial Stereotype—The Criminal Tribes and Castes of North India. *Indian Economic and Social History Review* 27, no. 2: 131–64.

———. 1990b. Disciplining and Policing the Criminals by Birth, Part 2: The Development of a Disciplinary System, 1871–1900. *Indian Economic and Social History Review* 27, no. 3: 257–87.

Nilsson, Usha. 2000. Grinding Millet but Singing of Sita: Power and Domination in Awadhi and Bhojpuri Women's Songs. In *Questioning Ramayanas,* ed. Paula Richman, pp. 137–58. Berkeley and Los Angeles: University of California Press.

Niranjana, Tejaswini. 1995. Banning "Bombayi": Nationalism, Communalism, and Gender. *Economic and Political Weekly* 30, no. 22: 1291–92.

Nugent, Neill. 1976. The Anti-immigration Groups. *New Community* 5, no. 3: 302–10.

Oberoi, Harjot. 1994. *The Construction of Religious Boundaries: Culture, Identity, and Diversity in the Sikh Tradition.* Chicago: University of Chicago Press.

O'Brien, D. J. T. 1895. *Grammar and Vocabulary of the Khowar Dialect (Chitrali) with an Introductory Sketch of Country and People.* Lahore: Civil and Military Gazette Press.

Omvedt, Gail. 1994. *Dalits and the Democratic Revolution: Dr. Ambedkar and the Dalit Movement in Colonial India.* New Delhi: Sage.

———. 1998. *Dalit Visions.* New Delhi: Orient Longman.

Ortner, Sherry L. 1973. Sherpa Purity. *American Anthropologist* 75: 49–63.

———. 1989. *High Religion: A Cultural and Political History of Sherpa Buddhism.* Princeton, N.J.: Princeton University Press.

———. 1991. Reading America: Preliminary Notes on Class and Culture. In *Recapturing Anthropology: Working in the Present,* ed. Richard G. Fox, pp. 163–90. Santa Fe, N.M.: School of American Research Press.

———. 1995. Resistance and the Problem of Ethnographic Refusal. *Comparative Studies in History and Society* 37, no. 1 (January): 173–93.

———. 1996. *Making Gender: The Politics and Erotics of Culture.* Boston: Beacon Press.

———. 1998. Identities: The Hidden Life of Class. *Journal of Anthropological Research* 54, no. 1 (Spring): 1–17.

———. 1999. *Life and Death on Mt. Everest: Sherpas and Himalayan Mountaineering.* Princeton, N.J.: Princeton University Press.

———. 2003. *New Jersey Dreaming: Capital, Culture, and the Class of '58*. Durham, N.C.: Duke University Press.

———. 2006. *Anthropology and Social Theory: Culture, Power and the Acting Subject*. Durham, N.C.: Duke University Press.

Osella, Filippo, and Caroline Osella. 2000. *Social Mobility in Kerala: Modernity and Identity in Conflict*. London: Pluto Press.

Oza, Rupal. 2001. Showcasing India: Gender, Geography, and Globalization. *Signs* 26, no. 4: 1067–96.

———. 2007. Showcasing India: Gender, Geography and Globalisation. In *Urban Women in Contemporary India,* ed. Rehana Ghadially, pp. 199–217. New Delhi: Sage.

Pachauri, S., and Joel Gittelsohn. 1994. Summary of Research Studies and Implications for Health Policy and Programmes. In *Listening to Women Talk about Their Health: Issues and Evidence from India,* ed. Joel Gittelsohn, M. E. Bentley, Pertti J. Pelto, Moni Nag, S. Pachauri, A. D. Harrison, and L. T. Landman, pp. 184–200. New Delhi: Ford Foundation and Har-Anand Publications.

Page, David, and William Crawley. 2001. *Satellites over South Asia*. New Delhi: Sage.

Pandey, Gyan. 1983. Rallying round the Cow: Sectarian Strife in the Bhojpuri Region, c. 1888–1917. In *Subaltern Studies II: Writings on South Asian History and Society,* ed. Ranajit Guha, pp. 60–129. Delhi: Oxford University Press.

———. 1990. *The Construction of Communalism in Colonial North India*. New York: Oxford University Press.

Pandian, M. S. S. 1992. *The Image Trap: MG Ramachandran in Film and Politics*. New Delhi: Sage.

Pandolfo, Stefania. 2000. The Thin Line of Modernity: Some Moroccan Debates on Subjectivity. In *Questions of Modernity,* ed. Timothy Mitchell, pp. 115–47. Minneapolis: University of Minnesota Press.

Pankaj, Ashok K. 2007. Engaging with Discourse on Caste, Class and Politics in India. *South Asia Research* 27, no. 3: 333–53.

Parameswaran, Radhika. 2004. Global Queens, National Celebrities: Tales of Feminine Triumph in Post-Liberalization India. *Critical Studies in Media Communication* 21, no. 4: 346–70.

Parker, Andrew, Mary Russo, Doris Sommer, and Patricia Yaeger, eds. 1992. *Nationalisms and Sexualities*. New York: Routledge.

Parkes, P. 2001. Alternative Social Structures and Foster Relations in the Hindu Kush: Milk Kinship and Tributary Allegiance in Former Mountain Kingdoms of Northern Pakistan. *Comparative Studies in Society and History* 43, no. 1: 4–36.

Parry, Jonathan. 1994. *Death in Banaras*. Cambridge: Cambridge University Press.

———. 2001. Ankalu's Errant Wife: Sex, Marriage and Industry in Contemporary Chhatisgarh. *Modern Asian Studies* 35, no. 4: 783–820.

Parry, Jonathan, Jan Breman, and Karin Kapadia, eds. 1999. The Worlds of Indian Industrial Labour. *Contributions to Indian Sociology.* Occasional Studies, 9. New Delhi: Sage.

Patel, Geeta. 1998. Home, Homo, Hybrid: Translating Gender. *College Literature* 24, no. 1: 133–50.

———. 2004. Homely Housewives Run Amok: Lesbians in Marital Fixes. *Public Culture* 16, no. 1: 131–57.

Patel, V., and N. Oomman. 1999. Mental Health Matters, Too: Gynaecological Symptoms and Depression in South Asia. *Reproductive Health Matters* 7, no. 14: 30–38.

Paul, Diane. 1985. *Women in Buddhism: Images of the Feminine in Mahayana Tradition.* Berkeley and Los Angeles: University of California Press.

Peace, Adrian. 1984. Constructions of Class, Images of Inequality: The Middle Class and the Urban Poor in a North Indian City. *Urban Anthropology* 13, no. 2–3: 261–94.

Peacock, James L., and Dorothy C. Holland. 1993. The Narrated Self: Life Stories in Process. *Ethos* 21: 367–83.

Perera, Sasanka. 1996. The Social and Cultural Construction of Female Sexuality and Gender Roles in Sinhala Society. Paper presented at the National Convention on Women's Studies, Centre for Women's Research [CENWOR], Colombo, Sri Lanka, March.

Perera, Vernon. 1998. Juki President Impressed by Local Workforce. *Sunday Observer* (Colombo), 11 October, Business: n.p.

Petech, Luciano. 1977. *A Kingdom of Ladakh.* Rome: Instituto per il Medio ed Estremo Oriente.

———. 1998. Western Tibet: Historical Introduction. In *Tabo: A Lamp for the Kingdom—Early Indo-Tibetan Buddhist Art in the Western Himalayas,* ed. Deborah Klimburg-Salter, pp. 56–103. London: Thames and Hudson.

Peterson, I. V. 1989. *Poems to Siva: The Hymns of the Tamil Saints.* Delhi: Motilal Banarsidass Publishers.

Pink, Daniel. 2004. The New Face of the Silicon Age: How India Became the Capital of the Computing Revolution. *Wired* (February): 96–103.

Pollock, Sheldon. 1993. Ramayana and Political Imagination in India. *Journal of Asian Studies* 52, no. 2: 261–97.

Povinelli, Elizabeth, and George Chauncey. 1999. Thinking Sexuality Transnationally: An Introduction. *GLQ* 5, no. 4: 439–50.

Prakash, Gyan. 1981. *Bonded Histories: Genealogies of Labor Servitude in Colonial India.* Cambridge: Cambridge University Press.

———. 1991. Becoming a Bhuinya: Oral Traditions and Contested Domination in Eastern India. In *Contesting Power: Resistance and Everyday Social Relations in South Asia,* ed. Douglas Haynes and Gyan Prakash, pp. 145–74. Berkeley and Los Angeles: University of California Press.

Prashad, Vijay. 1996. Desh: The Contradictions of "Homeland." In *Contours of the Heart,* ed. R. Srikanth and S. Maira, pp. 225–36. New York: Asian American Workshop.

Radhakrishnan, R. 1994. Is the Ethnic "Authentic" in the Diaspora? In *The State of Asian America,* ed. K. Aguilar-San Juan, pp. 219–23. Boston: South End Press.

Raheja, Gloria Goodwin. 1988. *The Poison in the Gift: Ritual, Prestation, and the Dominant Caste in a North Indian Village.* Chicago: University of Chicago Press.

———. 1995. The Limits of Patriliny: Kinship, Gender, and Women's Speech Practices in Rural North India. In *Gender, Kinship, Power: A Comparative and Interdisciplinary History,* ed. Mary Jo Maynes and Ann Waltner, pp. 149–76. London and New York: Routledge.

———. 1999. The Illusion of Consent: Language, Caste, and Colonial Rule in India. In *Colonial Subjects: Essays on the Practical History of Anthropology,* ed. Peter Pels and Oscar Salemink, pp. 117–52. Ann Arbor: University of Michigan Press.

———. 2002. The Erasure of Everyday Life in Colonial Ethnography. In *Everyday Life in South Asia,* 1st ed., ed. Diane P. Mines and Sarah Lamb, pp. 199–213. Bloomington: Indiana University Press.

Raheja, Gloria Goodwin, and Ann Grodzins Gold. 1994. *Listen to the Heron's Words: Reimagining Gender and Kinship in North India.* Berkeley and Los Angeles: University of California Press.

Rai, Amit S. 1995. India On-line: Electronic Bulletin Boards and the Construction of a Diasporic Hindu Identity. *Diaspora* 4, no. 1: 31–57.

Raj, Dhooleka. 2003. *Where Are You From? Middle-Class Migrants in the Modern World.* Berkeley and Los Angeles: University of California Press.

Rajagopal, Arvind. 1999. Thinking about the New Indian Middle Class: Gender, Advertising and Politics in an Age of Globalization. In *Signposts: Gender Issues in Post-Independence India,* ed. R. Sunder Rajan, pp. 57–99. New Delhi: Kali for Women.

———. 2001. *Politics after Television: Religious Nationalism and the Reshaping of the Indian Public.* Cambridge: Cambridge University Press.

Raman, Sita Anantha. 1996. *Getting Girls to School: Social Reform in the Tamil Districts 1870–1930.* Calcutta: Stree.

Ramanujan, A. K. 1970. Towards an Anthology of City Images. In *Urban India: Society, Space, and Image,* ed. Richard. G. Fox, pp. 224–44. Monograph and Occasional Papers Series, Monograph no. 10. Durham, N.C.: Duke University Program in Comparative Studies on Southern Asia.

———, ed. and trans. 1973. *Speaking of Siva.* New York: Penguin Classics.

———. 1975 [1967]. *The Interior Landscape: Love Poems from a Classical Tamil Anthology.* Bloomington: Indiana University Press.

———. 1981. Three Hundred Ramayanas: Five Examples and Three Thoughts on Translation. In *Many Ramayanas: The Diversity of a Narrative Tradition in South Asia,* ed. Paula Richman, pp. 22–49. Berkeley and Los Angeles: University of California Press.

———. 1985. *Poems of Love and War.* New York: Columbia University Press.

———. 1986. Two Realms of Kannada Folklore. In *Another Harmony: New Essays on the Folklore of India,* ed. Stuart Blackburn and A. K. Ramanujan, pp. 41–75. Berkeley and Los Angeles: University of California Press.

———. 1992 [1981]. *Hymns for the Drowning: Poems for Visnu by Nammalvar.* New York: Penguin Books.

Rao, M. S. A. 1979. *Social Movements and Social Transformation: A Study of Two Backward Class Movements in India.* New Delhi: Macmillan Co.

———. 1989. Some Conceptual Issues in the Study of Caste, Class, Ethnicity, and Dominance. In *Dominance and State Power in Modern India,* ed. Francine R. Frankel and M. S. A. Rao, pp. 21–45. Delhi: Oxford University Press.

Rashid, Sabina Faiz. 2007. *Durbolota* (Weakness), *Chinta Rog* (Worry Illness), and Poverty: Explanations of White Discharge among Married Adolescent Women in an Urban Slum in Dhaka, Bangladesh. *Medical Anthropology Quarterly* 21, no. 1: 108–132.

Ratti, Rakesh, ed. 1993. *A Lotus of Another Color: An Unfolding of the South Asian Gay and Lesbian Experience.* Boston: Alyson Publications.

Ray, Raka. 2000. Masculinity, Femininity, and Servitude: Domestic Workers in Calcutta in the Late Twentieth Century. *Feminist Studies* 26, no. 3: 691–718.

Reddy, Gayatri. 2003. "Men" Who Would Be Kings: Celibacy, Emasculation, and Re-Production of Hijras in Contemporary Indian Politics. *Social Research* 70, no. 1: 163–98.

———. 2005. *With Respect to Sex: Negotiating Hijra Identity in South India.* Chicago: University of Chicago press.

Reetz, Dietrich. 2002. The Busy World of the Tablighi-Jamaat: An Insight into Their System of Self Organization (*Intizam*). Paper presented at the 17th European Conference for Modern South Asia Studies, Heidelberg, September 9–13.

Rege, Sharmila. 1996. The Hegemonic Appropriation of Sexuality: The Case of the Lavani Performer of Maharashtra. In *Social Reform, Sexuality, and the State,* ed. Patricia Uberoi, pp. 23–38. New Delhi: Sage Publications.

Riaboff, Isabelle. 1997. Le Roi et le Moine: Figures et Principes du Pouvoir et de sa Légitimation au Zanskar (Himalaya occidental). Ph.D. diss., Laboratoires d'Ethnologie et de Sociologie Comparatif, Université de Paris X.

Richman, Paula, ed. 1991. *Many Ramayanas: The Diversity of a Narrative Tradition in South Asia.* Berkeley and Los Angeles: University of California Press.

———. 2000. *Questioning Ramayanas: A South Asian Tradition.* Berkeley and Los Angeles: University of California Press.

Ring, Laura A. 2006. *Zenana: Everyday Peace in a Karachi Apartment Building.* Bloomington: Indiana University Press.

Risseeuw, Carla. 1991. *Gender, Transformation, Power, and Resistance among Women in Sri Lanka: The Fish Don't Talk about the Water.* New Delhi: Manohar.

Robertson, G. S. 1899. *Chitral: The Story of a Minor Siege.* London: Methuen.

Rofel, Lisa. 1999. Qualities of Desire: Imagining Gay Identities in China. *GLQ* 5, no. 4: 451–74.

———. 2007. *Desiring China: Experiments in Neoliberalism, Sexuality and Public Culture.* Durham, N.C.: Duke University Press.

Rosaldo, Michelle. 1980. The Use and Abuse of Anthropology. *Signs* 5, no. 3: 389–417.

Rosenwald, George C., and Richard L. Ochberg, eds. 1992. *Storied Lives: The Cultural Politics of Self-Understanding.* New Haven, Conn.: Yale University Press.

Ross, J. L., S. L. Laston, P. J. Pelto, and L. Muna. 2002. Exploring Explanatory Models of Women's Reproductive Health in Rural Bangladesh. *Culture, Health and Sexuality* 4, no. 2: 173–190.

Rothenberg, Celia Elaine. 1998. Spirits of Palestine: Palestinian Village Women and Stories of the Jinn. Ph.D. diss., Anthropology, University of Toronto.

Roy, Beth. 1994. *Some Trouble with Cows: Making Sense of Social Conflict.* Berkeley and Los Angeles: University of California Press.

Roy, Kumkum. 1998. Unravelling the Kamasutra. In *A Question of Silence? The Sexual Economies of Modern India,* ed. Mary E. John and Janaki Nair, pp. 52–76. New Delhi: Kali.

Roy, Manisha. 1992. *Bengali Women.* Chicago: University of Chicago Press.

Rozario, Santi. 1992. *Purity and Communal Boundaries: Women and Social Change in a Bangladeshi Village.* London: Zed Books.

Rushdie, Salman. 1991. *Imaginary Homelands: Essays and Criticism.* London: Granta Books.

Rustomji-Kerns, Roshni, ed. 1994. *Living in America: Poetry and Fiction by South Asian American Writers.* Boulder, Colo.: Westview Press.

Sahlins, Marshall. 1985. *Islands of History.* Chicago: University of Chicago Press.

Said, Edward. 1978. *Orientalism.* New York: Pantheon Books.

Sanyal, Usha. 1996. *Devotional Islam and Politics in British India: Ahmad Riza Khan Barelwi and his Movement, 1870–1920.* Delhi: Oxford University Press.

Sarkar, Tanika. 1995. Heroic Women, Mother Goddesses: Family and Organisation in Hindutva Politics. In *Women and the Hindu Right: A Collection of Essays,* ed. Tanika Sarkar and Urvashi Butalia, pp. 185–219. New Delhi: Kali for Women.

———. 2001. *Hindu Wife, Hindu Nation: Community, Religion and Cultural Nationalism.* New Delhi: Permanent Black.

Sato, Ikuya. 1991. *Kamikaze Biker: Parody and Anomy in Affluent Japan.* Chicago: University of Chicago Press.

Saxenian, Anna Lee. 2000. Back to India: Indian Software Engineers are Returning with Enthusiasm and Entrepreneurial Know-How. *Wall Street Journal*, Technology Journal Asia, 24 January. http://interactive.wsj.com.

Schein, Louisa. 1999. Of Cargo and Satellites: Imagined Cosmopolitanism. *Postcolonial Studies* 2, no. 3: 345–75.

Scheper-Hughes, Nancy. 1992. *Death without Weeping: The Violence of Everyday Life in Brazil*. Berkeley and Los Angeles: University of California Press.

Scheper-Hughes, Nancy, and Margaret Lock. 1987. The Mindful Body: A Prolegomenon to Future Work in Medical Anthropology. *Medical Anthropology Quarterly* 1, no. 1: 6–41.

Schieffelin, Edward. 1985. Performance and the Cultural Construction of Reality. *American Ethnologist* 12: 704–24.

Schimmel, Anne-Marie. 1975. *Mystical Dimensions of Islam*. Chapel Hill: University of North Carolina Press.

Schuh, Dieter. 1976. *Urkunden und Zendschreiben aus Zentraltibet, Ladakh, und Zanskar. Monumenta Tibetica Historica*. Band 2, 4. St. Augustin: VGH Wissenschaftsverlag.

———. 1983. *Historiographische Dokumenta aus Zans-dkar*. Sankt Augustin: Archiv für Zentralasiatische Geschichts-Forschung Heft 6.

Scott, David. 1999. *Refashioning Futures: Criticism after Postcoloniality*. Princeton, N.J.: Princeton University Press.

Sedgwick, Eve Kosofsky. 1985. *Between Men: English Literature and Male Homo-social Desire*. New York: Columbia University Press.

———. 1990. *Epistemology of the Closet*. Berkeley and Los Angeles: University of California Press.

Seizer, Susan. 1995. Paradoxes of Visibility in the Field: Rites of Queer Passage in Anthropology. *Public Culture* 8, no. 1: 73–100.

———. 2000. Roadwork: Offstage with Special Drama Actresses in Tamilnadu, South India. *Cultural Anthropology* 15, no. 2: 217–59.

Sengupta, Somini. 2006. Is Public Romance a Right? The Kamasutra Doesn't Say. *New York Times*, 4 January 2006.

———. 2007. Careers Give India's Women New Independence. *New York Times*, 23 November 2007.

Seymour, Susan. 1999. *Women, Family, and Child Care in India: A World in Transition*. Cambridge: Cambridge University Press.

Shakabpa, Tsepon. 1967. *Tibet: A Political History*. New Haven, Conn.: Yale University Press.

Shanmugasundaram, S. 1997. *Bharatiraja: Mannum Makkalum*. Bangalore: Kaavya.

Sharma, Aradhana, and Akhil Gupta. 2006. Rethinking Theories of the State in an Age of Globalization. In *The Anthropology of the State: A Reader*, pp. 1–42. Malden, Mass.: Blackwell.

Sharma, O. P. 1994. *Universal Literacy: A Distant Dream (Based on the Census Data)*. New Delhi: Kar Kripa Publishers.

Sharma, O. P., and Robert D. Retherford. 1993. *Literacy Trends in the 1980s in India*. Faridabad: Government of India Press.

Sharma, Sanjay, John Hutnyk, and Ashwani Sharma. 1996. Introduction. In *Dis-Orienting Rhythms: The Politics of the New Asian Dance Music*, ed. Sanjay Sharma, John Hutnyk, and Ashwani Sharma, pp. 1–12. London: Zed Books.

Shome, Raka. 2006. Thinking through the Diaspora: Call Centers, India, and a New Politics of Hybridity. *International Journal of Cultural Studies* 9, no. 1: 105–24.

Shulman, David Dean. 1985. *The King and the Clown in South Indian Myth and Poetry*. Princeton, N.J.: Princeton University Press.

———. 2000. Bhavabhuti on Cruelty and Compassion. In *Questioning Ramayanas: A South Asian Tradition*, ed. Paula Richman, pp. 49–82. Berkeley and Los Angeles: University of California Press.

Siegel, Lee. 1978. *Sacred and Profane Dimensions of Love in Indian Traditions as Exemplified in the Gitagovinda of Jayadeva*. Delhi: Oxford University Press.

Siegel, James. 2003. *The Rope of God*. Ann Arbor: University of Michigan Press.

Singer, Milton. 1972. *When a Great Tradition Modernizes: An Anthropological Approach to Indian Civilization*. Chicago: University of Chicago Press.

Singh, Pashaura, and N. Gerald Barrier, eds. 1996. *The Transmission of Sikh Heritage in the Diaspora*. New Delhi: Manohar.

———. 1999. *Sikh Identity: Continuity and Change*. New Delhi: Manohar.

Sinha, Mrinalini. 1997. *Colonial Masculinity: The "Manly Englishman" and the "Effeminate Bengali" in the Late Nineteenth Century*. New Delhi: Kali.

Sisson, Richard, and Leo E. Rose. 1990. *War and Secession: Pakistan, India, and the Creation of Bangladesh*. Berkeley and Los Angeles: University of California Press.

Snellgrove, David, and Tadeusz Skorupski. 1980. *The Cultural Heritage of Ladakh: Zangskar and the Cave Temples of Ladakh*. Warminster, Wiltshire, England: Aris and Phillips.

Solon, Gary. 1992. Intergenerational Income Mobility in the United States. *American Economic Review* 83, no. 2: 393–408.

Southall Black Sisters. 1979. The Traditional Story of Ramayana. One-page program distributed at the Ramlila, 19 October.

Spencer, Jonathan. 1991. *A Sinhala Village in a Time of Trouble*. Delhi: Oxford University Press.

Spivak, Gayatri Chakravorty. 1995. Translator's Preface. In *Imaginary Maps: Three Stories by Mahasweta Devi*, pp. xxiii–xxix. New York: Routledge.

Sponberg, Alan. 1992. Attitudes toward Women and the Feminine in Early Buddhism. In *Buddhism, Sexuality, and Gender*, ed. Jose Cabezon, pp. 3–36. Albany: State University of New York Press.

Sridharan, E. 2004. The Growth and Sectoral Composition of India's Middle Class: Its Impact on the Politics of Economic Liberalization. *India Review* 3, no. 4: 405–28.

Srikanth, Rajni, and Sunaina Maira, eds. 1996. *Contours of the Heart: South Asians Map North America.* New York: Asian American Workshop.

Srinivas, M. N. 1976. *The Remembered Village.* Berkeley and Los Angeles: University of California Press.

Srinivas, Smriti. 2001. *Landscapes of Urban Memory: The Sacred and the Civic in India's High-Tech City.* Minneapolis: University of Minnesota Press.

Srinivasan, Amrit. 1985. Reform and Revival: The Devadasi and Her Dance. *Economic and Political Weekly* 20, no. 44: 1869–76.

Srivastava, Manoj. 1998. Promoting Adult Literacy in India through State-Society Synergy: A Comparative Study of Mass Literacy Campaigns in Kerala and Bihar. Master's thesis in Professional Studies, International Development, Cornell University.

Stetkevych, Jaroslav. 1996. *Muhammad and the Golden Bough: Reconstructing Arabian Myth.* Bloomington: Indiana University Press.

Stoler, Ann. 1995. *Race and the Education of Desire: Foucault's History of Sexuality and the Colonial Order of Things.* Durham, N.C.: Duke University Press.

Stone, Linda, and Caroline James. 1995. Dowry, Bride-Burning, and Female Power in India. *Women's Studies International Forum* 18, no. 2: 125–35. Reprinted in *Gender in Cross-Cultural Perspective,* ed. Caroline B. Brettell and Carolyn F. Sargent, pp. 307–16. Upper Saddle River, N.J.: Prentice-Hall, 2001.

Sudha, S., and S. Irudaya Rajan. 2003. Persistent Daughter Disadvantage: What Do Estimated Sex Ratios at Birth and Sex Ratios of Child Mortality Risk Reveal? *Economic and Political Weekly* 38, no. 41 (Oct. 11–17): 4361–69.

Suleri, Sara. 1989. *Meatless Days.* Chicago: University of Chicago Press.

Sunder Rajan, Rajeshwari. 1993. *Real and Imagined Women: Gender, Culture and Postcolonialism.* London: Routledge.

———. 1999. Introduction. In *Signposts: Gender Issues in Post-Independence India,* ed. Rajeshwari Sunder Rajan, pp. 1–16. New Delhi: Kali.

———. 1999. The Story of Draupadi's Disrobing. In *Signposts: Gender Issues in Post-Independence India,* ed. Rajeshwari Sunder Rajan, pp. 331–58. New Delhi: Kali.

Tambiah, Stanley J. 1991 [1986]. *Sri Lanka: Ethnic Fratricide and the Dismantling of Democracy.* Chicago: University of Chicago Press.

Tambiah, Yasmin. 1997. Women's Sexual Autonomy: Some Issues in South Asia. *Options* 9: 28–32.

Tamil Lexicon. 1982. 6 vols. Madras: University of Madras.

Tatla, Darshan Singh. 1999. *The Sikh Diaspora: The Search for Statehood.* London: Routledge.

Taylor, Stan. 1978. The National Front: Anatomy of a Political Movement. In *Racism and Political Action in Britain,* ed. Robert Miles and Annie Phizacklea, pp. 124–46. London: Routledge.

Tennekoon, Serena. 1986. "Macho" Sons and "Man-Made" Mothers. *Lanka Guardian,* 15 June.

Thadani, Giti. 1996. *Sakhiyani: Lesbian Desire in Ancient and Modern India.* London: Cassell.

Thapan, Meenakshi, ed. 1997. *Embodiment: Essays on Gender and Identity.* Delhi: Oxford University Press.

Tharu, Susie. 1989. Tracing Savitri's Pedigree: Victorian Racism and the Image of Women in Indo-Anglian Literature. In *Recasting Women: Essays in Colonial History,* ed. Kumkum Sangari and Sudesh Vaid, pp. 254–68. New Delhi: Kali.

———. 1997. The Impossible Subject: Caste in the Scene of Desire. In *Embodiment: Essays on Gender and Identity,* ed. Meenakshi Thapan, pp. 256–70. Delhi: Oxford University Press.

Tharu, Susie, and K. Lalita, eds. 1991. *Women Writing in India 600 B.C. to the Present.* Vol. 1. New York: Feminist Press.

Thiruchendran, Selvy. 1997. *Ideology, Caste, Class, and Gender.* New Delhi: Vikas.

Tilakaratne, W. M. 2006. Phasing Out of MFA and the Emerging Trends in the Ready Made Garment Industry in Sri Lanka. In *Employment in Ready-made Garment Industry in Post-MFA ERA: The Cases of India, Bangladesh and Sri Lanka,* ed. Mayumi Murayama. Institute of Developing Economies, Japan External Trade Organization, Joint Research Program Series, no. 140 (March 2006). Available at www.ide.go.jp/English/Publish/Jrp/ (accessed 7 January 2009).

Tinker, Hugh. 1974. *A New System of Slavery: The Export of Indian Labour Overseas 1830–1902.* Oxford: Oxford University Press.

Tolen, Rachel. 1996. Between Bungalow and Outhouse: Class Practice and Domestic Service in a Madras Railway. Ph.D. diss., University of Pennsylvania.

———. 2000. Transfers of Knowledge and Privileged Spheres of Practice: Servants and Employers in a Madras Railway Colony. In *Home and Hegemony: Domestic Service and Identity Politics in South and Southeast Asia,* ed. Kathleen M. Adams and Sara Dickey, pp. 63–86. Ann Arbor: University of Michigan Press.

Tontisirin, K., G. Attig, P. Winichagoon, and J. Yhoung-Aree. 2005. Asian Workshop on Nutrition Education—Sharing Expertise. Country Situations, Bangladesh. Food and Agriculture Organization. Electronic document, www.fao.org/docrep/T2860T/T2860T04.HTM.

Trawick, Margaret Egnor. 1986. Internal Harmony in Paraiyar Crying Songs. In *Another Harmony: New Essays on the Folklore of India,* ed. Stuart Blackburn and A. K. Ramanujan, pp. 294–344. Berkeley and Los Angeles: University of California Press.

———. 1988. Spirits and Voices in Tamil Songs. *American Ethnologist* 15: 193–215.

———. 1990. *Notes on Love in a Tamil Family.* Berkeley and Los Angeles: University of California Press.

———. 1991. Wandering Lost: A Landless Laborer's Sense of Place. In *Gender, Genre, and Power in South Asian Expressive Traditions,* ed. Arjun Appadurai, Frank J. Korom, and Margaret A. Mills, pp. 224–66. Philadelphia: University of Pennsylvania Press.

Trollope-Kumar, Karen. 1999. Symptoms of Reproductive Tract Infections—Not All That They Seem to Be. *Lancet* 354, no. 9192: 1745–46.

———. 2001. Cultural and Biomedical Meanings of the Complaint of Leucorrhea in South Asian Women. *Tropical Medicine and International Health* 6, no. 4: 260–66.

Tsering, Tashi, and Philippa Russell. 1996. An Account of the Buddhist Ordination of Women. *Cho Yang* 1, no. 1: 21–30.

Tsomo, Karma Lekshe. 1988. *Sakyadhita: Daughters of the Buddha.* Ithaca, N.Y.: Snow Lion Press.

———. 1996. *Sisters in Solitude.* Albany: State University of New York Press.

Turner, Stuart. 1996. Torture, Refugees, and Trust. In *Mistrusting Refugees,* ed. E. Valentine Daniel and John C. Knudsen, pp. 56–72. Berkeley: University of California Press.

Uberoi, Patricia. 1996. When Is a Marriage Not a Marriage? Sex, Sacrament and Contract in Hindu Marriage. In *Social Reform, Sexuality and the State,* ed. Patricia Uberoi, pp. 319–45. New Delhi: Sage.

Unnithan, Maya, and Kavita Srivastava. 1997. Gender Politics, Development, and Women's Agency in Rajasthan. In *Discourses of Development: Anthropological Perspectives,* ed. R. D. Grillo and R. L. Stirrat, pp. 157–81. New York: Berg.

Upadhyay, Anita, et al. 1995. *Prernā gīt aur chetan nāre.* Jaipur: Rajasthan Praurh Íikṣaṇ Samiti.

Van der Veer, Peter. 1992. Playing or Praying: A Sufi Saint's Day in Surat. *Journal of Asian Studies* 51, no. 3: 545–65.

———. 1994. *Religious Nationalism: Hindus and Muslims in India.* Berkeley and Los Angeles: University of California Press.

———. 2004. Transnational Religion: Hindu and Muslim Movements. *Journal for the Study of Religions and Ideologies* 7: 4–18.

Van der Veer, Peter, and Hartmut Lehmann. 1999. *Nation and Religion: Perspectives on Europe and Asia.* Princeton, N.J.: Princeton University Press.

Van Willigen, John, and Narender K. Chadha. 1999. *Social Aging in a Delhi Neighborhood.* Westport, Conn.: Bergin and Garvey.

Vanita, Ruth, ed. 2001. *Queering India: Same-Sex Love and Eroticism in Indian Culture and Society.* New York: Routledge.

Vanita, Ruth, and Saleem Kidwai, eds. 2000. *Same-Sex Love in India: Readings from Literature and History.* New York: St. Martin's Press.

Vasudevan, Ravi S. 2000. Shifting Codes, Dissolving Identities: The Hindi Social Film of the 1950s as Popular Culture. In *Making Meaning in Indian Cinema,* ed. Ravi S. Vasudevan, pp. 99–121. New Delhi: Oxford University Press.

Vatuk, Sylvia. 1980. Withdrawal and Disengagement as a Cultural Response to Aging in India. In *Aging in Culture and Society*, ed. Christine Fry, pp. 126–48. New York: Praeger.

———. 1990. "To Be a Burden on Others": Dependency Anxiety among the Elderly in India. In *Divine Passions: The Social Construction of Emotion in India*, ed. Owen Lynch, pp. 64–88. Berkeley and Los Angeles: University of California Press.

———. 1995. The Indian Woman in Later Life: Some Social and Cultural Considerations. In *Women's Health in India: Risk and Vulnerability*, ed. Monica Das Gupta, Lincoln C. Chen, and T. N. Krishnan, pp. 289–306. Bombay: Oxford University Press.

Vertovec, Steven. 1997. Three Meanings of "Diaspora," Exemplified among South Asian Religions. *Diaspora* 6, no. 3: 277–99.

Visram, Rozina. 1986. *Ayahs, Lascars, and Princes*. London: Pluto.

Visweswaran, Kamala. 1997. Diaspora by Design: Flexible Citizenship and South Asians in U.S. Racial Formations. *Diaspora* 6, no. 1: 5–29.

Wadley, Susan S. 1975. *Shakti: Power in the Conceptual Structure of Karimpur Religion*. University of Chicago Studies in Anthropology Series in Social, Cultural and Linguistic Anthropology, no. 2. Chicago: Dept. of Anthropology, University of Chicago.

———. 1994. *Struggling with Destiny in Karimpur, 1925–1984*. Berkeley and Los Angeles: University of California Press.

———. 1995a. No Longer a Wife: Widows in Rural North India. In *From the Margins of Hindu Marriage: Essays on Gender, Religion, and Culture*, ed. Lyndsey Harlan and Paul Courtright, pp. 90–118. New York: Oxford University Press.

———. 1995b. The "Village Indira": A Brahman Widow and Political Action in Rural North India. In *Women in India: Two Perspectives*, ed. Doranne Jacobson and Susan S. Wadley, pp. 225–50. Delhi: Manohar.

———. 2000. The Village in 1998. In *Behind Mud Walls: Seventy-Five Years in a North Indian Village*, ed. William Wiser and Charlotte Wiser; with chapters by Susan S. Wadley and David G. Mandelbaum, pp. 319–38. Berkeley and Los Angeles: University of California Press.

Wadley, Susan S., and Bruce W. Derr. 1993. Karimpur Families over 60 Years. In *Family, Kinship and Marriage in India*, ed. Patricia Oberoi, pp. 393–415. Delhi: Oxford University Press.

Warner, Michael, ed. 1993. *Fear of a Queer Planet: Queer Politics and Social Theory*. Minneapolis: University of Minnesota Press.

Weber, Max 1968. The Distribution of Power within the Political Community: Class, Status, Party. In Max Weber, *Economy and Society*, vol. 2, ed. Guenther Roth and Claus Wittich. New York: Bedminster Press.

Weeks, Jeffrey. 1981. *Sex, Politics, and Society: The Regulation of Sexuality since 1800*. London and New York: Longman.

Weerasinghe, Rohini. 1989. Women Workers in the Katunayake Investment Promotion Zone (KIPZ) of Sri Lanka: Some Observations. In *Women in*

Development in South Asia, ed. V. Kanesalingam, pp. 306–21. New Delhi: Macmillan India.

Westermarck, Edward Alexander. 1926. *Ritual and Belief in Morocco.* 2 vols. London: Macmillan.

Williams, Raymond. 1977. *Marxism and Literature.* London: Oxford University Press.

Willis, Jan. 1985. Nuns and Benefactresses: The Role of Women in the Development of Buddhism. In *Women, Religion, and Social Change,* ed. Yvonne Had-dad and Ellison Findly, pp. 59–86. Albany: State University of New York Press.

Willis, Paul. 1977. *Learning to Labour: How Working Class Kids Get Working Class Jobs.* Aldershot, UK: Grover.

Wilson, Ara. 2004. *The Intimate Economies of Bangkok: Tomboys, Tycoons, and Avon Ladies in The Global City.* Berkeley and Los Angeles: University of California Press.

Wiser, Charlotte V. 1978. *Four Families of Karimpur.* Foreign and Comparative Studies Program, South Asian Series, no. 3, Syracuse University. Syracuse, N.Y.: Maxwell School of Citizenship and Public Affairs, Syracuse University.

Wiser, William H. 1958 [1936]. *The Hindu Jajmani System: A Socio-economic System Interrelating Members of a Hindu Village.* Lucknow: Lucknow Publishing House.

Wiser, William, and Charlotte Wiser. 2001. *Behind Mud Walls: Seventy-Five Years in a North Indian Village.* Rev. and exp. ed. with chapters by Susan S. Wadley. Foreword by David G. Mandelbaum. Berkeley and Los Angeles: University of California Press.

Wolpert, Stanley. 1982. *A New History of India.* 2nd ed. Oxford: Oxford University Press.

Women of South Asian Descent Collective, ed. 1993. *Our Feet Walk the Sky: Women of the South Asian Diaspora.* San Francisco: Aunt Lute Books.

Yalman, Nur. 1962. The Ascetic Buddhist Monks of Ceylon. *Ethnology* 1, no. 3: 315–28.

Yuval-Davis, Nira. 1997. *Gender and Nation.* London: Sage.

Zaman, B. Q. 2002. *The Ulama in Contemporary Islam: Custodians of Change.* Princeton, N.J.: Princeton University Press.

Zarrilli, Phillip. 1996. Tooppil Bhaasi's Theatre of Social Conscience and the Kerala People's Arts Club. In *Memories in Hiding,* ed. Tooppil Bhaasi, pp. vii–xiii. Calcutta: Seagull Books.

Zelliot, Eleanor. 1992. *From Untouchable to Dalit: Essays on the Ambedkar Movement.* New Delhi: Manohar.

Žižek, Slavoj. 1989. *The Sublime Object of Ideology.* London: Verso.

BERNARD BATE is Associate Professor of Anthropology at Yale University. He is author of *Tamil Oratory and the Dravidian Aesthetic: Democratic Practice in South India.*

URVASHI BUTALIA is a publisher and writer based in India. Co-founder of Kali for Women, India's first feminist publishing house, she is now Director of Zubaan, an imprint of Kali. Among her published works are: *Women and the Hindu Right: A Collection of Essays* (edited with Tanika Sarkar); *Speaking Peace: Women's Voices from Kashmir* (edited), and the award-winning *The Other Side of Silence: Voices from the Partition of India.*

E. VALENTINE DANIEL is Professor of Anthropology at Columbia University. His books include *Fluid Signs: Being a Person the Tamil Way* and *Charred Lullabies: Chapters in an Anthropography of Violence.*

SARA DICKEY is Professor of Anthropology at Bowdoin College. She is author of *Cinema and the Urban Poor in South India* and co-editor of *Home and Hegemony: Domestic Service and Identity Politics in South and Southeast Asia.*

JOYCE BURKHALTER FLUECKIGER is Professor in the Department of Religion at Emory University. She is author of *In Amma's Healing Room: Gender and Vernacular Islam in South India* (Indiana University Press, 2006) and *Gender and Genre in the Folklore of Middle India,* and co-editor of *Oral Epics in India* and *Boundaries of the Text: Epic Performances in South and Southeast Asia.*

MICHELE RUTH GAMBURD is Professor of Anthropology at Portland State University. She is author of *The Kitchen Spoon's Handle: Transnationalism and Sri Lanka's Migrant Housemaids* and *Breaking the Ashes: The Culture of Illicit Liquor in Sri Lanka,* and co-editor of *Tsunami Recovery in Sri Lanka: Ethnic and Regional Dimensions.*

ANN GRODZINS GOLD is Professor in the Departments of Religion and Anthropology at Syracuse University. Her recent publications include *In the Time of Trees and Sorrows: Nature, Power and Memory in Rajasthan* (authored with Bhoju Ram Gujar) and a co-edited volume, *Women's Renunciation in South Asia*.

KIM GUTSCHOW is Lecturer at Williams College. Her book *Being a Buddhist Nun: The Struggle for Enlightenment in the Himalayas* won the Sharon Stephens Prize awarded by the American Ethnological Society in 2005.

KATHLEEN HALL is Associate Professor of Education and Anthropology at the University of Pennsylvania, where she is also Director of the South Asia Center. She is author of *Lives in Translation: Sikh Youth as British Citizens*.

PATRICIA JEFFERY is Professor of Sociology at the University of Edinburgh. Her publications include *Don't Marry Me to a Plowman! Women's Everyday Lives in Rural North India* (with Roger Jeffery); *Appropriating Gender: Women's Activism and Politicized Religion in South Asia* (with Amrita Basu); and *Degrees without Freedom: Education, Masculinities and Unemployment* (with Craig Jeffrey and Roger Jeffery).

ROGER JEFFERY is Professor of Sociology of South Asia at the University of Edinburgh. His publications include (with Patricia Jeffery) *Population, Gender, and Politics: Demographic Change in Rural North India*; (with Nandini Sundar) *Branching Out: Joint Forest Management in Four Indian States*; and (with Anthony Heath) *Change and Diversity: Economics, Politics and Society in Contemporary India*.

CARI COSTANZO KAPUR is Lecturer in the Department of Anthropology at Stanford University.

NAVEEDA KHAN is Assistant Professor of Anthropology at Johns Hopkins University. She is editor of *Beyond Crisis: Re-evaluating Pakistan*.

SARAH LAMB is Associate Professor and Chair of Anthropology at Brandeis University. She is author of *White Saris and Sweet Mangoes: Aging, Gender and Body in North India* and *Aging and the Indian Diaspora: Cosmopolitan Families in India and Abroad* (Indiana University Press, 2009).

MARK LIECHTY is Associate Professor of Anthropology and History at the University of Illinois at Chicago and author of *Suitably Modern: Making Middle Class Culture in a New Consumer Society*.

RITTY LUKOSE is Associate Professor in the Gallatin School of Individualized Study at New York University and author of *Liberalization's Children: Gender, Youth and Consumer Citizenship in Globalizing India*.

CAITRIN LYNCH is author of *Juki Girls, Good Girls: Gender and Cultural Politics in Sri Lanka's Global Garment Industry*. She is Assistant Professor of Anthropology at Olin College of Engineering and Visiting Research Associate in the Department of Anthropology at Brandeis University.

PURNIMA MANKEKAR is a professor in the Departments of Women's Studies and Asian American Studies at the University of California, Los Angeles. She is author of *Screening Culture, Viewing Politics: An Ethnography of Television, Womanhood, and Nation in Postcolonial India.*

MCKIM MARRIOTT, whose base is in Anthropology and the Social Sciences College of the University of Chicago, has researched cultures of South Asia for five decades. He edited *Village India* and *India through Hindu Categories,* and has written extensively on caste and other aspects of social organization.

MAGNUS MARSDEN is Senior Lecturer in Social Anthropology at the School of Oriental and Asian Studies, University of London and author of *Living Islam: Muslim Religious Experience in Pakistan's North-West Frontier.*

KALYANI DEVAKI MENON is Assistant Professor in the Department of Religious Studies at DePaul University and author of *Everyday Nationalism: Women of the Hindu Right in India.*

DIANE P. MINES is Associate Professor of Anthropology at Appalachian State University. She is author of *Fierce Gods: Inequality, Ritual, and the Politics of Dignity in a South Indian Village* (Indiana University Press, 2005) and *Caste in India,* and co-editor of *Village Matters.*

SERENA NANDA is Professor Emeritus of Anthropology at John Jay College, City University of New York, and is author of *Neither Man nor Woman: The Hijras of India; Gender Diversity: Cross Cultural Variations;* and *The Gift of a Bride: A Tale of Anthropology, Matrimony, and Murder.*

KIRIN NARAYAN is Professor of Anthropology at the University of Wisconsin–Madison. She is author of *Storytellers, Saints and Scoundrels: Folk Narrative in Hindu Religious Teaching; Love, Stars and All That; Mondays on the Dark Night of the Moon: Himalayan Foothill Folktales* (in collaboration with Urmila Devi Suud); and *My Family and Other Saints.*

ANAND PANDIAN is Assistant Professor in the Department of Anthropology at Johns Hopkins University. He is author of *Crooked Stalks: Cultivating Virtue in South India* and co-editor of *Race, Nature, and the Politics of Difference.*

STEVEN M. PARISH is Professor of Anthropology at the University of California at San Diego. He is author of *Moral Knowing in a Hindu Sacred City; Hierarchy and Its Discontents: Culture and the Politics of Consciousness in Caste Society;* and *Subjectivity and Suffering in American Culture.*

JEAN-LUC RACINE is Senior Fellow at the Centre for the Study of India and South Asia in Paris. He edited *Calcutta 1905–1971: Au Coeur des Creations et des Revoltes du Siecle* and *Peasant Moorings: Village Ties and Mobility Rationales in South India*. He is author (with Viramma and Josiane Racine) of *Viramma, Life of an Untouchable*.

JOSIANE RACINE resides in Paris and conducts research on popular culture in Tamil Nadu, South India. She is author (with Viramma and Jean-Luc Racine) of *Viramma, Life of an Untouchable*.

SMITHA RADHAKRISHNAN is Assistant Professor of Sociology at Wellesley College.

SABINA FAIZ RASHID is Associate Professor at the James P. Grant School of Public Health, at BRAC University in Dhaka.

GAYATRI REDDY is Associate Professor of Gender and Women's Studies and of Anthropology at the University of Illinois at Chicago, and author of *With Respect to Sex: Negotiating Hijra Identity in South India*.

PAULA RICHMAN is William H. Danforth Professor of the Religion Department at Oberlin College. Her books include *Extraordinary Child: Poems from a South Indian Devotional Genre; Questioning Ramayanas: A South Asian Tradition;* and *Ramayana Stories in Modern South India* (Indiana University Press, 2008).

LAURA RING is author of *Zenana: Everyday Peace in a Karachi Apartment Building* (Indiana University Press, 2006). She holds a Ph.D. in Anthropology from the University of Chicago.

SUSAN SEIZER is Associate Professor of Communication and Culture at Indiana University and author of *Stigmas of the Tamil Stage: An Ethnography of Special Drama Artists in South India*.

MARGARET TRAWICK is a sociocultural anthropologist who has done extensive ethnographic research in Tamil Nadu and more recently in Sri Lanka. She is author of *Notes on Love in a Tamil Family* and *Enemy Lines: Warfare, Childhood and Play in Batticaloa*.

VIRAMMA was a Dalit agricultural laborer and midwife in Karani, a village in southeast India. She passed away in her village in 2000.

SUSAN S. WADLEY is Ford Maxwell Professor of South Asian Studies at Syracuse University. She is author of several books, including *Struggling with Destiny in Karimpur, 1925–1984* and *Raja Nal and the Goddess: The North Indian Epic Dhola in Performance* (Indiana University Press, 2004).

INDEX

Page locators in italics refer to figures and tables